ASIAN YEARBOOK OF INTERNATIONAL LAW

Asian Yearbook
of
International Law

published under the auspices of the
Foundation for the Development
of International Law in Asia (DILA)

General Editors

B.S. Chimni – Miyoshi Masahiro – Surya P. Subedi

VOLUME 10
2001-2002

MARTINUS NIJHOFF PUBLISHERS
LEIDEN / BOSTON

A C.I.P. Catalogue record for this book is available from the Library of Congress.

ISBN **90 04 14639 3**

ASIAN YEARBOOK OF INTERNATIONAL LAW

TABLE OF CONTENTS

ASIAN AND INTERNATIONAL ORGANIZATIONS

CHRONICLE

LITERATURE

INTRODUCTION BY THE GENERAL EDITORS

We are proud to present this Tenth volume of the *Asian Yearbook of International Law* and pleased to have reached the stage where we are today. The continent of Asia is experiencing dramatic and breathtaking changes in almost all areas of human activity. Phenomenal economic growth is taking place across the continent, with the rare exceptions of certain South and Southeast Asian least developed States. These are exciting times for Asia and for the development of international law.

The world of international law has moved from the traditional Eurocentric and West-centric mode in its acquisition of a truly global character. Asian States are playing a leading role in developing and formulating new rules of international law and in shaping the future policies of our planet. Consequently, international law has become a discipline of growing interest in Asia with the new challenges posed by new developments, both political and economic. For instance, both the Caspian Sea and the South China Sea are emerging as foci not only in terms of the exploration and exploitation of natural resources, but also in terms of their volatility and vulnerability to potential conflict over these very natural resources. Competition for energy and fresh water resources is likely to become more acute in this region. The rapid degrada-tion of the environment currently taking place across Asia is a constant cause for concern. The challenge for international lawyers is to address these developments in a constructive manner and enable international law to manage these changes.

The key to advancing human civilization and to ensuring lasting peace and prosperity is through respect for the rule of law both at the regional and the international levels. This is where the community of international legal scholars have a role to play. Together, they have a role in ensuring that the exercise of power remains within the boundaries of international law, in creating awareness of both the impending problems and the solutions to such problems, and in disseminating the message of peace, freedom, tolerance, and harmony. This is particularly so for Asian scholars, who are at the heart of these changes.

As the *Yearbook* begins its new decade, we assure our readers that we will continue in our endeavour to promote international law in Asia, to reach out to as many scholars as possible, to join hands with the wider body of scholars in upholding international law, and to serve as a platform for discussion of the need for the timely reform and change of this body of law in order to meet the challenges posed by the new developments taking place around us.

The General Editors

ABBREVIATIONS

AJIL	-	American Journal of International Law
Am.U.J.Int'l.L&Pol'y	-	American University Journal of International Law and Policy
APEC	-	Asia-Pacific Economic Co-operation
ASEAN	-	Association of Southeast Asian Nations
Asian YIL	-	Asian Yearbook of International Law
BDFA	-	British Documents on Foreign Affairs
BJC	-	British Journal of Criminology
BYIL	-	British Yearbook of International Law
CEDAW	-	Convention on the Elimination of Discrimination Against Women
CTS	-	Consolidated Treaty Series (C. Parry, Ed.)
CWILJ	-	California Western International Law Journal
DJILP	-	Denver Journal of International Law and Policy
EJIL	-	European Journal of International Law
FO	-	Foreign Office, UK
GATS	-	General Agreement on Trade in Services
GATT	-	General Agreement on Tariffs and Trade
GYIL	-	German Yearbook of International Law
Hague Receuil	-	Receuil des cours de l'Académie de droit international de la Haye
HMSO	-	Her Majesty's Stationery Office, UK
HRLJ	-	Human Rights Law Journal
ICAO	-	International Civil Aviation Organization
ICJ	-	International Court of Justice
ICJ Rep	-	International Court of Justice Reports
ICLQ	-	International and Comparative Law Quarterly
ICRC	-	International Committee of the Red Cross
ICTY	-	International Criminal Tribunal for former Yugoslavia
IHT	-	International Herald Tribune
IJIL	-	Indian Journal of International Law
IJMCL	-	International Journal of Maritime and Coastal Law
ILA	-	International Law Association
ILM	-	International Legal Materials

Ind.JIL	-	Indian Journal of International Law
IYIA	-	Indian Yearbook of International Affairs
JIA	-	Journal of International Affairs
JAIL	-	Japanese Annual of International Law
JP	-	The Jakarta Post
McGill.L.J.	-	McGill Law Journal
NATO	-	North Atlantic Treaty Organization
OECD	-	Organization for Economic Cooperation and Development
RIAA	-	Reports of International Arbitral Awards
SAARC	-	South Asian Association for Regional Cooperation
SAFHR	-	South Asia Forum for Human Rights
SCMP	-	South China Morning Post
Tex.L.Rev.	-	Texas Law Review
TIAS	-	Treaties and other International Acts Series (US Department of State)
UNCED	-	United Nations Conference on Environment and Development
UNCLOS	-	United Nations Convention on the Law of the Sea
UNCTAD	-	United Nations Conference on Trade and Development
UNGA	-	United Nations General Assembly
UNTS	-	United Nations Treaty Series
UST	-	Treaties in Force, a List of Treaties and Other International Agreements of the United States
Va.J.Int'l.L	-	Virginia Journal of International Law
YaleJIL	-	Yale Journal of International Law
YILC	-	Yearbook of the International Law Commission

ARTICLES

THE JAPANESE SEIZURE OF KOREA FROM THE PERSPECTIVE OF THE UNITED KINGDOM NATIONAL ARCHIVE, 1904-1910

Anthony Carty*

1. INTRODUCTION

Between the years 1904 and 1910 the Japanese consolidated their hold on Korea in terms that have given rise to considerable tension between the two countries. The controversy surrounds especially the conclusion of a series of treaties in the years 1904 and 1905; these treaties Korean scholars judge to be invalidated by a measure of duress then exerted not only upon Korea as a State but also upon the Korean officials responsible for the signature of the treaties. The Korean view is that Korea was at that time recognized as a State by the international community, and that Japan violated that status through its policy of oppressive treaties and gradually increasing encroachment upon Korean sovereignty. The same considerations are also held to apply to the question of the validity of the final treaty of annexation in 1910.[1]

The present contribution to the discussion does not attempt to challenge either the Japanese or the Korean perspectives in these debates. However, given the huge importance of the British Empire at the relevant time, it is believed that the introduction of the British dimension will serve to show that the then character of Japanese-Korean international law relations was largely determined by openly and complacently held imperial and colonial assumptions. It was easily assumed that the principle of the equality of States applied not to all States, but only to those States which were judged by leading Powers to be equal. This should mean that the Japanese-Korean

---

* Professor at the School of Law, University of Westminster.

The author acknowledges the support of the Arts and Humanities Research Board of the United Kingdom in the research for this article.

[1] These debates are recorded in the July, August and September 1998 issues, the March, July and October 1999 issues, and the May, June and November 2000 issues of the monthly magazine, *Sekai,* in articles by Prof. Sakamoto Shigeki of Kansai University, Japan; Prof. Yi Tae-jin of Seoul National University; Prof. Sasakawa Norikatsu of the International Christian University; Japan, Prof. Unno Fukuju of Meiji University, and Arai Shin'ichi. These debates are translated into English and are also available from Prof. Yi Tae-jin, whose expertise and knowledge in these discussions is exemplary: tjyi@plaza.snu.ac.kr

Asian Yearbook of International Law, Volume 10 (B.S. Chimni *et al.,* eds.)
© 2005 Koninklijke Brill NV. Printed in The Netherlands, pp. 3-24.

conflict has to be seen in a much wider international context in which other States, and in particular the British Empire, played a decisive role. It might possibly be better for Koreans wishing to dispute the legality of Japanese conduct in the period 1904 to 1910 to challenge the responsibility of the Western-dominated international legal community for the suffering inflicted through an internationally sanctioned colonialism on their country, rather than to treat the Japanese seizure of Korea in terms of the treaty law of the time.

By way of conclusion some general remarks will be offered concerning the implications of the British archival record for the character of international law at the time. It will readily be seen that the British interest did not centre on whether the Japanese were coercing Korean officials and State institutions; the British officials seem to have had a very clear picture of what was happening. Rather, the question was whether, in British eyes, Korea really was a State in the sense required by the international community at the time. However, there is no doubt that Britain answered this question also in the context of its understanding of its own national interest, in particular in terms of what it thought to be the optimal policy to follow towards Japan. Both Britain and Japan considered there was from Russia a long-term and permanent threat to their respective interests. A final assessment of the place and character of the international law of the time will be attempted after consideration of all of these factors.

The style of presentation will be chronological and, as far as possible, it will scrupulously present the documentation, commenting on it only at the end. Although it is believed the legal implications of the correspondence are clear, the officials concerned only rarely consulted legal advice, so far as the record showed. Their decisive judgements were factual, concerning the character of the Korean entity. This is not to say that posterity is required to accept uncritically the judgements made by British officials and politicians at the time. Instead, some critical reflections will be offered in conclusion, particularly with respect to the systemic implications of the debate for the fundamental character of international law as a universal standard of behaviour. It is obvious that the British regarded Korea at the time as a failed State; perhaps that concept was as problematic at that time as it might be regarded now. Nonetheless, the issue of "failed States" is complex and continues to be a matter of open debate.

There are two separate dimensions to the chronology of the archival record. The first concerns a record of reports by the British Minister in Seoul, Sir J.N. Jordan. This is particularly illuminating in terms of first-hand reporting about Korea to London. The record shows that Jordan did have definite influence on the British assessment of the viability of the Korean State, a central issue. However, Korea was very much a part of a wider international scene that is reflected in the correspondence of the British Foreign Office with the Great Powers, especially Japan. This is evident in the archives of the British Embassy in Tokyo and the Japanese Embassy in London, besides a limited correspondence between the British Foreign Office and officials in Paris, Washington, Vienna, and other capitals. The two streams of archives only occasionally interlink. Thus, it is proposed to present these materials in two parts that lead up to the end of 1905 and culminate in the formal imposition of a Japanese

Protectorate over Korea. The first of these outlines the correspondence from Seoul leading to the Protectorate; the second considers the rest of the correspondence in the context of the conclusion of the second Anglo-Japanese Alliance in August 1905. The third part considers briefly the Annexation Agreement of 1910.

2.   THE VIEW FROM THE BRITISH MINISTER IN SEOUL

2.1.   February and March 1904: the first treaty encroachments upon Korean sovereignty

At Seoul in the winter-spring of 1904 the British Minister, J.N. Jordan, wrote a series of despatches directly to the British Foreign Secretary in London, the Marquess of Lansdowne, with copies to the Embassies in Peking and Tokyo. The first issue reported concerned an Agreement between the two countries made just before the Russo-Japanese war and concerning the status of Korea in that coming conflict. The controversy concerning whether Korea was freely consenting to the Agreement appears immediately. Jordan had many comments on this question.

In despatch No. 56 he transmitted a copy of the Agreement between Japan and Korea of 23 February 1904. The Minister for Foreign Affairs provided the copy, and he, Jordan, had checked for its accuracy. The Minister had signed it, and so had the Japanese Minister Plenipotentiary in Seoul, Mr G. Hayashi. Jordan commented, "I understand that the Corean [*sic*] Government demurred chiefly to signing Articles One and Four, and wished to introduce some modifications, but their objections were summarily overruled by the Japanese Minister".[2]

Article 1 provided that, in order to maintain the traditional friendship between Japan and Korea, and with a view permanently to establishing the peace of the Orient, the Korean Government, reposing full confidence in Japan, undertake to give full effect to the disinterested advice of the Imperial Japanese Government with regard to administrative reforms. This Article touches upon the organizational capacity of the Korean State and becomes a familiar theme. Article 4 was much more explicitly related to Korea's international position.

> "In the event of encroachment by a third power or internal disturbance threatening the security of the Imperial Household or the integrity of Corean Territory, the Japanese Government shall take immediately such action as circumstances may require and the Corean Government will at the same time afford every facility to the action of the Japanese Government. In order to attain this object, the Imperial Japanese Government may utilise, when circumstances require it, such strategic points as may be necessary."

---

[2] FO 17/1659. The spelling of Korea in these documents is with a "C".

Jordan comments at length on a conversation he had with Hayashi. The Agreement was a reproduction of a proposal recently made in negotiations with Russia, which the latter had rejected. Hayashi told Jordan that the Korean Minister, Yi Chi Yong, had said at the last moment that he could not sign the Agreement. When Hayashi asked for the refusal to be made in writing, the Minister consented to carry out the engagement, explaining that his reluctance had been due to the persistent and determined opposition of Yi Yong Ik. Hayashi objected, saying that he had the previous day explained the Agreement fully to Yi Yong Ik, and that it had been entirely accepted. Hayashi then had an audience with the Korean Emperor, attended by a large military staff and imposing retinue, where he suggested that Yi Yong Ik be sent to Japan "to enlarge his views and give him an opportunity to acquire some experience of foreign countries." This had happened; Jordan comments that Yi Yong Ik was to remain in Tokyo under surveillance. Jordan's conclusion to these conversations and to the despatch reads:

"The Agreement appears to be a flagrant violation of Corean neutrality, but it was obvious from the first that the Corean Declaration on that point was not likely, in the event of hostilities, to be capable of enforcement, and that she would be obliged to act at the dictation of the belligerent Power which first occupied her capital".[3]

Jordan followed this despatch on 7 March 1904 (No. 72) with a close commentary upon its operation. Korea had not been a voluntary partner to the Agreement, having been constrained, on the present occasion – as she had always been in her past history – to espouse the cause of the occupying Power who first obtained military control of her capital. The Koreans had a long experience of a national existence based upon the equipoise of the political forces around them, "and it is only when the preponderance is, as now, all on one side, that their congenial role of playing off one Power against another no longer serves its object".[4] Jordan observed that the population and what he calls "the Emperor and the Palace Part" were divided on the merits of the course being adopted. Bomb outrages were committed against the Foreign Minister signing the Agreement, which Jordan took to be a sign of the anti-Japanese ill-feeling that would show when Japanese troops were temporarily absent from Seoul. It indicated that the Japanese position rested upon a reserve of force. At the same time, the Foreign Minister had obtained the personal approval of the Emperor and the formal sanction of the Council of State for the signing. Jordan comments finally that the Emperor attempted to open contacts with the Russians in Shanghai, but had been blocked by Japanese police. Jordan quotes the Japanese Minister describing this as the Emperor's being "again at his old tricks".[5]

The same despatch comments extensively on the misgovernment of Korea, particularly the state of its finances plagued, as it was, by a debased nickel coinage. However, in the next preserved despatch (No. 82) of 16 March, Jordan comments:

---

[3] Ibid.
[4] FO 17/1659.
[5] Ibid.

"That Japan will succeed in Egyptianizing Corea no observer of her own national development can possibly doubt, but the task is a formidable one and in its accomplishment she will receive even less assistance from the native element than the British Authorities received in Egypt".[6]

The Japanese had already taken charge of the department of Communications and had their eyes on the War Ministry. There was said to be some idea of disbanding the Korean Army and utilising the men in a non-combatant capacity in connection with the present hostilities.[7]

It is worth noting that on 19 March Jordan was able to report the contents of a Russian communication, from the Ussuri Boundary Commissioner, commenting on Japan's general behaviour towards Korea:

"Japan's actions in Corea had been contrary to international law, and in the years 1895 and 1902 the Corean Government had made a declaration that, in the event of a conflict between those two countries, Corea would take no part therein. This declaration received the approval of both Russia and Japan. Notwithstanding this, however, three days before the declaration of war, the Japanese had instructed their representative in Seoul to request the Corean Emperor to acknowledge a Japanese protectorate over Corea. In the event of a refusal, Japanese troops would occupy the palace. The Corean troops were not equal to the task of resisting the Japanese, who arrived in due course at Seoul. The Japanese intimidated the Corean Emperor and Government, and, in defiance of the law of nations, deprived the country of her independence. This is a matter of common knowledge both to officials and people".[8]

2.2.   August to December 1904: the Japanese grip tightens

The next stage of Japanese encroachment upon Korea was less dramatic, but very significant. On 23 August 1904, Korea agreed to the appointment of a Japanese Financial Adviser, and the Japanese nominated a foreigner as Diplomatic Adviser. Finally, Korea agreed, through Article III, "When concluding any Treaty with a foreign Power or other important international transaction in the nature of Agreements granting special rights to individual foreigners, and so forth, the Corean Government will consult the Government of Japan." Jordan comments to the Marquess of Lansdowne that he regards these developments very positively. In particular, they will put an end to the practice of the Emperor and the Court "in continuing to make perfectly absurd Contracts with unscrupulous foreigners". Jordan describes very disparagingly the attempts of the Emperor to avoid signing this Agreement and

---

[6] Ibid.
[7] Ibid.
[8] Ibid.

comments that the latter's evasiveness "may be regarded as a measure of the difficulties which reform schemes are likely to encounter in this country".[9]

Jordan had already heavily commented on the coming of this Agreement in a slightly earlier despatch (No. 167) on 16 August 1904. All his sympathies are with the Japanese. Hayashi had explained everything to the Koreans "in studiously temperate language". In particular, the Korean army would be radically reduced, and this would help assure the Japanese a supply of coolies for military operations. There would be a withdrawal of Korean legations abroad, which had been flattering to the vanity of the Korean Emperor and affording him one of the keenest pleasures in his life. These steps are ostensibly to save money, but are presumably intended to assure Japanese control over the foreign relations of Korea. With an Adviser of their choice and business abroad done through their own legations, "the Japanese will control Corean foreign policy almost as effectively as the British Government did that of the late Transvaal Republic or as the Government of India does in the case of the Amer of Afghanistan".[10]

The sequel to this was the actual appointment of the two Advisers. There was an Agreement for a Japanese Financial Adviser on 15 October 1904, without whose consent the Korean Government could take no action. Again, Jordan comments that in drawing up the document, and in particular the above clause, the Japanese "would appear to have followed with some closeness the model set by the British in Egypt". As in Egypt the Adviser sits on the Council of State and can veto any decision. As Lord Milner comments on a similar power in Egypt, it makes the Financial Adviser master of the situation. When he also happens to be a citizen of the country which is in military occupation of the country, i.e., Egypt, then, writes Lord Milner, "there is no need to dwell at tedious length upon the magnitude of his powers".[11]

The Diplomatic Adviser, an American, Mr Stevens, under an Agreement of 27 December 1904 received a mandate similar to the Financial Adviser's except that the Japanese Government might terminate the arrangement at any time without consulting Mr Stevens. Article 2 provides, quite simply, that

> "(i)t will be the duty of Mr Stevens to examine and settle with the utmost faithfulness all questions which arise affecting the relations between the Corean Government and foreign Governments or between the Corean Government and the subjects and citizens of foreign Powers".[12]

It is difficult to see what is left of Korea's independence by the end of 1904. A Protectorate has been imposed.

---

[9] FO 17/1660, despatch No. 169, 24 August 1904.
[10] FO 17/1660.
[11] Ibid., despatch No. 199, 19 October 1904, Jordan to the Marquess of Lansdowne.
[12] FO 17/1660, despatch No. 231, Jordan to the Marquess of Lansdowne, 28 December 1904.

2.3. January to December 1905: Steps leading to the final imposition of a Protectorate following upon the renewal of the Anglo-Japanese treaty of 1902

The year begins with a number of currency and financial Agreements between the Corean Government and the First Bank of Japan, concluded in order to sort out the debased character of the currency circulating in the country. The credit of the Japanese Government is directly pledged for the successful re-organization of the currency. The Bank is responsible also for the receipt of the national revenue and the disbursement of Government expenditure, thereby practically functioning as the Government Bank of Korea. Jordan believes this will greatly relieve the ordinary Korean from the oppressive corruption of Korean fiscal and customs administration. Under these Agreements,

"Corea has lost her financial independence, and fallen under the economic, no less than the political, tutelage of Japan. For this she is herself largely responsible, but it is only fair to say that, as far as the currency disorganisation is concerned, the blame is shared to some extent with Japan. Japan owes it to herself and to the other treaty Powers who have commercial relations with Corea, to repair the mischief".[13]

Jordan continues to comment shortly afterwards that the Emperor has had to agree with the Japanese Minister to recall the Korean Ministers at Tokyo, Paris, and Berlin, preparatory to the closing of the delegations. He says that "the abolition of Corean representation abroad ... proposes to remove the last vestige of independence which Corea retains in her external affairs". Remarking also, at the same time, about the proposed loss of control over communications (postal and telegraphic), Jordan still claims that such an interference with a nominally independent country could be justified by the "marvellous transformation which Japanese energy has effected in the material condition of Corea".[14] The actual abandonment of control over postal, telegraphic and telephone communications came with an Agreement at the end of March. Jordan makes no mention of any coercive dimension in this complete sub-jugation of Korea. Instead, he remarks, almost nostalgically, about the new agreement that it is a severe blow to Koreans who regarded attendance at meetings of the International Postal Union as an outward manifestation of their national independence second in importance only to having legations abroad.[15]

Only in the course of June 1905 does Jordan first address the criticism being made of Japanese conduct in Korea. Korean is, admittedly, being overrun by large numbers of Japanese adventurers. Even leaving aside the element of exaggeration of the events, particularly by American missionaries, there is some element of truth about the levels of extortion of Koreans and about unscrupulous Japanese land grabs.

---

[13] FO 17/1692, despatch No. 16, 1 February 1905 with enclosures.
[14] Ibid., despatch No. 32, 27 February 1905.
[15] Ibid., despatch No. 52, 4 April 1905, referring to the agreement of 30 March 1905 to hand over control of the Korean system of communications to Japan.

Once again Jordan displays his usual understanding of the Japanese. They have taken some steps to restrain their nationals, but they can hardly be expected to exclude them from Korea. The situation between Britain and Egypt is not really comparable. Britain did not have the same need of an outlet for its surplus population and, anyway, Europeans would not be so attracted to settling on the Nile; nor was there to the same extent "the political necessity for England of having a population of her own race settled on the land as a bulwark against the aggression of a powerful neighbour". In any case, as with Britain and the Transvaal, extension of influence will come "by having a leavening of the dominant race settled permanently in the country". Of course, disputes between Koreans and Japanese could be more easily resolved if the Japanese took more trouble to develop a judicial system and one of law enforcement. However, one must be realistic about the tensions that have existed for centuries between Koreans and Japanese. "Except that there is no trace of religious animosity, the estrangement is not unlike that which prevails between Saxon and Celt in some parts of Ireland and is quite as unreasoning in its nature."[16]

Jordan saw the dilemma of Japan concerning the introduction of reforms in Korea. When critics warn the Japanese that the cornerstone of their policy must be the maintenance of Korean independence, the same critics complain, in the same breath, that the pace of reform in the country is too slow. Jordan comments firmly: "Now, it is the observance of the independence pledge which hampers the reform programme by the necessity it imposes of following a cumbersome and tortuous procedure." Then Jordan describes, in the most disparaging terms, the difficulties experienced by the Japanese in doing legal business with Korean officialdom. This is crucial to how one sees the whole argument about coercion of Korean officials to reach agreement. It will become central to the circumstances in which the Protectorate Agreement was concluded later in November 1905. It is therefore worth quoting at length how Jordan saw this process:

> "A measure is brought in the first instance before the Council of State, consisting
> of ten members, who cannot often be mustered in sufficient numbers to form a
> quorum. The Japanese Minister, or the Secretary of Legation, is generally present
> to take charge of the Bill and explain its object. A series of long discussions follows
> in which the Corean members indulge in harmless platitudes but take care to commit
> themselves to no expression of opinion which will give umbrage to the Emperor,
> who has his informants at the meeting. The difficulty is only half over when the
> measure finally emerges, often in emasculated form, from the Council of State. It
> is then submitted to the Emperor, who gives it his sanction, and, at the same time,
> lets it be known that any attempt to enforce it will meet with his severe dis-
> approval".[17]

---

[16] FO 17/1692, despatch No. 87, 19 June 1905. As the author of a work on the British justifications for their conquest of Ireland, I cannot help but be amused by this particular comment of Jordan. See Anthony Carty, *Was Ireland Conquered?* (1996). In particular in Chapters Two, Three and Four, I reconsider opinions about the ever-so-unreasonable squabbling of Celts with Saxons.

[17] Ibid., despatch No. 87, 19 June 1905.

Against this background, it is not surprising that, at the end of August 1905, Jordan acquiesced in the Japanese assumption of control of Customs Administration, actually handled by a British citizen, Mr McLeavy Brown, on behalf of Korea. This was at the instigation of the Japanese Minister, Hayashi, and of Mr Megata, the Financial Adviser. The Korean Emperor sent messengers to Jordan asking for assistance to avert the blow. The messengers stated that British acceptance of this change "was interpreted as an indication of our abandonment of all interest in Corea, and had on that account caused the Emperor peculiar pain. I did want to reassure them on this point, at the same time discouraging all idea of opposition to the change".[18]

There follows, by way of conclusion, the dramatic impact upon Korea of the publication of the Anglo-Japanese Agreement of 12 August 1905. It provided in Article III:

"Japan possessing paramount political, military, and economic interests in Corea, Great Britain recognizes the right of Japan to take such measures of guidance, control and protection in Corea as she may deem proper and necessary to safeguard and advance those interests, provided always that such measures are not contrary to the principle of equal opportunities for the commerce and industry of all nations."[19]

The Korean Foreign Minister protested to Jordan on 15 October 1905 that the Anglo-Japanese Treaty contradicted the Treaty between Great Britain and Korea. The latter states that "in case of differences arising between one of the High Contracting Parties and a third power, the other High Contracting party... shall exert its good offices to bring about an amicable arrangement" (Article I, para. 2), also that "both countries shall freely enjoy the same ... privileges as are enjoyed ... in other countries" (Article II). The protest note continued that the equality of States has been the ruling principle of recent years among the Powers, no matter how small a country is. "Why then should our country be made a solitary exception to this rule?" It called upon the British Government to rescind the Treaty. The heart of the protest becomes a plea against the unfairness of British conduct:

"Corea had never given Great Britain cause for complaint, besides the good faith and sincerity of Great Britain are well known all the world over; how is it that so little importance is now attached to our Treaty? If any other country made an arrangement with a third Power affecting Great Britain, would Great Britain consent?"[20]

---

[18] Despatch No. 121, Jordan to the Marquess of Lansdowne, Seoul, 30 August 1905, reproduced in Kenneth Bourne and D. Cameron Watt (general eds.), British Documents on Foreign Affairs: Reports and Papers from the Foreign Office Confidential Print, Part I, from the mid-19th Century to the First World War, Series E. Ian Nish (ed.), *East Asia, 1860-1914*, vol. 8: *Russo-Japanese War 1904-1905*, University Publications of America, 1989, Doc. 344, at 310-311. FO 17/1693.

[19] Reproduced, inter alia, by G.P. Gooch and Harold Temperley (eds.), in *British Documents on the Origins of the War 1898-1914*, Vol. IV: *The Anglo-Russian Rapprochement 1903-7*, London: HMSO, 1929, at 166 (semi-official archival document collection).

[20] British Documents on Foreign Affairs (BDFA), n.18, Doc.373, at 333.

Jordan recommends to the Marquess of Lansdowne that it does not seem to him desirable that any notice should be taken of this communication. "Even a mere formal acknowledgement might, in the present temper of the Coreans, be construed as a tacit acquiescence in the justice of their remonstrance, and would raise hopes which cannot possibly be fulfilled." Jordan intimated that the Japanese legation concurred in this view. If pressed, Jordan would inform the Foreign Minister verbally that the Treaty in question "contains nothing which had not already been conceded by Corea herself to Japan in the Agreements entered into between the two Powers on the 23rd February and 23rd August, 1904, and 1st April, 1905, and that they cannot reasonably object to the recognition by Great Britain of a state of things which owes its existence to their own act and deed".[21] Eventually, on 8 December 1905, Lansdowne authorizes a written response to the Koreans in the terms of this last paragraph of Jordan's despatch: "The reply should be put on record. In our opinion it is conclusive".[22]

The formal Protectorate was established by an Agreement between Japan and Korea finally signed on 18 November 1905. It provided that the control and direction of Korea's foreign relations shall be vested in the Japanese Government and shall be transferred to the Foreign Office in Tokyo (Article I). The Government of Korea engages not to conclude hereafter any act or engagement having an international character, except through the medium of the Government of Japan.[23]

Jordan devotes a lengthy despatch to describing the circumstances surrounding the conclusion of this Agreement. The despatch touches upon crucial ground, because the heart of the Korean legal argument against the legality of Japan's presence in Korea rests upon the duress employed to secure this Agreement. Jordan does confirm that duress was present. He relies upon Korean testimony, which he thought accurate. Firstly on 15 November, the Japanese Marquis Ito explained to the Korean Emperor the terms of the Peace Treaty between Japan and Russia, and the terms of Article III of the Anglo-Japanese Alliance. He urged upon the Emperor "the importance of having the rights accorded to Japan in these documents recognised and confirmed by a formal Arrangement between Japan and Corea". He stated in the plainest language that "Japan absolutely refused to contemplate the possibility of resumption of direct diplomatic relations between Corea and Russia". Most of the stipulations had already been conceded in more or less formal instruments in the last eighteen months.[24] Jordan commented that the Emperor, as usual, endeavoured to evade responsibility by referring the question to the consideration of the Council of State but, after four hours' discussion and the exercise of much pressure, he appears eventually to have accepted the proposals in principle; the Foreign Minister was instructed to elaborate the details in consultation with the Japanese Minister. The next day, 16 November, Marquis Ito spent four hours in full conference with all of

---

[21] Ibid., Doc.372, at 332-333. Despatch no.142, Jordan to Marquess of Lansdowne, 17 October 1905. Confidential Print 8703/67.

[22] Ibid., Doc. 381, at 337. Confidential Print 8703/75.

[23] BDFA, n.18, Docs. 364 and 366, telegram no. 41, Seoul, 18 November 1905, at 328-329.

[24] Ibid., Doc. 389, despatch No. 160, Jordan to the Marquess of Lansdowne, 18 November 1905, at 340-341. See also Confidential Print 8703/88.

the Cabinet Ministers, but confided in Jordan that he had made no effective impression.

On 17 November, Hayashi met the Council of State and demanded the signature of the Agreement. Meeting with a refusal, he sent a message to the Emperor requesting an audience, but was referred back to the Ministers. They said that in the absence of express instructions from His Majesty, they must adhere to their decision to withhold their signatures. Then, late in the evening, Hayashi appealed to Marquis Ito. Jordan notes "that the approaches to the Palace were strongly guarded by Japanese gendarmes, that Japanese troops patrolled the streets all the day, and that a very formidable display of force was visible in all the more important quarters of the city".[25] In response to Hayashi's request Marquis Ito, General Baron Hasegawa and others arrived at the Palace shortly before midnight and demanded an audience with the Emperor, threatening to force their way in, if necessary. This produced the desired effect and all of the Cabinet, except the Prime Minster, who had an opportune fit of mental derangement, agreed to the Japanese demands. "A telephone message was sent to the Foreign Office for the seal, and the Agreement was signed at 1.30 this morning." The Corean Ministers were sent to their homes, each with an escort of Japanese police.

Jordan's final comment is singularly unsympathetic to the Koreans. They appear depressed and in no mood to make the best of the situation or to endeavour to attain, through Japanese assistance, "to a state of national regeneration which they have so signally failed to reach by their own unaided efforts". He comments that a Japanese Lord Cromer might be able to appease the bitter feeling which has so long existed between the two races, but Japan's task in Korea is so formidable "that nothing but considerations for her own safety would, I imagine, justify her in undertaking it".[26]

3.   BRITISH-JAPANESE RELATIONS AND THE CONCLUSION OF THE
      ANGLO-JAPANESE AGREEMENT OF 12 AUGUST 1905

Anglo-Japanese diplomatic relations began in 1905 with a very strong statement that appears in the files of Viscount Hayashi. He was instructed to inform the Marquess of Lansdowne that one of the most important points involved in the final settlement of the present conflict between Japan and Korea concerned Korea. It was stated firmly that the Korean Peninsula "forms Japan's natural outer zone of defence and the Japanese Government believe it to be essential to their country's safety and repose that they should maintain intact Japan's predominance there". The message then goes on to elaborate more familiar material that was tirelessly repeated by Jordan. Notwithstanding their best efforts to eradicate evils, the Korean administration continues to constitute a hotbed of intrigue, conspiracies and corruptions. The conclusion is forced on the Japanese Government that to insure peace, order and improved Government "and to prevent a revival of sinister influences such as those

---

[25] Ibid.
[26] Ibid.

that menaced Japan's position at the outbreak of the war it will be necessary for them to place Corea entirely within the sphere of Japanese influence, and to assume complete protection, control and direction of the destiny of Corea".[27]

The whole history of the negotiation of the Anglo-Japanese Agreement is well known and exposed.[28] Here it is important only to highlight the particular place of Korea. When the negotiations were intensifying in July 1905, the British Ambassador in Tokyo, Sir Claude MacDonald, wrote to the Marquess of Lansdowne that the new alliance partook of the nature of a bargain in which, in return for our acquiescence in the Protectorate which Japan intended to establish over Korea at the conclusion of the war (with Russia), she would engage to assist Britain should the Indian Empire be attacked by a third Power. MacDonald said that he had pointed out to the Japanese that such acquiescence would entail a reconsideration of and an amendment to the pledge made in conjunction with Japan in the preamble and Article I of the now existing Anglo-Japanese Agreement, recognizing the territorial integrity and independence of the Empire of Korea.[29]

MacDonald went on to repeat his already expressed view that "as Japan would most certainly establish such a Protectorate whether we acquiesced or not, and as her assistance in the matter of an attack on the Indian Empire would render such an event a practical impossibility for generations to come, I thought that we should accept the terms of the Japanese reply without delay".[30]

Very significantly, MacDonald reinforces his argument about the inevitability of this Protectorate with reliance upon the reports from Jordan in Seoul. He refers to the fact that he himself was once His Majesty's Government's Representative in Korea in the 1980s, and that he thought no one more qualified than Jordan to judge the quality of the situation there. Jordan reports that the Japanese "are getting the entire administration of the country into their hands". The Japanese Prime Minister and Foreign Minister are stressing that they cannot accept a situation of continuing intrigues by the Koreans with the Russians. MacDonald says he had just received on 7 July a letter from Jordan stating that it may be heresy to say so (presumably because of the existing Anglo-Japanese Agreement), but he (Jordan) feels certain that nothing short of a Protectorate will save the situation. Jordan writes: "In the interests of the Coreans themselves this is the only possible solution, and the people, as distinguished from the officials, would, I believe, infinitely prefer it to the Government they have had during the last ten years of nominal independence".[31]

In fact, the main negotiating issues between London and Tokyo concerning the "Korean Article", Article III, soon became matters of detail. The British worried about the commercial and trading rights of other Powers, including themselves, and this led to a variety of formulations of third party rights. The Japanese concern was

---

[27] FO 46/600, at 11.
[28] For instance, Gooch and Temperley, n.19.
[29] FO 46/ 673, at 216, despatch No. 188, Sir C. MacDonald to the Marquess of Lansdowne, Tokyo, 15 July 1905.
[30] Ibid.
[31] Ibid.

that a Most Favoured Nation open-door policy would defeat the whole exercise of gaining control of the Peninsula. The Japanese persuaded the British to omit any reference to the Treaty Rights of other nations, but retained a general reference to equal opportunities for commerce and industry.[32] Still, before concluding the Agreement, the British felt it necessary to have American approval and this was sought. The Marquess of Lansdowne informed them that the Agreement would contain a clause under which Japan would obtain paramount influence in Korea, and that "it seemed to us inevitable that she should acquire such an influence". The American response was firm: "Both Mr Loomis and Mr Lodge replied unhesitatingly that the United States' Government saw no objection to the establishment of Japanese control in Corea, and Mr Lodge even added that in the view of the United States' Government it was much to be wished that such a preponderance should be created".[33] Britain was to seek the approval of other Powers after the Agreement was concluded.[34]

The second issue was one of presentation. How was Britain to present its change of policy and apparent gift to Japan to its own population and thus public opinion? MacDonald in Tokyo said that he had explained the issue to the Japanese Prime Minister. There was a problem with the extension of the second Anglo-Japanese Agreement beyond the first. Article II clearly foreshadowed a Japanese Protectorate over Korea, which meant His Majesty's Government "would have to a very great extent to 'go back' on the protestations they had frequently made respecting the maintenance of the independence and territorial integrity of the Corean Empire, protestations which had, so to speak, crystallized in the Preamble and Article I of the present Agreement".[35] Thus, Article IV, in the British first draft, mentioned that "Japan, on the other hand, equally recognises the special interests of Great Britain in the regions adjacent to the Indian frontier etc." MacDonald pointed out to the Japanese that such an Article, "about as harmless and non-committal to the Japanese as it was possible for any statement to be", was nonetheless inserted to meet whatever Parliamentary opposition as might occur – for "it must be remembered that Corea had an Article, and a very comprehensive one, all to herself, whereas no allusion whatever was made to India except in the Preamble".[36] A slightly different wording of Article IV eventually resulted in Japan's recognizing Britain's special interest in the Indian frontier.[37] At the same time, the effect of Article II and the Preamble

---

[32] Gooch and Temperley, n.19, esp. at 140-151 and 164-169 for various drafting stages of the Agreement.

[33] FO 46/ 673, despatch No. 195A, the Marquess of Lansdowne to Sir M. Durand, Foreign Office, 31 July 1905.

[34] See below.

[35] FO 46/673, despatch No. 199, Sir C. MacDonald to the Marquess of Lansdowne, Tokio, 25 July 1905.

[36] Ibid.

[37] Gooch and Temperley, n.19, at 166-167.

meant that Japan would have to come to Britain's defence if the latter were attacked on the Indian frontier.[38]

Closely following the conclusion of the Agreement on 12 August 1905, the Marquess of Lansdowne undertook the presentation of this policy to the other Powers. His own draft memorandum of 3 September 1905 explained the Korea Article in these words:

> "Article III, dealing with the question of Korea, is deserving of especial attention. It recognises in the most emphatic language the paramount position which Japan will henceforth occupy in Korea, and her right to take in that country such measures of safeguarding and advancing her political, military and economic interests in that country, provided always that such measures are not contrary to the principle of equal opportunity for the commerce and industry of all nations.
>
> In this respect the new Agreement differs conspicuously from that of 1903. It has however become evident that Korea, owing to its close proximity to the Japanese Empire, its inability to stand alone, and the danger arising from its weakness as well as from its chronic misgovernment, must fall under the control and tutelage of Japan.
>
> H.M. Government observes with satisfaction that this point was readily conceded by Russia in the treaty of Peace recently concluded with Japan, and they [the British Government] have every reason to believe that similar views are held by other Powers with regard to the relations which should subsist between Japan and Korea."[39]

It is well known that the final printed version of this despatch, for instance to the British Ambassador in Paris, Sir F. Bertie, modified this memorandum. Firstly, the words "as well as from chronic misgovernment" were not even in the printed memorandum.[40] Furthermore, in the memorandum itself the words "and the danger arising from its weakness" were actually pencilled out.[41] When the Ambassador met the French Foreign Minister on 8 September, the latter had already received a translation of the despatch from the French Embassy in London. On his instructions the Foreign Minister struck out of the French translation the equivalent of the words "and the danger arising from its weakness". The French Minister went on to comment at length on the effect of Article III:

> "He said that he did not see anything in the Agreement to which France could take exception; that Russia could not be expected to like it; and on my suggesting that

---

[38] Ibid., at 165-166. There is an interesting report from the General Staff at the War Office, to the effect that such a Japanese undertaking was not reliable. A State could be expected to observe a treaty obligation it had entered into only when it was clearly in its national interest to do so. Japan had no such interest in defending Britain's Indian frontier and could not be expected to move essential troops away from its home defences for this purpose. FO 46/673, the Negotiation of the Anglo-Japanese Agreement, 1905.

[39] FO 46/672, at 17.

[40] FO 46/672, at 83, the Marquess of Lansdowne to Sir F. Bertie, Foreign Office, 6 September 1905.

[41] Ibid.

there was nothing in it hostile to her unless she desired to disturb us in India, and that it might even help to simplify matters in discussion between the Russian and British Governments, M. Rouvier said that the French Government would be very glad indeed if they could be of service in bringing the two Governments together. Finally, he said that perhaps, on the whole, Russia might not see so much to object to."[42]

Very soon afterwards the Japanese came to the British to (as it were) cash their blank cheque on Korea. On 26 September 1905 the Japanese communicated to the Marquess of Lansdowne their usual concerns about the Koreans "intriguing with foreign Powers, particularly manipulating the influence of Russia in Korea". This was contrary to the Korea-Japan Agreement of 22 August 1904, under which Korea agreed to consult Japan before taking any steps regarding important diplomatic affairs. Indeed, Korea's policy of manipulations may be said to have been one of the direct causes of the war with Russia. Japan knows that, with the new Agreement, it can expect HMG's support in assuming the charge of Korea's external relations. This it intends to do very shortly. The Marquess of Lansdowne replied:

> "I told Viscount Hayashi that, as he was aware, His Majesty's Government were entirely favourable to the development of Japanese influence in Korea, and that, so far as they were concerned, the Japanese Government were not likely to encounter any difficulties in giving effect to their policy".[43]

There is a further record of a meeting in Tokyo on 1 November, between Marquis Ito and MacDonald, in which the former told the latter the Japanese had now the agreement of both the American and Russian Governments to a Japanese Protectorate over Korea. The Russians merely wanted assurances that there would be no interference with the Emperor and the Imperial Family. Thus, the Japanese intended to proceed at once to conclude a Protectorate Agreement and appoint a Japanese functionary of similar standing and invested with similar powers to those possessed by Lord Cromer in Egypt. MacDonald reminded the Marquis that the secret of British success in Egypt was that the very best people were sent there, particularly Lord Cromer. He administered Egypt in a statesmanlike manner in the interests of the Egyptians. The same would be required for Korea. Marquis Ito agreed that such was the Japanese intention in following the British example in Egypt.[44]

Finally, on 22 November 1905, the Marquess of Lansdowne reports to MacDonald that he has received a copy of the Japan-Korea Protectorate Agreement. Viscount Hayashi added that the Japanese intention was to place Korea in the position occupied

---

[42] FO 46/672, at 110, despatch no. 333, Sir F. Bertie to the Marquess of Lansdowne, Paris, 9 September 1905.

[43] FO 46/590, at 123, despatch no. 151, from the Marquess of Lansdowne to Sir C. MacDonald, Foreign Office, 26 September 1905.

[44] FO 46/593, at 293, despatch no. 263A, Sir C. MacDonald to the Marquess of Lansdowne, Tokyo, 1 November 1905.

by a British Colony towards the mother-country in respect of its external relations. An accompanying declaration by the Japanese Government ended the year 1905 as it began, with a reference to Japanese security interests:

> "Relations of propinquity have made it necessary for Japan to take and exercise, for reasons closely connected with her own safety and repose, a paramount interests and influence in the political and military affairs of Corea."

It had appeared that a merely advisory function for Japan could not achieve its object and so the Governments of the two countries were in accord as to the absolute necessity for the Protectorate Agreement.[45]

4.   THE JAPANESE ANNEXATION OF KOREA IN 1910

There is very little of interest in the British Archives on this final stage of the Japanese-Korean story. Obviously, the British Minister has been withdrawn, but there was now a Consul General Bonar, who was to continue with opinions on Korean political affairs, similarly to Jordan. However, a note of disquiet does enter into his observations on the developments in Japanese colonial strategy. MacDonald was still the Ambassador in Tokyo and Sir Edward Grey had replaced the Marquess of Lansdowne as British Foreign Secretary. There is, however, a factor of note in British reactions to the Japanese annexation plans: the British Foreign Secretary did show some hesitation in accepting the Japanese annexation policy and tried, mildly, to discourage it. However, after not much pressure from Japan, the British gave way.

When it was clear that annexation was pending, Gaston de Bernhardt, from the Treaty Department, prepared a legal opinion on the expiry of Treaties where one of the parties loses its existence as an independent State. He made reference to an opinion of the Law Officers on the effect of HMG's conquest of Upper Burmah in 1885. They said that the effect of conquest was to give the Crown the right to extinguish the independent existence of the State and, if the Crown thinks fit to exercise this right, all of the treaties which the King or his predecessors may have made with Foreign Powers will thereupon cease to exist. Germany equally claimed, with the annexation of the Sultan of Zanzibar's territories on the east African main-land in 1890 that all of the Sultan's Treaties had been extinguished; the claim had not been disputed. The cases of Madagascar and the Transvaal were also considered. In the former case the French appeared to undertake certain obligations towards other Powers, but Britain did not succeed in holding France to these obligations when

---

[45] BDFA, n.18, Doc. 368, despatch no. 190, from the Marquess of Lansdowne to Sir C. MacDonald, Foreign Office, 22 November 1905 and Doc. 369, Declaration by the Japanese Government respecting Corea.

France annexed the island. The conquest of the Transvaal by Britain ended its treaties.[46]

The Agreement of 17 November 1905 between Korea and Japan provided in Article II: "The Government of Japan undertakes to see to the execution of the Treaties actually existing between Corea and other Powers". Viscount Hayashi declared on 23 November to Sir F. Campbell (in London) that Japan, "undertaking the duty of watching over the execution of the existing Treaties of that Country, they will see that those Treaties are maintained and respected, and they also engage not to prejudice in any way the legitimate, commercial and industrial interests of those Powers in Corea".[47]

Britain concluded a Treaty of Friendship and Commerce with Korea on 26 November 1888. In the event of Japan's annexing Korea, she would no doubt argue that that Treaty had lapsed on annexation, just as the French argued that British Treaties with Madagascar came to an end when that island became a French colony.[48]

Perhaps strangely, Sir Edward Grey took the opportunity of this advice to argue with the Japanese Ambassador in London that the Madagascar precedent was appropriate for Korea. Annexation would lead to Britain's and, more importantly, to many other Powers', losing their Treaty rights in Korea; thus, Sir Edward Grey "wished the Japanese Government to consider very carefully whether the moment was opportune for annexing Corea".[49] Britain was similarly hampered by Treaties with respect to Zanzibar, over which it had a Protectorate: "but we had hitherto not thought it worthwhile to create friction with other Powers by annexing Zanzibar, and declaring that these Treaties were at an end".[50] Shortly after this the Japanese Ambassador reiterated the concerns that led Japan towards annexation. The Protectorate had not brought tranquillity to Korea, and the people of Korea regarded their situation as temporary and unsettled. The policy of Japan was to secure the peace of Asia "and to secure the safety of Japan".[51] When the time came to annex Korea, Japan would be ready to make a declaration guaranteeing all the economic interests of the Powers.[52] This statement was followed immediately by a formal note from the Japanese Foreign Ministry distinguishing the Madagascar case from that of Korea. France and Britain had made mutual concessions with respect to Madagascar and Zanzibar. The French then annexed the former and asked the British to withdraw consular jurisdiction; however, France insisted on similar rights in Zanzibar, until the British had established a proper court system there. Neither side contested the

---

[46] FO 371/ 877, at 323, Memorandum respecting British Treaty Rights in Corea in the event of its annexation by Japan, Gaston de Bernhardt, Foreign Office, 6 July 1910.
[47] Ibid.
[48] Ibid. This confirmed MacDonald's own view of the legal situation, despatch no.26, Sir. C. MacDonald to Sir Edward Grey, Tokyo, 4 July 1910, FO 371/877, at 326.
[49] FO 371/877, despatch no. 116, Sir Edward Grey to Sir C. MacDonald, 14 July 1910.
[50] Ibid.
[51] FO 371/877, despatch no. 122, Sir Edward Grey to Sir C. MacDonald, 19 July 1910.
[52] Ibid.

principle that annexation extinguished treaties with the annexed country.[53] Gaston de Bernhardt confirmed again, at Sir Edward Grey's request, his advice that whatever economic concessions Japan made with respect to existing Treaty rights with Korea would be a matter of grace on Japan's part.[54] This did not discourage the Foreign Secretary from requesting the Japanese to consider the arrangement between the US and Spain over the Philippines, which envisaged a ten-year continuance of economic benefits.[55]

Meanwhile, in Seoul, the British Consul General Bonar composed a despatch upon the extent of British interests in Korea. He remarked that the appropriate way to protect British interests was for Japan and Britain to conclude with respect to these a special convention. This approach would not be unreasonable and need not tie Japanese hands with respect to future legislation.

> "Japan is not entering conquered territory, as she did in Formosa, though by the recent institution of the Board of Colonisation, Corea is to take its place with other colonies. Japan annexes Corea by consent of the Powers, if I may be permitted thus to describe the process which brings about annexation at any moment she may choose for this step."[56]

Sir Edward Grey accepted Japanese economic counter-proposals on 3 August 1910[57] and communicated his acceptance to MacDonald in Tokyo on 5 August.

> "The principle of annexation of Corea by Japan has been accepted by us, after consultation with the Board of Trade as to the best means of protecting the commercial interests of this country after the event takes place."[58]

On 23 August 1910 the Japanese Embassy in London transmitted the *Declaration of the Imperial Government as to the Annexation of Corea to the Empire of Japan.* This Declaration based itself upon an Agreement between the Governments of Japan and of Korea, with the approval of the Emperor of Japan and the Emperor of Corea. They regarded the annexation as necessary to securing reforms responsive to the situation and to securing sufficient guarantees for the future. The Declaration offered as well the economic guarantees for which the British had asked.[59]

Sir Edward Grey then informed MacDonald in Tokyo of these developments in terms of law and the politics of Anglo-Japanese relations as set out in Article III of the Anglo-Japanese Agreement. This Article did not contemplate annexation and the Agreement therefore entailed no positive obligation upon Britain to support

---

[53] FO 371/ 877, Mr Takaaki Kato to Sir Edward Grey, Japanese Embassy, London, 25 July 1910.
[54] FO 371/ 877, Annexation of Korea, Gaston de Bernhardt, 27 July 1910.
[55] FO 371/ 877, Sir Edward Grey to Mr Kato, Foreign Office, 3 August 1910.
[56] FO 371/ 878, despatch No. 44, Consul General Bonar to Sir Edward Grey, 20 July 1910.
[57] FO 371/ 877, Sir Edward Grey to Mr Kato, 3 August 1910.
[58] FO 371/ 877, Sir Edward Grey to Sir C. MacDonald, 5 August 1910.
[59] FO 371/878, Mr Kato to Sir Edward Grey, 23 August 1910.

annexation: "On the other hand, it seemed to me that it would be inconsistent with spirit of agreement for us to oppose the annexation". The Foreign Secretary had already informed the Japanese Ambassador that if his views were requested from other powers he would say that "we had no political objection to annexation of Corea by Japan".[60]

From Seoul, Bonar wrote a final, long, despatch in which he expressed the usual disparaging remarks about Koreans; however, this time he accompanied them with some disquieting concerns about the direction of Japanese colonial and imperial policy. He spoke of "the disappearance of the make-believe entity of the Corean Empire" and added:

"It may seem cruel, perhaps, to ignore in this connection the position of the Corean people who have caused so much to be heard of them in the last thirty years, but who really have done so little to further their own cause. But few foreigners, however, not full of anti-Japanese prejudice, will lament their political disappearance and possibly amongst the Coreans themselves, if the truth were known. The events of the last few weeks, culminating in a treaty of annexation, which, I understand from the very best sources, the former and present Emperors regard with the utmost indifference, add the soothing effect of honours, money, and enforced political inaction, have already reconciled the official and upper classes to their fate. ... (O)ne may safely assume that of the very small fraction of the population of Corea which is able to ponder at all on political matters, some will sullenly, others cheerfully, but most with the utmost indifference, accept their entire subjugation to Japan which is to be inaugurated tomorrow...".[61]

However, Bonar concluded with a disquisition on *The Aspirations of Japan.* He begins:

"Apart from the actual period at which Corea was to become an integral portion of the Japanese Empire, no doubt ever existed, one presumes, as to the present sequel of the Russo-Japanese war. The term 'aspirations' is not intended to apply to the fulfilment of Japan's legitimate wish to acquire definitely the ownership of Corea, but it would be futile to disregard the fact that this entry into possession carries with it the possibilities and desires which Japan may also hereafter consider legitimate. If one is to understand that the present action of Japan has the approval of all the foreign Powers, this approval will become, I venture to think, a stepping stone to the formation of a conviction in the mind of Japan (which probably already exists) that liberty of action beyond the limits of Corea has now become her right".[62]

Thus, within ten years, Japan will advance the boundary of its Empire beyond the Yalu river by many miles. There are great strategic advantages to Japan in its

---

[60] FO 371/878, despatch No. 26, Sir Edward Grey to Sir C. MacDonald, 25 August 1910.
[61] FO 371/878, despatch No. 58, Consul General Bonar to Sir Edward Grey, 28 August 1910.
[62] Ibid.

annexing Korea. The power of Japan will be consolidated to an extent which as yet the world seems hardly willing to recognize. The annexation is not merely a "foregone conclusion": it is of the utmost importance from an international point of view. "I have in other despatches ventured to express the opinion that Japan on the Yalu and her railway to Mukden constitute a threat to the so-called territorial integrity of China."[63] The annexation "has placed Japan in a position to exact a far greater price for her friendship than hitherto – a price larger possibly than those who have been and could be her friends may be willing to pay".[64]

5.   CONCLUSION

The main weight of the Korean arguments about Japan's illegal seizure of Korea rests upon the invalidity of the Protectorate and Annexation Treaties. They were presented by Japan to the international community as voluntary arrangements freely entered into by Korea. On this basis Korea freely integrated itself into Japan. All of the evidence recently cited by Korean international lawyers and historians suggests that the Treaties were induced through coercion, indeed to the point that the Treaties may not have even been signed and sealed correctly by the Korean authorities.[65] It is perfectly understandable that such arguments should be mounted. The standard textbook *International Law* by Oppenheim, in its second edition of 1911, refers to the absorption of Korea into Japan as having occurred voluntarily as a result of a Treaty. In the same sentence Oppenheim contrasts this with subjugation.[66] Other British textbooks treat the matter similarly: Phillipson's fifth English edition of Wheaton's *Elements of International Law* refers to Korea's Declaration of Independence in 1895 and to the two Agreements of 1904 and 1905 giving Japan an advisory role in Korea's foreign affairs and establishing a Protectorate. Nonetheless, after recounting these developments Phillipson ends his discussion with the sentence: "In 1910, however, Japan annexed Korea".[67] It is undisputed that, after this, Korea had ceased to exist as a State.

The difficulty with the contemporary Korean international law arguments, taken alongside the evidence of the State practice of the Great Powers and in particular of Great Britain (or the British Empire), is that the central issue in Korean-Japanese relations was whether Korea, in the first place, qualified under international law as a State. This question, Korea's capacity to exercise the functions of a State, is prior to the question whether the exercise of a legally recognizable capacity has been abused by other States. The actual quality of Japanese-Korean relations, revealed also through the British archives, would not have been known to Oppenheim. His treatment of the issue must therefore be regarded as superficial. However, the exact

---

[63] Ibid.
[64] Ibid.
[65] See literature cited in n.1.
[66] L. Oppenheim, International Law, Vol. I, 2nd edition, 1911, at 127.
[67] Wheaton's Elements of International Law, fifth English edition by C. Phillipson (1916), at 68.

circumstances surrounding the conclusion of the Korean-Japanese Agreements and Treaties were fully known to British officials, who recognized in Japanese-Korean relations the dimension of coercion and even violence surrounding the conclusion of the Agreements and other treaties, but considered this to be of no significance. Instead, the British stressed the confusion and incompetence of the Korean authorities and, above all, their inability to manage Korean affairs effectively so as to ensure the independence of their country against pressures coming both from Russia and from Japan.

It might appear antithetical to the very idea of law to say that a State does not have a right to exist unless it is able to resist attempts to conquer it by neighbours that are overwhelmingly more powerful. However, the concept of international order and security at the time did suppose that where a country is unable to assure its own defence against one potential aggressor, some other "overwhelmingly powerful neighbour" will inevitably intervene, across its territory and against the other "overwhelmingly powerful neighbour", to defend the latter's own vital interests. Oppenheim himself described Japan's occupation of Korea during the Russo-Japanese war as necessitated by the inability of Korea to defend itself against Russian encroachment. He described Japan's action as an intervention in Japan's own vital interests, to liberate Korea from Russian occupation.[68]

Obviously, the question whether, at this time, British judgements on the topic of Korea were justified is completely open. The records kept in the National Archive are unusually tidy. While supposedly secret, they are in the form of so-called Confidential Prints, virtually a form of publication. It is possible to wonder whether the British could have chosen to see a different picture. There are glimpses in the private papers of Jordan that suggest a more complex picture of the quality of Japanese-Korean relations. For instance, a very significant figure in one of the Agreements was Mr Megata, appointed Japanese Financial Adviser. In a hand-written letter of 3 October 1905, Jordan confided to Campbell in the Foreign Office, that Megata was a curious choice for the Japanese to have made. Jordan described him as an enigma to everyone in Seoul:

> "He is a fidgety nervous sort of man who seems unable to concentrate his attention upon anything for any length of time. The explanation generally given is that he is a heavy drinker and I am afraid it is only too true. The Japs, while admitting his eccentricities, give him credit for great financial ability, but character is of more importance than ability in Japanese Agents in this country where finances are the pivot of the whole administration".[69]

It is quite possible that the failings of the Koreans were only slightly less significant than those of the Japanese, the more it appeared to the British that the Russians might succeed in occupying the country and displacing the Japanese. In that case, the main failing of the Koreans would have been an insufficiently focussed deterrence

---

[68] L. Oppenheim, International Law, Vol. II, 2nd edition, 1912, at 387-388.
[69] FO 350/3, at 80.

of Russians; Korea may have been making the best of the qualities of its Allies and friends, and the worst of those of unreliable strangers.

At the same time it was not only the British who considered Korea unable to survive as an independent State: Britain secured American agreement and the acquiescence of the other Powers. However wrong the view might have been, it was held effectively and put into force. Since the collapse of the moral intuitionism of the natural law tradition at the end of the eighteenth century, international law has been a predominantly positivist discipline, relying upon the force of those social convictions which actually hold sway in international society. Social convictions acquire legal character in the positivist tradition when they become so strong that society, here international society, is able and willing to apply coercion in carrying them out. What the record of the British National Archive shows is that Britain took a lead in encouraging Japan to exercise precisely such a force against a country whose perceived weakness was regarded as a serious source of instability and a potential threat to the peace. Undoubtedly, such a concept of international law needs to be challenged in its very foundations.

It is easy enough for histories of colonialism and international law to demonstrate that powerful countries use the law as a weapon to suppress the weak. What is much more difficult to mount is a criticism of a systematic approach to law, in this case, positivism, which rests upon a theory of validity immanent to actual social practice. Natural law theory offered a transcendent standard with which the arrogance of human consciousness could be challenged. However, its place is now profoundly contested. The question still remains: how can an individual, never mind a collective entity, have a sense of obligation that is not simply a socially or historically conditioned response to circumstances, whether immediately (in the sense of contemporaneously), external, or historically acquired? In another place I try to argue that the search for a way out of the inert body of unconscious prejudice is the real challenge for the "phenomenological international lawyer".[70] Whether there is an "ought" beyond the self is one of the first questions of metaphysics. Yet there is arguably an "ought" within the self that can, through an inter-subjective dialectic, reach beyond the closure of the self-as-object to the self-as-subject-in-relation. It is precisely such an inter-subjective dialectic that the contributors to the monthly magazine *Sekai* have undertaken.

---

[70] Anthony Carty, "Scandinavian realism and phenomenological approaches to statehood and general custom in international law", 14 EJIL (2003), at 817-841.

HUMAN RIGHTS IN SOUTH ASIA: ABUSE AND DEGRADATION[*]

Annapurna Waughray[**]

1. INTRODUCTION

This article is an expanded version of a paper[1] presented at a symposium held in March 2003 at Manchester Metropolitan University, Manchester, England. The purpose of the symposium was to examine, within the global context, the current situation regarding human rights in South Asia, to identify the obstacles to the full realization of human rights in the sub-continent, and to consider how those obstacles might be overcome. Four substantive papers[2] were presented, focusing on specific human rights issues in South Asia, the themes of which were explored and developed in small workshops. This article presents a detailed overview of the issues discussed in the symposium and in particular the areas addressed in three of the substantive papers.[3]

Two observations in a recent Indian publication on human rights address directly the reality of human rights in South Asia today: firstly, that "no progress will ever make human rights superfluous or out of date, so long as humans face poverty and cruelty"; secondly, that "upholding human rights is to reverse the tendency to eliminate people because they are different, as no one has the right to say that everybody

---

[*] This article bears the title of the symposium organized at Manchester Metropolitan University in March 2003 by Burjor Avari, Senior Lecturer in Indian and South Asian History, Department of History and Economic History, and Coordinator for Multicultural Studies, Manchester Metropolitan University.

[**] Senior Lecturer in Law, School of Law, Manchester Metropolitan University.

[1] A. Waughray, "Abuse and degradation: human rights in South Asia", unpublished, 2003.

[2] D.A. Ghanchi, "Human rights in a fractured society: frustrations and fulfilment of the Indian experiment", unpublished, 2003; N. Malik, "The treatment of religious communities in Pakistan: the erosion of Jinnah's Vision", unpublished, 2003; J. Rehman, "South Asian Association for Regional Cooperation (SAARC): constitutionalism, regional peace and human rights", unpublished, 2003; U. Baxi, "Globalisation and human rights: winners and losers", taken from U. Baxi, *People's Report on Human Rights Education: Introduction*, revised final text, 2002.

[3] *Ibid.,* Ghanchi, Malik and Rehman.

Asian Yearbook of International Law, Volume 10 (B.S. Chimni *et al.,* eds.)

© 2005 Koninklijke Brill NV. Printed in The Netherlands, pp. 25-56.

should be like himself [*sic*]."[4] These comments should not be considered as applicable only to the Indian experience. The reality of human rights across South Asia today is that millions face poverty and cruelty on a daily basis, whilst the tendency in the region to seek to eliminate 'the other' on grounds of religion, gender, caste, ethnicity, or nationality appears undiminished.

Constitutional and legislative protection of human rights is far from lacking in the region as a whole. Nevertheless, the South Asian experience illustrates the fact that "commitment on paper to human rights does not of itself change the reality on the ground".[5] If "failure to act is caused by not just lack of knowledge, but also a kind of immunity to realities",[6] the reality in the region, as evidenced by the speakers at the Manchester symposium, is that human rights violations are in large part due to a reluctance or inability to act in the face of realities, and in smaller but significant part to the wilful negation of human rights by the State and its agents, and by non-State actors – private individuals, organizations and corporations – from whose behaviour the State, under international human rights law and national legislation, has a duty to protect its citizens.

Section 2 of this paper presents an overview of the development and application of international human rights law and highlights those factors which continue to impede the full realization of human rights in South Asia. Section 3 considers the extent to which human rights and fundamental freedoms, particularly the rights of vulnerable groups and minorities, are respected in the context of South Asia. Sections 3.1 and 3.2 are based on the symposium paper by D.A. Ghanchi on the frustrations and fulfilments of the Indian experiment, and on Nadeem Malik's case study of the treatment of Ahmadi Muslims in Pakistan. Section 3.3 considers the issue of caste-based discrimination. The discussion in the first part of Section 4 is extracted from the symposium paper presented by Javaid Rehman and considers the role, both current and potential, of the South Asian Association for Regional Cooperation (SAARC) as a force for peace, security, development, and the protection of human rights. There follows an examination of the role and potential of existing fora for the promotion and protection of human rights in South Asia in working towards the establishment of a sub-regional human rights system for South Asia. Section 5 offers some concluding thoughts. It is hoped that the preliminary observations in this article will contribute towards the stimulation of further debate on human rights and the rule of law, the treatment of women and religious minorities, the issue of caste discrimination, and the possibilities for greater regional cooperation in South Asia on human rights issues.

---

[4] C.J. Nirmal (ed.), *Human Rights in India* (New Delhi: OUP India, 2000), at xxvii-xxviii.
[5] *Ibid.,* at xxvii.
[6] *Ibid.*

2.   INTERNATIONAL HUMAN RIGHTS LAW AND SOUTH ASIA

The *1993 Vienna Declaration and Programme of Action on Human Rights*[7] provides a useful starting point for our discussion. Unanimously endorsed by the one hundred and seventy-one states (including India, Pakistan, Bangladesh, Sri Lanka, Nepal, and Myanmar) represented at the UN-sponsored World Conference on Human Rights in Vienna in June 1993, the Declaration and Programme of Action categoric-ally affirms that all human rights derive from the dignity and worth inherent in the human person,[8] and that human rights and fundamental freedoms are the birthright of all human beings.[9] According to Article 1 of the Vienna Declaration, the universal nature of the rights and freedoms expressed in the Charter of the United Nations, human rights instruments and international law is beyond question.[10] At Article 5 the Vienna Declaration affirms that all human rights are universal, indivisible, interdependent, and interrelated; there can be no hierarchy or ranking of rights and no prioritizing of one category of rights over another. Notwithstanding the emphasis placed on "the significance of national and regional peculiarities and various historical, cultural and religious backgrounds" by leaders of Asian states, as expressed in the Final Declaration of the Regional Meeting for Asia of the 1993 World Conference on Human Rights (the "Bangkok Declaration"),[11] Article 5 of the Vienna Declaration explicitly addresses, and disposes of, two issues central to the debate on the universal-ity of human rights: firstly, whether there exists a core set of universally applicable fundamental rights (the answer is in the affirmative), and secondly, the nature of the interrelationship between the different types or 'generations' of rights.

It is widely acknowledged that no one civilization, religion or philosophy has a monopoly on the notion of the importance of human dignity and the protection thereof,[12] yet the origins of the modern human rights movement are generally traced to the articulation in the seventeenth and eighteenth centuries within the Western European liberal democratic tradition of certain specific rights and freedoms which derive from natural rights and natural law philosophies and which constitute the classic 'civil liberties' or so-called 'first generation' civil and political rights. The presumption was that such rights were natural, inherent and inalienable, the birthright of all men; although, as the foregoing suggests, these egalitarian ideals did not necessarily extend to women, children, slaves, the colonized, the poor, the handi-capped, or the mentally ill.

---

[7] 1993 Vienna Declaration and Programme of Action on Human Rights: UN Doc A/CONF.157/23 (1993).

[8] *Ibid.*, Preamble.

[9] *Ibid.*, Part I, Article 1.

[10] *Ibid.*

[11] Final Declaration of the Regional Meeting for Asia of the 1993 World Conference on Human Rights: UN Doc A/CONF.157/ASRM/8-A/CONF.157/PC/59, Article 8.

[12] *See* A. Robertson and J. Merrills, *Human Rights in the World* (Manchester: Manchester University Press, 1996), at Chapter 1, and A. Sen, "Human rights and Asian values", *The New Republic*, 14 – 21 July 1997.

While the late nineteenth century onwards saw an emerging recognition at national level of certain individual rights or protections for specific individuals,[13] the position at the international level was very different. Prior to World War II international law was, subject to very limited exceptions,[14] exclusively concerned with the facilitation and regulation of relations between States; its scope did not extend to the treatment by States of persons within their own borders, such matters being considered as falling strictly within the parameters of domestic jurisdiction.[15] A growing realization of the extent of the human rights violations perpetrated during the war provided the catalyst for change; the end of the war signalled the start of the use of international law to identify and set legally binding universal human rights standards and to create mechanisms to implement, monitor and enforce such rights. The 1945 Charter of the United Nations introduced for the first time in an international instrument the notion that the promotion and protection of fundamental human rights was a legitimate matter of concern of the international community and of international law.[16] From its inception in 1945 the United Nations has played a crucial role in the development of international human rights law.

The end of World War II also marked the start of a long process, beginning with the International Military Tribunals at Nuremberg and Tokyo and culminating in the recent creation of the International Criminal Court, of seeking to hold individuals accountable under international law for gross human rights violations committed both in war and in peacetime. This principle was reaffirmed and reinforced in the 1998 Rome Statute for the International Criminal Court which has, in addition to war crimes, jurisdiction over the crime of genocide and crimes against humanity regardless of whether commission occurs in the course of armed conflict or in peacetime.[17] The Rome Statute, which came into force on 1 July 2002, has been signed by 139

---

[13] For example, the 1829 British prohibition of the custom of *Sati* (widow immolation) in India; the United Kingdom's 1884 Reform Act which established the principle of "one man, one vote" and gave most, but not all, adult males the right to vote (universal male suffrage was not introduced in Britain until 1918, universal female suffrage in 1928).

[14] The abolition of slavery; the 1864 Geneva Convention for the Amelioration of the Condition of the Wounded on the Field of Battle and the subsequent development of international humanitarian law; the establishment in 1919 of the International Labour Organization and the subsequent promulgation of international standards for the protection of workers; the establishment by the League of Nations of mandated territories and agreements for the protection of minorities; *See* Robertson and Merrills, n. 12, at 15-23.

[15] *See* Robertson and Merrills, n. 12, at 1-2; *see* also D. McGoldrick, *The Human Rights Committee* (Oxford: Clarendon Press, 1996), at 4, and A. Steiner and P. Alston, *International Human Rights in Context* (Oxford: Oxford University Press, 2002), at 126-135.

[16] Charter of the United Nations 1945, Preamble, Article 1, Article 55, Article 56, Article 62, Article 68, Article 76. The inclusion in the Charter of references to human rights was largely at the behest of the Latin American and smaller states, NGOs and pressure groups. Suggestions that a "Bill of Rights" be incorporated in the Charter were rejected. *See* McGoldrick, n. 15, at 4 and J. Rehman, *International Human Rights Law: A Practical Approach* (Harlow: Longman, 2003), at Chs. 2 and 3.

[17] Rome Statute of the International Criminal Court, Articles 5-8. UN Doc A/Conf 183/9.

states and ratified by 92 to date.[18] The level of signing and ratification of the Rome Statute by South Asian states is poor: Afghanistan has acceded to the Statute; Bangladesh has signed but not ratified it, and India, Pakistan, Sri Lanka, and Nepal have neither signed nor ratified the Statute.

On 9 December 1948 the UN General Assembly adopted the Convention on the Prevention and Punishment of the Crime of Genocide.[19] This Convention defined the crime of genocide for the first time in an international instrument of binding nature and provided for individuals accused of genocide to be tried either in national courts or by a putative international criminal tribunal, although the Convention itself contained no provision for the creation of such an organ. Just a day later the Universal Declaration of Human Rights was adopted by the UN General Assembly as a "common standard of achievement for all peoples and all nations".[20] Intended as an authoritative interpretation of the human rights provisions of the United Nations Charter rather than as a legally-binding instrument, the Universal Declaration was adopted without dissenting votes, albeit eight abstentions,[21] despite encompassing a wide range of rights in addition to the classic civil and political rights: economic, social and cultural rights ('second generation' rights) such as the right to work, the right to social security, the right to an adequate standard of living, the right to education, and the right to leisure; and 'third generation' or group rights such as the right to a suitable social and international order.[22]

The intention of following the Universal Declaration with a single norm-setting instrument and a second instrument establishing mechanisms for enforcement was disrupted by the onset of the Cold War; in the arena of human rights, this manifested itself in the form of intense ideological disagreement over the nature and relative importance of civil and political *versus* economic and social rights, the justiciability of the two types of rights, and the methods for implementing, monitoring and enforcing them. At the same time, the post-WWII decolonization process resulted in the arrival on the world stage of newly independent States, primarily from the South, many of whom prioritized economic and social rights over civil and political rights.[23] The inability of the world community to reach agreement on a single, comprehensive rights instrument underwritten by uniform mechanisms for enforcement resulted in the adoption in 1966, a full eighteen years after the Universal Declaration, of two legally-binding standard-setting instruments, one on economic, social and cultural rights and the second on civil and political rights, each containing separate and

---

[18] *See* website of the Rome Statute of the International Criminal Court: http://www.un.org/law/icc/statute/romefra.htm.

[19] Adopted 9 December 1948. Entered into force 12 January 1951. GA Res. 206A III. 78 U.N.T.S. 277. The Genocide Convention has been ratified and/or acceded to by Afghanistan, Bangladesh, India, Nepal, Pakistan and Sri Lanka.

[20] Adopted 10 December 1948. GA Resolution 217 A(III). UN Doc.A/811.

[21] Byelorussia, Czechoslovakia, Poland, Ukraine, USSR, Yugoslavia, Saudi Arabia, and South Africa.

[22] See Rehman, n. 16, at Chap. 3.

[23] *See* McGoldrick, n. 15, at Chap. 1.

different mechanisms of monitoring and enforcement;[24] together with the Universal Declaration, they form the International Bill of Rights. It is noteworthy that in practice few States have ratified one Covenant yet not the other, an indication that States indeed generally consider the rights in both Covenants to be interrelated and indivisible.[25]

In 1965 the UN-sponsored International Convention on the Elimination of All Forms of Racial Discrimination (the "Race Convention") was adopted.[26] Over the course of the next three decades the series of UN-sponsored, specialized international human rights treaties that followed the Race Convention and the two Covenants provided for the elimination of discrimination against women,[27] the prohibition of torture,[28] and the rights of the child.[29] A further Convention, on the rights of migrant workers and their families, came into force on 1 July 2003.[30] This network of free-standing treaties complements an array of bodies and mechanisms that are part of, or derive from, the Charter and the UN structure itself. Between them these treaties, their monitoring bodies[31] and the various UN bodies and mechanisms[32] purport both to set universal international human rights norms, and to monitor and enforce them.

---

[24] International Covenant on Economic, Social and Cultural Rights. Adopted 16 December 1966. Entered into force 3 January 1976. GA Res. 2200A (XXI). UN Doc. A/6316 (1966). 999 *UNTS* 3. International Covenant on Civil and Political Rights. Adopted 16 December 1966. Entered into force 23 March 1976. GA Res. 2200A (XXI). UN Doc. A/6316 (1966). 999 *UNTS* 171.

[25] Amongst South Asian States, Pakistan is alone in having failed to ratify either Covenant. For full State-by-State ratification details *see* http://www.bayefsky.com/.

[26] Adopted 21 December 1965. Entered into force 4 January 1969. GA Res. 2106 (XX). 660 *UNTS* 195. Ratified by Afghanistan (6 July 1983); Bangladesh (11 June 1979); India (3 December 1968); Nepal (30 January 1971); Pakistan (21 September 1966); Sri Lanka (18 February 1982).

[27] Convention on the Elimination of All Forms of Discrimination Against Women. Adopted 18 December 1979. Entered into force 3 September 1981. GA Res. 34/ 180. UN Doc. A/34/46. 1249 *UNTS* 13. Ratified by Afghanistan (1 April 1987); Bangladesh (6 November 1984); India (9 July 1993); Nepal (22 April 1991); Pakistan (12 March 1996); Sri Lanka (5 October 1981).

[28] Convention Against Torture and other Cruel, Inhuman or Degrading Treatment or Punishment. Adopted 10 Dec.1984. Entered into force 26 June 1987. GA Res. 39/46. UN Doc. A/39/51 (1984). 1465 *UNTS* 85. Ratified by Afghanistan (1 April 1987); Bangladesh (5 October 1998); Nepal (14 May 1991); Sri Lanka (3 January 1994). Signed but not ratified by India (14 October 1997).

[29] Convention on the Rights of the Child. Adopted 20 November 1989. Entered into force 2 September 1990. GA Res. 44/25. UN Doc. A/44/49 (1989). 1577 *UNTS* 3. Ratified by Afghanistan (28 March 1994); Bangladesh (3 August 1990); India (11 December 1992); Nepal (14 September 1990); Pakistan (12 November 1990); Sri Lanka (12 July 1991).

[30] International Convention on the Protection of the Rights of All Migrant Workers and Members of Their Families. Adopted 18 December 1990. Entered into force 1 July 2003. GA Res. 45/148. UN Doc. A/48/49 (1993).

[31] Committee on the Elimination of All Forms of Racial Discrimination (CERD); Committee on Economic, Social and Cultural Rights; Human Rights Committee (HRC); Committee on the Elimination of All Forms of Discrimination Against Women (CEDAW); Committee Against Torture (CAT); Committee on the Rights of the Child (CRC). For a full discussion of the treaty monitoring bodies *see* Rehman, n. 16, at Ch. 4, 5, 10-15.

[32] *See* Rehman, n. 16, at Ch. 2.

Despite such achievements at international level in the setting of standards and the establishment of implementation, monitoring and enforcement mechanisms, the realization at regional and national level of universal human rights as envisaged in the 1993 Vienna Declaration remains impeded by a variety of factors, many of which are pertinent to the relatively poor progress of the enjoyment of human rights in the context of South Asia. Across the region there are widespread violations of international human rights treaty obligations; these may result from institutional failure, or from being committed by agents of the State such as the police and the military or by private individuals whose behaviour the State fails to prevent or punish. At national level the lack of accessible and effective remedies, coupled with a lack of political will on the part of national and local law enforcement bodies and, at times, also of the judiciary to implement remedies that are in theory available, continues to render basic rights illusory, whilst at international level enforcement mechanisms are often inaccessible, slow and ultimately ineffective since the power to reach a judicial settlement or impose sanctions is lacking. Universal ratification of international human rights treaties has still not been achieved, although some, such as the Convention on the Rights of the Child, have achieved near-universal status; conversely, where States have ratified, there is widespread failure fully to implement in their national legal systems the human rights obligations which they have undertaken at international level. Reservations incompatible with the object and purpose of the treaty[33] continue to be entered to international human rights treaties, a problem particularly acute in relation to the Convention on the Elimination of all Forms of Discrimination against Women (the "Convention on Women"). The practice of entering such reservations is commonly defended and justified on the grounds of culture, tradition or religion.[34] The 1993 World Conference on Human Rights urged both the universal ratification of international human rights treaties and the avoidance as far as possible of resort to reservations.[35]

3.   RESPECT FOR HUMAN RIGHTS IN SOUTH ASIA: CURRENT ISSUES

The issues examined by the Manchester symposium centre on the extent to which the current situation regarding human rights in South Asia is compatible with universal human rights and fundamental freedoms as articulated in the *1993 Vienna Declaration and Programme of Action*, the threat to human rights posed by the current wave of

---

[33] On treaty reservations generally, *see* Vienna Convention on the Law of Treaties, adopted 22 May 1969, entered into force 27 January 1980, 1155 *UNTS* 331; advisory opinion on *Reservations to the Genocide Convention*, ICJ Rep. 1951, at 15.
[34] *See* for example the reservation of Bangladesh to Articles 2 and 16(1)c of the CEDAW on the grounds that these Articles conflict with *Sharia* law.
[35] *See* n. 7, Part I, Article 26. Among South Asian states ratification of all but the Migrant Workers' Convention is universal, apart from India, which has signed but not ratified the Torture Convention, and Pakistan, which has neither signed nor ratified the two International Covenants and the Torture Convention.

globalization,[36] and how respect for and effective enjoyment of human rights in the sub-continent might be improved. South Asia is home to one in five of the world's population. It has huge diversities of language, religion, race, and culture. It has experienced invasion, conquest, immigration and emigration, colonialism, partition, conflict, territorial disputes, and terrorism; it now finds itself at the epicentre of the phenomenon known as globalization. It exhibits, and permits, extremes of poverty, social exclusion, wealth, and power. It is also a region where the human rights of its inhabitants are regularly violated and where remedies for such violations are all too frequently denied, despite *de jure* protection provided at national level under State Constitutions[37] and by a complex web of legislation, regulations, and statutory and constitutional bodies and institutions.

3.1.   Globalization, poverty and the right to development

Many millions in the region lack a standard of living adequate for their health and well-being, including housing, access to clean and safe water, medical care and access to basic education; these in turn result in social exclusion.[38] Security of food and nutrition is of crucial importance in the region as a whole, particularly for the most impoverished. Production is generally good, but equality of access to food, and to distribution, remains poor. Whilst starvation deaths are relatively rare, chronic under-nourishment and malnourishment, especially amongst children, are endemic across the region. The 1993 World Conference on Human Rights affirmed that extreme poverty and social exclusion constitute a violation of human dignity.[39] All States have a duty to promote the human rights of the poorest and to foster participation by the poorest people in the decision-making processes of the communities where

---

[36] *See* U. Baxi, *The Unreason of Globalization and the Reason of Human Rights* (Mumbai: Dept. of Sociology, University of Mumbai, 1999); *see* also UN Sub Commission on the Promotion and Protection of Human Rights, Preliminary Report by J. Oloka-Onyango and D. Udagama on Globalisation and its impact on the full enjoyment of human rights (E/CN.4/Sub.2/2000/13); Committee on Economic, Social and Cultural Rights, Statement on globalisation and economic, social and cultural rights, 11 May 1998.

[37] The constitutions of Bangladesh, India, Nepal, Pakistan, and Sri Lanka distinguish between civil and political rights, typically justiciable and expressed as fundamental rights; and economic, social and cultural rights, typically non-justiciable and expressed as fundamental or directive principles of State policy.

[38] *See* for example the 2001 India Census according to which there are 321 million illiterate people in India out of a population of 1 billion; only 12.3% of rural households have electricity, toilet and safe drinking water; half of all children are malnourished; one third of the population lives below the national poverty line. *See* P. Radhakrishnan, *India Development Report* (New Delhi: OUP India, 2002); Pakistan has a population of some 140 million, 59% of whom are illiterate; one third do not have access to safe water; 38% of children under five are malnourished and 34% of the population lives below the national poverty line.

[39] *See* n. 7, Part I, Article 25; *see* also n. 7, Part I, Article 14: "The existence of widespread extreme poverty inhibits the full and effective enjoyment of human rights; its immediate alleviation and eventual elimination must remain a high priority for the international community."

they live.[40] The World Conference on Human Rights also reaffirmed the right to development, as established in the UN Declaration on the Right to Development,[41] as a universal and inalienable right and as an integral part of fundamental human rights, and called on the world community to help alleviate the external debt burden of developing countries in order to supplement the efforts of the governments of such countries.[42] Conversely, a lack of development is no excuse for human rights failures and abuses; the right to development requires effective policies at national level as well as equitable economic relations and a favourable economic environment at the international level, and the lack of development should not be invoked to justify the abridgment of internationally recognized human rights.[43]

3.2.   Human rights in a fractured society: democracy, the rule of law, governance and human rights[44]

Democracy, development and respect for human rights and fundamental freedoms are interdependent and mutually reinforcing.[45] The strengthening by national governments of national legislation, institutions and infrastructures that uphold the rule of law and democracy is a prerequisite to the individual enjoyment of universal human rights and fundamental freedoms.[46] The discussion in this sub-section is extracted from the symposium paper presented by D.A. Ghanchi, former Pro-Vice-Chancellor of North Gujarat University,[47] in which he examines the impact of sectarian friction, polarization and societal fragmentation on democracy, the rule of law and human rights in India. Ghanchi presents examples of violations of the right to life in its broadest sense as a means of examining the fault-lines in Indian society. Describing India as "a fractured society", he argues that administrative inefficiency, corruption, the arbitrary exercise of power by State authorities, and divisive, manipulative and self-serving politics threaten to undermine the rule of law, democracy, and human rights.

The Indian Constitution of 1950 laid the foundation for a pluralistic, multi-cultural, secular, democratic society. Its building blocks were to be a polity based on the rule of law; a society based on freedom, justice, equality, social security, and non-discrimination; an economy based on the equity, egalitarianism and prosperity of all; a government free from corruption, nepotism, favouritism, communalism, and inefficiencies; and an education system that should be universal, compulsory and free

---

[40] *See* n. 7, Part I, Article 25.
[41] Adopted 4 Dec.1986. GA Res. 41/128. U.N. Doc. A/41/53 (1986).
[42] *See* n. 7, Part I, Article 12.
[43] *Ibid.*, Article 10.
[44] Ghanchi, n. 2.
[45] *See* n. 7, Article 8.
[46] *Ibid.*, Article 34.
[47] Ghanchi, n. 2.

at the primary stage, and which should act as a tool of national development: economic, social, cultural, moral, and spiritual. Civil and political rights were enshrined in Articles 12-35 of the Indian Constitution as "Fundamental Rights" and made enforceable by law,[48] while economic and social rights were listed as "Directive Principles of State Policy".[49] However, Ghanchi finds that whilst India has one of the most democratic Constitutions in the world, "its institutions – the legislature, the executive and the judiciary, and their operators, namely the politicians, the bureaucracy and the functionaries in every domain of administration, government and management – have proved abysmally short in performance".[50]

3.2.1.   The right to life

At its most elementary level the right to life refers to bare physical existence. In its most comprehensive form it signifies life with dignity, comprising the availability of adequate food, clean water, shelter and clothing, access to health and medical care, education, a safe and clean environment, good governance, and freedom from corruption as well as freedom from ill-treatment, discrimination and persecution. Violation of any of these elements entails abridgement of the right to life.

3.2.2.   Mass killings, the role of the state and the responsibility of the judiciary

Mass killings such as have occurred in the recent past in Bosnia Herzegovina and Kosovo are not unknown in India. Countless people have been killed in communal riots that have occurred year after year since Partition in 1947. The right to life of religious minorities is regularly violated as a result of sectarian violence, such as the massacre of Sikhs in Delhi in 1984, and the recent communal violence in Gujarat which has claimed upwards of three thousand lives and destroyed businesses and property worth billions of rupees. At least as great a disaster as the loss of life and property is the damage to the psyche of minorities wrought by fear, hatred, exclusion, and persecution. Communal violence, with the displacement it entails, has resulted in tens of thousands of Indian citizens' becoming refugees in their own country. Muslims are the largest religious minority in India and constitute 12% of the population or around 150 million people. During the violence in Gujarat in 2002 an estimated five hundred thousand Muslims fled their homes. When the temporary relief camps provided by the State government closed, the displaced were left with no help from the State yet fearful of returning to their demolished homes and businesses in the face of hostility and socio-economic exclusion.[51] In specific cases the State itself has been found wanting not only for failing to prevent or control com-

---

[48]   Constitution of India, Part III.
[49]   Constitution of India, Part IV.
[50]   Ghanchi, n. 2, at 2.
[51]   Ghanchi, n. 2, at 1-3.

munal violence, but even for direct involvement in it.[52] Ghanchi is critical of the role of the judiciary for their perceived failure in restraining and punishing the perpetrators of violations of the right to life of the Muslim minority in Gujarat. He cites the observations of a leading lawyer and human rights activist in Gujarat on the role and responsibility of the judiciary:

> "As democracy and human rights of all do not depend upon majoritarianism alone, it is the constitutional responsibility and obligation of the judiciary to prevent and deter the latter from encroaching upon and undermining the former."[53]

The development of effective national legal systems was identified by the 1993 World Conference on Human Rights as being central to the achievement of human rights.[54] In the light of this, Ghanchi argues that the apparent reluctance of the State and the judiciary to defend the interests of the Muslim minority in India represents a serious challenge to the rule of law.[55]

3.2.3. *Detained persons: violation of the right to life by state agency*[56]

Aside from what he terms "the phenomenon of mass frenzy" Ghanchi identifies the security forces, police and prison authorities as a significant source of violation of the right to life. An estimated four hundred people a year are killed in incidents involving the police, euphemistically known as "encounters", which occur both inside and outside police stations and jails. Similarly, it is estimated that custodial deaths – deaths and disappearances of prison inmates at the hands of the prison authorities – claim a further four hundred lives a year. The torture and ill-treatment of prison inmates are widespread and have "become a regular part of jail administration".

---

[52] Report of the Citizens' Tribunal on the Gujarat Killings, chaired by Mr. Justice Krishna Aiyar, cited in Ghanchi, n. 2, at 2.

[53] Mr. Girish Patel, "The Lawyer's Stance": letter of 10th January 2003 to the *Times of India*, Ahmadabad, cited in Ghanchi, n. 2, at 3.

[54] *See* n. 7, Part I, Article 27: "Every state should provide an effective framework of remedies to redress human rights grievances or violations. The administration of justice, including law enforcement and prosecutorial agencies and, especially, an independent judiciary and legal profession....are essential to the full and non-discriminatory realisation of human rights and indispensable to the processes of democracy and sustainable development."

[55] There are notable exceptions to the criticisms of the judicial system in relation to human rights, for example, the development of Public Interest Litigation, and the judicial activism of the Supreme Court of India in upholding human rights; *see* V. Vijyakumar in Nirmal, n. 4, at 213-215; S. Sathe, *Judicial Activism in India* (New Delhi: Oxford University Press, 2002); M. Saharay, *Public Interest Litigation and Human Rights in India* (Allahabad: Premier Publishing Company, 2000); S. Ahuja, *People, Law and Justice: Casebook on Public Interest Litigation*, Vols. I and II (Hyderabad: Orient Longman, 1997); K. Verma, *Fifty Years of the Supreme Court of India: Its Grasp and Reach* (New Delhi: Oxford University Press, 2000), at Chs. 1, 4, 8 and 13; *Zahira Habibulla H Sheikh and Another v State of Gujarat and Others*, 2004 *SCCL.COM* 507 (Criminal Appeal Nos. 446-449 of 2004), known as the "Best Bakery" case, arising out of the communal violence in Gujarat in 2000.

[56] Ghanchi, n. 2, at 4-5.

Women and children in detention are particularly vulnerable to human rights abuses.[57] The investigation of custodial deaths and ill-treatment falls within the remit of the National Human Rights Commission (NHRC), established by the 1993 Human Rights Act. Although constituted and funded by central government, the NHRC functions as an independent statutory body. The establishment and work of the NHRC have raised awareness of the extent of police and prison brutality; it has also provided an additional forum for victims to have their complaints heard and addressed.

3.2.4. *Threats to the right to life with dignity: poverty, economic deprivation and lack of education*[58]

Endemic poverty and economic deprivation resulting in malnutrition, disease and death constitute in themselves a gross violation of the right to life. According to a recent report of the National Council of Applied Economic Research,[59] Thirty per cent of India's population live below the official poverty line and have a daily intake of 1800 calories or less. Infant mortality in India is 71 per 1000 live births. This figure compares poorly with China (30 per 1000), Thailand (25 per 1000) and Sri Lanka (18 per 1000). Child mortality in the first year of life is 111 per 1000. The same report notes India's high level of incidence of diseases such as tuberculosis (TB) and AIDS. Every year there are three million cases of infectious TB and twelve million of the non-infectious type; some five hundred thousand people die from TB alone every year. There are three-and-a-half million HIV-positive persons in India. By 2015 India will have the highest number of HIV-positive persons in the world. Ghanchi cites a report by the Mumbai-based Strategic Foresight Group. It sounds a warning in respect of economic disparities and their impact on human rights in India:

> "The disparities engendered by India's current development model have given rise to three broad kinds of economies; the Business Class economy, which gives access to luxuries, constitutes a bare 2% of the population restricted to fifteen cities. Next comes the Bike economy comprising 15% of the population. The remaining 83% belong to the Bullock Cart economy, half of whom barely manage to survive".[60]

Education plays a crucial role in personal empowerment, providing individual and social competencies and imparting dignity to a person's life. However, despite India's constitutional commitment to the provision of education for all six- to four-

---

[57] "The plight of parents": interview of 10th November 2002 with Pervoz Imroz, founder of the Association of Parents of Disappeared Persons, *The Times of India*, Ahmadabad, at 12, cited in Ghanchi, n. 2, at 4; "Women prisoners and whistle blowers", in the column 'Out of Court', *The Times of India*, Ahmadabad, 19 January 2003, at 10, cited in Ghanchi, n. 2, at 4.

[58] Ghanchi, n. 2, at 5-8.

[59] *Ibid.,* at 5.

[60] Ghanchi, n. 2, at 6.

teen-year-olds, 66% of girls and 50% of boys in this age group do not attend school, and of those who do, some 50% drop out by the fourth year of the primary stage. The drop-out rate for girls is higher. One hundred and twenty-five thousand of the six hundred and fifty thousand state primary schools have just one room, and eighty-five thousand have no room at all. According to the 2001 Census the general literacy level in the country is 65%, that among men being 76% and women 54%. The regional disparities in literacy levels, however, are vast. The literacy rate in Uttar Pradesh is 41%, in Rajasthan 38% and in Bihar 38%, but 65% in Tamil Nadu, 76% in Goa and 90% in Kerala. Compare these with the literacy rates in other Asian countries such as Thailand (94%), Sri Lanka (89%), Indonesia (84%), and China (78%). Literacy among women in certain Indian States is extremely low: 25% in Uttar Pradesh, 22% in Bihar and 29% in Rajasthan. India, consequently, has the largest number of illiterate people in the world. The right to life with dignity is seriously jeopardized by the poor average level of education in the country.

3.2.5. Gender discrimination: violation of the right to life of women and girls

Under international human rights law it is the duty of States, notwithstanding national and regional particularities and differences in historical, cultural and religious backgrounds, to promote and protect all human rights and fundamental freedoms regardless of their political, economic and cultural systems.[61] This includes a specific duty to protect the human rights of women and girls, including the elimination of gender-based violence and discrimination, and harmful cultural practices:

> "The human rights of women and of the girl child are an inalienable, integral and indivisible part of universal human rights [...] [g]ender-based violence and all forms of sexual harassment and exploitation, including those resulting from cultural prejudice and international trafficking, are incompatible with the dignity and worth of the human person and must be eliminated."[62]

In the sub-continent as a whole, violations of the human rights of women and girls occur on a daily basis in both the public and private spheres, exemplified by practices such as sexual assault and harassment, rape, sexual abuse, child prostitution, forced marriage, domestic violence, dowry killings, so-called "honour killings", and *sati* – all of which are prohibited under national legislation, as well as under international human rights law. The prevailing culture of son-preference across the sub-continent ensures that discrimination against women and girls is entrenched even before birth, a reality reflected in the incidence of female foeticide, female infanticide, with higher malnutrition and death rates, and lower levels of education amongst girl children. The following examples of gender discrimination as a violation of the right

---

[61] *See* n. 7, Part I, Article 5.
[62] *Ibid.*, Article 18.

to life of women in India are taken directly from the symposium paper presented by Ghanchi.[63]

A woman's right to life is violated from the conception stage. Sex testing of foetuses and sex selection abortion is increasing in India despite recent directions by the Supreme Court to various state governments for them to regulate sonogram centres to prevent sex testing of foetuses.[64] Census figures for the twentieth century reveal a progressive worsening of the sex ratio of women to men. According to the 2001 Census, in the state of Gujarat the sex ratio of women for every 1000 men was 919. In the 0-6 years age group the ratio was 878, and in the Mehansa district of Gujarat the ratio was just 798. At the same time violence and sexual assaults on women are increasing. It is not just illiteracy and backwardness that perpetuate a patriarchal system which discriminates against women. A number of surveys show an even stronger son-preference among the literate and wealthy than among the economically weaker sections. Even in a progressive state like Kerala, despite its history of women's emancipation, the favourable sex ratio of 1058 is slowly changing in favour of men.[65] Only genuine social and political empowerment can reverse this negative mindset.

Once born, argues Ghanchi, the Indian girl child is subjected to injustices year after year in matters of nutrition, healthcare, education, marriage, and property rights. Early marriage and frequent pregnancies are a threat to girls' physical health and social adjustment. Dowry is a great curse resulting in humiliation, domestic violence and even death. In Delhi alone there are an estimated three hundred and fifty victims of bride burning every year for dowry. Surveys by the International Centre for Research on Women reported in *The Times of India* of 17 February 2003 estimate that 60% of women face domestic violence at some point in their marriage, with women from all socio-economic backgrounds affected. Many women are reluctant to go to court for fear of losing custody of their children.[66]

Rape is also prevalent. As many as 15,000 cases were reported in the year 2002. Ghanchi cites Ms. Rhonda Copelon, Director of the International Women's Human Rights Clinic and a panel member on the International Institute for Justice in Gujarat, speaking to *The Times of India* in January 2003:

> "In every society women still fear the stigma of rape. When justice doesn't respond, it pushes them back into the realms of secrecy and shame, and when rapists are allowed to roam free in the community, there is more terror."[67]

---

[63] Ghanchi, n. 2, at 9-11.
[64] *Ibid.,* at 9.
[65] *Ibid.*
[66] *Ibid.,* at 10.
[67] "Discounting Women ", *The Times of India*, Ahmadabad, 10 December 2002, at 12, cited in Ghanchi, n. 2, at 10.

The communal violence in Gujarat in 2002 witnessed a great increase in incidents of rape, including group rape, against Muslim women. Ghanchi cites further from the same interview:

"Great progress in international law has been made in recent years in respect of rape, and it should be applied to Gujarat, for International Criminal Tribunals recognize rape as a crime against humanity, a form of torture, and an act that contributes to genocide."[68]

Prostitution is also rife, and is inextricably linked to poverty. India has around one million prostitutes, of whom three hundred thousand are children. Poverty, famine, unemployment and man-made (*sic*) disasters such as riots encourage this institution. It is estimated that the annual business of prostitutes amounts to Rs.50,000 crore [a crore is ten million], of which Rs.11,000 crore derives from child prostitution. Child prostitution is rising by 10% every year.

Ghanchi finds a "compensatory solace" in representative democracy. The constitution amended under the regime of the late Prime Minister Rajiv Gandhi in 1986 reserves 30% of the seats in local civic authorities for women. The lower house of the Indian Parliament (the "Lok Sabha") has had around 4% to 7% women members since its inception. However, the achievement of women's equality in society, in the economy and in the *polit* will take a much longer time. Until then, Ghanchi argues, education, mobilization and agitation must be stepped up.[69]

3.3.   Caste-based discrimination[70]

The caste system is one of the most urgent and challenging human rights issues facing the region today. Caste-based discrimination, or discrimination on the basis of work and descent (described as the "hidden apartheid"), affects an estimated two hundred and fifty million people in India alone.[71]

Dalits (those belonging to the Scheduled Castes,[72] or so-called "Untouchables")

---

[68]   *Ibid.*

[69]   *Ibid.*, at 11.

[70]   I am grateful to the Socio-Legal Studies Association, which has enabled me to conduct funded research on the subject of caste discrimination and international human rights law.

[71]   *See* Human Rights Watch, *Caste: A Global Concern* (New York: Human Rights Watch, 2001); *see* also S. Narula, *Broken People: Caste Violence Against India's "Untouchables"* (New York: Human Rights Watch, 1999); M. Srinivas (ed.), *Caste: Its Twentieth Century Avatar* (New Delhi: Penguin, 1996).

[72]   "Scheduled Castes" is the legal term adopted by the Constitution of India; " 'Scheduled Castes' means such castes, races or tribes or parts of or groups within such castes, races or tribes as are deemed under Article 341 to be Scheduled Castes for the purpose of this Constitution": Constitution of India, Article 366 (24); "The President may with respect to any State or Union territory, and where it is a State, after consultation with the Governor thereof, by public notification, specify the castes, races or tribes or parts of or groups within castes, races or tribes which shall for the purposes

number one hundred and sixty million in India – more than the entire population of Pakistan. Caste is a phenomenon that occurs not only in India, but across South Asia, in Bangladesh, Nepal, Pakistan, and Sri Lanka, and throughout the South Asian diaspora. Caste-type systems are also found in Japan and parts of Africa.[73] India, however, contains the greatest number of those affected due to the sheer size of the Indian population; accordingly, this section focuses on the South Asian, specifically the Indian, aspects of the issue.

Notwithstanding academic debate over the origins and definition of caste, it is generally accepted that the caste system is at least two thousand years old and derives from the Hindu division of society into four hierarchical categories, known as the *varna* system: this has the priests at top of hierarchy, the serfs, cultivators and artisans at the bottom, and the rulers, landowners and warriors, and commoners and traders, in between. Within this framework are some three thousand castes and sub-castes, traditionally social, occupational or territorial in origin, all broadly falling within one of the *varnas*. In addition there is a large category of people – about one in six of the Indian population – who fall outside the *varna* system.[74] These are the people known as "Untouchables" or Dalits, as they choose to call themselves, meaning "the oppressed" or "broken people". Caste is a hierarchical system of institutionalized inequality based on "rigid social stratification into ranked groups defined by descent and occupation".[75] The connection between caste and occupation is not, however, infallible: people of the same caste have always performed different occupations, and people in the same occupation may belong to different castes. What is *not* disputed is that caste is based on descent, is thus hereditary and is inalienable. Regardless of occupation, the position of an individual within the caste system is irrevocable. Caste identity is not fluid and the system, certainly in its current form, admits no possibility of caste mobility within an individual's lifetime. No individual can escape the caste of their birth through education, marriage, the acquisition of fame or fortune, or through conversion to another religion. In daily life, caste is the

---

of this Constitution be deemed to be Scheduled Castes in relation to that State or Union territory, as the case may be.": Constitution of India, Article 341.

[73] *See* Sub Commission on the Promotion and Protection of Human Rights, Working Paper by Mr. Rajendra K.W. Goonesekere on Discrimination based on Work and Descent, E/CN.4/Sub.2/2001/16, 14 June 2001, Part I: Communities where discrimination based on work and descent is experienced; *see* also Expanded Working Paper on Discrimination based on Work and Descent by Mr. Asbjorn Eide and Mr. Yozo Yokota, E/CN.4/Sub.2/2003/24, 26 June 2003, Part I: some affected communities outside of Asia.

[74] *See* T. Zinkin, *Caste Today* (London: Oxford University Press, 1962); J. Hutton, *Caste in India* (Cambridge: Cambridge University Press, 1946); G.S. Ghurye, *Caste and Race in India* (Bombay: Popular Prakashan, 1969); M. Srinivas, *Caste in Modern India* (New Delhi: Asia Publishing House, 1962); G. Flood, *An Introduction to Hinduism* (Cambridge: Cambridge University Press, 1998).

[75] *See Caste Discrimination: A Global Concern* (New York: Human Rights Watch, 2001), at 1; M. Mendelsohn and M. Vicziany, *The Untouchables: Subordination, Poverty and the State in Modern India* (Cambridge: Cambridge University Press, 1998), at 15 and Ch. 9; D. Quigley, in M. Searle, M. Chatterjee and U. Sharma (eds.), *Contextualising Caste: Post-Dumontian Approaches* (Oxford: Blackwell, 1994), at 30-31.

principal means through which individuals 'place' themselves and others within the social hierarchy. The concept of caste is deeply ingrained in the South Asian psyche, and in the psyche of the diaspora.

Central to the caste system is the notion of *Untouchability.* This derives from the Hindu concept of ritual purity and pollution.[76] "Untouchables" are deemed polluted from birth and were, hence, historically assigned and restricted to those occupations, invariably the most menial, deemed 'polluting'. The concept of Untouchability resulted in the development of strict practices of social and physical segregation, caste endogamy, and ritual restrictions on the sharing of food and drink. These rules were stringently enforced by social, economic, religious, political, psychological and physical means. Following Independence, Untouchability was abolished in India by the 1950 Constitution,[77] but it continues to be practised in the public, social and private spheres in myriad forms across the country, particularly in rural areas. Modern manifestations of Untouchability range from the shockingly violent to the very subtle. In many villages, to this day, Untouchables are forced to live in segregated settlements in the least attractive areas or on the outskirts of a village. They are refused access to public cremation facilities or burial grounds, are forbidden from using roads within caste Hindu areas, and they may not use the same wells and bathing ghats as caste Hindus. In the social sphere, Untouchability continues to be practized in the denial of access to temples and places of worship, the refusal of service in hotels and restaurants, and the social ostracism or exclusion of Dalits in the workplace and in other social situations. The practice of making Dalits use separate drinking glasses is decreasing, yet it still persists in some areas. At the private level, social interaction and integration with caste Hindus remains limited even in urban areas; inter-caste marriage is virtually taboo. In education and employment Dalits suffer discrimination and humiliation. Monitoring groups around the country continue to record incidents of atrocities, often extremely violent, against individual Dalits and against Dalit communities.[78] Overt caste discrimination is less pronounced in metropolitan areas, where individuals are not known to each other, as caste is not automatically discernible from physical appearance and characteristics. Furthermore, the avoidance of physical contact is impossible, at least in public spaces; but where the cloak of anonymity is removed, discrimination both overt and covert remains widespread. Dalit women and girls suffer the dual oppression of caste and gender, characterized by female infanticide, reduced access to food and education,

---

[76] *See* P. Kolenda, *Caste in Contemporary India: Beyond Organic Solidarity* (Illinois: Waveland Press, 1978), Ch. 4; G. Flood, n. 74, at Chs. 1 and 3, and 219-220.

[77] Constitution of India, Article 17.

[78] *See* for example Sakshi Human Rights Watch, *Dalit Human Rights Monitor Andhra Pradesh 2002-2003* (Secunderabad: Sakshi Human Rights Watch, 2003); M. Macwan and H. Desai, *atrocities on Dalits in Gujarat 1990-3: a Documentation and Evaluation* (Surat: Centre for Social Studies, South Gujarat University, 1997).

rape and sexual assault by high caste men, and by socially-sanctioned child prostitution and sex slavery in the form of the *Devadasi* system.[79]

Caste is as much an economic as a social phenomenon. The caste system and in particular the practice of Untouchability are intimately linked to poverty. Despite the economic reforms initiated in the 1990s, and the wealth and opulent lifestyle enjoyed by a privileged few, India is still a poor country; according to the 2001 Census, one third of all Indians live below the national poverty line. India is also still predominantly an agricultural society: roughly 70% of the population live in rural areas. Around half of India's poor are landless agricultural labourers, the majority of whom are Dalits. Three quarters of Dalits live below the poverty line, mostly in rural India. They constitute the poorest and most vulnerable section of Indian society. A high proportion of the rural landless are Dalit women, the lowest-paid section of agrarian society. Furthermore, of an estimated forty million bonded labourers of which fifteen million are children, the majority are Dalits.[80] A Human Rights Watch study of bonded labour in the silk industry found children aged between six and fourteen working ten to fourteen hours a day, six days a week, the majority of whom were Dalits. Similarly, a recent UNICEF study found that 71% of children working in brick kilns were Dalits or low castes. Dalits continue to be employed in the most menial of occupations, including occupations such as manual scavenging (the manual removal of night soil from dry latrines), prohibited by law but still accounting for the employment of around one million Dalits, primarily women.[81]

In 1947 India gained its independence and in 1950 a democratic constitution was adopted, drafted by a Committee chaired by Dr. B.R. Ambedkar, himself an Untouchable, one of India's foremost economists and lawyers, and an activist for social justice.[82] India has an impressive and progressive domestic legal framework in relation to caste that includes constitutional prohibitions on caste discrimination and the practice of Untouchability,[83] constitutional affirmative action provisions,[84] a network of legislation banning bonded labour[85] and the practice of manual scavenging,[86] and providing for the criminalization of untouchability[87] and atrocities against scheduled castes;[88] in addition are a range of constitutional and statutory bodies at national and State level concerned with the promotion and protection of human

---

[79] Under the Devadasi system young Dalit girls are dedicated to a temple where they are forced to act as prostitutes for upper caste men; *see* Human Rights Watch, n. 71; *see* also S. Narula, n. 71, at Ch. IX.
[80] *See* Human Rights Watch, n. 71.
[81] *Ibid.*
[82] *See* B. Chandra *et al, India After Independence: 1947-2000* (New Delhi: Penguin, 2000).
[83] Constitution of India, Articles 15 and 17.
[84] *Ibid.*, Articles 15(4) and 16(4).
[85] Bonded Labour System (Abolition) Act 1976.
[86] Employment of Manual Scavengers and Construction of Dry Latrines (Prohibition) Act 1993.
[87] Protection of Civil Rights Act 1976 (formerly the Untouchability (Offences) Act 1955).
[88] SC and ST (Prevention of Atrocities) Act 1989.

rights, including the rights of Dalits.[89] Unfortunately, despite the existence of these extensive provisions designed to eliminate caste discrimination and the practice of Untouchability, both remain rife primarily because the existing domestic provisions are neither implemented nor enforced. Victims of discrimination and violence often lack any knowledge of the relevant legal provisions designed to protect them. There is reluctance on the part of victims of discrimination to resort to the law. This is mainly because of the cost, the fear of reprisal, and a lack of confidence in the police and the legal process. The police and lawyers themselves are frequently deficient in familiarity with the relevant law and legal processes. On the part of the police there may be a reluctance, due to caste prejudice, to initiate investigations into allegations of caste discrimination or violence. In its statement to the UN-sponsored World Conference on Racism held in Durban in 2001, the National Human Rights Commission representative referred to the problems of implementation thus:

> "[I]t is widely recognised that much remains to be done to bring an end to the discrimination and inequality that have been practised for centuries and that this requires both sustained effort and time. There are manifest inadequacies in implementation which are deeply frustrating and painful to the Scheduled Castes and Scheduled Tribes and, indeed, to all Indians who strive to end the injustice that persists in several forms and the atrocities that occur."[90]

Educational and economic empowerment and elevation are also the key tools in the fight against the promulgation of the caste system; these were highlighted by the NHRC[91] and by numerous Dalit academics, intellectuals and activists. Ambedkar himself was deeply committed to education as the primary vehicle for the empowerment of Dalits, combined with improvements in their economic status.

At the international level, awareness and understanding of caste-based discrimination have been increasing in recent years, particularly as a result of the efforts of NGOs and activists to raise the profile of this form of human rights violation at the UN-sponsored World Conference on Racism held in Durban in 2001. Article 1(1) of the International Convention on the Elimination of All Forms of Racial Discrimination (CERD) prohibits discrimination *inter alia* on grounds of descent, a ground proposed by India during the drafting of the Convention. An analysis of the Summary Records of the Monitoring Committees established under the two International Covenants and of the international conventions on race, women and children reveals both an awareness, on the part of those countries affected, of caste-type systems as a source of discrimination, and the extent of concern of the treaty bodies at the *de facto* perpetuation of caste systems and the practice of Untouchability in various countries around the world. Despite the failure of Dalit activists and their supporters to secure official recognition at Durban that caste discrimination falls within the ambit

---

[89] National Human Rights Commission; State Human Rights Commissions and Committees; National Commission for Scheduled Castes and Scheduled Tribes.

[90] *Journal of the National Human Rights Commission*, India, 2002, at 256.

[91] *Ibid.*, at 258.

of the Race Convention, developments at the UN level since Durban have been encouraging. In August 2002 the Committee on the Elimination of Racial Discrimination adopted for the first time a General Recommendation on Descent-Based Discrimination, reaffirming the Committee's view that discrimination based on descent, prohibited under Article 1(1) of the Race Convention, includes "discrimination against members of communities based on forms of social stratification such as caste and analogous systems of inherited status which nullify or impair their equal enjoyment of human rights."[92] In August 2003 the UN Sub-Commission on the Promotion and Protection of Human Rights, recalling the two expert working papers on discrimination based on work and descent submitted to it in 2001 and 2003 respectively,[93] adopted a Resolution on Discrimination based on Work and Descent[94] calling for the preparation of a third expert working paper to examine legal, judicial, administrative, and educational measures taken by the Governments concerned, to identify additional communities affected by this form of discrimination, and to prepare a draft set of principles and guidelines for all relevant actors in cooperation and collaboration with, *inter alia,* the Race Committee, the International Labour Organization and UNESCO. The resolution further calls on States to formulate and implement at the national, regional and international level new and enhanced policies and plans of action to effectively eliminate discrimination based on work and descent, taking into account the measures proposed in General Recommendation XXIX and to give widespread publicity to the General Recommendation. Caste-based discrimination is also actively being addressed by the UN Working Group on Contemporary Forms of Slavery[95] and by the International Labour Organization. The issue of caste-based discrimination, particularly the issue of inadequate implementation and enforcement of domestic provisions and fulfilment of international human rights obligations pertaining to caste, demands to be addressed with a continued sense of urgency at the national, regional, and international levels and requires to be tackled simultaneously on political, legal, social, cultural, economic, and religious fronts.

3.4. Religious minorities: a case study of the treatment of the Ahmadiyya Muslim community in Pakistan[96]

International human rights law imposes on States a duty to protect the rights of religious, linguistic, racial, and ethnic minorities, and
an obligation to ensure that persons belonging to minorities may exercise fully and effectively all human rights and fundamental freedoms without discrimination. This

---

[92] CERD General Recommendation XXIX; CERD/C/61/Misc 29.
[93] *See* UN Sub-Commission on the Promotion and Protection of Human Rights, Working Paper by A. Eide and Y. Yokota on Discrimination Based on Work and Descent (E/CN.4/Sub.2/2003/24).
[94] UN Sub-Commission on the Promotion and Protection of Human Rights; Resolution 2003/22 of 13 August 2003. Discrimination based on work and descent.
[95] *See* Report E/CN.4/Sub.2/2003/31.
[96] Malik, n. 2.

includes the right of religious minorities to profess and practice their own religion.[97] Nevertheless, discrimination against and the persecution of religious minorities, and the rise of sectarian politics, constitute a serious threat to the rule of law and to peace and stability in the region. The following discussion is extracted from the symposium paper by Nadeem Malik;[98] it examines the progressive decline in religious rights in Pakistan since 1947, focussing on the treatment of the Ahmadiyya Muslim Community as a case study.[99]

Ahmadi Muslims number around four million in Pakistan and have always considered themselves as belonging to the Muslim *ummah*, or wider "community of Muslims".[100] The Ahmadiyya Muslim community has been described as "the most persecuted Muslim religious group today",[101] unique as a religious community, Malik claims, because the discrimination that Ahmadis suffer has been made entirely legal – indeed, it has been written into the national Constitution. The Ahmadiyya Community was founded in India in the late 1880s by the Muslim theologian and scholar Hazrat Mirza Ghulam Ahmad of Qadian (1835-1908) against a backdrop of declining Muslim fortunes in India exacerbated by the social and cultural insularity, anti-modernity and anti-British stance of the Muslim religious leaders, the orthodox clergy or *ulema*. As Malik explains, Hazrat Mirza Ghulam Ahmad espoused a fundamentally different interpretation of the identity of the Promised Messiah to that of the Sunni Muslim majority; alarmed by his unorthodox doctrinal interpretations and religious writings – and by the popularity of his teachings, which threatened their political authority and grip on the general body of Muslims – the orthodox clergy declared Hazrat Mirza Ghulam Ahmad a heretic and denounced his followers as apostates.

Muhammed Ali Jinnah, the first President of independent Pakistan, conceived of Pakistan as a liberal, secular nation rather than as a theocracy. Malik cites Jinnah's first address to the new Constituent Assembly of Pakistan in August 1947 in which the non-sectarian character of Pakistan was addressed:

> "You are free. You are free to go to your temples. You are free to go to your mosques or to any other places of worship in this State of Pakistan. You may belong to any religion or caste or creed – that has nothing to do with the business of the State. We are starting in the days when there is no discrimination, no distinction between one community and another, no discrimination between one caste or creed and another. We are starting with this fundamental principle, that we are all citizens and equal members of one state".[102]

---

[97] *See* n. 7, Part I, Art 19.

[98] Imperial College, University of London, United Kingdom.

[99] Malik, n. 2.

[100] *See* A.M. Khan, "Persecution of the Ahmadiyya community in Pakistan: an analysis under international law and international relations", 16 *Harvard Human Rights Journal* (2003), at 217.

[101] Donna E. Artz, "Heroes or heretics: religious dissidents under Islamic law", 14 *Wisconsin International Law Journal* (1996), 349, at 408, cited in Malik, n. 2, at 2.

[102] Malik, n. 2, at 6.

Khan recounts how this vision was reflected in the approach of Pakistan during the drafting of the Universal Declaration of Human Rights, adopted in 1948. Whereas the Saudi representative opposed the right contained in Article 18 of the UDHR to change one's religion as contrary to Islamic law (or *Shari'a*) and a product of western thinking, the Pakistani representative – Pakistan's first foreign minister and an Ahmadi – embraced the right to freedom of conscience as entirely consistent with Islam's rejection of any compulsion in matters of faith.[103]

Pakistan is a country of one hundred and fifty-five million people divided on religious and ethnic lines. Sunni Muslims form 77% of the population, 20% are Shias and one per cent Ahmadi, with Hindus and Christians together amounting to between two and three per cent. At its inception, the modern Pakistan was ethnically, linguistically and religiously diverse, a situation requiring astute and delicate handling if the country were to develop in peace and harmony. Malik argues that with Jinnah at the helm the centrifugal forces inherent in a nation with such strong ethnic and religious diversity were subdued. With the premature death of Jinnah in 1948, however, came a more or less permanent crisis of leadership and a progressive erosion of the vision of a modern, secular, tolerant, and inclusive Muslim country. In parallel with religious intolerance, ethnic struggles also emerged. Fifty-five per cent of the population are Punjabi and the remainder a mixture of Pathan (10%), Sindhi (18%), Mohajir (10%), and Baluchi (2%). In 1947 the Punjab was more advanced than other regions of Pakistan in terms of general educational and political development; consequently, Punjabis dominated the political, economic and military landscape. The ethnic minorities felt increasingly marginalized by the majority Punjabis, and secessionist tendencies that were mild at Pakistan's inception have reached crisis point in recent years.[104]

In March 1949, following the death of Jinnah, the Constituent Assembly passed the so-called "Objectives Resolution" which declared that the first Constitution of Pakistan should be based on the "ideals of Islam", although religious freedom for non-Muslims would be provided for.[105] Malik refutes the denials of the government at the time that the resolution implied a theocratic State, arguing that it was clear that the resolution was indeed the first step in that direction. Consequently, he argues, demands by Muslim separatists that Ahmadis be declared non-Muslim became both a rallying point for fundamentalist parties and the principal weapon in the campaign to transform the country into an Islamic theocracy.[106] In 1962 the so-called 'repugnancy clause' was added to the Constitution, a significant move, Malik contends, towards theocracy: "No law shall be repugnant to the teachings and requirements of Islam as set out in the Qur'an and Sunnah, and all existing laws shall be brought into conformity therewith."[107]

---

[103] Khan, n. 100.
[104] Malik, n. 2, at 7-9.
[105] The "Objectives Resolution" was incorporated into the Constitution of Pakistan as Article 2 by Presidential Order No.14 of 1985; *see* Malik, n. 2, at 14.
[106] *Ibid.*
[107] Constitution of Pakistan, Part IX, Article 227.

In 1973 the new Constitution, introduced following the secession in 1971 from West Pakistan of East Pakistan to become Bangladesh, was amended by the inclusion of a legal definition of non-Muslims that covered Ahmadis as well as Christians, Hindus, Sikhs, Buddhists, Parsis, the Baha'i community, and the Scheduled Castes.[108] Ahmadis were thus explicitly deprived by law of their identity as Muslims. In 1978, electoral reforms were introduced providing for separate electorates for non-Muslims in the National and Provincial Assemblies. Members of minority religions could vote only for candidates from a minority list. As a result, Malik argues, majority Muslim candidates had no incentive to appeal to religious minorities. This has severely affected Christians, Hindus and other religious communities by further diminishing the already weak voice that these communities had in politics. According to Malik, the impact of these reforms on Ahmadis, who consider themselves to be Muslims and who therefore refuse to register or vote as non-Muslims, has been complete disenfranchisement, yet in 2002 President Musharraf confirmed that the separate electoral system and the legal status of Ahmadis under the Constitution would remain unchanged.

In 1984 President Zia ul Huq, in power since 1977 following a military *coup*, pushed through parliament a number of ordinances targeting religious minorities, of which two (collectively referred to as Ordinance XX) amended Pakistan's Penal Code and were aimed specifically at Ahmadis.[109] Ordinance XX provided for the imposition of a prison sentence and a fine for blasphemy defined, in relation to Ahmadis, as the use of Islamic terminology and references whether spoken, written or by "visible representation", directly or indirectly posing as Muslims, referring to their faith as Islam or in any manner whatsoever "outraging the feelings of Muslims". Ahmadis were thus prohibited from behaving and conducting themselves as Muslims; their very existence as Ahmadi Muslims was criminalized. With the introduction in 1986 of the Criminal Law Act, together with ordinance XX known as the "Blasphemy Law", the penalty for blasphemy was increased to death.[110]

Malik argues that once a culture of discrimination and persecution is engendered in a society it seldom remains confined to a specific target, particularly where it has the explicit backing of the Constitution and the law; the terminology of the "Blasphemy Law" in Pakistan is such that even though Ahmadis were the intended targets the law can be used against anyone who "outrages the religious feelings of Muslims". Ahmadis have been subjected on religious grounds to decades of persecution in Pakistan. It was inevitable that Christians and Hindus would also become targets of the rising extremist Muslim groups. Thus, in parallel with the state-supported persecution of Ahmadis in Pakistan there has been increased agitation against Christians, Hindus, and Shia Muslims over the same period.[111]

Christians and Hindus in Pakistan suffer widespread discrimination in all areas of public and private life. The vast majority of Christians and Hindus belong to the

---

[108] *Ibid.*, Part XI1, Ch. 5, Article 260(3)(a) and (b).
[109] Pakistan Penal Code, Sections 298(b) and 298(c).
[110] Pakistan Penal Code, Section 295(c).
[111] Malik, n. 2, at 22-23.

poorest social classes in Pakistan, a situation compounded by the social segregation and isolation of Pakistan's various religious and ethnic communities, which further alienates minority communities from the mainstream. Christians and Hindus face problems at every level. Even if they can afford schooling for their children they continue to suffer religious discrimination and poor career prospects. Since Partition in 1947 the Hindu population of Pakistan has shrunk considerably, primarily through migration and through conversion to Christianity or Islam. At various periods of conflict with India large numbers of Hindus, fearing for their lives, have migrated across the border; few have returned. Anti-Muslim communal violence in India exacerbates this situation, leading to revenge attacks on Hindus in Pakistan. Hindus once accounted for more than five per cent of the population of Pakistan, but now they amount to no more than about one per cent, mostly in the Sind province. Christians suffer greater targeted violence from extremist Muslim groups because they are perceived as 'Westerners', an image bolstered in the minds of extremist groups by the fact that numerous Christian churches based in the West are active in Pakistan, particularly among poor villagers. Christians are especially vulnerable during times of anti-Western sentiment. Following the American invasion of Afghanistan in 2002 and the Anglo-American invasion of Iraq in 2003 numerous Christian churches in Pakistan were attacked and dozens of Christians were killed or injured by extremist Muslim groups. Yet Christians benefit from the fact that there are many highly respected and well-funded Christian schools, financed by churches based in the West, which provide a high level of education. Although some Christians attend these schools, the vast majority are Muslim children from rich families for whom attendance at such schools has become a status symbol. Malik explains that Shias have not been declared non-Muslims and hence still enjoy a better position than Ahmadis; in the prevailing climate of religious intolerance, however, the Shias have increasingly come under attack. The *ulema* largely follow the Wahabi faith of Saudi Arabia, associated with an anti-Shia stance, and the re-emergence of Shia Iran as a regional power has fuelled a divide with ancient roots in the history of Islam.[112] This has led to violent clashes in some parts of Pakistan, particularly in Karachi during the 1990s.

Today, argues Malik, religious discrimination is enshrined in Pakistan's constitution. In parallel with the persecution of Ahmadi Muslims other religious communities have also come under increasingly violent attack. Repeal of the laws and Constitutional amendments that infringe upon religious rights and a return to the first Constitution of Pakistan would comprise the first step in the reversal of that trend.

4.   REGIONAL COOPERATION, PEACE AND HUMAN RIGHTS[113]

The fundamental link between human rights, on the one hand, and stability and peace, on the other, first identified in the Charter of the United Nations, is reiterated

---

[112] *Ibid.,* at 24-25.
[113] Rehman, n. 2.

in the 1993 Vienna Declaration. It declares that efforts towards the universal respect for and observance of human rights and fundamental freedoms contribute to the stability and well-being necessary for peaceful and friendly relations among nations.[114] As Javaid Rehman[115] reminds us, in Europe regional organizations such as the European Union, the Council of Europe, and the Organization on Security and Cooperation in Europe (OSCE) have been the driving force for economic development, security and greater protection of human rights.[116] The following sub-section is extracted from the symposium paper presented by Javaid Rehman[117] on the role and contribution of regional institutions in facilitating cooperation and dialogue as a means of resolving conflicts and disputes and of combating terrorism and human rights abuses, and the possibility of South Asia's following the European example of regional cooperation.

4.1.   South Asian Association for Regional Cooperation (SAARC): Constitutionalism, Regional Peace and Human Rights

4.1.1. Background

South Asia is beset by political and constitutional instability, largely a heritage of the colonial period and the subsequent process of decolonization, compounded by boundary and territorial disputes, conflict along ethnic, religious and linguistic lines, widespread violations of civil and political, economic, social and minority rights, and also by international and regional terrorism, which presents a major challenge to stability in the region. British India, which formed the core of present day South-Asian States, was a conglomeration of around 600 autonomous principalities and princely states of varying sizes, along with unified provinces. The partition of India led the way to decolonization in the rest of South Asia and cost a million lives.[118]

---

[114] *See* n. 7, Article 6.

[115] Javaid Rehman, Professor of International Law, University of Ulster, United Kingdom.

[116] *See* T. Hartley, *The Foundations of European Community Law* (Oxford: Clarendon Press, 3rd edn., 1994); D. Wyatt and A. Dashwood, *European Community Law* (Oxford: Clarendon Press, 3rd edn.); S. Weatherill and P. Beaumont, *EC Law* (London: Penguin Books, 2nd edn., 1995); J. Steiner, *Textbook on EC Law* (London: Blackstone Press, 4th edn., 1994); A.H. Robertson, *The Council of Europe: Its Structure, Functions and Achievements* (London: Stevens, 1956); J.G. Merrills, *Human Rights in Europe: A Study of the European Convention on Human Rights* (Manchester: Manchester University Press, 4th edn., 2001); A. Bloed (ed.), *The Conference on Security and Co-operation in Europe: Basic Documents 1993 – 1995* (The Hague: Martinus Nijhoff, Publishers, 1997); J. Maresca, *To Helsinki–The Conference on Security and Co-operation in Europe 1973–75* (Durham, N.C.: Duke University Press, 1985); A. Bloed and P. Van Dijk, *Essays on Human Rights in the Helsinki Process* (Dordrecht: Martinus Nijhoff, Publishers, 1985); A. Bloed and P. Van Dijk, *The Human Dimension of the Helsinki Process* (Dordrecht: Maritinus Nihjoff, Publishers, 1991); all cited in Rehman, n. 2, at 1-2.

[117] Rehman, n. 2.

[118] *Ibid.,* at 2-3.

In the words of Rehman, "the new States that emerged, in common with those that had not been directly colonized, such as Afghanistan and Nepal, have had a tumultuous relationship with constitutional development, economic growth, democracy and human rights."[119] Afghanistan's political and constitutional history has been one of conflict and civil war. The repression and human rights violations characterizing the ten-year rule of the Taliban were a consequence of the support given to fundamentalist groups, who married opposition to the Soviet occupation with extremist ideology. Notwithstanding the replacement of the Taliban regime with a new government Afghanistan "remains a constitutional quagmire". Large-scale and systematic human rights violations continue, committed by local and regional warlords who, according to Human Rights Watch, "now represent the primary threat to peace and security in the country".[120] Afghanistan has a tense relationship with Pakistan, which has itself experienced military rule, lack of democracy and human rights violations for much of its independent history. However, the principal source of tension in the region lies in the conflict between its two nuclear powers, Pakistan and India, particularly in the territorial dispute over the predominantly Muslim province of Jammu and Kashmir, and in mutual allegations of state-sponsored terrorism and human rights abuses.[121] Though a constitutional democracy, India has undergone periods of crisis where constitutional and political development has been badly affected by domestic terrorism (such as the assassination of two Prime Ministers, Indira Gandhi and her son Rajiv Gandhi), the declaration of a State of Emergency in 1975, regular outbreaks of communal violence, dissension over the rights of Adivasis or tribals, Dalits, minority rights, and the recognition of regional languages.

4.1.2.　SAARC: its role and remit

As can be seen from the experience of the Council of Europe, the European Union, the African Union (formerly the Organisation of African Unity) and the Inter-American System of Human Rights, regional institutions can play a significant role in developing norms of democratic governance, constitutionalism, the rule of law, and human rights. Regional agencies have also traditionally been valued in dispute resolution and in attempts to eradicate terrorism.[122] The pre-eminent regional organization for South Asia is the South Asian Association for Regional Cooperation,

---

[119] *Ibid.,* at 3. *See* also C. Baxter, Y.K. Malik, C.H. Kennedy, and R.C. Oberst, *Government and Politics in South Asia: Pakistan, India, Bangladesh and Sri Lanka, Nepal, Bhutan and the Maldives* (Lahore: Vanguard), at 62; M. Hutt (ed.), *Nepal in the Nineties: Versions of the Past, Visions of the Future* (London: Oxford University Press, 1994); H. Skar, "Nepal, Indigenous Issues and Civil Rights: The Plight of the Rana Tharu", in R. Barnes, A. Gray and B. Kingsbury (eds.), *Indigenous Peoples of Asia* (Ann Arbor, MI: Association of Asian Studies, 1993), at 173–194; all cited in Rehman, n. 2, at 3.

[120] Rehman, n. 2, at 4.

[121] *Ibid.,* at 5.

[122] *See* C. Gray, "Regional arrangements and the United Nations collective security system" in H. Fox (ed.), *The Changing Constitution of the United Nations* (London: British Institute of International and Comparative Law, 1997), at 91-116: cited in Rehman, n. 2, at 7.

or SAARC, established in December 1985 on the basis of a document drafted by the late president of Bangladesh, President Zia-ur-Rahman, and with a current membership of Bangladesh, Bhutan, India, Maldives, Nepal, Pakistan, and Sri Lanka.[123] Its remit is to promote, *via* the mechanism of dialogue and cooperation, regional peace and stability (including the eradication of terrorism) and the welfare of the peoples of South Asia through economic growth and development, social and cultural progress, and the promotion of mutual trust and understanding.[124] It operates through a hierarchical institutional structure involving, at different levels, the participation of Heads of State, Foreign Ministers, Foreign Secretaries, civil servants, and technical experts in Summit Meetings, Council Meetings, and a variety of finance, co-ordinating and technical Committees. In addition, it has established a number of institutions and agreements designed to assist the achievement of its economic objectives. Through the framework of SAARC as an organization, Member States have, at least in principle, been able to agree on some of the fundamental principles affecting human rights and regional peace and security.

4.1.3. The regional convention on the suppression of terrorism

Under the auspices of SAARC a Regional Convention on the Suppression of Terrorism was adopted in 1987. Rehman observes that

> "Regional terrorism has been an endemic aspect of the political relationships of South-Asian States.... [N]ot only have non-State actors conducted terrorist acts but organs of States themselves have been implicated in terrorism and gross human rights violations."[125]

He goes on to note that all States of the region have been affected by domestic militancy, and by cross-border or internal opposition movements that have resorted to terrorism:

> "The crime of terrorism represents the culmination of fundamental human rights violations. Whatever definition is accorded to terrorism, it violates the principal human rights as enshrined in the International Bill of Rights."[126]

---

[123] Rehman, n. 2, at 9.

[124] Note however that SAARC's remit does not specifically include the promotion of human rights as such; *see* full text of the SAARC Charter at http://www.nepaldemocracy.org/saarc_charter.html (1 September 2003).

[125] Rehman, n. 2, at 12.

[126] *See* e.g. *United States Diplomatic and Consular Staff in Tehran (United States of America v. Iran)*, Judgment 24 May 1980, *ICJ Rep. 1980*, at 3, where the International Court notes: "Wrongfully to deprive human beings of their freedom and to subject them to physical constraint in conditions of hardship is in itself manifestly incompatible with ... the fundamental principles enunciated in the Universal Declaration of Human Rights", cited in Rehman, n. 2, at 15.

Given that finding a definition of terrorism has proved highly controversial, the Convention adopts a broad approach towards definition. In addition, Rehman notes, Member States are given further discretion "to expand the scope of terrorist acts, by recognising other serious violent offences as terrorist acts and denying these the stature of political offences" – provisions which, whilst expanding the scope of the Convention, risk creating ambiguity and confusion, given the varying nature and scope of criminal offences in the different legal systems.[127] The Convention is also mindful of the principles of cooperation of the SAARC Charter as well as of the seriousness of the problem of terrorism that has dogged the region. Thus, while re-affirming the principles of international law, the Preamble acknowledges that "cooperation among SAARC states is vital if terrorism is to be prevented and eliminated from the region".

4.1.4. Assessment

Since its creation SAARC has provided a valuable forum for regional inter-state dialogue at the highest level. However, despite notable achievements such as the adoption of the Regional Convention on the Suppression of Terrorism, Rehman describes SAARC as remaining "a minor player in generating the spirit of constitutionalism, democracy and human rights."[128] Crucially, SAARC's effectiveness is significantly reduced by its lack of legislative and enforcement powers. A more prominent role for SAARC, including the greater visibility and extension of its existing activities in the fields of human rights and democracy, would require an increase in its legislative and enforcement powers. Such a development would depend in particular on the willingness of its Member States to accord it greater legislative power.

4.2.   A sub-regional human rights system for South Asia?

Asia is today the only region in the world without a regional human rights system. The need for States in those areas in which regional human rights arrangements do not already exist to consider the establishment of regional and sub-regional arrangements for the promotion and protection of human rights was emphasized in the 1993 Vienna Declaration and Programme of Action[129] and has subsequently been re-iterated in a succession of UN Human Rights Commission and General Assembly resolutions on regional arrangements for the promotion and protection of human rights.[130]

---

[127] Rehman, n. 2, at 14.

[128] *Ibid.,* at 17.

[129] *See* n. 7, Article 37.

[130] For example General Assembly Resolutions of 7 March 1995: A/RES/49/189; 3 March 1997: A/RES/51/102; 10 March 1999: A/ RES/53/148; 14 March 2001: A/RES/ 55/105.

In addition to SAARC there are a number of other fora for regional human rights cooperation in South Asia. Three of these, the Asia Pacific Forum for National Human Rights Institutions, the UN Asia Pacific Workshops on Cooperation for the Promotion and Protection of Human Rights, and the South Asia Forum for Human Rights will be considered briefly. The Asia Pacific Forum for National Human Rights Institutions was established in 1996 following the first Asia Pacific regional meeting of national human rights institutions convened by the United Nations Office of the High Commissioner for Human Rights.[131] The Forum consists of national human rights institutions that conform to the standards set out in the 1993 UN General Assembly "Paris Principles" relating to the status of national human rights institutions.[132] The bulk of the Forum's twelve member institutions are from East Asian, South East Asian and Pacific Rim states; South Asia is poorly represented, the only member institutions being the National Human Rights Commissions of India, Nepal and Sri Lanka. The object of the Asia Pacific Forum is to protect and promote the human rights of the people of the Asia Pacific region[133] by supporting, through regional cooperation, the establishment and development of independent national human rights institutions, and by promoting cross-sector cooperation and joint activity on human rights. As an organization for regional dialogue and cooperation rather than an embryonic regional human rights system, the Forum has no judicial or quasi-judicial function or powers. Its activities at regional level include specialist training programmes and thematic regional workshops for member institutions, with annual meetings intended to serve as a mechanism for the practical advancement of human rights in the region. At international level, representatives of the Forum's member institutions together with NGO (non-governmental organization) representatives participate as observers in the intergovernmental Asia Pacific Workshops on Cooperation for the Promotion and Protection of Human Rights in the Asia Pacific region, convened regularly by the United Nations since 1982.[134] Through these UN Workshops a regional consensus has been reached on what is described as a "step by step" "building-blocks" approach, involving extensive government consultation, concerning the establishment of regional human rights arrangements in Asia. The Framework for Regional Technical Cooperation adopted at the 1998 Regional Workshop in Tehran (the "Tehran Framework") confirmed the "step by step" process towards establishing regional

---

[131] The Asia Pacific Forum of National Human Rights Institutions was established under Australian law as a non-profit company limited by guarantee. It is funded primarily by the UN Office of the High Commissioner for Human Rights and the governments of Australia and New Zealand.

[132] A/ RES/48/134 of 20 December 1993.

[133] Article 2 of the Constitution of the Asia Pacific Forum of National Human Rights Institutions, adopted at the sixth annual meeting of the Forum in Colombo, Sri Lanka in September 2001.

[134] The UN Regional Workshops bring together senior government representatives from governments in the Asia Pacific region with responsibility for human rights issues, with national human rights institutions and NGOs participating as observers.

human rights arrangements[135] and identified four key areas for regional cooperation in human rights.[136]

The South Asia Forum for Human Rights (SAFHR), established in 1993, is a regional public forum for the promotion of universal standards of human rights. It aims, through mechanisms such as people-to-people dialogue and the development of regional communications networks, to expose human rights abuses in the region, to provide a forum for the exchange of ideas on human rights, and through education and study programmes to raise awareness of human rights issues and the links between human rights, peace and democracy.[137]

Existing regional human rights systems vary considerably. Typically, though, they comprise a regional instrument backed up by monitoring and enforcement mechanisms in the form of a Commission or similar body and a Court. South East Asian and East Asian NGOs have already drawn up two regional human rights instruments, the Declaration on Basic Rights and Duties of ASEAN Peoples and Governments,[138] and the Asian Human Rights Charter.[139] A similar exercise could be undertaken by South Asian NGOs with a view to producing a sub-regional instrument for South Asia as a basis for tripartite discussions between governments, NGOs and national institutions in the South Asia region.[140] SAFHR has already highlighted the need for South Asian states to develop and adopt a regional charter or protocol for the protection of refugees and displaced persons. The combined expertise of the Asia Pacific Forum's member institutions, its government and NGO participants, together with those parties involved in the UN Asia Pacific Regional Workshops, SARRC and SAFHR, must be combined to chart the way forward for the creation of a sub-regional human rights system in South Asia, which should be accorded from

---

[135] Sixth Workshop on Regional Arrangements for the Promotion and Protection of Human Rights in the Asian and Pacific Region (28 Feb – 2 March 1998): Tehran Workshop Conclusions. UN Doc. E/CN.4/1998/50 Annex I.

[136] Development of national plans of action for the promotion and protection of human rights and the strengthening of national capacities; human rights education; development of national institutions for the promotion and protection of human rights; development of strategies for the realization of the right to development and economic, social and cultural rights.

[137] Mission Statement of South Asia Forum for Human Rights (SAFHR) adopted by the founding body of SAFHR on 19 February 1993 at Kathmandu, Nepal.

[138] Declaration adopted by the First General Assembly of the Regional Council on Human Rights in Asia on 9 December 1983, in Jakarta, Indonesia and presented to the ASEAN Secretariat on the same day.

[139] Charter drafted by the Asian Human Rights Commission, Hong Kong and formally declared on 17 May 1998 in Kwangju, South Korea.

[140] The notion of a specifically Asian approach to human rights which emphasises the particularities of the Asia-Pacific region, highlighted in the 1993 Report of the Regional Meeting for Asia of the World Conference on Human Rights and challenged by the 1993 Bangkok NGO Declaration for its downplaying of civil and political rights at the expense of economic, social and cultural rights (the so-called "Asian values" debate), is particularly associated with the viewpoint of South East and East Asian states.

the outset adequate legislative and enforcement powers along the lines of the European regional human rights system.[141]

5.   CONCLUSION

As the papers summarized in this article show, South Asia's record to date on the promotion and effective protection of human rights and fundamental freedoms is poor, but the potential for change exists if national governments are willing to accept the challenge. At the international level, the ratification of universal human rights instruments by all States in the region must be achieved, ideally without resort to reservations. At the national level, States are failing in their duty to eliminate all violations of human rights and their causes, and obstacles to the enjoyment of these rights. The consequence of this failure is incalculable human misery across the region. The development and strengthening of independent national justice systems and law enforcement agencies is a prerequisite to the provision of effective remedies for human rights violations. States must work towards the creation of a human rights culture in all aspects of society through education on human rights, democracy and the rule of law. At the regional level, channels for inter-governmental dialogue and for dialogue between governments, national institutions and NGOs already exist. This dialogue must be deepened and developed with a view to drafting and adopting a regional human rights system for South Asia – one that must be accorded adequate legislative and enforcement powers. There can be no advancement of human rights in the region in the absence of genuine political commitment on the part of States. If South Asian States are to tackle the human rights crisis confronting the region, as analyzed in this overview, they must be willing to take the steps indicated above.

---

[141] Established in 1951 by the Council of Europe; *see* Rehman, n. 16, at Chap. 6.

APPRECIATING COMPLIANCE WITH INTERNATIONAL ENVIRONMENTAL LAW TREATIES: LESSONS FROM A DEVELOPING COUNTRY – MALAYSIA*

Azmi Sharom**

> *"[A] World Order based on the Rule of Law thinly hides from sight the fact that social conflict must still be solved by political means and that even though there may exist a common legal rhetoric among international lawyers, that rhetoric must, for reasons internal to the ideal itself, rely on essentially – political – principles to justify outcomes to international disputes."*[1]

In a world where international law is often breached by those with the power or the nerve, it would be tempting to subscribe to the Realist view above, then compliance with international law would appear to be merely an ideal of the naïve. However, is such pessimism justified? In this article, it will be shown that such a cynical approach is not entirely accurate and that despite the recalcitrant acts of the few, there is still reason to strive towards the achievement of better compliance with international law. There is a case to be made in support of compliance as a valid and important concern with sound theories to encourage greater adherence to the principle. Here, the focus shall be on international environmental law.

1. IS CYNICISM JUSTIFIED?

At the core of Realist argument is the fact that international law can be separated neither from politics nor from power play. The principle of State sovereignty means that the very nature of international law making (treaties, for example) is a reflection of State will. There is no distinction therefore between what a State wants and what they choose with which to govern themselves. Although this may provide the

---

* This paper is drawn from a Ph.D. thesis by A. Sharom, entitled "Compliance with International Environmental Law: Three Malaysian Case Studies", University of London, 2002.
** Lecturer in Law, University of Malaya.
[1] M. Koskenniemi, "The politics of international law", 1 *EJIL* 4 (1990), at 7.

Asian Yearbook of International Law, Volume 10 (B.S. Chimni *et al.,* eds.)
© 2005 Koninklijke Brill NV. Printed in The Netherlands, pp. 57-93.

semblance of a legal order, in fact it merely veils the political will and force of the State players. Realists would argue that the study of compliance and the theories with which to improve it is a waste of time. This is because States comply not because of treaty obligations *per se*, but because of political or economic reasons. Therefore, no matter what a treaty contained, this would make no difference to State behaviour because the State would ultimately do what is best for its interest.

It is true that self-interest governs much of international law. The making of treaties is after all a reflection of State will. Furthermore, even domestic law making in a democratic society is to a certain extent a reflection of the will of its subjects. The issue here is whether, although politics do play a major role in international law, the latter should then be viewed with total cynicism? Should cynicism then colour the discussion of compliance even *once* the laws have been made? Overt pessimism implies that since international law ultimately, regardless of the ratification of treaties and the like, will always take a back seat to self-interest, compliance therefore happens as an accident rather than as a legal obligation.

However, the *realpolitik* position, above, where the concept of law takes a back seat to political realities, does have one glaring weakness. A subtle argument is put forward by Oppenheim,[2] who says about the precious State sovereignty that nations guard so carefully,

> "(I)t is only by reference to a higher legal rule in relation to which they are all equal, that the equality and independence of a number of sovereign States can be conceived. Failing that superior legal order, the science of law would be confronted with the spectacle of some sixty sovereign States,[3] each claiming to be the absolute highest and un-derived authority".

In short, in order to exist in the form that they wish, States already have to make a concession to the *idea of law* – without which the present system, imperfect as it is, would simply crumble.

Furthermore, there are writers such as Oran Young who dispute that States act purely on political self-interest alone. Young devised a method through which to examine the efficiency of international institutions or regimes (this would include treaty regimes) to prove that realist ideology is not without its flaws.[4] According to this test, one has to look at what have been described as "hard cases". These are situations where:

  a. One or more prominent members of the group are predisposed to dislike the decisions of the international institution;

---

[2] Quoted in I. Brownlie, *Principles of Public International Law*, 4th edn., Oxford: Clarendon Press, 1990, at 33.

[3] This was written in 1938.

[4] O.R. Young, "The effectiveness of international institutions: hard cases and variables", in J.N. Rosenau and E.O. Czempiel, (eds.), *Governance Without Government: Order and Change in World Politics*, Cambridge University Press, 1992.

b. It is comparatively easy to violate the rules of the international institution in such a way that it is hard to prove that the breach occurred, and

c. Ongoing changes in international society raise doubts about the relevance or underpinnings of the regime.

If the international institution can survive a situation with one or all of the above characteristics then it can be deemed to be working; it does in fact change behaviour despite obstacles, therefore it is not merely the plaything of States' wills. An example is the Whaling Convention (1946). Despite the changes to society and the regime (from a mere regulatory approach to an anti-whaling sentiment), the opposition of key members to any real control of whaling (of Norway and Japan, in particular) and the difficulties of enforcement, the Convention still managed to adopt the 1986 moratorium banning whaling and put pressure on so-called "scientific whaling".

However, another view veers away from simple one-upmanship. Chayes and Chayes argue that there is actually no empirical evidence to indicate that States comply only when it is in their interest to do so; this in turn, conversely, suggests that they comply even when it is not in their interest to do so.[5] Such "evidence" is merely anecdotal and there is no statistical or empirical data to support either view. Instead, they imply that these two opposing points of view are "background assumptions". The method with which one approaches compliance would thus depend on the type of assumption being used.

Chayes and Chayes go on to argue that Realist assumptions are not helpful when attempting to study ways with which to improve compliance. The Realist assumption is that a State's primary motivation is, they say, economic and military in nature. Any improvement in compliance would therefore require action along the lines of economic or military sanctions. Both methods are expensive, hard to mobilise, of doubtful efficacy, and probably politically unpopular. On the other hand, using a background assumption that States will generally comply, regardless of the self-interest of each, is more illuminating when attempts are made to devise a framework for understanding and improving compliance.

Other writers have also reached conclusions that support the approach of Chayes and Chayes. Mitchell's study on the regimes governing international oil pollution found that parties to a treaty not only abide by treaty provisions; by and large, they do so even at a significant cost to themselves.[6] Sands argues that the sheer bulk of international environmental dispute settlement in various fora (not necessarily the International Court of Justice) has meant that Realists such as Koskenniemi are no longer relevant, for greater dispute settlement efforts through activities such as

---

[5] A. Chayes and A.H. Chayes, "On compliance", 47 *International Organization* 175-205 (Spring 1993).

[6] R.B. Mitchell, *Intentional Oil Pollution at Sea: Environmental Policy and Treaty Compliance*, Massachusetts: The MIT Press, 1994.

arbitration reflects a greater faith not only in the international dispute settlement mechanisms but also in the laws with which that system is to apply.[7]

Furthermore, it is submitted that States do not as a general rule ratify treaties in order not to comply. In their article "On Compliance" Chayes and Chayes argue that the voluntary and consensual nature of treaties means that States become party to them because it is believed by these States that it is in their interest to do so.[8] The treaty-making process involves a great deal of discussion and negotiations at the national, regional, and international levels. During these discussions the specialized wishes of a State can by and large be accommodated. These wishes can be pushed forward either individually or collectively. It is true that the political realities of the world mean that stronger States have a greater influence on the treaty-making process. For example, the United States by itself almost put a stop to the United Nations Convention on the Law of the Sea despite ten years of negotiations. However, using the same treaty as an example, the relatively weak coalition of land-locked States managed to have their interests represented and reflected in the treaty despite being small players amongst the sea-going nations.[9] In other words, the treaty-making process allows through its participatory elements for checks and balances to occur. This ultimately leads to a situation where the treaty is a compromise of interests. It may result in a weak treaty – yet a weak treaty is, arguably, better than no treaty at all. Besides, a treaty should be an organic entity, constantly growing, changing and evolving; thus, it has the potential to become stronger.

Taking these factors into consideration Chayes and Chayes argue that two factors can be concluded: firstly, that States will not take part in lengthy and expensive negotiations in order routinely to violate treaty provisions; secondly, that if there is no compliance, then it is because the treaty does not accurately reflect the needs and wishes of States, rather than because non-compliance is a deliberate action on their part.[10]

2.   COMPLIANCE THEORY

Working therefore on the premise that compliance matters, what follows is a study of compliance theory. To summarize: compliance theory is the body of ideas and principles that aim towards the improvement of compliance with international treaties. Before compliance theory is examined, however, there should first be a discussion of the definitions of 'compliance'.

---

[7] P. Sands, "Compliance with international environmental obligations: existing international legal arrangements", in J. Cameron, J. Werksman and P. Roderick, (eds.), *Improving Compliance with International Environmental Law*, London: Earthscan Publications, 1996, at 81.

[8] *See* n. 5, at 179-180.

[9] *See* especially Part X of the United Nations Convention on the Law of the Sea that is entitled "Right of Access of Land-Locked States to and from the Sea and Freedom of Transit".

[10] *See* n. 5, at 183.

2.1.   Definition of 'compliance'

'Compliance' is defined in the Ninth Edition of the Concise Oxford Dictionary as "the act or an instance of complying; obedience to a request, command, etc.". In short, compliance, in its common, everyday meaning, is the act of obeying, of doing what one is told to or has agreed to. For the purposes of this article, though, there has to be somewhat more clarity than that. What is meant, after all, by such terms as "obeying" and "obedience"? How are these terms relevant when treaty obligations are addressed? When discussing compliance issues in international law as to the parameters of the discussion have to be absolutely certain. This is important because there can be many interpretations over the implications of compliance.

Firstly, compliance has to be distinguished from mere "implementation". Implementation consists of the formal legislation or regulations adopted by countries for them to comply with treaties. According to Brown Weiss and Jacobson:

> "Implementation refers to measures that States take to make international accords effective in their domestic law. Some accords are self-executing; that is, they do not require national legislation to become effective. But most international accords require national legislation or regulations to become effective".[11]

They go on to say:

> "Compliance goes beyond implementation. It refers to whether countries in fact adhere to the provisions of the accord and to the implementing measures that they have instituted. The answer cannot be taken as given even if laws and regulations are in place. Measuring compliance is more difficult than measuring implementation. It involves assessing the extent to which governments follow through on the steps that they have taken to implement international accords. In the end, assessing the extent of compliance is a matter of judgment.
>
> Compliance has several dimensions. Treaties contain specific obligations, some of which are procedural, such as the requirement to report, and others that are substantive, such as the obligation to cease or control an activity. In addition, preambles or initial articles in treaties place these specific obligations in a broad normative framework, which we refer to as the "spirit of the treaty".[12]

This definition is slightly different from one offered by R.B. Mitchell,[13] who defines 'compliance' as "behaviour that conforms to a treaty's explicit *rules*".[14] An example of such behaviour would be the adoption of national implementation measures, such as the passing of relevant legislation if existing legislation is in-

---

[11] E. Brown Weiss and H.K. Jacobson (eds.), *Engaging Countries: Strengthening Compliance with International Environmental Accords*, MIT Press, 1998, at 4.
[12] Brown Weiss and Jacobson, n. 11, at 4.
[13] R.B. Mitchell, "Compliance theory: an overview", in Cameron, Werksman and Roderick, n. 7.
[14] Emphasis added.

sufficient. In this definition, note the emphasis on the "explicit rules" of a treaty. This definition excludes two methods of examining compliance, and these are:

a. Examining the treaty as a whole when discussing compliance, as this definition is concerned only with specific provisions. For example, if a treaty were to have 100 articles or sections, the study of compliance according to Mitchell would be a matter of examining each and every article (or part) and seeing whether they are individually being complied with or not, without being concerned with whether the treaty as a whole is being complied with.[15]
b. Examining the role of the subtext, general norms or "spirit" of the treaty and the intentions of the parties that can be deduced from sources such as the preamble and the *travaux preparatoires.*

This is a rather technical method of study. Mitchell defends his approach as being necessary for the purposes of empirical research. It is easier, after all, to gauge compliance at this very objective level. Studying a treaty as a whole can also be counter-productive. Too much time may be spent pedantically pointing to instances of non-compliance with particular provisions as being indicative of treaty failure. This is especially true in the light of the work done by Chayes and Chayes, who argue that non-compliance with a few provisions need not necessarily mean that the treaty has failed.[16] Compliance can never be perfect: what is sought is substantial or acceptable compliance; therefore, any insistence on the faultless compliance with every single article of a treaty would be unrealistic. In the words of Mitchell:

> "Evaluating compliance against treaty provisions also makes more sense than speaking of compliance with the treaty as a whole. Parties often comply with some treaty provisions while violating others. Within a nation, different actors – governments, industry and non-governmental organisations (NGOs) – may well be responsible for implementing different treaty provisions. To speak of 'treaty compliance' therefore loses valuable empirical information by aggregating violation of one provision compliance with another. It also deserves mention that measuring compliance by strict reference to legal standards suggests that compliance is binary, either one complies or one violates: in fact[,] treaties can induce considerable beneficial be-havioural change that either falls short of actual compliance, *strictu sensu,* or goes beyond minimum treaty requirements".[17]

There are other benefits with Mitchell's approach, which was also adopted by Sands.[18] The sheer subjectivity of concepts such as "intentions" can lead to a separate quagmire of debate within which the researcher can get bogged down to such an extent that the primary questions regarding compliance *per se* gets lost in

---

[15] *See* n. 13, at 5-6.
[16] *See* n. 5.
[17] *See* n. 13, at 6.
[18] *See* n. 7.

the secondary questions and interpretations as to what constitutes "intentions", and other similarly theoretically challenging discussions. Admittedly, even specific provisions are open to interpretation. However, the constant interpretation and re-interpretation of provisions is a normal part of treaty-based law. This process is to be expected and is fundamentally different from examining a treaty in the light of more intangible concepts such as "intention". The former involves the study of rules that are determined and laid out clearly on paper while the latter depends on more circumstantial authorities.

The problem with this definition is that it is possible that *any* implementing action done by a State may be deemed as compliance. This is clearly not good enough. For implementation to have meaning, that is to say, if it can be deemed as compliance, then there is a need to assess the extent to which governments ensure that their implementation measures sufficiently meet the objectives of the treaty. Surely it cannot be deemed compliance if a government establishes a monitoring body as demanded by the treaty, but then fails to staff it with qualified people (such detail is normally not included in treaties, but it is certainly implied). It is therefore insufficient merely to study treaty provisions and their specific demands: one must look also at the "spirit" behind those demands.[19]

Given that the purpose of this study is determining ways of improving compliance, a certain degree of subjectivity can enter into the definition used. This is similar to the approach taken by Edith Brown Weiss and Harold K. Jacobson (see above) and for the purposes of this article there will be a combination of both these definitions. The common sense of the Weiss and Jacobson approach will provide the basis, while certain elements of Mitchell's definition, in particular the aspect of emphasising individual treaty provisions rather than the treaty as a whole, will also be used. In short, 'compliance' shall be defined as: "The actions which conform to the explicit rules and the broad norms or spirit of a treaty".

2.2.   Compliance distinguished from effectiveness and enforcement

Two further points of definition needs to be made, namely, to distinguish the term "compliance" from the terms "effectiveness" and "enforcement". Effectiveness is related to compliance, yet is not identical with it. Compliance with a treaty need not necessarily mean that it is effective and similarly, any effectiveness need not be found merely because of compliance. For example, there may be good compliance with a treaty regarding international trade in a particular endangered species. However, due to domestic consumption of that species, the problem that the treaty was designed to address, the prevention of extinction, is not effectively met. Conversely, a country

---

[19] It should be noted that one of the reasons for this disparity in approach is because Mitchell's definition was designed with the specific intention of maximising the empirical element of his research. This is due to the fact that one of the tenets of his argument is that treaties change behaviour; in other words, that compliance is the result of treaty law. It constitutes a challenge to realist thinking, which assumes that compliance is accidental and independent of the treaty.

may not be in compliance with a pollution treaty, but due to other factors, for example, an economic collapse, there are left no factories that may pollute. This study is concerned not with the effectiveness of international environmental law *per se*, because effectiveness can be influenced by factors other than the treaty. Thus, in order to determine how compliance can be improved, the study needs to concentrate on compliance itself., As a general rule, furthermore, it can be said that greater compliance should lead to greater effectiveness.[20]

The term 'enforcement' can also be confused with compliance, but there is an important distinction: compliance means that a duty has been carried out, while enforcement comes into play only if that duty was not carried out – in other words, if there was no compliance. Of course there is a relationship between the two, for tighter enforcement should encourage greater compliance, but, as can be seen, they are rather different. The two terms are not interchangeable and should be kept separate.

Enforcement is, however, seen as the normal method through which to elicit compliance. Respected international environmental law textbooks, such as Birnie and Boyle's *International Law and the Environment*[21] and Philippe Sands' *Principles of International Environmental Law Vol. 1*[22] both have chapters on compliance and both focus primarily on enforcement measures, *i.e.* what can be done when compliance has not occurred. There is no denying the importance of this approach. It is vital to ensure that enforcement measures are robust and ever expanding [to meet growing needs]. That is not, though, within the scope of this article. Moreover, it is submitted that compliance is of greater importance than enforcement, particularly with regard to the environment: once enforcement measures have to come into play, generally, it can safely be said that the damage has already been done. In the field of the environment, this is not the ideal situation. It is more pertinent to consider the fact that international dispute settlement (the usual form of enforcement measures) can take a long time to conduct. Furthermore, the traditional remedies of damages may not be able to put right the environmental damage done. No amount of money can, for example, bring back to life an extinct species or a destroyed ecosystem.

2.3.   Why states comply and why they do not

In order to examine compliance there has to be an understanding of the reasons *why* States comply and, conversely, why they do not. If this can be established then, theoretically, improving compliance becomes a matter of encouraging the positive and limiting the negative which, as can be seen later, is what compliance theory tries to achieve.

---

[20]   Brown Weiss and Jacobson, n. 11, at 5.
[21]   Patricia Birnie and Alan Boyle, *International Law and the Environment*, Oxford: Oxford University Press, 1992.
[22]   Philippe Sands, *Principles of International Environmental Law*, Vol. 1, Manchester: Manchester University Press, 1994.

In their book *Engaging Countries: Strengthening Compliance with International Environmental Accords*, Brown Weiss and Jacobson identify several factors that could influence a State's compliance.[23] These factors take into account the treaty itself as well as considerations beyond the actual document.

With regard to the treaty, consideration has to be given to the actual treaty-making process. This would include factors such as who drafted the treaty, the form taken by negotiations, and the depth and extent of agreement. One can reason that the greater a nation's involvement in the process and the more its views were taken into consideration, the greater is the likelihood that the State would be compliant. This idea matches the one put forward by Chayes and Chayes above: that States become involved with the treaty process because they wish for it to achieve their objectives.

The nature of the treaty provisions could also play a part in compliance, whether they are substantive or procedural, and whether they are specific or vague. The sort of compliance mechanism that exists within the treaty will, of course, have an important role to play. It follows that the clearer are a treaty's obligations and the stronger is its compliance mechanism, compliance is more likely to occur.

The way that a treaty treats non-members is another factor to be considered. That is, to ask whether member States may continue to deal with non-member countries or whether there is a bar against their doing so. If a government is of the opinion that joining a treaty will offer no differences from when they are not a party, this perspective may prove to be a disincentive to joining. Conversely, if a State believes that by being a party to and complying with the treaty there is to be gained a definite advantage that to remain outside the regime would not offer, then it will be an incentive for joining and for complying with the treaty obligations.

Compliance-influencing factors beyond the treaty proper can be further divided into two types. Firstly, there is the international environment, by which is meant the action and attitude of other States towards the treaty. Is there generally a good degree of compliance? Is there pressure applied among States for fellow Members to comply? Is the practice of 'free riding', i.e., when party members do not comply yet enjoy the benefits of the treaty nonetheless because sufficient numbers do comply, prevalent? Furthermore, the relationship between the States and international organizations related to the treaty (for example, the Secretariat) can be a significant factor. It is submitted that if Member States and any relevant international organiza- tion were to behave in a positive and pro-active manner, this would induce greater compliance.

The second question concerns factors at the national level. A country with a strong economy and a sound democratic system would, fundamentally, be more likely to comply. This is because it would be able to afford the necessary expenditure to comply and its citizens would have avenues with which to apply pressure on the government if it failed to do so. However, the idea that democracy automatically equals better compliance cannot be relied on. Vogel and Kessler argue that greater democracy does not necessarily mean wider environmental compliance.

---

[23] Brown Weiss and Jacobson, n. 11, at 7.

"In the former Soviet Union, democratisation reduced national compliance with some international environmental agreements. What democratisation does offer citizens is a greater voice in shaping a wider array of public policies, including environmental regulation. If the citizens of democratic or relatively democratic nations strongly support the objectives of the environmental treaties their government has signed, as appears to be the case in the United States and Northern Europe, compliance is likely to be enhanced. On the other hand, if they value other objectives, such as profit from the sales of endangered species or inexpensive refrigeration, then compliance is likely to prove more difficult."[24]

In his book *Intentional Oil Pollution at Sea*, Mitchell offers further analysis on the sources of compliance and non-compliance. Whilst he does not take a Realist viewpoint, he does acknowledge the political aspects of treaty behaviour and these are reflected in his conclusions. Many States comply with treaty law, for example, simply because it is good for them or because there can be no loss arising from their compliance. It is possible that a State already has such stringent laws on the environment within its own jurisdiction that treaty compliance entails no significant change in behaviour. It does, howeve,r give them a moral high ground over non-party States and [influence the] legitimization of policy and legislation at the national level. It is also possible that States comply because the treaty provisions themselves are so vague that even inaction would not be seen as non-compliance, or the treaty is attempting to control behaviour that is beyond the ability of States to carry out.[25]

However, there are also sources of compliance that do not fall conveniently within the Realist-type explanations. Non-compliance may have an unknown effect on the future of the treaty and on future treaty relationships. Such an uncertainty could act as a deterrent to non-compliance. This fear of the unknown is related to another source of compliance: that once the rules of a treaty are set in place and the bureaucracy established, it might actually be difficult to stop complying in order to violate a condition. That is to say, it becomes easier simply to comply, as compliance can be habit forming; also, decision-making becomes so much simpler when following a set of established rules and procedure.[26]

Furthermore, treaties can cause publicity. Non-compliance that is highly publicised may have a serious shaming effect on the offending State. This goes hand in hand with the next source of compliance: political pressure. Treaties provide a convenient rallying ground for environmental lobbyist and activist groups on which they can focus their pressure on States at a domestic and international level, giving their campaign legal weight and authority, and making it hard for States to be inactive – since they have already agreed to a particular course of action.

---

[24] D. Vogel and T. Kessler, "How compliance happens and doesn't happen domestically", in Brown Weiss and Jacobson, n. 11, at 34.

[25] For example, nodule mining in the deep-sea bed under United Nations Convention on the Law of the Sea as governed by Article 151.

[26] A point also supported by Chayes and Chayes, n. 5.

Compliance may also occur because of what Mitchell terms 'interdependent self-interest'. This is a situation where compliance is seen by States as being an option preferable to non-compliance because it encourages other States to comply; in turn, this will improve the situation for a complying State. Therefore, to violate treaty provisions or not to comply brings very little good, ultimately. Unfortunately, interdependent self-interest can encourage the problem of 'free riding'.

Apart from 'free riding', other reasons why States may not comply can range from the relatively "innocent" to the more cynical. "Innocent" non-compliance would be due to problems such as incapacity, where a State cannot afford to comply or does not have the necessary tools (technology, trained staff, or institutional mechanisms) for compliance, and inadvertence where a State tried in good faith yet failed to comply, for whatever reason (usually associated with non-capacity).

Vogel and Kessler state that making laws and directives without taking into account the capacity of regulatory bureaucracies to implement them would lead to poor compliance. For example, the American Environmental Protection Agency was given too much to do in too little time, leading to long delays before legislative initiatives took concrete form. If such problems arise in a country as wealthy as the United States, then such requirements would be even more problematic in developing nations. However, as a general rule, Vogel and Kessler assert, "compliance tends to be greatest in nations whose government bureaucracies are the most competent and powerful."[27]

There is also the possibility that States have acted cynically in signing and/or ratifying a treaty and had no intention, in the first place, of complying. A State may sign or even ratify a treaty for many self-serving reasons, such as the positive publicity of being part of a treaty, or even to show political support to allies by signing a treaty as a favour to them. It is also possible that the State had never intended to comply. This could be because it realizes that enforcement measures are too weak to be used effectively against them; also, value systems might differ, where the State agrees in principle with the aims of the treaty but in practice finds other, more important, matters that require attention. Needless to say, there is a plethora of reasons why States do not comply. The issue now to be addressed is to ask what can be done about non-compliance.

In the face of non-compliance the international community has traditionally seen two types of action that may be taken in order to elicit compliance. These are, on the one hand, positive inducements, implying financial and technological help along with the provision of educational aid and training; on the other hand, negative sanctions include taking enforcement measures; the shaming of offending States by exposure to the press or at least to the Conference of Parties; the forcing of compliance by powerful States, and reciprocity where non-compliance by State A would result in a similar action by State B (this is useful only in small multilateral or bilateral treaties). Some negative sanctions are perhaps particularly unattractive to enforce, and may even lead to counter-productive results. The thought of a powerful

---

[27] Vogel and Kessler, n. 24, at 22-23.

State from the North 'punishing' a small State from the South may in itself be enough to raise Third World hackles to the point that the actual issues become confused; attention may be directed away from the environmental concern at hand. It is, after all, only wealthy and powerful States which have the strength to take such action, often unilaterally. As it stands, only the United Nations Charter and the Organization of American States Charter allow for the use of harsh negative sanctions, be they economic or military, in order to force compliance. Both methods come at a high cost, administratively, economically and politically.

Taking into account the reasons why States do and do not comply, and considering the limitations of more "traditional" methods of eliciting compliance, it is submitted that it is possible to design a theory to encourage the creation of a system that actually supports compliance with treaties without the need for confrontational methods of enforcement.

2.4.   Compliance through a system of management

Supporters of compliance theory do not dispute the Realist argument that external factors can influence compliance; their differing opinion is based on the belief that treaty provisions *can* have an effect *as well*. Whether the provisions of a treaty can induce compliance depends on the treaty's own compliance system. A compliance system consists of the provisions within the treaty itself that determine the methods with which compliance can be induced. Chayes and Chayes describe the system as compliance through management.

> "We believe that effective compliance management requires establishing and maintaining a transparent information system and a response system. The information system must produce adequate and accurate information about actors' behaviours under the treaty. The managerial response system must then produce discriminating responses to different types of non compliance, using both multilateral, treaty based and unilateral actions to induce change".[28]

In *Intentional Oil Pollution at Sea*, Mitchell distinguishes three types of compliance systems and they are: the primary rule system; the compliance information system, and the non-compliance response system. This falls within the Chayes and Chayes concept, with the added factor of being concerned also with the primary rules of the treaty. For the purposes of this article the Mitchell framework will be used when a treaty management/compliance system is examined.

The *primary rule system* sets the basic parameters of the treaty. It determines the players who will be involved, the changes in behaviour required of them, and the new regulations by which they will have to abide. The *compliance information system* identifies the players involved in reporting on parties' compliance or lack

---

[28] A. Chayes, A.H. Chayes and R. Mitchell, "Managing compliance: a comparative perspective", in Brown Weiss and Jacobson, n. 11, at 42.

of it, as well as the mechanisms to be used in gathering and disseminating that information. The *non-compliance response system* determines the type and degree of action that should be taken in the event that non-compliance should occur.

These three work together. Primary rules establish the new boundaries; the information system sees whether those boundaries are being adhered to, and the response system is to act if the information points towards non-compliance. It takes no leap of faith to see that the clearer and better are defined the primary rules, the more stringent is the information gathering, and the more efficient is the response system, then the better the compliance should be. In the absence of any external factors influencing or enforcing compliance, the workings of a treaty's compliance system should be examined by a researcher in order to determine precisely those factors within the treaty provisions that induce the parties to behave appropriately.

2.4.1. Primary rule system

The primary rules laid down by a treaty are highly influential on compliance. They determine the standards that have to be set, as well as the new behaviour patterns that have to be followed. This would mean the determination of costs and new activities. The way such rules are structured and the burden they place on parties will have an influence on compliance, thus if there is a greater burden on developed States, this may mean greater compliance because these States have the resources and perhaps the internal pressures (as incentive) to do what they have agreed to do.

If the primary rules encourage transparency in the treaty processes, so much the better: if it is easy to see when there is non-compliance, this should have a two-fold effect. Firstly, transparency would encourage compliance because of the parties' fear of discovery of non-compliance and, secondly, because transparency would ensure that those who do comply do so for all to see. These aspects make it easier to deal with the 'bad' and reward the 'good'. It is important, therefore, to make sure that the acts to be regulated are those that are the most straightforward to monitor.

Specificity is a factor to encourage compliance. The clearer are the rules, the more certain the parties will be as to where they stand. This, again, will make it easier for those who wish to comply and harder for those who may try to avoid compliance through so-called 'misunderstandings' and 'misinterpretations'. Of course, establishing very specific rules throughout the treaty may be difficult because of the nature of treaty making;[29] however, it is an ideal towards which the treaty should aim, so that even if not all of the provisions are specifically worded, a good proportion is clearly defined.

At this point, it is submitted that taking Mitchell's logic to its conclusion, surely if higher levels of compliance are required, the optimum type of primary rules would be those that are most clearly worded and easiest to follow. There lies in this approach the danger that rules may be designed to elicit compliance for compliance's sake:

---

[29] If States feel a treaty provision may be too burdensome to them, then it is possible that they will either not agree or make moves for reservations.

it would render the treaty a working and respected law, yet would do nothing for the problem it seeks to rectify.

2.4.2.   *Compliance information system*

The intention of a compliance information system can be summed up in one word: 'transparency'; it is:

> "[T]he adequacy, accuracy, availability, and accessibility of knowledge and information about the policies and activities of parties to the treaty, and of the central organisations established by it on matters relevant to compliance and effectiveness, and about the operations of the norms, rules and procedures established by the treaty".[30]

A sound compliance information system has therefore to collect a wide range of relevant, accurate, reliable, and legitimate information on compliance and effectiveness, which is also made available to the public.

Transparency is vital to the good management of treaty compliance because it plays several important functions. Without good transparency it would be difficult to co-ordinate actions. It is also a reassurance for Member States to learn of the levels of compliance of the other Members to a treaty. It is necessary for States to feel secure in the fact that the other States are making efforts to accomplish that which is required of them. 'Free riding' would also be harder to achieve if transparent checks were able to show that some States were simply not fulfilling their obligations. Such openness has the further advantage of being a deterrent to States to fail to comply.[31]

The major issue here is that it is often difficult to obtain information: not necessarily from the point of view of recalcitrance, but from an inability to do so well.[32] It is important that the treaty take into account certain points when demanding data. Obtaining data from large groups is harder to achieve than from small groups; therefore, if the same data can be obtained from a source with fewer actors, gathering data would be made much easier.[33] Furthermore, the type of information required has to be within the technological capability of the States involved.[34]

---

[30]   Chayes, Chayes and Mitchell, n. 28, at 43.

[31]   Charney, "Non-legal sanctions in commercial relationships" 104 *Harvard Law Review* 373-467, and Koehane, *Hegemony: Co-operation and Discord in the Political World Economy*, Princeton: Princeton University Press, 1984, suggest that negative reputation impacts and diffuse reciprocity may be adequate in deterring non-compliance.

[32]   An International Labour Organisation Working Group as reported in Chayes, Chayes and Mitchell, n. 28, at 46.

[33]   Vogel and Kessler, n. 24, at 24-25.

[34]   In his book, *Intentional Oil Pollution at Sea*, Mitchell notes how monitoring of the dumping of oil from ships became easier when the monitoring shifted from actual polluting acts to ensuring that each ship is equipped with the required pollution control devices. It was technically very hard to trace discarded oil to the culprit, whereas it is easier to check that ships are properly equipped.

This still leaves the issue of the actual data gathering. Self-reporting is the easiest method applied by a treaty for demanding data, but it really needs to be supplemented by other means. The Convention on International Trade in Endangered Species of Wild Fauna and Flora 1973 (CITES), for example, has a double reporting system: one report comes from the exporting State and one from the importing State. This serves to act as a self-checking mechanism. It is submitted that what is required is to open the entire process to include as many bodies as possible in the task, rather than limiting data collection to the States themselves. In practical terms, this would entail the involvement of Non-Governmental Organisations (NGOs).

The expertise of NGOs should be exploited to the full when gathering data. Bodies such as Traffic and Wetlands International are vital cogs in the smooth working of CITES and RAMSAR.[35] However, NGOs are more important than as mere data-gatherers. If transparency is to be taken seriously, the concept should include the entire international environmental law system.

Cameron[36] argues for greater openness in the international legal process. This would include treaty processes, i.e., the phases from the forming of the treaty through to its actual application. Basing the process on a constitutional law model, he argues in favour of the importance of transparency and public (in Cameron's case, the emphasis is on NGO) participation.

The participation of non-governmental bodies has been acknowledged by the United Nations in its Charter, particularly Article 71, which states:

"The Economic and Social Council may make suitable arrangements for consultation with non-governmental organisations which are concerned with matters within its competence. Such arrangements may be made with international organisations and where appropriate, with national organisations after consultation with the Member of the United Nations concerned".

The UN has in many conferences and treaty-making exercises used this facility. The watershed for NGO participation came with UNCED where the precedence was set to accommodate NGOs by simplifying accreditation rules,[37] as well as by giving NGOs opportunities to make their views available to participants through the publishing of statements in all of the official UN languages. This broadening of participation has been carried on into post-UNCED events such as HABITAT II in Istanbul 1996. In the context of designing a transparent treaty system, this sort of encouragement towards non-governmental bodies should be embraced. Apart from the monitoring role and the information-gathering/dissemination role, NGOs may often have at their disposal expertise useful to governments with a limited capacity.

---

[35] RAMSAR Convention on Wetlands of International Importance, Especially as Waterfowl Habitat, 1982.
[36] "Compliance, citizens and NGOs" in Cameron, Werksman and Roderick, n. 7.
[37] UNCED Rules of Procedure, Rule 65 Decisions 1/1: Role of NGO[s] in the Preparatory Process for UNCED.

To summarize, a compliance information system is intimately linked to transparency. Monitoring by self-reporting and the empowerment of NGOs are vital to this aim. On-site monitoring is another method of improving a compliance information system. The treaty provisions should be designed so as to enhance the flow of information between and among parties. The provisions should also increase the resources that would allow for maximum monitoring. The more effective a treaty is to be in this sense, the greater the number of groups and individuals that should be given the ability to participate in the monitoring and information system. The wider the range of actors who can process, disseminate and analyze data, the better, as sources of compliance and non-compliance can be identified – and rewarded or punished, as the case may be.

2.4.3. *Non-compliance response system*

The treaty should also include provisions that facilitate compliance and sanctions non-compliance. Sanctioning violations need not mean the treaty's providing for aggressive acts. The provision of a regular conference of parties could have an important effect. It allows all States to be recognized, 'good' or compliant States to be acknowledged and 'bad' or non-compliant States publicly to be exposed and shamed. Information could be shared and new developments discussed.

It is possible that disputes may have arisen over the respective duties of States. Dispute resolution helps to clarify norms and to remind parties of their duties. It is also desirable that a treaty provide specific enforcement measures in the event of non-compliance. It is also possible, as with the United Nations Convention on the Law of the Sea, to have a compulsory dispute settlement mechanism.[38] Non-contentious methods of dispute settlement are to be aimed at.[39]

A treaty should also make it hard for violations to occur. For example, with pollution control, instead of trying to apply a limit on effluent, a treaty should instead make it compulsory for pollution control devices to be installed. In this way pollution does not become an option.[40] Most disputes are settled by negotiation. But what if negotiations fail? Binding arbitration/litigation has had a relatively small role in solving environmental law disputes. The processes are costly, contentious, cumbersome, and slow. Furthermore, far more work needs to be done if smaller, less-developed countries are to be able to face richer partners in court on equal terms (it may be argued that negotiation faces the same problem and is possibly less helpful because there are few rules of engagement – nor is there a judge to ensure fair play). Negotiations also raise the political visibility of the problem yet are often not subject to the control of the parties involved.

The method of dispute settlement matters less than the fact that the parties accept the outcome as authoritative. The Convention on International Civil Aviation 1944 has a Council that deals on a rather informal basis with questions of interpretation;

---

[38] Annex VII of the Convention.
[39] Chayes, Chayes and Mitchell, n. 28, at 54-56.
[40] *See* n. 34.

it favours settlement by political and diplomatic means, rather than through confrontational arbitration. The trend now is towards binding arbitration, as used by the WTO after the Uruguay Round. A middle ground is comprised of compulsory conciliation culminating in a non-binding recommendation from the conciliators if the parties fail themselves to come to an agreement. Even though the conciliators' decision is not binding, it is still influential and is likely to carry weight with those parties in dispute as well as all parties in general.

Another method is the authoritative or semi-authoritative interpretation by a designated body of the international organization, for example, the Secretariat. This provides a less contentious method of treaty interpretation. Furthermore, it can also prevent parties from failing to comply by arresting the States from committing themselves to activities that clash with the goals of the regime. The non-formal and non-confrontational nature of such a system also means that it is highly probable that States will submit questions of interpretation. An on-going process such as this would go some way towards rendering the treaty a vital and "live" one. Furthermore, it is unlikely that States would reject the answers to questions that they themselves had submitted.

2.4.4. *Other actions to encourage compliance*

With regard to facilitating compliance: the main concern should be capacity building for Member States who may, without help, otherwise not be able to comply. This includes financial, technological[41] and educational help. Apart from the direct benefits such help may provide, party States may be encouraged to report if they believed that they would obtain assistance as a result of the said reporting. For example, a State may be less reluctant to report its failures if it knew that such reporting could lead to some form of help and thus benefit for itself.

The problem here, of course, is to find sources of financing for such capacity-building exercises. Treaties now ought to have a mechanism that allows for wealthier nations to help poorer ones. The Montreal Protocol Multilateral Fund, the Climate Fund of the Framework Convention on Climate Change, and the Global Environmental Facility proceed on the premiss that developing countries need financial and technical assistance. All of these mechanisms are designed not just for operating projects, but for education and training, the improvement of scientific capacity, assistance to planning departments, the enhancement of data systems, and the like.

The treaty should be open to change and adaptation in order for it to remain vital. Traditional change would mean a slow process involving amendments. The possible adverse effects of delay can be overcome in several ways. Framework treaties provide skeleton of a law which can then be fleshed out in future documents, and constitute one such way. This has been successful with the 1985 Vienna Convention for the Protection of the Ozone Layer and its more substantial sister treaty, the 1987 Montreal

---

[41] Care has to be taken to ensure that aid such as technology transfer is not only compatible with the nations receiving it, but is also up to date: technology transfer would be reduced to a farce if developed States used it as an opportunity to 'dump' defunct technology on needy countries.

Protocol. However, in contrast, the 1992 Climate Change Convention has experienced great difficulty in seeing any significant flesh added onto its skeletal frame.

Other methods include for the treaty to provide a body that can 'interpret' the Articles of the treaty, as is done by the IMF Agreement. Special provisions for changing the "technical" regulations, allowing for a simpler method for changing "technical" aspects of the treaty, is a helpful way of making changes relatively quickly: a majority vote, for example, to a change that affects the annex of a treaty, as in CITES.

Changes in the treaty depend on the parties' view of the success of the treaty. If compliance is good then it may wish further to improve the standard; f compliance is poor, then an investigation is required into why this is so. There is no point in amending the treaty to become more specific when the problem is a financial one. What must be noted is that change is necessary for the ultimate survival and relevance of a treaty.

Brown Weiss and Jacobson[42] contend that the following measures should be taken to improve compliance in the short term. Creating communities of interested parties, especially scientists and specialists in the topic, or what has been termed "epistemic communities". More scientists lead to more information, greater understanding and therefore better compliance. Involving domestic officials and bureaucracies, so that their personal interests and reputations become issues at stake, also increases the motivation to comply. Encouraging greater personal involvement and wider networking with international peers mean that individual government servants are more likely to do their best.

To conclude this part of the article, there is a sense that looking towards an authoritarian figure or some form of harsh treatment of offenders is not the preferred approach of eliciting compliance. The writer concurs with this. It would seem that the way forward is to be found in the serious democratization of the international law processes. This means the use of human rights, both substantive and procedural, to empower citizens in the taking of legal and political action themselves without their having to depend on States to do so. It means also the opening up of the treaty processes, allowing as many actors into these as possible, to encourage transparency and a constitutional model of international law.

Treaty design may have an important task to play, too. If the Chayes and Chayes and Mitchell theory is correct, the shape and form of the treaty should play a major role in State compliance. This theory will now be applied to the Malaysian scenario. It is hoped that this will shed more light on the topic by seeing how and why a developing nation complies and how viable are the theories discussed above when applied to the context of the said country. The treaties chosen for further study are the Washington Convention on International Trade in Wild Flora and Fauna 1973 (CITES),[43] the Basel Convention on the Control of Transboundary Movement of Hazardous Wastes and their Disposal 1989 (Basel)[44] and the Ramsar Convention

---

[42] Brown Weiss and Jacobson, n. 11, at 10.
[43] 12 ILM 1088 (1973).
[44] 28 ILM 657 (1989).

on Wetlands of International Importance Especially as Waterfowl Habitat 1971 (Ramsar).[45] These Treaties are all established instruments; thus, it would be easier and fairer to examine the Malaysian government's performance of them, because sufficient time has passed for consideration prior to ratification and for necessary post-ratification action to have been taken.[46]

These Treaties are also sufficiently specific in nature and the responsibilities placed on the parties reflect this.[47] They are also (as their full titles suggest) quite diverse. It is therefore hoped that such diversity will imbue the paper with a broad enough spectrum to provide a satisfactory overview of compliance – and the application of compliance theory – with international environmental law in Malaysia.

3.   COMPLIANCE WITH *CITES* IN MALAYSIA

As its full title suggests CITES is about the control of international trade in rare species of plants and animals. It is not limited to live specimens, but also concerns dead specimens or parts of specimens (Article I). The main method through which trade is controlled is by a system of appendices and permits. If a species is placed on any one of the three appendices provided for by the treaty, then trade in this species is controlled. Appendix I is reserved for endangered species and trade for commercial reasons[48] may not take place (Article III). Appendix II is for species that are not yet endangered, but which could become so if trade is not controlled (Article IV). This being the case, then some method of regulation is required to keep international trade in these species limited. Appendix III is basically a list of species that individual parties can insert without the need of approval from the other members (Article V). In other words, if Country A wishes to protect one of its domestic species yet is uncertain whether it can obtain the necessary support of other members to vote that species into either Appendix I or II, then it can unilaterally place it into Appendix III, thus providing it with some form of trade protection which the other parties are

---

[45] 11 ILM 969 (1972).

[46] Malaysia ratified these treaties in 1977, 1994 and 1993 respectively.

[47] Furthermore, it is submitted that the other treaties to which Malaysia is do not raise sufficient compliance issues. The Convention Concerning the Protection of the World Cultural Heritage does not demand very much action on the part of its parties. The same applies to the Vienna Convention for the protection of the Ozone Layer (along with its protocols) and the United Nations Framework Convention on Climate Change. These last two treaties require no action from countries that are still developing; Malaysia falls into that category. The Convention on Biological Diversity is a vague framework treaty that also places no serious obligations, and the Convention to Combat Desertification is quite easy to comply with in a country with a tropical climate.

[48] Resolution 5.10 of the Conference of Parties: Definition of Primary Commercial Purposes, states that commercial purpose would mean an activity whose purpose is to obtain economic benefit, including profit. "Commercial purpose" is also more about the use of the specimen once it has been obtained. It is possible that a commercial transaction may take place in the acquisition of the specimen, but this need not mean that once acquired, the specimen will be used for commercial purposes.

not only obliged to respect but are also obliged to take practical measures to ensure that trade in the said species is controlled.

In order to obtain a permit to export a specimen listed in Appendix I, the approval of the Management Authority (MA) and the Scientific Authority (SA) must first be obtained. The MA will determine that the specimen was not obtained illegally, that the transport of any live specimen is safe and will not harm it, and that its export is not for commercial purposes. The SA will give its approval only if the export of the specimen is not detrimental to the survival of the species. For Appendix I species, there is also a need for an import permit to be obtained. The import permit is granted by the SA and MA of the importing country; its criteria are similar to those of the exporting State. In other words, there is a system of double-checking to ensure that the export is totally above board.

For Appendix II specimens, the criteria are similar, but there is no need to ensure that the export is carried out for non-commercial purposes: Appendix II specimens may be traded. There is also no need for an import permit. The primary obligation of parties is to ensure a working MA and SA along with the necessary legislation so that the permit system can be implemented. Another important obligation is the duty to publish annual reports with which the Secretariat and the Conference of Parties can monitor the activities of individual States.

Malaysia has by and large been able to put in place the necessary laws and institutions for it to comply with CITES.[49] The main pieces of legislation making it illegal to procure specimens without prior consent are the Protection of Wildlife Act 1972 (PWA)[50] and the Fisheries Act 1985 (FA).[51] The PWA has lists of animals and birds, classifying them as "protected" and "totally protected". It is an offence to take, harm or even be in possession of these species without the approval of the government in the form of licenses for "protected" species and of ministerial approval for "totally protected" species. With regard to fish, the Fisheries (Control of Endangered Species of Fish) Regulations 1999,[52] made by virtue of the FA, lists several species of aquatic life that cannot be taken, harassed, possessed or harmed without permission from the Department of Fisheries. Naturally, considering it is a treaty about trade, customs officials and customs legislation form a vital part of the implementation of CITES. In Malaysia the Customs Act 1967[53] governs this aspect of law enforcement. The Act provides that restricted goods may not be

---

[49]   The Malaysian legal system is quite unique in that the states of Sarawak and Sabah have constitutionally provided extra legislative powers. Therefore, with regard to wild flora and fauna, they have their own separate legislation and implementing bodies, whereas in Peninsular Malaysia these matters are in the purview of the Federal Government. To avoid confusion, however, this article will focus primarily on the laws and institutions of Peninsular Malaysia. Reference to Sarawak and Sabah will, of course, be made when relevant. It is submitted, though, that by and large the issues faced by the authorities on Peninsular Malaysia are similar to those faced by their Borneo cousins.

[50]   Laws of Malaysia, Act 76.

[51]   Laws of Malaysia, Act 317.

[52]   P.U.(A) 409/99.

[53]   Laws of Malaysia, Act 235 (Revised 1980).

exported from or imported into the country (Section 31). By virtue of Section 31, CITES specimens will thus need the requisite permits in order to be allowed through customs. Within the PWA and the FA provisions are made to punish those who commit offences under them.

Regarding the CITES institutions, the Management Authority in Peninsular Malaysia is the Department of Wildlife and National Parks (PERHILITAN), which is a Federal department under Ministry of Science, Technology and the Environment (MOSTE). Although PERHILITAN is the Management Authority, it does not bear the entire burden of this responsibility by itself. PERHILITAN as a body is expert primarily in land-based animals. Therefore, when it comes to flora and marine life, it requires the help of the Department of Agriculture (DOA) and the Department of Fisheries (DOF) respectively. These two bodies aid PERHILITAN in the granting of permits. The DOF grants the permits for all fish specimens, while the DOA grants the permits for all flora specimens.

The Scientific Authority is officially the Ministry of Science, Technology and the Environment (MOSTE). Specifically, the Environmental Protection and Management Division of MOSTE holds this responsibility. The most important point to be made here is that MOSTE is by no means a scientific organization. It is a government bureaucracy and as such lacks the necessary expertise to do what is required of it by CITES. This problem is circumnavigated by the CITES Committee, consisting of several bodies, each with its own expertise. Theoretically, what the committee should have is enough knowledge collectively to perform the function of a CITES Scientific Authority. The members of the committee include the Department of Agriculture, the Department of Wildlife and National Parks, the Fisheries Department, the Ministry of Primary Industry, the Ministry of Foreign Affairs, the Department of Customs and Excise, and the Malaysian Forest Research Institute.

What is particularly striking about this mix of bodies is that although some of them seem clearly relevant others do not; they may in fact even appear slightly sinister. Looking at the job of the Scientific Authority, its primary concern is to ensure that if a particular specimen is exported, this action will not create a danger to the species as a whole. One can see where the Fisheries Department or the Department of Agriculture might have the ability to determine this fact. However, where does the Ministry of Foreign Affairs fit into this? Worse still, the Ministry of Primary Industry's ambit is the exploitation of natural resources such as timber, so what role does it play as part of the "Scientific Authority"?

This leads to the issue of compliance. On the surface it does appear that the necessary actions have been taken by the Malaysian government to implement CITES. The permit system is active and is very much part of the established bureaucracy. The problem with CITES in Malaysia is not one of non-compliance, but instead it is really one of poor compliance. The reasons for this are examined below.

3.1. Problems with Malaysian CITES Compliance

The weaknesses in Malaysian compliance with CITES can be summarized as
a lack of expertise, poor legislation, a lack of resources, and poor environmental
awareness. These points are discussed in detail below. Much of the information is
obtained through interviews with officials in the various governmental bodies entrusted
with the implementation of CITES.

3.1.1. Lack of expertise

The most prominent problem with the implementation of CITES in Malaysia
is, arguably, the lack of expertise. This is not to say that there are no capable individuals working on CITES obligations. When discussing the matter of expertise, there
are two strands to the issue. Firstly, it has to be said that there exist bodies that are
simply incapable of carrying out the job which they are supposed to be doing, be
it through a lack of training or simply through being the wrong sort of entity in the
first place. Secondly, although expertise does exist, it exists in different forms and
in different places. There is, therefore, the issue of bringing these disparate bands
of expertise together in a coherent fashion so as to enable better CITES compliance.

As pointed out earlier, the Scientific Authority is more of an administrative body
and not a scientific one as such. Decisions made by the CITES committee tend to
be of a broad policy nature.[54] The CITES committee is more concerned with the
listing exercises of CITES: that is, to say when a new species is to be added into
any of the appendices. Decisions made on these exercises appear to be political and
economic rather than environmental in nature. Domestic interests take precedence,
thus when it was proposed that Merbau and Ramin wood be included in the
Appendices, this was soundly opposed by the MOSTE, prompted largely by the
Ministry of Primary Industries (which would explain the presence of its representatives in the committee). Other considerations taken into account by the committee
includes the maintenance of cordial ties with fellow developing countries, particularly
the G77. Therefore, Malaysia objected to the inclusion of Mahogany into Appendix
I even though it is not an indigenous plant and has no economic relevance to the
country. Mahogany is, however, economically important for Brazil – a G77 country
and an ally who has to be supported.

One objectionable factor regarding the CITES committee is not that it is making
decisions based on political or economic expediency which, to a certain extent, is
to be expected of any government; the issue here is the lack of a proper Scientific
Authority capable of doing the main duty the treaty has set out for it to do. That
is to say, the body should ensure that any export or import will not be detrimental
to the survival of the species as a whole (Article III (3)(a), IV (2)(a) and IV (6)(a)
of CITES).

---

[54] Interview with MOSTE, 14 July 1997.

In Malaysia, for all practical purposes, the Scientific Authority is PERHILITAN, the same body that is the Management Authority. This is also not a completely satisfactory circumstance. Although it is much better to have a body with some scientific expertise doing the job of the Scientific Authority, it should be pointed out that PERHILITAN's expertise is limited to wild animals and birds, and the situation is far from ideal. Even within their own area of expertise, there are problems: there is no baseline information regarding the species available for trade; the approximate numbers that are available is limited to large mammals.[55] Yet these animals are not the ones being traded, given that they appear in Appendix I. Without this baseline information, there is no real scientific basis to make the decision as to whether it is safe for the species as a whole to allow trade to continue. The situation is even worse regarding fish and fauna: the relevant bodies with the expertise, the Fisheries Department and the Department of Agriculture, are not agencies with protection as their primary concern; their greater concerns lie with the fishing and agricultural industries and not with the protection of fish and fauna. Furthermore, having one body doing the work of both the Management and the Scientific Authority diminishes the double protection of having two separate bodies determining the wisdom of allowing a particular specimen an import or export permit.

The problem of a lack of expertise manifests itself in the way that CITES works in Malaysia. From the earlier descriptions, it can be seen that the system depends on a variety of bodies all working together. For example, PERHILITAN may turn to the DOA when faced with a decision regarding a plant specimen; and a case of marine life will have to be referred to the DOF. This is not a criticism *per se*, for many countries, particularly smaller developing countries, simply do not have the resources to establish one central body to work specifically on CITES. However, the problem that arises is one of co-ordination.[56] With so many bodies each working on a small part of the greater whole, there is a need for strong central body and an efficient co-ordinating mechanism to ensure that decisions are made quickly, accurately and efficiently. Unfortunately, neither of these elements exists in the Malaysian context. The Environmental Protection and Management Division of MOSTE consists of the head, one officer and a handful of clerical staff. This small number of staff, along with their other non-CITES related duties mean that they simply do not have the resources to play the role of a pro-active CITES co-ordinator.

The system which exists regarding co-operation is also very *ad hoc* in nature. Although interviews with officials from PERHILITAN, DOF, DOA and Customs and Excise did not disclose any dissatisfaction with the system, the fact remains that the lack of a formal framework is a serious shortcoming. The *ad hoc* way in which the day-to-day running of CITES currently occurs may suit government officers for the moment, as a comfortable pattern of practice would normally emerge. However, any changes or improvements to the system become difficult to implement without proper organization.

---

[55] Interview with PERHILITAN, 28 November 2001.
[56] Interview with Chen Hin Keong, Director of TRAFFIC Southeast Asia, 25 July 1997.

An example would be new training. In July 1996, the CITES Secretariat with the co-operation of MOSTE held a training seminar in Malaysia. There were 60 participants, mainly from various relevant government departments. The seminar was about the implementation of CITES and it was in general well received. Most of the officers interviewed had attended this seminar and found it of help. An interesting point is the question of the dissemination of knowledge. In an interview with an official from Customs and Excise, it was asked how the new knowledge that had been gained from the seminar would be disseminated across the Department.[57] The method used is for the officer who had attended the training seminar to write a report; this would then be submitted to a superior who would then decide whether the recommendations in the report should be acted upon or not. It is true that this system of hierarchical decision-making is usual and should be expected; the point is rather, that with regard to CITES, without a strong co-ordinating central body responsible for CITES as a whole with a rebit for action, all that is left are the perseverance and interest of individual officers, if any changes are to be made. A CITES co-ordinating body could provide the extra authority and systematic methods through which changes can occur.

Another problem with an *ad hoc* system of operations is that it makes data gathering a haphazard exercise. Without a proper data-gathering mechanism under the administration of a single responsible body, the results could be less than satisfactory, especially now since the Fisheries Department and the Department of Agriculture are to process permits themselves. As it stands, data gathering is erratic and not entirely satisfactory.

3.1.2. Weakness in legislation

The most serious shortcoming in Malaysian wildlife legislation is the complete lack of any specific law for flora. The legislative protection that exists for the protection of plant life is secondary in nature. For example, the National Forestry Act 1984[58] has provisions preventing the taking of plants without a permit, but this depends on the prior protection of a specific area of land. Thus, if a forest reserve is set aside, then the plants on that land cannot be taken. This is not good enough, as plants are subject to a great deal of over-exploitation and unsustainable harvesting. An example would be the slipper orchid (*Paphiopedilum*) and cycads taken from the wild and openly sold in nurseries.[59] There are insufficient laws properly to stop this practice; even if a provision of the the National Forestry Act were broken, officers are more concerned with timber products than with decorative plants (such as cycads) to take much action over the unlawful taking of flowers. Furthermore, there is no legislative power to take action against individuals who have transported flora.[60] This is naturally a serious setback with regard to CITES enforcement and compliance.

---

[57] Interview with Royal Malaysian Customs and Excise, 22 July 1997.
[58] Laws of Malaysia, Act 313.
[59] Interview with Forest Research Institute Malaysia, 24 July 1997.
[60] Interview with Plant and Plant Quarantine Division, Department of Agriculture, 24 July 1997.

A rather strange legal anomaly is the Fisheries (Control of Endangered Species of Fish) Regulations 1999. This regulation lists species of whales, dolphins, manatees and clams (which are mammals and shellfish), but the only fish species in the list is one species of whale shark. Considering that the CITES species that are found in Malaysia include some rare and endangered fish, this does seem to be a serious shortcoming. Furthermore, the Fisheries Act deals only with marine fish; river fish, many of which are endangered, do not by virtue of the Malaysian constitution's division of legislative powers fall under the jurisdiction of the Fisheries Act and instead are within the purview of regional governments. These fail to provide any sort of protectionist legislation.

Another issue concerns the low penalties imposed on lawbreakers. This has two effects. Firstly, the penalties do not act as a sufficient deterrent to those involved in such illegal activity, and secondly, they give the impression that such crimes are not very serious. Furthermore, the low penalties may have an adverse effect on the attitude of law officers towards such crimes. For example, one PERHILITAN officer complained that the courts tend to be too lenient on offenders. It is not within the ambit of this research to examine the cause and effect of low penalties as deterrence. However, an examination of the records shows that low penalties constitute an issue that needs to be addressed:

1996: 4528 fines with a total of RM 231,095 collected (an average fine of RM 51)
1997: 4079 fines with a total of RM 218,275 collected (an average fine of RM 53)
1998: 4378 fines with a total of RM 316,170 collected (an average fine of RM 72)
1999: 3578 fines with a total of RM 190,515 collected (an average fine of RM 53)

The following figures are those of the total fines collected from compound offences as well as those from court decisions. The number of court cases is itself very small:

1996: 39 fines with a total of RM 8,970 collected (an average fine of RM 230)
1997: 42 fines with a total of RM 32,350 collected (an average fine of RM 770)
1998: 21 fines with a total of RM 62,750 collected (an average fine of RM 2988)
1999: 14 fines with a total of RM 43,590 collected (an average fine of RM 3113)

From these figures it can be seen that once a case goes to court, the sentences meted out are significantly higher than the total average. However, it can be argued that the severity of the cases should warrant sterner punishment due to the endangered nature of the species involved. Furthermore, the vast majority of cases are compound offences, even for protected and totally protected species. In compound cases, the average fine is very low. For example, compound cases involving protected species in 1999 totalled 1403. The fines collected amounted to RM 171,931. The average fine was RM 123.[61]

---

[61] Figures obtained from the *Wildlife Department Annual Report* 1996, 1997, 1998 and 1999.

3.1.3. Lack of resources

This is a problem endemic in many areas of Malaysian environmental protection. Looking at the CITES-related bodies, one can see that a shortage in manpower is chronic. As pointed out above, the Environmental Protection and Management Division of MOSTE, the main co-ordinating body for CITES enforcement, consists of two officers and a handful of clerical staff. The shortage of finance and trained personnel also means that there are insufficient people to fulfil basic requirements such as data gathering, monitoring and reporting. For example, there has been no study conducted on any illegal trade in Malaysia; therefore, there are no available figures at all. There are suspicions that Malaysia is a transit point for illegal trading, but again, there is no concrete evidence as no study has confirmed or refuted this.

Whatever evidence exists comes from the occasional cases where an illegal shipment of specimens is found. In February 2000 smugglers were caught with 901 snakes, brought into Malaysia from Thailand *en route* to Singapore and thence to China, Taiwan and Hong Kong. In the same month, 1000 snakes were seized at a roadblock. It is believed the snakes are from Thailand, bound for Penang, where they will be processed before being exported.[62]

Perhaps more important is the lack of data on the numbers of each species of animals and plants in the country. Without such hard data it is difficult to make decisions regarding the viability of their trade. Species that are clearly endangered are protected because they will be in Appendix I; therefore, no trade is allowed at all. However, species that are still relatively abundant can still be traded under Appendix II. The number that may be exported has to be determined by the Scientific Authority, yet in order to do this effectively and with the safety of the survival of the species in mind, there has to be some baseline information regarding the numbers of the species as a whole.

3.1.4. Lack of environmental awareness

Proper training is vital in the enforcement of CITES; the lack of training is most notable in the Customs and Excise Department. Customs officers are simply not sufficiently well trained in recognizing specimens. Their role in CITES appears to be limited to the checking of permits. This is clearly not enough. Admittedly, when in doubt, customs officers refer to bodies with the necessary expertise, such as the Wildlife Department or the Department of Agriculture. However, interviews with both these bodies show that although such steps may be effective when situations of doubt occur, there is on the whole still a major problem, namely, that of identification of what is on the permit and what is actually before the officer's eyes. It is possible that the two do not match; with insufficient training, the discrepancies will not be spotted. This is especially important in cases of specimens in transit because

---

[62]   *TRAFFIC Bulletin*, Vol. 18, No. 2 (2000).

these then lie completely within the control of the customs officers (Article VII (1) of CITES).

In a way, this is not surprising, as environmental matters do not constitute the priority of the Malaysia customs service. The emphasis is on the monitoring of imports which are a threat to culture and religion, and on the collecting of revenue from duty. Exports are not closely monitored since they bring in revenue into the country and are thus encouraged. Customs officers also receive very minimal training on environmental matters. The official course for customs officers at the Royal Malaysian Customs Academy in Melaka has no courses designed for environmental awareness, with the exception of timber identification.[63] Training related to CITES is irregular and limited to the occasional attachment to other government departments or to specific short courses like the 1996 CITES seminar. Even then, the seminar was not geared towards customs officials.

The lack of awareness is, of course, not limited to customs officers. There is a lack of environmental awareness in the entire legal system from the Attorney General's Chambers to judges.[64] This raises the point that the laws are only as effective as those who enforce them. Some type of training in the form of consciousness raising is required – especially in an area where the damage done by the lawbreakers is not patently obvious to everyone.

4.   COMPLIANCE WITH *BASEL* IN MALAYSIA

The Basel treaty is primarily concerned with the exportation of hazardous wastes to countries that do not have the capacity to treat it safely. It is the result of many shocking practices, primarily in the early nineteen-eighties when developed nations were dumping their waste in developing nations because this was cheaper than treating it at home. Poor nations desperate for money would accept these wastes as an easy way of boosting their finances, resulting in environmental damage and unacceptable risks to life.[65]

---

[63] The Malaysian Royal Customs Academy's *Training Programme Syllabus 2000* has no environmental component.

[64] The Attorney General's Chambers, as well as the Judicial Service, confirmed that there is no environmental awareness training given to their personnel. The author asked these bodies on 20 November 2001 and 15 November 2001 respectively.

[65] *See Toxic Terror: Dumping of Hazardous Wastes in the Third World*, Third World Network, Penang, 1988, D.P. Hackett, "An assessment of the Basel Convention on the Control of Transboundary Movements of Hazardous Waste and Their Disposal", 5 *American U.J.Int'l Law & Policy* 291 and D.J. Abrams, "Regulating international hazardous waste trade", 28 *Columbia Journal of Transnational Law* 801 (1990).

The main principles of Basel can be summarized as follows:[66]

a. All generation of hazardous wastes should be kept to a minimum;
b. If this cannot be done, disposal should preferably be done as close as possible to the source;
c. In the following cases, waste cannot be exported at all: to Antarctica, to non-parties of Basel (unless there is a separate bilateral treaty), or to parties which have banned the import of hazardous wastes;
d. Transboundary movement of hazardous waste is a 'last resort' measure that can take place only if the movement complies with the rules and regulations established by the treaty, if it is the best option from an environmental perspective, and if it is done under the principle of non-discrimination and according to the principle of environmentally sound management;
e. The foundation of the Basel regime is the system of Prior Informed Consent (PIC) of the potential importing State and all transit States, and
f. Hazardous waste exported illegally and that which cannot be treated safely in the country of destination is to be shipped back to the source.

In order to implement Basel, a party State would have to put into place a mechanism that would enable the PIC system to work. According to the treaty, this would mean the establishment of a competent authority and a focal point (Article 5). These bodies will be responsible for the dissemination of information regarding the movement of wastes from their country and also for approving (or rejecting) the importation and transit of wastes.

According to Article 4(9) of the treaty, hazardous waste can be exported only for the following reasons:

a. The exporting State does not have the capacity to dispose of it in an environmentally sound manner;
b. The waste in question is required for as a raw material for recycling or recovery industries in the importing state, and
c. The Transboundary movement falls into any criteria determined by the parties, as long as it does not contradict the objectives of the treaty.

Any traffic that falls under one of the following descriptions is illegal traffic and Parties must ensure that they have the necessary laws to punish the wrong doers (Article 4(3)):

a. Without notification as set out by the treaty to all parties concerned;
b. Without the consent of a state concerned;
c. With consent obtained through fraudulent means;
d. That does not match up to the documents, or

---

[66] K. Kummer, *International Management of Hazardous Wastes: The Basel Convention and Related Legal Rules*, New York: Oxford University Press, 1995, at 47.

e. That results in disposal which is in contravention with the treaty or any other
    international law.

On the domestic front States are required generally to ensure, as far as their local
conditions (economic, social and technological capacities) allow, minimizing the
production of wastes. They are also to provide for adequate disposal facilities within
their own borders and to control the persons involved in the management of hazardous
wastes from causing pollution. The export of hazardous waste ought to be kept to
a minimum (Article 4(2)(a)(b)(c)(d)).

Malaysia has an entire system of laws that is used in the control of the import
and export of hazardous wastes. The main laws that are used for implementing Basel
are the Environmental Quality Act 1974 (EQA), Environmental Quality (Scheduled
Wastes) Regulations 1989,[67] the Environmental Quality (Prescribed Premises)
(Scheduled Wastes Treatment and Disposal Facilities) Order 1989,[68] and the Environmental Quality (Prescribed Premises)(Scheduled Wastes Treatment and Disposal
Facilities) Regulations 1989.[69]

The Act and these Regulations work together. Section 34 of the EQA makes it
an offence to dump any sort of waste on Malaysian soil or waters, unless it is on
specified and licensed premises. It is also an offence to export or import or allow
for the transit of hazardous waste without obtaining prior permission from the Director
General of the DOE. If the 'consent' is a forgery or is obtained through fraudulent
means, this, too, is an offence. These offences carry a maximum fine of RM500,000
and/or a maximum jail sentence of five years.

The Scheduled Wastes Regulations establishes a list of "scheduled wastes". It
also establishes the treatments and control of these wastes. The Prescribed Premises
Order determines the types of premises that are allowed to handle such wastes and
the Prescribed Premises Regulations control the running of these places through a
system of licences.

Malaysia is both an exporter and importer of hazardous wastes. Due to a lack
of facilities properly to treat or dispose of wastes, exports are made to countries such
as the United States, Japan, Singapore, and the United Kingdom. The types of wastes
exported are sludge containing heavy metals, spent solvents, spent catalysts and PCB-
containing transformers and capacitors. Conversely, Malaysia imports wastes as raw
materials for various industrial processes. Examples include: used lead acid batteries,
copper slag and waste plastics.[70]

---

[67] P.U. (A) 139/89.
[68] P.U. (A) 140/89.
[69] P.U. (A) 141/89.
[70] A.R. Awang and I. Shafii, "Country Report – Malaysia", *Proceedings of Regional Seminar on
the Implementation of the Basel Convention on the Control of Transboundary Movements of
Hazardous Wastes and Their Disposal*, Department of the Environment, 11–13 April 1994, Kuala
Lumpur.

Waste exported from Malaysia

Year	Amount (metric tons)
1993	496
1994	1284.1
1995	3734.81
1996	3734.81
1997	2694.04
1998	7161

Most of the wastes are exported to Japan and the United States. Imports of hazardous wastes, on the other hand, are not a common occurrence. The total requests for importation between 1993 and 1998 number 63. The breakdown of the figures is as follows:

Requests for the importation of waste

Year	Requests
1993	13
1994	9
1995	5
1996	8
1997	10
1998	18

To facilitate enforcement and in order to comply with Basel's requirements regarding the import and export of hazardous wastes, two amendments were made to the Orders under the Customs Act 1967.[71] These were the Customs (Prohibition of Export)(Amendment)(No.2) Order 1993[72] and the Customs (Prohibition of Import)(Amendment)(No.3) Order 1993.[73]

The role of customs officials is to ensure that no export or import of scheduled wastes occurs without the approval of the Director General of the DOE (in the form of the necessary documents). The approval of the DG of the DOE for either imports or exports is dependent on the guidelines'[74] issued by the Department being followed.

In Malaysia the only justification for importing wastes is if it is to be used for the purposes of industry, for example, in the recycling industry. To import scheduled wastes, the importer must fill in the relevant form. The types of information required are: a justification for the importation, and methods of handling the hazardous waste,

---

[71] Laws of Malaysia, Act 235.
[72] P.U. (A) 209/93.
[73] P.U. (A) 271/93.
[74] *Guidelines on the Export, Import and Storage of Scheduled Wastes in Malaysia* CD Rom, Department of Environment, Ministry of Science, Technology and the Environment.

including its collection, packaging, labelling, mode of transportation, and transportation route. This process requires about two months from start to finish. The DOE also examines the environmental impact that such an importation may cause.[75]

The only wastes that can be exported are those that cannot be safely managed (either disposed of or treated) by the facilities in Bukit Nenas, Port Dickson. The necessary forms need to be filled in, and the following information provided: justification for the export; information on the planned methods for the handling of waste, which includes the packaging, and labelling; and the transportation routes (as determined by international law).

The exporter must also provide the written agreements between, firstly, the waste generator and inland waste transporters and, secondly, between the waste generator and recipient. In line with the rules of the PIC there have to be documents, certified true copies, from the competent authority of the receiving country stating that the latter has the facility to dispose of the waste and is competent to do so. A list of all transit countries is also required.

For proper monitoring and accountability purposes, the complete Curriculum Vitae of each of the personnel involved in the export must be submitted. In the event of an accident liability is covered through insurance and bank guarantees. There has to be evidence of both a bank guarantee and an insurance policy before the export can be approved.

4.1.   Problems with Malaysian *Basel* compliance

The most obvious problems are the lack of staff and training. The DOE has to deal with fifty to sixty applications for the import and export of hazardous waste per year. It is a lengthy and complex procedure requiring considerable work. One problem is the length of time necessary to obtain answers from importing and transit states. Yet there is in Malaysia only one officer in charge of all Basel business, and even then his duties are not limited only to Basel-related activities.

More serious perhaps is the lack of training amongst customs officers. This is particularly true in cases where expert identification of wastes is necessary. Customs officers face difficulty when identifying wastes. They might mix wastes with actual goods and products, given the nature of some of these wastes. The DOE has provided training for Customs officers,[76] but the practice of the Royal Customs and Excise is that officers may be transferred from one post to another. Thus, a person who might have obtained training may be posted not to entry points but to Customs Headquarters. This lack of expertise can have serious consequences especially if hazardous waste is not classified as such (thus falling under Art 9(1)(d) of Basel as illegal trade).

---

[75] I. Shafii, "Principles of the Basel Convention", *Workshop on Scheduled Wastes Management in Malaysia*, Department of Environment, Ministry of Science, Technology and the Environment, Petaling Jaya, Malaysia, 25 July 1995.

[76] Awang and Shafii, n. 70.

As pointed out before, Basel is not just about the control of the transboundary movement of wastes; it is also about the minimization of wastes. In this sense, Malaysia still has a long way to go. The EQA Regulations, for example, have only a rather vague section encouraging the minimization of waste. Therefore, there is no strong legal authority to make sure that this minimization is practised.

Furthermore, industry is given no financial incentive to improve its production methods such that they minimize wastes. The current methods of production and disposal are relatively cheap and it is more economically viable to continue in the present fashion rather than make improvements. The Malaysian Agenda for Waste Reduction programme (MAWAR) conducted by the DOE in the mid 1990s received a very poor response, partly for these reasons.

5.   COMPLIANCE WITH *RAMSAR* IN MALAYSIA

The Ramsar Convention is unique in that it requires substantial moves towards compliance before a State can even become a party. In short, a State would have to select a wetland site, based on certain criteria set out in the treaty, to be included in the Ramsar List of Wetlands of International Importance (the List) before it could join (Article 2). This site would then have to be subject to the principle of "wise use" which, in effect, means its protection and care (Articles 3 and 4).

Other obligations include the co-operation and exchange of information with other parties, especially in the case of shared wetlands (Article 5). Member States are also encouraged to substitute the name of another site if they were to remove their selected site from the list (Article 4(2)).

Generally speaking, Ramsar does not comprise detailed law, as CITES and Basel do. The obligations of Ramsar are rather vague; much is left to the individual parties to do what they can. However, despite its seeming simplicity, to comply with the spirit of the treaty is more complex than it would appear. It is in this sense that the Malaysian experience is quite interesting.

The Ramsar site in Malaysia is Tasek Bera.[77] Tasek Bera is a lake situated in south-west Pahang, a state on the Malaysian peninsula. It is part of an alluvial peat swamp system. It is about twenty-five kilometres from the nearest town, Bahau. The lake has a catchment area of 61,383 hectares, with the southern part of the area being in the state of Negri Sembilan. The catchment area is not pristine, having been exploited for logging and forest conversion (to oil palm cultivation).

Tasek Bera is the largest fresh water lake and swamp system in Malaysia, covering 6,150 hectares. It lies at the centre of the three drainage basins of the Pahang, Rompin and Muar rivers. Tasek Bera was probably formed as a result of changes in the course of the Pahang River and its tributaries, followed by a blocking of the river channel, probably by the plant Rasau. The swamp developed because

---

[77] Information about Tasek Bera is obtained from P. Benstead, C. Jeffs and R. D'Cruz, *Tasek Bera: The Wetland Benefits of the Lake System and Recommendations for Management*, Asian Wetland Bureau, 1993.

of the waterlogged environment and consists of three main habitats: peat swamp forest, extensive reed beds, and open water with beds of submerged plants.[78]

The area is rich with plant life that includes *Utricularia flexuosa, Lepirironia*, ferns, screw pines, orchids and sedges. The fauna are equally impressive. There are ninety-five species of fish, including the endangered Asian Arowana and Ikan Temerloh. Approximately 200 species of birds were recorded. The endangered Crested and Crestless Fireback, Masked Finfoot and the Malaysian Night Heron are among them. Tasek Bera is not, however, an important haven for waterfowl due to the naturally acidic nature of the water.

There is no complete list of mammals in the area, but the following species have been sighted: the Clouded Leopard, Leopard, Tiger, Asian Elephant and the Tapir. All of these species are rare and the Tiger, Tapir and Elephant are endangered.

The legal issue here is that the establishment of a protected site is under the ambit of the regional state government, in this case the Pahang state government. Therefore, the administration of the site lies in its hands. The problem was that the Pahang state government did not have the necessary expertise to devise a management plan for the area. This was overcome by turning to the non-governmental organization (NGO), Wetlands International.

With funding from the Danish Government, Wetlands International set about drawing up a cross-sectoral management plan for the site. There is now in place an administrative and management structure for the protection of the site. The responsible authority for the administration of the site is the Pahang State Director of Forests. However, the Department of Wildlife and National Parks is the lead management agency in view of its conservation remit and the fact that the Ministry of Science, Technology and the Environment is the national administrative authority for the Ramsar Treaty. Other government agencies do play a part by providing their expertise when necessary.

The management authority staff is under the supervision of a Chief Officer, who reports to the Ramsar Management Executive Body – the main policy and decision-making body of the system. The Secretary General of the Ministry of Science, Technology and the Environment chairs it. Aiding the Executive Body are two supportive committees: the Scientific Advisory Committee, which provides technical information about the site's management and research activities, and a Consultative Committee chaired by the Pahang State Economic Planning Unit. This Consultative Committee provides a formalized mechanism for consultation with stakeholders and to co-ordinate site management with government planning processes.[79]

In the day-to-day running of the site staff will be seconded from relevant government agencies. These include the Department of Wildlife and National Parks, the Forestry Department, the Fisheries Department, the Department of Environment, the Pahang State Tourism Agency, and the Department for Orang Asli[80] Affairs. The

---

[78] *Integrated Management of Tasek Bera, Support for the Implementation of Obligations under the Ramsar Convention: Project Brief*, Wetlands International, at 1.
[79] Wetlands International is to sit on both of these committees.
[80] Indigenous Peoples.

Management Authority also has the power to employ local people in roles such as rangers and wardens.

This cross-sectoral management body is to be applauded, as the issues involved in the protection of an eco-system like a wetland are numerous. For example, the presence of the Department of the Environment is potentially useful if the area is faced with the problem of pollution from the oil palm plantations surrounding the Tasek Bera site. Furthermore, the site has now been earmarked to be gazetted under the National Forestry Act 1984 as a Permanent Reserved Forest, thus ensuring that it has special legal protection.

6.   IN SUPPORT OF COMPLIANCE THEORY

It is submitted that the Malaysian experience supports the ideas in compliance theory. It shows that once a country has agreed to be part of a treaty regime, any non-compliance is not simply a matter of self-interest *versus* international obligations. Furthermore, the theories as to what encourages compliance also appear to be justified.

First and foremost, there has been much effort made to comply with these treaties. It is illogical to believe that States would take the trouble and the effort to be part of a treaty regime only not to comply. This is particularly true with treaties in which States believe. What can also be seen from this case study is that treaties that are properly formulated, with clear goals, objectives and methods of achieving them, are more likely than not to experience compliance. It is impossible to be part of CITES without the establishment of a Management and Scientific Authority; it is impossible to be part of Basel without clear laws against illegal traffic, and it is impossible to be part of Ramsar without having first chosen a site to be placed on the List.

Once the institutions and mechanisms are put into place, compliance has a tendency to become habit-forming. The 'way things are done' becomes compliance with the treaty. It then becomes a matter of following the set procedure in order to comply. If Malaysia were to make a decision based on economic and/or military considerations each time the government is faced with a choice whether to allow import or export of hazardous wastes, it would be a time-consuming and laborious exercise of constantly weighing the *pros* and *cons* of such an application. It is far easier merely to allow the mechanisms in place to do the decision-making. In other words, the Realist argument that self-interest comes first all the time is in reality not practical.

What this case study also shows is that the problems faced by Malaysia in complying with the three Treaties discussed above are rather about capacity than recalcitrance. The lack of expertise and training arise time and again. With regard to CITES the poor baseline data on species make it hard for a Scientific Authority, the *ad hoc* body that it is, to make truly sound decisions. In both CITES and Basel implementation, the lack of training amongst front-line officers, particularly customs officers, means that border checks are not as sound as they should be.

These types of problems do not lead to non-compliance *per se*, but together are perhaps better described as 'poor' compliance. The encouraging factor is, however, that these are not insurmountable problems. One way around difficulties of this sort is, of course, for the regime itself to provide help. This can be in monetary form or even in the form of training. The CITES Secretariat, for example, does provide seminars for the identification of species. However, these seminars could benefit from being more specific to the needs of individual nations.

The way that Ramsar was implemented in Malaysia provides an interesting solution. The Pahang State Government entrusted with the management of the Ramsar site was not well equipped to do the job. Therefore, help was obtained through two methods: funds were obtained through a Danish Aid Programme, and Wetlands International, an NGO, provided the expertise. It is this sort of imaginative problem-solving solution that perhaps environmental treaty regimes should explore further.

It is submitted as well that treaties with a sound reporting mechanism and good transparency encourage compliance. They take the form of obligating regular reports, frequent Conferences of Parties that are open to as many parties as possible, and an active secretariat. All three treaties studied have these mechanisms in place and result in greater consideration of compliance on the part of the Malaysian government.

The argument used is that with greater transparency, the 'good' states can be recognized and 'bad' States shamed. This is true because without transparency and public criticism, then non-compliance would go "unpunished". However, there is another aspect to transparency: the human factor.

During the course of the interviews conducted, there was an interesting incident where the officer being questioned expressed embarrassment that the country report that should have been prepared by his department was not yet ready. This desire to do a job well in the light of international scrutiny can also be seen in the frantic activity currently being experienced in the Ministry of Science, Technology and the Environment regarding wetlands. The Ramsar Conference of Parties in Seville in 2002 provided a spur for the Ministry and its officials to take more pro-active measures for wetland protection. These include the urgent implementation of the Malaysian Wetland Policy and the search for more sites to add to the Ramsar List.[81]

7.   CONCLUSION

In conclusion, it is submitted that the theories put forward by the likes of Chayes and Chayes, Mitchell, and Brown Weiss and Jacobson ring true. The reasons for compliance and non-compliance are not a simple matter of States being 'bad' and 'selfish'. Taking such a cynical stand would lead to the conclusion that either it was not worth the effort to try to improve compliance or to believe that the only way to improve compliance was through purely political means, with economic and military sanctions as enforcement measures.

---

[81] Three more sites have now been earmarked as Malaysian Ramsar sites.

Yet from what has been discussed, it has been shown that compliance either happens or does not happen for a variety of complex reasons, and not all of them can simply be explained away as a matter of self-interest. Therefore, environmental treaty regimes would do well to take into consideration these complex factors, which include the form of the treaty, the methods through which to achieve the objectives of the treaty, and the capacity of the parties, when determining how to improve compliance.

To summarize, if a treaty is to succeed, then it should have the following characteristics: the treaty-making process should be as democratic as possible, with all interested parties being able to participate in a meaningful way towards the formation of the treaty; the treaty itself should be clear, and the obligations imposed should be made as clear and as definite as possible. If compliance can be obtained through bureaucratic methods, such an approach should be encouraged, because bureaucracies are habit-forming.

Treaty regimes must either make aid (financial and practical) available to poorer members, or the latter should be imaginative in their approach to obtaining the said help. While the Secretariat may not have unlimited wealth, it should have enough funds to be as pro-active as possible, establishing close ties with the relevant officers, being sensitive and quick to respond to any changes or to any requirements of treaty members. However, this help must be dictated by the needs of the parties. Expert advice and training would be really helpful only if they were directed to the places in greatest need.

Transparency and inclusiveness should be of paramount priority. Reporting on a regular basis is a must (along with the necessary help, if so required), as are regular Conferences of Parties. Non-governmental bodies should be as involved as closely as possible in the entire regime, from its formation to its implementation. This is not just for the usual reasons of the existence of such groups: playing watchdog and public decriers of foul play; NGOs can also be vital on the ground, either in helping enforcement bodies by being an extra pair of eyes (as TRAFFIC, the wildlife trade NGO, is to PERHILITAN) or even by helping governmental agencies ill-equipped to do the work at hand (as Wetlands International is to the Pahang State Government).

Finally, what must not be forgotten is the human factor. PERHILITAN have been attempting for years to change legislation in order for CITES species automatically to be included in the Protection of Wildlife protected species lists. The Legal Adviser for the department was closely involved in the process which, until recently, seemed as though it would become a reality. However, recent administrative changes saw the Legal Adviser leaving PERHILITAN, to be replaced by another officer who reportedly does not have the same enthusiasm for the project, thus leaving it stalled.

It is submitted that such an occurrence illustrates the overlooked fact that governments and government agencies are not faceless entities; they consist of real men and women, who behave in a myriad of ways. No international document, no matter how well crafted, can change this fact. Yet this human factor cannot and must not be overlooked. People can make a difference; how they do their duty is one such way that this can be achieved – nor can we forget the power of the public in pushing their governments towards positive action. Compliance ultimately lies therefore in the hands of the people; those with the duty to their jobs, and those who care enough to make sure the jobs are done well.

UNILATERAL USE OF ARMED FORCE AND THE CHALLENGE OF HUMANITARIAN INTERVENTION IN INTERNATIONAL LAW

Mohammad Taghi Karoubi[*]

1   INTRODUCTION

Apart from the important provision of Article 51 which admits unilateral forcible action in the exercise of the right of individual and collective self-defence against an armed attack, the use of force under the United Nations Charter is intended to be monopolized by the Organization.[1] This monopoly finds its expression in the provision concerning the prohibition of the unilateral resort to force by states in Article 2(4) of the UN Charter where, for the first time, direct reference was made to not resorting to force, which has a broader meaning than not resorting to war, the formula used in the Pact of Paris.[2] The principle of the prohibition on the use of force or threat of force has been repeatedly stressed in United Nations General Assembly (UNGA) resolutions.[3] The principle, today, is not only a conventional general principle, but it has also become a principle of customary international law as indicated by the International Court of Justice (ICJ) in its decision in the Nicaragua

---

[*] Lecturer in Law, Tehran, Iran. LLB, Tehran University, LLM. and Ph.D., Hull University (UK).
[1] *See* H. Waldock, "The regulation of the use of force by individual states in international law", 81 *RCADI*, 1952, 455. *See* also H. McCoubrey and N.D. White, *International Law and Armed Conflict*, Aldershot: Dartmouth Press, 1992; I. Claude, "The Blueprint", *International Conciliation*, No. 532, March 1961; *Id.*, "United Nations Use of Military Force", 7-2 *JAC*, June 1963; R. Hoggins, *United Nations Peacekeeping 1946-1967: Documents and Commentary*, Vol. 1, London: Oxford University Press, 1969; A. James, *The Role of Force in International Order and United Nations Peace-keeping*, The Ditchley Foundation, May 1969; W.J. Durch, (ed.), *The Evaluation of UN Peacekeeping*, New York: St Martin's, 1993; D.W. Bowett, *United Nations Force*, London: Stevens and Sons, 1964; F. Seyersted, *United Nations Forces in the Law of Peace and War*, Leiden, London: A.W. Sijthoff, 1966; D.J. Scheffer, *Law and Force in New International Order*, Boulder: Westview Press, 1991.
[2] For more details about the Pact of Paris, *see* J.L. Brierly, "Some implications of the Pact of Paris", 10 *BYIL* (1929) 208. *See* also Q. Wright, "The meaning of the Pact of Paris", 27 *AJIL* (1933); F. Kellogg, "The war prevention policy of the U.S.A.", 22 *AJIL* (1928).
[3] *See Declaration on Friendly Relations* (1970), GA Res. 2625; *Definition of Aggression* (1975), GA Res. 3314; *Declaration on the Non-Use of Force* (1988), GA Res. 42/22.

Asian Yearbook of International Law, Volume 10 (B.S. Chimni *et al.*, eds.)

Case[4] and the *Legality of the Threat or Use of Nuclear Weapons*.[5] It is also included by many writers in the commanding principles of international law (*jus cogens*).[6]

In spite of this restriction and deep transformation in the legal system,[7] however, some unilateral military actions in the final decade of the twentieth century took place under claims of protecting innocent people from mass human rights violation by oppressive Governments. This kind of justification can be seen in the US statement regarding the US's military action in Iraq in 1996, as well as in the rationale given by NATO leaders during the Kosovo crisis in 1999.[8] For example, US President Clinton and UK Prime Minister Blair, during NATO's action in March 1999, emphasized that the humanitarian catastrophe led the allies to act, and the choice

---

[4] The International Court of Justice upheld the authority of the Charter prohibition contained in Article 2(4). The Court in its decision in the *Nicaragua Case* held that the principles of Article 2(4) were not only treaty law but the substance of customary international law as well. *Military and Paramilitary Activities in and Against Nicaragua (Nicar. v. US)* (Merits), ICJ Rep. 1986 at 14, paras 187-192. States have on many occasions expressed their individual support for the Article, and such expressions of support have come from many different sectors of the community of states. *See* R. Higgins, "The attitude of western states towards legal aspect of the use of force", in A. Cassese (ed.), *The Current Legal Regulation of the Use of Force* (1986), at 435; B. Szego, "The attitude of socialist states towards the international regulation of use of force", *ibid*.

[5] *See* the *Legality of the Threat or Use of Nuclear Weapons* case, ICJ Rep. 1996, at 226, para 70.

[6] *See* B. Simma, "NATO, the UN and the use of force: legal aspects", 10 *EJIL* (1999), at 1-4. *See* also A.C. Arend and R.J. Beck, *International Law & the Use of Force*, London, New York: Routledge Press, 1993, at 31-6; G. Christenson, "The World Court and *jus cogens*", 81 *AJIL* (1987); N. Ronzitti, "Use of force, *jus cogens* and state consent", in Cassese, n. 4.

[7] In the period between the League of Nations and the United Nations a profound change occurred in international law in regard to the use of armed force in international relations among states. For more information about the issue, *see* F. Northedge, *The League of Nations: Its Life and Times 1920-46*, Leicester: Leicester University Press, 1986. *See* also H. Miller, *The Drafting of the Covenant*, Vol. I; A.E. Hindmarsh, *Force in Peace, Force Short of War in International Relations*, Cambridge, Mass.: Harvard University Press, 1933; G. Scott, *The Rise and Fall of the League of Nations*, London: Hutchinson, 1973; E.H. Carr, *International Relations between the Two World Wars 1919-1933*, New York: St Martin Press. 1967; S. Mark, *The Illusion of Peace, International Relations in Europe 1918-1933*, London: Macmillan Press, 1976.

[8] The US President, Clinton, tried to justify the US's action for the protection of innocent Kurdish people and stated that, "Saddam's ... methods are always the same – violence and aggression, against the Kurds ...". *See* Clinton speech at *http://www.the-times.co.uk/cgi-bin/BackIssue?* Available in September 2000. *See* also *The Times*, "US threatens to attack again", September 3, 1996, at *http://www.the-times.co.uk/cgi-bin/BackIssue?* Available in September 2000. *See* the Prime Minster of Great Britain, John Major, when he said, "we are concerned about any external threats he produces and repression of his own people and it is against that the United States acted". *See* N.D. White, "Commentary on the protection of the Kurdish safe-haven: Operation Desert strike", 2 *Nottingham JACL* (December 1996), at 201. *See* also C. Antonopoulos, "The unilateral use of force by states after the end of the cold war", 4 *Nottingham JACL* (June 1999), at 152; S.P. Subedi, "The doctrine of objective regimes in international law and the competence of the United Nations to impose territorial or peace settlements on states", 36 *GYIL* (1994); D.P. O'Connell, "Continuing limits on United Nations intervention in civil war", 67 *Ind.LJ* (1992).

was to do something or do nothing.[9] President Clinton stated that the action was designed to avert a humanitarian catastrophe, to preserve stability in a key part of Europe, and to maintain the credibility of NATO.[10] The US emphasized the goals of the NATO action, rather than a basis in international law, for authorization of the use of force.[11] The permanent representative of the UK in the United Nations Security Council, Jeremy Greenstock, also stated:

> We have taken this action with regret, in order to save lives. It will be directed towards disrupting the violent attacks being committed by the Serb security forces and weakening their ability to create a humanitarian catastrophe.[12]

Solana, the NATO Secretary General, in a press statement emphasized, rather than legality, the moral duty of NATO to "stop the violence and bring an end to the humanitarian catastrophe", and concluded that, "we have a moral duty to do so."[13]

The place of the doctrine of humanitarian intervention in international law in the light of the views of adherents of the doctrine, namely, Wolff,[14] Kant,[15] Vattel,[16] Woolsey,[17] and Arntz,[18] and of those who opposed the doctrine, such as Hobbes,[19] Wildman[20] and Reddie,[21] will be examined briefly in this article. In doing so, the paper will analyze the tension between sovereignty and human rights in the established international legal order which manifest in the opening words of the United Nations Charter, as well as the attempts of recent scholars such as Cassese

---

[9] *See* Clinton's Address on Air-strikes against Yugoslavia in the *New York Times* on 24 March 1999. *NYT* also cited the full text of Tony Blair's statement on the Kosovo bombing. *See* also R. Sylvester, "The Blair doctrine: This is an ethical fight ", *The Independent*, 28 March 1999.

[10] *See* Statement by President Clinton confirming NATO air strikes against the Serbs on 24 March 1999 in the *New York Times* at *www.nytimes.com* NYT.

[11] *Ibid.*

[12] *See* Statement in the United Nations Security Council by Jeremy Greenstock, KCMG, Permanent Representative of the UK on 24 March 1999, at *http://www.fco.gov.uk/news/newstext.asp?2157,* Available in October 2000.

[13] *See* J. Solana, NATO Secretary-General, Press Statement on 24 March 1999 at *http://www.nato.int/ docu/pr/1999/p99-041e.htm,* Available in October 2000.

[14] *See* C. Wolff, *Jus Gentium Methodo Scientifica Peractatuma* (tr. J.B. Scott), Washington: Carnegie Endowment for International Peace, Vol. II, 1934.

[15] *See* F.X. De Lima, *Intervention in International Law*, Uitgeverij Pax Nederland, 1971, at 14-15.

[16] *See* E. Vattel, *The Law of Nations: Principles of the Law of Nature, Applied to the Conduct and Affairs of Nations and Sovereigns* (tr. Fenwick), Washington: Carnegie Endowment for International Peace, 1916.

[17] *See* T.S. Woolsey, *Introduction to the Study of International Law*, (4th ed.), London: Sampson, Low, Marston, Low and Searle, 1875.

[18] *See* Arntz's view in S. Chesterman, *Just War or Just Peace,* Oxford: Oxford University Press, 2001.

[19] *See* T. Hobbes, *Leviathan*, London: Den, 1914.

[20] *See* R. Wildman, *Institutes of International Law*, London: William Benning, 1849.

[21] *See* J. Reddie, *Inquiries in International Law: Public and Private*, Edinburgh: William Blackwood and Sons, 1851.

who tried to justify the doctrine in some circumstances, based on legal or moral grounds.

2.   THE QUESTION OF HUMANITARIAN INTERVENTION BEFORE
      WORLD WAR II

Intervention by states for the protection of the lives of their nationals in another state has been a controversial issue among writers from the past until now. Wolff (1679-1754), for example, in his remarkable work, *Jus Gentium Methodo Scientifica Peractatuma,* rejected the interference of a state in the sovereignty and government of another state based on the equality of states in natural law.[22] He argued that by nature all nations are equal to one another, for nations are considered as individuals, free persons living in a state of nature.[23] Therefore, since by nature all men are equal, all nations are equal to one another.[24] Wolff further concluded that equality of nations bestows on them equal rights and duties, for the same reason that men's equality gives them the same rights and obligations.[25] In his view: "Since by nature the rights and the obligations of all nations are the same, and since that is lawful which we have the right to do and lawful which we are alleged not to do or to omit; what is lawful by nature for one nation, that likewise is also lawful for another, and what is not lawful for one is also not lawful for another."[26] Wolff, in his belief that states have equal rights and duties, went a step further than his predecessors by deliberating upon "interference" by a state with the exercise of sovereignty of another, which he conceded is a delicate issue in international law, as international law bestows equal rights and duties on all states.[27] For the same reason he maintained that interference in the government of one state by the government of another state is not permissible.[28] The principle of non-intervention in the sovereignty of a state by another state was strongly supported by Wolff.

In the eighteenth century, Kant, who was largely influenced by the French Revolution in 1789 and by the writings of Rousseau, supported the principle of non-intervention of a state in another state where the state has a republican government.[29] He stated that, "No state should interfere in the constitution or the government of another state."[30] It is significant to note that Kant, however, qualified his idea by holding that intervention is illegal only in the case of republican governments;

---

[22] *See* Wolff, n. 14, part 8, at 15. *See* also Reddie, n. 21; Wildman, n. 20, at 62-63.
[23] *Ibid.*
[24] *Ibid.*
[25] *Ibid.*
[26] *Ibid.,* 170, part I, at 16.
[27] *Ibid.*
[28] *Ibid.*
[29] *See* De Lima, n. 15, at 14. *See* also K. Lowenstein, *Political Reconstruction of Europe*, 1946, at 17-19.
[30] *Ibid.*

therefore, in other cases, intervention is permissible.[31] In other words, in his view, the principle of non-intervention was applicable only in relations between republican governments and not in relations between republican governments on the one hand and monarchical governments on the other. For Kant, the intervention of republican governments in the affairs of monarchical governments was justified to bring re-publican rule in such states.[32] Two centuries later, in 1990, Weigel and Reisman in some aspects approached the Kant doctrine.

Weigel, in his work, "From Last Resort to End Game", approaches the criterion of right authority from a more secular standpoint, and defines this authority according to the secular political processes that validate it.[33] Weigel argues that only demo-cratically oriented states or transnational organizations qualify as authorities competent to declare a just war.[34] To him, in modern times, "democratic election" is a criterion of competent authority. According to this approach, the competent authority require-ment was met in all recent wars because the United States authority was "demo-cratically elected" and supported by "open and vigorous debate that directly engaged the moral issues."[35] It is submitted that the authority required for a state to resort to and wage a just war is often so loosely defined in traditional theory that it may be tempting to discount this requirement. Undoubtedly, this is a specification more tightly construed than in traditional just war criteria. The fact that the requirement does not, in practice, discriminate very specifically among possible configurations of authority should not obscure the very important fact that it has the capability to discriminate *per se*. Here the question is: Does justification of the war directly correspond to the rank order of legitimacy, if the war-making authority of some states is more strongly legitimized than the authority of other states? According to Weigel's terminology, the more democratic state possesses greater legitimacy and therefore, in the case of armed conflict between the US – as the most democratic state in the world – and the rest of the world, while both parties admit the possibility of both sides having a just cause and all other conditions appear to be equal, the US side is more legitimate because it is more democratic! He, indeed, argues in favour of democracy, but we know that the question of what constitutes democracy is subjective rather than objective. The unilateral use of force which recently took place by the US and the UK against Iraq renders the attack to be held to be not only less legit-imate, but actually illegitimate. Indeed, military action cannot be justified on the basis that the states concerned are more democratic than the Iraqi regime, itself based on

---

[31] *Ibid.*

[32] Kant used the concept of republicanism; today, the concept of democracy is used by some writers in order to justify some interventions. Weigel, in regard to right authority, argues that a more democratic authority possesses greater legitimacy yet he ignored the fact that the question of democracy is subjective rather than objective. Weigel, "From last resort to end game", in E. Decosse (ed.), *But Was It Just?,* New York, 1992.

[33] *Ibid.,* 23.

[34] *Ibid.*

[35] *Ibid.*

military power, but an important point is that the mere existence of a democracy cannot justify war.

Reisman also argued that the term 'sovereignty' constituted an anachronism when applied to undemocratic governments or leaders.[36] He argued that unilateral intervention to support or restore democracy did not violate sovereignty.[37] Reisman then concluded that it was "anachronistic" to say that the US violated Panama's sovereignty in 1989 by launching an invasion to capture its illegitimate head of state.[38] It is submitted that this is an extreme conclusion presented by Reisman. How is it possible to violate sovereignty of states while the sovereignty still has important roles and a place in contemporary international law? His view is not acceptable and it is illegitimate for one state to interfere in the affairs of another state by the use of force to install a new and more legitimate state; such action is not condoned by jurists.

The exercise of intervention, however, has been recognized and considered in the nature of self-defence or self-preservation,[39] in the past, by some writers such as Vattel and Wheaton. Vattel, for example, in this regard said, "Whoever wrongs the state, violates its rights, disturbs its peace, ignores it in any manner whatever, becomes its enemy and is in a position to be justly punished. Whoever ill-treats a citizen indirectly injures the state, which must protect that citizen. The sovereign of the injured citizen must avenge the deed and if possible, force the aggressor to give full satisfaction or punish him, since otherwise the citizen will not obtain the chief end of a civil society, which is protection."[40] Accordingly, the state extends itself through its nationals who are a vital part of the concept of statehood and, consequently, the state has a right to protect its nationals. At that time, states exercising this right were free to use whatever means they considered just. Hence, a state could utilize armed force against another state that had violated the rights of its nationals residing in the territory of the latter.

In the nineteenth century, three important interventions took place that merit attention. The earliest example of humanitarian intervention occurred in 1827 by the joint intervention of Great Britain, France and Russia to the aid of Greek insurgence against the Turks.[41] Stowell argues that it has usually been classed as an instance of humanitarian intervention motivated by the "uncivilized methods" by which that war was being conducted.[42] The Treaty between Great Britain, France and Russia for the Pacification of Greece, signed at London on 6 July 1827, set forth in the

---

[36] *See* M. Reisman, "Sovereignty and human rights in contemporary international law", 84 *AJIL* (1990), at 866.
[37] *Ibid.*
[38] *Ibid.*
[39] *See* De Lima, n. 15, at 115.
[40] *See* Vattel, n. 16, sects. 18-21.
[41] *See* C. Fenwick, "Intervention: individual and collective", 39 *AJIL* (1945), at 650. *See* also J.P. Fonteyne, "The customary international law doctrine of humanitarian intervention: its current validity under the UN Charter", 4 *CWILJ* (1974).
[42] *See* E.C. Stowell, *Intervention in International Law*, Washington, DC.: John Byrne and Co, 1921, at 126-127.

preamble the specific ground on which they justified their intervention.[43] The second intervention took place following a meeting in Paris on 31 July 1860, of the ambassadors of Austria, Great Britain, France, Prussia and Russia, with a representative of Turkey, when a protocol was adopted and incorporated into a convention signed on 5 December 1860 in order to support Christian minorities in Lebanon and Damascus who were attacked by Druzes and Muslims.[44] French-occupied parts of Great Syria[45] and its warships policed the coast from August 1860 to June 1861.[46]

The last intervention was carried out by the US in Cuba at the end of the nineteenth century, in response to reports of atrocities committed by Spanish Military authorities attempting to suppress the insurrection that took place in 1895.[47] This was the closest example of unilateral humanitarian intervention in the pre-charter state practice. According to Ferrel, approximately 200,000 Cubans died in the camps when the Spanish authorities forced the disaffected population into concentration camps in order to identify revolutionaries, an action which caused genuine outrage in the US.[48] President Mckinley, in his message to Congress on 11 April 1898, justified the intervention for "the cause of humanity"[49] and then outlined the following justifications for US intervention in the conflict: the protection of US citizens and their property in Cuba, the protection of US commercial interests, and self-defence.[50] However, the character of the action has been questioned by writers.[51] Bowett,[52] Moore[53] and Buergenthal,[54] on the one hand, argued that the US intervention took place for the protection of nationals, property, and as abatement of a nuisance. Fonteyne[55] and Woolsey,[56] on the other hand, thought it lacked a clearly humanitarian motive.[57] They noted that the US acted not on the score of humanity alone, but that American interests were deeply involved and the action might be properly regarded as self-defence.[58]

---

[43] *See* E. Hertslet, *The Map of Europe by Treaty*, Vol. 1, London: Butterworths, 1875, at 769-770.

[44] *See* id., *The Map of Europe by Treaty*, Vol. 2, 1875, at 1451-1455.

[45] *Ibid.*

[46] *Ibid.*

[47] *See* R. Ferrell, *American Diplomacy: A History*, (3rd edn.), New York: Norton Press, 1975, at 350.

[48] *Ibid.*

[49] Cited in J.B. Moore, The Principles of American Diplomacy, New York: Harper and Brothers, 1918, at 219-220.

[50] *Ibid.*

[51] For more discussion *see* I. Brownlie, *International Law and the Use of Force by States*, Oxford: Clarendon Press, 1963, at 46.

[52] *See* D.W. Bowett, *Self-Defence in International Law*, Manchester: Manchester University Press, 1958, at 97.

[53] *See* Moore, n. 49, at 208.

[54] *See* T. Buergenthal, "The Copenhagen CSCE meeting: a new public order for Europe", 11 *HRLJ* (1990).

[55] *See* Fonteyne, n. 41, at 206

[56] *See* Woolsey, n. 17, at 76.

[57] *See* Fonteyne, n. 41, at 206.

[58] *See* Woolsey, n. 17, at 76.

The status of humanitarian intervention in the first half of the twentieth century becomes more problematic. Collective action on the part of the international community being politically difficult, the notion of unilateral intervention by a state or group of states sat uncomfortably with the increasing emphasis on the inviolability of the domestic jurisdiction. The League of Nations neither prohibited nor explicitly supported humanitarian intervention. By acceptance of obligations not to resort to war and "the maintenance of justice and a scrupulous response for all treaty obligations in the declaring of organized reports with one another", the Covenant aimed at peace. The use of force was not outlawed as such, but war was made a matter of concern to the entire League; members were required in the first instance to submit any dispute to arbitration, judicial settlement, or to enquiry by the Council. It is at least arguable that internal human rights violations could have constituted such a dispute, though the Council explicitly disclaimed any capacity to make recommendations on a matter that "by international law is solely within the domestic jurisdiction of [a] party". The Pact of Paris also said nothing of humanitarian intervention, though its tenor is clearly inconsistent with any such right. State parties stated their conviction that "all changes in their relations" should be sought only by pacific means, condemned recourse to war for the "solution of international controversies", and renounced it as an instrument of national policy. There was considerable diplomatic activity concerning reservations to this prohibition, but the reservations were limited to the right of legitimate defence or self-defence.

A group of jurists at the time argue that humanitarian intervention existed as a legal right. They tried to define the theory as the attempt to give a juridical basis to the right of one state to exercise control over the internal acts of another state.[59] Woolsey[60] and Arntz[61] approached Grotius' conception of punitive war and adopted the view that it was representative of civilized government intervening in the affairs of other states. Bluntschli,[62] and Creasy[63] recognized the legality of humanitarian intervention based on a state entitled to assert the rights of subjects *vis-à-vis* their sovereign in certain circumstances. This was the modern equivalent of Grotius' right to wage war on behalf of the oppressed. However, some writers, such as Hobbes,[64] Wildman,[65] Reddie,[66] and Bernard,[67] were opposed to a right of humanitarian intervention. They rejected all intervention in the sovereignty of another state because

---

[59] Chesterman in his work, *Just War or Just Peace,* cited Antoine Rougier's description of the theory as an attempt to give a juridical basis to the right of one state to exercise control over the affairs of another state. *See* n. 18, at 36.

[60] *See* Woolsey, n. 17, at 32.

[61] Cited in Chesterman, n. 18, at 36.

[62] *Ibid.*

[63] *See* E.S. Creasy, *First Platform of International Law*, London: John Van Voorst, 1876.

[64] *See* Hobbes, n. 19.

[65] *See* Wildman, n. 20, at 62-63.

[66] *See* Reddie, n. 21.

[67] *See* M. Bernard, *On the Principle on Non-Intervention*, Oxford: J.H. and J. Parker, 1860. *See* also T.E. Holland, *Lectures on International Law,* London: Sweet and Maxwell, 1933.

any intervention on their behalf, no matter how great the moral claim, is incompatible with sovereignty.[68]

3.   HUMANITARIAN INTERVENTION AFTER WORLD WAR II

A strong tendency to the principle of non-intervention was seen at the end of World War II, with its even more terrible results than the First World War. At that time, people once again thought more seriously about confronting the use of force issue at the international level, to prevent war. In this way the international community in general and the major Allied Powers in particular became convinced that yet another effort should be made to establish a universal international organization charged with the management of international conflict. The League had failed in this task, but the new organization, it was believed, would be different. The conduct of Japan in China (1931), Italy in Ethiopia (1935), Germany in both Austria (1938) and Czechoslovakia (1938-9), and of the USSR in Finland (1939-40) and the invasion of Poland by Germany (1939),[69] repudiated everything for which the League stood. The joint Declaration of Roosevelt, the President of the USA, and Churchill, the Prime Minster of Great Britain, on 14 August 1941,[70] proclaimed the abandonment of unilateral resort to force and the "... establishment of a wider and permanent system of general security".[71] They also declared their hope that after the final destruction of the Nazis, a system would be established which would afford to all nations the means of dwelling in safety within their own boundaries and would "bring about the fullest collaboration between all nations in the economies field with the object of securing, for all, improved labour standards, economic advancement and social security."[72] In the Declaration of the United Nations of 1 January 1942, the USA, the UK, the USSR, China and other states in a state of war with the Axis Powers subscribed to the Atlantic Charter of 14 August 1941, stating that they were engaged in a "common struggle" against the Axis.[73] They also declared that they would pursue the war in co-operation with each other.[74] This declaration had the effect of attributing to the armed struggle of the anti-Axis coalition the character of a collective war of sanction.

---

[68]   *Ibid.*

[69]   The invasion of Poland by Germany in September, 1939, and the subsequent state of war between Germany, on the one hand, and the UK and France, on the other, is widely accepted as the starting point of the Second World War.

[70]   Text is available in 35 *AJIL,* Suppl. 191 (1941).

[71]   *Ibid.*

[72]   *Ibid.*

[73]   Text is available in 36 *AJIL,* Suppl. 191 (1942).

[74]   *Ibid.*

The United Nations[75] Charter in its preamble declares that the new organization was established "to save succeeding generations from the scourge of war, which twice in our lifetime has brought untold sorrow to mankind". It emphasized that the means to end such catastrophe was "… by acceptance of principles and institution of methods, that armed force shall not be used, save in the common interest." The principle of non-intervention generally recognized in the provisions of Article 2(1) on sovereign equality, Article 2(4) on the non-use of force, and Article 2(7) on domestic jurisdiction. According to the San Francisco Conference the principle of sovereign equality contains some elements including a) that states are juridically equal; b) that each state enjoys the rights inherent in full sovereignty; c) that the personality of the state is respected, as well as its territorial integrity and political independence; and d) that the state should, under international order, comply faithfully with its international duties and obligations.[76]

The UNGA through its 1970 Friendly Relations Declaration proclaimed sovereign equality, non-use of force and non-intervention, along with four other principles of the UN Charter, to constitute basic principles of international law.[77] The Declaration also declares that each state enjoys the rights inherent in full sovereignty, has the duty to respect the personality of other states, and has the right freely to choose and develop its political, social, economic and cultural systems.[78] According to the Declaration, the territorial integrity and political independence of the state are inviolable.[79]

> No state or group of states has the right to intervene, directly or indirectly, for any reason whatever, in the internal or external affairs of any other state. Consequently, armed intervention and all other forms of interference or attempted threats against the personality of the state or against its political, economic and cultural elements are in violation of international law. … no state shall organize, assist, foment, finance, invite or tolerate subversive, terrorist or armed activities directed towards the violent overthrow of the regime of another state or interfere in civil strife in another state.[80]

The principles of non-use of force and non-intervention have received international judicial recognition in the ICJ twice: in the *Corfu Channel* case, and in the *Case*

---

[75] The victorious countries established a new international organization called the United Nations Organization. The UN Charter, sponsored by the United States, Britain, the Soviet Union and China, and originally signed by fifty-one states, was designed to introduce law and order and an effective collective security system into international relations. The charter was approved in 1945 at the San Francisco Conference and entered into force on 24 October 1945.

[76] *See* UNCIO, Doc. Vol. VI, at 457.

[77] *See* the principle of non-use of force in the *Declaration on Friendly Relations* in GA. Res. 2625 (XXV), GAOR 25th session, Suppl. No 28 (1970), at 121. *See* also the *Definition of Aggression* in GA. Res.3314 (XXIX), GAOR 29th session, Suppl. No 31 (1974), at 142.

[78] *Ibid.*

[79] *Ibid.*

[80] *Ibid.*, 3rd principle.

Concerning Military and Paramilitary Activities in and against Nicaragua. In the former case the Court stated that:

> The Court can only regard the alleged right of intervention as the manifestation of a policy of force, such as has, in the past, given rise to most serious abuses and such as cannot, whatever be the present defects in international organization, find a place in International Law. Intervention is perhaps less admissible in the particular form it would take here; for from the nature of things, it would be reserved for the most powerful States and might easily lead to preventing the administration of international justice.[81]

In the latter case, the ICJ recognized the customary law basis of the principles of non-use of force and non-intervention as evidenced by both state practice and *opinion juris*, and stated that:

> The principle of non-intervention involves the right of every sovereign State to conduct its affairs without outside interference; though examples of trespass against these principles are not infrequent, the Court considers that it is part and parcel of customary international law. As the Court has observed: 'Between independence States, respect for territorial sovereignty is an essential foundation of international relations' (*ICJ Reports 1949*, p.35) and international law requires political integrity also to be respected.[82]

After World War II, the tension between sovereignty and human rights in the established international legal order is manifest in the opening words of the United Nations Charter. War is to be renounced as an instrument of national policy and human rights are to be affirmed. Under Article 2(4) of the Charter, the threat or use of force is prohibited and protection of human rights is observed in the provisions of Articles 55 and 56. Chesterman noted that the most recent writers who pay attention to humanitarian intervention recount this tension;[83] he then proceeds to consider a series of alleged instances of intervention on humanitarian grounds, in order to conclude whether or not such a right exists in practice.[84]

The place of humanitarian intervention in the contemporary modern legal system is a controversial issue among jurists.[85] Some jurists have doubted the legality of

---

[81] *See* the *Corfu Channel* case, ICJ. Rep. 1949, 4, at 35. *See* also *ibid.* at 26-31.

[82] *See* the *Military and Paramilitary Activities in and Against Nicaragua (Nicaragua v. United States)* Jurisdiction and Admissibility, ICJ. Rep. 1984, at 392, para. 85; 429, para. 79; 431, para. 90; 432, para. 93; 433-434, para. 94; 434.

[83] *See* Chesterman, n. 18, at 45.

[84] *Ibid.*

[85] *See* E. Borchard, *The Diplomatic Protection of Citizens Abroad*, New York Banks Law, 1922. *See* also L. Oppenheim, *International Law*, Vol. 2 (7th edn., ed by H. Lauterpacht), London, 1948; H. Lauterpacht, "The Grotian tradition in international law", 23 *BYIL* (1946); *id., International Law and Human Rights,* London: Stevens and Sons, 1950; J.L. Brierly, *The Law of Nations: An Intro-*

the doctrine as part of modern international law and attempted to reject it on a number of legal and moral grounds. Waldock, for example, doubted the doctrine's legitimacy because "its basis was [possibly] sheer power rather than law."[86] It has also been claimed that the principle is supported simply as the ultimate sanction against human rights violations, thus as the only means of enforcing an international minimum standard. The argument was used to allow the temporary or permanent substitution of sovereign rule in the "offending" state, "in the name of the society of nations", a collective rather than unilateral endeavour in the 1920s.[87] In regard to the status of the doctrine of humanitarian intervention, Lauterpacht pointed out that:

> There is a substantial body of opinion and practice in support of the view that ... when a state renders itself guilty of cruelties against and persecution of its nationals in such a way as to deny their fundamental human rights and to shock the conscience of mankind, intervention in the interest of humanity is legally permissible.[88]

Lauterpacht, however, states that this doctrine "has never become a fully acknowledged part of positive international law",[89] and admits that it is, in fact, a "precarious doctrine".[90]

4.   INTERVENTION FOR THE PROTECTION OF HUMAN RIGHTS

The idea of intervention for the protection of human rights dates back to the seventeenth century when some writers, namely Grotius,[91] Vattel[92] and Wolff,[93] began to consider the validity of intervention by a state in the affairs of another for the protection of those rights. Grotius, on the one hand, admitted that a state's form of Government was its own concern, but on the other hand he supported action taken by other rulers in the affairs of other states.[94] He stated that:

---

duction to the International Law of Peace (6th edn. ed. by H. Waldock), Oxford: Clarendon Press, 1963.

[86] *See* Waldock, n. 1, at 403. *See* also Brierly, n. 85.
[87] *See* Borchard, n. 84, at 14.
[88] *See* Oppenheim, n. 85, at 279.
[89] *See* Lauterpacht, "The Grotian tradition in international law", n. 85, at 46.
[90] *See* Lauterpacht, *International Law and Human Rights*, n. 85, at 31-32.
[91] *See* Grotius, Bk. II, Ch. XXV, sect. 8.
[92] *See* n. 16.
[93] *See* n. 14.
[94] Grotius in regard to punitive war supported civilized government intervention in the affairs of other States. At the beginning of the twentieth century, Theodore Roosevelt along the lines of Grotius supported intervention as a police measure. He stated that "[c]hronic wrongdoing, or an impotence which results in general loosening ties of civilized society, may in America, as elsewhere, ultimately require intervention by some civilized nation, and in the Western Hemisphere the adherence of the United States to the Monroe doctrine may force the United States, however, reluctantly, in flagrant cases of such wrongdoing or impotence, to the exercise of an international police power". Cited

If a tyrant ... practises atrocities towards his subjects which no just man can approve, the right of human social connection is not cut off in such a case ... Constantine took arms against Maxentius and Lucius; and several of the Roman Emperors took or threatened to take arms against the Persians if they prevented not the Christians from being persecuted on account of their religion.[95]

Vattel confirmed intervention in the affairs of other states for the protection of human rights in the following manner:

[I]f a prince by violating the fundamental laws, gives his subjects a lawful cause for resisting him, if by his un-supportable tyranny, he brings on a national revolt against him, any foreign power may rightfully give assistance to an oppressed people who ask for aid ... foreign nations may assist one of the two parties which seems to have justice on its side.[96] (emphasis added)

The idea of protection of certain fundamental rights by sovereign states, which was propagandized by those writers, eventually appeared in the behaviour of some states in the form of important provisions in their respective constitutions and other national instruments. The *Habeas Corpus* Act and the Petition of Rights Act in 1679, the Bill of Rights in 1689, and the French Declaration of the Rights of Man and Citizen are good examples. Later, the collective protection of the rights of minorities was asserted in and exercized through bilateral and multilateral treaties which gave the right to groups of states to interfere in the affairs of another state failing to observe guarantees undertaken by it. Such treaties gave to the collective system the right of intervention in the affairs of other states for safeguarding the human rights of minorities. The basic criterion of these treaties remained the protection of religious or ethnic minorities.

During the seventeenth century, various treaties were undertaken for the protection of Catholic minorities living in states with Protestant majorities. An important landmark for the protection of a religious minority living within the territory of other states was the Treaty of Westphalia in 1648. Parties undertook to protect the rights of their respective subjects forming religious minorities on parity with the majority.[97] Following the Treaty of Westphalia for the protection of the religious minorities living in states with another majority religion, other treaties were and established, such as the Treaty of Velau (Wehlau) between Poland and Brandenburg in 1657,[98] the Treaty of Peace among Poland, Austria, Sweden and Brandenburg in 1660,[99] and the Treaty of Nijmegen between the Holy Roman Empire and France in 1679.[100] For the pro-

---

in Chesterman, n. 18, at 36-37.

[95] *See* Grotius, n. 91, II, Ch. XXX, sect. 8.

[96] *See* Vattel, n. 16, II, Ch. IV, 56.

[97] *See* De Lima, n. 15, at 104-106.

[98] *Ibid.*

[99] *Ibid.*

[100] *Ibid.*

tection of Christians living in the Ottoman Empire, few treaties undertaken by European states[101] gave the signatories to the respective treaties the right to intervene, in concert or individually, in the affairs of the guaranteeing power, in response to the non-observance of the undertaking.[102] The protection of these rights in practice, however, remained chiefly the concern of the powerful states when these states met at the crossroads of power, the main issue was mostly allowed to go into abeyance. The protection of such rights acquired under treaty provisions, after the end of the First World War, became the chief concern of the League of the Nations. The Principal and Associated Powers concluded a series of treaties with Poland, Czechoslovakia, the Serb-Croat-Slovene state, Romania, Greece, Austria, Bulgaria, and Hungary in order to safeguard the rights of minorities by giving them equal treatment to that accorded to the rest of their populations.[103] The general pattern of these treaties was that all the inhabitants of these states were accorded full and complete protection of life, liberty and free exercise of creed, religion or belief.[104]

In the League Covenant, the protection of human rights appears only in the provision regarding the mandate territories, which was a result of pre-League experience, such as the treaty rights obtained from Turkey to protect the rights of the Christians. The League of Nations, as evidenced, became the guarantor for the application of the terms of the minority treaties. In this sense the League replaced the powers that intervened to protect minority rights,[105] individually or collectively, as expediency demanded.[106]

The protection of human rights has been keenly debated in the United Nations. Therefore, the UN Charter has made considerable reference to the promotion of these rights on a universal scale and they are mentioned repeatedly throughout the Charter, unlike in the League Covenant where human rights were protected in the mandated territories only. Art 1 (3) provides for the co-operation of the member states to realize certain fundamental human rights. It referred to "promoting and encouraging respect

---

[101] The treaty gave Russia the right to intervene in the affairs of Turkey in the case of denial of the rights of Christians. The first collective intervention to protect a treaty right took place in 1827 when Turkey failed to protect the rights of Greek Orthodox Christians. Russia started the Crimean War under the terms of the Treaty of Kutchuk-Kainardji. *See* n. 15, at 104-106.

[102] *See* H. Rosting, "Protection of minorities by the League of Nations", 17 *AJIL* (1923), at 641.

[103] *Ibid.*

[104] *Ibid.*

[105] For more details about protection of minority at that time, *see* M.K. Ganji, *International Protection of Human Rights*, Paris: Minard Press, 1962; H. Kelsen, *Principles of International Law* (2ⁿᵈ edn. ed. by R. W. Tucker), New York, etc.: Holt, Rinehart and Winston, Inc., 1966.

[106] *See* the Polish Treaty on 28 June 1919, partly quoted in 17 *AJIL*. For the protection of minority rights, Article 12 of the Treaty states that: "Poland agrees that the stipulations in the foregoing Articles, so far as they affect persons belonging to racial, religious, or linguistic minorities, constitute obligations of international concern and shall be placed under the guarantee of the League of Nations. ... any member of the Council of the League of Nations shall have a right to bring to the attention of the Council any infraction or any danger of infraction of any of these obligations, ... the Council thereupon take such action and give such direction as it may deem proper and effective in the circumstances."

for human rights and for fundamental freedoms for all without distinction". Article 55 (c) repeats the same principle in general terms and calls for "universal respect for, and observance of, human rights and fundamental freedom for all without distinction as to race, sex, language, or religion". Article 76(c) also emphasises this point and asserts an aim: "to encourage respect for human rights and for fundamental freedoms for all without distinction as to race, sex, language, or religion, and encourage recognition of the interdependence of the people of the world".

Here, this question may arise: do the UN Charter provisions on human rights create mandatory obligations of a legally binding character? The legally binding character of the provisions of the Charter on human rights is a controversial question among jurists. In this regard, among authorities on international law various opinions are observed, which can be divided into two categories. The first school of thought, represented by scholars such as Lauterpacht[107] and Jessup,[108] is that the UN Charter provisions on the human rights issue have created "mandatory obligations" of a legally binding character. Lauterpacht emphasized the "mandatory obligations" and referred to Article 13 of the UN Charter, which provides that the Assembly shall make recommendations for the purpose of assisting in the realization of human rights and freedoms.[109] He also cited Article 55 (c) of the UN Charter which requires "universal respect for, and observance of, human rights and fundamental freedoms" and Article 56, which states that "all members pledge themselves to take joint and separate action in co-operation with the organization for the achievement of the purposes set forth in Article 55".[110] On the other hand, Kelsen in his work, *The Law of the United Nations*,[111] rejects the "mandatory obligations"[112] and argues that Charter provisions are only in the nature of declarations and goals to be realized and are, at most, "imperfect obligations" without any binding force.[113] He argues that the Charter provisions do not impose upon the members a strict obligation to grant to their subjects the rights and freedoms mentioned in the Preamble or the text of the Charter.[114]

It seems that there are three main reasons why the UN Charter provisions on the human rights issue are deemed not to have created "mandatory obligations" of a legally binding character:

---

[107] *See* Lauterpacht, *International Law and Human Rights*, n. 85, at 148.

[108] *See* P.C. Jessup, *A Modern Law of Nations*, (3rd edn.), New York: Macmillan Press, 1949, at 87-92.

[109] *See* Lauterpacht, *International Law and Human Rights*, n. 85, at 148.

[110] *Ibid.*

[111] *See* H. Kelsen, *The Law of the United Nations*, London: Stevens and Sons, 1950. *See* also *id.*, "Collective security and collective self-defence under the Charter of the United Nations", 42 *AJIL* (1948).

[112] *Ibid.*, at 29.

[113] *Ibid.*

[114] *Ibid.*

-   First, the language of the UN Charter does not support the interpretation that the Members are under a legal obligation regarding the rights and freedoms of their subjects. All the formulae concerned establish the purposes or functions of the Organization, not the obligations of Members, and the Organization is not empowered by the Charter to impose upon the governments of Member states the obligation to guarantee their subjects the rights referred to in the Charter. Lauterpacht has referred to Articles 13, 55 and 56 of the UN Charter as evidence for "mandatory obligations", but the language used in those articles does not lend itself to this kind of interpretation. Article 13, for example, requests that the General Assembly initiates studies and makes recommendations for the purpose of promoting international co-operation in the political, economic, and cultural fields, and assisting in the realization of human rights and fundamental freedoms. Clearly, those recommendations cannot create "mandatory obligations", because UN provisions do not impose upon the Members a strict obligation to obey them.[115]

-   Secondly, supporting the idea of the legally binding character of the provisions of the Charter on human rights would give rise to anarchy in the international community, which would certainly not achieve the main purposes of the UN Charter. Indeed, the lack of clear criteria for the concept of human rights would allow states to interfere in the behaviour of others in the name of human rights when motivations other than human rights were involved, as we have seen on some occasions, such as the intervention of the US in Grenada in 1983[116] and in Panama in 1989.[117] There were few interventions solely for human rights, such as the intervention of the US in Rwanda, which the present author does not want to ignore. There were, however, many cases in which states interference in the behaviour of others in the name of human rights when motivations other than human rights were involved.

-   Thirdly, the history of Articles 55 and 56 of the UN Charter shows that none of the delegates made any direct statement about mandatory obligations. The short historical review of Article 55 of the UN Charter demonstrates that only during the discussion about the article did a few delegates demand a separate action when grave infringement of basic human rights occurred and co-operation from the states concerned was not forthcoming. However, they emphasized that the International Organization should take such action in order to protect basic human rights.[118] It is significant that even the US delegates supported the view

---

[115] The General Assembly shall initiate studies and make recommendations for the purpose of: "... b. promoting international co-operation in the economic, social, cultural, educational, and health fields, and assisting in the realization of human rights and fundamental freedoms for all without distinction as to race, sex, language, or religion." UNCIO, Vol. X. at 340. UNCIO. Vol. VI, at 439.

[116] *UNYB*, 1983, at 211. *See* General Assembly Resolution 38/7 (1983), para. 1.

[117] *UNYB*, 1989, at 175. *See* General Assembly Resolution 44/20 (1989).

[118] *See* the view of the representative of the former Soviet Union during the discussion on Article 56. UNCIO, Vols. 6 and 10. *See* also the view of the Australian delegate in the course of the drafting of the provisions of the application of the enforcement measures under Chapter VII as an exception

that, in such a case, only the International Organization could intervene in domestic affairs, even though unilateral interventions by the United States in the course of time proved that there is a serious discrepancy between theory and reality in the US policy.

At the San Francisco Conference on International Organization, those delegates certainly intended to authorise only the International Organization, in extreme circumstances, to intervene in the case of grave infringements of basic human rights by a state, in order to prevent such infringements; unilateral armed intervention by states for the protection of human rights had no place at that time.

Attempts to justify incidents of the unilateral intervention of states in the affairs of another state for the protection of human rights in some circumstances have been seen by scholars as based on legal or moral arguments. They presented different arguments for the same aim – protecting innocent people – which in this paper will be divided into three categories.

4.1. Intervention under a higher ranking law

The advocates of the first category argue that if the lives of people are at stake, the formal law ought to be violated to save thousands of lives to achieve the higher goal, even if the Security Council does not authorize force.[119] This is a view of some scholars who consider humanitarian intervention to be a moral imperative.[120] They note that the identification of human rights, and the protection of the inherent dignity

---

to the general rule of non-intervention by the Organization in the domestic jurisdiction over human rights, who called the fundamental freedoms a matter of international concern and as such not falling within the "essentially" domestic jurisdiction of the state concerned. In a comment on the issue, the Australian representative pointed out that "... the clause in its wide form is needed in order to enable the Security Council to deal with grave infringements of basic rights within a state".

[119] Some politicians including the Czech President in the light of the human tragedy in the Balkans in the final decade of the twentieth century have chosen a different approach to the question of the "territorial integrity and political independence of states". They refer to NATO air strikes against Serbia in 1999 and argue that, even though NATO acted with no authority from the UN Security Council, this violation of the UN Charter did not constitute an act of aggression or disrespect for international law, but took place under another law (human rights), one that ranks higher than the law which protects the sovereignty of states. In their view, to breach and ignore the territorial integrity and political independence of states in order to protect human life is permissible and applicable in many cases. If this view is accepted, however, there is no respect left for Article 2 (4). The phrase "territorial integrity and political independence" has been the object of controversy as to its meaning in relation to the prohibition of the use of armed force in Article 2(4) of the Charter.

[120] *See* A. Cassese, *"Ex iniuria ius oritur*: are we moving towards international legitimation of forcible humanitarian countermeasures in the world community?"*, 10 *EJIL* (1999), at 25. *See* also *id.*, "A follow-up: forcible humanitarian countermeasures and *opinio necessitates*", 10 *EJIL* (1999); A.D. D'Amato, "The invasion of Panama was a lawful response to tyranny", 84 *AJIL*, 1990, at 516-520; *id.*, *International Law: Process and Prospect*, New York: Transnational Publishers, 1987.

and equality of all members of the human family, are acknowledged in the Universal Declaration of Human Rights (UDHR) and UN Charter. Hyndman, for example, asserts those purposes and states that they "are essential prerequisites for true and firm foundations for freedom, justice and peace in the world."[121] In this regard, the editors of *Oppenheim*, Jennings and Watts, also argued that involvement of the international community on both a global and a regional basis "with the protection of human rights diminishes any need for states to retain or exercise an individual right of humanitarian intervention."[122] *Oppenheim* stressed that "if humanitarian intervention is ever to be justified, it will only be in extreme and very particular circumstances."[123]

In regard to the legality of humanitarian intervention, advocates claim that unilateral force is permitted to enforce the human rights provisions in the Charter. Since promotion of human rights is one of the primary purposes of the Charter, then the use of force to compel compliance would not violate Article 2(4) of UN Charter. This claim is not for enforcement, but for the "self-enforcement" of human rights provisions. It is precisely the argument favouring humanitarian intervention as a unilateral right. This argument ignores the possibility that force to uphold human rights might be inconsistent with the maintenance of peace. It even requires the assumption that the intervenor has ascertained the true wishes of the people, is willing to effect these wishes, and does so without violating the state's integrity and independence. Here, also this question was propounded: does it imply that every single UN purpose stated in Article 1 of the Charter can be pursued through the unilateral use of force? Clearly, the unilateral use of force has no place in this respect. In the current international legal system, collective security, which has the character of enforcement action on behalf of the international community, fulfils a general interest shared by all states. It has been entrusted to the United Nations through the SC, which has the primary responsibility for the maintenance of international peace and security, and through the GA by virtue of the 'Uniting for Peace' Resolution.[124] Therefore, it is correct to say that under modern international law, the unilateral use of force for maintaining international peace and security, as well as for vindicating international law, is inadmissible. The reactions of some states against the UK and French Governments' ultimatum over the 1956 Suez crisis and NATO in the 1999 Kosovo crisis demonstrate this fact. In the former case, following the Israeli aggression over the Suez Canal on 26 October 1956, the UK and French Governments issued a joint ultimatum and demanded the cessation of hostilities and withdrawal of the forces of both belligerents from the Canal.[125] The ultimatum also demanded the temporary

---

[121] Hyndman, "Sri Lanka: a study in microcosm of regional problems and need for more effective protection of human rights", 20 *DJILP* (1992), at 303.

[122] *See* 1 *Oppenheim's International Law* (9th edn. ed. by Jennings and Watts), Longman Group Ltd, 1992, at 443-444.

[123] *Ibid.*

[124] GA Res. 377 A (v) (1950).

[125] *See* S/3712, *SCOR*, 11th yr. Suppl. October-December 1956, at 11.

occupation of certain key positions of the Canal area on Egyptian territory by the UK and French forces.[126] It also threatened that:

> Failing an answer by 6:30, Cairo time, on 31 October 1956, the Governments of the UK and France would intervene in whatever strength they might deem necessary to secure compliance.[127]

The legal status of the ultimatum was discussed and rejected by many states, including the US. Among the arguments the statements of the representatives of Yugoslavia and the US were remarkable. The representative of Yugoslavia stated that:

> While the Security Council, the organ of the United Nations which bears primary responsibility for the maintenance of peace and security, is considering the action to be taken in the face of Israel aggression against Egypt, two Member States of the United Nations have apparently decided to embark upon what can be described as the unilateral application of force. They have done so clearly without any kind of authorization from the United Nations.[128]

The representative of the US also emphasized that his government believed that if the draft resolution were adopted and promptly carried out, the reason for the twelve-hour United Kingdom and French ultimatum would be invalid as its basis would have disappeared.[129] He further concluded that "we do not imply that in any circumstances this ultimatum would be justifiable or be found to be consistent with the purposes and principles of the Charter."[130]

Following the collapse of the Rambouillet negotiations[131] (in France on 29 January 1999, co-chaired by the UK and France) between the Kosovo Liberation Army (KLA) and the Federation Republic of Yugoslavia (FRY) in the middle of March, air strikes were launched on 24 March 1999, and continued for 78 days by NATO. The action

---

[126] *Ibid.*

[127] *Ibid.* The representative of the UK in the Security Council, Mr Pierson Dixon, tried to justify the objective of the Anglo-French action for stopping the fighting and safeguarding the free passage of shipping through the Suez Canal in the general interest and in the interest of security and peace. *SCOR*, 11th yr., 749th mtg., para 11.

[128] *SCOR* 11th yr., 749th mtg., para.25.

[129] *Ibid.*, para. 22.

[130] *Ibid.*

[131] The first round of negotiations in Rambouillet started from 6 to 23 February 1999, followed by a second round in Paris, from 15 to 18 March 1999. The proposed settlement at Rambouillet, dictated by the West, required: Yugoslavia to withdraw its forces from Kosovo, the KLA to lay down their arms, NATO peace-keeping troops on the ground to enforce the agreement, and a three-year period to settle the political future of Kosovo. *See* H. McCoubrey, 'Kosovo, NATO and international law', 14 *International Relations* (August 1999), at 31-38.

met with the strong opposition of some states,[132] including two permanent members of the SC, Russia and China, who believed the UN Security Council had not authorized military action against Serbia. They raised considerable objections to NATO's action.[133] Universal condemnation of the joint Anglo-France action in Suez that purported to restore international peace and security in the area by unilateral means, and considerable objections to NATO's action in Kosovo, demonstrated these objections. Therefore, it can be said that no purpose of the UN can be realized by resort to the unilateral use of force.

Intervention as an ethical obligation
The second category of our study concerns those people whose support of humanitarian intervention is based on an ethical viewpoint. Since the international community has witnessed mass violations of human rights in the late twentieth century, a few scholars such as Cassese rely on the ethical viewpoint; they argue that unilateral intervention without Security Council authorization in order to stop such violation is, in extreme circumstances, permissible, even though it is contrary to the UN Charter.[134] Cassese in his work, *"Ex iniuria ius oritur*: Are We Moving towards International Legitimization of Forcible Humanitarian Countermeasures in the World Community?"* tries first, to demonstrate the place of human rights in the present world;[135] second, seeks to justify NATO action in Kosovo, and third, expresses his support for similar cases in the future. He, as a prominent example of this school, refers to the massacres and other Serb violations in Kosovo; Cassese then argues that resort to armed force may become justified under certain strict conditions, even in the absence of any authorization by the Security Council.[136] Next, he poses these questions: "Should one sit idly by and watch thousands of humans being slaughtered or brutally persecuted?[137] Should one remain silent and inactive only because the

---

[132] *See* R.G.C. Thomas, "NATO and international law", May 1999, at *http://jurist.law.pitt.edu/ thomas.htm*. Available in October 2000. *See* also McCoubrey, n. 131, at 32-34.

[133] Apart from Russia and China, some other states expressed opposition. Among them, the representative of India to the Security Council well expressed his objection to NATO's act. He emphasized that this attack directly violated Article 53 of the Charter, and stated that "No country, group of countries or regional arrangement, no matter how powerful, can arrogate to itself the right of taking arbitrary and unilateral military action against others. That would be a return to anarchy where might is right .... The attacks now taking place on Yugoslavia have not been authorized by the Council, acting under Chapter VII, and are therefore completely illegal." *Ibid.*

[134] *See* Cassese, *"Ex iniuria ius oritur..."*, n. 120, at 25-27. It should be noted that many years ago, such human tragedy happened in Bosnia and Kosovo. Nardin accepts and supports this position. *See* T. Nardin, *Law, Morality, and the Relations of States*, Princeton: Princeton University Press, 1983, at 93-94.

[135] In regard to the place of human rights in the present world he says, "human rights are increasingly becoming the main concern of the world community as a whole. There is a widespread sense that they cannot and should not be trampled upon with impunity in any part of the world." *See* n. 120.

[136] *Ibid.*

[137] *Ibid.*

existing body of international law proves incapable of remedying such a situation?[138] Or, rather, should respect for the Rule of Law be sacrificed on the altar of human compassion?".[139]

In order to answer those questions, he argues that resort to armed force was justified from an ethical viewpoint, though this moral action is contrary to the current international legal system.[140] Then, Cassese introduces the criterion of extreme circumstances in order to prevent misuse of the concept of human rights, as follows:

i gross and egregious breaches of human rights involving loss of life of hundreds or thousands of innocent people, and amounting to crime against humanity, are carried out in the territory of sovereign State, either by the central governmental authorities or with their connivance and support, or because the total collapse of such authorities cannot impede those atrocities;

ii if the crime against humanity results from anarchy in a sovereign state, proof is necessary that the central authorities are utterly unable to put an end to those crimes, while at the same time refusing to call upon or to allow other states or international organizations to enter the territory to assist in terminating the crimes. If, on the contrary, such crimes are the work of the central authorities, it must be shown that those authorities have consistently withheld their co-operation from the United Nations or other international organizations, or have systematically refused to comply with appeals, recommendations or decisions of such organizations;

iii the Security Council is unable to take any coercive action to stop the massacres because of disagreement among the Permanent Members or because one or more of them exercises its veto power. Consequently, the Security Council either refrains from any decision or only confines itself to deploring or condemning the massacres, plus possibly terming the situation a threat to the peace;

iv all peaceful avenues which may be explored consistent with the urgency of the situation to achieve a solution based on negotiation, discussion and any other means short of force have been exhausted, notwithstanding which, no solution can be agreed upon by the parties to the conflicts;

v a group of states (not a single hegemonic Power, however strong its military, political and economic authority, nor such a Power with the support of a client state or an ally) decides to try to halt the atrocities, with the support or at least the non-opposition of the majority of Member States of the UN;

vi armed force is exclusively used for the limited purpose of stopping the atrocities and restoring respect for human rights, not for any goal going beyond this limit and purpose. Consequently, the use of force must be discontinued as soon as this purpose is attained. Moreover, it is axiomatic that use of force should be commensurate with and proportionate to the human rights exigencies on the ground. The more urgent the situation of killings and atrocities, the more intensive

---

[138] *Ibid.*
[139] *Ibid.*
[140] *Ibid.*

and immediate may be the military response thereto. Conversely, military action would not be warranted in the case of a crisis which is slowly unfolding and which still presents avenues for diplomatic resolution aside from armed confrontation.[141]

The present author completely agrees with Cassese that, nowadays, the international community cannot view mass violations of human rights as being acceptable merely because the Security Council is unable to take any coercive action to stop them; failure on the part of the SC to halt them may be as a result of disagreement among its Permanent Members or exercises of veto power. My concern is, however, that Cassese's criteria could all too easily be broadly interpreted by certain superpowers and in the end misapplied to military intervention in the name of human rights, even though Cassese, in his categories, tries to introduce the criterion of extreme circumstances specifically in order to prevent such misuse of the concept of humanitarian intervention. In his final conditions, Cassese argues for example that "armed force is exclusively used for the limited purpose of stopping the atrocities and restoring *respect for human rights*", yet he ignores the fact that different people approach the concept in different ways. "Respect for human rights" is a principle accepted and confirmed by all human beings, but there are different interpretations of this "respect". There are many concepts such as violence, pacifism, human rights, freedom, reform, and democracy that can be and are interpreted in different ways. It is not the purpose of this work to enter into discussion, but I wish only to remind readers of this difference by offering an example. As we know, violence against human beings is seen as wrong from the pacifist point of view. In this regard, some pacifist philosophers[142] renounce all types of violence absolutely, and support the absolutist position.[143] Others,[144] however, reject only certain types of organized violence, such as warfare and violent revolution.[145] As we have seen, the concept of pacifism is defined in different ways amongst its philosophers. Therefore, how is it possible that the military intervention of states in the internal affairs of others be offered through reasons of "respect for human rights?" There is no consensus on some concepts, such as "respect for human rights." It is hard to accept unilateral intervention, without authorization from the Security Council, simply by invoking respect for human rights.

---

[141] *Ibid.*

[142] *See* J. Meyerding, "Feminism and pacifism: doing it our way", *WIN* (October 1979), at 10.

[143] *See* the argument of J. Meyerding, as one of the absolutist pacifists. She rejects all forms of violence and defines all kinds of violence in this manner: "Pacifism is opposed to violence in all forms, including physical, emotional, intellectual, and economic coercion ... because violence denies the value of its victims' lives." *Ibid.*

[144] *See* G. Sharp, *Gandhi as a Political Strategist: With Essays on Ethics and Politics*, Boston: Porter Sargent, 1979, at 205-206. *See* also G. Sharp, *Social, Power and Political Freedom*, Boston: Porter Sargent, 1973.

[145] G. Sharp supports this idea and defines pacifists as "those persons and groups who, as the minimum, refuse participation in all international or civil wars or violent revolutions, and base this refusal on moral, ethical, or religious principle." *Ibid.*

The concept of human rights also has often been used as a pretext for unilateral armed intervention by major powers in other states. The intervention of the US in the name of human rights in Nicaragua is a prominent example. In this intervention the US destroyed certain economic resources of the Sandinista Government, in order ostensibly to protect human rights. The ICJ in the *Nicaragua Case* clearly did not accept the US's argument and ruled:

> [W]here human rights are protected by international conventions, that protection takes the form of such arrangements for monitoring respect for human rights as are provided for in the conventions themselves.[146]

> *[T]the use of force could not be the appropriate method to monitor or ensure such respect. With regard to the steps actually taken, the protection of human rights, a strictly humanitarian objective, cannot be compatible with the mining of ports, the destruction of oil installations, or again, with the training, arming and equipping of the contras …* (emphasis added).[147]

Nowadays the view prevails, particularly amongst developing countries, that human-itarian intervention may be a pretext for intervention by major powers for political purposes or motivations other than human rights protection. Mani rightly says "a cursory look at the history of international relations is enough to reveal that the "facility" of intervention has been repeatedly utilized by big powers against small powers."[148] Therefore, it is true to say that the history of most interventions in the past created a fear of abuse, in the view of the international community. Frank and Rodley well demonstrated the fear in this manner:

> When States wish to intervene, they will reach for convenient humanitarian justifica-tions that extend from genocide to electoral irregularities. When nations wish to avert their eyes, even millions dying in concentration camps or under the treads of tanks are perceived as merely local problems to be left to those in charge, often by States which have themselves pleaded the right of humanitarian intervention in other instances.[149]

4.3. Intervention for human rights and Article 2(4)

The final group of our study in this paper is supported by Anthony D'Amato[150]

---

[146] ICJ. Rep. 1986, at 134, para 267.

[147] *Ibid.*, at 134-5, para 268.

[148] *See* V.S. Mani, "Humanitarian intervention and international law", *Ind.JIL* (1996), at 25.

[149] *See* T. Frank and Nigel Rodley, "After Bangladesh: the law of humanitarian intervention by military force', 67 *AJIL* (1973), at 294.

[150] D'Amato advocates a restricted sense of Article 2(4) of the Charter and permits limited inter-vention. Despite the clear intention of States Parties to the San Francisco Conference, including the United States delegate, who emphasized that there were "no loopholes in the provisions",

and Fernando Teson.[151] They argue that humanitarian intervention on the basis
of the protection of human rights is not a violation of the "territorial integrity and
political independence" of the target state.[152] They support a restricted sense of
Article 2(4) of the Charter and then present the idea that a war waged in a good cause
would violate neither the territory integrity nor the political independence of the state.
Teson, for example, argues that genuine humanitarian intervention does not result
in territorial conquest or political subjugation.[153]

In order to respond to the claims of those writers who have argued that forceful
humanitarian intervention does not comprise force against the territorial integrity
or political independence of the target state, it is submitted that the military intervention of one state against another state on humanitarian grounds is directly opposed
to the territorial integrity of states, as we have seen in many cases such as the Indian
intervention in East Pakistan/Bangladesh in 1971;[154] the Vietnamese intervention
in Cambodia in 1978;[155] the Israeli intervention in Uganda in 1976;[156] the Belgian
and French intervention in Zaire in 1978;[157] the Tanzanian interventions in Uganda
in 1978[158] and 1979;[159] the US intervention in Granada in 1983;[160] the US intervention in Panama in 1989-90,[161] and finally, the NATO intervention in Kosovo
in 1999; these culminated in the territorial violation of Pakistan, Cambodia, Uganda,
Zaire, Granada, Panama, and Serbia, respectively.

D'Amato, after examining the *travaux preparatoires* of the article, argues that the delegates to the
San Francisco Conference simply did not understand the words they were using. Later he also
claimed that the US invasion of Panama in 1989 complied with Article 2 (4) because the US did
not intend to, and has not, colonialized, annexed or incorporated Panama. *See* A. D'amato, "The
invasion of Panama was a lawful response to tyranny", n. 120, at 516-520.

[151] *See* F.R. Teson, *Humanitarian Intervention: An Inquiry into Law and Morality*, 22nd edn., New
York: Transnational Publishers, 1997, at 150.

[152] *See* D'Amato, *International Law: Process and Prospect*, n. 120, at 57-70.

[153] *See* Teson, n. 116, at 151.

[154] S/PV.1606 (1971), para 186. GA Res. 2793 (XXVI) (1971), paras. 4 & 8. SC Res. 303 (1971).
See also D.W. Bowett, "The use of force for the protection of nationals abroad", in A. Cassese (ed.),
The Current Legal Regulation of the Use of Force, Dordrecht: Martinus Nijhoff, 1986.

[155] *See* T. Avirgan and Martho Honey, *War in Uganda: the Legacy of Idi Amin*, Westport: Lawrence
Hill, 1982. *See* also *Vietnam's Intervention in Cambodia in International Law*, Canberra: AGPS,
1989.

[156] For more details *see* S/PV. 1939 (1976), paras. 106-15; S/PV. 1941 (1976), para. 77; S/12139
(1976).

[157] *See* Chesterman, n. 18, at 76-77.

[158] *Ibid.*

[159] *Ibid.*

[160] *UNYB* (1983), at 211. The Security Council failed to protest the intervention only by reason
of a US veto. In this regard the General Assembly adopted resolution 38/7 in 1983 and emphasized
that it deeply deplore[d] the intervention as a flagrant violation of international law. *See* para 1.

[161] *UNYB* (1989), at 175. Again, a Security Council resolution was blocked by veto. The General
Assembly in this regard adopted the resolution by an overwhelming majority and condemned the
unilateral action by the US. *See* GA Res. 44/20 (1989).

Again, the military intervention of one state in the affairs of another state on humanitarian grounds is directly opposed to the notion of the territorial integrity of states. In the case of Pakistan, the Indian action resulted in the secession of the Eastern Province, that is, in the permanent territorial impairment of the country. In the cases of Cambodia and Uganda, it resulted in the violent overthrow of the Government of each of these countries. It may thus be questioned what indeed constitutes force against the territorial integrity or political independence of a state, if the above instances are not seen as doing so. Our claim is supported by states of the General Assembly *Declaration on Friendly Relations*,[162] Security Council and General Assembly resolutions,[163] and ICJ decisions[164] which concern the meaning of non-intervention and condemnation of the unauthorized use of force by a state.

Moreover, the UN Charter is a multilateral treaty and is therefore subject to many of the same customary law rules of interpretation as are other treaties. The Vienna Convention on the Law of Treaties,[165] now applied as custom by ICJ in the *Maritime Delimitation and Territorial Questions* case *(Qatar/Bahrain)*,[166] provides that "A treaty shall be interpreted in good faith in accordance with the ordinary meaning to be given to the terms of the treaty in their context and in the light of its object and purpose".[167] Therefore, such an interpretation of Article 2(4) is unreasonable as it directly ignores the aim of the article.

5.   INTERVENTION AND STATE PRACTICE

State practice does not support the existence of unilateral intervention in the light of the humanitarian intervention doctrine. A quick look at the Indian intervention in East Pakistan and the Vietnamese intervention in Cambodia has shown that representatives of third states did not support those actions, even though both states tried to justify their actions in humanitarian terms. Regarding the Indian intervention in East Pakistan, the international community not only did not accept its action and argument, which emphasized "the purest of motives and the purest of intentions: to rescue the people of East Bengal from what they are suffering",[168] but also urged

---

[162]   *See* GA Res. 2625 (XXV) (1970).

[163]   *See* GA Res. 45/150 (1990); 2625 (1970).

[164]   *See* the *Corfu Channel* case, ICJ. Rep. 1949, 4, at 35. *See* also *ibid.* at 26-31. *Military and Paramilitary Activities in and Against Nicaragua* (*Nicaragua v. United States*), Jurisdiction and Admissibility, ICJ. Rep. 1984, at 392, para. 85; 429, para. 79; 431, para. 90; 432, para. 93; 433-434, para. 94; 434.

[165]   *See* Vienna Convention on the Law of Treaties of 1969.

[166]   ICJ Rep. 1995, 6, at 18, para. 33. Cf. *Territorial Dispute (Libyan Arab Jamahiriya/Chad)*, ICJ. Rep. 1994, 6, at 21-22, para. 41.

[167]   Article 31 (1).

[168]   *See* SCOR, 26th yr., 1606th and 1608th mtgs., paras. 185 and 262. The Indian representative in the Council, Mr. Sen, made a reference to considerations of humanity as the basis of India's action in East Pakistan. However, India's justification was far from being the central argument for action. During the debate, the point was made repeatedly: "Provocation and aggression of various kinds

India to cease hostilities and withdraw from East Pakistan.[169] On 25 December 1978, the Vietnamese took military action in Cambodia. As a result of the action the Khmer Rouge Government, which had perpetrated horrific atrocities against the Cambodian population between 1975 and 1978, was overthrown.[170] The majority of states considered Vietnam's action as unlawful intervention.[171] In this regard, some representatives expressly indicated their objection against the use of force in order to protect human rights. For example, the representative of Singapore stated that:

> No other country has a right to topple the Government of Democratic Kampuchea, however badly that Government may have treated its people. To hold to the contrary principle is to concede the right of a foreign Government to intervene and overthrow the Government of another country....[172]

The representative of France stated that:

> The notion that because a regime is detestable foreign intervention is justified and forcible overthrow is legitimate is extremely dangerous. That could ultimately jeopardize the very maintenance of international law and order and make the continued existence of various regimes dependent on the judgment of their neighbours.[173]

---

by Pakistan from 25 March onwards is a reality. As a result, retaliation had followed in exercise of the right of self-defence, and we have warned that we shall exercise this right without hesitation". For more details *see SCOR*, 1680th mtg., para. 272.

[169] *Ibid.*, The US representative emphasized that the action is contrary to the UN Charter (1606th mtg., paras. 193-194). *See* also para. 237 (China), paras. 201-213 (Italy), paras. 220-227 (France), paras. 279-292 (Belgium).

[170] As a result of the action, a new Government was formed, composed of Members of a "Cambodian National Front" that appears to have been formed under the patronage of the replacement Vietnamese Government. By that time, relations between Cambodia and Vietnam had been severely strained because of repeated border incidents perpetrated by the Cambodian armed forces since 1975. During the debate at the Security Council the Vietnamese representative pointed out, "In order to draw a clear picture of the problem of Kampuchea, it is appropriate to make a clear distinction between two wars: one, the border war ... against Vietnam, which the Vietnamese people have been forced to deal with; the other, the revolutionary war of the Kampuchean people against the dictatorial rule of the Pol Pot-Leng Sary clique .... Like any other country in a similar situation, Vietnam is determined to exercise its right of legitimate defence recognized by the Charter of the United Nations and by International law in order to defend its independence, sovereignty and territorial integrity."

[171] *See SCOR*, 34th yr., 2109th mtg., para. 18 (Norway); *SCOR*, 34th yr., 2109th mtg., para. 36 (France); *SCOR*, 34th yr., 2110th mtg., para. 49 (Singapore); *SCOR*, 34th yr., 2110th mtg., paras. 27-29 (Portugal); *SCOR*, 34th yr., 2110[h] mtg., para. 58 (New Zealand). It should be noted that only the former Soviet Union and Czechoslovakia supported Vietnam's action.

[172] *SCOR*, 34th yr., 2110th mtg., para. 49.

[173] *SCOR*, 34th yr., 2109th mtg., para. 36.

The UK also took the view that:

> Whatever is said about human rights in Kampuchea, it cannot excuse Vietnam, whose human rights record is deplorable, for violating the territorial integrity of Democratic Kampuchea, an Independent State Member of the United Nations....[174]

The US military action without Security Council authorization against Iraq on 3-4 September 1996 met with considerable opposition from many states,[175] including three of its permanent members: France,[176] Russia,[177] and China.[178] Moscow called the US action "unacceptable" and described the situation as "an inadequate and inadmissible response".[179] The Kremlin statement also stated that "Russia insists on ending all military actions in Iraq threatening the sovereignty and territorial integrity of that country".[180] Binyon notes that Moscow, in its statement, used some of the strongest anti-American language since the Cold War.[181] France, one of the three countries patrolling the no-fly zones, was not satisfied with the action. In this regard a spokesman for its Foreign Ministry affirmed "France's commitment to Iraq's territorial integrity"[182] and noted that "Paris did not believe Saddam had violated United Nations resolutions."[183] Therefore, as Mani says, "under modern international law, there is no place for humanitarian intervention and contrary views in the Western doctrine are untenable in terms of state practice and the ruling of International Court".[184]

6. CONCLUSION

The legitimacy and validity of the right of humanitarian intervention is in international law still disputed amongst jurists. Adherents of this doctrine argue that the right survived or emerged after the enactment of the UN Charter and that humanitarian

---

[174] *SCOR*, 34th yr., 2110th mtg., para. 65.

[175] Most Arab nations, apart from Kuwait, strongly condemned the operation. Spain and New Zealand were also concerned that America was acting hastily. Indonesia, the world's most populous Muslim state, regretted the violence.

[176] *See http://www.the-times.co.uk/cgi-bin/BackIssue?* Available in September 2000.

[177] The Kremlin in its statement stated: "Russia insists on ending all military actions in Iraq threatening the sovereignty and territorial integrity of that country". *See http://www.the-times.co.uk/cgi-bin/BackIssue?* Available in September 2000. *See* also M. Binyon, "Alarmed Russians call on America to show restraint" in *The Times,* at *http://www.the-times.co.uk/cgi-bin/BackIssue,* 4 September 1996. Available in September 2000.

[178] *Ibid.*

[179] *Ibid. See* also *http://www.the-times.co.uk/cgi-bin/BackIssue?* Available in September 2000.

[180] *Ibid.*

[181] *See* Binyon, n. 177.

[182] *See* n. 177.

[183] *Ibid.*

[184] *See* Mani, n. 148, at 25.

action in Kosovo in 1999 for human rights is compatible with Article 2(4) of UN Charter. However, none of the arguments upon the legitimacy of humanitarian intervention by commentators and politicians – that the right survived or emerged after the enactment of the UN Charter and that recent humanitarian action for human rights is compatible with Article 2 (4) of UN Charter – could be persuasive that it is compatible with the article and purpose of the Charter because:

- The doctrine of humanitarian intervention was repudiated by the ICJ in its judgement in the South-West Africa Case.[185]
- A cursory look at *Legality of Use of Force Case* in 1999[186] where FRY instituted proceedings against ten NATO members before the ICJ, alleging that their acts were unlawful violations of Article 2(4), reveals, contrary to the claim of NATO leaders, that Counsel in the joint hearings avoided making any reference to humanitarian intervention; instead, Counsel replied that intervention took place in order to protect fundamental values insured in the *jus cogens*, such as the right to life,[187] and also to prevent "an impending catastrophe recognized as such by the Security Council".[188] Apart from the Kingdom of Belgium[189] which relied on the right of humanitarian intervention before an international tribunal, other NATO members including the UK used the language of Security Council resolution 1199, "humanitarian catastrophe", and did not refer to the humanitarian intervention doctrine.[190]
- State practice does not support the existence of unilateral intervention in the light of the humanitarian intervention doctrine even in the best cases, as discussed in this paper, where intervening states tried to justify their actions in humanitarian terms.

The present legal system does not nowadays recognize the enforcement, by an individual military force, of any claim, except in self-defence because, on the one hand, the text of the Charter contains no express justification of resort to force on humanitarian grounds. Action in self-defence under Article 51 of the Charter cannot be invoked in justifying humanitarian intervention, for there is no necessity of self-defence on the part of the intervening state. The admissibility of protection of nationals in exercising the right to self-defence is an argument not valid for the protection of the nationals of another state. Indeed, as the international community currently stands, that is, largely composed of sovereign states, the general regime

---

[185] *See* ICJ Rep. 1966, at 6.
[186] *See Legality of Use of Force (Provisional Measures)*, ICJ, CRs (1999).
[187] *Ibid.* CR 99/15 (10 May 1999).
[188] *Ibid.*
[189] The Kingdom of Belgium took the view that humanitarian intervention is compatible with Article 2 (4). It said, "… Belgium takes the view that this is an armed humanitarian intervention, compatible with Article 2, paragraph 4, of the Charter, which covers only intervention against the territorial integrity or political independence of a state." *See* Belgium's arguments on the legality of armed humanitarian intervention under the UN Charter in *Legality of Use of Force (Provisional Measures)*, CR 99/15 (10 May 1999).
[190] *Ibid.*, CR 99/23 (11 May 1999).

of law on the use of force is applicable exclusively between states. Hence, the right of self-defence is recognized as admissible for the protection of the entirety of a territorial, political and populated community, the state.[191] Indeed, the claim of the right to use force for the protection of the human rights of the citizens of another state has the difficult task of surmounting the provision of Article 2(4) of the Charter. On the other hand, as we are aware, under the dominant doctrine on the law of state responsibility developed by the UN International Law Commission, the obligation of states to respect and protect the basic rights of all human persons is the concern of all states; that is, they are owed *erga omnes*. According to the judgment of the Court in the *Barcelona Traction* case[192] this duty is owed to entire international communities with regard to certain human rights. Thus, in the event of material breaches of such obligations, every state is obliged to respond to violations, individually and collectively, by the use of non-forcible actions and resort to "countermeasures" against the perpetrator. What does "countermeasures" mean under international law? Does international law permit the use of armed force by foreign states, individually or collectively, to stop violations of international human rights – as some permanent members of the Security Council did in the Persian Gulf in 1996 and Kosovo in 1999? According to modern international law, since 1945, countermeasures must not involve the threat of or use of armed force. This fact was also confirmed in 1970 by the General Assembly's *Declaration on Friendly Relations*.[193] Clearly, response to those violations, whether individually or collectively, must be made by states in a non-forcible manner.

It seems that humanitarian intervention by military means is permissible only when mass violations of human rights occurring within a country constitute a threat to peace, as determined by the Security Council, so that the latter finally authorises an enforcement action in order to stop the violations. The ICJ in the *Legality of Use of Force* case in 1999 reaffirms that "when such a dispute gives rise to a threat to the peace, breach of the peace or act of aggression, the Security Council has special responsibility under Chapter VII of the Charter."[194] Therefore, humanitarian intervention involving the threat or use of military force and undertaken without the mandate or authorization of the Security Council will, as a matter of principle, remain in breach of the UN Charter. Nevertheless, this prohibition of the UN Charter does not mean that the sovereignty of the target state stands higher than human rights in the scale of values of contemporary international society. The law that prohibits unilateral humanitarian intervention has reflected the judgement of the community that the justification for humanitarian intervention is often ambiguous and accompanied by other motivations. In other words, the law against unilateral intervention

---

[191] *See* Kahn, "From the Nuremberg to The Hague: The United States' position in *Nicaragua v. United States* and the development of international law", 12 *YaleJIL* (1987), at 47.
[192] See ICJ Rep. 1970, paras. 33-34.
[193] *See* GA Res. 2625. *See* also *Declaration on the Inadmissibility of Intervention*, GA. Res.2131 (XX), UN Doc. A 6014 (21 December 1965).
[194] *See Legality of Use of Force Case* (1999), *supra* n. 5. *See* also ICJ website at *www.u-paris2.fr/cij/ icjwww/ipres...ss1999/ipresscom9923_iyall_19990602.htm.*

established in the UN Charter emphasises that no individual state can be entrusted with the authority to judge and determine wisely. The situation in the world today, particularly since the two catastrophes in Bosnia and Kosovo, and the fact that the international community has moved toward the creation of stronger international human rights law, has led some writers such as Charney[195] to suggest that the development of a new rule of law that permits intervention by regional organizations to stop such crimes without the Security Council's authorization would be appropriate. In my view there is a need neither to change the current rule nor to create allowing humanitarian intervention a new rule that could provide a pretext for abusive intervention under international law. The present ambiguous situation or acquiescence in a violation considered necessary and desirable in the particular circumstances are preferable to the adoption of a new rule which, by allowing unilateral intervention without Security Council authorization, would be wide open to abuse.

---

[195] *See* J.I. Charney, "Anticipatory humanitarian intervention in Kosovo", 93 *AJIL* (1999), at 834-845.

UNIVERSAL PERMISSIVE JURISDICTION FOR THE VIOLATION OF COMMON ARTICLE 3 OF THE GENEVA CONVENTIONS FOR THE PROTECTION OF THE VICTIMS OF WAR OF 12 AUGUST 1949[*]

Takhmina Karimova[**]

INTRODUCTION

It has been estimated that more than 250 conflicts of a non-international character, internal conflicts, and tyrannical regime victimization have occurred since World War II.[1] While the law applicable to international conflicts has been widely accepted and comprises the necessary enforcement mechanisms, the law of non-international armed conflicts remains limited to common Article 3 of the Geneva Conventions for the protection of the victims of war of 12 August 1949, and to the Additional Protocol II relating to the protection of victims of non-international armed conflicts of 8 June 1977. Provisions mentioned indeed represent a minimum set of standards and do not encompass the notion of "grave breaches" since it was viewed that the grave breaches provisions would constitute an encroachment on state sovereignty.[2]

However, the recent developments in international humanitarian law and international criminal law have changed the situation; new approaches are evolving in order to put an end to the long existent impunity[3] of the perpetrators of the most heinous crimes committed in internal conflicts. When, due to the failure of the domestic structure, to political unwillingness or to the weakness of a state[4] the perpetrators go unpunished, the concept of universal jurisdiction offers the means

---

[*] This article won the Sata International Law Prize for 2003.

[**] Intern at the International Criminal Court in The Hague; LL.M. Essex University, UK, 2003.

[1] C. Bassiouni, "Universal Jurisdiction for international crimes: historical perspectives and contemporary practice", 42 *Va.J.Int'l.L* 1., 2001 (Lexis-nexis).

[2] T. Graditzky, "Individual criminal responsibility for the violations of humanitarian law committed in non-international armed conflicts", *IRRC,* No. 322 (1998), 29-56 at 30.

[3] J. Dugard, "Bridging the gap between human rights and humanitarian law: punishment of offenders, *IRRC,* No. 324 (1998), 445-453 at 447.

[4] Bassiouni, n. 1.

Asian Yearbook of International Law, Volume 10 (B.S. Chimni *et al.,* eds.)

© 2005 Koninklijke Brill NV. Printed in The Netherlands, pp. 125-143.

of repression of serious violations of the law applicable in internal armed conflicts.[5] The major challenge in this sphere would be the determination of whether international law as it stands today gives states the authority to prosecute and try[6] those in charge of the internal atrocities or, in other words, whether the notion of universal jurisdiction extends to the violation of common Article 3 of the Geneva Conventions, and if it does, what form of jurisdiction it takes. The work will focus on jurisdiction over violations of common Article 3 as Protocol II, due to the fact that its higher threshold of applicability rarely comes into effect and, therefore, a universally recognized norm such as Article 3 remains a primary source of the law applicable in non-international armed conflicts.[7] The first section of the present work considers the concept of universal jurisdiction in the first instance, its scope, and the forms it may take. This is essential in order to give a general overview of what universal jurisdiction is meant to be and its forms, in particular universal permissive jurisdiction. The second section reflects on the content of Article 3 and its specific provisions: the core of the main question whether the violation of these provisions would give rise to universal permissive jurisdiction. Such an analysis will be made in the third section; specifically, it will explore the existing *opinio juris* and state practice that evidence criminalization of Article 3, i.e., whether it can be assumed that an international custom has been formed to provide a universal mechanism of enforcement of the Article. Lastly, the fourth section aims at briefly describing the implications of the Rome Statute of International Criminal Court on common Article 3, particularly the role of the Rome Statute with regard to criminalization in Article 3 of the Geneva Conventions.

1. UNIVERSAL JURISDICTION

1.1. General aspects of Jurisdiction

The term 'jurisdiction' can have different meanings, yet it is generally accepted that it embraces the "power to prescribe, adjudicate and enforce".[8] The power to prescribe refers to legislative jurisdiction, the environment for making the law applicable to actors, events, or things.[9] The authority of the state to subject certain actors or things to the processes of its judicial or administrative tribunals,[10] i.e., the application of the law, constitutes adjudicatory jurisdiction. Lastly, the power to take action to compel the actors to comply with laws and to redress non-compliance is called 'enforcement jurisdiction'. Bassiouni suggests that these powers derive from the

---

[5] Graditzky, n. 2, at 30.

[6] *Ibid.*

[7] A.G. Peterson, "Order out of the chaos: domestic enforcement of the law of armed conflict", 171 *Mil.L.Rev.* (2002), 1-91, at 17.

[8] Bassiouni, n. 1, f. 31.

[9] K.C. Randall, Universal jurisdiction under international law, 66 *Tex.L.Rev.*, 1988 (Lexis-nexis).

[10] *Ibid.*

principle of state sovereignty, where legislative jurisdiction is closely linked with the sovereignty of the state, while adjudicative and enforcement jurisdiction may not necessarily be connected with sovereignty as this jurisdiction can directly affect jurisdictional conflicts between the states; Bassiouni sees the best way to resolve any such conflict as being by means of extraterritorial jurisdiction in the case of valid legal nexus.[11] International law indeed provides several principles as legal bases for such an extraterritorial jurisdiction.

These include the principle of territoriality, under which the jurisdiction is claimed by the court where the offence is committed;[12] through the nationality or active personality principle, which gives jurisdiction to the state over the crimes committed by the person having the same nationality as that state;[13] through the passive personality principle, i.e., when the victim is a national of the state, the protective principle provides jurisdiction over the crimes affecting the security of state,[14] and lastly, through the universality principle. The principles listed, with the exception of the universality principle, are limited; that is, for jurisdiction to be claimed, there is a necessity to establish a link, either considering the act that has been committed – in which case principle of territoriality is exercised – or the offender, justified by the nationality principle, or with the victim, under the passive personality principle, or else a link with the interests of a state, as provided by the protective principle.

1.2.   Universal jurisdiction: concept and scope

The foremost of the significant features of the universality principle, unlike the other principles of jurisdiction, lies in the absence of any requirement of any kind of link between the act committed and the state exercising jurisdiction; in other words, "universal jurisdiction transcends national sovereignty".[15] Being an exception to the traditional forms of jurisdiction, it provides that "every state has jurisdiction over a limited category of offences generally recognized as of universal concern, regardless of the situs of offence and the nationality of the offender and the offended".[16] As a consequence, states have the authority to prosecute a crime without the presence of any connection between the place of the crime committed, the perpetrator's nationality, the victim's nationality, and the enforcing state.[17]

International conventional and customary law are primary sources of international criminal law. Conventional law is deemed to be more easily adaptable to the require-

---

[11] Bassiouni, n. 1, f. 36.

[12] M. Hudson, "Case of SS 'Lotus'", *World Court Reports*, Vol. II: 1927-1932, New York: Oceana Publishers, 1969, at 20.

[13] ICRC fact sheet on National Enforcement of International Humanitarian Law, http://www.icrc.org/ Web/eng/siteeng0.nsf/iwpList74/39587781F62FF7F4C1256B66005C8CF1 (accessed 27.02.2003)

[14] I. Brownlie, *Principles of Public International Law*, Oxford: Clarendon Press, 1998, at 307.

[15] Bassiouni, n. 1, f. 54.

[16] Randall, n. 9.

[17] *Ibid.*

ments of legality, the principles of *nullum crimen sine lege* and *nulla poena sine lege*; however, this aspect does not diminish the status of customary law as a substantial source.[18] Thus, the applicability of universal jurisdiction can be invoked with reference to 1) national legislation; 2) conventional law determining whether there are legal norms providing application of universal jurisdiction.[19] For example, the United Nations Convention on the Law of the Sea grants the states the right to seize any pirate ship or aircraft in any place outside their jurisdiction,[20] and 3) as has already been mentioned, customary law.

Among the 27 categories of crimes in international law evidenced by 276 conventions, only a few of them provide universal jurisdiction.[21] Universal jurisdiction cannot therefore be exercised in relation to any and all crimes, but only in respect of particular crimes; it is at present universally recognized that piracy, slavery, war crimes, crimes against humanity, genocide, apartheid and torture are based on customary and conventional international law and, as such, are "construed as reflecting universal jurisdiction".[22]

An assessment of different theories of universal jurisdiction by Bassiouni leads him to the conclusion that the standpoint of each theory is found in the assertion that there are certain commonly shared values in and interests of the international community that necessitate the expansion of enforcement mechanisms to counter serious breaches of these values; there also exists an assumption that the enforcement of these mechanisms will provide deterrence, world order, peace and justice.[23] Taking this further, Randall points out that every state has an interest in exercising jurisdiction over the crimes that have been universally condemned[24] and which violate norms of international concern. As a consequence, a state exercises *actio popularis* against persons who are *hostis humanis generis* and thus acts as a "surrogate for the international community".[25] Broomhall suggests that universal jurisdiction "fills the gap left where other more basic doctrines of jurisdiction provide no basis for the national proceedings".[26] Thus, this point is essential with regard to the suppression of breaches of common Article 3, as there is indeed no mechanism in force under the conventional law. Where there is a risk that the domestic enforcement system may be ineffective, the universality principle acts as a safety net in the prosecution of crimes of international concern.

---

[18] Bassiouni, n. 1.
[19] *Ibid.*
[20] UN Convention on the Law of the Sea of 1982, Art. 105.
[21] Bassiouni, n. 1.
[22] *Ibid.*
[23] *Ibid.*
[24] Randall, n. 9.
[25] Bassiouni, n. 1.
[26] B. Broomhall, "Towards the development of an effective system of universal jurisdiction for crimes under international law", 35-2 *N.Eng.L.Rev.* 400 http://www.nesl.edu/lawrev/Vol35/35-2/broomhall.pdf (accessed 02.03.2003).

1.3. Forms of universal jurisdiction

While this is not a subject of uniformity, there exist assertions among the scholars dealing with the forms of universal jurisdiction known as mandatory and permissive universal jurisdiction; these assertions are founded on the logic of the interpretation of the "must and may" possibilities of actions taken by states. Therefore, when universal jurisdiction is permissive, a state has the right and "may" exercise the authority to prosecute or try perpetrators. When the jurisdiction is mandatory, it is more than a mere right: rather, it is an obligation of the state to prosecute and try the offenders. The famed formula for the mandatory universal jurisdiction reads *aut dedere aut judicare,* i.e., either extradite or punish.

It is claimed that the distinction between the mandatory and permissive jurisdictions draws a parallel between customary law and conventional law.[27] Treaty law usually defines the crime and obliges the states parties to investigate and prosecute, or otherwise extradite the perpetrators to a state willing to do so. An appropriate example is the "grave breach" provisions of the Geneva Conventions of 1949. According to the relevant article of each of the conventions a state must search for the alleged offenders and consider either bringing them to its national courts or handing them over to another state party.[28] There is a speculation that when the language of the treaty is based on the *aut dedere aut judicare* formula, the jurisdiction is not truly "universal"; it is further maintained that in such cases the treaty more closely resembles a regime of "jurisdictional rights and obligations arising among a close set of states parties".[29]

In contrast with the mandatory form, the permissive universal jurisdiction mainly originates in customary international law; therefore, there is no ground to assert that states are required to exercise jurisdiction under customary international law.

An example of permissive jurisdiction can be found in the law of armed conflicts, where there is a clear requirement to repress grave breaches; Article 86 of Additional Protocol I states that "the high contracting parties *shall* repress grave breaches, and *take measures necessary* to suppress all other breaches of the Conventions or the Protocol which result from a failure to act when in duty to do so"[30] (emphasis added). Here, a duty can be revealed in the wording of "shall", and a right that is permission under the wording of "take measures necessary". There is, therefore, no obligation as such. Hence, with respect to war crimes that do not constitute grave breaches, the states "may" exercise universal jurisdiction in order to repress the violations.

Having discussed some relevant issues on universal jurisdiction, it is now necessary to come closer to the main subject of this work and to illustrate the rationale for examining the universal permissive jurisdiction applicable to the violation of

---

[27] *Ibid.*, 401.
[28] Geneva Convention Relative to the Treatment of Prisoners of War of 12 August 1949, Art. 129.
[29] Broomhall, n. 26, at 401.
[30] Protocol Additional to the Geneva Conventions of 12 August 1949 relating to the Protection of the Victims of International Armed Conflicts, Art. 86.

common Article 3. Since neither common Article 3 nor Protocol II contain provisions requiring states to punish serious violations of the law of internal conflicts, there appears to be no ground to invoke universal jurisdiction under international conventional law.[31] However, due to the recent changes in international law (which will be analysed later in greater detail), there are bases for ascertaining that serious violations of Article 3 are punishable: if a crime is condemned and found as criminal in international conflicts, there is no reason why it should not be condemned in the context of internal conflicts.[32] These grounds are viewed as being based on customary international law. Before resorting to polemics on customary law, first of all it is for reasons of comprehensibility necessary to illustrate the context of Article 3 itself.

2.   COMMON ARTICLE 3 OF THE GENEVA CONVENTIONS OF 1949

Article 3 appears in the text of each of the Geneva Conventions of 1949 and contains provisions that are applied in the armed conflicts of non-international character. The article "sets forth the minimum protections and standards of conduct to which the state and its armed opponents must adhere".[33]

Under the provisions of Article 3 each party to the conflict shall be bound to apply, as a minimum, the following provisions:

1) Persons taking no active part in the hostilities, including members of armed forces who have laid down their arms and those placed *hors de combat* by sickness, wounds, detention, or any other cause, shall in all circumstances be treated humanely, without any adverse distinction founded on race, colour, religion, faith, sex, birth or wealth or any other similar criteria.

   To this end the following acts are and shall remain prohibited:
   a) violence to life and person, in particular murder of all kinds, mutilation, cruel treatment and torture;
   b) taking of hostages;
   c) outrages upon personal dignity, in particular humiliating and degrading treatment;
   d) passing of sentences and carrying out executions without previous judgement pronounced by a regularly constituted court, affording all judicial guarantees which are recognized indispensable by civilized people.[34]

---

[31] M. Griffin, "Ending the impunity of perpetrators of human rights atrocities: a major challenge for international law in the 21st century", *IRRC*, No. 838, 369-389, at 372.
[32] C. Enache-Brown and A. Fried, "Universal crime, jurisdiction and duty: the obligation of *aut dedere aut judicare* in international law", 43 *McGillL.J.*(1998), 613 (Lexis-nexis).
[33] S. Ratner, "International v. internal armed conflict", http://www.crimesofwar.org/thebook/intl-vs-internal.html (accessed 13.03.2003).
[34] Geneva Convention III, n. 28, Art. 3.

Common Article 3 sets out the fundamental principles of humanity that apply in internal armed conflict and is binding on each party to the conflict, including the insurgent forces.[35] However, the binding nature of the provisions does not presume a recognition of the status of the insurgents.

Article 3 was, rather, meant only to establish fundamental humanitarian standards, not to define status.[36] The International Court of Justice in the *Nicaragua* case has determined that Article 3 contains the rules that "constitute a minimum yardstick" applicable even in international conflicts.[37] Notwithstanding the minimum requirements and the lack of status recognition, the parties very often do not apply these standards.

When discussing a norm within the framework of international law, the issue of customary rules becomes relevant; it is accepted that Article 3 has reached the status of customary international law.[38] The International Criminal Tribunal for the former Yugoslavia (hereinafter the ICTY) held that the law governing internal conflicts developed on two levels: in customary and in conventional law, and some treaty rules have become customary, which was for the most part true in relation to common Article 3. Furthermore, the tribunal confirmed its position by referring to the authoritative decision held by the ICJ in *Nicaragua v. United States of America* (a case concerning the military and paramilitary activities of the US in and against the interests of Nicaragua).[39]

In considering the provisions regulating conflicts of internal character, one point should be mentioned: that the conflict in question is presumably limited to the area within the frontiers of a particular state, which has sovereign authority over its territory. Consequently, offences committed within the boundary of a particular state fall under the national jurisdiction of that state. Most of the violations of the rules of war also "violate rules of general criminal law namely those relating to homicide, bodily assault, or other offences against physical or sexual integrity, offences against property".[40]

Accordingly, it would not be incorrect to assume that violations of the law applicable to internal conflicts, specifically of Article 3, may be considered a crime under the general criminal law provisions of the state concerned.[41] Thus, domestic mechanisms conduct the suppression of breaches of Article 3. However, experience shows that most of the violations – on the part of the government, for instance –

---

[35] J. Pictet, *The Geneva Conventions of 12 August 1949: Commentary*, Vol. I, ICRC, 1952, at 38-61.

[36] Peterson, n. 7, at 18.

[37] *Nicaragua v USA Military*, ICJ Rep. 1986, 14, at 114, para. 218. http://www.icjcij.org/icjwww/icases/inus_ijudgment/inus_ijudgment_19860627.pdf (accessed 06.03.2003).

[38] *Prosecutor v. Tadic*, case IT-94-1-AR72, Appeal on Jurisdiction (2 October 1995), para. 98; *Prosecutor v. Delalic et al.*, case IT-96-21, judgment (16 November 1998) http://www.un.org/icty/celebici/trialc2/judgement/index.htm ; *Prosecutor v. Akayesu*, case ICTR-96-4 (2 September 1998), para. 608 http://www.ictr.org/wwwroot/default.htm (accessed 07.03.2003).

[39] *Prosecutor v. Tadic,* n. 38, para. 98.

[40] M. BOTHE, "War crimes in non-international armed conflicts" in Y. Dinstein and M. Tabory (eds.), *War Crimes in International Law*, Martinus Nijhoff Publishers, 1996, 293-305, at 295.

[41] *Ibid.*

will be justified by the excuse of the maintenance of the rule of law and order required by the legal system of that state.[42] It is therefore argued that "there is no moral justification ... for treating the perpetrators of atrocities in internal conflicts more leniently than those engaged in international wars";[43] universal permissive jurisdiction can act as a substitute for an enforcement mechanism.

From the text of Article 3 it is obvious that most of its provisions overlap with those of international human rights law provisions, and that violation of the prohibitions can amount to crimes against humanity or genocide; as a result, apparently, crimes committed in the context of internal conflicts will not go unpunished. Nonetheless, due to difficulties in definition and other requirements, such as proof of the systematic or deliberate nature of the crime,[44] some of the killings or other serious violations can fall outside the scope of the crimes mentioned. For example, according to Article 7 of the Rome Statute for International Criminal Court, an act can constitute a crime against humanity if it is proved that the act committed was a part of *widespread or systematic* (emphasis added) attack against any civilian population with the knowledge of the attack,[45] while in order to establish a violation of Article 3 there is no need to ascertain the systematic or widespread character of the crime.

Thus, the next issue to be addressed is the determination in what circumstances universal jurisdiction is applicable since there is a risk that a domestic legal system, out of policy or other considerations, fails to respond accurately to the violation of common Article 3 – the minimum humanitarian standards applicable in internal conflicts. In relation to universal permissive jurisdiction, it must be noted that we should hypothetically assume, pending a thorough discussion, that for such jurisdiction to be exercised in the absence of relevant treaty provision we must determine the existence of customary international law criminalizing breaches of Article 3.

3. CRIMINALIZATION OF COMMON ARTICLE 3 UNDER CUSTOMARY INTERNATIONAL LAW AND UNIVERSAL JURISDICTION

The process of a rule acquiring the status of customary law is uneven.[46] Nonetheless, "international humanitarian law has developed faster since the beginning of atrocities in the former Yugoslavia than in half-century since the Nuremberg tribunals and the adoption of Geneva Conventions for the protections of victims of war of

---

[42] *Ibid.*

[43] *Ibid.* 238.

[44] T. Meron, "International criminalization of internal atrocities", in T. Meron (ed.), *War Crimes Law Comes of Age*, Oxford: Clarendon Press, 1998, 228-262, at 234.

[45] Rome Statute of ICC (A/CONF.183/9), entered into force 1 July 2002 http://www.icc.org (accessed 13.03.2003) Art. 7.

[46] Peterson, n. 7, at 26.

12 August of 1949".[47] In this respect the practice of the International Criminal Tribunal for the former Yugoslavia is a particularly valuable source of assessment of Article 3 and its criminalization (i.e., the prosecution of breaches of Article 3 under international law).

It is a tenet of international law that in order for a rule to become a customary norm two elements are essential: state practice and *opinio juris*;[48] the latter is believed to be a conviction held by states that a certain form of conduct is required under international law.[49] The Tribunal in Appeal on Jurisdiction (*Tadic* case) has pointed out that in relation to the establishment of the general practice in such an area as the law of internal armed conflict, it is difficult to "pinpoint the actual behaviour of the troops in the field for the purpose of establishing whether they in fact comply with, or disregard, certain standards of behaviour";[50] the court has reasoned its position by lack of access to the theatre of military operations, a lack of information, etc. and thus "on account of the inherent nature of this subject-matter, reliance must primarily be placed on such elements as official pronouncements of States, military manuals and judicial decisions",[51] i.e., *opinio juris*. The position of the tribunal on this question has been contested; the counterargument was that the training, education, and disciplining of a state's soldiers are also a reliable evidence of state practice.[52] Another interesting position concerning the court's approach was brought forward by Theodor Meron. He observes in particular that the tribunal used statements as an evidence of both practice and *opinio juris*, and expresses the view that the tribunal relied mainly on human rights methodology, whereas *opinio juris* is deemed to compensate for insufficiency of practice.[53]

3.1. *Opinio juris*

The International Committee of the Red Cross (hereinafter the ICRC) in its comment on the draft statute for the Yugoslavia tribunal admitted that "in accordance with the International Humanitarian Law as it stands today, the idea of war crimes is limited to the situations of international armed conflict";[54] furthermore, in the course of establishing the ICTY it was perceived that Article 3 and Protocol II "were not the rules of international humanitarian law which are beyond doubt part of

---

[47] T. Meron, "War crimes law for the twenty-first century: the law of armed conflict into the next millennium", in Schmitt and Green, *US Naval War College International Studies*, Vol. 71 (Rhode Island: Newport, 1998), 325-335, at 326.

[48] P. Malanczuk, *Akehurst's Modern Introduction to International Law* , London: Routledge, 2001, at 44.

[49] *Ibid.*

[50] *Prosecutor v. Tadic*, n 38, para. 99.

[51] *Ibid*

[52] Peterson, n. 7, at 46.

[53] T. Meron, "The continuing role of custom in the formation of international humanitarian law", T. Meron (ed.), *War Crimes Law Comes of Age*, Oxford: Clarendon Press, 1998, 262-278, at 264.

[54] Mcron, n. 44, at 236.

customary international law".[55] Yet long before, the International Court of Justice had not only established the customary status of common Article 3 in the *Nicaragua* case, but held that Article 3 should be considered in light of Article 1 of the Geneva Conventions given that states are obliged to "respect" and "ensure respect" of the conventions.[56] In view of the latter the obligation to respect implies penal measures to suppress war crimes.[57]

In contrast to the opinion of the International Court of Justice, the political will of the international community as expressed by some representatives of leading countries was in favour of the criminalizing norms applicable in internal conflicts. In particular, the US permanent representative to the United Nations stated that the US understanding of the "laws and customs of war" in Article 3 of the ICTY Statute are such that they "include all obligations under humanitarian law agreements in force in the territory of the former Yugoslavia at the time the acts were committed, including common Article 3 of 1949 Geneva Conventions".[58] Statements to a similar effect were made by the representatives of a number of other states.[59] It is therefore concluded that these statements entail the existence of universal jurisdiction.[60]

In looking for the sources of *opinio juris*, the Security Council resolutions addressing internal conflicts should not be ignored. For instance, Security Council - resolution 794 concerning Somalia "strongly condemns all violations of international humanitarian law ... and affirms that those who commit or order the commission of such acts will be individually held responsible".[61] The Security Council resolutions in relation to the conflicts in Rwanda also contain similar provisions and stress the need to take effective measures to bring to justice those in charge of the commission of the crimes.[62] Hence, the resolutions adopted by the Security Council constitute evidence that the Security Council regards as an established principle of international law the criminal responsibility of the individuals who have committed or ordered to be committed those violations of international humanitarian law in the context of internal conflicts.[63]

The developments in the field of the law applicable in internal armed conflicts occurred mainly owing to the establishment and further proceedings of International

---

[55] Secretary General's Report to the Security Council on the establishment of the ICTY, UN Doc. S/25704, 3 May 1993, para. 34, cited in *Prosecutor v. Akayesu*, para. 608. 2 September 1998. http://www.ictr.org/wwwroot/default.htm (accessed 06.03.2003).

[56] *Nicaragua v USA*, n 38, at 114, para. 220.

[57] Meron, n. 44, at 251.

[58] UN Doc. S/PV.3217 (25 May,1993), at 15, cited in John R.W.D. Jones, *The Practice of International Criminal Tribunals for the Former Yugoslavia and Rwanda*, Irvington-on-Hudson, NY: Transnational Publishers, Inc., at 35.

[59] *Ibid.*

[60] Graditzky, n. 2, at 35.

[61] UN Doc. S/RES/794 (1992), 47 U.N. *SCOR*, at 63, http://www1.umn.edu/humanrts/peace/docs/scres794.html (06.03.2003).

[62] UN Doc. S/RES/978 (1995) http://ods-dds-ny.un.org/doc/UNDOC/GEN/N95/054/92/PDF (16.03.2003).

[63] Graditzky, n. 2, at 49.

Tribunals of the former Yugoslavia and Rwanda when developments in the sphere of the law applicable in internal conflicts were reflected in the decisions of the tribunals. An illustration of some points of its jurisprudence is essential.

The Statute of the ICTY was drafted to deal with the conflict in the territory of the former Yugoslavia as being international in nature, as the offences listed in Articles 2 and 3 of the Statute indicate;[64] nevertheless, it is believed that nothing in the Statute denies the possibility of criminalization of the serious violations of the law of non-international conflicts.[65] It was mainly the mixed character of the conflict that forced the drafters to draw up the Statute with discretion. The explanation for this cautious approach is that "the Security Council intended that to the extent possible, the subject matter jurisdiction of the International tribunal should extend to both internal and international armed conflicts".[66] The progressive step taken by the tribunal was an extension of the applicability of article 3 of its Statute. The Appeal Chamber by a majority held that "violations of the laws and customs of war" covered also violations of common Article 3 of the Geneva Conventions of 1949 and other customary rules of internal conflicts.[67] However, these violations must meet the specific conditions set, in order for Article 3 of the International Criminal Tribunal for former Yugoslavia Statute to be applied:

1) The violation must constitute an infringement of a rule of international humanitarian law;
2) The rule must be customary in nature, or if it belongs to treaty law, the required conditions must be met ...;
3) The violation must be "serious", that is to say, it must constitute a breach of a rule protecting important values, and the breach must involve grave consequences for the victim. Thus, for instance, the fact of a combatant simply appropriating a loaf of bread in an occupied village would not amount to a "serious violation of international humanitarian law";
4) The violation of the rule must entail, under customary or conventional law, the individual criminal responsibility of the person breaching the rule.[68]

In the case of the tribunal for Rwanda and in view of the nature of the conflict which was classified as being of a non-international character, the Security Council elected to take a more "expansive approach to the choice of the applicable law than the one underlying the Statute of the Yugoslav Tribunal, and included within the subject-matter jurisdiction of the Rwanda Tribunal international instruments regardless of whether they were considered part of customary international law or whether they have customarily entailed the individual criminal responsibility of the perpetrators

---

[64] Meron, n. 44, at 231.
[65] Graditzky, n. 2, at 49.
[66] *Prosecutor v. Tadic*, n. 38, para.78.
[67] *Ibid.* para. 89.
[68] *Ibid.*, para. 94.

of the crime. Article 4 of the Statute ... [thus it] for the first time criminalizes [violations of] common Article 3 of the four Geneva Conventions."[69]

The International Law Commission, a body set up by the General Assembly for the development of international law, plays an important role in forming legal doctrines in international law, and one of the areas of the work of the International Law Commission has been the Draft code on crimes against the peace and security of mankind. Article 20 of the Draft code deals with war crimes; in particular, paragraph (f) lists as war crimes certain violations of the international humanitarian law applicable in the conflicts of a non-international character.[70] The enumerated violations are analogous to the context of common Article 3. Furthermore, in the commentary of its Report on the work of its Forty-Eighth session, the International Law Commission considers paragraph (f) significant in the light of the frequency of non-international conflicts, and states that the International Criminal Tribunal for the former Yugoslavia had "reaffirmed" the principle of individual criminal responsibility.[71] The word "reaffirmed" may imply that it had been already an existing principle prior to the decision and also may imply that the principle is generally recognized.

The Security Council Resolutions, *ad hoc* tribunals and the International Law Commission stress the establishment of principle of individual criminal responsibility, a significant factor with regard to universal jurisdiction. Present international law prescribes individual criminal responsibility for the serious crimes that are of universal concern. The Draft Code of Crimes against the Peace and Security of Mankind and the Rome Statute of International Criminal Court are worthy of note, listing the crimes widely accepted as being those entailing individual criminal responsibility. Article 2 of the Draft Code provides individual criminal responsibility for aggression, genocide, crimes against humanity, war crimes and crimes against the United Nations and associated personnel,[72] while Article 1 of the Rome Statute of International Criminal Court emphasizes the purpose of the establishment of the court to exercise jurisdiction over the persons committing the most serious crimes: namely, genocide, crimes against humanity, war crimes and crimes of aggression, with Article 25 laying down individual responsibility for their commission.[73] Offences listed as international crimes in these authoritative sources encompass the notion of universal jurisdiction; thus, universal jurisdiction and individual criminal responsibility are interrelated elements of the most serious international crimes. It can consequently be assumed that giving rise to individual criminal responsibility in the context of non-international conflicts necessitates recognition of universal jurisdiction and that, accordingly, violations of Article 3 seem to be regarded as war crimes.

---

[69] *Prosecutor v. Akayesu*, n. 38, para. 604.
[70] ILC Draft Code of Crimes against Peace and Security of Mankind 1996, art. 20 http://www.un.org/law/ilc/texts/dcodefra.htm (18.03.2003).
[71] *Report of the International Law Commission on the Work of its Forty-Eighth Session*, 6 May to 26 July 1996 (A/51/10), http://www.un.org/law/ilc/reports.htm, (accessed 7.03.2003), at 119.
[72] ILC Draft Code, n. 70, Art. 2.
[73] Rome Statute, n. 45.

3.2.   Establishment of state practice

In the field of customary international law the view of what states regard as a rule is not enough to deem it such. Article 38, paragraph (b), of the Statute of the International Court of Justice provides that *opinio juris* must be confirmed by general state practice.[74] As mentioned earlier with reference to the *Tadic* case, the behaviour of the parties in the theatre of military operations is not the only evidence; evidence of state practice can also be found in military manuals and national legislation. Even government statements to the press and international conferences can constitute state practice.[75]

3.2.1. *Military manuals*

The value of the military manuals derives from the fact that these regulate the conduct of the armed forces, who are the primary participants in all kinds of armed conflict. The Appeal Chamber in the *Tadic* case drew attention to the Military Manual of Germany of 1992, which has included, under the rubric of "grave breaches of the international humanitarian law", "criminal offences" against persons protected by common Article 3, such as "willful killing, mutilation, torture or inhumane treatment including biological experiments, willfully causing great suffering, serious injury to body or health, taking of hostages", as well as "the fact of impeding a fair and regular trial".[76] In addition to this the Appeal Chamber submits examples of the military manuals of New Zealand in which the violation of common Article 3 is treated as a war crime. The manuals of the United States of America and of Great Britain were placed under scrutiny, as their interpretation of war crimes includes the infringement of common Article 3.[77] Most military manuals do not draw a distinction regarding the nature of the conflict to which the international humanitarian law is applied, but some recognize the applicability of international humanitarian law to all situations involving armed conflict.[78]

3.2.2. *Domestic legislation*

A recent study carried out by Amnesty International on universal jurisdiction identifies different categories of national legislations, namely, legislations providing universal jurisdiction over the general definition of "war crime" which can be interpreted as also implying crimes committed in internal conflicts; another category comprises

---

[74] Bassiouni, n. 1.
[75] Malanczuk, n. 48, at 44.
[76] *Prosecutor v. Tadic*, n 38, para. 131.
[77] *Ibid.*
[78] T. Meron, "Humanization of humanitarian law", 94 *AJIL* (2000), 239-279, at 261.

the legislations expressly giving courts the authority to exercise universal jurisdiction over crimes committed in non-international conflicts.[79]

Among the most prominent national legislations criminalizing and providing universal jurisdiction is the Belgian Law of 16 June 1993 regarding the grave breaches of the Geneva Conventions. This law qualifies as "war crimes" violations of specific norms applicable in internal conflicts: Article 2, section 3, lists the offences against protected persons under the Geneva Conventions and Additional Protocols I and II.[80] Article 7 of the law provides universal jurisdiction; specifically, it states that the Belgian courts do not need to establish their territorial or national link with the perpetrator.[81] Yet a point is raised that reveals doubts concerning the threshold of internal conflicts.[82] It is well known that Protocol II puts a higher threshold of applicability than does Article 3. As a consequence, from the context of the Belgian law it is not clear whether there can be grave breaches of Article 3.

The Spanish Penal Code follows the same path as the Belgian legislation by including innovative provisions for criminalizing certain acts committed in armed conflicts of a non-international character. Thus, Article 608 includes in the category of "protected persons" those who are covered by the provisions of Additional Protocol II of 1977. Norms governing violations of the law of internal armed conflicts are grouped under the provisions regulating conflicts generally, which are in their turn classified under the heading of "crimes against [the] international community".[83]

The United States War Crimes Act of 1996 is applicable in situations when the crime is committed by or the victim of the crime is a member of the armed forces or a national of the United States. In comparison with the two previous examples, the context of "war crimes" in this law covers violations of common Article 3.[84] The inclusion of common Article 3 in war crimes is evaluated as a demonstration "that the United States of America considers criminal accountability for violation of this article as customary international law".[85] It is further argued that the Act does not simply represent an implementing legislature, but reflects the state practice of the United States of America. Despite the fact that the law mentioned makes no reference to the exercise of universal jurisdiction for the violation of common Article 3, what matters in this context is the establishment of the state practice in relation

---

[79] Legal Memorandum on Universal Jurisdiction, AI 53/005/2001 Chapter 3 http://web.amnesty.org/web/web.nsf/pages/legal_memorandum (accessed 12.03.2003).

[80] Loi du Juin 16, 1993 relative à la répression des violations graves du droit international humanitaire, (avec les amendements de 10 février 1999) http://www.worldpolicy.org/globalrights/treaties/Belgique-loi.html (accessed 08.03.2003).

[81] *Ibid.*

[82] Graditzky, n. 2, at 39.

[83] Spanish Criminal Code of 23 November 1995, Articles 608-614, http://www.universaljurisdiction.info/index/Laws/Law_Summaries/80179,79779 (accessed 12.03.2003).

[84] J. Aldykiewsz, "Authority to court-martial non-U.S. military personnel for serious violations of international humanitarian law committed during internal armed conflicts", 167 *Mil.L.Rev.* (Lexisnexis), f. 150.

[85] *Ibid.*

to criminalization of Article 3, i.e., the prosecution of the perpetrators for the violation of the provision of this article.

The Swiss Military Penal Code of 13 June 1927, with the recent amendments, also provides for universal jurisdiction for violations of the law applicable in internal conflicts. Article 2 (9) of the Code provides that the civilians who have committed crimes against the law of nations in the course of armed conflict can be prosecuted under the military penal code.[86]

The Netherlands Wartime Criminal Act provides jurisdiction over violations of the laws and customs of war including Geneva Conventions and Protocol I. Article 8 of this law criminalizes all violations of the laws and customs of war. It is established that the reach of the article is limited neither to grave breaches of the Geneva Conventions nor to armed conflicts of an international character.[87] Article 1, paragraph 3, of the Wartime Act indicates that the term "war" includes civil wars.[88]

Other examples include the Nicaraguan Penal Code, which provides universal jurisdiction over violations of international humanitarian law regardless of the character of the conflict, and the Irish Geneva Convention Act, criminalizing violations of the Geneva Conventions including Article 3.[89] Many other states pursue the line of the criminalization of international humanitarian law. Their respective legislatures address violations of the law applicable to conflicts of both an international and a non-international character, but a weakness may be seen in the failure of these examples of legislation to provide pure universal jurisdiction; conditions are attached in order to make them applicable extra-territorially. This is true, for example, with regard to the Portuguese Penal Code, which extends jurisdiction beyond its territory and [beyond its treatment of] non-nationals only, for instance, in the event of an international treaty provision imposing such a jurisdiction.[90] It should be noted here that the nature of the jurisdiction authorized by national legislations is permissive as there is no requirement deriving from any binding treaty. Rather, it is a conviction of the states that the fact that Article 3 lacks an enforcement mechanism should be understood to be tantamount to a crime giving rise to universal permissive jurisdiction.

3.3.3. Judicial decisions

Some points of interest were raised in the course of the torts claim brought in the case of *Kadic v. Karadzic* by Bosnian victims under the US Alien Tort Act against Radovan Karadzic. The complainants alleged that they are victims of acts of rape,

---

[86] Swiss Military Penal Code of 13 June 1927, Art.2, http://www.admin.ch/ch/f/rs/321_0/index.htmlh (accessed 12.03.2003).

[87] J. Kleffner "Jurisdiction over genocide, crimes against humanity, war crimes, torture and terrorism in the Netherlands", to be published in A. Cassese and M. Delmas-Marty (eds.), *Crimes internacionaux et jurisdiction nationals: Étude comparée*, Presses Universitaire de France, 2002, 8 http://www1.jur.uva.nl/acil/jann_kleffner1.PDF (accessed 12.03.2003).

[88] *Ibid.*, 10

[89] Graditzky, n. 2, at 43.

[90] *Ibid.*

forced prostitution, torture, summary executions, etc. The US Courts of Appeal for the Second Circuit determined that the alleged violations constitute violations of the law of nations. When considering the alleged crimes within the scope of war crimes, the court examined the context of common Article 3 confirming the existence of individual criminal responsibility, referring to the judgement of the post-WWII Military Tribunals.[91] To quote the latter, "the court seemed convinced that the notion of war crimes together with universal jurisdiction also covered certain violations of the law applicable in non-international conflicts".[92]

On 30 April 1997, the Swiss Military Tribunal found the former Rwandan mayor of Mushubati guilty of committing war crimes as well as of a violation of common Article 3 of the Geneva Conventions, on the basis of the Swiss Military Penal Code. It is determined that this decision was the first conviction in Switzerland to provide universal jurisdiction for war crimes in the context of non-international conflict.[93]

The case of *Knezevic* is an interesting precedent of application of the norms of the Netherlands legislation that was mentioned earlier. The magistrate of Arnhem had to establish a preliminary judicial enquiry requested by the public prosecutor in respect of war crimes committed in the territory of the former Yugoslavia in 1992.[94] In this respect Knezevic was suspected of implication in the commission of a number of war crimes. The public prosecutor qualified the conflict as a non-international conflict and described the alleged offences as violations of common Article 3 of the Geneva Conventions of 1949. The magistrate held that the Netherlands had no jurisdiction and, soon after, an appeal was brought to the District Court (Military Division). The District Court found that the Dutch courts did indeed have the authority to try the case and that the alleged offences if proved would constitute violations of common Article 3. The court justified the existence of jurisdiction on the basis of Article 1 of the Wartime Criminal Act, section 1 of which provides for the prosecution of the crimes committed in armed conflicts, including civil wars, and section 3 providing for the universal jurisdiction.[95]

The *Knezevic* case is noteworthy since the District Court went through a very detailed examination of the Wartime Act provisions relating to the jurisdiction. In the second appeal, the Supreme Court returned to the issue of jurisdiction and came to the conclusion that section 3 of the Wartime Act expressly gives jurisdiction over war crimes irrespective of where and by whom they have been committed.[96]

The evaluation of whether each and every element of the rule is in compliance with the general requirements of customary law is complex. Thus, the task of conducting the work within the borders of the issues at stake forces one to omit a detailed examination of all the aspects of the customary nature of the rule, such as consistency, repetition, etc. The Appeals Chamber stated that reliance must be put upon *opinio*

---

[91] *Kadic v. Karadzic*, 70 F. 3ᵈ 232 (2ⁿᵈ Cir. 1995), Federal Reporter, at 243.
[92] Graditzky, n. 2, at 44.
[93] Legal Memorandum, n. 79.
[94] J. Kleffner, n. 87, at 9.
[95] *Ibid.*, 11.
[96] *Ibid.*, 13.

juris due to an insufficiency of state practice, yet military manuals, state legislature and judicial decisions are indicative of existing state practice. Even though military manuals address only the conduct of armed forces, existing domestic legislations not only criminalize breaches of Article 3, but provide jurisdiction on the basis of the universality principle; furthermore, the judicial decisions provide evidence that the system in fact operates, hence: "All of these factors (i.e., *opinio juris* and state practice) confirm that international law imposes criminal liability for serious violations of common Article 3, as supplemented by other general principles and rules on the protection of victims of internal armed conflict".[97]

By enforcing relevant laws, states acknowledge that crimes committed in the context of internal conflicts are subject to universal reach whatever their nature, and that the form of the jurisdiction exercised is permissive, as there is no provision under conventional international law requiring states to prosecute perpetrators of internal conflicts regardless of any jurisdictional links, i.e., states would not be in breach of their obligations under international law.

4. THE ROLE OF THE ROME STATUTE OF INTERNATIONAL CRIMINAL COURT IN THE CRIMINALIZATION OF COMMON ARTICLE 3

The establishment of the International Criminal Court is not a result of the efforts of recent years: in fact, the process dates back to the era of the League of Nations, succeeded by the United Nations. The International Law Commission was the body put in charge of formulating the draft statute for the ICC.[98] The political atmosphere in the Cold War period impeded effective work on the draft statute; the work was resumed in 1989. The years following the end of the Cold War were promising in terms of consensus and mutual understanding reigned between the former opponents. However, the emergence of new conflicts forced the world community to respond to large-scale human rights violations in the former Yugoslavia and in Rwanda through the creation of *ad hoc* tribunals.

Their establishment had a constructive impact. They "provided a final spur to the emergence of the ICC, an organ of global reach and thus potentially able to respond to violations occurring everywhere",[99] neither temporally nor geographically limited. In 1994, subsequent to the submission of the Draft Statute of International Criminal Court to its Forty-Ninth session, the General Assembly set up a Preparatory Committee on the Establishment of the ICC which worked until the Diplomatic Conference at Rome of 15 June-17 July 1996 that in turn led to the adoption of the Rome Statute for the International Criminal Court.[100]

---

[97] *Prosecutor v. Tadic*, n. 38, para. 134.

[98] A. Cassese, P. Gaeta and J.R.W.D. Jones, *The Rome Statute of the International Criminal Court: Commentary*, Oxford University Press, 2002, at 6.

[99] *Ibid.*, 16.

[100] *Ibid.*

The first permanent international court has jurisdiction over genocide, crimes against humanity, war crimes and crimes of aggression.[101] Even though the reach of the ICC is universal, its jurisdiction is not so, with the exception of those referrals of the Security Council that are based on the theory of universality.[102] This fact by no means undermines the right or in some cases the duty of states to exercise their universal jurisdiction over international crimes. In affirmation of the latter, the preamble of the Rome Statute recalls "the duty of every state to exercise its criminal jurisdiction over those responsible for international crimes" and emphasizes that the International Criminal Court is complementary to national criminal jurisdiction.[103] The Rome Statute is the first international treaty criminalizing serious violations of common Article 3, including this in the category of war crimes and thus prescribing individual criminal responsibility. The question of prior criminalization of Article 3 in the International Criminal Tribunal for the Rwanda Statute cannot be raised since the latter was established by a Security Council resolution under Chapter VII of the United Nations Charter.

Article 8, section 2 (c), of the Rome Statute of International Criminal Court includes in "war crimes" provisions serious violations of common Article 3 and other serious violations of the laws and customs of war applicable in non-international armed conflicts. The context of the provisions concerning Article 3 is analogous to the prohibitions listed in Article 3 itself.

It is argued that prior to the adoption of International Criminal Court Statute, only few countries would exercise universal jurisdiction over crimes committed in internal conflicts, as there were no treaty provisions authorizing such exercise.[104] Further, it is suggested that the states should avail themselves of the opportunity to review their respective legislations and ensure that their courts are able to exercise universal jurisdiction over the crimes listed in the ICC Statute.[105] Meron showed his recognition of this idea when he stated that the International Criminal Court "may thus become a model for national laws to be enforced under the principle of universality".[106]

Thus, the basic implication of the Rome Statute of International Criminal Court in relation to the serious violations of common Article 3 is in fact that the adoption of the Rome Statute is an "authoritative and largely customary statement of international humanitarian and criminal law".[107] Indeed, the reflection of Article 3 in the Rome Statute represents the finalization of the criminalization of the law applicable in internal conflicts under international customary law; in particular, the inclusion of the violation of common Article 3 into the category of war crimes in article 8

---

[101]   Rome Statute, n. 45, article 5.
[102]   Bassiokuni, n. 1.
[103]   Rome Statute, n. 45.
[104]   Y. Iwasawa, "Final report on the exercise of universal jurisdiction in respect of gross human rights offences", *ILA report of 69ᵗʰ session in London* (2000), at 12.
[105]   *Ibid.*
[106]   Meron, Epilogue, n. 44, at 305.
[107]   *Ibid.*

of the Statute evidences this statement. The International Criminal Court does not give rise to universal jurisdiction, and according to Article 1 of the Rome Statute it is complementary to national courts. However, once again it should be stressed that its significance is concluded in its representation of an "authoritative and customary statement of the international humanitarian law". As a consequence such a statement determines that the violation of common Article 3 is a crime under international customary law and that this in turn gives rise to universal permissive jurisdiction.

5.   CONCLUSION

Thus, it is no longer incongruous that the international community regards serious breaches of common Article 3 as acts leading to individual criminal responsibility, and as crimes of universal concern and subject to universal condemnation. The consideration of *opinio juris* and more significantly, state practice, evidence the emergence of a customary rule criminalizing violations of Article 3. The latter is supported by the adoption of the ICC Statute. Despite the fact that the jurisdiction of the International Criminal Court is not universal, it reflects the current position of states on the subject matter and constitutes a significant development in determining breaches of Article 3 as war crimes.

As a consequence, in the absence of a legally binding treaty provision, customary international law becomes the basis for the application of universal permissive jurisdiction over serious violations of Article 3. State sovereignty cannot constitute a barrier to the non-addressing of serious violations of the minimum humanitarian standards set in Article 3. Crimes remain crimes regardless of the context of the conflict. Recent developments in this sphere have prompted the assertion that serious breaches of common Article 3 lead to universal jurisdiction; at present, though, the jurisdiction is only permissive, until a relevant treaty provision requiring mandatory universal jurisdiction is adopted.

SHORT ARTICLES AND NOTES

NEPAL'S ROAD TO THE WORLD TRADE ORGANIZATION: A PRAGMATIC OVERVIEW

Rudra P. Sharma[*]

It is Nepal where an executive order of a selected (not elected) government superseded the mandatory constitutional provisions. A pragmatic consensus is said to have been created to form the basis of the executive order to ratify the WTO membership. This is food for thought for the international community: to look into the WTO membership of Nepal and thereby draw inferences as to how and when it conforms to international law.

1. BACKGROUND

As the Nepalese Constitution requires a two-thirds majority in parliament, Nepal's fourteen-year effort to obtain membership in the World Trade Organisation (WTO) culminated in an executive order at cabinet level that paved the way for this.[1] Nepal formally became the 147th member of the WTO one month after depositing the ratification of the accession protocol, thus on 23 April 2004. This article is about the Nepalese perspective on international law; it focuses on the dichotomy between domestic law and international law, on the one hand, and a state's commitment to the international community on the other.

Nepal's proposal for accession to the WTO was accepted by the 146 WTO members on 11 September 2003 during the fifth WTO ministerial meeting in Cancun, Mexico. Further, Nepal had to ratify the accession by 31 March 2004.[2] Although the protocol of accession fails to mention which authority (parliament, cabinet or any other government authority) has the power to ratify the accession protocol, it can be inferred from Article 126 of the Constitution of the Kingdom of Nepal 1990

---

[*] Advocate practising at the Supreme Court of Nepal and Consultant at the Federation of Nepalese Chambers of Commerce and Industry (FNCCI).

[1] *See* http://www.wto.org. *See* also *The Kathmandu Post*, 24 March 2004. Also available in http://www.nepalnews.com.

[2] *See Report of the Working Party on the Accession of the Kingdom of Nepal to the World Trade Organisation*, 28 August 2003, at 75-76.

Asian Yearbook of International Law, Volume 10 (B.S. Chimni *et al.,* eds.)

(hereinafter: the Constitution) that the WTO membership should be ratified by a two-thirds majority of the parliament.[3] However, there was no possibility of ratification of the WTO membership by the parliament as King Gyanendra Bir Bikram Shah Deva had dissolved the House of Representatives on 4 October 2002 following the eight-year rebellion of the Communist Party of Nepal, the Maoist (CPN-Maoist) party.[4]

In this article, I shall attempt to put my views, in the context of a parliamentary democracy, regarding Nepal's membership of the WTO. In a parliamentary democracy, a treaty with or membership of a multilateral trading organization such as the WTO is supposed to be ratified, acceded to, accepted or approved by the parliament of the nation. This claim can be made if such provisions are guaranteed by the Constitution of the nation. However, it may be wrong to generalize this proposition to include the case of Nepal, also provided the context is the membership of Nepal in the WTO. The Constitution of Nepal is the fundamental law of the land and it guarantees that membership of a multilateral trading organization such as the WTO should be ratified, acceded to, accepted or approved by a two-thirds majority of the parliament. However, this fundamental law happened to be superseded by an executive order in the name of addressing the need of the day and fulfilling a commitment to the international community.

Here, I shall attempt to present an overview of the historical perspective of Nepal's entry into the WTO. This constitutes the background to an analysis of the core legal issues that follow, including those of international trade law, focusing on Article 126 of the Constitution and the Treaty Act 1990 of Nepal in the context of Nepal's membership of the WTO. These two provisions in Nepalese law have long been subjected to analysis, as the decisions of the Supreme Court of Nepal based on these Nepalese laws have contributed to the development of some new trends in international law.

The relevant decisions of the Nepalese Supreme Court concern the issue of when a treaty becomes a treaty in law.[5] The arguments of the author in this paper are, however, based on the aforesaid Nepalese laws as these relate to Nepal's membership of the WTO and certain other related issues. Lastly, I conclude that the saying "Need does not know law" applies to some extent to Nepal's membership of the WTO. I am attempting to point out the fundamental flaw in Nepal's WTO membership: it has posed a threat to the due process of law. I conclude that international law is now no more a remote aspect of law: it is, rather, being developed as an indispensable part of domestic law since almost all of the spheres and aspects of domestic laws are either overlapping with or being superseded by international law.

---

[3] *See* Article 126 of *The Constitution of the Kingdom of Nepal 1990*, His Majesty's Government Ministry of Law, Justice and Parliamentary Affairs, Law Books Management Board, at 104-105.
[4] *See The Kathmandu Post*, 5 October 2002. Also available at www.nepalnews.com.
[5] *See* Surya P. Subedi, "When is a treaty a treaty in law? An analysis of the views of the Supreme Court of Nepal on a bilateral agreement between Nepal and India", 5 *Asian YIL* (1995), at 201-210.

2.   HISTORICAL OVERVIEW

In 1989, Nepal applied for membership in the General Agreement on Tariffs and Trade (GATT). Nepal was unable to become a member of GATT for miscellaneous reasons.[6] After the establishment of the WTO, Nepal again applied for admission to membership of the multilateral trading regime. Upon application, a comprehensive document called the Memorandum of Foreign Trade Regime (MFTR) was to be submitted. It took about two years to prepare the document, finalized only in 1998. The document includes the following three aspects:

a)   Legal provisions of the nation especially focusing on trade regime;
b)   Economic policies, and institutional structure for the implementation of the same; and
c)   Mechanism of its delivery, mandate and process to implement (a) and (b).

This document was distributed to all WTO member-nations. The responding nations asked approximately four hundred questions on the basis of the MFTR. Nepal responded to and defended the questions. Nepal also had to make a commitment to enact many of the provisions of Nepal's legal regime to render it compatible with the WTO regime. This process took a long time for Nepal.[7]

A formal committee, the Working Party, was set up to deal with the membership issues of Nepal. The Party had three formal and three informal meetings regarding Nepal's accession. After the conclusion of six such meetings on 15 August 2003, the Working Party concluded a paper regarding Nepal's membership of the WTO. This document included all of the conditions for accession. As the 146 members of the WTO agreed the document in the 5th Ministerial meeting held in Cancun, a contract based on the paper was accepted by one of the parties. The contract was later provided to Nepal on condition that if Nepal deposited a signature to ratify the same by 31 March 2004, accepting all the conditions of the document, then Nepal would formally become a member of the WTO within thirty days after the ratification. If Nepal had not deposited the signature within the said time limit, Nepal would not have become a WTO member.

Nepal had been participating in the WTO ministerial meetings as an observer since 1996. A succession of ministers took part in all of these, including the function held in 1998 to celebrate the establishment of the GATT.[8] They strongly pleaded for Nepal's membership of the WTO.[9] In 2003, Hari Bahadur Basnet, Commerce

---

[6]   Rudra Sharma, "How to ratify the membership of WTO?", *Kantipur*, 12 November 2003. The reality is that it has been 14 years since Nepal applied for membership of the WTO. First, Nepal applied for membership of GATT especially with the objective of getting a space in international trade once India imposed an economic blockade in 1989.

[7]   *See* Rudra Sharma, "Nepal's accession to World Trade Organisation – 1", *The World Trade Review*, fortnightly from Islamabad (Pakistan.), Vol. 3, No. 24, 16–31 December 2003.

[8]   *Ibid.*

[9]   *Ibid.*

Minister of the Surya Bahadur Thapa government (which was not responsible to the parliament, nor did it have the full support of its own party, the National Democratic Party, since its members were selected by the King) went to Geneva and signed the protocol of accession.

The constant participation of ministers in the WTO ministerial meetings shows that Nepal made a series of commitments between 1995 and 2003 towards membership of the WTO. This also proves that all of the political parties of Nepal which were in the government after the restoration of democracy in 1990 had agreed on Nepal's accession to the WTO.

3.   THE ISSUES

Nepal's accession to the WTO raised serious legal and constitutional questions from the perspective of international law and its application. These also revolve around the dichotomy between jurisdictions of domestic law and those of international law. The dichotomy pervades almost all legal discourses all over the world, sometimes involving the issue of the sovereignty of a nation state when the jurisdiction of international law contradicts that of domestic law.

There are contradictions between the respective jurisdictions of international law and of domestic law right from the time when international law evolved. Even though international law is said to be a remote aspect of law, it is superseding domestic laws in every sphere of life, due to the ever-developing globalization and liberalization of state affairs, especially after the 1990s[10] when Nepal embarked on liberalization. This contradiction between the jurisdictions of international law and domestic law, along with widely discussed phenomena such as globalization and liberalization, has pervaded Nepalese legal, political and economic scenarios especially since the restoration of democracy in 1990.[11] Further, the effects and impacts of Nepal's WTO entry have pervaded almost all walks of life. Therefore, it is clearer if each and every sector is examined to see how the issues have pervaded them. Nepal intends to amend or enact about 42 laws. However, it is not the WTO which required Nepal to amend all of these 42 laws. The WTO makes it mandatory only to make four laws. They are:

---

[10] Nepal is the sole country on the globe which has never been under the colonization of a foreign power. However, Nepali politics has always been under the influence of her neighbouring countries, especially India, and Western countries such as the USA, in recent years. King Prithivi Narayan Shah founded the Kingdom of Nepal by conquering over 50 tiny Kingdoms in the Southern Part of the Himalayas 250 years ago. The Kings of Nepal remained as titular heads of the state during the reign of the Ranas, who ruled Nepal for 104 years before democracy was established in 1950. The Kings ruled again about 40 years before democracy was restored in 1990.

[11] Rudra Sharma, "A pragmatic approach of liberalism: some observations", *Nepal Law Review* (Faculty of Law, Tribhuvan University, Kathmandu, Nepal), 2003.

a) Customs valuations;
b) Technical barriers to trade;
c) Quarantine (sanitary and phyto-sanitary) measures; and
d) Intellectual property rights.

For this Nepal has asked for a grace period of four years. Other laws are to be made to protect our stakeholders from the vulnerability that results from joining the global mainstream of trade, for example, as regards an anti-dumping Act. If another state dumps any goods on Nepal, we can take anti-dumping measures. Similarly, Nepal's industries may not compete with multi-national companies. We need to enact a Competition Law to give protection to our stakeholders.

4. THE CONSTITUTIONAL AND DEMOCRATIC PERSPECTIVE

It is said that a constitution governs the state affairs of a country. However, the ever-increasing scope of international trade and the jurisdiction of international law are slowly and gradually encroaching on the very concept of sovereignty. States also seem readily to enter into a compromise with this. Further, the binding nature of the WTO has accelerated this trend. Therefore, the terms and conditions accepted and made by Nepal during the accession and ratification process are also no less important than the constitution of the kingdom of Nepal itself. These provisions are capable of influencing domestic, as well as international, trade in the years to come.

We know the validity of and statutes governing the role, function and importance of trade in a parliamentary democracy. Trade in a parliamentary democracy is governed by domestic laws made by the representatives of the people and by international law, as well as by custom practised among the nation states. The rule of law and the sovereignty of people are upheld in a parliamentary democracy while carrying out any activities of a state; the same applies to the trade and trading policies of a nation state. Therefore, it can be concluded that the sovereignty of the people is probably the greatest principle of a parliamentary democracy; it can be assumed that a Constitution followed by a representative parliament is the fundamental law of the land and as such is supposed to govern every function of the state.

However, it may be an innovation in the history of international law that a constitution of a 'nation state' which is expressly mentioned as a fundamental law of the land is superseded by an executive order. By mentioning here 'nation state', I intend to indicate that a state happened to take such decision in the interests of fulfilling its international responsibilities as a member of the international community, and in an effort to align itself to mainstream trends in the multilateralism caused by globalization and the WTO. In Nepal, it so happened that an executive order superseded the mandatory constitutional provisions in the name of carrying out trade and of fulfilling the commitment made within the international community. Thus, Nepal's accession to the WTO has raised a series of issues in terms of the representation of a state, the sovereignty of a state, the responsibility of each and every stakeholder in this regard and, furthermore, the capacity and resources to address post-WTO challenges.

From a jurisprudential perspective, Nepal's accession to the WTO provides a pedestal for international trade jurisprudence to formulate new principles and, at least, provides a level playing field on which scholars of trade may gauge the systematic development of other principles of international trade law. It happened thus because Nepal became the first LDC to ratify the WTO accession, as Cambodia (another LDC to accede to the WTO together with Nepal) could not accomplish the ratification in time. The document of accession protocol is also said to be the best package in the history of the WTO.[12] When Nepal acceded to the WTO in the 2003 Cancun ministerial conference, there was an outcry in Nepal among the representatives of political parties and even civil society as to how the accession could be ratified in the absence of the parliament.[13] However, Nepal ratified its WTO membership on the ground that all political parties had duly consented to the WTO accession/ratification. Some quarters of civil society and some key lawyers lobbied to prove that Nepal as a nation has a consensus in favour of accession to and ratification of the WTO.[14] Nepal is a good example of those countries that have consented to WTO accession as to how such a consensus can be developed. As the application of international law depends heavily upon consensus, this may serve as a useful example in international trade law in the future. Despite tremendous contemporary resistance to perceived attacks on democracy and sovereignty, such voices were slowly and gradually placated through the efforts of certain opinion builders and civil society, towards a considered opinion.

5.   THE NEPALESE LEGAL SYSTEM AND THE WTO

The core legal aspects of Nepal's membership of the WTO should be viewed from the perspective of how the Nepalese legal system, including through the courts, liberalized itself in order to cope with international conventions and principles of international law. This should also be viewed against the background of how the Nepalese economy reached a balance with the Nepalese legal system and courts that

---

[12]   *See The Kathmandu Post* 24 April 2004. Nepal and Cambodia were allowed accession to the WTO together in the last Cancun ministerial. However, Cambodia could not ratify it within the prescribed time of six months and thereby asked for another six months' time for ratification.

[13]   Although the Nepali monarch is a constitutional monarch, King Gyanendra dismissed the democratically elected Prime Minister on 4 October, 2002 and thereby dissolved parliament. Then, the King himself appointed another Prime Minister at his discretion by applying Article 127 of the Constitution that allows certain provisional arrangements. Therefore, the major political parties of Nepal have been pleading that no major decision can be made by the government through a representative appointed at the King's discretion. They were also pleading that WTO membership cannot be ratified until and unless a democratically elected parliament is restored. Parliamentary elections could not, though, be held due to the ongoing insurgency in the country.

[14]   Some articles written by this author in the widely read Nepali national daily *Kantipur* and some of the programs organized by civil society like SAWTEE helped to build a consensus on this matter.

became lenient slowly and gradually. It should also be considered that Nepal has signed sixteen human rights conventions and nine ILO conventions. Furthermore, Nepal has been a member of the World Intellectual Property Organisation (WIPO) since 4 February 1997; it acceded to the Paris Convention on 22 June 2001. Nepal, while acceding to the WTO, has agreed in the Working Party Report of the Accession Protocol that it will examine other IP-related Conventions such as the Geneva Phonograms Convention, the Union for the Protection of the New Varieties of Plants (UPOV) 1991, the WIPO Copyright Treaty, and the WIPO Performers and Phonograms Treaty, in terms of national interest; Nepal will also explore the possibility of joining them in future as appropriate.[15] It is worth noting here that the civil society in Nepal heavily protested against the possible inclination of the Nepal government to accept the UPOV; the government later agreed to its adoption. Similarly, preparations are in the final stage to accede to the Patent Co-operation Treaty (PCT) and the Madrid Protocol.[16]

The WTO became necessary in order for Nepal to be linked to the global mainstream. If we had not obtained membership, we would have been left out of the mainstream and would thus have been more vulnerable. It has provided us with an alternative means of protection, as part of the global mainstream.

It may be argued that an individual has the right to choose and thereby plead for a referendum to decide such an important issue. Article 108 of the Constitution of the Kingdom of Nepal 1990 ensures the people's right to choose as a *sine qua non* of democracy. However, a group of ideologues argues that Article 108 of the Constitution is the very root cause of all anomalies and aberrations that have shown up during the last twelve years[17] after the restoration of democracy.

Had there been no WTO, there would have been another multilateral body to regulate international trade. Still, we may consider the line of argument that the failure of the WTO ministerial meeting in Cancun, Mexico last September suggests that the WTO may fail some time in the future. However, the process of liberalization will continue, and the accelerating globalization will subject all elements to global competition. Therefore, the post-ratification challenges of Nepal are concerned with the process of disciplining ourselves along the path towards liberalism and multilateralism, doing the needful to achieve these.

A global format of law is being developed all over the world. It has also extended to the trade sector of Nepal as her legal system has been exposed to the free trade

---

[15] *See Report of the Working Party on the Accession of the Kingdom of Nepal to the World Trade Organisation*, at 40.

[16] The author is confident about these facts on the basis of his own experiences while working as a project co-ordinator at the National Human Rights Commission and as a consultant at the FNCCI itself.

[17] Rudra Sharma, "The present confusion reels around the electoral provisions of the Constitution", *Essays on Constitutional Law*, March 2001, at 138. To conclude, the time has come to review Article 108 of the Constitution which has been providing room for any governing party to influence the whole election procedure in its favour and thereby causing all the distortions and malpractice, including political criminalization.

regime over the past decades.[18] The existing legal regime offers many facilities and privileges for foreign investment: the one-window policy of the government and other privileges are offered as a package to foreign investors.[19] Foreign investment can easily be made in Nepal and may thus influence the market in this region. As easily-influenced cross-border relations exist, one instance of foreign investment in Nepal can make a difference to this whole South Asian region. There would have been less significance to Nepal's entry into the WTO if Nepal had not been exposed to liberalism in the late 1980s.

In the history of international trade law, we find no significant mention of Nepal. However, scholars of international trade law all over the world have been studying Nepal for the last few years. For the past year, the ideologues of international trade law are busy analyzing Nepal's entry into the WTO.

Considering the volume of trade of Nepal in the world market, Nepal's entry into the WTO may not have major significance. However, this may prove more important to global trade if the strategic presence of Nepal in the world market is examined, especially in connection with its compliance with intellectual property rights. Taking intellectual property as the power tool of economic growth,[20] compliance in Nepal with intellectual property laws makes a significant difference within South Asian economic development due to Nepal's strategic location between the two largest markets of the world.[21] In this regard, South Asia is a region of dazzling opportunity.[22]

---

[18] Bal Bahadur Mukhia, "Trade Jurisprudence and overview on trade law in Nepal", *Nepal Law Review*, Vol.16, Nos. 1 & 2 (2003). The trade regime in Nepal is more liberal and open. Anybody can now import from overseas with no quantitative restrictions and import licence requirements. The only requirement is that of opening of a letter of credit through commercial banks. VAT has been implemented under which exports are zero-rated and all import taxes refunded.

[19] *See* Mukhia, n. 18. Foreign Investment and Technology Transfer Act 1992 (First Amendment 1996) is in line with open and liberal economic policies. Foreign investment and the one-window policy have been introduced. It has opened up FDI. Nepal has followed the principles of foreign investment: namely, (i) the theory of non-discrimination; (ii) the principle of national treatment; (iii) the theory of guarantee of repatriation.

[20] Kamil Idris, *Intellectual Property: A Power Tool for Economic Growth*, Geneva: World Intellectual Property Organization, at 4. For many years, economists have tried to provide an explanation as to why some economies grow fast while others do not; in other words, why some countries are rich and others are not. It is generally agreed that knowledge and inventions have played an important role in economic growth. The renowned economist Paul Romer suggests that the accumulation of knowledge is the driving force behind economic growth.

[21] As Nepal is a landlocked country between India and China, it has no direct access to seaports. However, it does have huge populations on the other sides of her borders. It constitutes the largest market in the world and the industrious people domiciled there may be crucial to determining the fate of world trade in the years to come.

[22] Christina B. Rocca (US Assistant Secretary for South Asian Affairs), "Why South Asia matters", *The Kathmandu Post*, 12 February 2004. South Asia is a region of both enormous danger and dazzling opportunity. It is a region struggling against international terrorism, regional nuclear confrontation and proliferation, social instability and humanitarian 'crises'; and yet it is a region that is home to nearly a fifth of the world's population, a huge and growing market whose industrious

6.   THE INCEPTION AND ADOPTION OF INTERNATIONAL LAW IN NEPAL

Nepal embarked on liberalization after the 1980s; the liberal mood of this land-locked kingdom was institutionalized when it adopted a liberal constitution as a result of a popular movement in 1990. The constitution is in tune with protecting human rights of the individual as envisaged by most of the principles of human rights adopted in the international instruments. These principles of the constitution and the open environment after the restoration of democracy and the growth of proactive civil society have led the Supreme Court of Nepal to adopt the major principles of inter-national human rights instruments in its decisions. It has adopted such principles in the cases of *Annapurna Rana v. Kathmandu District Court*, *Chanda Bajracharya v. His Majesty's Government,* and so on.[23] The trend has flourished over the years, leading to the development of a proactive and rights-based culture that has been a proponent of monism in terms of complying with international instruments. Interpreta-tion of the Treaty Act of Nepal occurs in a manner to ensure the enforcement of international instruments ratified by Nepal notwithstanding the Constitution and other laws.[24] This has further increased the contradiction between monism and dualism in terms of complying with international instruments ratified by Nepal and in terms of complying with the Constitution of the Kingdom of Nepal 1990. The Treaty Act 2047 of Nepal is lenient in order for it to comply with the international instruments ratified by Nepal.[25]

However, the proponents of monism also have strong arguments in terms of complying with international instruments. They argue that monism is not allowed by the Constitution since the latter is the Supreme Law of the land.[26] They argue that the Treaty Act 1990 is merely a law made under the Constitution and such law cannot supersede the Constitution, which is the fundamental law of the land. They also argue that no international instruments ratified by Nepal can supersede the Constitution of Nepal until and unless Article 1 of the Constitution is amended to make a space for them. The Supreme Court has merely adopted the international instruments ratified by Nepal and has remained silent on its comparative relevance

---

citizens are keen to build better future for themselves and their families. This region is now, and will long remain, at the forefront of America's foreign policy concern.

[23] *See* Rudra Sharma and others, "Summary of the leading cases relating to human rights held by the Supreme Court of the Kingdom of Nepal", a paper presented at a seminar organized by the Informal Sector Service Centre (INSEC) and the International Centre for the Legal Protection of Human Rights (INTERIGHTS), Kathmandu, 2001.

[24] Nepal has ratified 16 international human rights instruments and some other ILO conventions. This is probably the greatest number in South Asia.

[25] Section 9 of the Treaty Act 2047 states that the international instrument prevails in the event of contradiction between the domestic law and international instruments ratified by Nepal.

[26] *The Constitution of the Kingdom of Nepal 1990*, n. 3, Article 1 (1). This Constitution is the fundamental law of Nepal and all laws inconsistent with it shall, to the extent of such inconsistency, be void.

with Clause 9 of the Treaty Act and Article 1 of the Constitution. Therefore, a constitutional question, serious in international law terms, still remains unanswered.

Despite the Treaty Act 1990 and the lenient mood of the Supreme Court to adopt international treaties, Nepal nowhere declares the supremacy of international law. A clear, strong wall of separation between domestic and international law still exists. The Nepalese legal system is dualist, not monist.[27] The contention of Article 1 of the Constitution as the fundamental law of the land proves this proposition. However, the Treaty Act provides for the primacy of treaty law over domestic law. Nepal's membership of the WTO in the absence of parliament has further given momentum to the spirit of the Treaty Act.

7.   LAWS APPLICABLE IN NEPAL'S WTO RATIFICATION

During the Fifth WTO ministerial meeting held in Cancun in September 2003, Nepal agreed to ratify the accession protocol by the end of March 2004.[28] After this development, the debate about the ratification of the Protocol on Accession achieved new heights due on the one hand to the absence of parliament, and there were no gestures towards forming a parliament in the then immediate future. Legal as well as trade scholars sat together to discuss the interpretation of the Constitution and other existing laws of Nepal. While interpreting the legal constitutional issues, some international laws were also involved.

There were four main kinds of laws applicable to the ratification of the WTO.

a)   Articles XII, IX, XI and XV of the Agreement Establishing the WTO;[29]
b)   Article 126 of the Constitution of the Kingdom of Nepal 1990;[30]

---

[27] Annanda Mohan Bhattarai, *Displacement and Rehabilitation in Nepal, Law Policy and practice*, New Delhi: Anmoal Publication Pvt. Ltd, 2001, at 148-157.

[28] *Report of the Working Party on the Accession of the Kingdom of Nepal to the World Trade Organisation: World Trade Organisation on the Accession of Nepal*, 28 August 2003, Sect. 7, at 76. This protocol shall be open for acceptance, by signature or otherwise, by the Kingdom of Nepal until 31 March 2004.

[29] *See* http://www.wto.org.

[30] *See* n. 26, at 104. (126) Ratification of Accession to, Acceptance of or Approval of Treaty or Agreement:

(1) The ratification of, accession to, acceptance of or approval of treaties or agreements to which the Kingdom of Nepal or His Majesty's Government is to become a party shall be as determined by law.

(2) The laws to be made pursuant to clause (1) shall, *inter alia*, require that the ratification of, accession to, acceptance of or approval of treaties or agreements on the following subjects to be done by a majority of two-thirds of the members present at a joint sitting of both Houses of Parliament: (a) Peace and friendship; (b) defence and strategic alliance; (c) boundaries of the Kingdom of Nepal; and (d) natural resources and the distribution of their uses.

Provided that out of the treaties and agreements referred to in sub-clauses (a) and (d), if any treaty or agreement is of an ordinary nature, which does not affect the nation extensively, seriously or in the long term, the ratification of, accession to, acceptance of or approval of such treaty or

c) Clauses 3, 4, 6, 7 and 14 of the Treaty Act 1990;[31] and
d) Articles 14, 15, 26, 27, 46 and 47 of the Vienna Convention on the Law of Treaties 1969.[32]

We have to analyze the legal regime of WTO accession on the basis of these laws. According to Article XII of the Agreement Establishing the WTO, the accession negotiations for the original members were not very difficult, in comparison with the process as practised for those nations which become members through accession. There is the WTO text on the one side, whereas there are agreed terms on the other. The accession process in accordance with agreed terms is very difficult. Nepal had to deal with the agreed terms as it failed to become an original member of the WTO by virtue of its being a member of GATT.

According to Article XII.2 of the WTO Establishing Agreement, the two-thirds majority of the WTO ministerial meeting, or of the General Council at a time when the ministerial conference is not in session, should approve the report of the Working Party. The Cancun WTO ministerial conference approved our accession by consensus.[33]

WTO Article XIV.1 has used the word "acceptance". According to the Vienna Convention on the Law of Treaties, acceptance, accession, ratification, and approval have the same meaning. Therefore, acceptance also means ratification. A short provision about acceptance says that those states which have completed the accession process will formally become members 30 days after depositing the instrument of acceptance.[34]

Article XI says that if any country wants to withdraw from WTO membership, it has to notify the WTO, and the membership will be withdrawn six months after such notification. If any condition of the WTO appears to be unbearable, one can withdraw from the WTO, yet, in practice, it is next to impossible.[35] Article 126 of the Constitution says that ratification, accession to and acceptance of an international treaty shall be determined by law. Furthermore, the law is the Treaty Act 1990. According to Article 126 (2) of the Constitution, any treaty or agreement relating to four factors such as peace and friendship, defence and strategic alliance, the boundaries of the kingdom of Nepal and natural resources, and distribution of

---

agreement may be done at a meeting of the House of Representatives by a simple majority of the members present.

(3) After the commencement of this Constitution, unless a treaty or agreement is ratified, acceded to, accepted or approved in accordance with this Article, it shall not be binding on his Majesty's Government or the Kingdom of Nepal.

(4) Notwithstanding anything contained in clauses (1) and (2), no treaty or agreement shall be concluded in detrimental to the territorial integrity of the Kingdom of Nepal.

[31] Treaty Act 1990.
[32] *See* 1155 *UNTS* 331.
[33] *See* n. 7.
[34] *Ibid.*
[35] *See* Rudra Sharma, "The saga of Nepal's membership in WTO", 8 *Business Age* (April 2004), at 21.

their uses requires a two-thirds majority of the joint sitting of the members of parliament.[36]

This Article also provides that if the nature of the treaty relating to peace and friendship and natural resources is of an ordinary nature, it can be approved by a simple majority of the House of Representatives. According to Article 126 (3), if any treaty is not ratified according to this Constitution, that treaty shall not be binding on His Majesty's Government. It cannot create any obligation on Nepal.

8.   LAWS ABOUT THE PROCEDURE OF RATIFICATION AND
        ACCESSION

In international law, there are two aspects of a treaty: the procedure to become a signatory, and that to become a party. Section (3) of the Treaty Act 1990 deals with the procedure to become a signatory and with matters concerning the conclusion of a treaty. After signing the accession protocol of the WTO, Nepal became a signatory to the WTO, not a party. Article 4 (1) of the Treaty Act 1990 provides for the acceptance, approval or ratification of any treaty which is not covered by Article 126 of the Constitution. Article 4 (3) of the Treaty Act provides that Nepal will be party to a particular international treaty after depositing the acceptance. Article 4 (4) of the said Act states that membership of any inter-governmental agency or body can be approved only by the House of Representatives.

Section 14 of the Treaty Act deals with transitional provisions. Although the provision is for an interim period, this states that the government can ratify a treaty at the time when there is no parliament. Nepal is still not a party to the Vienna Convention on the Law of Treaties. However, the WTO has accepted the Vienna Convention as the instrument to be applied in interpreting the texts of the WTO. As this Convention applies to all WTO members while interpreting the WTO texts, this will *ipso facto* also be applicable to Nepal.

Articles 14 and 15 of this Convention are similar to section 4 of our Treaty Act, which refers to the ratification of a treaty. Article 26 of the same Act states *pacta sunt servanda*. By this, a treaty is ratified in good faith and such a treaty is enforced irrespective of domestic law. Article 27 of the Vienna Convention further states that no domestic law can be invoked so as not to enforce a treaty ratified on the basis of *pacta sunt servanda*.

Articles 46 and 47 of the Convention are more important. A treaty once ratified by a state cannot be revoked simply because some domestic laws were infringed while an international treaty was being ratified. Article 47 states that one cannot after ratification argue that some specific restrictions made in domestic laws were not fulfilled during the process of ratification.

---

[36] *Ibid.*

9.   LAWS ABOUT RATIFICATION IN THE ABSENCE OF PARLIAMENT

The absence of a parliament is possible in the life of a nation. The Treaty Act 1990 has envisaged and Article 14 has provided for transitional provisions. For this, section (4) of the Treaty Act may be amended to give a space for the ratification of a treaty when there is no parliament. There is another possibility about bringing a special ordinance for ratification of the WTO.

However, after the accession voices were raised, saying that there might have been numerous problems if Nepal had chosen to become a WTO member through ordinance, which should be presented in the parliament within six months. There will be no legal validity if this is not ratified by parliament within six months. Yet, considering Articles 46 and 47 of the Vienna Convention, we cannot avoid compliance with the WTO simply because there were certain errors in the compliance with domestic laws at the time of ratification of WTO.

Articles 46 and 47 of the Vienna Convention may support this proposition, which may not constitute the finest domestic procedure. However, this does not fulfil the concept of the rule of law in its strict sense. Therefore, the best option was to opt for parliament. Another alternative was to amend Section 4 (4) of the Treaty Act, authorizing the ratification of the treaty in the absence of a parliament. Section 4 (4) should also include a provision that the ratification should even be sealed by the head of the state, so that controversies may be avoided in the future. The legitimacy of a government may be questioned while that of a head of a state will not. This fact will strengthen the legal validity of the ratification. Then, the document should be submitted to the parliament when it is formed.

10.   FINAL LEGAL ARRANGEMENTS MADE BY NEPAL

Despite several issues and their pertinent legal impacts, Nepal's WTO membership led Nepal towards a situation of complexity and responsibility. There were two prominent issues: the state's commitment as a member of the international community, and Nepal's internal politics. On the one hand, Nepal had responsibilities towards the international community to fulfil the commitments made in the international arena. However, it was difficult for Nepal to fulfil its international commitment due to the internal state of affairs. There was a conflict between these factors. Still, the conflict should work for a good, if it is for the betterment of the society.[37] There was a question of responsibility regarding the extent to which internal politics can become involved in the process of fulfilling the international commitments of a state.

---

[37] Rudra Sharma, "Conflict transformation by peaceful means", *The Sunday Post*, 15 December 2002. Conflict is inevitable and pervades everywhere – in a group of people in society, among families, even within the family and between the spouses. However, the victim of conflict cannot be every individual if the conflict is a 'responsible' conflict, as it were, and if it is for the betterment of the society.

It is not merely a matter of international trade law. As long as there are indeed states, there may be issues of internal conflict within a state. Just before it deposited its ratification on 23 March, Nepal appears to have made a consensus opinion that a state should keep on fulfilling its international responsibilities and commitments irrespective of its internal conflicts. Nepal's WTO accession concerned about the welfare of the people more than international trade law. The vulnerability of risk in the absence of WTO membership was assessed to be more pertinent than the arithmetic of profit and loss. Therefore, Nepal finally amended the Treaty Act 1990 to pave the way for the ratification of the WTO. The following are some key provisions of the Treaty Act 1990 and its amendment for the membership of WTO. Section 9 (1) of the Treaty Act 1990 reads as follows:

> If any provision of the treaty of which His Majesty's Government or the Kingdom of Nepal is a party, after such treaty is ratified, acceded, accepted or approved, is inconsistent with any law in force, such law to the extent of such inconsistency, shall be void and the provision of the treaty shall come into force as law of Nepal.[38]

Section 4 of the said Treaty Act, 1990 reads as follows:

> (4) Regarding the establishment of any intergovernmental organisation or obtaining membership of any such organisation or subject to a treaty which is inconsistent with the prevailing law, His Majesty's Government or the Kingdom of Nepal shall not be a party of such treaty even as the provision for ratification, accession, acceptance or approval is not made for such treaty.[39]

Finally, His Majesty's Government of Nepal published the following amendment of the aforesaid section 4 of the Treaty Act to provide a space for the ratification of Nepal's WTO accession[40] in (4 A) Special provision about ratification or accession:

> 1) Notwithstanding anything contained in section 4 or 4(1), if, in the absence of the parliament, an immediate ratification, acceptance or approval or accession is required for obtaining of the membership of an international organisation established under a multilateral treaty, His Majesty's Government should submit the matter to His Majesty the King.
>
> 2) If the treaty submitted by His Majesty's Government to His Majesty the King pursuant to sub-section (1) is ratified, accepted or approved or provided an approval for the accession to the same, such treaty shall be deemed as ratified, accepted or approved or acceded to.

---

[38] *See* n. 31, at 204.
[39] *See ibid.*
[40] *See Nepal Gazette* Section 53, Extraordinary, 76 *Nepal Rajpatra*, Part II, date 2060/12/4.

3) If a treaty is ratified, accepted or approved or acceded to pursuant to sub-section (2), the information of the same should, within seven days, be submitted to the meeting of the parliament that is held just after accomplishment of such task.

4) Notwithstanding anything stated elsewhere in this section, no treaty shall be ratified, accepted or approved or the same shall be acceded to pursuant to this section after the fixation of the date of election.

This is the road travelled by Nepal for fourteen years in order to become a member of the WTO. At this juncture, His Majesty's Government sent a letter to the WTO headquarters in Geneva on 23 March applying to become the 147th member of the WTO.

11. CONCLUDING REMARKS

Membership alone is not the end of Nepal's road to the WTO. Obviously, the obtaining of membership of the WTO by a land-locked least developing country (LLDC) like Nepal is a matter of paramount importance for the country. Therefore, such membership raises many issues in the country. Nepal's WTO membership can, of course, be considered as one of the most prominent events in the history of Nepal since the Kingdom of Nepal was established some 250 years ago.

I have attempted in this paper to deal with the relationship between domestic law and customary international law. It seems that there is still a clear dichotomy between international law and domestic law. It seems that Nepal's legal and judicial system is nearer to the British and Indian approach, which prefers domestic legislation to apply international law.[41]

However, the wall of separation of domestic from international law is being dismantled for several reasons, coupled with accelerating globalization and liberalisation in every sphere of life. This is not the time for a debate between the free world and socialist countries. Therefore, there is no option other than the WTO. It is time to look at the experiences of other states and then to do our best. China, for example, was supposed to be a socialist country; it is now ahead of us in terms of trade liberalization.

The nation has been under violence for a decade, with internal conflict and rebellion. Elections were not held, even after the expiration of the term of the parliament. However, we should accept that we are in a transitional stage socially and economically. Not only the rebels but also the industrious young generation want to see a change in the socio-economic spheres of the nation. What we need to do is to make political decision to dissociate politics from business and thereby address the challenges of the WTO. Therefore, we need political decisiveness. Such decision making should be a democratic and pragmatic decision.

---

[41] *See* n. 27, at 154.

A government in power may put things on the right track. The international community nevertheless seeks its legitimacy, too, concerned how far the people or successive governments would continue to make progress. This is an important point in the present context of Nepal. We have to go between two conflicting propositions: on the one hand, fulfilling international commitments, and on the other, respecting national laws. If there had been a parliament in the soonest possible time, that would have helped address the problem. However, we have to resolve the situation whether there is a parliament or not. Trade and commerce continue whether or not there is a parliament. Industries keep on running irrespective of a change of government.

We need not take the WTO as a remedy for everything. Rather, Nepal, as a fully-fledged member of the WTO, needs to consider that WTO membership should be an aid to improving the condition of poor people. Simultaneously, we need to be cautious about the facts that are laid before us. Numerous promises have been made over the last 50 years regarding the amelioration of the condition of the poor. However, the data before us reveal that the betterment of the poor is next to impossible.[42] Further, this has also not decreased the gap between rich and poor.[43] This WTO ratification should create an environment in which the poor can be assisted: educate the people to adapt to any situation of life.[44]

There may be discussions about the attempts made by this Himalayan kingdom to accede to the WTO; those concerned with this field may have their own opinions about the manner and matter of Nepal's accession to the WTO. There may be unending discussions and debates about the ratification of Nepal's membership in the absence of a parliament. However, this is now history. The lengthy and strenuous accession and ratification process will long be remembered as a matter of importance in the history of international law, especially for two reasons: first, Nepal became the first LDC to complete the arduous accession procedure; second, Nepal had to

---

[42] Rudra Sharma, "Efforts to alleviate poverty", *The Kathmandu Post*, 1 January 2001. In 1981 the first Conference on Least Developed Countries (LDDc) decided on annual GDP growth target of 7.2 per cent for the LDCs. Now, almost 20 years later, the actual average rate of annual GDP growth rate is 2.2 per cent. In 1981, the number of LDCs was 32. Today, that number has increased to 48. In 1981, the richest 20 per cent of the world's population had an income 30 times greater than the poorest 20 per cent. Now, the richest 20 per cent earn 60 times as much. Today, the poorest 20 per cent of the world's people survive on 1.4 per cent of the world's total income, and the assets of the top three billionaires exceed the combined GNP of all the least developed countries. This means the top three billionaires of the world have more assets than the GNP of the 48 LDCs.

[43] *See ibid.* Two hundred and fifty years ago, the difference in *per capita* income between the richest and poorest countries was, approximately 5:1 and the difference between Europe and East or South Asia was around 2:1. Today, the gap between the richest industrial nation and the poorest non-industrial country is about 400:1 and it is still growing. Some countries are growing poorer relatively and even absolutely.

[44] Rudra Sharma, "Constitutionalism holds key to democratic governance", in *Essays on Constitutional Law*, Kathmandu: Nepal Law Society. The most important problem of today's society is not economic development, as Marx believed; it is not the problem of religion, as religious preacher, believe; it is not the problem of ideology, as political leaders believe: it is rather the problem of education which enables individuals to adapt themselves to any adversity or prosperity in life.

ratify the WTO accession protocol in the absence of a parliament despite mandatory constitutional provisions.

Over the decades, there have been talks about the WTO. However, such talks were mainly focused on the accession and ratification of Nepal to the multilateral trading system. The post-ratification talks need to focus on the competitiveness of Nepalese enterprises and their viability in the context of accelerating globalization coupled with the WTO regime. By obtaining WTO membership, Nepal has become a part of the global multilateral trading system. This is a paradigm shift. Neither state affairs, nor business activities, can be carried on in the way they were. We need to keep our own house in order. Competitiveness cannot be developed if rampant corruption and over-assiduous bureaucracy continues. I do not mean to suggest that there is no corruption or over-assiduous bureaucracy in the countries that have already become members of the WTO. However, the nations to have cast themselves under the WTO regime have developed a cadre system in administration, trade, international affairs, and so on. Cadres should be developed even among bureaucrats, provided we want to compete with other WTO member countries. If we are to develop the competitiveness of the private sector under the multilateral trading system, we must consider the competitiveness of the people who identify themselves as 'civil servants.' They should prepare themselves to deliver service at a par with their counterparts in those foreign countries with which Nepal needs to carry on its business trans-actions. Nepal in its post-ratification period should commercialize on the huge and immense potential of natural resources through the maximum exploitation of intel-lectual property. Establishment of a 'knowledge-based industry' by exploiting intel-lectual property rights is the key way towards prosperity in twenty-first century Nepal. Creating a way forward along these lines is another challenge of post-WTO-ratifica-tion Nepal.

Post-WTO Nepal needs to work for its institutional development. Nepal needs an independent commission to enforce competition law. Similarly, there are many institutions to be established in order to meet the challenges of the post-ratification period. The cost of establishing and operating such institutions is immense.

Last but not least, Nepal's WTO membership follows the process of dismantling the wall between international law and domestic law. Nepal will be adopting monism some time in the future, though; the length of time may not now be predicted. Any law, whether it is competition law or criminal law, is tending towards global adapta-tion. A global format may be prescribed for any kind of law today. Nepal's integration within the WTO and other regional Free Trade Agreements such as SAFTA and BIMSTAC may lead this kingdom to become part of a borderless regional or even global territory. It is possible in the future, if we are optimistic, to consider South Asia as a region with potentiality similar to that of the European Union. The establish-ment, development and expansion of the European Union indicate that it may be expanded in future irrespective of any boundary or historical and political back-ground.[45]

---

[45] *See* M.R. Josse, "EU: Quantum Leap forward", *The Kathmandu Post*, 28 April 2004, at 4.

The expansion of the EU by ten more states including Poland has dismantled the buffer zone between the EU and the former Russian Federation. Soon, the EU is expected to include other countries, such as Turkey. At this point, one can imagine what the political map of the world some 30 years from now will be. As the EU is now in the fifth stage of liberalization,[46] the success stories of the EU will certainly be replicated in other Free Trade Areas (FTA) such as SAFTA and BIMSTAC. As the stages of trade liberalization are developed in other FTAs, as happened in the EU, there will be no conflict between monism and dualism. The wall of separation between domestic law and international law will be dismantled and eliminated for ever once such FTAs are expanding and entering into the progressive stages of liberalization. Nepal's membership of the WTO should be considered as the prelude to such developments being made in the future. Nepal's WTO membership even in the absence of the parliament gives a strong message to scholars of international law that such developments will not be obstructed or postponed due to the internal conflicts within a nation state.

---

[46] The EU adopted preferential trade in the first stage. The second was free trade; the third, customs union; the fourth, economic union; and the fifth and last is monetary union with the common Euro.

LEGAL MATERIALS

STATE PRACTICE OF ASIAN COUNTRIES IN THE FIELD OF INTERNATIONAL LAW[*]

BANGLADESH[1]

Bangladesh has recently enacted the Arbitration Act 2001 (the Act). It came into force on 10 April 2001,[2] repealing the Arbitration (Protocol and Convention) Act 1937 and the Arbitration Act 1940,[3] legacies of the British Raj in India. Such a legislative step was urgent in the face of increasing foreign investment in Bangladesh in various sectors, especially in natural gas and power, and the ever-growing export trade with the rest of the world. The Act, principally based on the UNCITRAL Model Law,[4] consolidates the law relating to both domestic and international commercial arbitration. It thus creates a single and unified legal regime for arbitration in Bangladesh. This modernization gives Bangladesh a facelift as an attractive place for dispute resolution in the field of international trade, commerce and investment.

The Act has 59 sections organized into 14 chapters. Chapter I (s1) deals with introductory matters; Chapter II (ss2-8), general provisions; Chapter III (ss9-10), the arbitration agreement; Chapter IV (ss11-16), composition of the tribunal; Chapter V (ss17-22), jurisdiction of arbitral tribunals; Chapter VI (ss23-35), conduct of proceedings; Chapter VII (ss36-41), the making of the award and termination of proceedings; Chapter VIII (ss42-43), recourse against an award; Chapter IX (s44), enforcement of awards; Chapter X (ss45-47), recognition and enforcement of certain foreign awards; Chapter IX (s48), appeals; Chapter XII (ss49-56), miscellaneous (deposit of costs, dispute as to arbitrator's remuneration or costs, bankruptcy, limitations, etc.); Chapter XIII (ss57-58), supplementary provisions (power of the Govern-

---

[*] Edited by B.S. Chimni. However, the responsibility for the veracity of the materials included is that of the individual contributors alone.
[1] Contributed by A.F.M. Maniruzzaman, Professor of International and Business Law, University of Portsmouth, United Kingdom.
[2] The official authentic English text has not yet been published.
[3] By s 59(1).
[4] Available at *http://www.uncitral.org/en-index.htm*.

Asian Yearbook of International Law, Volume 10 (B.S. Chimni *et al.,* eds.)
© 2005 Koninklijke Brill NV. Printed in The Netherlands, pp. 167-264.

ment or of the Supreme Court to make rules), and Chapter XIV (s59), repeals and savings.

The salient features of the Act are:

a) The preamble specifically mentions that it is "[a]n Act to enact the law relating to international commercial arbitration, recognition and enforcement of foreign arbitral awards and other arbitrations." However, the Act is also applicable to domestic arbitration.

b) In an international commercial dispute one of the parties to the dispute must be either a firm registered abroad or a foreign national.

c) The dispute in question must arise out of a legal relationship, whether contractual or not, but considered as a commercial dispute under the law in force in Bangladesh.

d) The parties are free to determine the number of arbitrators. If they fail to do so, the tribunal is to consist of three.

e) The parties may choose arbitrators of any nationality and the chairman of the tribunal may be of any nationality if that factor is accepted by the parties.

f) The courts (i.e., the District Judge's Court in respect of domestic commercial arbitration and the High Court Division of the Supreme Court of Bangladesh in respect of international commercial arbitration) can intervene in regard to appointments of the arbitrators on behalf of the parties as well as of the chairman of the arbitral tribunal within sixty days from the receipt of a party's application, to facilitate the arbitral process.

g) The court shall respect the parties' agreement to arbitrate and refer any party to such agreement to arbitration and stay any legal proceedings that may have been commenced against the other party.

h) The parties are free to agree on the venue, failing which the tribunal shall determine it, having regard to the circumstances of the case, including the convenience of the parties.

i) In the absence of the parties' agreement as to the language of the proceedings, the tribunal can use any language it deems appropriate.

j) The Act preserves the doctrines of severability of the arbitration agreement and *competence-compétence*, so that the tribunal can rule on its own jurisdiction.

k) The tribunal is not bound to follow the Code of Civil Procedure 1908 or the Evidence Act 1872. Subject to the parties' agreement, it may adopt any procedure for conducting the proceedings.

l) With respect to the substance of a dispute, the parties are free to choose the rules of law or legal system of any country. In the context of the substantive law chosen by the parties, the Act expressly discards *renvoi*, unless the parties agree to the contrary.

m) If the parties do not choose the applicable substantive law, the Act authorizes the tribunal to apply the rules of law – anything short of a legal system, such as transnational commercial rules or the rules of *lex mercatoria* – which the tribunal deems most appropriate in the circumstances.

n) If all the parties agree, the tribunal may use mediation, conciliation or any other procedure at any time during the arbitral proceedings to encourage settlement.

o) Although the Act makes provision for the tribunal to make interim orders in respect of the subject-matter of the dispute, a similar provision has not been made for the court, whose intervention may still be needed in an emergency even before the tribunal is constituted.

p) No appeal lies against the tribunal's order of interim measure of protection.

q) The tribunal can summon any persons to appear before it, albeit through the competent court, to give evidence or to submit materials if they do not do so of their own accord.

r) The tribunal has no power to act in respect of consolidation of arbitral proceedings and concurrent hearings, unless it is given by the parties on agreed terms. The parties are free to agree on these matters.

s) The tribunal must deal with any dispute submitted to it as quickly as possible and act fairly and impartially by giving each party 'reasonable opportunity' to participate in the proceedings, and in deciding its procedure and evidence and in exercising other powers conferred upon it.

t) Subject to the parties' agreement, the tribunal may appoint experts, legal advisers or assessors to assist it on specific issues.

u) The tribunal may continue the proceedings in the absence of a party and make an award on the basis of the evidence before it.

v) The tribunal must make its award without undue delay and the award will have the same force of law as if it were a decree of a court.

w) An award shall be made by the majority of the arbitrators and shall be in writing and signed at least by the majority where the tribunal consists of more than one arbitrator.

x) An award can be challenged in the court only on specified grounds.

y) The Act makes provision for appeal against an order of the court setting aside or refusing to set aside an award, or refusing to recognize or enforce any foreign arbitral award. All these appeals go to the Appellate Division of the Supreme Court of Bangladesh.

INDIA[5]

JUDICIAL DECISIONS

Maritime Liens and Maritime Claims under Indian Law *vis-à-vis* various related International Conventions – the extent of adaptations of these conventions into Indian law

M.V. AL. QUAMAR v. TSAVLIRIS SALVAGE (INTERNATIONAL) LTD. AND OTHERS

Supreme Court of India, 17 August 2000
AIR 2000 Supreme Court 2826

Facts

The Petitioner was the owner of the ship M.V. Al. Quamar. Respondent No. 1 company M/s Tsavliris Salvage (International) Ltd. had obtained a decree from the Admiralty Court in England against this ship pursuant to a contract of salvage entered into by it with Respondent No. 2 who was the owner of the ship at that point of time (the ship was named M.V. Al Tabish). Respondent No.1 Company had, pursuant to a Salvage Contract with Respondent No. 2, mobilized its tug for salvaging and towing the aforesaid vessel which had met rough weather in the high seas. The English Admiralty Court had passed the decree holding Respondent No. 2 liable. The money decree passed by the English Court was a decree *in personam* against Respondent No. 2. The ship in question was found located in the territorial waters of the state of Andhra Pradesh, India and consequently within the Admiralty Court of Andhra Pradesh, being the High Court of Andhra Pradesh, as a successor to the Chartered High Court of Madras.[6] Respondent No. 1, decree-holder, having come to know about the anchoring of the said ship at Visakhapatnam (in the state of Andhra Pradesh in India) filed an execution petition invoking section 44A of the Indian Civil Procedure Code for the arrest and detention of the ship and for recovering the decretal amount from Respondent No. 2.[7] The master of the ship (Petitioner, who is the

---

[5] Contributed by V.G. Hegde, Associate Professor, School of International Studies, Jawaharlal Nehru University, New Delhi.

[6] The Admiralty jurisdiction was a British legacy. The Court, while tracing the historical antecedents of this development noted, albeit briefly, "…This special admiralty jurisdiction was saved by the Government of India Act, 1915 as also that of 1935 and subsequently protected in terms of Article 225 of the Constitution". The Court further noted "…these three Presidency towns (Calcutta, Madras and Bombay) were conferred with the same jurisdiction as was vested in the High Court of England…". Article 225 of the Indian Constitution seeks to save the jurisdiction of the existing High Courts. It, *inter alia*, provides that "…shall be the same as immediately before the commencement of this Constitution".

[7] Section 44A of the Indian Civil Procedure Code provides for the execution of decrees passed by courts in reciprocating territories which included the United Kingdom.

present owner of the ship) challenged these execution proceedings before the Supreme Court.[8]

State Practice and Implementation:

The Court, while referring to the concept and scope of application of maritime lien and claim, noted that India had not adapted into its legal system the Brussels Convention relating to the Arrest of Seagoing Ships, 1952. While on this issue, the Court repeated its general observations in the case of *MV Elisabeth* in 1993:[9]

> Indian legislation has not [...] progressed, notwithstanding the Brussels Protocol of 1968 adopting the Visby Rules or the United Nations Convention on the Carriage of Goods by Sea, 1978 adopting the Hamburg Rules. The Hamburg Rules prescribe the minimum liabilities of the carrier far more justly and equitably than the Hague Rules so as to correct the tilt in the latter in favour of the carriers. The Hamburg Rules are acclaimed to be a great improvement on the Hague Rules and far more beneficial from the point of view of the cargo owners. India has also not adopted the International Convention relating to the Arrest of Seagoing Ships, Brussels, 1952. Nor has India adopted the Brussels Convention 1952 on civil and penal jurisdiction in matters of collision; nor the Brussels Conventions of 1926 and 1967 relating to maritime liens and mortgages. India seems to be lagging behind many other countries in ratifying and adopting the beneficial provisions of various conventions intended to facilitate international trade. Although these conventions have not been adopted by legislation, the principles incorporated in the conventions are themselves derived from common law of nations embodying the felt necessities of international trade and are as such part of common law of India and applicable for the enforcement of maritime claims against foreign ships.

Displacement and rehabilitation of tribals and other persons – applicability of ILO Convention 107 to which India is a signatory – Resolution of the United Nations Water Conference 1977

NARMADA BACHAO ANDOLAN v. UNION OF INDIA AND OTHERS

Supreme Court of India, 18 October 2000
AIR 2000 Supreme Court 3751

---

[8] The Court, *inter alia*, held that "Both the English Admiralty Court, which is, admittedly, a Court of competent jurisdiction, as well as the Andhra Pradesh High Court being a corresponding Court of Competent admiralty jurisdiction, could not only entertain such a suit in the first instance but could equally be competent to execute such a decree of Admiralty Court.

[9] *M.V. Elisabeth v. Harwan Investment and Trading Pvt. Ltd.*, AIR 1993 Supreme Court 1014

Facts

The case related to construction of various hydropower and irrigation projects and the consequent displacement of a large population on the river Narmada, one of the largest rivers flowing in Central India. The issue also involved, *inter alia*, the decision on the height of one of the dams known as the Saradar Sarovar Project. These projects on the river had been taken up for basin-wise development of the river with flood control, irrigation, power and extension of the navigation. This resulted in the large-scale displacement of people, particularly the tribal population located in different village clusters. The Petitioner, a non-governmental organization working for the rehabilitation of the tribal villages in the Narmada Valley, had put forward three strands of arguments relating to (a) the environment; (b) relief and rehabilitation; and (c) the necessity for reviewing the whole project.[10]

State Practice and Implementation:

The Court, while on the issue of relief and rehabilitation of the tribals, noted:

> While accepting the legal proposition that International Treaties and Covenant can be read into domestic laws of the country the submission of the respondents was that Article 12 of the ILO Convention No. 107 stipulates that "the populations concerned shall not be removed without their free consent from their habitual territories except in accordance with national laws and regulations relating to national security, or in the interest of national economic development or of the health of the said populations".[11] The said Article clearly suggested that when the removal of the tribal population is necessary as exceptional measure, they shall be provided with land of quality at least equal to that of the land previously occupied by them and they shall be fully compensated for any resulting loss or injury.[12]

---

[10]   The Court did not agree to the review of the whole project.

[11]   With regard to the aspects of relief and rehabilitation (R&R), the Court elaborated further "...Displacement of people living on the proposed project sites and the areas to be submerged is an important issue. Most of the hydrology projects are located in remote and inaccessible areas, where local population is, like in the present case, either illiterate or having marginal means of employment and the per capita income of the families is low. It is a fact that people are displaced by projects from their ancestral homes. Displacement of these people would undoubtedly disconnect them from their past, culture, custom and traditions, but then it becomes necessary to harvest a river for larger good. A natural river is not only meant for the people close by but it should be for the benefit of those who can make use of it, being away from it or nearby. Realising the fact that displacement of these people would disconnect them from their past, culture, custom and traditions, the moment any village is earmarked for take over for dam or any other development activity, the project implementing authorities have to implement R&R programmes".

[12]   The Court also refers to various internal mechanisms such as Rehabilitation Committees, monitoring of rehabilitation programmes by concerned Government Agencies, and various forms of Grievance Redressal Mechanisms for the assistance of the project affected population.

Referring to 'water availability' as a basic need and a human right, the Court observed:

> Water is the basic need for the survival of human beings and is part of right of life and human rights as enshrined in Article 21 of the Constitution of India[13] and can be served only by providing a source of water where there is none. The Resolution of the UNO in 1977 to which India is a signatory, during the United Nations Water Conference resolved unanimously *inter alia* as under:
> "All people, whatever their stage of development and their social and economic conditions, have the right to have access to drinking water in quantum and of a quality equal to their basic needs"

Extradition – Extradited person can be tried only for offences mentioned in the extradition decree and for no other offences – Doctrine of Speciality under International Law – Evolution of extradition conventions and practices

DAYA SINGH LAHORIA v. UNION OF INDIA AND OTHERS

Supreme Court of India, 17 April 2001
AIR 2001 Supreme Court 1716

Facts

The Petitioner contended that the criminal courts in the country had no jurisdiction to try in respect of offences that did not form a part of the extradition judgment by virtue of which the petitioner was brought to this country, and he could be tried only for the offences mentioned in the extradition decree. Therefore, he could not be tried for offences other than the offences mentioned in the extradition order issued pursuant to an extradition treaty between India and USA.

The Petitioner also referred to Section 21 of the Extradition Act of India, 1962[14] (as amended in 1993) which provided:

> Whenever any person accused or convicted of an offence, which, if committed in India would be an extradition offence, is surrendered or returned by a foreign State, such person shall not, until he has been restored or has had an opportunity of returning to that State, be tried in India for an offence other than (a) the extradition offence in relation to which he was surrendered or returned; or (b) any lesser offence disclosed by the facts proved for the purposes of securing his surrender or return other than an offence in relation to which an order for his surrender or return could not be

---

[13] Article 21 provides "No person shall be deprived of his life or personal liberty except according to procedure established by law".
[14] The original Extradition Act, 1962 was amended in 1993 by Act 66 of 1993.

lawfully made; or (c) the offence in respect of which the foreign State has given its consent.

Reference was also made to Article 7 of the Extradition Treaty between India and USA[15] according to which:

> A person surrendered can in no case be kept in custody or be brought to trial in the territories of the High Contracting Party to whom the surrender has been made for any other crime or offence, or on account of any other matters, than those for which the extradition shall have taken place, until he has been restored, or has had an opportunity of returning, to the territories of the High Contracting Party by whom he has been surrendered. The stipulation does not apply to crimes or offences committed after the extradition.

State Practice and Implementation:

While noting that Section 21 of the Extradition Act was in consonance with Article 7 of the Extradition Treaty, the Court observed:

> ...Extradition is a great step towards international cooperation in the suppression of crime. It is for this reason the Congress of Comparative Law held at [The] Hague in 1932, resolved that States should treat extradition as an obligation "resulting from the international solidarity in the fight against crime". In Oppenheim, *International Law*, the expression is defined as "Extradition is a delivery of an accused or a convicted individual to the State on whose territory he is alleged to have committed or to have been convicted of a crime, by the State on whose territory the alleged criminal happens for the time to be". There is no rule of international law which imposes any duty on a State to surrender a fugitive in the absence of an extradition treaty. The law of extradition, therefore, is a dual law. It is ostensibly a municipal law; yet it is a part of international law also, inasmuch as it governs the relations between two sovereign States over the question whether or not a given person should be handed over by one sovereign State to another sovereign State. This question is decided by national Courts on the basis of international commitments as well as on the rules of international law relating to the subject. A number of attempts have been made to conclude a convention governing extradition requests among nations. The Pan American Conference of 1902 produced a treaty of extradition signed by twelve States, but it was not ratified. In 1933 the Seventh Pan American Conference concluded an Extradition Convention, which was ratified by number of States, including

---

[15] This was a treaty between the USA and the UK made applicable to India pursuant to section 2 (d) of the Extradition Act of India, 1962 according to which 'extradition treaty' means "a treaty (agreement or arrangement) made by India with a foreign State relating to the extradition of fugitive criminals and includes any treaty relating to the extradition of fugitive criminals made before the 15th day of August 1947 which extends to and is binding on India". The present Extradition Treaty between India and USA came into force on 21 July 1999.

United States of America, but the League Codification Committee had doubted the feasibility of the general convention on extradition. In 1935, the Harvard Law School brought out a draft convention on the subject. The International Law Association has also considered legal problems relating to extradition in the conference held at Warsaw. In 1928 the draft convention on extradition was approved but nothing has materialized in concluding a universal convention on extradition, notwithstanding the fact that most States earnestly believe in the efficacy and usefulness of extradition proceedings which each State has to resort to at one time or the other. The Asian-African Legal Consultative Body also prepared a draft convention on extradition at its meeting in Colombo in 1960. In September 1965, the Commonwealth Conference of Law Ministers and Chief Justices expressed the desire for a Commonwealth Convention on Extradition. In March 1966, the Commonwealth Law Ministers reached an agreement in London for the speedy extradition of fugitive between Commonwealth Counties. But, in the absence of any extradition convention, nations have resorted to bilateral extradition treaties by which they have agreed between themselves to surrender the accused or convict to the requesting State in case such person comes under the purview of the given treaty. Bilateral treaties at the international level are supplemented by national laws or legislation at the municipal level. Extradition treaties between nations, draft conventions and national laws and practices have revealed that some customary rules of international law have developed in the process. The doctrine of Speciality is yet another established rule of international law relating to extradition. Thus, when a person is extradited for a particular crime, he can be tried for only that crime. If the requesting State deems it desirable to try the extradited fugitive for some other crime committed before his extradition, the fugitive has to be brought to the *status quo ante*, in the sense that he has to be returned first to the State which granted the extradition and a fresh extradition has to be requested for the latter crime. The Indian Extradition Act makes a specific provision to that effect.

…The doctrine of speciality is in fact a corollary to the principles of double criminality, and the aforesaid doctrine is premised on the assumption that whenever a State uses its formal process to surrender a person to another State for a specific charge, the requesting State shall carry out its intended purpose prosecuting or punishing the offender for the offence charged in its request for extradition and none other.

Interpretation of Article II (2) of the New York Convention on Recognition and Enforcement of Foreign Arbitral Awards, 1958 – Scope of application of 'agreement in writing' in the context of an arbitration agreement – the contours of 'public policy' in the context of Indian law

SMITA CONDUCTORS v. EURO ALLOYS LTD

Supreme Court of India, 31 August 2001
AIR 2001 Supreme Court 3730

Facts

This case raised issues relating to the interpretation of Article II (2) of the New York Convention on the Recognition and Enforcement of Foreign Arbitral Awards, 1958 (hereinafter 'The New York Convention'). Article II of the Convention referred to "agreement in writing" and as to what constituted "agreement in writing".

In this case, a contract to supply certain items was proposed by the respondent to the appellant with an accompanying letter to complete the formalities of signing and returning a copy for the sake of good order. The Appellant neither signed nor returned the contract format. Reminders were also sent to which there was no response from the Appellant. Even the second contract was not signed. Shipments were, however, made by the Appellant on the basis of certain irrevocable letters of credit. In March 1991, the Reserve Bank of India (RBI) placed certain restrictions on the import of goods. In another notification, RBI modified the margins for opening letters of credit. The Appellant sent a telex to the Respondent to the effect that severe restrictions had been imposed by the RBI due to an unprecedented foreign exchange crisis. Accordingly, the Appellant further noted, RBI had not cleared his application for a letter of credit. Accordingly, the Appellant invoked the *force majeure* clause cancelling shipment for both the contracts.

The Respondent initiated arbitration proceedings with respect to both the contracts before the London Metal Exchange. While the arbitration proceedings continued before the London Metal Exchange, the Appellant had pursued litigation in India seeking revocation of the arbitration proceedings. Indian courts refused to intervene. Meanwhile, the arbitration proceedings before the London Metal Exchange were concluded and an award was issued against the Appellant. The Respondent filed a suit before the Mumbai High Court seeking enforcement of the said award. The Appellant filed this case seeking a declaration that there was no valid agreement between the parties as there was no 'agreement in writing' (in terms of Article II (2) of the New York Convention) and that the arbitration before the London Metal Exchange was void.

State Practice and Implementation:

The Appellant's contention was that a foreign award could be enforced if it was in pursuance of an agreement in writing for arbitration *vide* the New York Convention.[16] The arbitration award in the present case was not pursuant to an agreement in terms of Article II of the New York Convention. The expression 'agreement in

---

[16] India became a party to the New York Convention for the Enforcement of Foreign Arbitral Awards, 1958 on 13 July 1960. The New York Convention had been given effect by a separate legislation in India, namely the Foreign Arbitral Awards (Recognition and Enforcement) Act, 1961. This Act has been repealed in the new Arbitration and Conciliation Act, 1996 which is based on the United Nations Commission on International Trade Law (UNCITRAL) Model Law on International Commercial Arbitration, 1985. The New York Convention now forms part of the new 1996 Act and appears in the first schedule of the Act.

writing', according to Article II (2) of the New York Convention, would include an arbitral clause in a contract or an arbitration clause signed by the parties or contained in the exchange of letters or telegrams.[17]

The Respondent, on the other hand, argued that the correspondence between the parties and the conduct of the Appellant clearly established that there existed an arbitration clause between the parties and, therefore, there was full compliance with Article II of the New York Convention. The Court noted the submission of the Respondent in the following way:

> ...the definition of what constitutes a written arbitration agreement given in Article II (2) can be deemed to be an internationally uniform rule which prevails over any provisions of Municipal law regarding the form of the arbitration agreement in those cases where the Convention is applicable. The Courts in the contracting States have generally affirmed the uniform rule character of Article II (2).[18]

The Appellant contended that the award was contrary to public policy of India and RBI had issued certain circulars imposing restrictions on imports and, therefore, attracted the *force majeure* clause. The Court noted:

> The question of what is the 'public policy' has been considered by this Court in Renusagar's case by interpreting the words in section 7 (1) (b) (ii) of the Act to mean 'public policy of India and not of the country whose law governs the contract or of the country of place of arbitration'. In doing so, this Court took note of the fact that under Arbitration (Protocol and Convention) Act, 1937 the expression 'public policy of India' had been used, whereas the expression 'public policy' is used in the Act; that after the decision of this Court in V.O. Tractoroexport, Moscow v. Tarapore & Co. (1970) 3 SCR 53, S.3 was substituted to bring it in accord with the provisions of New York Convention on Arbitration, 1958 which seeks to remedy the defects in the Geneva Convention of 1927 that hampered the speedy settlement of disputes through arbitration; that to achieve this objective by dispensing with the requirement

---

[17] The Appellant in support of his argument cited several decisions of different Courts reported in the Year Book of International Commercial Arbitration, with particular reference to the interpretation of Article II of the New York Convention on 'agreement in writing'. Notable among them were: a case decided by the US District Court between *Sen Mar Inc (US) v. Tiger Petroleum Corporation N.V.* (1993) in which the Respondent's responsive telexes were held to be devoid of arbitration language; Italian Court of Appeal in *Finagrain Compagnie Commerciale Agricole et Financiere S.A. v. Patano Snc* (Italy) (1996) in which case there were three contracts and the Court upheld the validity of two contracts for the purpose of enforcement as per Article II of the New York Convention and found the third contract short of that requirement; Decision of the Swiss Court in *Gaetano Butera (Italy) v. Pietro e Romano Pagnan* (Italy) (1979) wherein arbitral clause was held to be void as it was signed by one of the parties.

[18] Reference has also been made to an earlier decision of the Indian Supreme Court in the case of *Renusagar Power Co. Ltd. v. General Electric Company* (1994) AIR 1994 Supreme Court 860. In this case the Supreme Court of India held that the New York Convention controlled the proceedings in arbitration.

of the leave to enforce the award by the Courts where the award is made and thereby avoid the problem of double exequatur; that the scope of enquiry is restricted before the Court enforcing the award by eliminating the requirement that the award should not be contrary to the principles of the law of the country in which it is sought to be relied upon; that enlarging the field of enquiry to include public policy of the country whose law governs the contract or of the country of place of arbitration would run contrary to the expressed intent of the legislation. Therefore, it was held that the words 'public policy' [are] intended to broaden the scope of enquiry so as to cover the policy of other countries, that is, the country whose law governs the contract or the country of the place of arbitration. In the absence of a definition of the expression 'public policy', it is construed to mean the doctrine of public policy as applied by the Courts in which the foreign award is sought to be enforced and this Court referred to a large catena of cases in this regard. Therefore, we will proceed on the basis that the expression 'public policy' means public policy of India, and the recognition and enforcement of foreign award cannot be questioned on the ground that it is contrary to the foreign country pubic policy and this expression has been used in a narrow sense must necessarily be construed as applied in private international law which means that a foreign award cannot be recognized or enforced if it is contrary to (1) fundamental policy of Indian law; or (2) the interests of India; or (3) justice or morality.

The Court rejected the contentions of the Appellant and decided not to interfere or modify the award made by the arbitrators.

Appointment of Arbitrators by the Court – Article 11 of the UNCITRAL Model Law on International Commercial Arbitration vis-à-vis section 11 of the Indian Arbitration and Conciliation Act, 1996 – Issues of compatibility

M/S KONKAN RAILWAY CORPORATION LTD v. M/S RANI CONSTRUCTION PVT LTD.

Supreme Court of India, 30 January 2002
AIR 2002 Supreme Court 778

Facts

The issue before the Constitution Bench of the Supreme Court was whether an order under Section 11 of the Arbitration and Conciliation Act, 1996[19] to appoint (or refuse to appoint) an arbitrator by the Chief Justice or any person designated by

---

[19] Section 11 deals with the appointment of arbitrators. If the parties fail to agree on the appointment of arbitrators, the Chief Justice or any other person designated by him could be requested to make the appointment. This provision is based on the UNCITRAL Model Law on International Commercial Arbitration.

him to take the necessary measure in this regard was an administrative order or a judicial order, and whether it was amenable to the jurisdiction of the Supreme Court under Article 136 of the Constitution.[20]

State Practice and Implementation:

The Section 11 of the Indian Arbitration and Conciliation Act, 1996 with regard to the appointment of arbitrators was based on Article 11 of the UNCITRAL Model Law. The Court noted:

> ...The Statement of Objects and Reasons of the Act states, "Though the said UNCITRAL Model Law and Rule are intended to deal with international commercial arbitration and conciliation, they could, with appropriate modifications, serve as a model for legislation on domestic arbitration and conciliation. The present Bill seeks to consolidate and amend the law relating to domestic arbitration, international commercial arbitration, enforcement of foreign arbitral awards and to define the law relating to conciliation, taking into account the said UNCITRAL Model Law and Rules". That the Model Law was only taken into account in the drafting of the said Act is, therefore, patent. The Act and the Model Law are not identically drafted. Under Section 11 the appointment of an arbitrator, in the event of a party to the arbitration agreement failing to carry out his obligation to appoint an arbitrator, is to be made by "the Chief Justice or any person or institution designated by him", under clause 11 of the Model Law it is to be made by a Court. Section 34 of the Act is altogether different from clause 34 of the Model Law. The Model Law and judgments and literature thereon are, therefore, not a guide to the interpretation of the Act and, especially of Section 11 thereof.

The Court, in conclusion, held that "...the order of the Chief Justice or his designate under section 11 nominating an arbitrator is not an adjudicatory order and the Chief Justice or his designate is not a tribunal".

---

[20] Article 136 of the Indian Constitution empowers the Supreme Court to grant special leave to appeal from any judgment, decree, sentence or order in any cause or matter passed or made by any Court or tribunal in the territory of India.

INDONESIA[21]

JUDICIAL DECISIONS

Crimes against humanity; universal jurisdiction

Injunction Decision No. 01/Pid HAM Ad Hoc/2002/PN JAKPUS dated 4 April 2002

PROSECUTOR OFFICE OF THE REPUBLIC OF INDONESIA v. ABILIO JOSE OSARIO SOARES

In this case Abilio Jose Osario Soares was accused of crimes against humanity under Law No. 26 of 2000. One of the arguments put forward by Soares in his defence was that the *ad hoc* Human Rights Court of the Central Jakarta Court did not have the competence to examine his case since the alleged crime was not considered as an act of crime when it happened and, thus, this was against the principle of *nullum crimen sine lege*.

The Court rejected Soares's argument, stating that crimes against humanity constitute an international crime. As an international crime the principle of universal jurisdiction applies. As a consequence, the principle *Nullum Crimen Sine Lege* can be put aside.

Injunction Decision No. 02/AD HOC/2002 dated 28 March 2002

PROSECUTOR OFFICE OF THE REPUBLIC OF INDONESIA v. TIMBUL SILAEN

In this case Timbul Silaen was accused of crimes against humanity under Law No. 26 of 2000. One of the arguments put forward by Silaen on the issue of jurisdiction was that the *ad hoc* Human Rights Court of the Central Jakarta Court did not have the jurisdiction to examine his case since the alleged crime occurred in East Timor, which was not in Jakarta.

The Court rejected Silaen's argument since crimes against humanity constitute an international crime. As an international crime the principle of universal jurisdiction applies. Under this principle any court may exercise jurisdiction to examine any alleged international crime.

---

[21] Contributed by Hikmahanto Juwana, Professor of International Law, University of Indonesia.

NATIONAL LAWS ON INTERNATIONAL LAW MATTERS

Anti-Terrorism Law

Republic of Indonesia, Government Regulation in Lieu of Law No. 1 of 2002 – "Combating Criminal Acts of Terrorism"[22]

On October 18, 2002 the President issued Government Regulation in Lieu of Law (hereinafter referred to as GRL) No. 1 of 2002 concerning the Eradication of Criminal Acts of Terrorism. This was a response to the Bali Bombing on 12 October 2002 which killed almost 200 holidaymakers, mostly foreigners.

The GRL provides several reasons for its promulgation. First, terrorism had claimed human lives intolerably and raised widespread fear among the community. It had also caused loss of freedom and damage to property. Therefore, measures need to be taken to eliminate the act of terrorism. In addition, the government acknowledged that terrorism has maintained extensive networks, such that it poses a threat to national and international peace and security. In order to meet national and international commitments to combat terrorism it was important to pass a national legislation with reference to international conventions relating to terrorism. Lastly, the GRL was a matter of urgency since there was as yet no legislation in Indonesia dealing comprehensively or adequately with combating criminal acts of terrorism.

The GRL applies to any person who commits or intends to commit a criminal act of terrorism in the territory of the Republic of Indonesia and/or another nation that has jurisdiction and expresses an intention to prosecute that person.

The GRL also applies to criminal acts of terrorism which are committed: (a) against the citizens of the Republic of Indonesia outside the territory of the Republic of Indonesia; (b) against the state facilities of the Republic of Indonesia overseas, including the premises of the diplomatic officials and consuls of the Republic of Indonesia; (c) with violence or threats of violence to force the Government of Indonesia to take or not to take an action; (d) to force any international organization in Indonesia to take or not take an action; (e) on board a vessel sailing under the flag of the Republic of Indonesia or an aircraft registered under the laws of the Republic of Indonesia at the time when the crime is committed; and (f) by any stateless person who resides in the territory of the Republic of Indonesia.

Under the GRL, the act of terrorism is divided into those who are committing the act of terrorism and those who have the intention to commit an act of terrorism.

There are various acts of terrorism defined under GRL. The most important is any person who intentionally uses violence or the threat of violence to create a widespread atmosphere of terror or fear in public or to create mass casualties, by forcibly taking the freedom, life or property of others or causes damage or destruction to vital strategic installations or the environment or public facilities or international facilities. Those who commit these kinds of acts of terrorism can be sentenced in

---

[22] The English translation is available at: http://www.law.unimelb.edu.au/alc/indonesia/gr_1.html (last visited 23 January, 2003)

the form of death penalty, life imprisonment, or a minimum sentence of 4 years and a maximum of 20 years. Those who have the intention to commit act of terrorism can be sentenced to a maximum of life imprisonment.

Other acts of terrorism are: (a) destroying, rendering inoperational or damaging facilities associated with air traffic and aviation security or causes the operation of such facilities to fail; (b) causing the destruction, inoperability or damage to facilities associated with aviation security or causes the operation of such facilities to fail; (c) intentionally and illegally destroying, damaging, removing or moving signs or equipment associated with aviation security, or causing the operation of said signs or equipment to fail, or erecting incorrect signs or equipment; (d) due to his or her negligence aviation security signs or equipment are destroyed, damaged, removed or moved or incorrect aviation security signs or equipment are erected; (e) intentionally and illegally destroying or rendering inoperational any aircraft partly or wholly belonging to another party; (f) intentionally and illegally causing the crash, destruction, rendering inoperational or damage to an aircraft; (g) through his or her negligence causes an aircraft to crash, be destroyed, in-operational or damaged; (h) for the purposes of self-enrichment or the enrichment of another person, illegally obtains insurance and then causes arson or explosion, crash, destruction, damage or renders inoperational an aircraft insured against danger or its contents or profit are insured against danger; (i) while aboard an aircraft uses illegal means to takeover, defend a takeover or otherwise control an aircraft in flight; (j) while aboard an aircraft uses violence or threats of violence or threats in any other form, takes over or defends a takeover or takes on control of an aircraft in flight; (k) jointly engages in a criminal plot, with prior planning, to cause serious injuries to any person, resulting in damage to an aircraft that could endanger the flight, committed with the intention of takeover of the freedom or of infringing upon the freedom of any person; (l) intentionally and illegally committing violence against a person in an aircraft in flight, where the act could endanger the safety of the aircraft; (m) intentionally and illegally damaging an aircraft on duty or causing damage to an aircraft that renders the aircraft incapable of flight or endangers the safety of the flight; (n) intentionally and illegally placing or causing to be placed aboard an aircraft on duty, by any means whatsoever, an object or substance capable of destroying an aircraft, rendering it incapable of flight or causing to the aircraft damage capable of endangering the flight; (o) jointly committing with two or more other persons as part of previously planned plot resulting in serious injuries to a person any act in point (l), (m) and (n); (p) providing information known to be false and thereby endangering the safety of an aircraft in flight; (q) while aboard an aircraft committing an act capable of endangering the safety of the aircraft in flight; and (r) while aboard an aircraft committing an act capable of disturbing law and order on the aircraft in flight.

Those who are found guilty of the above acts of terrorism can be sentenced in the form of the death penalty, life imprisonment, or a minimum prison sentence of four years and a maximum of 20 years.

It should be noted that the GRL provides that the various acts of terrorism will not be applicable to politically criminal acts nor to criminal acts relating to political crimes nor to criminal acts with political motives nor to criminal acts with the political objective of obstructing an extradition process.

The GRL also provides that any person who unlawfully imports into Indonesia, makes, receives, attempts to acquire, delivers or attempts to deliver, controls, carries, has the stock of his own or has in his possession, stores, transports, hides, uses, or carries in or out of Indonesia any firearm, ammunition, explosive substance or other dangerous material with the intention to commit any act of terrorism is a criminal act. The sentence for those found guilty can be in the form of death penalty, life imprisonment, or a minimum prison sentence of three years and a maximum of 20 years.

In addition, a person will be criminally charged under the GRL if such person intentionally uses chemical or biological weapons, radiology, micro-organisms, radioactivity or its components to create an atmosphere of terror or fear in the general population, causes large number of casualties, causes danger to health, to cause chaos to life, security, and other people's rights, or to cause damage and destruction to vital strategic installations or the environment or public facilities, or international facilities. The sentence for those found guilty can be in the form of death penalty, life imprisonment, or a minimum prison sentence of four years and a maximum of 20 years.

Furthermore, those who intentionally provide or collects funds with the objective that they be used or there is a reasonable likelihood to be used partly or wholly for criminal acts of terrorism will bear criminal responsibility under the GRL. Those who are found guilty can be sentenced of a minimum of four years of imprisonment or a maximum of 15 years.

Moreover, a person can be qualified as committing an act of terrorism if such person intentionally provides or collects assets with the objective to be used or there is a reasonable likelihood to be used partly or wholly for: (a) committing any unlawful act of receiving, possessing, using, delivering, modifying or discarding nuclear materials, chemical weapons, biological weapons, radiology, micro-organism, radio-activity or its components that causes death or serious injuries or causes damage to assets; (b) stealing or seizing nuclear materials, chemical weapons, biological weapons, radiology, micro-organism, radioactivity or its components; (c) embezzling or acquiring illegally nuclear materials, chemical weapons, biological weapons, radiology, micro-organism, radioactivity or its components; (d) requesting nuclear materials, chemical weapons, biological weapons, radiology, micro-organism, radio-activity or its components; (e) threatening to: (1) use such nuclear materials, chemical or biological weapons, radiology, micro-organisms, radioactivity or its components to cause death or injuries or damage to properties; or (2) commit criminal acts as stipulated in (b) with the intention to force another person, an international organiza-tion, or another country to take or not to take an action; (f) attempting to commit any criminal act as stipulated in (a), (b) or (c); and (g) participating in committing any criminal act as stipulated in (a) to (f).

The sentence for those found guilty is imprisonment within a minimum prison sentence of three years and a maximum of 15 years.

The GRL also provides that any person who intentionally provides assistance to any perpetrator of criminal acts of terrorism by: (a) providing or lending money or goods or other assets to any perpetrator of criminal acts of terrorism; (b) harbouring any perpetrator of any criminal act of terrorism; or (c) hiding any information on any criminal act of terrorism will be criminally charged. The sentence for those found guilty is imprisonment with a minimum sentence of three years and a maximum of 15 years.

Furthermore, any person who plans and/or incites other person to commit any criminal act of terrorism can be sentenced either to the death penalty or to life imprisonment.

Moreover, any person who conducts any plot, attempt, or assistance to commit any criminal act of terrorism will be sentenced the same as those who are committing any such act of terrorism.

One interesting point to note is the GRL can also be applied to those who provide any assistance, facilities, means or information for the committing of any criminal act of terrorism which are outside the territory of the Republic of Indonesia. The sentence is the same as the sentence for those committing the act of terrorism.

Another interesting point is the GRL provides for criminal responsibility of corporations involved in any act of terrorism. It is stipulated that in the event an act of terrorism is committed by or on behalf of a corporation, the prosecution and sentencing shall be carried out against such a corporation or its management. An act of terrorism shall be deemed to have been committed by a corporation if the criminal act is committed by persons who, based on their work relationship or other relationships, act in the environment of such corporation either individually or jointly. In the event the prosecution is brought against a corporation, then its management shall represent the corporation.

The GRL also stipulates other criminal offences related to acts of terrorism. To take an example, any person who uses violence or the threat of violence or who intimidates detectives, investigators, public prosecutors, solicitors and/or judges who are handling any criminal act of terrorism, so as to hamper the judicial process, will be criminally charged. The sentence is a minimum imprisonment of three years to a maximum of 15 years. Another example is a person who provides false testimonies, submits false material evidence, and unlawfully influences witnesses during a court session or attacks the witnesses, including the court officials in the trial of a criminal act of terrorism, can also be criminally charged. The sentence is imprisonment of a minimum of three years and a maximum of 15 years.

The GRL introduces a novel procedure from ordinary criminal procedure, that is, an investigator may use any intelligence report as preliminary evidence. However, the GRL provides that the adequacy of the preliminary evidence obtained must be determined through an inquiry process by the Head or its Deputy of the District Court. The inquiry process is conducted in closed session within a maximum period of 3 (three) working days.

The GRL provides various extraordinary powers to investigators, public prosecutors and judges.

Investigators may detain any person strongly suspected of committing a criminal act of terrorism based on adequate preliminary evidences for a maximum period of seven times twenty-four hours.

Investigators, public prosecutors or judges are authorized to order banks and other financial institutions to freeze the assets of any individual whose assets are known or reasonably suspected to be the proceeds of any criminal act connected to terrorism.

In addition the GRL provides that for the purpose of investigation, the investigators, public prosecutors or judges are authorized to request information from banks and other financial institutions regarding the assets of any person who is known or strongly suspected of having committed a criminal act of terrorism.

Furthermore, investigators are authorized (a) to open, examine and confiscate mail and packages by post or other means of delivery; and (b) to intercept any conversation by telephone or other means of communication suspected of being used to prepare, plan and commit a criminal act of terrorism. However, investigators may intercept only when based on an order of the Head of the District Court for a maximum period of one year.

The GRL stipulates protection for those involved in the criminal process of terrorism case. Witnesses, investigators and judges and their families are entitled to protection by the State from any possible threat endangering themselves, their lives and/or properties including before, during or after the investigation process.

The Court may examine and render a decision even if the defendant is not present (in absentia). This occurs if the defendant has been officially and appropriately summoned but without valid reason does not appear before the court.

The GRL also imposes an obligation on the state to pay compensation and restitution to victims of terrorist acts. It provides that any victim and the family of victims of a wrong act of terrorism shall be eligible for compensation and/or restitution. In addition, any individual shall be entitled to rehabilitation if he/she is discharged of all legal charges by the court with permanent legal power.

The GRL obligates Indonesia to conduct international cooperation with other nations in the areas of intelligence, the police department and other technical cooperation connected with anti-terrorism measures in accordance with the applicable legislative provisions.

The GRL stipulates that provisions of the GRL may be applied retroactively to acts of terrorism that occurred prior to the promulgation of this GRL, provided that such application is determined by legislation in the form of an Act of a GRL.

Republic of Indonesia, Government Regulation in Lieu of Law No. 2 of 2002 – "The Enactment of Government Regulation in Lieu of Legislation Number 1, 2002 on Combating Criminal Acts of Terrorism, in relation to the Bombing in Bali on 12 October 2002"[23]

---

[23] The English translation is available at: http://www.law.unimelb.edu.au/alc/indonesia/gr_2.html (last visited 23 January 2003).

On the same day the Government issued GRL 1 of 2002, another GRL was issued known as GRL No. 2 of 2002. The GRL is issued by taking into account the retroactive provision provided under GRL 1 of 2002. GRL 2 of 2002 is issued to give legal basis for the perpetrator of the Bali bombing to be prosecuted based on GRL 1 of 2002.

GRL 2 of 2002 contains only two articles. Article 1 provides that the provisions of GRL 1 of 2002 are deemed to take effect in relation to the bombing incident which occurred in Bali on 12 October 2002. Article 2 provides that the GRL take effect on the date it was enacted.

The reason for applying GRL 1 of 2002 retroactively is found in the elucidation of GRL 2 of 2002. It is stated that terrorism is considered as a crime against humanity and civilization.

AIR LAW

Republic of Indonesia, Government Regulation No. 3 of 2001 – "Aviation Security and Safety"

On February 5, 2001 Indonesia issued Government Regulation (hereinafter abbreviated as "GR") No. 3 of 2001 concerning Aviation Security and Safety as implementing regulation of provisions under Law 15 of 1992 concerning Aviation.

The GR provides detailed rules on aviation security and safety. The Minister in charge of civil aviation has the responsibility to assure aviation security and safety. The GR gives the Minister the power to regulate, control and supervise a range of activities from designing, manufacturing, operating and maintenance of aircraft to navigation service and airport operation, as well as determining the requirement for aviation personnel.

To take an example, the Minister has the responsibility to determine the requirements for aircraft reliability and, thus, provides guidelines in the design, manufacturing, operation and maintenance of aircraft.

Furthermore, the GR stipulates in detail provisions on the use and operation of an aircraft. It provides that the commercial operation of the aircraft for air transport purposes can be carried out only by aircraft operators holding a certificate issued by the Minister.

The GR also regulates Indonesia's air space and traffic, and contains provisions on search and rescue in the event of an aircraft accident, as well as protection regarding pollution of the air.

SPACE LAW

Republic of Indonesia, Law No. 16 of 2002 – "The Ratification of Treaty on Principles Governing the Activities of States in the Exploration and Use of Outer Space, Including the Moon and Other Celestial Bodies, 1967"

On April 17, 2002, Indonesia finally ratified the Treaty on Principles Governing the Activities of States in the Exploration and Use of Outer Space, Including the Moon and Other Celestial Bodies (Space Treaty 1967). The main reason for Indonesia's not acceding earlier to the Space Treaty of 1967 was due to Indonesia's claim over the Geo-stationery Orbit (hereinafter abbreviated as "GSO").

For many years Indonesia along with other equatorial countries has been struggling for their claim of the GSO. In December 3, 1977 in Bogotá, the equatorial countries issued a declaration known as the Bogotá Declaration to claim the GSO above their territories.

The ratification of the Space Treaty of 1967 has put an end to the long struggle by Indonesia over the GSO.

LAW OF THE SEA

Republic of Indonesia, Government Regulation No. 37 of 2002 – "The Rights and Obligations of Foreign Ships and Aircraft when Exercising the Right of Archipelagic Sea Lanes Passage through Established Archipelagic Sea Lanes"[24]

On June 28, 2002 the Government issued GR No. 37 of 2002. The GR is intended to serve as implementing regulation of Law 6 of 1996 concerning Indonesian Waters. Under Law 6 of 1996 it is provided that the government has the authority to determine the sea lanes, including flight routes above the sea lanes. In addition, it has the responsibility to regulate the rights and obligations of foreign ships and aircraft when exercising the right of sea lanes passage in the archipelagic waters.

Under GR 37 of 2002, foreign ships and aircraft may exercise the right of archipelagic sea lanes passage in order to sail or fly from one part of the high seas or an exclusive economic zone to another part of the high seas or an exclusive economic zone through or over the Indonesian territorial sea and its archipelagic waters.

The archipelagic sea lane that may be used for exercising the right of archipelagic sea lanes passage for sailing from the South China Sea to the Indian Ocean or *vice versa* through the Natuna Sea, the Karimata Strait, the Java Sea and the Sunda Strait is Archipelagic Sea Lane I.

The archipelagic sea lane that may be used for exercising the right of archipelagic sea lanes passage for sailing from the Sulawesi Sea to the Indian Ocean or *vice versa* through the Makassar Strait, the Flores Sea and the Lombok Strait is Archipelagic Sea Lane II.

The archipelagic sea lane that may be used for exercising the right of archipelagic sea lanes passage for sailing from the Pacific Ocean to the Indian Ocean or *vice versa* through the Maluku Sea, the Seram Sea, the Banda Sea, the Ombai Strait and the Sawu Sea is Archipelagic Sea Lane IIIA.

---

[24] The English translation is available at http://www.law.unimelb.edu.au/alc/assets/ships_aircraft.doc (last visited 23 January 2003).

The Archipelagic Sea Lane IIIA, includes (a) Archipelagic Sea Lane Branch IIIB, which joins Archipelagic Sea Lane IIIA at point IIIA-8, for sailing from the Pacific Ocean to the Indian Ocean or *vice versa* through the Maluku Sea, the Seram Sea, the Banda Sea and the Leti Strait, of which the axis is the line that joins connecting points IIIA-8, IIIB-1 and IIIB-2; Archipelagic Sea Lane Branch IIIC, which joins Archipelagic Sea Lane Branch IIIB at point IIIB-1, for sailing from the Pacific Ocean to the Arafura Sea or *vice versa* through the Maluku Sea, the Seram Sea and the Banda Sea, of which the axis is the line that joins connecting points IIIB-1, IIIC-1 and IIIC-2; Archipelagic Sea Lane Branch IIID, which joins Archipelagic Sea Lane IIIA at point IIIA-11, for sailing from the Pacific Ocean to the Indian Ocean or *vice versa* through the Maluku Sea, the Seram Sea, the Banda Sea, the Ombai Strait and the Sawu Sea, of which the axis is the line that joins connecting points IIIA-11 and IIID-1; Archipelagic Sea Lane Branch IIIE, which joins Archipelagic Sea Lane IIIA at point IIIA-2, for sailing from the Indian Ocean to the Sulawesi Sea or *vice versa* through the Sawu Sea, the Ombai Strait, the Banda Sea, the Seram Sea and the Maluku Sea, or for sailing from the Timor Sea to the Sulawesi Sea or *vice versa* through the Leti Strait, the Banda Sea, the Seram Sea and the Maluku Sea, or for sailing from the Arafura Sea to the Sulawesi Sea or *vice versa* through the Banda Sea, the Seram Sea and the Maluku Sea, of which the axis is the line that joins connecting points IIIA-2, IIIE-1 and IIIE-2.

It should be noted that a provision under the GR stated that the list could be amended and adjusted. The government will renew it routinely to improve and complete the shortcomings of the geographical coordinates of outer points drawing the archipelago baselines. In addition if there are new data or there are changes to the baselines, the list will be amended and adjusted accordingly.

HUMAN RIGHTS

Republic of Indonesia, Government Regulation No. 2 of 2002 – "Procedures on Protection of Victims and Witnesses for Gross Violations of Human Rights"

The GR provides that victims and witnesses of gross violations of human rights have the right to obtain protection from the law enforcer and security apparatus. The protection is rendered at the beginning of investigation process, prosecution and examination before the court.

The forms of protection include safeguarding personal safety, concealing identities, and the provision of court testimony without being seen by the accused.

Protection of victims and witnesses is rendered based on the discretion of the law enforcer and security apparatus, or request by the victims and witnesses. If a request is made, such request has to be addressed to the National Commission on Human Rights in the investigation phase; to the Attorney General Office at the prosecution phase; and to the Court at the examination phase. The request will be passed through the security apparatus by those institutions. Law enforcement and security apparatus upon receiving a request will verify the ground for such request and identify the form of protection necessary.

Protection will be terminated if the victims or witnesses submit a request for termination, the victims of witnesses die or, based on the decision of the law enforcer or security apparatus, the protection is no longer necessary .

The GR provides that victims or witnesses shall not be charged any fees for the protection rendered. The cost of protections is borne by the law enforcers or security apparatus.

Republic of Indonesia, Government Regulation No. 3 of 2002 – "Compensation, Restitution and Rehabilitation for Victim of Gross Violations of Human Rights"

The GR provides for compensation, restitution and rehabilitation for victims of gross violations of human rights.[25] Compensation is defined as money paid by the state if the perpetrator found guilty by the Court could not afford to pay compensation to the victims. The Court defines restitution as money paid by the perpetrator found guilty. Rehabilitation is defined as to rehabilitate a victim to his or her position, such as dignity, good name, position and other rights.

In the event the victim of gross violation of human rights has died, the heirs and successors are entitled to receive the restitution or compensation.

The state is required to provide compensation in the event the person responsible is unable to provide for the remuneration set by the court. The execution of payment will become the responsibility of the Ministry of Finance.

JAPAN[26]

JUDICIAL DECISIONS

Detention of a Korean fishing boat engaging in the fisheries activities within the maritime area newly incorporated into the Japanese territorial sea following the adoption of straight baselines; Effect on the prior fisheries agreement of the new straight baselines for the delimitation of the territorial sea

---

[25] Under Law 26 of 1999 the term "gross violation of human rights" consisted of crimes against humanity and genocide. The two are commonly referred to as "international crimes".

[26] Contributed by Yakushiji Kimio, Ritsumeikan Asia Pacific University, member of the Study Group on Decisions of Japanese Courts Relating to International Law.

X v. STATE OF JAPAN

Supreme Court, 30 November 1999[27]
**Keishu [Supreme Court Reports: Criminal Cases] Vol.53 No.8 (1999) 1045;
Hanrei Jiho [Law Cases Reports] No.1694 (1999)155; Hanrei Times [Law Times
Reports] No.1017 (1999) 114**

Since the Hiroshima High Court, Matsue Branch reversed the original judgment
and remanded the case to the Matsue District Court, X made a *jokoku* appeal to the
Supreme Court, arguing that the decision of the Hiroshima High Court erred in its
judgment with regard to the legality of the drawing of the straight baseline in question
in this case as well as in the interpretation of the Korean-Japanese Fisheries Agreement [1965] and, therefore, the decision of the Hiroshima High Court violated article
98 (2) of the Japanese Constitution, which provides that the treaties concluded by
Japan shall be faithfully observed. The Supreme Court dismissed the appeal on the
ground that the object of the appeal was to argue a mere violation of laws and
regulations even if the Appellant invoked the Constitution, and consequently that
the argument did not constitute the statutory ground for *jokoku* appeal.[28] However,
the Supreme Court held as follows:
The original judgment (of the Hiroshima High Court) is to be duly approved, which
held that the exercise of Japan's adjudicatory jurisdiction over an illegal act committed
in the area concerned[29] was not to be restricted by the Japanese-Korean Fisheries
Agreement [1965] (the one before its nullification on 22 January 1999)[30] since the
maritime area in question where the accused was held to have engaged in fishing
activities on 9 June 1997 in violation of article 3, paragraph 1, of the Law for
Regulation of Fishing Operations by Foreign Nationals had been newly incorporated
into the Japanese territorial sea since 1 January 1997, in accordance with articles
1 and 2 of the Law on the Territorial Sea and the Contiguous Zone [1996] and article
2, paragraph 2, of its Enforcement Order (Cabinet Order).

**Disqualification of a child born out of lawful wedlock but acknowledged by the
father as his own in respect of child support allowance; Discrimination against
a child born out of wedlock**

---

[27] Through appeal from Hiroshima High Court, Matsue Branch, 11 September 1998, 8 AsYIL 154.
See also the 15 August 1997 Decision of the Matsue District Court, Hamada Branch, 7 AsYIL 287.
[28] Article 405 of the Law of Criminal Procedure limits the compulsory grounds for *jokoku* appeal
to the Supreme Court to a violation of the Constitution; a violation of a treaty has been deemed
as a violation of an ordinary law enacted by the Diet.
[29] The point where the fishing boat was seized was approximately 18.9 miles north-west of Hamada,
Shimane Prefecture and had been outside the Japanese territorial sea until Japan adopted straight
baselines for the delimitation of its territorial sea.
[30] The Japanese-Korean Fisheries Agreement of 1965 was replaced by the new Japanese-Korean
Fisheries Agreement, which was signed on 28 November 1998 and entered into force on 22 January
1999.

THE GOVERNOR OF KYOTO PREFECTURE v. X

Osaka High Court, 16 May 2000
Shomugeppo [Monthly Bulletin on Law Suits] Vol.47 No.4 (2001) 917

The Appellee (the plaintiff of the first instance) gave birth to a child out of lawful wedlock and was provided with a child support allowance by Kyoto Prefecture in 1987. However, the Appellant (the defendant of the first instance) decided to disqualify her for the child support allowance in September, 1995 for the reason that the child had been recognized by his father in January, 1994. Though she lodged an objection against this decision, the Appellant dismissed her claim. Then she brought her case before the Kyoto District Court for the annulment of the said decision.

Article 1 of the Child Support Allowance Law provides that the purpose of the Law is to promote children's welfare by providing children unsupported by their fathers with a child support allowance. For this purpose article 4, paragraph 1, of the Law obligates the local governor to provide any mother taking care of a child whose parents have dissolved their marriage or whose father is dead. Any mother taking care of children placed under a similar situation and defined as such by a cabinet order is also included in the beneficiaries of the child support allowance (article 4, paragraph 1, item 5). The Order for Enforcement of the Child Support Allowance Law defined the category of children qualified for child support allowance pursuant to the delegation of authority prescribed in article 4, paragraph 1, item 5, of the Child Support Allowance Law. According to article 1-2, item 3, of the said Order for Enforcement (before it was amended in accordance with the Cabinet Order No. 224 of 1998[31]) "any child who was conceived by the mother out of lawful wedlock (or under circumstances similar to de facto marriage although marriage is not registered)" qualifies for child support allowance "(except any child acknowledged by the father as his own)".

The Kyoto District Court held that the exception in parentheses that excludes "any child acknowledged by the father as his own" from any child who was conceived by the mother out of lawful wedlock was illegal and thus invalid, on the ground that the exception deviated from the scope of delegation of authority set forth under the Child Support Allowance Law, article 1 of which designated any child unsupported by his or her father as a beneficiary of the child support allowance.

Contrary to this, the Osaka High Court held that the said exception did not violate article 14 of the Constitution[32] or did not manifestly deviate from or abuse the discretionary powers given to the government under the Child Support Allowance Law, given that the government was empowered under the Law to decide by its

---

[31] The Cabinet Order No. 224 of 1998 deleted the words "(except any child acknowledged by the father as his own)" in article 1-2, item 3, of the Order for Enforcement of the Child Support Allowance Law.

[32] Article 14 of the Constitution provides: "All of the people are equal under the law and there shall be no discrimination in political, economic or social relations because of race, creed, sex, social status or family origin."

discretion the range of beneficiaries of the child support allowance among the children unsupported by their father or under a similar situation and that the living conditions of those children who were recognized by their father could be considered improved in the eyes of the law. In this litigation the Appellee (plaintiff) argued that the exception in question violated articles 2, 24 and 26 of the International Covenant on Civil and Political Rights (hereinafter referred to as the ICCPR), and article 2, paragraph 1, and article 26 of the Convention on the Rights of Child (hereinafter referred to as the CRC), as well as the Convention on the Elimination of Discrimination against Women. The Osaka High Court dismissed these arguments, holding as follows (in summary):

Since Japan has not ratified the Optional Protocol to the ICCPR and has not declared under article 41 of the ICCPR that it recognizes the competence of the Human Rights Committee (hereinafter referred to as the HRC) to receive and consider communications from other States Parties, its obligation under the ICCPR is limited to submitting reports set forth in article 40. The general comments [especially on articles 2 and 26[33] in this case] have no binding force upon the States Parties and are expected to be referred to only as a guideline when they interpret and implement the ICCPR. In addition, the right to child support allowance in question is a social right and thus falls under the International Covenant on Economic, Social and Cultural Rights (hereinafter referred to as the ICESCR). Article 9 of the ICESCR does not require that States Parties recognize the right to social security as a concrete right to be realized immediately. Certainly, article 2, paragraph 2, requires a social right to be equally implemented. However, whether or not a specific social security system shall be established should be judged and decided, taking into account the economic and social conditions of the time as well as the general living conditions of citizens. Furthermore, in materializing a specific legislation on social security allowance, one cannot disregard the financial conditions of the State and such legislation needs complex and highly technical considerations for various issues to be solved. Therefore, choice and decision of particular legislation is left to a wide discretion of the Diet. The ICESCR declares that States Parties have political responsibility to positively promote their social security policy in order to realize the rights enumerated in the Covenant, and does not lay down that individuals be provided immediately with specific rights. Since the government did not manifestly deviate from or abuse its discretionary powers under the Child Support Allowance Law in this case, there is no violation of the ICCPR.

Though article 2, paragraph 1, of the CRC stipulates that States Parties shall respect and ensure the rights set forth in the Convention without discrimination of any kind, its article 26 [paragraph 2[34]] provides that the benefits should, where appropriate, be granted, taking into account the resources and circumstances of the child and persons responsible for the support of the child, as well as any other consideration relevant to an application for benefits made by or on behalf of the child. Thus the Convention does not require States Parties to provide all fatherless families

---

[33] Added by the author.
[34] Added by the author.

uniformly with the right to the benefits of the child support allowance. The concluding observations of the Committee on the Rights of the Child concerning Japan's first report is of a nature of "suggestions and general recommendations" based on article 45 of the Convention and therefore has no legally binding force on the Japanese domestic jurisdiction. Furthermore, the said concluding observations say nothing about whether or not article 1-2, item 3, of the Order for Enforcement of the Child Support Allowance Law contravenes the Convention. Thus it cannot be held that this provision violates the CRC.

Since the child support allowance is not provided for female children in a discriminatory way, no problem arises in respect of the Convention on the Elimination of Discrimination against Women.[35]

Sovereign Immunity of the Republic of Nauru and the Republic of Nauru Finance Corporation from the civil law jurisdiction of Japanese Courts; Waiver of the immunity made in the bond documents

KLESCH & COMPANY LIMITED v. THE REPUBLIC OF NAURU FINANCE CORPORATION *ET AL*

Tokyo District Court, 30 November 2000
Hanrei Jiho[Law Times Reports] No.1740 (2001) 54

The defendant, the Republic of Nauru Finance Corporation (hereinafter referred to as "RONFIN"), was created under the Republic of Nauru Finance Corporation Act in 1972. The plaintiff, Klesch & Company Limited (hereinafter referred to as "Klesch"), is a privately owned British company created in 1990. On 27 July 1989, RONFIN issued bearer bonds called RONFIN Japanese Yen Bonds Series C (hereinafter referred to as Series C Bonds), having an aggregate face value of five billion yen. Another defendant, the Republic of Nauru, unconditionally secured the repayment of the principal of the Series C Bonds and its interest. Although the RONFIN Series C Bonds were originally due for repayment on 27 July 1994, by agreement of the original bondholders the maturity date was postponed stage by stage to 27 April 1995. However, RONFIN made no payment of the bond debt from 27 July 1994 and the bond became defaulted on 27 April 1995. Klesch purchased certain Series C Yen Bonds with a face value of one billion yen before the bonds were to have matured and registered its ownership of the Series C Bonds in Japan on 18 May 1995. Klesch filed suit against RONFIN and the Republic of Nauru for repayment of the bond debt on 1 June 1995. While RONFIN and the Republic initially refused

---

[35] The Appellee made a *jokoku* appeal against this decision to the Supreme Court. The Supreme Court held on 31 January 2002 that the exception of article 1-2, item 3, of the Order for Enforcement of the Child Support Allowance Law was illegal and invalid on the ground that the stipulation deviated from the scope of delegation of authority set forth under the said Law. The decision says nothing about whether the said exception violates the ICCPR and CRC.

to accept the service of a summons sent through diplomatic channels on the ground that RONFIN and the Republic were immune from Japanese courts' jurisdiction, RONFIN and the Republic asserted sovereign immunity under international customary law before the Tokyo District Court through their counsel.

Series C Bonds include commitments that any lawsuit against RONFIN may be filed with Tokyo District Court and other higher courts competent to accept appeals from Tokyo District Court to the jurisdiction of which RONFIN is to be unconditionally and irrevocably subject and that RONFIN unconditionally and irrevocably waives immunities it has and would have from the proceedings arising out of Series C Bonds debt and filed against it, including service, adjudgment, attachment and execution, to the extent that the applicable law permits. The Republic of Nauru made the same commitments in connection with its security of RONFIN's bond in the same Series C Bonds.

Tokyo District Court held that neither the Republic of Nauru nor RONFIN enjoys sovereign immunity from the jurisdiction of the court for the following reasons:

Both the Republic and RONFIN expressed explicitly their intention to submit to the jurisdiction of the Tokyo District Court in the proceedings relating to Series C Bonds as well as the intention to waive immunity from the proceedings in Japan including judgments on merits. The cause of this lawsuit relates to economic activities extensively and widely performed in the international society in these days. Furthermore, the intention to choose courts other than the Republic of Nauru's courts as competent courts to deal with disputes arising out of the Series C Bonds, as well as to waive immunity from the jurisdiction of such courts, is explicitly expressed in the clauses of commitments written in the said bonds. In these circumstances, the court cannot affirm that to give the foreign State and its organ immunity from the jurisdiction of domestic courts is required by customary rules of international law, which Japan shall observe as "established laws of nations" under article 98, paragraph 2, of the Constitution.

Having traced the historical development of the theory on immunity from the so-called doctrine of absolute immunity to that of restrictive immunity, as well as the recent tendency of national legislation and the European Convention of 1972 to adopt restrictive immunity, the Tokyo District Court concluded as follows:

Based on the economic nature of the cause of this claim, that is, the flotation of bonds secured by the government as well as the explicit waiver made in the commitment written in the bonds, the Court cannot accept the argument that the Defendants shall be immune from the jurisdiction of Japanese courts in the proceedings of this case according to customary international law on sovereign immunity. Therefore, the court need not consider whether or not RONFIN is a genuine State organ, the purpose of the flotation of the Series C Bonds and the other issues posed by the Defendants.

KOREA[36]

JUDICIAL DECISIONS*

Recognition of Refugee Status and Its Legitimacy
Seoul Administrative Court, 16 August 2001
99Gu1990 Judgment

A.M.A.M. v. MINISTER OF DEPARTMENT OF JUSTICE

1. The plaintiff was a foreigner holding an Iraqi passport. He entered Korea on 14 May 1995 after getting a tourist visa at the Korean embassy in Jordan. He worked at the city of Incheon before finally applying for refugee status to the Ministry of Department of Justice in accordance with Article 76, para. 2 of the Immigration Control Law of Korea.

The application for refugee status was however rejected by the Minister of Department of Justice on 30 December 1998 because the plaintiff could not prove the condition of a 'well-founded fear of being persecuted' as laid down at Article 1 of the 1951 Convention relating to the Status of Refugees (hereinafter, The 1951 Convention).

The Plaintiff then instituted a lawsuit against the Minister of Department of Justice for revoking the decision of not granting refugee status.

2. Decision on 'Well-Founded Fear of Being Persecuted'

The 1951 Convention defines a 'refugee' as a person who 'owing to a well-founded fear of being persecuted for reasons of race, religion, nationality, membership of a particular social group or political opinion, is outside the country of his nationality and is unable or, owing to such fear, is unwilling to avail himself of the protection of that country; or who, not having a nationality and being outside the country of his former habitual residence as a result of such events, is unable or owing to such fear, is unwilling to return to it'.[37] In this case whether the plaintiff had a 'well-founded fear of being persecuted' in his country was the most controversial question.

Since Saddam Hussein took office on 16 July 1979, the domestic and human rights situation in Iraq had been serious; many people were illegally arrested, tortured and confined under his dictatorial rule.

The Plaintiff contended that he had carried out anti-government activities including the distribution of printed matters and criticizing the Hussein regime as a member of a secret student organization of Baghdad University which was a sub-organ of

---

[36] Contributed by Eric Yong-Joong Lee, Assistant Professor, Seoul National University College of Law, Korea.

* Contributed by Eric Yong-Joong Lee, Dongguk University College of Law, Korea

[37] Art. 1(A) of the 1951 Convention. This definition was slightly expanded at the meeting of the Organization of African Unity in 1969, but its substance still revolves around the concept of political defection. For details, see P. Kourula, *Broadening the Edges: Refugee Definition and International Protection Revisited* (The Hague: Kluwer Law International, 1997), pp. 49-62.

the Kurd Democratic Party. He also asserted that he participated in an anti-Hussein demonstration around March 1991. If the insistence of the Plaintiff was true, he should have been arrested and punished by the Iraqi government. If the Plaintiff was a member of anti-government organization involved in anti-Hussein activities he would have been watched by the secret police of Iraq. However, the Plaintiff completed military service between September 1988 and May 1991 and obtained a passport for emigration without any difficulties.

The Plaintiff also contended that he was severely discriminated against by the Iraqi government because he is a Kurd. He maintained that he was arrested at a park by the police while dating his girl friend when he was a senior college student. At the police station, he was tortured and threatened just because he was a Kurd. Although Kurds were actually not in a good position in Iraq, they were not severely discriminated against if they did not directly participate in the liberation movement.

3. The Plaintiff did not go back to Iraq even after the term of validity of the passport had expired. He then altered the term on the passport illegally. However, despite his insistence, there is no clear evidence that would prove that the Plaintiff was involved in the liberation movement of the Kurds and took part in anti-Hussein regime activities. Considering that the Plaintiff graduated from Baghdad University and was granted a veterinarian license as well as serving in the military forces of Iraq, he was presumably not persecuted due to his ethnic origin.

4. The Plaintiff did not therefore have a 'well-founded fear of being persecuted' as laid down at Article 1 of the 1951 Convention. Therefore, the Plaintiff could not be regarded as a refugee under Article 2(2)(2) of the Immigration Control Law. Following this reasoning the Court turned down the Plaintiff's request for cancelling the original decision of the defendant regarding the non-granting of refugee status.

Direct Application of Treaty

Supreme Court, 22 October 2002, 2002Da32523, 32530 Judgment

ARAH MARINE CO. v. MARINE JEWELRY

1. The so-called contracting carrier who made the transportation contract with passengers, senders or their representatives according to the Warsaw Convention for the Unification of Certain Rules Relating to International Carriage by Air as amended at The Hague of 1955 (hereinafter, the Warsaw Convention), and who mandated its implementation to the actual carrier is a carrier under the Warsaw Convention.

Considering that the Plaintiff made the transportation contract with the Defendant to convey the freight from the Kimpo airport of Korea to Los Angeles airport, issued the transportation invoice and then made a separate air transportation contract with Asiana airlines co. for the transportation of goods, the transportation of freight in this case is the international air transportation under the revised Warsaw Convention and the Plaintiff is the transporter in the contract. Therefore, it is right that the revised Warsaw Convention is applied to the contract between the Plaintiff and the Defendant. The reason for appeal is unacceptable.

2. Pursuant to Article 19 of the revised Warsaw Convention, the transporter is responsible for the damage occasioned by delay in the carriage by air of passengers, luggage or goods. In this case, the damage occasioned by delay covers not only the damage in the course of air transportation as laid down in Article 18, para. 2 of the revised Warsaw Convention, but also the damage which occurred through delay caused by the late loading of baggage or freight. In addition, Article 26 of the revised Warsaw Convention states that "in the case of delay the complaint must be made at the latest within twenty-one days from the date on which the baggage or cargo have been placed at his disposal. Failing complaint within the times aforesaid, no action shall lie against the carrier, save in the case of fraud on his part."

The Supreme Court accepts that the original decision is right for the following reasons: Due to the accumulation of export freight, the transportation contract-making between the Plaintiff and the Asiana Airlines Co. was delayed. Accordingly, the freight was transported one day later than the date on the first document of carriage and five days later than the date on the second document of carriage of the Plaintiff. As a consequence, the responsibility of the damage compensation of the Plaintiff was extinct.

3. This court shall reject the appeal.

Cancellation Conditions for Foreign Arbitration Decision

Supreme Court, 16 February 2003, 2001Da 77840 Judgment

YOU HOON-KEUN v. MAJESTIC WOODCHIPS INC.

The following is the original decision. Donghae Pulp Co. and the Defendant Majestic Woodchips Inc., established under the state law of Louisiana of the United States, made a contract in 1994 that the Defendant would provide pieces of wood for making pulp, the raw material for paper. The two sides agreed to settle the disputes relating to the contract by Korean law and the Rules of Conciliation and Arbitration of the International Chamber of Commerce.

When a dispute arose between the Defendant and Donghae Pulp Co. regarding the implementation of the aforesaid contract, the Defendant and its domestic branch, TKT Co., called for arbitration. Following the request, the arbitration court appointed Neil Kaplan (living in Hong Kong) as the arbitrator on 4 August 1996 and decided Singapore as the arbitration region. The arbitrator filled out the Terms of Reference stating the arbitrator can change the arbitration region and that the arbitration will be processed by the national laws in force of the arbitration region and the Rules of Conciliation and Arbitration of the International Chamber of Commerce as amended on 1 January 1988. The parties concerned signed the Terms of Reference. Afterwards, the arbitrator changed the arbitration region to Hong Kong and conducted the arbitration proceedings there. On 14 July 1998 the arbitrator decided that Donghae

Pulp Co. should compensate the damage of the Defendant as it had violated the contract.

According to the original judgment, this arbitration case is not a domestic award under the arbitration law because this is the judgment made in Hong Kong concerning a commercial dispute. Thus, the New York Convention on the Recognition and Enforcement of Foreign Arbitral Awards (hereinafter, New York Convention) in which Korea and United States have joined should be applied for the recognition and enforcement of this arbitral award.

Article 5, para. 1(e) of the New York Convention stipulates the cancellation of the award as a reason for refusing the recognition and the enforcement of the arbitration award. Following this regulation, the arbitration award shall be cancelled by the country in which that award was made or the competent authority of the country under the law of which that award was made. In this case, by the way, Donghae Pulp Co. and the Defendant agreed merely to resolve the disputes regarding the abovementioned contract by arbitration. However, they did not clearly agree on the standard law of the arbitration process, but agreed only to follow Korean law and the Rules of Conciliation and Arbitration of the International Chamber of Commerce. Pursuant to Article 11 of the Rules of Conciliation and Arbitration of the International Chamber of Commerce and in conformity of the parties concerned, the arbitrator decided the laws in force of the arbitration region and the Rules of Conciliation and Arbitration of the International Chamber of Commerce as the standard laws. Because Hong Kong laws in force and the Rules of Conciliation and Arbitration of the International Chamber of Commerce were mainly applied in the arbitration process, the Korean court is not a competent authority.

This court shall reject the appeal.

Constitutionality of the Present Extradition Procedure
Constitutional Court, 30 January 2003, 2001 HunBa95 Decision

Claimant: KANG, X K.

Re-appeal to the Supreme Court's Decision (2001MO272) regarding extradition permission

The claimant was a Korean-American citizen who was indicted for rape and other crimes by the State Court of California and was found guilty by the verdict of juries in February 1999. He fled from the United States into Korea on 1 March 1999 just before the final adjudication of the State court and was finally sentenced to 271 years' servitude at the California court. On 4 June 2001, the US Department of Justice required the extradition of the claimant. Accordingly, the Seoul High Prosecutor Office referred the matter regarding the extradition of the claimant to the Seoul High Court, and that Court permitted the extradition on September 25, 2001. The claimant re-appealed to the Supreme Court against this decision, but the Supreme Court denied his appeal again. Then the claimant applied for the examination of the constitutionality of Article 3 of the Extradition Law[38]* to the Constitutional Court.

The following were the assertions of the claimant. The provision of this case regulates the single-trial system; this would pursue the public interests as does transnational cooperation, through obtaining the quick investigation and adjudication procedure for criminals. However, the single-trial system would give the claimant a heavy psychological burden as well as block the possibility of re-trying the decision from the beginning. Thus, this regulation will not be consistent with the principles of the Constitution regarding Dignity, Pursuit of Happiness (Article 10), Personal Liberty and Integrity and Due Process of Law (Article 12, paragraph 1), Right to Trial (Article 27, paragraph 1) and No Infringement of Essentials (Article 37, paragraph 2).

The Constitutional Court's decision was as follows. The Extradition Law applies the Criminal Procedural Law with appropriate modification; grants the claimant the right to ask for the aid of a lawyer; gives the accused a chance to express a personal opinion; and allows extradition to be denied when necessary. Although the Extradition Law regulates a single-trial system, it is undeniable this process has the rationality and legitimacy that the due process of law generally requires. Moreover, the extradition examination is a measure of international judicial cooperation. It is one of the procedures for deciding the extradition of a criminal following the request of a foreign country which has entered into an extradition treaty with Korea. The principle of reciprocity is strictly observed in this process.

The Extradition Law has several regulations which prevent unjust extradition or an extradition that involves human rights violation. Considering all the statements, the single-trial system as laid down in Article 3 of the Extradition Law does not imply a limitation on the dignity and fundamental freedom of citizens. Thus, the Constitutional Court decided that there was no violation of relevant Constitutional regulations.

Conclusively, Article 3 of the Extradition Law was not unconstitutional.

---

[38] * It reads: "The Seoul High Court and the Seoul High Prosecutor Office shall have the executive jurisdiction over the case regarding the extradition examination and the request concerned."

MALAYSIA[39]

JUDICIAL DECISIONS

Enforcement of Foreign Judgment

[2002] 7 MLJ 703

BANQUE NATIONAL DE PARIS v. TING KAI HOON[40]

[2002] 2 MLJ 353

COMMERZBANK (SOUTH EAST ASIA LTD) v. TOW KONG LIAN[41]

The enforcement of foreign judgements in Malaysia can take place in two ways: either by using the principles of common law or through the Reciprocal Enforcements of Judgments Act 1958[42] (REJA).

Both of these cases concern the statutory enforcement of foreign judgments. The REJA lays down the rules with which a party can enforce a foreign judgment here. This is done basically by registering the foreign judgment in Malaysia. The foreign judgment is then treated as if it is a Malaysian judgement and enforcement is done accordingly.

Naturally, there are defences to the enforcement of foreign judgments.[43] The party against whom the judgment is being carried out can, for example, claim that the initial case heard in the foreign court was not valid as it did not have the original jurisdiction to hear the case in the first place; otherwise, the party can even argue that the enforcement of the foreign judgment would be contrary to Malaysian public policy.[44]

In the cases of *Banque National de Paris v Ting Kai Hoon* and *Commerzbank (South East Asia Ltd) v Tow Kong Lian* the defendants were both Malaysians trying to stop a Singaporean judgment enforced against them in Malaysia. They both tried to use the provisions in the REJA to achieve this, but with different levels of success.[45]

---

[39] Contributed by Azmi Sharom, Associate Professor, University of Malaya, Faculty of Law
[40] [2002] 7 MLJ 703.
[41] [2002] 2 MLJ 353.
[42] Revised in 1972. Act 99.
[43] In particular sections 5 and 6 of REJA.
[44] There are of course other justifications in REJA which can be used not to enforce a foreign judgment.
[45] In both cases there were several lines of argument to justify their application. However, for the purpose of this survey, only the points with greatest relevance to Conflict of Laws principles will be discussed.

In *Banque National de Paris* the Defendant argued that the Singaporean judgment should not be enforced in Malaysia based primarily on two grounds: firstly because the Singaporean judgment was void for uncertainty, and secondly, because to enforce the judgment would be against Malaysian public policy.

Regarding the first line of argument, the judge held that when a foreign judgment is registered in Malaysia, it is treated as though it is a Malaysian judgment. It does not become a Malaysian judgment. Therefore any judgment on the actual merits of the case would have to be sought in the court where it was heard, in this case, the Singaporean court.

On the grounds of public policy, the Defendant had argued that the Plaintiffs, by offering credit facilities to the Defendant, acted unlawfully in that they had breached the rules of Exchange Control Act 1953[46] and the Banking and Financial Institutions Act 1989.[47] The judge found both arguments to be without merit. The Defendant's application was thus dismissed.

In the *Commerzbank* case the Defendant tried to get out of the foreign judgment by arguing that the Singaporean court had no original jurisdiction to hear the case and the enforcement of the foreign judgment would be against Malaysian public policy. With regard to the matter of jurisdiction, the Defendant relied on section 5(2)(a)(i) of REJA which states that for the foreign court to be deemed to have had jurisdiction to hear the case, then the Defendant must have submitted to its jurisdiction. This the Defendant did not do and the Singaporean judgment was given in default.

However, the judge was not convinced of this argument because the Defendant, in the guarantee to the loan being made, had agreed to the Singapore courts' being the proper forum to determine any problems that may arise. He had therefore contractually submitted to the Singapore Court's jurisdiction and his non-appearance made no difference to this.[48]

But the Defendant in *Commerzbank* was successful in his claim that to enforce the Singaporean judgment would be contrary to Malaysian public policy. This argument was accepted because the service of writ for the trial on the Defendant by the Singapore court was not carried out according to the procedure laid out by Malaysian law.

There are two ways to serve a writ in Malaysia in situations where the case is being heard in a foreign jurisdiction. A letter of request from the court or foreign tribunal requesting service upon a person in Malaysia must be received by the Minister who then sends it to the High Court with a request that this service take place. Alternatively, where there is a Civil Procedure Convention between the foreign

---

[46] Revised 1969. Act 17.

[47] Act 372.

[48] It is strange that the Defendant tried this line of argument because in section 5(2)(a)(iii) of REJA it clearly states that a foreign court will be deemed to have jurisdiction "if the judgment debtor, being a defendant in the original court, had before the commencement of the proceedings agreed, in respect of the subject matter of the proceedings to submit to the jurisdiction of that court or of the courts of the country of that court".

country and Malaysia, the request may be made directly to the registrar by way of a request from a consular or any other authority of that foreign country.

Neither of these procedures was followed; by serving its writ on the Defendant with no heed to the procedures of Malaysian law the Singapore Court had acted in a way that was contrary to the sovereignty of Malaysia and thus as a matter of public policy the case following the wrongful service of writ could be neither recognized nor enforced in Malaysia.

SOVEREIGNTY OVER PULAU LIGITAN AND PULAU SIPADAN[49]

On 17 December 2002 the International Court of Justice (ICJ) delivered its judgment in the case concerning *Sovereignty over Pulau Ligitan and Pulau Sipadan (Indonesia/Malaysia)*. The facts of the case can be summarized as follows. Pulau Ligitan and Pulau Sipadan are two islands located in the Celebes Sea off the north-east coast of the island of Borneo. Ligitan is uninhabited whilst Sipadan has a scuba diving resort on it. Both Indonesia and Malaysia claimed sovereignty over the islands.

On 2 November 1998, the two countries notified the Registrar of the Court that a Special Agreement between the two States was signed on 31 May 1997 and came into force on 14 May 1998. According to this Agreement, Malaysia and Indonesia agreed to have their dispute settled by the ICJ. Hearings were held from 3 to 12 June 2002.Indonesia's claims were based on three grounds:

a. A Convention concluded between Great Britain and the Netherlands in 1891 (the 1891 Convention) had defined the boundaries for British and Dutch territories and the islands that fell within the Dutch area. Upon Independence from Holland, Indonesia would therefore inherit those islands.
b. In the alternative, they claim sovereignty over the islands as successors to the Sultan of Bulungan who possessed authority over the islands and who had contracted the islands to the Dutch.
c. A series of *effectivites* or activities which express an interest on the control of these islands have been conducted by the Dutch and Indonesian governments.

Malaysia's claims were based on two grounds:

a. Sovereignty over the islands were obtained through the transmission of title from the Sultan of Sulu, to Spain, to the United States of America, to Great Britain on behalf of the State of North Borneo, to the United Kingdom of Great Britain (when North Borneo became a colony) and then finally to Malaysia when North Borneo became part of Malaysia.
b. A series of *effectivites* or activities which express an interest on the control of these islands have been conducted by the British and Malaysian governments.

---

[49] Judgment obtained from the International Court of Justice website, http://212.153.43.18/icjwww/icj002.htm

The decision of the ICJ, with 16 votes for Malaysia and one against is as follows: With regard to the 1891 Convention, the Court held that the Indonesian government was mistaken in its interpretation of the treaty, namely Article IV which reads:

> From 4'10" north latitude on the east coast the boundary-line shall be continued eastward along that parallel, across the Island of Sebittik: that portion of the island situated to the north of that parallel shall belong unreservedly to the British North Borneo Company, and the portion south of that parallel to the Netherlands.

The Indonesians contended that the boundary line extended into the ocean and seeing as Sipadan and Ligitan were south of the parallel 4'10", it therefore belonged to Indonesia as an inheritance from the Netherlands.

Having examined the object and purpose of the 1891 Convention, the ICJ held that it was of the opinion that the Convention was about the delimitation of the boundaries between the parties' possession *within* the island of Borneo itself and it could not find anything to suggest that the parties intended to delimit the boundary between their possessions to the east of Borneo and the island of Sebatik or to determine the sovereignty of any other islands.

With regard to the alternative ground that Indonesia inherited the islands from the Dutch who had contractually acquired them from the Sultan of Bulungan, it was held that the contract referred to mentions the islands of Nanukan and Sebatik, and the islets belonging thereto. The Court was reluctant to include within the definition of "islets" Sipadan and Ligitan which are 40 nautical miles away.

The ICJ was equally dismissive of the Malaysian historical claims on the islands. The supposed succession of the islands depended on their belonging to the Sultan of Sulu in the first place. This was not proved to the Court's satisfaction and it held that in all relevant documents, reference was never made to the two islands by name. Instead the Sultanate of Sulu was described as "the Archipelago of Sulu and the dependencies thereof" or "the Island of Sooloo with all its dependencies".

In the Protocol with Spain[50] where the Sultan of Sulu transferred title of his lands, again there was no mention of the two islands and there is no evidence that Spain considered Ligitan and Sipadan to be part of the agreement. Going further down the chain of succession from Spain to the United States to Britain, the Court found that there could be no certainty that the islands were part of the agreements.

The ownership of the islands was therefore decided on the effectivites.[51] The Court did not accept the Indonesian claims that their activities which included navy patrols (by the Dutch navy and Indonesian navy), along with the activities of

---

[50] Protocol between Spain and Sulu Confirming the Bases of Peace and Capitulation of 22 July 1878.

[51] The dissenting judge, Judge Franck, who was appointed by Indonesia, described making a decision based on the *effectivites* as akin to trying to guess the weight of a handful of grass and a handful of feathers. He decided in favour of Indonesia maintaining that the 1891 Convention, in delimiting the entire frontier between Britain and Holland, had established a line intended to ensure that future conflicts over territory do not occur. This would logically include islands in the area.

Indonesian fishermen on the islands, were sufficient to establish sovereignty. The Court instead was impressed with the Malaysian *effectivites* which were, although modest in nature, diverse in character, including legislative, administrative and quasi-judicial acts and covering a considerable period of time that shows a pattern which reveals an intention to exercise State functions with respect to the two islands. These activities included control over the taking of turtle eggs, allegedly the most important economic activity on Sipadan for many years, the establishment in 1933 of a bird sanctuary on Sipadan, and the construction and maintenance of lighthouses on both islands in the 1960s. Furthermore, when these activities were carried out, there was no protest from either the Dutch or subsequently the Indonesian governments. Ligitan and Sipadan were declared as falling within Malaysian sovereignty.

NATIONAL LAWS ON INTERNATIONAL LAW MATTERS

Anti-Personnel Mines Convention Implementation Act 2000

Act 603

This is an act to implement the Convention on the Prohibition of the Use, Stock-piling, Production and Transfer of Anti-Personnel Mines and on their Destruction 1997 (Mine Ban Treaty) which Malaysia acceded to on 22 April 1999 and which came into force for the nation on 1 October 1999.

The act basically bans the use of anti-personnel mines.[52] This includes the placing of mines, the development and production of mines and the possession of mines.[53] There are exceptions[54] for the purpose of training or when possession is for the purpose of disarming the mines. Any mines in Malaysia which are stockpiled, laid or surrendered will be destroyed.

In the event there is an international fact finding mission sent to Malaysia (as authorized under Article 8 of the Mine Ban Treaty), a certificate shall be issued to each member of the fact-finding mission, stating their identity, status, immunities, privileges and any conditions applicable to the mission.[55] The fact finding mission may be accompanied by the Malaysian police or the military[56] when conducting

---

[52] Which is defined in section 2 as "a mine that is designed to be exploded by the presence, proximity or contact of a person and that is capable of incapacitating, injuring or killing one or more persons; but a mine that is designed to be detonated by the presence, proximity or contact of a vehicle as opposed to a person, and that is equipped with anti handling devices, is not considered to be an anti-personnel mine as a result of being so equipped."

[53] Section 3.

[54] Section 4.

[55] Section 10.

[56] Section 13.

their work which is fundamentally limited to inspection of premises which are relevant to determining compliance with the treaty.[57]

Search warrants can be issued by magistrates if there is reasonable cause to believe there are premises where activities in contravention of the treaty are being conducted, to enable a fact-finding mission to carry out its duties or if necessary information is believed to be available in the premises.[58] However, if a police officer not below the rank of Inspector is convinced that evidence would be destroyed if the procedure for obtaining a warrant is followed, then the premises may be entered without one.[59]

If there is no specific provision for penalties, then the general penalty for committing an offence under this act is a fine not exceeding RM 20000 or a five-year prison sentence or both.

NEPAL[60]

JUDICIAL DECISIONS

Rights of the Child – Registration of an Association – UN Convention on Rights of the Child

TILOTAM POUDYAL v. HMG MINISTRY OF HOME AND OTHERS

Writ Petition No. 174 of 2000 decided by a Full Bench of the Supreme Court of Nepal on 19 July 2001

The petitioner and other persons were minors while applying for registration of a Non-Governmental Organisation (NGO) named "Children Awakening Club Nepal" (*Jagriti Bal Club Nepal*) before the District Administration Office, the concerned authority to register NGOs. The petitioner master Tilotam Poudyal and his friends had applied before the Nawalparasi District Administrative Office for registration of the Children Awakening Club Nepal (hereinafter Club) in early 1997. The District Administration Office had asked for directions from the Ministry of Home regarding registration of an NGO where the applicants were minors. The Home Ministry decided in December 1997 that only citizens were eligible for registering an NGO under the

---

[57] Section 12.
[58] Section 14.
[59] Section 15.
[60] Contributed by Mr. Surendra Bhandari, Advocate, Supreme Court of Nepal.

Association Registration Act, 1978.[61] The Home Ministry noted that the applicants were minor and had not attained the age for obtaining citizenship and therefore were not eligible to register an NGO in their name and directed the District Administration Office Nawalparasi to deny the registration of NGO to minors.

The petitioner applied to the Supreme Court of Nepal in early 1998 for issuance of writs of *certiorari* and *mandamus* to quash the decision of Ministry of Home and direct the District Administrative Office Nawalparasi to grant registration of the proposed NGO. The Division Bench of the Supreme Court of Nepal decided the case in November 2000. The judges of the Division Bench forwarded the matter to the Full Bench which unanimously decided it in July 2001.

There were the following legal questions to be decided by the court:

i. Whether minors are eligible to register an NGO
ii. Whether the Ministry of Home was free to give discriminatory decisions
iii. Whether the denial of registration of a NGO to minors showed disrespect to the UN Convention on the Rights of Child.

The Full Bench of the Supreme Court of Nepal[62] decided that the minors are also citizens of Nepal capable of obtaining a citizenship certificate through a legal process and could not be discriminated against in exercising those rights conferred on citizens by any law only because they are minors. The domestic laws of Nepal, particularly the Association Registration Act, 1978, cannot restrict the right to association granted by the Constitution of the Kingdom of Nepal as a fundamental right. Moreover, Nepal was a party to the UN Convention on the Rights of the Child, 1989, which under Section 9 of the Treaty Act, 1990 of Nepal, prevails over conflicting domestic laws. Article 15 of the UN Convention on the Rights of Child[63] requires Contracting Parties to provide the right of association to children without any discrimination. The Ministry of Home had also permitted minors to register an NGO in

---

[61] The Association Registration Act, 1978 and Association Registration Rules, 1979 do not prescribe that only the citizens are eligible for registration of an association but Article 12 (2) of the Constitution of the Kingdom of Nepal prescribes that all the citizens shall have rights including freedom to assemble peaceably and freedom to form unions and associations. Further the Association Registration Act does not discriminate between minor and the persons who have attained age. The Citizenship Act of Nepal, 1964 and Citizenship Rules 1992 do not impose any condition or limitation of age for citizenship. However, according to the Children Act, 1992 those are "children" who have not attained sixteen years of age.

[62] The Full Bench was composed of Justice Kedar Nath Upadhyaya, Justice Kedar Nath Acharya and Justice Rajendra Raj Nakhwa.

[63] Article 15 of the UN Convention on the Rights of Child provides:

1. States Parties recognize the rights of the child to freedom of association and to freedom of peaceful assembly.

2. No restrictions may be placed on the exercise of these rights other than those imposed in conformity with the law and which are necessary in a democratic society in the interests of national security or public safety, public order (*ordre public*), the protection of public health or morals or the protection of the rights and freedoms of others.

Kathmandu District Administration Office in 1995. The Ministry could not make discriminatory decisions for minor registration of an NGO inside and outside Kathmandu. Therefore, the decision of the Ministry was inconsistent with Article 11 (1) and (2)[64] of the Constitution of the Kingdom of Nepal, 1990 and Article 15 of the UN Convention on the Rights of the Child. On these grounds the Supreme Court invalidated the decision of the Ministry and directed it to register the proposed NGO.

Right to Clean Drinking Water – Compliance with WHO Standards

ADVOCATE PRAKASH MANI SHARMA v. DRINKING WATER CORPORATION NEPAL AND OTHERS

Writ Petition No. 2237 of 2000 decided by Division Bench of the Supreme Court of Nepal in June 2001

The petitioner had filed a public interest litigation before the Supreme Court of Nepal asking for the issuance of a Writ of Mandamus against the respondent Nepal Drinking Water Corporation ordering it to provide clean drinking water to the consumers. The petitioner claimed that the drinking water distributed by Nepal Drinking Water Corporation, which is responsible for distribution of clean drinking water under Drinking Water Corporation Act, 1989, was below the standards prescribed by the WHO. Due to the consumption of unhygienic water common people suffered from many types of diseases. The activities of the respondent had therefore seriously affected the right to live in a clean and healthy environment. The respondent Drinking Water Corporation denied the claim of the petitioner stating that it was distributing water to the consumers in compliance with WHO standards.

There were the following legal questions to be decided by the court:

I. Whether the Drinking Water Corporation was responsible to supply clean drinking water

II. Whether the court could exercise jurisdiction to examine evidences in Public Interest Litigation to verify the contentions between the parties to the case

III. Whether the WHO Standards would apply as mandatory rules.

The Division Bench[65] of the Supreme Court of Nepal decided the case in June 2001. The Supreme Court of Nepal acknowledged that the petitioner and the defendant had made opposing statements regarding the quality of the drinking water and

---

[64] *See Constitution of the Kingdom of Nepal*, (1990). Article 11(1) of the Constitution provides, "All citizens shall be equal before the law. No person shall be denied the equal protection of the laws." Article 11 (2) provides, "No discrimination shall be made against any citizen in the application of general laws on grounds of religion, race, sex, caste, tribe or ideological conviction or any of these."

[65] The Bench was composed of Justice Kedar Nath Acharya and Justice Bhairab Prasad Lamsal.

therefore there was a need to verify the contentions. However, the Court denied examination of any evidences while exercising extraordinary jurisdiction in a public interest litigation case; however, the court received the WHO Standards and the Report of Institute of Medicine, Tribhuvan University. The Court did not specifically speak about the legal validity of the WHO Standards but said that the Drinking Water Corporation was an autonomous body that was not required to act upon the direction of anyone. However, the Court directed to the Drinking Water Corporation to realize the objectives of a Welfare State and to be aware of the responsibility of the Corporation to provide clean drinking water to the consumers. The Court denied issuing the Writ Petition.

PAKISTAN[66]

JUDICIAL DECISIONS

Private International Law
Execution and enforcement of decrees passed by foreign court within Pakistan.

MUNAWAR ALI KHAN (APPELLANT) v. MARFANI AND CO. LTD (RESPONDENTS)

High Courts of Appeal Nos. 76 to 79 of 1995. Case Heard on 20 August 2002

In 1989, the Respondents filed a suit against the Appellants claiming that the Appellants had agreed to sell and the Respondents had agreed to purchase an immovable property in central London. A number of ancillary charges were to be provided by the Appellants as part of the sale. The Appellants failed to provide for these service charges, despite the sale of the property having been completed. The respondent company filed a suit in London, and the writs of summons were issued to the Appellants, all of whom were resident in Pakistan.

The Appellants did not submit to the jurisdiction of the trial court in London and the Respondents' suits were decreed upon. One of the Appellants responded to the summons seeking further time to prepare his arguments, but did not appear on the date of the hearing. A subsequent application by the Appellants for the setting aside of the order was dismissed on 6 July 1990. A subsequent appeal by the Appellants was also dismissed in July 1991. In a subsequent ruling in August 1995 a court ordered the execution of the aforementioned orders.

---

[66] Contributed by Javaid Rehman, Professor of International Law, University of Ulster, UK.

In the present case before the High Court of Justice in Karachi, the Appellants were challenging the order of enforcement and execution of judgment as pronounced by the English court on the basis that:

(a) the foreign judgment was not pronounced by a Court of Competent jurisdiction as provided by S.13(a) of the Civil Procedure Code (V of 1908).
(b) notwithstanding the fact that one of the Appellants did respond to the summons served upon him, none of the Appellants submitted to the jurisdiction of the English court.

The counsel for the Appellants argued that the judgment of the United Kingdcm court was unenforceable, when the aforementioned exception to S.13 is taken into account. The counsel argued fervently before the court that the mere fact that the cause of action according to the procedural law of the country arose within its territorial jurisdiction should be of little significance in determining whether such Court had jurisdiction to deal with the matter. The counsel also relied upon Cheshire and North on Private International Law (13th Edition) where the authors note at p. 420:

> According to the decisions that have dealt with the matter up to the present, it is undoubted that the various circumstances considered above exhaust possible cases in which foreign Court possesses international competence. Thus it is not sufficient that the cause of action, as for instance a breach of contract or a commission of a tort accrued in foreign country.

The counsel for the Respondents argued that the once the courts in the United Kingdom had exercised jurisdiction, the decision of the court should be treated as conclusive and binding. It was not disputed that the cause of action of accrued within a foreign jurisdiction where the contract between the parties had been entered and payment had to be made by the Appellants. The Respondents further relied upon Order 11, Rule 1 of the Supreme Court Rules whereby the United Kingdom courts could exercise jurisdiction over non-resident foreigners in matters where the cause of action accrued within their jurisdiction. The instant case summons were served upon the Appellants one of them, having responded to the same, sought additional time, but in the end failed to appear on the date of the hearing.

After detailed examination of the case-law and the arguments from the learned counsels for the Appellants the Court made the following pronouncements:

(a) having regard to the existing legislation namely S.13(a) of the Civil Procedure Code (V of 1908) an action on the basis of a foreign judgment could only be maintained if the defendant in the aforesaid judgment was a resident or at least physically present in the foreign country at the time of commencement of pro-ceedings or had submitted to or had agreed to submit to the jurisdiction of such foreign Court. The mere fact that the cause of action had accrued within the jurisdiction would not confer competence upon such Court in an international sense so as to make its judgments recognisable and enforceable in Britain.

(b) A distinction needs to be drawn in instances where the defendant has appeared before a foreign court only to protest against assumption of jurisdiction *vis-à-vis* those situations where he takes up defences on the merits of the case or applies to have a default judgment set aside and appeals to the merits of such claims. In view of the court, while the latter instances were examples of submission and acknowledgement of the court's jurisdiction, the former could not be so regarded. The present case fell in the former category, whereby there was a failure on the part of foreign court to successfully assume jurisdiction.

(c) The application of S.13(a) of the Civil Procedure Code (V of 1908) would *prima facie* lead to an anomalous situation in that a decree of a Court in United Kingdom which is directly executable as a decree of a District Court in Pakistan may become unexecutable merely because that Court was not considered to possess jurisdiction in an 'international' sense notwithstanding the fact that under its own system of laws it had full powers to pass such decree. The High Court of Karachi directed that a copy of the judgement highlighting the present anomalous situation be presented to the Secretary, Ministry of Law Government of Pakistan and Secretary Pakistan Law Commission to consider the desirability of amending the relevant provisions of the Civil Procedure Code (V of 1908) in the light of anomalies as highlighted by the Court.

In the light of the aforementioned considerations, the High Court of Karachi allowed this appeal. The Court did not make any order as regards costs. Copies of the judgment were sent out respectively to the Secretary, Ministry of Law Government of Pakistan and to the Secretary, Pakistan Law Commission for a review and amendment of the relevant provisions of the Civil Procedure Code (V of 1908).

PHILIPPINES[67]

JUDICIAL DECISIONS

Extraditee's right to bail; when exceptions to no-bail rule apply

GOVERNMENT OF THE UNITED STATES OF AMERICA, represented by the Philippines Department of Justice, petitioners, v. HON. GUILLERMO G. PURGANAN, Presiding Judge, Regional Trial Court of Manila, Branch 42, and MARK JIMENEZ a.k.a. MARIO BATACAN CRESPO, respondents

[G.R. No. 148571. 17 December 2002.]

---

[67] Contributed by Harry Roque Jr, Faculty Member, College of Law, University of Philippines, Diliman, Quezon City.

The Supreme Court denied the respondent Manila Congressman Mark Jimenez's motion that the High Court reconsider its decision nullifying the lower court's grant of bail to him. In this case, Jimenez was subject of an extradition proceeding to the United States for election fraud.

The Supreme Court brushed aside the petitioner's plea that he deserves bail under the exception laid down in its earlier decision, namely, "(1) that, once granted bail, the applicant will not be a flight risk or a danger to the community; and (2) that there exists special, humanitarian and compelling circumstances including, as matter of reciprocity, those cited by the highest court in the requesting state when it grants provisional liberty in extradition cases therein."

It said that there has been no clear and convincing showing as to the absence of flight risk and the non-endangerment of the community, or as to the existence of special, humanitarian and compelling circumstances justifying grant of bail.

The Supreme Court said that the procedure adopted by the Extradition Court of first notifying and hearing a prospective extraditee before the actual issuance of the warrant for his arrest is tantamount to giving notice to flee and avoid extradition. "Whether a candidate for extradition does in fact go into hiding or not is beside the point. In the final analysis, the method adopted by the lower court was completely at loggerheads with the purpose, object and rationale of the law, and overlooked the evils to be remedied," observed the Supreme Court.

The Supreme Court said that contrary to Jimenez's claims, the Extradition Court did not negate the flight risk posed by him; neither did it make a finding on flight risk as it considered the issue irrelevant, having already determined bail to be a matter of right. Without making any finding on flight risk, it found the capacity to flee subservient to "the benefits that respondent may be able to deliver to his constituents" despite the absence from the records of evidence showing the existence of such benefits.

It said that arguments (1) that the Extradition Court exercised due discretion in its grant of bail and (2) that the High Court's "ruling that bail is not a matter of right in extradition cases is contrary to prevailing law and jurisprudence" are neither novel nor deserving of further rebuttal.

It also stressed that the contention that the High Court's decision violates his due process rights is false, because as discussed in an earlier decision, in its simplest concept, due process is merely the opportunity to be heard – which opportunity need not always be a prior one. "In point of fact, private respondent has been given more than enough opportunity to be heard in this Court as well as in the Extradition Court."

The Supreme Court reiterated an earlier suggestion that private respondent can avoid arrest and detention which are the consequences of the extradition proceeding simply by applying for bail before the courts trying the criminal cases against him in the USA. "He himself has repeatedly told us that the indictments against him in the United States are bailable. Furthermore, he is capable, financially and otherwise, of producing the necessary bail in the US. Why then has he not done so? Otherwise stated, Respondent Jimenez has the actual power to lift his arrest and detention arising from his extradition by simply and voluntarily going to and filing bail in the USA."

Constitutionality of joint RP-US war exercises under the Visiting Forces Agreement; interpretation of treaties; municipal v. international law

ARTHUR D. LIM and PAULINO R. ERSANDO, Petitioners, v. HONORABLE EXECUTIVE SECRETARY as *alter ego* of HER EXCELLENCY GLORIA MACAPAGAL-ARROYO, and HONORABLE ANGELO REYES in his capacity as Secretary of National Defense, Respondents.
SANLAKAS and PARTIDO NG MANGGAGAWA, Petitioners-Intervenors, v. GLORIA MACAPAGAL-ARROYO, ALBERTO ROMULO, ANGELO REYES, Respondents.

[G.R. No. 151445. April 11, 2002.]

Beginning January 2002, personnel from the armed forces of the United States of America started arriving in Mindanao to take part, in conjunction with the Philippine military, in "Balikatan 02-1." These so-called "Balikatan" exercises are the largest combined training operations involving Filipino and American troops. In theory, they are a simulation of joint military manœuvres pursuant to the Mutual Defense Treaty, a bilateral defence agreement entered into by the Philippines and the United States in 1951.

The last "Balikatan" was held in 1995. This was due to the paucity of any formal agreement relative to the treatment of United States personnel visiting the Philippines. In the meantime, the respective governments of the two countries agreed to hold joint exercises on a reduced scale. The lack of consensus was eventually cured when the two nations concluded the Visiting Forces Agreement (VFA) in 1999.

The arrival of US troops was seen as part of the international anti-terrorism campaign declared by President George W. Bush in reaction to the tragic events that occurred on 11 September 2001. On that day, three commercial aircraft were hijacked, flown and smashed into the twin towers of the World Trade Center in New York City and the Pentagon building in Washington, D.C. by terrorists with alleged links to al-Qaeda ("the Base"), a Muslim extremist organization headed by the infamous Osama bin Laden. With no comparable historical parallels, these acts caused billions of dollars'-worth of destruction of property and the incalculable loss of hundreds of lives.

One group operating in the Philippines, the Abu Sayyaf terrorist organization, is suspected to have links with Bin Laden's organization. The RP-US exercises were set in Basilan, where the Abu Sayyaf has bases.

The Department of Foreign Affairs and its American counterpart drafted a Terms of Reference (TOR)[68] document to provide guidelines for the conduct of the ex-

---

[68] The TOR provides:
1. POLICY LEVEL
1. The Exercise shall be consistent with the Philippine Constitution and all its activities shall be in consonance with the laws of the land and the provisions of the RP-US Visiting Forces Agreement (VFA).

2. The conduct of this training Exercise is in accordance with pertinent United Nations resolutions against global terrorism as understood by the respective parties.

3. No permanent US basing and support facilities shall be established. Temporary structures such as those for troop billeting, classroom instruction and messing may be set up for use by RP and US Forces during the Exercise.

4. The Exercise shall be implemented jointly by RP and US Exercise Co-Directors under the authority of the Chief of Staff, AFP. In no instance will US Forces operate independently during field training exercises (FTX). AFP and US Unit Commanders will retain command over their respective forces under the overall authority of the Exercise Co-Directors. RP and US participants shall comply with operational instructions of the AFP during the FTX.

5. The exercise shall be conducted and completed within a period of not more than six months, with the projected participation of 660 US personnel and 3,800 RP Forces. The Chief of Staff, AFP shall direct the Exercise Co-Directors to wind up and terminate the Exercise and other activities within the six month Exercise period.

6. The Exercise is a mutual counter-terrorism advising, assisting and training Exercise relative to Philippine efforts against the ASG, and will be conducted on the Island of Basilan. Further advising, assisting and training exercises shall be conducted in Malagutay and the Zamboanga area. Related activities in Cebu will be for support of the Exercise.

7. Only 160 US Forces organized in 12-man Special Forces Teams shall be deployed with AFP field commanders. The US teams shall remain at the Battalion Headquarters and, when approved, Company Tactical headquarters where they can observe and assess the performance of the AFP Forces.

8. US exercise participants shall not engage in combat, without prejudice to their right of self-defense.

9. These terms of Reference are for purposes of this Exercise only and do not create additional legal obligations between the US Government and the Republic of the Philippines.

II. EXERCISE LEVEL

1. TRAINING

a. The Exercise shall involve the conduct of mutual military assisting, advising and training of RP and US Forces with the primary objective of enhancing the operational capabilities of both forces to combat terrorism.

b. At no time shall US Forces operate independently within RP territory.

c. Flight plans of all aircraft involved in the exercise will comply with the local air traffic regulations.

2. ADMINISTRATION & LOGISTICS

a. RP and US participants shall be given a country and area briefing at the start of the Exercise. This briefing shall acquaint US Forces on the culture and sensitivities of the Filipinos and the provisions of the VFA. The briefing shall also promote the full cooperation on the part of the RP and US participants for the successful conduct of the Exercise.

b. RP and US participating forces may share, in accordance with their respective laws and regulations, in the use of their resources, equipment and other assets. They will use their respective logistics channels.

c. Medical evaluation shall be jointly planned and executed utilizing RP and US assets and resources.

d. Legal liaison officers from each respective party shall be appointed by the Exercise Directors.

3. PUBLIC AFFAIRS

a. Combined RP-US Information Bureaus shall be established at the Exercise Directorate in Zamboanga City and at GHQ, AFP in Camp Aguinaldo, Quezon City.

b. Local media relations will be the concern of the AFP and all public affairs guidelines shall be jointly developed by RP and US Forces.

c. Socio-Economic Assistance Projects shall be planned and executed jointly by RP and US Forces in accordance with their respective laws and regulations, and in consultation with community and

ercises. On February 1, 2002, petitioners Arthur D. Lim and Paulino P. Ersando filed a petition for *certiorari* and prohibition, attacking the constitutionality of the joint exercise, arguing in addition that the exercises contravene even the spirit and intent of the VFA. They were joined subsequently by SANLAKAS and PARTIDO NG MANGGAGAWA, both party-list organizations, who filed a petition-in-intervention on February 11, 2002.

The Supreme Court disposed the issue of whether "Balikatan 02-1" is covered by the Visiting Forces Agreement by citing Section 3 of the Vienna Convention on the Law of Treaties, which contains provisions on the interpretation of international agreements.[69] The Supreme Court noted that the VFA permits United States personnel to engage, on an impermanent basis, in "activities", in the Philippines during war exercises, "the exact meaning of which was left undefined. The High Court said the expression is ambiguous, permitting a wide scope of undertakings subject only to the approval of the Philippine government." But the Supreme Court said that based on the Vienna Convention, the cardinal rule of interpretation must involve an examination of the text, which is presumed to verbalize the parties' intentions. The Convention likewise dictates what may be used as aids, to deduce the meaning of

---

local government officials.

Contemporaneously, Assistant Secretary for American Affairs Minerva Jean A. Falcon and United States Chargé d'Affaires Robert Fitts signed the Agreed Minutes of the discussion between the Vice-President and Assistant Secretary Kelly.

[69] SECTION 3. – INTERPRETATION OF TREATIES
Article 31
General rule of interpretation
1. A treaty shall be interpreted in good faith in accordance with the ordinary meaning to be given to the terms of the treaty in their context and in the light of its object and purpose.
2. The context for the purpose of the interpretation of a treaty shall comprise, in addition to the text, including its preamble and annexes:
(a) any agreement relating to the treaty which was made between all the parties in connection with the conclusion of the treaty;
(b) any instrument which was made by one or more parties in connection with the conclusion of the treaty and accepted by the other parties as an instrument related to the party.
3. There shall be taken into account, together with the context:
(a) any subsequent agreement between the parties regarding the interpretation of the treaty or the application of its provisions;
(b) any subsequent practice in the application of the treaty which establishes the agreement of the parties regarding its interpretation;
(c) any relevant rules of international law applicable in the relations between the parties.
4. A special meaning shall be given to a term if it is established that the parties so intended.
Article 32
Supplementary means of interpretation
Recourse may be had to supplementary means of interpretation, including the preparatory work of the treaty and the circumstances of its conclusion, in order to confirm the meaning resulting from the application of article 31, or to determine the meaning when the interpretation according to article 31:
(a) leaves the meaning ambiguous or obscure; or
(b) leads to a result which is manifestly absurd or unreasonable

terms, to which it refers as the context of the treaty, as well as other elements, may be taken into account alongside the aforesaid context. Hence, a careful reading of the TOR would arrive at the conclusion that it rightly falls within the context of the VFA. It declared:

> After studied reflection, it appeared farfetched that the ambiguity surrounding the meaning of the word 'activities' arose from accident. In our view, it was deliberately made that way to give both parties a certain leeway in negotiation … In this manner, visiting US forces may sojourn in Philippine territory for purposes other than military. As conceived, the joint exercises may include training on new techniques of patrol and surveillance to protect the nation's marine resources, sea search-and-rescue operations to assist vessels in distress, disaster relief operations, civic action projects such as the building of school houses, medical and humanitarian missions, and the like.

It further held:

> Under these auspices, the VFA gives legitimacy to the current Balikatan exercises. It is only logical to assume that "Balikatan 02-1," a "mutual antiterrorism advising, assisting and training exercise," falls under the umbrella of sanctioned or allowable activities in the context of the agreement. Both the history and intent of the Mutual Defense Treaty and the VFA support the conclusion that combat-related activities – as opposed to combat itself – such as the one subject of the instant petition, are indeed authorized.

But on the second issue of the constitutionality of allowing US troops on Philippine soil under the new arrangement, the Supreme Court demurred. First, it asked itself, granting that "Balikatan 02-1" is permitted under the terms of the VFA, what may US forces legitimately do in furtherance of their aim to provide advice, assistance and training in the global effort against terrorism?

"Differently phrased, may American troops actually engage in combat in Philippine territory?" "In our considered opinion," said the High Court, "neither the MDT nor the VFA allows foreign troops to engage in an offensive war on Philippine territory."

The Supreme Court observed that the Mutual Defense Treaty and the Visiting Forces Agreement, as in all other treaties and international agreements to which the Philippines is a party, must be read in the context of the 1987 Constitution. In particular, the Mutual Defense Treaty was concluded long before the present Charter, though it nevertheless remains in effect as a valid source of international obligation. It noted that the present Constitution contains key provisions useful in determining the extent to which foreign military troops are allowed in Philippine territory, particularly in the Declaration of Principles and State Policies,[70] and its provisions regulating the foreign relations powers of the Chief Executive when it provides that "[n]o treaty or international agreement shall be valid and effective unless concurred in by at least two-thirds of all the members of the Senate."[71] "Even more pointedly," the Supreme Court noted that the Transitory Provisions of the 1987 Charter also state:

> Sec. 25. – After the expiration in 1991 of the Agreement between the Republic of the Philippines and the United States of America concerning Military Bases, foreign military bases, troops or facilities shall not be allowed in the Philippines except under a treaty duly concurred in by the Senate and, when the Congress so requires, ratified by a majority of the votes cast by the people in a national referendum held for that purpose, and recognized as a treaty by the other contracting state.

The Philippine Constitution, the High Court had noted, "betrays a marked antipathy towards foreign military presence in the country, or of foreign influence in general. Hence, foreign troops are allowed entry into the Philippines only by way of direct exception. Conflict arises then between the fundamental law and our obligations arising from international agreements."It had then discussed the relation of international law *vis-à-vis* municipal law in Philippine jurisprudence – that is, whether the High Court may invalidate a treaty on the ground of unconstitutionality – by citing the case of *Philip Morris, Inc. v. Court of Appeals,* where the Court held that:

> ... Withal, the fact that international law has been made part of the law of the land does not by any means imply the primacy of international law over national law in the municipal sphere. Under the doctrine of incorporation as applied in most countries, rules of international law are given a standing equal, not superior, to national legislation.

It also cited the case *Ichong v. Hernandez,*[72] where the High Court ruled that the provisions of a treaty are always subject to qualification or amendment by a subsequent law, or that it is subject to the police power of the State, and the case of *Gonzales v. Hechanova,*[73] where it made the declaration that:

---

[70] Citing the following provisions in the 1987 Charter:
SEC. 2. – The Philippines renounces war as an instrument of national policy, adopts the generally accepted principles of international law as part of the law of the land and adheres to the policy of peace, equality, justice, freedom, cooperation, and amity with all nations.
SEC. 7. – The State shall pursue an independent foreign policy. In its relations with other states the paramount consideration shall be national sovereignty, territorial integrity, national interest, and the right to self-determination.
SEC. 8. – The Philippines, consistent with the national interest, adopts and pursues a policy of freedom from nuclear weapons in the country.
[71] Sec. 21, Art. VII.
[72] G.R. No. L-7995, 101 PHIL 1155 (1957).
[73] G.R. No. L-21897, 9 SCRA 230 (1963).

... As regards the question whether an international agreement may be invalidated by our courts, suffice it to say that the Constitution of the Philippines has clearly settled it in the affirmative, by providing, in Section 2 of Article VIII thereof, that the Supreme Court may not be deprived "of its jurisdiction to review, revise, reverse, modify, or affirm on appeal, certiorari, or writ of error as the law or the rules of court may provide, final judgments and decrees of inferior courts in – (1) All cases in which the constitutionality or validity of any treaty, law, ordinance, or executive order or regulation is in question." In other words, our Constitution authorizes the nullification of a treaty, not only when it conflicts with the fundamental law, but, also, when it runs counter to an act of Congress.

However, after discussing its own power to nullify treaties which run counter to the fundamental law, the Supreme Court refused to look into the issue of whether American troops are indeed actively engaged in combat alongside Filipino troops under the guise of a war exercises held under the auspices of the VFA and in contravention of the constitutional prohibition. It said such an issue is a question of fact which it is "understandably loath to do."

OTHER RELEVANT STATE PRACTICES

Opinions of the Secretary of Justice[74]

Opinion no. 041, s. 2001, 25 July 2001, "The Legal Status of the 1971 Technical Cooperation Agreement Between the Republic of the Philippines and the Federal Republic of Germany"

The National Economic Development Authority (NEDA) sought the opinion of the Department of Justice (DOJ) on the "legal status" of the 1971 Technical Cooperation Agreement between the Republic of the Philippines and the Federal Republic of Germany as to whether it is an executive agreement or a treaty.

For over 30 years now, the Agreement has been invoked by Project Arrangements as a basis for tax exemptions and other privileges for materials and services imported or purchased for German government-assisted projects. Its legal status was questioned when the German government proposed in 1999 some revisions to the 1987 Project Arrangement pertaining to the establishment in Manila of a Project Administrative Service (PAS), a German government agency tasked to support technical cooperation projects in administrative and commercial matters in Manila.

The proposal called for the inclusion of Value Added Tax exemption for materials and services, accommodation and rentals.

The DOJ Secretary held that the document is an executive agreement. Citing the case of Commissioner of *Customs v. Eastern Sea Trading*[75] the DOJ Secretary

---

[74] Executive Pronouncements
[75] 3 SCRA 351 (1961)

outlined the distinctions between treaties and executive agreements. In that case the Court had held that:

> International agreements involving political issues or changes of national policy and those involving international arrangements of a permanent character usually take the form of treaties. But international agreements embodying adjustments of details carrying out well-established national policies and traditions and those involving arrangements of a more or less temporary nature usually take the form of executive agreements.

According to the High Court, treaties are formal documents which require ratification with the approval of two/thirds of the Senate but executive agreements become binding through executive action without the need of a vote by the Senate or by Congress.

It said that the right of the Executive to enter into binding agreements without the necessity of subsequent Congressional approval has been confirmed by long usage. "From the earliest days of our history we have entered into executive agreements covering such subjects as commercial and consular relations, most-favoured-nation rights, patent rights, trademark and copyright protection, postal and navigation arrangements and the settlement of claims," the Court said in the case. "The validity of these has never been seriously questioned by our courts."

Based on the Court's pronouncement, the Justice Secretary said the 1971 Technical Cooperation Agreement is an executive agreement. For one, the Agreement, which aims to intensify the technical and economic development of both parties, does not in any way involve political issues or changes of national policy, according to the DOJ Secretary. "On the contrary, the Agreement, as well as its revisions in 1987 and, as proposed, in 1999, provides for details in carrying out the purpose of supporting development cooperation between the two (2) countries." Also, the 1971 Technical Cooperation Agreement and the consequent Arrangements provide for a definite period within which they shall remain in force. "Thus, said agreements/arrangements are not of a permanent character but only temporary in nature."

Nevertheless, the DOJ secretary said the fact that the 1971 Technical Cooperation Agreement embodies provisions on tax exemptions which ordinarily should be found in a treaty does not necessarily detract from its nature as an executive agreement on the assumption that the tax exemptions granted therein are based on provisions of existing laws and that the Agreement only seeks to effectuate or implement these provisions insofar as they may apply to the situations contemplated in the Agreement.

NATIONAL LAWS ON INTERNATIONAL LAW MATTERS

Republic Act No. 9168 "Philippine Plant Variety Protection Act."

Signed into law by the President of the Philippines on 7 June 2002, the Philippine Plant Variety Protection Act (PVPA) of 2002 intends to provide protection to new plant varieties by establishing a plant variety protection (PVP) system, an administrative procedure with which an applicant must comply to secure a form of intellectual property right called the "plant breeder's right".

The new Law essentially conforms to the 1991 UPOV Convention[76] (the French acronym for the Union for the Protection of New Plant Varieties) with respect to the granting of plant breeder's rights. It also creates the National Plant Variety Protection Board, mandated to promulgate guidelines for the effective implementation of the Law, and having original jurisdiction over petitions for compulsory licensing, nullification and cancellation of Certificates of Plant Variety Protection.

To support national genetic conservation activities, the Law further establishes a Gene Trust Fund for the benefit of organizations or institutions managing and operating an accredited gene bank. It also encourages farming communities and organizations to build an inventory of locally bred varieties.

The PVPA provides that the certificate of Plant Variety Protection shall be granted to varieties that are: a) new, b) distinct, c) uniform, and d) stable.

The Law provides that a variety shall be deemed new if the propagating or harvested material of the variety has not been sold, offered for sale or otherwise disposed of to others, by or with the consent of the breeder, for purposes of exploitation of the variety:

(a) In the Philippines for more than one year before the date of filing of an application for plant variety protection; or
(b) In other countries or territories in which the application has been filed, for more than four years or, in the case of vines or tress, more than six years before the date of filing of an application for Plant Variety Protection.

However, the requirement of novelty provided for in the law does not apply to varieties sold, offered for sale or disposed of to others for a period of five years before the approval of the law, provided that application for PVP is filed within one year from the approval of the law.

Under the law, a variety shall be deemed distinct if it is clearly distinguishable from any commonly known variety. Moreover, the filing of an application for the granting of a plant variety protection or for the entering of a new variety into an official register of variety in the Philippines or in any country, makes the said variety a matter of public knowledge from the date of the filing of the application, as long as the application leads to the granting of a Certificate of Plant Variety Protection

---

[76] Entered into force 24 April 1998. The original UPOV convention was created in 1961 and provided for protection of plant varieties and created "breeders rights." The 1991 convention enlarges the monopoly privileges of "breeders." Under the 1991 Convention, UPOV member states are required to give plant breeders a right over "all production of seed or other planting material". UPOV is a part of the international conventions and treaties under the the World Intellectual Property Organization (WIPO).UPOV 1991 was negotiated at a diplomatic conference under WIPO auspices in Geneva.

or the entering of the said other variety into the official register of variety, as the case may be.

The Law deems a variety uniform "if, subject to the variation that may be expected from the particular features of its propagation, it is sufficiently uniform in its relevant characteristics."

The Law deems a variety stable "if its relevant characteristics remain unchanged after repeated propagation or, in the case of a particular cycle of propagation, at the end of each such cycle." These are called the DUSN criteria, set forth by UPOV.

Under the PVP system put in place by the new Law, a plant breeder could apply for a PVP certificate over a new plant variety from the board.
A certificate and all attendant ownership rights would be given to the plant breeder if the plant variety has passed the test of distinctness, uniformity, stability, and newness.

Holders of a certificate of plant variety would have the right to authorize the production or reproduction, conditioning for the purpose of propagation, offering for sale, selling or other marketing strategies, exporting, importing and stocking of the plant variety.

However, any person who believes that the applicant is not entitled to the grant of the Certificate of Plant Variety Protection may file an opposition thereto within the period prescribed by the Board from the date of its publication and before the issuance of the Certificate of Plant Variety Protection. Opposition to the application may be made on the following grounds:

(a) that the person opposing the application is entitled to the breeder's right as against the applicant;
(b) that the variety cannot be registered under the law.

If the opposition is based on the conditions of Plant Variety Protection, such opposition shall be considered together with the examination of the application.

A holder of a certificate also has rights over:

(a) Varieties which are essentially derived from the protected variety, where the protected variety is not itself an essentially derived variety;

(b) Varieties which are not clearly distinct from the protected variety; and
(c) Varieties whose production requires the repeated use of the protected variety.

The law considers a variety as essentially derived from the initial variety when:

(a) It is predominantly derived from the initial variety, or from a variety that is itself predominantly derived from the initial variety, while retaining the expression of the essential characteristics that result from the genotype or combination of genotypes of the initial variety;
(b) It is clearly distinguishable from the initial variety;

(c) Except for the differences which result from the act of derivation, it conforms to the initial variety in the expression of the essential characteristics that result from the genotype or combination of genotypes of the initial variety.

A provision on exemption to plant variety protection acknowledges the traditional right of the farmer to save, use, replant and sell his produce from a protected variety, provided that propagation is not being done for commercial purposes.

The law defines a "breeder" as one who "discovered ... a new plant variety". Specifically, a "breeder" may be:

1) The person who bred, or discovered and developed a new plant variety; or
2) The person who is the employer of the aforementioned person or who has commissioned the work; or
3) The successors-in-interest of the foregoing persons as the case may be; or
4) The holder of the Certificate of Plant Variety Protection.

The law penalizes infringement of a Certificate of Plant Variety Protection. An infringer is defined in the law as any person who, without being entitled to do so, performs the following acts:

(a) Sell the novel variety, or offer it or expose it for sale, deliver it, ship it, consign it, exchange it, or solicit an offer to buy it, or any other transfer of title or possession of it; or
(b) Import the novel variety into, or export it from, the Philippines; or
(c) Sexually multiply the novel variety as a step in marketing (for growing purposes) the variety; or
(d) Use the novel variety in producing (as distinguished from developing) a hybrid or different variety therefrom; or
(e) Use seed which had been marked "unauthorized propagation prohibited" or "unauthorized seed multiplication prohibited" or progeny thereof to propagate the novel variety; or
(f) Dispense the novel variety to another, in a form which can be propagated, without notice as to being a protected variety under which it was received;
(g) Fails to use a variety denomination the use of which is obligatory under Section 15; or
(h) Perform any of the foregoing acts even in instances in which the novel variety is multiplied other than sexually, except in pursuance of a valid Philippine plant patent; or
(i) Instigate or actively induce performance of any foregoing acts, may be sued by the holder, who may also avail of all such relief as are available in any proceeding involving infringements of other proprietary rights.

Under the law, any person who violates any of the rights of the holder may also suffer the penalty of imprisonment of not less than three years but not more than six years and/or a fine of up to three times the profit derived by virtue of the infringement but which in no case should be less than one hundred thousand pesos (P100,000.00).

Republic Act No. 9160 "An Act Defining the Crime of Money Laundering, Providing Penalties Therefor and for other Purposes"

The new law on anti-money laundering was passed on 29 September 2001.[77] It sets out as the Philippine government's declared policy "to protect and preserve the integrity and confidentiality of bank accounts and to ensure that the Philippines shall not be used as a money laundering site for the proceeds of any unlawful activity. Consistent with its foreign policy, the State shall extend cooperation in transnational investigations and prosecutions of persons involved in money laundering activities whenever committed."

Sec. 4 of the law defines money laundering as "a crime whereby the proceeds of an unlawful activity are transacted, thereby making them appear to have originated from legitimate sources."

Under the law, money laundering is committed by the following:

(a) Any person knowing that any monetary instrument or property represents, involves, or relates to the proceeds of any unlawful activity, transacts or attempts to transact said monetary instrument or property.

(b) Any person knowing that any monetary instrument or property involves the proceeds of any unlawful activity performs or fails to perform any act as a result

---

[77] The Paris-based Financial Action Task Force (FATF), established by the world's industrialized countries in 1989, labelled the Philippines a 'non-cooperative country' in global efforts to combat money laundering in June 2000. The Philippines has a Bank Secrecy Law, which virtually guarantees the complete privacy of the depositor. Banks are not required to make a careful check on the identity of the individual opening the account, nor are they under any obligation to report any suspicious financial transactions. Moreover, FCDUs (Foreign Currency Deposit Unit) were completely protected by another law.

The FATF action compelled the Philippine Central Bank to take initial actions against money laundering. Circular No. 251, dated 7 July 2000, outlined the framework of countermeasures. This was followed by many circulars issued in an attempt to strengthen the provisions but their failure to address the issue was only highlighted by the the impeachment proceedings held against former President Estrada who was himself accused of using false name accounts to launder money from illegal gambling. In June, 2001, the FATF once again included the Philippines on its list, warning that if the Philippines did not legislate money laundering countermeasures by the end of September, financial sanctions would be imposed.

The FATF laid down five minimum conditions for inclusion in the new law: (1) the criminalization of money laundering, (2) the establishment of a system for the reporting of suspicious transactions, (3) obligatory confirmation of the customer's identity (when opening a new account), (4) the elimination of excessive bank secrecy, and (5) international cooperation. Threatened with economic sanctions, the Philippines' legislature rushed to pass a law on anti-money laundering just a day before the 30 September 2001 deadline set by the international body.

of which he facilitates the offence of money laundering referred to in paragraph (a) above.

(c) Any person knowing that any monetary instrument or property is required under this Act to be disclosed and filed with the Anti-Money Laundering Council (AMLC), fails to do so.

The new law covers transactions by:

(1) banks, non-banks, quasi-banks, trust entities, and all other institutions and their subsidiaries and affiliates supervised or regulated by the Bangko Sentral ng Pilipinas (BSP);

(2) Insurance companies and all other institutions supervised or regulated by the Insurance Commission; and

(3) (i) securities dealers, brokers, salesmen, investment houses and other similar entities managing securities or rendering services as investment agent, advisor, or consultant, (ii) mutual funds, close and investment companies, common trust funds, pre-need companies and other similar entities, (iii) foreign exchange corporations, money changers, money payment, remittance, and transfer companies and other similar entities, and (iv) "other entities administering or otherwise dealing in currency, commodities or financial derivatives based thereon, valuable objects, cash substitutes and other similar monetary instruments or property supervised or regulated by Securities and Exchange Commission."

Under the new law, a covered transaction is any "single, series, or combination of transactions involving a total amount in excess of four million pesos (P4,000,000) or an equivalent amount in foreign currency based on the prevailing exchange rate within five (5) consecutive banking days except those between a covered institution and a person who, at the time of the transaction was a properly identified client and the amount is commensurate with the business or financial capacity of the client; or those with an underlying legal or trade obligation, purpose, origin or economic justification."

It likewise refers to a single, series or combination or pattern of unusually large and complex transactions in excess of four million pesos (P4,000,000) especially cash deposits and investments having no credible purpose or origin, underlying trade obligation or contract. However, those deposits made before the law took effect are not covered by the law.

The new law ''criminalizes' money laundering by penalizing those who obtain funds through kidnapping, smuggling, drug-trafficking, illegal gambling, hijacking, graft, plunder, extortion, piracy, theft, swindling, E-commerce violations, arson and murder and securities fraud and "felonies of similar nature under the penal codes of other countries." Violators face a maximum penalty of 14 years in prison and a fine of three million pesos.

Under the new law, other than money laundering related to 14 types of illegal activity, the failure to keep the required records, submission of false reports and leaking of confidential information are all liable to punishment by fines or imprisonment. Unauthorized public disclosures of AMLA proceedings are punishable by a maximum of four years in prison and five hundred thousand pesos (P500,000) in fines.

The law also made the opening of anonymous accounts or accounts with fictitious names illegal, although peso and foreign currency non-checking numbered accounts are allowed. A separate section details requirements imposed on banks, quasi-banks and other financial institutions covered by the law for record-keeping – for five years – reporting and client identification as a means of preventing money laundering. Covered institutions are now required by law to report to the AMLC all covered transactions within five working days from the date the transactions were made, unless the Supervising Authority concerned prescribes a longer period not exceeding ten working days.

The law established an Anti-Money Laundering Council (AMLC), composed of the BSP governor and the chief commissioner of the Security Exchange Commission and the head of the Insurance Commission as members. The AMLC is responsible for the execution of anti-money laundering countermeasures and is authorized to freeze deposit accounts that it deems likely to be connected to illegal activity, for up to 15 days. No court may un-freeze the accounts, except the Supreme Court and the Court of Appeals. The Council can even act at the behest of foreign governments. It may also institute forfeiture proceedings against laundered money.

The law also created an oversight committee composed of seven senators and seven congressmen supposedly to safeguard confidentiality and guard against harassment particularly during an election period, when candidates have deep pockets let alone substantial accounts.[78]

Republic Act 9147 "An Act Providing for the Conservation and Protection of Wildlife Resources and Their Habitats, Appropriating Funds Therefor and For Other Purposes"

Signed into law on 30 July 2001, the Wildlife Resources Conservation and Protection Act expressly acknowledges Philippine commitments to international conventions on the protection of wildlife and their habitats.

The new law covers all wildlife species found in all areas of the country, including protected areas under Republic Act No. 7586, otherwise known as the National Integrated Protected Areas System (NIPAS) Act, and critical habitats. It also applies to exotic species which are subject to trade, are cultured, maintained and/or bred in captivity or propagated in the country.

---

[78] The new law failed to get the full agreement of the FATF, principally because of what the international body views as a serious inadequacy: it covers only accounts of more than four million pesos, a threshold figure much too high than the FATF-recommended figure of P500,000. Also, the new law still requires the order of a competent court before deposit accounts suspected of having connections to money laundering may be investigated.

The new law aims to protect the country's fauna from illicit trade, abuse and destruction, through (1) conserving and protecting wildlife species and their habitats, (2) regulating the collection and trade of wildlife, (3) pursuing, with due regard to the national interest, the Philippine commitment to international conventions, protection of wildlife and their habitats, and (4) initiating or supporting scientific studies on the conservation of biological diversity.

Under the law, all designated critical habitats shall be protected, in coordination with the local government units and other concerned groups, from any form of exploitation or destruction which may be detrimental to the survival of species dependent upon these areas.

The law allocates jurisdiction to the Department of Environment and Natural Resources (DENR) over all terrestrial plant and animal species, all turtles and tortoises and wetland species, including but not limited to crocodiles, waterbirds and all amphibians and dugong. Meanwhile, the Department of Agriculture (DA) has jurisdiction over all declared aquatic critical habitats, all aquatic resources including but not limited to all fishes, aquatic plants, invertebrates and all marine mammals, except dugong. The secretaries of the DENR and the DA shall review, and by joint administrative order, revise and regularly update the list of species under their respective jurisdiction. In the Province of Palawan, jurisdiction is given to the Palawan Council for Sustainable Development pursuant to Republic Act No. 7611.

Under the law, the DENR issues wildlife farm culture permits for the breeding or propagation of wildlife for commercial purposes, subject to the condition that only progenies of wildlife raised, as well as unproductive parent stock, shall be utilized for trade and that commercial breeding operations for wildlife, whenever appropriate, shall be subject to an environmental impact study.

The DENR Secretary is mandated by law to establish, within one (1) year after it takes effect, to establish a list of economically-important species. A population assessment of such species shall be conducted within a reasonable period and shall be regularly reviewed and updated by the Secretary.

The DENR Secretary will allow the collection of certain species only when the results of official assessments show that, despite certain extent of collection, the population of such species can still remain viable and capable of recovering its numbers. For this purpose, the Secretary shall establish a schedule and volume of allowable harvests.

And whenever an economically important species become threatened, any form of collection shall be prohibited except for scientific, educational or breeding/propagation purposes. The law provides that introduction, reintroduction or re-stocking of endemic and indigenous wildlife shall be allowed only for population enhancement or recovery. Any introduction shall be subject to a scientific study. The introduction of exotic species into protected areas and critical habitats is prohibited. If and when introduction is allowed, it shall be subjected to environmental impact assessment and the informed consent from local stakeholders.

Under the law, conservation, breeding or propagation of threatened species shall be encouraged to enhance its population in its natural habitat. Breeding shall be done simultaneously with the rehabilitation and protection of the habitat where the captive-bred or propagated species shall be released or reintroduced. When economically important species become threatened, collection shall be limited to scientific, educational or breeding purposes.

The law penalizes the following acts:

a. killing and destroying wildlife species, except when it is done as part of the religious rituals of established tribal groups or indigenous cultural communities, when the wildlife is afflicted with an incurable communicable disease, when it is deemed necessary to put an end to the misery suffered by the wildlife, or when it is done to prevent an imminent danger to the life or limb of a human being; when the wildlife is killed or destroyed after it has been used in authorized research or experiments
b. inflicting injury which cripples and/or impairs the reproductive system of wildlife species
c. effecting any of the following acts in critical habitats: dumping of waste products detrimental to wildlife; squatting or otherwise occupying any portion of the critical habitat; mineral exploration and/or extraction; burning; logging; and quarrying
d. the introduction, reintroduction, or restocking of wildlife resources.
e. the trading of wildlife.
f. collecting, hunting or possessing wildlife, their by-products and derivatives
g. gathering or destroying of active nests, nest trees, host plants and the like
h. maltreating and/or inflicting other injuries not covered by the preceding paragraph; and
i. the transporting of wildlife.

The law imposes stiff penalties and fines: a maximum of 12 years in prison and a fine of one million pesos is imposed, if harm is inflicted or undertaken against species listed as critical.

The fines collected will go into a Management Fund, along with damages awarded, fees, charges, donations, endowments, administrative fees or grants. The fund is administered by DENR as a special account in the National Treasury. It will be primarily earmarked for the rehabilitation or restoration of habitats. The Fund will also support scientific research, enforcement and monitoring activities, as well as enhancement of capabilities of relevant agencies.

Signed into law on 8 June 2001, RA 9139, otherwise known as the Administrative Naturalization Act of 2000, lays down administrative procedures for granting citizenship to aliens.

Under the law, an alien must meet the following requirements to qualify as an applicant for naturalization through administrative proceedings:

(a) The applicant must be born in the Philippines and have been a resident since birth;

(b) The applicant must be not less than eighteen (18) years of age, at the time of filing of his/her petition;
(c) The applicant must be of good moral character and believe in the underlying principles of the Philippine Constitution, and must have conducted himself/herself in a proper and irreproachable manner during his/her entire period of residence in the Philippines in his/her relation with the duly constituted government as well as with the community in which he/she is living;
(d) The applicant must have received his/her primary and secondary education in any public school or private educational institution duly recognized by the Department of Education, Culture and Sports, where Philippine history, government and civics are taught and prescribed as part of the school curriculum and where enrollment is not limited to any race or nationality: *Provided,* That should he/she have minor children of school age, he/she must have enrolled them in similar schools;
(e) The applicant must have a known trade, business, profession or lawful occupation, from which he/she derives income sufficient for his/her support and if he/she is married and/or has dependants, also that of his/her family: *Provided, however,* That this shall not apply to applicants who are college degree holders but are unable to practise their profession because they are disqualified to do so by reason of their citizenship;
(f) The applicant must be able to read, write and speak Filipino or any of the dialects of the Philippines; and
(g) The applicant must have mingled with the Filipinos and evinced a sincere desire to learn and embrace the customs, traditions and ideals of the Filipino people.

However, the following are not qualified to be naturalized as Filipino citizens:

(a) Those opposed to organized government or affiliated with any association of group of persons who uphold and teach doctrines opposing all organized governments;
(b) Those defending or teaching the necessity of or propriety of violence, personal assault or assassination for the success or predominance of their ideas;
(c) Polygamists or believers in the practice of polygamy;
(d) Those convicted of crimes involving moral turpitude;
(e) Those suffering from mental alienation or incurable contagious diseases;
(f) Those who, during the period of their residence in the Philippines, have not mingled socially with Filipinos, or who have not evinced a sincere desire to learn and embrace the customs, traditions and ideals of the Filipinos;
(g) Citizens or subjects with whom the Philippines is at war, during the period of such war; and
(h) Citizens or subjects of a foreign country whose laws do not grant Filipinos the right to be naturalized citizens or subjects.

Petitions for citizenship under this law are filed with the Special Committee on Naturalization, which is composed of the Solicitor General as chairman, the Secretary of Foreign Affairs, or his representative, and the National Security Adviser, as members, with the power to approve, deny or reject applications for naturalization. A forty thousand peso (P40,000) filing fee is charged from each applicant. If the petition is approved the Committee charges the applicant a naturalization fee of one hundred thousand pesos (P100,000) payable as follows: fifty thousand pesos (P50,000) upon the approval of the petition and fifty thousand pesos (P50,000) upon the taking of the oath of allegiance to the Republic of the Philippines; forthwith, a certificate of naturalization shall be issued. Within sixty days from the issuance of the certificate, the petitioner shall take an oath of allegiance in the proper forum upon proof of payment of the required naturalization processing fee and certificate of naturalization. Should the applicant fail to take the abovementioned oath of allegiance within the said period of time, the approval of the petition shall be deemed abandoned.

Applicants under the law shall file with the Special Committee on Naturalization created under Section 6 hereof, a petition of five copies legibly typed and signed, thumb-marked and verified by him/her, with the latter's passport-sized photograph attached to each copy of the petition, and setting forth the following:

(a) The petitioner's name and surname, and any other name he/she has used or by which he/she is known;

(b) The petitioner's present and former places of residence;

(c) The petitioner's place and date of birth, the names and citizenship of his/her parents and their residences;

(d) The petitioner's trade, business, profession or occupation, and if married, also that of his/her spouse;

(e) Whether the petitioner is single or married or his/her marriage is annulled. If married, petitioner shall state the date and place of his/her marriage, and the name, date of birth, birthplace, citizenship and residence of his/her spouse; and if his marriage is annulled, the date of decree of annulment of marriage and the court which granted the same;

(f) If the petitioner has children, the name, date and birthplace and residences of his/her children;

(g) A declaration that the petitioner possesses all the qualifications and none of the disqualifications under this Act;

(h) A declaration that the petitioner shall never be a public charge; and

(i) A declaration that it is the petitioner's true and honest intention to acquire Philippine citizenship and to renounce absolutely and forever any prince, potentate, State or sovereign, and particularly the country of which the applicant is a citizen or subject.

(2) The application shall be accompanied by:

(a) Duplicate original or certified photocopies of the petitioner's birth certificate;

(b) Duplicate original or certified photocopies of the petitioner's alien certificate of registration and native born certificate of residence;

(c) Duplicate original or certified photocopies of the petitioner's marriage certified, if married, or the death certificate of his spouse, if widowed, or the court decree annulling his marriage, if such was the fact;

(d) Duplicate original or certified photocopies of birth certificates, alien certificate of registration or native born certificate of residence if any, of the petitioner's minor children, wherever applicable;
(e) An affidavit of financial capacity by the petitioner, and sworn statements on the good moral character of the petitioner by at least two (2) Filipino citizens of good reputation in his/her place of residence stating that they have personally known the petitioner for at least a period of ten (10) years and that the said petitioner has in their own opinion all the qualifications necessary to become a citizen of the Philippines and is not in any way disqualified under the provisions of this Act;
(f) A medical certificate that petitioner is not a user of prohibited drugs or otherwise drug dependent and that he/she is not afflicted with acquired immune deficiency syndrome (AIDS);
(g) School diploma and transcript of records of the petitioner in the schools he/she attended in the Philippines. Should the petitioner have minor children, a certification that his children are enrolled in a school where Philippine history, government and civics are taught and are part of the curriculum; and
(h) If gainfully employed, the income tax returns for the past three years.

Within fifteen days from the receipt of the petition, the Committee shall determine whether the petition is complete in substance and in form. If such petition is complete, the Committee shall immediately publish pertinent portions of the petition, indicating the name, qualifications and other personal circumstances of the applicant, once a week for three consecutive weeks in a newspaper of general circulation, and have copies of the petition posted in any public or conspicuous area.

The Committee shall immediately furnish the Department of Foreign Affairs (DFA), the Bureau of Immigration (BI), the civil registrar of the petitioner's place of residence and tile National Bureau of Investigation (NBI) copies of the petition and its supporting documents. These agencies shall have copies of the petition posted in any public or conspicuous area in their buildings, offices and premises, and shall, within thirty days from the receipt of the petition, submit to the Committee a report stating whether or not the petitioner has any derogatory record on file or any such relevant and material information which might be adverse to the petitioner's application for citizenship.

If the petition is found by the Committee to be wanting in substance and form, the petition shall be dismissed without prejudice. The Committee is mandated by law to act on the petition within a sixty-day period.

Once the applicant's petition is approved, his alien wife and minor children may then file a petition for cancellation of their alien certificates of registration with the Committee subject to the payment of the filing fee of twenty thousand pesos (P20,000) and naturalization fee of forty thousand pesos (P40,000) payable as follows: twenty thousand pesos (P20,000) upon the approval of the petition and twenty thousand pesos (P20,000) upon the taking of the oath of allegiance to the Republic of the Philippines.

If the applicant is a married woman, the approval of her petition for administrative naturalization will not benefit her alien husband; however, her minor children may file a petition for cancellation of their alien certificates of registration with the Bureau of Immigration, subject to the requirements of existing laws.

The Special Committee may cancel certificates of naturalization issued under this Act in the following cases:

(a) If it finds that the naturalized person or his/her duly authorized representative made any false statement or misrepresentation or committed any violation of law, rules and regulations in connection with the petition for naturalization, or if he/she otherwise obtains Philippine citizenship fraudulently or illegally, the certificate of naturalization shall be cancelled;

(b) If the naturalized person or his wife, or any of his minor children who acquire Filipino citizenship by virtue of his naturalization shall, within five years next following the grant of Philippine citizenship, establish permanent residence in a foreign country, that individual's certificate of naturalization or acquired citizenship shall be cancelled or revoked: *Provided,* That the fact of such person's remaining for more than one year in his country of origin, or two years in any foreign country, shall be considered *prima facie* evidence of intent permanently to reside therein;

(c) If the naturalized person or his wife or child with acquired citizenship allows himself or herself to be used as a dummy in violation of any constitutional or legal provision requiring Philippine citizenship as a condition for the exercise, use or enjoyment of a right, franchise or privilege, the certificate of naturalization or acquired citizenship shall be cancelled or revoked; and

(d) If the naturalized person or his wife or child with acquired citizenship commits any act inimical to national security, the certificate of naturalization or acquired citizenship shall be cancelled or revoked.

In case the naturalized person holds any hereditary title, or belongs to any order of nobility, he shall make an express renunciation of his title or membership in this order of nobility before the Special Committee or its duly authorized representative, and such renunciation shall be included in the records of his application for citizenship.

OTHER RELEVANT STATE PRACTICE

The RP-PRC Extradition Treaty and the RP-Hong Kong Mutual Legal Assistance Pact

The Philippines signed a new extradition treaty with the People's Republic of China.[79] The treaty, under Article 2, para. 1, contains the double criminality principle, a well-established principle of international law that requires that for an offence to be extraditable, it must be "punishable under the laws of both parties." The article carries a list of the crimes for which a person can be extradited.

However, Article 4 of the treaty acknowledges the political offence exception, which prevents a state from using extradition as a weapon to bring back political rebels and dissenters within its coercive power.

The treaty also has a Rule of Specialty. Under Article 16, when the Philippine authorities extradite a person to China for a specified offence, that person can be tried by China only for that offence, and for no other. The rule ensures that the requesting state does not defeat the "political offence exception": it requests extradition for a common crime, then amends the accusation and charges the extraditee for another offence.

Also, the treaty provides for the non-extradition of a party's own nationals under Article 3, para. 1. The treaty moreover has a surrender provision obligating the two parties to arrest and surrender fugitives from the requesting state.

The RP-HONG KONG Agreement on Mutual Assistance on Legal and Criminal Matters

While the RP-China Treaty pertains to extradition alone, the RP-HK Agreement[80] covers to a wider range of judicial cooperation – serving of documents, obtaining evidence, searches and seizures, effecting testimony of witnesses. However, it excludes extradition, and allows cooperation between the two countries to the task of "identifying and locating persons" and "effecting the temporary transfer of persons in custody to appear as witnesses."

The agreement, however, carries the same safeguards found in the RP-China Extradition Treaty: the political offence exception (Article IV, *Limitations on Compliance*, para. 1.b, 1.c, and 1.d), and the double criminality requirement (id., para. 1.g).

The Agreement also expressly designates the Department of Justice as the executing authority in the Philippines – a feature that is only assumed in the RP-China Extradition Treaty.

---

[79] Signed by the two parties on 23 February 2001. The Agreement complements a memorandum of agreement signed by the two parties on 30 October 2001 on cooperation against illicit traffic and abuse of narcotic drugs, psychotropic substances and control of precursor chemicals.

Negotiated by both parties as early as 1998, the agreement allows the two governments to cooperate and provide mutual assistance in the investigation and prosecution of criminal offenses and in proceedings related to criminal matters.

Under the agreement, the governments pledge to help each other in identifying and locating persons, serving documents, obtaining evidence, articles or documents, executing requests for search and seizure, and facilitating the appearance of witnesses. The agreement also enables the two parties to effect the temporary transfer of persons in custody to appear as witnesses; to obtain judicial or official records; to trace, restrain, forfeit and confiscate the proceeds and instruments of criminal activities; to recover pecuniary penalties for offenses, and to provide information, documents and records, as well as to deliver property.

SRI LANKA[81]

JUDICIAL DECISIONS

Fundamental Rights – Provincial Council elections – unlawful poll at 23 polling stations – failure to declare the poll void and to appoint a re-poll – Articles 12(1) and 14(1) of the Constitution

MEDIWAKE AND OTHERS v. DAYANANDA DISSANAYAKE, COMMISSIONER OF ELECTIONS AND OTHERS
[(2001) 1 SRI LANKA LAW REPORTS PAGE 177, SUPREME COURT, FERNANDO J, WADUGODAPITIYA J AND ISMAIL J]

The four petitioners were registered voters of the Kandy District, one of the three districts in the Central Province. They were members of a particular political party; the first petitioner was a candidate for the Kandy District and the fourth petitioner was a polling agent.

Provincial Council elections in the Province took place on 6 April 1999 under the Provincial Council Elections Act. The petitioners alleged that on the day of the elections at 25 named polling stations in the District various incidents took place which affected the validity of the election results. They pleaded that the failure of the first and second respondents to conduct a proper poll at these polling stations and the failure of the first respondent to declare the poll at those stations void and order a re-poll violated their fundamental rights under the Constitution. The Court granted them leave to proceed in respect of the alleged infringement to Articles 12(1) and 14(1)(a) of the Constitution. These Articles read as follows.

---

[81] Contributed by Camena Guneratne, Senior Lecturer, Department of Legal Studies, Open University of Sri Lanka.

Article 12 (1) – All persons are equal before the law and are entitled to the equal protection of the law.

Article 14 (1) (a) – Every citizen is entitled to the freedom of speech and expression including publication.

On the facts of the case, the Court concluded that incidents of ballot stuffing, harassment and chasing away of polling agents of a particular political party had taken place. The Court considered the impact of these incidents on the fundamental rights of the petitioners.

The Court held that the petitioners, being registered voters of the Kandy District, had a legal right to vote in that election. In an earlier case it had been held that voting, in the exercise of that legal right, was a form of "expression" guaranteed by Article 14 (1) (a).[82] The Court further held that the requirement that elections must be free, equal and by secret ballot is fundamental to any election in any nation which respects the sovereignty of the people, representative democracy and the rule of law. The Court therefore took the view that "the right to a free, equal and secret ballot is an integral part of the citizen's freedom of expression when he exercises that freedom through his right ... to vote".

However, although it was clear that many voters had been unable to exercise their right to a free, equal and secret ballot, none of the petitioners claimed that they themselves had been prevented from voting. Therefore, while the irregularities complained of directly infringed the right of others to vote, the question arose as to whether this alone constituted an infringement of the *petitioners'* rights under Article 12(1) and 14(1)(a).

The Court stated that in order to decide that question it was necessary to consider the true nature of a citizen's right to vote, and Article 25 of the International Covenant on Civil and Political Rights was a useful starting point. Article 25 was quoted as follows:

> Every citizen shall have the right and the opportunity without any of the distinctions mentioned in Article 2 and without unreasonable restrictions:
> (a) To take part in the conduct of public affairs, directly or through freely chosen representatives;
> (b) To vote and to be elected at genuine periodic elections, which shall be by universal and equal suffrage and shall be held by secret ballot, guaranteeing the free expression of the will of the electors...

The Court went on to hold:[83]

> Sri Lanka is a party to that Covenant and its sister Covenant, which together constitute the international Bill of Human Rights. It would be idle to argue that our election laws pertaining to Provincial Council elections are not founded on guarantees to every

---

[82] Karunatilleke v. Dissanayake (1999) 1 Sri Lanka Law Reports, page 157.

[83] (2001) Sri Lanka Law Reports, at page 211.

citizen of the right to "take part" in public affairs, through representatives *freely chosen* by him, at *a genuine* election, by universal and equal suffrage, held by *secret ballot*, ensuring the *free expression* of the will of the electorate. Article 27 (15) [of the Constitution] requires the State "to endeavour to foster respect for international law and treaty obligations in dealings among nations." Accordingly, in interpreting the relevant provisions of an enactment regulating *any* election a Court must, unless there is compelling language, favour a construction which is consistent with the international obligations of the State, *especially* those imposed by the international Bill of Human Rights. I hold that those guarantees are an essential part of the freedom of expression recognised by Article 14(1)(a).

The citizen's right to vote includes the right to freely choose his representative, through a genuine election which guarantee the free expression of the will of *the electors*; not just his own. Therefore, not only is a citizen entitled *himself* to vote at a free, equal and secret poll, but he also has a right to a genuine election guaranteeing the free expression of the will of the entire electorate to which he belongs. Thus if a citizen desires that candidate X should be his representative and if he is allowed to vote for X but other like-minded citizens are prevented from voting for X, then his right to the free expression of the will of the elector has been denied. If 51% of the electors wish to vote for X, but ten per cent are prevented from voting – in consequence of which X is defeated – that is a denial of the rights not only of the ten per cent but of the 41% as well. Indeed, in such a situation, the 41% may legitimately complain that they might as well not have voted. To that extent, the freedom of expression of like-minded voters when exercised through the electoral process is a collective one, although they may not be members of any group or association.

A citizen's freedom of speech guaranteed by article 14(1)(a) is violated not only when he is not permitted to speak, but even when others are prevented from listening to him. A corollary of A's freedom of speech is A's right that those to whom he wishes to speak should be permitted to listen to him – provided of course that they want to listen to him. If a part of his audience is driven away, the effectiveness of the exercise of his freedom of speech is impaired, and thereby his right is infringed.

NATIONAL LAWS ON INTERNATIONAL LAW MATTERS

Civil Aspects of International Child Abduction Act No. 10 of 2001

This Act was passed to give effect to The Hague Convention on Civil Aspects of International Child Abduction adopted at The Hague on 25 October 1980. The Preamble to the Act refers to the Convention and states that as Sri Lanka has acceded to the Act it is necessary to make legal provision to enable Sri Lanka to fulfil its obligations under it.

The Act comes into operation on such date as the Minister certifies as the date on which the Convention enters into force in respect of Sri Lanka. The Minister may also specify the countries in respect of which the provisions of the Act shall apply and the date on which such provisions will start coming into force. These countries are known as specified countries.

The Act defines what is meant by the wrongful removal from or retention in Sri Lanka of a child. It designates the Secretary to the Ministry of Justice as the Central Authority for the purposes of this Act and specifies the powers and duties of such Authority. The appropriate Authority of a specified country or a person, institution or other body who claims that a child has been wrongfully removed to and retained in Sri Lanka may apply to the Central Authority for assistance in securing the return of such child. The Authority may apply to the High Court of the Western Province for an order ordering the return of such child to the specified country in which he or she habitually resided.

Where the High Court is satisfied that the child has been wrongfully removed to and retained in Sri Lanka and less than a year has elapsed between the wrongful removal and the application, it shall forthwith order the return of the child to the country where he/she habitually resides. It may also do so even where more than one year has elapsed since the removal of the child, unless it is satisfied that the child is settled in his or her new environment.

The Court may refuse to order the return of the child if the person or institution from whom the child was taken was not exercising rights of custody at the time, or had subsequently consented to or acquiesced in the removal of such child, or where there is grave risk that the child's return may expose him/her to physical or psychological harm or otherwise place him/her in an intolerable situation. The Court may also refuse the application if the child objects to being returned and if the Court is satisfied that the child has reached an age and degree of maturity where his/her views should be taken into account.

An order made by the High Court shall not be deemed to be a determination on the merits of any issue of custody of the child. Where the Central Authority has received a notice that a child has been wrongfully removed to Sri Lanka from a specified country, no court in Sri Lanka shall make such a determination until after the High Court or the Central Authority has refused an application to return a child to that country, or until six weeks have passed since the date of such notice and no application for the return of the child has been made.

The Court must dispose of an application within six weeks of its date. Where the Court fails to do so, the Central Authority may request from it reasons for the delay. The Authority may do so on its own volition or on the request of the appropriate authority in the specified country. Where an order has been made for the return of a child, the Central Authority shall facilitate such return.

Where any person, institution or other body in Sri Lanka claims that a child has been wrongfully removed from the country, and is residing in a specified country in breach of the rights of custody of that person or institution or body, such person, institution or body may apply to the Central Authority for assistance to ensure the return of the child to Sri Lanka. The Central Authority shall apply to the appropriate Authority in the specified country in which the child is residing for assistance in securing his/her return to Sri Lanka.

REGULATIONS

United Nations Regulations No. 1 of 2001 (dated 11 October 2001)

These Regulations were made by the Minister of Foreign Affairs under the United Nations Act No. 45 of 1968. Section 2 (1) of the Act provides that

> If, under Article Forty-one of the Charter of the United Nations signed at San Francisco on the twenty-sixth day of June, Nineteen hundred and forty-five, (being the Article which relates to measures not involving the use of armed force) the Security Council of the United Nations call upon the Government of Sri Lanka to apply any measures to give effect to any decision of that Council, the Minister in charge of the subject of Foreign Affairs may by regulations make such provision as appears to him necessary or expedient for enabling those measures to be effectively applied, including (without prejudice to the generality of the preceding provisions of this subsection) provision for the apprehension, trial and punishment of persons offending against the regulations.

Clause 2 of the Regulations states "The Security Council of the United Nations acting under Chapter VII of the Charter of the United Nations, unanimously adopted Resolution 1371 (2001) and has re-affirmed the principle established by the General Assembly in its declaration of October 1970 (Resolution 2625 (XXV) and reiterated by the Security Council in its Resolution 1189 of 18th August 1998, namely, that every State has the duty to refrain from organizing, instigating, assisting or participating in a terrorist act in another State, or acquiescing in organized activities within its territory directed towards the commission of such act and has decided that all States take necessary and effective measures to give effect to such decision."

These regulations were passed to give effect to this Resolution.

The Minster is empowered to appoint a Competent Authority by name or by office for the purpose of these Regulations. The Minister may also, in consultation with the Minister in charge of Defence, issue the necessary directions to implement these regulations. On information received, he/she, in consultation with the Minister in charge of Defence, shall determine the organizations or person in respect of whom these Regulations should be enforced, inform the Competent Authority of such determinations and forward to him/her the material on which the determination was made.

The Regulations prohibit any citizen of Sri Lanka (whether living in Sri Lanka or not) or any non-citizen living in Sri Lanka from doing any act which may directly or indirectly assist in the collection of funds for any terrorist organization or which may assist in any terrorist act. The funds, financial assets or resources of any person who engages in these acts shall be frozen with immediate effect.

No person shall within Sri Lanka make available, directly or indirectly, any funds or financial or economic resources for the benefit of any person or organization engaged in or attempting to engage in any terrorist act.

Any person who contravenes these provisions shall, on conviction by the High Court of Colombo be liable to imprisonment for a minimum period of five years and a maximum period of ten years. His/her funds, financial assets or resources shall also be forfeited to the State.

If any person knows or to has reasonable cause to believe that any person has committed an offence under these regulations or is about to do so, or has information relating to the movement or whereabouts of any such person, he/she must report it to the police. Failure to do so is an offence which carries a punishment of imprisonment of between two and seven years on conviction.

The term "terrorist act" has also been defined in the Regulations. It includes the use or threat of actions which involves:

(a) the use or threat of action which is designed to influence the government, or to intimidate the public or a section of the public;
(b) the use or threat of action which is made for the purpose of advancing a political, religious or ideological cause;
and that the action envisaged
    (i) involves serious violence against a person;
    (ii) involves serious damage to property;
    (iii) endangers the life of another person, other than the person committing the action;
    (iv) creates a serious risk to health or safety of the public or a section of the public; or
    (v) is designed seriously to interfere with or seriously to disrupt an electronic system.
"Terrorist organisation" means an organisation:
(a) which does any act, or causes any act to be done; or
(b) which is directly or indirectly connected with the collection of funds, and which assists, promotes or facilitated or is intended to assist, promote or facilitate the commission of a terrorist act.

NATIONAL LAWS ON INTERNATIONAL LAW MATTERS

Mutual Assistance in Criminal Matters Act No. 25 of 2002

The long title to this Act states that it is meant to provide for the rendering of assistance in criminal matters by Sri Lanka and specified countries and for matters connected therewith or incidental thereto.

This Act applies primarily in respect of any Commonwealth country which the Minister may declare by Order published in the Gazette.

Where an agreement has been entered into between Sri Lanka and any non-Commonwealth country, (whether before or after this Act), the Minister may by Order published in the Gazette declare that the provisions of the Act shall apply to such country. The Order shall specify the limitations and conditions which the Minister may decide to specify in the Order, having regard to the terms of the agreement. Every such order shall specify the terms of such agreement on which it was based. The Order shall remain in force only so long as the agreement remains in force.

All Orders in relation to any country (i.e., a specified country) shall be brought before Parliament as soon as convenient.

According to Section 3, the object of the Act is to facilitate the provision and obtaining by Sri Lanka of assistance in criminal matters, including:

(a) the location and identification of witnesses and suspects;
(b) the service of documents;
(c) the examination of witnesses;
(d) the obtaining of evidence, documents or other articles;
(e) the execution of requests for search and seizure;
(f) the effecting of a temporary transfer of a person in custody to appear as a witness;
(g) the facilitation of the personal appearance of witnesses;
(h) the provision of documents and other records;
(i) the location of the proceeds of any criminal activity;
(j) the enforcement of orders for the payment of fines or for the forfeiture or freezing of property.

The Secretary to the Ministry of Justice shall be the Central Authority for the purposes of this Act.

The appropriate authority of a specified country may make an application to the Central Authority requesting assistance in elation to a criminal matter failing within the jurisdiction of a criminal court in that country. Such a request may be refused wholly or partly if the Central Authority believes that the request relates to an act or omission that falls within any of the following categories.

(a) It would not constitute an offence under Sri Lankan law;
(b) The offence is of a political character;
(c) The act or omission would constitute an offence only under the military law of Sri Lanka.

The request may also be refused if it relates to the prosecution of a person for an offence for which that person has already been acquitted or convicted under Sri Lankan law. If compliance with the request would be contrary to the Sri Lankan Constitution or be prejudicial to the national security, international relations or public policy it could also be refused. Another basis for refusal would be where compliance would facilitate the prosecution or punishment of any person on account of his/her race, religion, language, caste, sex, political opinion or place of birth,

The Act makes provision for the following:

(a) Part II – assistance in relation to location and identifying persons;
(b) Part III – assistance in relation to the service of summons and other documents;

(c) Part IV – assistance in relation to taking of evidence and production of documents or other articles;

(d) Part V – arrangements for persons to give evidence or assist investigations;

(e) Part VI – assistance in relation to search and seizure;

(f) Part VII – tracing proceeds of crime and enforcement of orders.

OTHER RELEVANT STATE PRACTICE

Recommendations of the Human Rights Commission

Voting rights of migrant workers

The Human Rights Commission of Sri Lanka Act No. 21 of 1996 established the Human Rights Commission which consists of five members appointed by the President on the recommendation of the Constitutional Council. The Commission has a wide mandate and provides an alternative system to the judicial process in protecting human rights. The Commission's functions are to investigate complaints regarding the infringements or imminent infringements of fundamental rights, and to provide for the resolution of such complaints by conciliation and mediation.

The Commission's mandate also includes advising and assisting the government in drafting legislation as well as administrative directives and procedures, to strengthen and protect fundamental rights. It can also advise the government on necessary measures to ensure that national laws and administrative practices conform to international human rights norms and make recommendations to the Government on the need to accede to treaties and other international instruments in the field of human rights.

A significant recommendation was made by the Commission in the year under review in response to an application filed by a trade union, the National Workers' Congress, on behalf of migrant workers.[84] These workers number about one million and their earnings abroad now amount to one of the three highest sources of foreign exchange for the country. One of their long-standing demands was to be granted overseas voting rights while employed abroad.

In response to the application, the Commission recommended that Sri Lankans who have left the country to take up employment overseas and who intend to return to Sri Lankan within five years be given overseas voting rights. The Commission based its recommendation on the fact that Sri Lanka is a signatory to the United Nations Convention on the Protection of the Rights of All Migrant Workers and Members of their Families, and referred to Article 41 which addresses this issue.

---

[84] Information obtained from "Human Rights" a publication of the Ministry of Justice, Law Reform and National Integration, Volume 2002, Issue No. 3.

TAJIKISTAN[85]

JUDICIAL DECISIONS[86]

The Constitutional Court of the Republic of Tajikistan
Resolution of the Constitutional Court of the Republic of Tajikistan, 12 June 2001[87]
ESTABLISHMENT OF THE ACCORDANCE OF ARTICLES 329.5 AND 339.2 OF CRIMINAL PROCEDURE CODE TO THE CONSTITUTION OF TAJIKISTAN[88]

The Constitutional Court having considered the report of the Judge of the Constitutional Court, and having investigated the materials of the case, established:

The Supreme Court of the Republic of Tajikistan on the basis of requirements set by Article 33 of Penal Code, and fulfilling its authority to take to its own deliberation the cases of particular complexity or cases of special social importance, in its verdict of 24 November 2000 declared S.S. Sharipov guilty of the charges provided in Articles 186.1, 249.4 clauses (b) and (c), 181.3 clause (a), and 110.3 clause (a). In the verdict of 9 April 2001 the court also declared guilty B.I. Minboev of the commission of crimes according to Articles 104 and 195.1 of the Penal Code. In relation to both, the Supreme Court imposed the exceptional form of punishment: the death penalty.

According to Article 329.5 of the Criminal Procedural Code decisions of the Supreme Court are not subject to the cassational appeal and protest; those sentenced do not have the opportunity of bringing a cassational appeal against the decisions of the Supreme Court of Tajikistan. As a consequence, the constitutionality and substantial nature of its decisions remain unmonitored. Additionally, in accordance with Article 339.2 of the Criminal Procedural Code of Tajikistan, the question of the presence of the person sentenced during the deliberation of the court in examining the case regarding a cassational order is resolved by the same court. Furthermore, according to the same Criminal Procedural Code, authorities, namely the chairman of the Supreme Court and the General Prosecutor, have the right to enter a protest against the verdict, while the individual sentenced does not possess this right.

---

[85] Contributed by Tahmina Karimova, Intern, International Criminal Court, The Hague.
[86] The Tajik Judicial System stands for a well structured and complex organization. The Constitutional Court, Supreme Court and Supreme Economic Court are set at the top of the judicial hierarchy in accordance with the Constitution of Tajikistan. Each of the courts has its own place in the system and is endowed with competencies that are pertinent exclusively to it. [Article 1 of the Law *"On Constitutional Court of Republic of Tajikistan"*, adopted 2 November 1995 Ahbori Majlisi Olii Jumhurii Tojikiston (Registry of the Tajik Parliament) Issue 21, p. 223].
[87] Article 47 of the Law on Constitutional Court states that Resolutions of Constitutional Court cannot be appealed against.
[88] NB Unofficial Translation of the Case cited in the "Collection of the Legal – Normative Acts and the Decisions of Constitutional Court of Republic of Tajikistan" (Sbornik Normativno-pravovih Actov i Resheniy Konstitucionnogo Suda Respubliki Tadjikistan), Dushanbe 2002

The persons sentenced have pleaded before the court that they take partial responsibility for the commission of the crimes. According to their statements the investigation was conducted unilaterally; they were accused without sufficient evidence, and despite this fact they indeed have the right through a cassational order to appeal against the verdicts. This has not been granted and therefore their constitutional rights have been violated.

The sentenced S.S. Sharipov pleaded before the Constitutional Court through his legal representative that Article 329.5 should be proclaimed unconstitutional and as one without further legal effect. Additionally, Minboev with the help of his counsel appealed to the Constitutional Court of Republic of Tajikistan and requested the determination of Articles 329.5 and 339.2 of the Criminal Procedural Code as being non-compliant with the Constitution and thus without further legal effect.

The special representative of the Majlisi Namoyandagon of Majlisi Oli (lower house of the Tajik Parliament) M.Z. Rahimov explained that the Criminal Procedural Code of Tajikistan was adopted in 1961 and some of its articles do not meet the requirement of the Constitution and international standards recognized by Tajikistan. The Constitutional Court having investigated the disputed matters had come to the resolution that according to Article 17 of the Tajik Constitution each person is equal before the law and the court.

Furthermore, in accordance with Article 19.1 each person has a guarantee of judicial defence, and has a right to claim that his case be adjudicated by a competent and impartial court. The right to appeal against the judicial decisions is one of the democratic principles of criminal procedure; relying upon this principle and according to Article 329.1 of the Criminal Procedural Code, all participants of criminal procedure have a right to freely appeal against the decisions of court in cassational order.

To appeal regarding a cassational order is one of the means of assessing the legality and substantial nature of judicial decisions. It is directed at the timely disclosure of the committed violations of law, at verification of the implementation of the presumption of innocence principle, and at application of the law in High Instances, in order to ensure that crimes do not remain unpunished and the innocent are not charged wrongly for crimes they did not commit.

Whilst examining the case in the first instance, the Supreme Court is under the duty to provide the defendant simultaneously with the opportunity to realize the democratic principles concerning cassational instance, i.e., the right freely to appeal against the sentence, verification of the legality and substantial nature of sentences, provision of new evidence, etc.

In accordance with Article 20 of the Constitution of the Republic of Tajikistan no one is recognized as being guilty of having committed a crime prior to the moment the court decision is given legal effect; i.e., in accordance with the general rules of court examination, if no appeal or protest is brought against the latter within the time limit of seven days, then it comes into legal effect. Hence, the instance of cassation represents one of the most important stages of the judicial process and must be exercised. However, Article 329.5 of the Criminal Procedure Code of Tajikistan deprives the person sentenced of his right to appeal against the court decision and this circumstance is contradictory to the provision of Articles 17, 19 and 20 of the Tajik Constitution.

Moreover, Article 10.3 of the Tajik Constitution provides that international legal norms recognized by Tajikistan are a part of the legal system of Tajikistan. In the case of contradiction of Tajik laws with international legal acts, the latter have priority over the former.

According to the International Covenant of Civil and Political Rights adopted by UN GA Resolution (XXI) of 16 December 1966 and on the basis of the Resolution adopted by Majlisi Oli of the Tajik Republic from 1 November 1998, this Covenant has been in force in the territory of Tajikistan since 4 April 1999. In particular Article 14.5 of the Covenant provides that "every one who is sentenced for commission of a crime has a right for the sentence to be revised by the higher judicial instance in accordance with law".

Article 339.2 of the Criminal Procedural Code provides that court of cassational instance can decide whether the sentenced can take part in the court examination. In the event that the sentenced is not given such an opportunity, he is deprived of making use of the procedural rights provided by Articles 341-342 of the Criminal Procedural Code. These procedural rights include: the right to reject, the right to speech and to provide additional materials, or the right to revise materials provided by third parties; also, the person sentenced can be deprived of the right to be informed of the conclusion of the prosecutor. Such circumstances illustrate a violation of the requirement of Article 17 of the Constitution that provides equality of everyone before the law. The state of affairs also contradicts Article 88 of the Constitution that guarantees contestation and the equality of parties.

Further, according to Article 14.3 of International Covenant on Civil and Political Rights every one has a right as minimum for the following equal guarantees when he is charged with a criminal offence:

"d) to be tried in his presence, and to defend himself in person or through legal assistance of his own choosing".

Taking into account the above and other circumstances expressed in relation to the sentenced, he has as much a right to appeal in cassational order against the decision of the Supreme Court as do the other parties.

On the basis of the abovementioned, the Constitutional Court of the Republic of Tajikistan has come to a resolution to recognize Article 329 part 5 of the Criminal Procedural Code to be contradictory to Articles 17, 19 and 20 of the Constitution and therefore of no further legal effect. Moreover, all the normative acts that were based on Articles 329.5 and 339.2 of the Criminal Procedural Code or contained the provisions of these Articles should be considered as void.

NATIONAL LAWS ON INTERNATIONAL LAW MATTERS

Law "On the Usage and Protection of the Red Cross and Red Crescent Emblems and Appellations in the Republic of Tajikistan" adopted on 12 May 2001[89]

In accordance with the international obligations of the Republic of Tajikistan that flow from the Geneva Conventions on the Protection of the Victims of War of 12 August 1949 and Additional Protocols to them, and also according to the Rules of using the emblems of Red Cross or Red Crescent by national societies,[90] Tajikistan has enacted relevant law that regulates the usage and protection of the emblems of the Red Cross and the Red Crescent. The law accepts the same definitions of an armed conflict, medical personnel, sanitary and transport means and emblem as provided in the Geneva Conventions and Additional Protocols.

The objects that fall under the protection of the above-mentioned law are: the emblems of the Red Cross and the Red Crescent; the appellations "Red Cross" and "Red Crescent"; and distinguishing symbols identifying medical personnel and sanitary/transport means. Article 5 of the law provides that the emblem is the symbol of alleviation of the suffering of the wounded and sick in times of armed conflicts and emergency situations.

The emblem can be used only in circumstances envisioned in the law, Geneva Conventions and Additional Protocols. The emblem is specifically used as a protection sign in times of armed conflict and is used to distinguish medical personnel, medical and sanitary transportation in peacetime.

The law further refers to the usage of the emblem of the Red Crescent by the medical services of the armed forces of Tajikistan, other armed formations, by the civil medical service and by the national societies of the Red Cross and the Red Crescent; additionally, it determines the distinguishing symbols used by medical and sanitary transportation of the Red Cross and Red Crescent societies.

The usage of the emblem in contradiction to the law is a violation and hence criminal responsibility is provided for.

Law "On the Import and Export of Cultural Valuables" adopted 31 July 2001[91]

The law establishes a legal framework aimed at the preservation of the cultural heritage of peoples, the protection of cultural valuables from illicit import and export, the establishment of unified procedure of import and export, and at facilitating international cooperation in the field. It is provided that in cases where the present

---

[89] Ahbori Majlisi Olii Jumhurii Tojikiston (Registry of the Tajik Parliament for 2001) Issue #4, 2001, pp. 202-205.
[90] Adopted in the International Conference of the Red Cross and the Red Crescent in 1965, with amendments from 1991.
[91] *Ahbori Majlisi Olii Jumhurii Tojikiston* (Registry of the Tajik Parliament) Issue # 7 p. 511

law contradicts international treaty provisions ratified by Tajikistan, the latter will take precedence over the former.

The following cultural objects fall within the jurisdiction of the Act:

- cultural valuables created by nationals of Tajikistan;
- valuables created in the territory of Tajikistan by foreign nationals or by persons without a state;
- cultural objects found in the territory of Tajikistan;
- valuables collected in museums, libraries, archives, and galleries;
- cultural objects acquired by archaeological, ethnographical, folklore and by any other scientific expeditions;
- valuables acquired as a result of voluntary exchange;
- cultural objects received as a part of an inheritance or gift, or legally acquired with the agreement of the authorized agencies of a state to which cultural valuables belong; and
- cultural valuables imported to Tajikistan by foreign corporate bodies.

The Ministry of Culture and the Customs Committee are the two state agencies authorized by the Act to deal with the cases in the sphere of import and export of cultural valuables. More specifically, the Ministry is competent to specify categories of objects that qualify as a cultural valuable and is authorized to decide matters of import and export. It is in charge of the registration of imported and exported cultural valuables and additionally takes other measures relevant to the fulfilment of the abovementioned competencies. The Customs Committee exercises control over the importation and exportation of the cultural objects.

The owner or other authorized person of the cultural valuable can export the object on the basis of a certificate granted by the Ministry of Culture. It is forbidden to export cultural valuables created more than 50 years ago, objects that are registered in the state protection books, and objects that are permanently kept in state and public museums, archives and libraries.

The law allows temporary export of cultural objects for the purposes of international exhibitions, restoration and scientific research or export of valuables related to theatrical or artistic activity, etc. Temporarily exported cultural objects cannot be used as a credit guarantee or as an object of bail.

The Tajik diplomatic corps provides protection to temporarily exported cultural valuables. Objects that are aimed at subverting the constitutional system and state sovereignty or the violation of territorial integrity, objects that propagate war, terrorism, violence, religious extremism, racism and, additionally, materials of pornographic content cannot be brought into Tajikistan in the guise of cultural objects.

The law regulates the prevention of illegal import and export of cultural valuables and sets the legal framework for the transit of cultural objects, considering additionally their postage *via* mail. Finally, the Act sets the rules on returning cultural objects to Tajikistan and the process of compensation to *bona fide* owners of the returned cultural valuables.

Law "On Informing (Informatization)" adopted on 6 August 2001[92]

The Tajik authorities have endeavoured to create positive conditions in order to satisfy informational demands of corporate bodies, individuals and state agencies. Therefore, it was deemed essential to create a modern informational infrastructure that will be integrated into the international informational system. These and other reasons necessitated the adoption of a law that will regulate the legal conditions of the formation and utility of documented information and informational resources. The Act has established a legal framework for the creation of informational technology and for the determination of rights and duties of subjects taking part in the process of informing in society.

The law anticipates a new concept, i.e., "informatization" to understand the process of elaboration, creation and development of the informational technologies and resources. The so-called informatization is based on the principles of accessibility of information, and the effectiveness, completeness and precision of the presented information. Additionally, the law provides for the protection of property in the informational sphere.

The law outlines the responsibility of the state. The foremost obligation of the state in the field is to create necessary legal, economic, organizational and other conditions that will facilitate the development of informatization, at the same time bearing in mind the rights and interests of individuals.

The functions of state agencies in the sphere of informatization are confined to the creation of conditions for the comprehensive fulfilment of informational needs of the population, national informational structure facilitation, and the granting of support to the development of international and universal information network and systems, etc. The law provides that the objects of ownership in the sphere of informatization are informational resources, documented information, informational technology, a complex of programme and technical means and, in addition, informational systems and networks.

It must be noted that the law on "informatization" lays down a very comprehensive set of rules in the field of *informatization* and attempts to cover all significant areas in the field so as to provide a well-structured legal regime.

For instance, Chapter II of the Act is dedicated to the informational resources area. The law envisions that informational resources should primarily be used to satisfy the informational needs of society and state and should be directed at the establishment of unified informational space and its integration into the international informational community. The Chapter outlines the basics of the legal regime for informational resources and further specifies the directives on the usage of documented information.

However, the implementation of the right to receive information may not violate the civil, political, economic, social, spiritual and other rights and legal interests of other individuals and corporate bodies. Informational resources are classified according

---

[92] *Ahbori Majlisi Olii Jumhurii Tojikiston* (Registry of the Tajik Parliament for 2001) Issue # 7 p. 502.

to their level of accessibility. State informational resources are open and accessible, with the exception of information that is confined by the law to the category of "limited access".

Another significant part of the law on informatization is dedicated to infrastructure and informational systems. Particular attention is also given to the protection of informational resources and the rights of subjects in the sphere of information. The latter represents a very significant component in the development of such an area as information, since it provides protection from illegal interference in informational resources, and from unauthorized acts directed at the copying, modification, destruction, etc. of the information. However, the above-mentioned does not represent an exhaustive list of objectives to be achieved. Furthermore, protection is essential in order to preserve the precision, completeness, integrity of documented information, to protect the constitutional rights of individuals against any violation of confidentiality and private life, and additionally to preserve state secrecy, and lastly and generally, the rights of subjects participating in legal conditions concerning information.

Since information has become a significant part of international cooperation, the legislators have contemplated provisions regulating bilateral and multilateral cooperation in the area of information. Integration into international informational network is encouraged and relevant measures of precaution and protection from illicit acts are regulated.

Law "On the Status of Refugees" adopted on 10 May 2002[93]

As part of the implementation of its obligation in accordance with the International Convention on the Status of Refugees of 28 July 1951,[94] Tajikistan has adopted its second legislative act on "The Status of Refugees".[95] The previous law on the same matter adopted in July 1994 was subsequently declared as being without further legal effect.

The law provides provisions envisioning the scope of the Refugee Law. The law provides the definition of a "refugee", which does not differ substantially, except for the technical differences, from the definition provided in the Convention.

The law on Refugees identifies categories of people that are excluded from the scope of refugee status. These categories include:

1. persons who have allegedly committed crimes against peace, war crimes or crimes against humanity;

---

[93] *Ahbori Majlisi Olii Jumhurii Tojikiston* (Registry of the Tajik Parliament for 2002) Issue # 4 part I, p. 305.
[94] Ratified by the Government of Tajikistan in 1993.
[95] *Rights of Refugees: International and National Standards*, (compilation of international conventions and Tajik Law relating to the status of refugees) eds. UNHCR, Ministry of Labour and Social Protection of Tajikistan and "Law and Society" NGO. Dushanbe-2002 pp. 109-128.

2. persons against whom there are reasons to assume that they have committed serious crimes of non-political character beyond territory of Tajikistan prior to their seeking of the status of a refugee;
3. persons who are allegedly connected to the special agencies of their country of nationality, to international terrorist organizations or to drug-dealing structures;
4. persons in relation to whom there are reasons to purport that they are guilty of misconduct contravening with the principles and goals of UN organization and OSCE.

Furthermore, the law provides the details of the procedure of recognizing a person as a refugee. The subsequent provisions of the Act reflect the rights and duties and the most important guarantees available to a refugee. The guarantees include the principle of *non-refoulement*.

Law "On the Electronic Document" adopted on 10 May 2002[96]

The Law on the Electronic Document is the first legal act adopted in the sphere in Tajikistan. It establishes the legal basis of electronic document management, lays down the rules governing the basic requirements of such documents, and envisages the rights and duties of the parties in the context of relations resulting from the circulation of electronic documents.

According to this Act, an electronic document is allowed to be used in all the spheres involving informational and technical means that are necessary for the preparation and preservation of incoming and outgoing information. More specifically, electronic documents can be used in the conclusion of contracts, payments, carrying on correspondence and information transmission.

The law underlines the necessity for control and regulation in this sphere in order to ensure the protection of the rights and legal interests of the subjects and to ensure the protection of information as well. For this purpose the government of Tajikistan is endowed with the right to control the field of circulation of the electronic document.

A set of requirements must be met by a document in order for it to qualify as an electronic document. The first and foremost requirement is that the electronic document must be created, worked on, received and sent by technical and pro-gramming means. Further, the Act establishes the structure, and external and internal form of the electronic document.

The electronic document possesses the same legal effect as the hard format of the document. However, the reflection of the electronic document on paper, i.e., copy of electronic document must be appropriately certified in order to provide this with the legal effect. The law regulates other aspects of electronic format such as digital signatures, and lays down detailed rules dealing with the purpose and usage of personal keys to the signature.

---

[96] *Supra*, n. 15, at p. 308.

Dissemination of the electronic document that contains state, commerce or other types of secret and other information is forbidden or limited by the law. As a consequence, state agencies, corporate bodies and individuals that use the above-mentioned information are obliged to transmit such documents through certified and protected connection channels.

Furthermore, the law on electronic documents encompasses such areas as the licensing of the circulation of electronic documents and provides provisions regulating circulation of the e-documents in banking activity. Violation of the provisions of the law and dissemination of the information of limited access is penalized. The concluding part of the law envisions international cooperation in the sphere of electronic documents.

Law "On Information Protection" adopted 2 December 2002[97]

The role of information as a significant and major determinant of modern society is indisputable. Hence, realizing the threat of the information's being leaked, misappropriated, distorted, forged, illegally blocked, copied, etc., appropriate legal frameworks have been drawn up. The law on information protection establishes the fundamental principles of protection and regulates the legal conditions that emerge in this area.

The object of the legal protection provided in the present law is the documented information in relation to which certain rules and limitations have been set by the Tajik laws for the owner or proprietor. The latter is being further specified in terms of subjects of the legal conditions mentioned: that is, state institutions, corporate bodies and individuals can act in the capacity of proprietor. Moreover, it is anticipated that the subjects of legal conditions in the area of information have rights for protection from acts resulting in the destruction, misappropriation, and modification of information.

It is established by the law that organizational, technical, physical and cryptographical means can be used as a means of protecting the information. It is emphasized by the Act that authorized state agencies need to undertake protection through the administration of a unified technical policy on information protection. The implementation of such a policy in the area should be accompanied by a number of other measures and rules specified further in the law.

---

[97] *Ahbori Majlisi Olii Jumhurii Tojikiston* (Registry of the Tajik Parliament for 2002) Issue # 11, p. 696

OTHER RELEVANT STATE PRACTICE

Decree No. 855[98]

Presidential Decree No. 855, called otherwise "humanization of the criminal law" relating to "Reformation of Criminal and executive system of Tajikistan" was issued in July 2002. Aiming at the promotion of respect for human rights and improvement of the system of criminal punishment, it was established by the decree to start a transmission of the authority over criminal cases from the Ministry of Internal Affairs to the Ministry of Justice. Such a transmission requires a detailed and comprehensive legal regulation. Therefore, the Presidential Decree has also requested legislators to ensure adoption of relevant laws in fulfilment of the decree and to assist in the facilitation of reforms in the area of criminal law.

THAILAND[99]

JUDICIAL DECISIONS

Extradition; Political offence exception

PUBLIC PROSECUTOR v. SOK YOUEN A.K.A. SOK YUEN
[Black Case No. Phor. 6 / 2543; Red Case No. Phor. 7 / 2545, 28 November 2002, CRIMINAL COURT, JJ. POL ANUWATNITIKARN and TERDSAK INTARA-PREECHA]

The Defendant was accused by the Cambodian authorities of committing two offences: (a) the attempted murder of Prime Minister Hun Sen of Cambodia on 24 September 1998, as a result of which some houses were damaged, one child killed and three other persons injured; and (b) the illegal possession of weapons of war. The Cambodian military court issued a warrant for his arrest. The first offence is punishable with imprisonment of ten to twenty years, while the second one is punishable with imprisonment of six months to three years. The Defendant went into hiding in Cambodia and, a year later, escaped to Thailand. The Cambodian Government sought his extradition from Thailand in a series of diplomatic notes addressed to the Thai Ministry of Foreign Affairs in 1999 and 2000.

Pursuant to Section 4 of Thailand's Extradition Act B.E. 2472 (1929 A.D.), the Royal Thai Government may at its discretion surrender to foreign States with which no extradition treaties exist persons accused or convicted of crimes committed within the jurisdiction of such States, provided that by Thai laws such crimes are punishable

---

[98] Data provided by the Ministry of Justice of the Republic of Tajikistan.
[99] Contributed by Patcharapa Thawinyarti, Barrister-at-Law, Bangkok.

with imprisonment of not less than one year. Under Section 8, unless the Royal Thai Government decides otherwise, the extradition request together with the accompanying documents shall be transmitted to the Ministry of Interior in order that the case may be brought before the Court by the Public Prosecutor. Section 12 (3) stipulates that the offence for which extradition is sought must not be of a "political character". Section 17 makes clear that appeals in extradition cases lie with the Court of Appeal whose decision on all questions both of fact and of law shall be final.

There was no extradition treaty between Thailand and Cambodia in force at the time of the extradition request. The offences allegedly committed by the Defendant are punishable under the law of Thailand with imprisonment of not less than one year.

The Defendant argued, *inter alia*, that the crimes for which he was being sought by Cambodia were not ordinary crimes. The target of the alleged attempted murder was the Prime Minister of Cambodia, who had been in power for twenty-one years. Any person attempting to murder the Prime Minister, contended the Defendant, must have had ulterior political motives to overthrow the Government of Cambodia. The Defendant himself was a member of an armed group that fought Prime Minister Hun Sen's group during the armed conflict in Cambodia prior to the United Nations-supervised general election in 1993. Hence, the Defendant argued, the offences were of a political character. He further contended that his extradition was being sought for him to be punished for his membership of a political party in the Opposition in which he had played a leading role. Once in the hands of the Cambodian authorities, according to the Defendant, he would be compelled to implicate the leader of that opposition party as the mastermind of the attempted murder. He also argued that extraditing him to Cambodia would violate both his right to a fair trial before an impartial tribunal under Article 10 of the Universal Declaration of Human Rights of 1948, Article 14 of the International Covenant on Civil and Political Rights of 1966, as well as his refugee status granted by the UNHCR under Article 33 of the United Nations Convention relating to the Status of Refugees of 1951.

The Criminal Court held that the Defendant was the person named in the extradition request, that his offences were extraditable offences under the Extradition Act of 1929, and that the Royal Thai Government had decided to exercise its discretion to extradite the Defendant to Cambodia.

The Criminal Court then dealt at length with the Defendant's contention that his offences were of a political character. The Criminal Court alluded to the fact that there had been armed conflicts in Cambodia up to the Paris Conference of 1991 which resulted in the United Nations-supervised general election in 1993, and that after that election political situations were far from peaceful. There were clashes among opposing parties and Prince Norodom Ranaridth, Prime Minister Hun Sen's Co-Prime Minister, and Mr. Sam Rainsy, leader of the political party to which the Defendant belonged, had to escape from Cambodia. The United Nations had to organize another general election in 1998, with Mr. Hun Sen emerging as the winner. Prime Minister Hun Sen was on his way to take an oath as the newly elected and only Prime Minister of Cambodia when he and his entourage were fired upon allegedly by the Defendant. The Criminal Court reasoned that the assassination of a head of government would result in a change of the person of the head of government but not in a change in a political regime under a political party system of democracy. Therefore, even assuming for the sake of argument that the Defendant had political motives in committing his crimes, by deciding that such offences were of a political character the Court would seriously endanger the safety of Heads of State. It came as no surprise that the International Law Association resolved in 1892 that ordinary offences with political motives such as murder and attempted murder shall not be deemed political offences. Moreover, the Treaty between the Kingdom of Thailand and the Kingdom of Cambodia on Extradition, signed in Bangkok on 6 May 1998, provides in Article 3 (1) that a political offence for which the Requested State shall not grant an extradition "shall not include the taking or attempted taking of the life or an attack on the person of a Head of State or a Head of Government or a member of his or her family". Although the Treaty was not then in force at the time of the extradition request in this case, it manifested the intention of the two States to adhere to the aforesaid principle in accordance with State practice, which treats this kind of offences as ordinary crimes of a terrorist nature. The Court also rejected the Defendant's contention that he would be compelled to implicate the leader of his political party. This was because the Defendant himself had conceded that two of his alleged accomplices who had been previously arrested by the Cambodian authorities were now acquitted by the Cambodian military court after the Prosecution's failure to present evidence to the military court within the requisite period of six months of their arrest, and that the two alleged accomplices had not been forced to implicate the leader of the Defendant's political party.

The next contention of the Defendant disposed of by the Criminal Court concerned the refugee status accorded to the Defendant by the UNHCR which, according to the Defendant, would protect him from being sent back to Cambodia where he had a well-founded fear of persecution. The Criminal Court, however, ruled that Thailand was not a State Party to the 1951 Refugee Convention and had no obligation to respect the provisions of the Convention.

Finally, the Criminal Court held that the Defendant's argument that he would not get a fair trial before an impartial tribunal in Cambodia was irrelevant to the extradition process. By virtue of Section 13 of the Extradition Act of 1929, the Court need not hear evidence for the accused in his defence except on the following: (1) that he is not the person wanted; (2) that the offence is not extraditable or is of a political character; (3) that his extradition is in fact being asked for with a view to punishing him for an offence of a political character; and (4) his nationality. Section 14 of the same Act provides that if there is insufficient evidence, the Court shall order that the accused be discharged. The right to a fair trial in the court of the Requesting State is therefore not a ground for the Court not to extradite the Defendant. Whether the Defendant was guilty as charged depended on the evidence before the court that tried him, and which court would try him depended on the law of Cambodia.

The Criminal Court stated, *obiter*, that the Defendant's fear that he would not get a fair trial might be unfounded. The Court opined that even human rights NGOs called by the Defendant as witnesses testified that the Cambodian legal and judicial systems had been reformed by the United Nations to comply with universal standards. The death penalty had been abolished. Judicial appointments had to be approved by the King. The Defendant would have the right to legal counsel and to appeal to a higher court. In the absence of sufficient evidence to prove his guilt, the Defendant would be set free as in the case of his two alleged accomplices. Besides, there were numerous human rights NGOs operating in Cambodia which would be ever ready to render assistance to the Defendant.

The Criminal Court was therefore satisfied that the evidence was sufficient for the Defendant's extradition, and made an order pursuant to Section 15 of the Extradition Act of 1929 authorizing him to be detained with a view to being extradited.

The Defendant subsequently lodged an appeal before the Court of Appeal.[100]

OTHER RELEVANT STATE PRACTICE

Opinion of the Department of Treaties and Legal Affairs

Vienna Convention on Diplomatic Relations of 1961; summons of foreign embassy personnel to appear as witnesses before a criminal court of the receiving State

In September 2001, the Criminal Court issued a summons for Mr. P., Attaché of the New Zealand Embassy in Bangkok, and Ms. B., clerk of the Embassy, to appear before the Court as witnesses. The Department of Protocol, Ministry of Foreign Affairs of Thailand, transmitted the summons to the Embassy by a diplomatic note.

The Embassy sent Diplomatic Note No. 2001/245 dated 5 October 2001 in reply. The Note stated that the Embassy, under instruction from the Ministry of Foreign Affairs and Trade Wellington, sought dispensations from the summons for the two said persons to appear before the Criminal Court. For Mr. P., dispensation was sought in his capacity as a diplomatic agent of the Embassy. For Ms. B., who is a Thai national, dispensation was sought on the grounds that such appearance as witness would be inconsistent with her role as an employee of the Embassy who takes instructions from the diplomatic agents of the Embassy. In other words, compelling Ms. B., a locally engaged staff member, to testify in court would interfere unduly with the performance of the functions of the Embassy in violation of the Vienna Convention on Diplomatic Relations of 1961.

The Department of Treaties and Legal Affairs, Ministry of Foreign Affairs of Thailand, adopted the following legal position on this matter in its Memorandum No. 0602/35/2545 dated 10 January 2002 in reply to the request for legal opinions from the Department of Protocol of the same Ministry:

Thailand and New Zealand are States Parties to the 1961 Convention. Article 1 (c) of the Convention defines "members of the mission" as "the members of the

---

[100] The Court of Appeals rendered its judgment on 30 September 2003 upholding the judgment of the Criminal Court.

diplomatic staff, of the administrative and technical staff and of the service staff of the mission". Therefore, both Mr. P. and Ms. B. are members of the New Zealand diplomatic mission in Thailand.

However, while the position of Mr. P. is covered by Article 37 (2) of the Convention, that of Ms. B. comes under Article 38 (2) of the same Convention.

By virtue of Article 37 (2), Mr. P., who is not a national of or permanently resident in Thailand, the receiving State, enjoys the privileges and immunities specified in Articles 29 to 35 of the Convention, including the exemption stipulated in Article 31 (2) from an obligation to give evidence as a witness.

Pursuant to Article 38 (2), Ms. B., who is a Thai national, enjoys privileges and immunities only to the extent admitted by Thailand, the receiving State, although Thailand must exercise its jurisdiction over Ms. B. in such a manner as not to interfere unduly with the performance of the functions of the New Zealand Embassy. Under Thailand's normal practice, which it considers consistent with customary international law, Thailand construes the proviso "in such a manner as not to interfere unduly with the performance of the functions of the mission" in Article 38 (2) of the Convention to mean that any measure taken by the receiving State should not affect important operations of the mission and/or should not cause serious inconvenience to the member of the mission subjected to such measure. In Ms. B.'s case, the Criminal Court summonses her to appear as a witness in her capacity as interpreter of an offender who is a New Zealand national. It is true that the New Zealand Embassy has assigned Ms. B. to be interpreter as part of the Embassy consular functions to protect the interests of New Zealand nationals. In this light, Thailand concedes that (a) Ms. B. can make a request not to testify on matters relating to official information acquired in the course of her employment at the Embassy, and that (b) if necessary, Ms. B. may request a hearing schedule to accommodate her convenience. Otherwise, Ms. B.'s appearance as a witness before the Criminal Court would not result in any undue interference with the performance of the functions of the New Zealand Embassy, but should be considered as an act of cooperation between Thailand and New Zealand in their diplomatic relations.

International Agreement

Memorandum of Understanding between the Royal Thai Government and the Royal Government of Cambodia regarding the Area of their Overlapping claims to the Continental Shelf, 18 June 2001

In 1972, Cambodia proclaimed the continental shelf boundary in the Gulf of Thailand. Thailand followed suit in 1973. Cambodia's claim overlapped those of Thailand and Vietnam.

On 9 August 1997, Thailand and Vietnam concluded the Agreement on the Delimitation of the Maritime Boundary between the Two Countries in the Gulf of Thailand, which entered into force on 27 February 1998. As a result of this Agreement, Vietnam no longer claims any maritime area which is also claimed by both

Thailand AND Cambodia. The area under the Thai-Cambodian overlapping maritime claim is thereby narrowed down to approximately 26,000 square kilometres in all.

The most significant dispute between the two States lies in Cambodia's lateral maritime boundary line. The line is based on Cambodia's interpretation of Clause 1 of the Protocol annexed to the 1907 Franco-Siamese Treaty of 23 May 1907 which stipulates in its pertinent part: "The frontier between French Indo-China and Siam starts from the sea at a point opposite the highest point of the island of Koh Kut. From this point it follows a north-easterly direction to the ridge of Prom-Krevanh ..." Cambodia draws the boundary line starting from the terminus of the common land boundary between Thailand and Cambodia abutting the Gulf of Thailand in the direction of the highest point of Thailand's Koh Kut, located approximately 19 nautical miles offshore. The Cambodian boundary line then stops when it touches the eastern side of Koh Kut's landmass before the line continues its projection from the western side of the island's landmass in the same direction to the middle of the Gulf of Thailand where it meets the segment of Cambodia's median line drawn between the opposite Thai and Cambodian coasts in disregard of Thailand's major islands in the vicinity of the relevant Thai coasts. Thailand, on the other hand, interprets the said provision of the Protocol to mean that France and Siam (as Thailand then was) agreed on the course of the land frontier between Siam and French Indochina which started at the point opposite the highest point of Koh Kut. In other words, Koh Kut was intended as a point of reference for the land frontier which starts on the coast and then follows a north-easterly direction inland to the ridge of a mountain. Thailand also disputes Cambodia's median line drawn between the opposite coasts of the two States. Thailand considers its maritime boundary based on equidistance and median line equitable in light of the prevailing geographical circumstances of the two States.[101]

In 1978, Cambodia proclaimed an exclusive economic zone of 200 nautical miles measured from its baselines. Thailand followed suit in 1981. However, only Thailand proclaimed the geographical coordinates of the outer limit of the exclusive economic zone, on 16 February 1988. The coordinates coincide with those of the continental shelf proclaimed by Thailand in 1973.

Thailand and Cambodia are States Parties to the four Geneva Conventions on the Law of the Sea of 1958. Neither of them is party to the 1982 United Nations Convention on the law of the Sea.

Article 74 (3) and Article 83 (3) of the 1982 Convention provide, *inter alia*, that pending agreement on the delimitation of the exclusive economic zone and the continental shelf, respectively between States with opposite or adjacent coasts,

> [T]he States concerned, in a spirit of understanding and co-operation, shall make every effort to enter into provisional arrangements of a practical nature and, during this transitional period, not to jeopardize or hamper the reaching of the final agreement. Such arrangements shall be without prejudice to the final delimitation.

---

[101] See Kriangsak Kittichaisaree, *The Law of the Sea and Maritime Boundary Delimitation in South-East Asia* (1987) pp. 37-41, 51-54, 63-66.

Thailand and Malaysia had entered into this kind of provisional arrangements of a practical nature in their Memorandum of Understanding on the Establishment of a Joint Authority for the Exploitation and Exploitation of the Resources of the Sea-Bed in a Defined Area of the Continental Shelf of the Two Countries in the Gulf of Thailand, dated 21 February 1979. The 7,222 square kilometres of continental shelf disputed between the two States have become a joint development area (JDA) subject to the exploration and exploitation by the Joint Authority of the non-living natural resources for a period of fifty years commencing from the date of the entry into force of this Memorandum. Australia and Indonesia concluded similar arrangements in the Timor Gap in 1988, which are now superseded by the arrangements between Timor Lest and Australia.

With such precedents in mind, Cambodia proposed that Thailand and Cambodia enter into a joint development regime for the maritime area under their overlapping claims. Thailand was more circumspect, being convinced of the legal justifiability of its claim. The compromise appears in the Memorandum of Understanding between the Royal Thai Government and the Royal Government of Cambodia regarding the Area of their Overlapping Maritime Claims to the Continental Shelf, signed in Phnom Penh, Cambodia, on 18 June 2001 and in force on the date of its signature.

Under the Memorandum of Understanding ('MOU'), the Parties consider it desirable to enter into "provisional arrangements of a practical nature" in respect of the territorial sea, continental shelf and exclusive economic zone under their overlapping claims ("Overlapping Claims Area"). They intend, through accelerated negotiation, simultaneously to: (a) conclude an agreement for the joint development of the hydrocarbon resources located in the overlapping area below 11 Degrees Latitude North ("Joint Development Area"); and, as "an indivisible package", (b) agree on a mutually acceptable delimitation of the maritime area claimed by both Parties above 11 Degrees Latitude North ("Area to be Delimited"). The Area to be Delimited mostly involves the lateral delimitation between the Parties' adjacent coasts, including the maritime area in the vicinity of Thailand's Koh Kut. The MOU sets up a Joint Technical Committee, comprising officials of Thailand and Cambodia to be separately nominated, responsible for drawing up: (a) the agreed terms of the Joint Development Treaty, including a mutually acceptable basis for sharing the costs and benefits of the exploitation of hydrocarbon resources located in the Joint Development Area; and (b) an agreed delimitation of the maritime area between their respective current claims in the Area to be Delimited in accordance with applicable principles of international law. Subject to the entry into force of the delimitation of the Parties' respective maritime claims in the Area to be Delimited, this MOU and all actions taken pursuant to it are without prejudice to the maritime claims of either party.

In 2001 and 2002, the Parties met several times under the framework of the MOU, but could not reach any agreement on either the delimitation or the joint development.

Thailand and Laws to Counter International Terrorism[102]

As a Member State of the United Nations, the Royal Thai Government is bound by Article 25 of the United Nations Charter, which stipulates that all Member States of the United Nations must agree to accept and carry out the decision of the Security Council in accordance with the Charter.

I. **Thailand's domestic legal basis to implement the asset freeze required by UN Security Council Resolution 1267 (1999), and paragraphs 1 and 2(a) of UN Security Council Resolution 1390 (2002) as well as impediments under Thailand's domestic law in this context and steps taken to address them**

*   The Thai government has issued instructions to all authorities concerned to comply with UN Security Council resolutions on freezing of transfer of funds or financial resources belonging to the Taleban, Osama Bin Laden and Al-Qaeda network.

*   Pursuant to the Money Laundering Act of 2000, financial institutions, government units under the Department of Lands and traders engaging in businesses involving the operation of or consultation in a transaction related to the investment or mobilization of capital are required to report any suspicious transactions to the Anti-Money Laundering Office.

*   Section 3 of the Act defines "financial institution" as:
    -   The Bank of Thailand, a commercial bank and such banks as specifically established by law;
    -   Finance companies, credit financier companies and securities companies under the law on securities and stock exchange;
    -   The Industrial Finance Corporation of Thailand and small industrial finance corporations;
    -   Life insurance companies and insurance companies;
    -   Savings co-operatives; or
    -   Juristic persons carrying on such other businesses related to finance as pre-scribed in a Ministerial Regulation.

*   Therefore, under the sixth definition, "financial institution" can be broadly interpreted to cover intermediaries outside the main financial sector.

*   The penalty for non-compliance with the requirement to report suspicious trans-actions is a fine of up to 300,000 Baht.

---

[102] Based on Thailand's implementation report pursuant to paragraphs 6 and 12 of UN Security Council Resolution 1455 (2003), submitted to the United Nations in June 2003.

- However, the Money Laundering Act does not provide a legal basis for the authorities concerned, such as the Bank of Thailand or the Anti-Money Laundering Office, to freeze the transfer of funds or financial resources belonging to persons or entities suspected of committing or facilitating the commission of terrorist acts. This is because the object and purpose of the Money Laundering Act are to suppress the use of money for whatever purpose if the money is derived from certain specified unlawful activities. The Act was not intended to suppress the use of money deriving from lawful activities although such use is for unlawful purposes.

- Under the Money Exchange Control Act of 1942, all persons or legal entities that provide services for the transmission of money or valuables must be approved by the Ministry of Finance under the recommendation of the Bank of Thailand. Any persons or legal entities that provide such services in violation of the Act of 1942 shall be liable to a fine of up to 20,000 Baht or to imprisonment of up to three years or both.

- According to Notification No. 13 issued by the Bank of Thailand under the authority of the Money Exchange Controls Act of 1942, any person (except authorized banks, companies or persons) shall not buy, sell, lend, exchange or transfer foreign money or other foreign mediums of exchange without permission.
  In the context of anti-terrorism, the Bank of Thailand has applied the following administrative measures to ensure that Thailand comply with the relevant Security Council Resolutions:

  - Issued a circular requesting the Thai Bankers' Association, the Association of Finance Companies and the Foreign Banks' Association to distribute the UN Security Council's list of proscribed terrorists to all commercial banks and financial institutions. All commercial banks and financial institutions have been requested promptly to report their suspicions if any transactions that may be linked, or related, to terrorism, terrorist acts or terrorist organizations are carried out.
  - Issued a notice to financial institutions regarding the correct practices in accepting a deposit for opening a bank account, and prohibits the use of an assumed name or alias. Financial institutions are required to follow the "Know Your Customer" Policy by having their customers identify themselves.
  - In accordance with Thailand's existing exchange control law,
    - The transfer of funds into or out of Thailand has to be reported to the Bank of Thailand; and
    - Foreign exchange must be supported by relevant documents justifying the transactions in question.

- Although circulars of the Bank of Thailand have no legal binding force, in practice all commercial banks and monetary institutions based in Thailand follow the guidelines in such circulars and report their actions to the Bank of Thailand.

  No asset has been frozen in accordance with UN Security Council Resolution 1455 (2003). None of the financial assets or economic assets previously frozen are related to Usama Bin Laden or members of Al-Qaeda or the Taleban or associated individuals or entities, pursuant to UN Security Council Resolution 1452 (2002).

- In order to close the existing legal lacuna under Thai domestic laws, on 11 December 2001 the Council of State submitted to the Cabinet draft amendments to the Penal Code and to the Money Laundering Act.

- The draft amendment to the Penal Code defines the scope of terrorism and prescribes the act of terrorism as a serious offence under Thai criminal law. The proposed punishment ranges from a fine of between 200,000 and 1,000,000 Baht to the death sentence. Any person who threatens to commit such an offence or is an accomplice thereto would receive the same punishment as the principal perpetrator of the crime of terrorism. Persons engaging in various forms of attempted commission of the crime are subject to a lesser punishment, ranging from a fine of between 60,000 and 300,000 Baht to 3-15 years of imprisonment. Accomplices include persons or entities making funds or financial assets available to *principal perpetrators.* The draft amendment states that any person providing *or procuring* "force, arms, assets or any support for the commission of terrorism" is considered to be committing an act of terrorism. If found guilty, that person will be subject either to the death penalty, life imprisonment or imprisonment ranging from three years to 20 years, and shall also pay a fine of between 60,000 and 1,000,000 Baht.

- The thrust of the draft amendment to the Money Laundering Act is to make terrorist offences under the Penal Code as amended predicated offences under the Money Laundering Act, which will enable the Anti-Money Laundering Office to freeze the funds, financial assets and other economic resources of entities and persons who support terrorism.

- The Money Laundering Act as amended would empower the Transaction Committee, appointed by the Anti-Money Laundering Office, to examine a transaction or asset relating to the commission of an act of terrorism, as one of the predicated offences under the Act. According to Section 48, the Committee can withhold for a maximum of 90 days authorization for those transactions believed to be related to terrorism. The amended law will further enable the Committee to order the seizure or attachment of any property or asset found to be connected with the commission of any of the presently listed offences under the Money Laundering Act.

- The two draft amendments to the Penal Code and the Anti-Money Laundering Act mentioned above have taken into account the requirements of the International Convention for the Suppression of the Financing of Terrorism of 1999, which Thailand signed on 18 December 2001.

II. Travel Ban

- Article 12(7) of the Immigration Act of 1979 stipulates that the competent Thai authority has the right to deny entry into the Kingdom of any person or persons whose conduct is deemed to be harmful to the peace and safety of the public or to national security, or who is/are being sought under a warrant of arrest issued by a competent authority of a foreign government.

- Intelligence and security agencies in Thailand have been on high alert since the 11 September 2001 incident. Tight measures are in place to inspect and monitor any movement of terrorists. A watch list of persons who have any connection with terrorist groups is shared among all agencies concerned so that they can cooperate to prevent suspects from entering the country.

- The immigration procedures start with the application for a visa at Thai Embassies and Consulates abroad. Thailand has reduced the number of countries eligible for visa exemption from 57 to 38 and the number of countries whose nationals may apply for a visa at the immigration checkpoint upon arrival has been reduced from 96 to 15. The Royal Thai Government has also introduced stricter visa application procedures for certain target groups. The requirement for visa application allows more time for authorities to check the identification of applicants to ensure that those who want to travel to Thailand are not on the watch list. Therefore, it is very important that the database be constantly updated.

- Terrorist suspects often travel with counterfeit documents and identification. The information received is often incomplete. Thai authorities may be informed of only the name of the suspected person without other relevant information, such as his/her last name or birth date. Incomplete information, such as lack of data on gender or passport number, makes it impossible for authorities concerned to include such information in the official watch list. In cases where there are many persons using the same name, which is not unusual for people of Arab origin, complete information is necessary to help confirm the true identification of the suspect.

- In an effort to enhance its capability to control the movement of people more effectively, the Immigration Bureau of Thailand has carried out the following actions:

- The Bureau has installed a computerized system to monitor and collect information on incoming and outgoing passengers at all international airports.
- Black List or Watch List diskettes with names of terrorist groups proscribed by the United Nations are distributed to all 53 immigration border checkpoints as well as to the Thai Embassies and Consulates abroad to improve the efficiency of inspection of incoming and outgoing travellers. These diskettes are updated on a bi-monthly basis.
- The Bureau has installed a system linking all ports of entry with online data.
- The Bureau has also installed passport machines to check, prevent and arrest suspected terrorists and targeted persons in the Black List or Watch List, including persons who are under arrest warrants.
- Passport inspection equipment has also been installed at all international airports and key border checkpoints, such as the ones along the border with Malaysia.

III. Legal Framework for International Cooperation

- The Mutual Assistance in Criminal Matters Act of 1992 provides a broad framework for cooperation with other countries in criminal matters – taking testimony and statements of persons; providing documents, records and evidence for prosecution and search and seizure of assets. The thrust of the law is based on principles of double criminality and reciprocity that allow Thailand to extend assistance in criminal matters to virtually every country. The law is supplemented by the Treaties of Mutual Assistance in Criminal Matters that Thailand has concluded with five countries; namely, the United States, Canada, the United Kingdom, France and Norway.

- The Extradition Act of 1929 provides another channel of international judicial cooperation. As is the Act on Mutual Assistance in Criminal Matters, the main thrust of the Act of 1929 is also based on the two basic principles of double criminality and reciprocity. It is supplemented by 14 bilateral extradition treaties with friendly countries; namely, the United Kingdom, Belgium, Indonesia, the Philippines, the United States, the People's Republic of China, the Republic of Korea, Laos, Bangladesh, Cambodia, Malaysia, Fiji, Canada, and Australia.

- Thailand has also signed a Memorandum of Understanding on Counter Terrorism Cooperation with Australia and has acceded to the Agreement on Information Exchange and Establishment of Communication Procedures between Malaysia, Indonesia, the Philippines, and Cambodia. Besides, the Anti-Money Laundering Office has been a member of the EGMONT Group since 2000, thereby enabling the Office to have access to and exchange information with all the 57 members of the Group.

IV. Arms Embargo

Measures have been implemented to prevent the acquisition of conventional arms and weapons of mass destruction (WMD) by Osama Bin Laden, members of the Al-Qaeda organization and the Taleban, and other individuals, groups, undertakings and entities associated with them, along with Export Controls to prevent the above targets from obtaining the items and technology necessary for weapons development and production.

Measures to criminalize the violation of the arms embargo directed at Osama Bin Laden, members of Al-Qaeda organization and the Taleban, and other individuals, groups, undertakings and entities associated with them.
Arms/arms broker licensing system/Safeguards of weapons and ammunition produced within Thailand

- The Ministry of Defence reports to the UN Register on Conventional Arms (UNSCR) through the Thai Ministry of Foreign Affairs on an annual basis on the import and export of seven kinds of conventional arms; namely, battle tanks, armoured combat vehicles, artillery systems, combat aircraft, attack helicopters, warships, missiles and missile launchers. The UNSCR controls the import and export of conventional arms that belong to its Member States.

- As a State Party to the Chemical Weapons Convention (CWC) of 1993, Thailand has complied with its obligations and is committed to the international and non-discriminatory verification activities of the Organization for the Prohibition of Chemical Weapons (OPCW). The Royal Thai Government has already enacted legislation for the full implementation of the CWC. The Ministry of Industry has now concluded the Initial Declaration and is now expediting the process of its approval by the Cabinet, as required by the Constitution, before submitting it to the OPCW.

- Thailand is a State Party to the Nuclear Non-Proliferation Treaty (NPT) of 1968 and has its Safeguards Agreement with the International Atomic Energy Agency (IAEA). Thailand supports the recent proposals by the IAEA on the issue of protection against nuclear terrorism. Thailand's Office of Atom for Peace is accelerating the process to conclude the Additional Protocol with the IAEA.

- The proposed amendment to the Penal Code would punish any person who, inter alia, provides or procures arms or stockpiles weapons in order to commit a terrorist act.

- The relevant laws that regulate the domestic manufacture, sale, possession and disposition of weapons are:
  - The Munitions of War Control Act of 1987, which prohibits a person from importing, procuring, manufacturing or possessing weapons except

with the permission of the Permanent Secretary of the Department of Defence. The Act also states that permission shall not be given to any person who may cause any disturbance to the public peace.

- Under the Firearms, Ammunition, Explosive Articles and Fireworks and Imitation of Firearms Act 1974, a person shall not manufacture, purchase, possess, use, or import guns, bullets or explosives without permission from the firearms registrar. The permission shall not be given to any person who may cause any violence to the public peace.

• Furthermore, the Act on Export Control of Armaments and Materials of 1952 and the Decree on the Export Control of Armaments and Materials of 1992 subject an export or transshipment of weapons and explosives to the permission of the Minister of Defence or a person designated by the Minister, and to the following conditions of the export or transshipment:

- A foreign government shall request such export or transshipment pursuant to an agreement with the Royal Thai Government.
- The subjects of the export or transshipment shall be the Government's armaments and materials used in wartime, authorized by the Minister of Defence.
- The export or transshipment shall be undertaken publicly as a business authorized by the Minister of Defence.

• In the interest of enhancing Thailand's abilities to combat terrorism, on 19 August and 31 October 2002, the Ministry of Interior and the Ministry of Defence issued orders to various agencies to take all measures within their competence for strict compliance with the law by all handlers of firearms. These new measures include closer monitoring of sensitive materials by all provincial administrations. In addition, each province is entrusted with preparing a detailed report on the use of explosive materials on every first day of each month. The Permanent Secretary of the Interior has been authorized to approve all movements of sensitive materials across provincial borders. Armed military personnel must accompany movement of these materials.

• It is widely accepted that a large-scale terrorist attack requires extensive planning and includes the acquisition of explosive materials such as ammonium nitrate, TNT, power-gel and/or C4 as well as detonators. Taking the above into account, the Royal Thai Government has intensified its control and regulation of sensitive explosive materials and has tightened its surveillance of foreign persons that have irregular patterns of movement in Thailand.

• Imports and exports of prohibited and restricted goods are criminal offences and offenders are liable to punishment in accordance with the relevant laws governing the import and export of such goods. The Customs Act of 1926 also provides for punishment of those who submit false information on goods to be imported and exported. Offenders are liable to up to ten years' imprisonment.

- Generally, customs officers check on spot goods to be exported and imported that are not subject to any restrictions or duties. Imports and exports of prohibited and restricted goods are subject to a thorough inspection. After 11 September 2001, Thailand has enforced more stringent measures for both imports and exports, especially those goods going to and coming from target countries, which are also thoroughly checked.

- In June 2003, Thailand and the United States signed a Declaration of Principles, paving the way for the implementation of the "Container Security Initiative" or the CSI. Under the CSI, Thai customs officers will work closely with their US counterparts to detect "suspect" containers, and stringent procedures for cargo shipment will be implemented.

- Thailand is also member of the Asia-Pacific Regional Intelligence Liaison Office, which has its headquarters in Tokyo. The Customs Services of 27 countries from Asia-Pacific and South Asia, including those of 18 Asian Regional Forum (ARF) countries, participate in this forum. It provides a good opportunity for customs officers in the region to share their experiences and intelligence. Past cooperation has focused on the issue of narcotic drugs, but it could be expanded to other issues relating to terrorism which has become a serious concern to the international community, such as illegal arms, chemicals and WMD.

PARTICIPATION IN MULTILATERAL TREATIES[*]

Editorial introduction

This section records the participation of Asian states in open multilateral law-making treaties which mostly aim at world-wide adherence. It updates the treaty sections of earlier Volumes until 31 December 2002. New data are preceded by a reference to the most recent previous entry. In case no new data are available, the title of the treaty will be listed with a reference to the latest Volume containing such data.

For the purpose of this section states situated broadly west of Iran, north of Mongolia, east of Papua New Guinea and south of Indonesia will not be covered. The Editors wish to express their gratitude to all international organizations that have so kindly made available information on the status of various categories of treaties.

Note:
- Where no other reference to specific sources is made, data are derived from Multi-lateral Treaties deposited with the Secretary-General - Status as at 31 December 2002 (ST/LEG/SER.E/21).
- No indication is given of reservations and declarations made.
- Sig. = signature; Cons. = consent to be bound; Eff. date = effective date; E.i.f. = entry into force; Ratif. registered = ratification registered; Min. age spec. = minimum age specified.

TABLE OF HEADINGS

Antarctica	Finance
Commercial arbitration	Health
Cultural matters	Human rights, including women and
Cultural property	children
Development matters	Humanitarian law in armed conflict
Dispute settlement	Intellectual property
Environment, fauna and flora	International crimes
Family matters	International representation

---

[*] Compiled by Karin Arts, Associate Editor, Associate Professor in International Law and Development, Institute of Social Studies, The Hague.

Asian Yearbook of International Law, Volume 10 (B.S. Chimni *et al.,* eds.)

© 2005 Koninklijke Brill NV. Printed in The Netherlands, pp. 265-290.

International trade
Judicial and administrative
cooperation
Labour
Narcotic drugs
Nationality and statelessness
Nuclear material
Outer space
Privileges and immunities

Refugees
Road traffic and transport
Sea
Sea traffic and transport
Social matters
Telecommunications
Treaties
Weapons

ANTARCTICA

Antarctic Treaty, Washington, 1959: *see* Vol. 6 p. 234.

COMMERCIAL ARBITRATION

Convention on the Recognition and Enforcement of Foreign Arbitral Awards, 1958
(Continued from Vol. 8 p. 174)

State	Sig.	Cons.
Iran		15 Oct 2001

CULTURAL MATTERS

Agreement for Facilitating the International Circulation of Visual and Auditory Materials of an Educational, Scientific and Cultural Character, Beirut, 1948: *see* Vol. 7 pp. 322-323.
Agreement on the Importation of Educational, Scientific and Cultural Materials, Florence, 1950: *see* Vol. 8 p. 174.
Convention concerning the International Exchange of Publications, 1958: *see* Vol. 6 p. 235.
Convention concerning the International Exchange of Official Publications and Government Documents between States, 1958: *see* Vol. 6 p. 235.
International Agreement for the Establishment of the University for Peace, New York, 1980: *see* Vol. 6 p. 235.

Regional Convention on the Recognition of Studies, Diploma's and Degrees in Higher Education in Asia and the Pacific, Bangkok, 1983
(Continued from Vol. 6 p. 235 and corrected from Vol. 9 p. 282).

State	Sig.	Cons.
India		2 Aug 2000

CULTURAL PROPERTY

Convention for the Protection of Cultural Property in the Event of Armed Conflict, 1954
(Continued from Vol. 7 p. 323 and corrected from Vol. 9 p. 282).
(Status as provided by UNESCO)

State	Sig.	Cons.
China	14 May 1954	5 Jan 2000

Protocol for the Protection of Cultural Property in the Event of Armed Conflict, 1954
(Continued from Vol. 6 p. 236 and corrected from Vol. 9 p. 282).
(Status as provided by UNESCO)

State	Sig.	Cons.
China	14 May 1954	5 Jan 2000

Convention on the Means of Prohibiting and Preventing the Illicit Import, Export and Transfer of Ownership of Cultural Property, 1970
(Continued from Vol. 7 p. 323)
(Status as provided by UNESCO)

State	Sig.	Cons.	State	Sig.	Cons.
Bhutan		26 Sep 2002	Japan		9 Sep 2002

Convention concerning the Protection of the World Cultural and Natural Heritage, 1972
(Continued from Vol. 7 p. 323)
(Status as provided by UNESCO)

State	Sig.	Cons.
Bhutan		17 Oct 2001

DEVELOPMENT MATTERS

Charter of the Asian and Pacific Development Centre, 1982, *see* Vol. 7 pp. 323-324.
Agreement to Establish the South Centre, 1994, *see* Vol. 7 p. 324.

Amendments to the Charter of the Asian and Pacific Development Centre, 1982
Kuala Lumpur, 16 July 1998

State	Sig.	Cons.	State	Sig.	Cons.
China		14 Sep 2001	Vietnam		9 Jul 2001
Malaysia		14 May 2001			

DISPUTE SETTLEMENT

Declarations recognizing as compulsory the jurisdiction of the International Court of Justice under Article 36, paragraph 2, of the Statute of the Court, *see* Vol. 6 p. 238.

Convention on the Settlement of Investment Disputes between States and Nationals of Other States, 1965
(Continued from Vol. 6 p. 238)
(Status as at 31 December 2002, provided by the World Bank)

State	Sig.	Cons.	State	Sig.	Cons.
Brunei	16 Sep 2002	16 Sep 2002	Timor-Leste	23 Jul 2002	23 Jul 2002
Kazakhstan	23 Jul 1992	21 Sep 2000			

ENVIRONMENT, FAUNA AND FLORA

International Convention for the Prevention of Pollution of the Sea by Oil, as amended, 1954: *see* Vol. 6 p. 238.
International Convention Relating to Intervention on the High Seas in Cases of Oil Pollution Casualties, 1969: *see*
Vol. 9 p. 284.
Convention on the Prevention of Marine Pollution by Dumping of Wastes and Other Matter, 1972, as amended: *see* Vol. 7 p. 325.
Protocol Relating to Intervention on the High Seas in Cases of Pollution by Substances Other Than Oil, 1973: *see* Vol. 6 p. 239.
Protocol to amend the 1971 Convention on Wetlands of International Importance especially as Waterfowl Habitat, 1982: *see* Vol. 6 p. 240.
International Convention on Oil Pollution Preparedness, Response, and Cooperation, 1990: *see* Vol. 9 p. 285.

International Convention on Civil Liability for Oil Pollution Damage, 1969
(Continued from Vol. 9 p. 284)
(Status as included in IMO doc. 8687, as at 31 December 2003)

State	Denunciation	E.i.f.	State	Denunciation	E.i.f.
Brunei	31 Jan 2002		Papua New Guinea	23 Jan 2001	22 Jan 2002

Convention on Wetlands of International Importance especially as Waterfowl Habitat, 1971
(continued from Vol. 7 p. 325)
(Status as provided by UNESCO)

State	Cons. (deposit)	State	Cons. (deposit)
Kyrgyzstan	12 Nov 2002	Uzbekistan	8 Oct 2001
Tajikistan	18 Jul 2001		

International Convention on the Establishment of an International Fund for Compensation for Oil Pollution Damage, 1971
(Continued and corrected from Vol. 9 p. 284)
(Status as included in IMO doc. 8687, as at 31 December 2003)

State	Denunciation	E.i.f.	State	Denunciation	E.i.f.
China	5 Jan 1999	5 Jan 2000	Papua New		
India	21 Jun 2000	21 Jun 2001	Guinea	23 Jan 2001	23 Jan 2002

Protocol to the International Convention on Civil Liability for Oil Pollution Damage, 1976
(Continued from Vol. 6 p. 239)
(Status as included in IMO doc. 8687, as at 31 December 2003)

State	Cons.	E.i.f.
Cambodia	8 Jun 2001	6 Sept 2001

Protocol Relating to the 1973 International Convention for the Prevention of Pollution from Ships, as amended, 1978
(Continued from Vol. 8 p. 176).
(Status as included in IMO doc. 8687, as at 31 December 2003)

State	Cons. (deposit)	Excepted Annexes	State	Cons. (deposit)	Excepted Annexes
Bangladesh	18 Dec 2002		Philippines	15 Jun 2001	
Iran	25 Oct 2002	III and IV			

Convention for the Protection of the Ozone Layer, 1985
(Continued from Vol. 9 p. 284)

State	Cons.
Cambodia	27 Jun 2001

Protocol on Substances that Deplete the Ozone Layer, 1987
(Continued from Vol. 9 p. 284)

State	Cons.
Cambodia	27 Jun 2001

Amendments to Articles 6 and 7 of the 1971 Convention on Wetlands of International Importance especially as Waterfowl Habitat, 1987
(Continued from Vol. 6 p. 240)

State	Cons. (deposit)
Uzbekistan	8 Oct 2001

Convention on the Control of Transboundary Movements of Hazardous Wastes and Their Disposal, 1989
(Continued from Vol. 7 p. 325)

State	Sig.	Cons.	State	Sig.	Cons.
Cambodia		2 Mar 2001	Brunei		16 Dec 2002
Bhutan		26 Aug 2002			

Amendment to the Montreal Protocol, 1990
(Continued from Vol. 8 p. 177)

State	Cons.
Kazakhstan	26 Jul 2001

Framework Convention on Climate Change, 1992
(Continued from Vol. 9 p. 285)

State	Sig	Cons
Afghanistan	21 Jun 1992	19 Sep 2002

Convention on Biological Diversity, 1992
(Continued from Vol. 7 p. 326)

State	Sig.	Cons.
Afghanistan	12 Jun 92	19 Sep 2002

Amendment to the Montreal Protocol, 1992
(Continued from Vol. 9 p. 284)

State	Cons.	State	Cons.
Maldives	27 Sep 2001	Philippines	15 Jun 2001

Protocol to amend the 1969 International Convention on Civil Liability for Oil Pollution Damage, 1992
(Continued from Vol. 8 p. 176)
(Status as included in IMO doc. 8687, as at 31 December 2003)

State	Cons.	E.i.f.	State	Cons.	E.i.f.
Brunei	3 Jan 2002		Papua New		
Cambodia	8 Jun 2001	8 Jun 2002	Guinea	23 Jan 2001	23 Jan 2002

UN Convention to Combat Desertification in those Countries Experiencing Serious Drought and/or Desertification, Particularly in Africa
Paris, 14 October 1994
Entry into Force: 26 December 1996

State	Sig.	Cons.	State	Sig.	Cons.
Afghanistan		1 Nov 1995	Mongolia	15 Oct 1994	3 Sep 1996
Bangladesh	14 Oct 1994	26 Jan 1996	Myanmar		2 Jan 1997
Brunei		4 Dec 2002	Nepal	12 Oct 1995	15 Oct 1996
Cambodia	15 Oct 1994	18 Aug 1997	Pakistan	15 Oct 1994	24 Feb 1997
China	14 Oct 1994	18 Feb 1997	Papua New		
India	14 Oct 1994	17 Dec 1996	Guinea		6 Dec 2000
Indonesia	15 Oct 1994	31 Aug 1998	Philippines	8 Dec 1994	10 Feb 2000
Iran	14 Oct 1994	29 Apr 1997	Singapore		26 Apr 1999
Japan	14 Oct 1994	11 Sep 1998	Sri Lanka		9 Dec 1998
Kazakhstan	14 Oct 1994	9 Jul 1997	Tajikistan		16 Jul 1997
Korea (Rep.)	14 Oct 1994	17 Aug 1999	Thailand		7 Mar 2001
Laos	30 Aug 1995	20 Sep 1996	Turkmenistan	27 Mar 1995	18 Sep 1996
Malaysia	6 Oct 1995	25 Jun 1997	Uzbekistan	7 Dec 1994	31 Oct 1995
Maldives		3 Sep 2002	Vietnam		25 Aug 1998

Amendment to the Convention on the Control of Transboundary Movements of Hazardous Wastes and Their Disposal, 1995
(Continued from Vol. 8 p. 178)

State	Sig.	Cons.	State	Sig.	Cons.
Brunei		6 Dec 2002	Malaysia		26 Oct 2001
China		1 May 2001			

Amendment to the Montreal Protocol, 1997
(Continued from Vol. 9 p. 285)

State	Cons.	State	Cons.
Bangladesh	27 Jul 2001	Malaysia	26 Oct 2001
Iran	17 Oct 2001	Maldives	27 Sep 2001
Japan	30 Aug 2002	Mongolia	28 Mar 2002
Korea (DPR)	13 Dec 2001		

Protocol to the Framework Convention on Climate Change, 1997
(Continued from Vol. 8 p. 177)

State	Sig.	Cons.	State	Sig.	Cons.
Bangladesh		22 Oct 2001	Malaysia	12 Mar 1999	4 Sep 2002
Bhutan		26 Aug 2002	Papua New		
Cambodia		22 Aug 2002	Guinea	2 Mar 1999	28 Mar 2002
China	29 May 1998	30 Aug 2002	Sri Lanka		3 Sep 2002
India		26 Aug 2002	Thailand	2 Feb 1999	28 Aug 2002
Japan	28 Apr 1998	4 Jun 2002	Vietnam	3 Dec 1998	25 Sep 2002
Korea (Rep.)	25 Sep 1998	8 Nov 2002			

Amendment to the Montreal Protocol, 1999
Beijing, 3 December 1999
Entry into force: 25 February 2002

State	Cons.	State	Cons.
Japan	30 Aug 2002	Malaysia	26 Oct 2001
Korea (DPR)	13 Dec 2001	Sri Lanka	27 Nov 2002

Cartagena Protocol on Biosafety to the Convention on Biological Diversity
Montreal, 29 January 2000
Entry into force: not yet

State	Sig.	Cons.	State	Sig.	Cons.
Bangladesh	24 May 2000		Malaysia	24 May 2000	
Bhutan	26 Aug 2002		Maldives	3 Sep 2002	
China	8 Aug 2000		Myanmar	11 May 2001	
India	23 Jan 2001		Nepal	2 Mar 2001	
Indonesia	24 May 2000		Pakistan	4 Jun 2001	
Iran	23 Apr 2001		Philippines	24 May 2000	
Korea (DPR)	20 Apr 2001		Sri Lanka	24 May 2000	
Korea (Rep.)	6 Sep 2000				

FAMILY MATTERS

Convention on the Recovery Abroad of Maintenance, 1956: *see* Vol. 6 p. 243.
Convention on the Law Applicable to Maintenance Obligations Towards Children, 1956: *see* Vol. 6 p. 244.
Convention on the Conflicts of Law Relating to the Form of Testamentary Dispositions, 1961: *see* Vol. 7 p. 327.
Convention on Consent to Marriage, Minimum Age for Marriage and Registration of Marriages, 1962: *see* Vol. 8 p. 178.
Convention on the Law Applicable to Maintenance Obligations, 1973: *see* Vol. 6 p. 244.
Convention on Protection of Children and Co-operation in respect of Intercountry Adoption, 1993: *see* Vol. 9 p. 285.

FINANCE

Agreement Establishing the Asian Development Bank, 1965: *see* Vol. 7 p. 327.

Convention Establishing the Multilateral Investment Guarantee Agency, 1988
(Continued from Vol. 9 p. 286)
(Status as at 31 December 2002, provided by the World Bank)

State	Sig.	Cons.	State	Sig.	Cons.
Tajikistan		9 Dec 2002	Timor-Leste		23 Jul 2002

HEALTH

Protocol Concerning the Office International d'Hygiène Publique, 1946: *see* Vol. 6 p. 245.

HUMAN RIGHTS, INCLUDING WOMEN AND CHILDREN

Convention against Discrimination in Education, 1960: *see* Vol. 7 p. 328.
International Covenant on Civil and Political Rights, 1966: see Vol. 9 p. 287.
Optional Protocol to the International Covenant on Civil and Political Rights, 1966: *see* Vol. 8 p. 179.
International Convention on the Elimination of All Forms of Racial Discrimination, 1966: *see* Vol. 8 p. 179.
International Convention against Apartheid in Sports, 1985: *see* Vol. 6 p. 248.
Convention on the Rights of the Child, 1989: see Vol. 7 p. 329.

Convention on the Political Rights of Women, 1953
(Continued from Vol. 9 p. 286)

State	Sig.	Cons.
Cambodia	11 Nov 2001	

Convention on the Nationality of Married Women, 1957
(Continued from Vol. 9 p. 286)

State	Sig.	Cons.
Cambodia		11 Nov 2001

International Covenant on Economic, Social and Cultural Rights, 1966
(Continued from Vol. 9 p. 287)

State	Sig.	Cons.
China	27 Oct 1997	27 Mar 2001

Convention on the Elimination of All Forms of Discrimination against Women, 1979
(Continued from Vol. 8 p. 180)

State	Sig.	Cons.
Korea (DPR)		27 Feb 2001

Convention against Torture and Other Cruel, Inhuman or Degrading Treatment or Punishment, 1984
(Continued from Vol. 8 p. 180)

State	Sig.	Cons.
Mongolia		24 Jan 2002

International Convention on the Protection of the Rights of All Migrant Workers and Members of Their Families, 1990
(Continued from Vol. 8 p. 180)

State	Sig.	Cons.
Tajikistan	7 Sep 2000	8 Jan 2002

Amendment to article 8 of the International Convention on the Elimination of All Forms of Racial Discrimination, 1992
(Continued from Vol. 6 p. 247)

State	Sig.	Cons.
China		10 Jul 2002

Optional Protocol to the Convention on the Elimination of All Forms of Discrimination against Women, 1999
(Continued from Vol. 9 p. 287)

State	Sig.	Cons.	State	Sig.	Cons.
Cambodia	11 Nov 2001		Mongolia	7 Sep 2000	28 Mar 2002
Kazakhstan	6 Sep 2000	24 Aug 2001	Nepal	18 Dec 2001	
Kyrgyzstan		22 Jul 2002	Sri Lanka		15 Oct 2002

Optional Protocol to the Convention on the Rights of the Child on the Involvement of Children in Armed Conflict, 2000
(Continued from Vol. 9 p. 287)

State	Sig.	Cons.	State	Sig.	Cons.
China	15 Mar 2001		Mongolia	12 Nov 2001	
Indonesia	24 Sep 2001		Pakistan	26 Sep 2001	
Japan	10 May 2002		Vietnam	8 Sep 2000	20 Dec 2001
Maldives	10 May 2002		Tajikistan		5 Aug 2002

Optional Protocol to the Convention on the Rights of the Child on the Sale of Children, Child Prostitution and Child Pornography, 2000
(Continued from Vol. 9 p. 287)

State	Sig.	Cons.	State	Sig.	Cons.
Afghanistan		19 Sep 2002	Mongolia	12 Nov 2001	
Cambodia	27 Jun 2000	30 May 2002	Pakistan	26 Sep 2001	
China	6 Sep 2000	3 Dec 2002	Sri Lanka	8 May 2002	
Japan	10 May 2002		Tajikistan		5 Aug 2002
Kazakhstan	6 Sep 2000	24 Aug 2001	Vietnam	8 Sep 2000	20 Dec 2001
Maldives	10 May 2002	10 May 2002			

HUMANITARIAN LAW IN ARMED CONFLICT

International Conventions for the Protection of Victims of War, I-IV, 1949: *see* Vol. 6 p. 249.

Protocol I Additional to the Geneva Conventions of 12 August 1949, and Relating to the Protection of Victims of International Armed Conflicts, 1977: *see* Vol. 7 p. 330.

Protocol II Additional to the Geneva Conventions of 12 August 1949, and Relating to the Protection of Victims of Non-International Armed Conflicts, 1977: *see* Vol. 7 p. 329.

INTELLECTUAL PROPERTY

Convention for the Protection of Literary and Artistic Works, 1886 as amended 1979, *see* Vol. 9 p. 289.

Universal Copyright Convention, 1952: *see* Vol. 6 p. 251.

Protocols 1, 2 and 3 annexed to the Universal Copyright Convention, 1952: *see* Vol. 6 p. 251.
International Convention for the Protection of Performers, Producers of Phonograms and Broadcasting Organizations, 1961: *see* Vol. 6 p. 252.
Multilateral Convention for the Avoidance of Double Taxation of Copyright Royalties, 1979: *see* Vol. 6 p. 252.

Convention for the Protection of Industrial Property, 1883 as amended 1979
(Continued from Vol. 9 p. 288)
(Status as included in WIPO doc. 423(E) of 15 Jan 2003)

State	Party	Latest Act to which State is party
Nepal	22 Jun 2001	Stockholm

Convention Establishing the World Intellectual Property Organization, 1967
(Continued from Vol. 6 p. 252)
(Status as included in WIPO doc. 423(E) of 15 Jan 2003)

State	Membership		State	Membership
Iran	14 Mar 2002		Myanmar	15 May 2001

Convention for the Protection of Producers of Phonograms against Unauthorized Duplication of their Phonograms, 1971
(Continued from Vol. 8 p. 181)

State	Sig.	Cons.		State	Sig.	Cons.
Kazakhstan		3 May 2001		Kyrgyzstan		12 Jul 2002

INTERNATIONAL CRIMES

Convention on the Prevention and Punishment of the Crime of Genocide, 1948: *see* Vol. 8 p. 182.
Slavery Convention, 1926 as amended in 1953, *see* Vol. 7 p. 331.
Supplementary Convention on the Abolition of Slavery, the Slave Trade, and Institutions and Practices Similar to Slavery, 1956, *see* Vol. 7 p. 331.
Convention on Offences and Certain Other Acts Committed on Board Aircraft, 1963: *see* Vol. 9 p. 289.
Convention on the Non-Applicability of Statutory Limitations to War Crimes and Crimes Against Humanity, 1968: *see* Vol. 6 p. 254.
Convention for the Suppression of Unlawful Seizure of Aircraft, 1970: *see* Vol. 8 p. 289.
Convention for the Suppression of Unlawful Acts Against the Safety of Civil Aviation, 1971: *see* Vol. 8 p. 290.

International Convention on the Suppression and Punishment of the Crime of Apartheid, 1973: *see* Vol. 7 p. 331.
International Convention against the Recruitment, Use, Financing and Training of Mercenaries, 1989: *see* Vol. 8 p. 184.

Convention on the Prevention and Punishment of Crimes Against Internationally Protected Persons Including Diplomatic Agents, 1973
(Continued from Vol. 8 p. 183)

State	Sig.	Cons.	State	Sig.	Cons.
Laos		22 Aug 2002	Vietnam		2 May 2002
Tajikistan		19 Oct 2001			

International Convention Against the Taking of Hostages, 1979
(Continued from Vol. 9 p. 290)

State	Sig.	Cons.	State	Sig.	Cons.
Korea (DPR)		12 Nov 2001	Tajikistan		6 May 2002
Laos		22 Aug 2002			

Convention for the Suppression of Unlawful Acts Against the Safety of Maritime Navigation, 1988
(Corrected and continued from Vol. 9 p. 290)
(Status as included in IMO doc. 8687, as at 31 December 2003)

State	Cons	E.i.f.
Vietnam	12 Jul 2000	10 Oct 2002

Protocol for the Suppression of Unlawful Acts Against the Safety of Fixed Platforms Located on the Continental Shelf, 1988
(Corrected and continued from Vol. 8 p. 183)
(Status as included in IMO doc. 8687, as at 31 December 2003)

State	Cons	E.i.f.
Vietnam	12 Jul 2002	10 Oct 2002

**Protocol for the Suppression of Unlawful Acts of Violence at Airports Serving
International Civil Aviation, Supplementary to the Convention for the Suppression of
Unlawful Acts Against the Safety of Civil Aviation, 1988**
(Continued from Vol. 9 p. 290)
(Status as at 31 December 2002 provided by the ICAO Secretariat)

State	Cons.	Eff. date.	State	Cons.	Eff. date.
Brunei	20 Dec 2000	19 Jan 2001	Papua New		
Iran	14 Feb 2002	16 Mar 2002	Guinea	11 Jul 2002	10 Aug 2002
Laos	7 Oct 2002	6 Nov 2002			

Convention on the Marking of Plastic Explosives for the Purpose of Detection, 1991
(Continued from Vol. 8 p. 291)
(Status as at 31 December 2002 provided by the ICAO Secretariat)

State	Sig.	Cons.	State	Sig.	Cons.
Korea (Rep.)	2 Jan 2002	3 Mar 2002	Sri Lanka	11 Oct 2001	10 Dec 2001

Convention on the Safety of United Nations and Associated Personnel, 1994
New York, 9 December 1994
Entry into force: 15 January 1999

State	Sig.	Cons.	State	Sig.	Cons.
Bangladesh	21 Dec 1994	22 Sep 1999	Pakistan	8 Mar 1995	
Brunei		20 Mar 2002	Philippines	27 Feb 1995	17 Jun 1997
Japan	6 Jun 1995	6 Jun 1995	Singapore		26 Mar 1996
Korea (Rep.)		8 Dec 1997	Turkmenistan		29 Aug 1998
Laos		22 Aug 2002	Uzbekistan		3 Jul 1996
Nepal		8 Sep 2000			

International Convention for the Suppression of Terrorist Bombings, 1997
New York, 15 December 1997
Entry into force: 23 May 2001

State	Sig.	Rat.	State	Sig.	Rat.
Brunei		14 Mar 2002	Mongolia		7 Sep 2000
China		13 Nov 2001	Myanmar		12 Nov 2001
India	17 Sep 1999	22 Sep 1999	Nepal	24 Sep 1999	
Japan	17 Apr 1998	16 Nov 2001	Pakistan		13 Aug 2002
Kazakhstan		6 Nov 2002	Philippines	23 Sep 1998	
Korea (Rep.)	3 Dec 1999		Sri Lanka	12 Jan 1998	23 Mar 1999
Kyrgyzstan		1 May 2001	Tajikistan		29 Jul 2002
Laos		22 Aug 2002	Turkmenistan	18 Feb 1999	25 Jun 1999
Maldives		7 Sep 2000	Uzbekistam	23 Feb 1998	30 Nov 1998

Statute of the International Criminal Court, 1998
Rome, 17 July 1998
Entry into force: 1 July 2002

State	Sig.	Rat.	State	Sig.	Rat.
Bangladesh	16 Sep 1999		Philippines	28 Dec 2000	
Cambodia	23 Oct 2000	11 Apr 2002	Tajikistan	30 Nov 1998	5 May 2000
Iran	31 Dec 2000		Thailand	2 Oct 2000	
Korea (Rep.)	8 Mar 2000	13 Nov 2002	Timor-Leste		6 Sep 2002
Kyrgyzstan	8 Dec 1998		Uzbekistan	29 Dec 2000	
Mongolia	29 Dec 2000	11 Apr 2002			

International Convention for the Suppression of the Financing of Terrorism
New York, 9 December 1999
Entry into force:
10 April 2002

State	Sig.	Rat.	State	Sig.	Rat.
Bhutan	14 Nov 2001		Mongolia	12 Nov 2001	
Brunei		4 Dec 2002	Myanmar	12 Nov 2001	
Cambodia	11 Nov 2001		Philippines	16 Nov 2001	
China	13 Nov 2001		Singapore	18 Dec 2001	30 Dec 2002
India	8 Sep 2000		Sri Lanka	10 Jan 2000	8 Sep 2000
Indonesia	24 Sep 2001		Tajikistan	6 Nov 2001	
Japan	20 Oct 2001	11 Jun 2002	Thailand	18 Dec 2001	
Korea (DPR)	12 Nov 2001		Uzbekistan	13 Dec 2000	9 Jul 2001
Korea (Rep.)	9 Oct 2001		Vietnam		25 Sep 2002

INTERNATIONAL REPRESENTATION
(*see also*: Privileges and Immunities)

Vienna Convention on the Representation of States in their relations with International Organizations of a Universal Character, 1975: *see* Vol. 6 p. 257.

INTERNATIONAL TRADE

Convention on Transit Trade of Land-locked States, 1965: *see* Vol. 6 p. 257.
Convention on the Limitation Period in the International Sale of Goods, 1974: *see* Vol. 6 p. 257.
UN Convention on Contracts for the International Sale of Goods, 1980: *see* Vol. 8 p. 184.
UN Convention on the Liability of Operators of Transport Terminals in International Trade, 1991: *see* Vol. 6 p. 257.

JUDICIAL AND ADMINISTRATIVE COOPERATION

Convention Relating to Civil Procedure, 1954: *see* Vol. 6 p. 258.
Convention on the Service Abroad of Judicial and Extrajudicial Documents in Civil or Commercial Matters, 1965: *see* Vol. 9 p. 291.
Convention on the Taking of Evidence Abroad in Civil or Commercial Matters, 1970: *see* Vol. 9 p. 292.

Convention Abolishing the Requirement of Legalisation for Foreign Public Documents, 1961
(Corrected from Vol. 9 p. 332)
(Status as provided by The Hague Conference on Private International Law)

State	Sig.	Cons.
Kazakhstan	5 Apr 2000	30 Jan 2001

LABOUR

Freedom of Association and Protection of the Right to Organise Convention, 1948 (ILO Conv. 87): *see* Vol. 9 p. 292.
Discrimination (Employment and Occupation) Convention, 1958 (ILO Conv. 111): *see* Vol. 8 p. 185.
Employment Policy Convention, 1964 (ILO Conv. 122): see Vol. 8 p. 186.

Forced Labour Convention, 1930 (ILO Conv. 29)
(Continued from Vol. 7 p. 333)
(Status as at 31 December 2002 as provided by the ILO)

State	Ratif. Registered		State	Ratif. Registered
Kazakhstan	18 May 2001		Nepal	3 Jan 2002

Right to Organise and Collective Bargaining Convention, 1949 (ILO Conv. 98)
(Continued from Vol. 8 p. 185)
(Status as at 31 December 2002 as provided by the ILO)

State	Ratif. Registered
Kazakhstan	18 May 2001

Equal Remuneration Convention, 1951 (ILO Conv. 100)
(Continued from Vol. 8 p. 185)
(Status as at 31 December 2002 as provided by the ILO)

State	Ratif. Registered	State	Ratif. Registered
Kazakhstan	18 May 2001	Singapore	30 May 2002
Pakistan	11 Oct 2001		

Abolition of Forced Labour Convention, 1957 (ILO Conv. 105)
(Continued from Vol. 9 p. 292)
(Status as at 31 December 2002 as provided by the ILO)

State	Ratif. registered
Kazakhstan	18 May 2001

Minimum Age Convention, 1973 (ILO Conv. 138)
Entry into force: 19 June 1976
(Corrected from Vol. 9 p. 293)
(Status as at 31 December 2002 as provided by the ILO)

State	Ratif. Reg.	Min. age spec.	State	Ratif. Reg.	Min. age spec.
Cambodia	23 Aug 1999	14	Mongolia	16 Dec 2002	15
China	28 Apr 1999	16	Nepal	30 May 1997	14
Indonesia	7 Jun 1999	15	Papua New		
Japan	5 Jun 2000	15	Guinea	2 Jun 2000	16
Kazakhstan	18 May 2001	16	Philippines	4 Jun 1998	15
Korea (Rep.)	28 Jan1999	15	Sri Lanka	11 Feb 2000	14
Kyrgyzstan	31 Mar 1992	16	Tajikistan	26 Nov 1993	16
Malaysia	9 Sep 1997	15			

Worst Forms of Child Labour Convention, 1999 (ILO Conv. 182)
(Continued from Vol. 9 p. 293)
(Status as at 31 December 2002 as provided by the ILO)

State	Ratif. registered	State	Ratif. registered
Bangladesh	12 Mar 2001	Nepal	3 Jan 2002
China	8 Aug 2002	Pakistan	11 Oct 2001
Iran	8 May 2002	Singapore	14 Jun 2001
Japan	18 Jun 2001	Sri Lanka	1 Mar 2001
Korea (Rep.)	29 Mar 2001	Thailand	16 Feb 2001
Mongolia	26 Feb 2001		

NARCOTIC DRUGS

Agreement Concerning the Suppression of the Manufacture of, Internal Trade in, and Use of, Prepared Opium and amended by Protocol, 1925, amended 1946: *see* Vol. 6 p. 261.

Agreement Concerning the Suppression of Opium Smoking, 1931, amended by Protocol, 1946: *see* Vol. 6 p. 261.

Protocol Amending the Agreements, Conventions and Protocols on Narcotic Drugs, concluded at The Hague on 23 January 1912, at Geneva on 11 February 1925 and 19 February 1925 and 13 July 1931, at Bangkok on 27 November 1931 and at Geneva on 26 June 1936, 1946: *see* Vol. 6 p. 261.

Protocol bringing under International Control Drugs outside the Scope of the Convention of 1931, as amended by the protocol of 1946: *see* Vol. 6 p. 262.

Convention for the Suppression of the Illicit Traffic in Dangerous Drugs, 1936, amended 1946: *see* Vol. 6 p. 262.

Protocol for Limiting and Regulating the Cultivation of the Poppy Plant, the Production of, International and Wholesale Trade in, and Use of Opium, 1953: *see* Vol. 6 p. 262.

International Opium Convention, 1925, amended by Protocol 1946: *see* Vol. 7 p. 334.

Convention for Limiting the Manufacture and Regulating the Distribution of Narcotic Drugs, 1931, and amended by Protocol, 1946: *see* Vol. 7 p. 334.

Single Convention on Narcotic Drugs, 1961: *see* Vol. 7 p. 334.

Convention on Psychotropic Substances, 1971: *see* Vol. 9 p. 294.

United Nations Convention Against Illicit Traffic in Narcotic Drugs and Psychotropic Substances, 1988: *see* Vol. 9 p. 294.

Single Convention on Narcotic Drugs, 1961, as Amended by Protocol 1972
(Continued from Vol. 9 p. 294)

State	Sig.	Cons.
Iran		18 Dec 2001

Protocol amending the Single Convention on Narcotic Drugs, 1972
(Continued from Vol. 8 p. 186)

State	Sig.	Cons.
Iran	25 Mar 1972	18 Dec 2001

NATIONALITY AND STATELESSNESS

Convention relating to the Status of Stateless Persons, 1954: *see* Vol. 6 p. 264.

Optional Protocol to the Vienna Convention on Diplomatic Relations concerning Acquisition of Nationality, 1961: *see* Vol. 6 p. 265.

Optional Protocol to the Vienna Convention on Consular Relations concerning Acquisition of Nationality, 1963: *see* Vol. 8 p. 187.

NUCLEAR MATERIAL

Convention on Civil Liability for Nuclear Damage, 1963: *see* Vol. 6 p. 265.
Joint Protocol Relating to the Application of the Vienna Convention (and the Paris Convention on Third Party Liability in the Field of Nuclear Energy), 1980: *see* Vol. 6 p. 265.
Convention on Early Notification of a Nuclear Accident, 1986: *see* Vol. 9 p. 295.
Convention on Assistance in the Case of a Nuclear Accident or Radiological Emergency, 1986: *see* Vol. 9 p. 295.
Protocol to amend the Convention on Civil Liability for Nuclear Damage, 1997: *see* Vol. 8 p. 188.
Convention on Supplementary Compensation for Nuclear Damage, 1997: *see* Vol. 8 p. 189.

Convention on the Physical Protection of Nuclear Material, 1980
(Continued from Vol. 9 p. 295)
(Status as at 31 December 2002, provided by IAEA)

State	*Sig.*	*Cons. (deposit)*
India		12 Mar 2002

Convention on Nuclear Safety, 1994
(Continued from Vol. 8 p. 188)
(Status as at 31 December 2002, provided by IAEA)

State	*Sig.*	*Cons. (deposit)*
Indonesia		12 Apr 2002

Joint Convention on the Safety of Spent Fuel Management and on the Safety of Radioactive Waste Management, 1997
Entry into force: 18 Jun 2001
(Continued from Vol. 8 p. 188)
(Status as at 31 December 2002, provided by IAEA)

State	*Sig.*	*Cons. (deposit)*
Korea (Rep.)		16 Sep 2002

OUTER SPACE

Treaty on Principles Governing the Activities of the States in the Exploration and Use of Outer Space, Including the Moon and Other Celestial Bodies, 1967: *see* Vol. 6 p. 266.

Agreement governing the Activities of States on the Moon and other Celestial Bodies, 1979
(Continued from Vol. 6 p. 267)

State	Sig.	Cons.
Kazakhstan		11 Jan 2001

Convention on Registration of Objects Launched into Outer Space, 1974
(Continued from Vol. 7 p. 337).

State	Sig.	Cons.
Kazakhstan		11 Jan 2001

PRIVILEGES AND IMMUNITIES

Convention on the Privileges and Immunities of the Specialized Agencies, 1947: *see* Vol. 7 p. 338.
Vienna Convention on Diplomatic Relations, 1961: *see* Vol. 6 p. 268.
Optional Protocol to the Vienna Convention on Diplomatic Relations concerning the Compulsory Settlement of Disputes, 1961: *see* Vol. 6 p. 269.
Vienna Convention on Consular Relations, 1963: *see* Vol. 8 p. 189.
Optional Protocol to the Vienna Convention on Consular Relations concerning the Compulsory Settlement of Disputes, 1963: *see* Vol. 6 p. 269.
Convention on Special Missions, 1969: *see* Vol. 6 p. 269.
Optional Protocol to the Convention on Special Missions concerning the Compulsory Settlement of Disputes, 1969: *see* Vol. 6 p. 269.

Convention on the Privileges and Immunities of the United Nations, 1946
(Continued from Vol. 9 p. 296)

State	Sig.	Cons.
Tajikistan		19 Oct 2001

REFUGEES

Convention relating to the Status of Refugees, 1951: *see* Vol. 8 p. 190.
Protocol relating to the Status of Refugees, 1967: *see* Vol. 8 p. 190.

ROAD TRAFFIC AND TRANSPORT

Convention on Road Traffic, 1968: *see* Vol. 7 p. 338.
Convention on Road Signs and Signals, 1968: *see* Vol. 7 p. 338.

SEA

Convention on the Territorial Sea and the Contiguous Zone, 1958: *see* Vol. 6 p. 271.
Convention on the High Seas, 1958: *see* Vol. 7 p. 339.
Convention on Fishing and Conservation of the Living Resources of the High Seas, 1958:
see Vol. 6 p. 271.
Convention on the Continental Shelf, 1958: *see* Vol. 6 p. 271.
Optional Protocol of Signature concerning the Compulsory Settlement of Disputes, 1958:
see Vol. 6 p. 272.

United Nations Convention on the Law of the Sea, 1982
(Continued from Vol. 9 p. 296)

State	Sig.	Cons.
Bangladesh	10 Dec 1982	27 Jul 2001

Agreement relating to the Implementation of Part XI of the United Nations Convention on the Law of the Sea of 10 December 1982, 1994
(Continued from Vol. 8 p. 190, corrected from Vol. 9 p. 296)

State	Sig.	Cons.		State	Sig.	Cons.
Bangladesh	10 Dec 1982	27 Jul 2001		Maldives	10 Oct 1994	7 Sep 2000

Agreement for the Implementation of the Provisions of the United Nations Convention on the Law of the Sea (...) relating to the Conservation and Management of Straddling Fish Stocks and Highly Migratory Fish Stocks, 1995
(Continued from Vol. 8 p. 191)
Entry into force: 11 December 2001

SEA TRAFFIC AND TRANSPORT

Convention Regarding the Measurement and Registration of Vessels employed in Inland
Navigation, 1956: *see* Vol. 6 p. 273.
International Convention for the Safety of Life at Sea, 1960: *see* Vol. 6 p. 273.
International Convention on Load Lines, 1966: *see* Vol. 6 p. 274.
International Convention on Tonnage Measurement of Ships, 1969: *see* Vol. 6 p. 274.
Special Trade Passenger Ships Agreement, 1971, *see* Vol. 6 p. 275.
Protocol on Space Requirements for Special Trade Passenger Ships, 1973: *see* Vol. 6
p. 275.
Convention on a Code of Conduct for Liner Conferences, 1974: *see* Vol. 6 p. 276.
UN Convention on the Carriage of Goods by Sea, 1978: *see* Vol. 6 p. 276.
Protocol Relating to the International Convention for the Safety of Life at Sea, 1974 (as
amended) 1978: *see* Vol. 6 p. 276.

Convention on Facilitation of International Maritime Traffic, 1965 as amended
(Continued from Vol. 8 p. 191)
(Status as included in IMO doc. J/8687, as at 31 December 2003)

State	Cons.	E.i.f.	State	Cons.	E.i.f.
Indonesia	4 Nov 2002		Korea (Rep)	6 Mar 2001	5 May 2001

Convention on the International Regulations for Preventing Collisions at Sea, 1972 as amended
(Continued from Vol. 6 p. 275)
Status as included in IMO doc. J/8687, as at 31 December 2003)

State	Cons.	E.i.f.
Mongolia	26 Jun 2002	26 Jun 2002

International Convention for Safe Containers, as amended 1972
(Continued from Vol. 6 p. 275)
Status as included in IMO doc. J/8687, as at 31 December 2003)

State	Cons.	E.i.f.
Iran	11 Oct 2001	11 Oct 2001

International Convention for the Safety of Life at Sea, 1974, as amended
(Continued from Vol. 6 p. 276)
Status as included in IMO doc. J/8687, as at 31 December 2003)

State	Cons.	E.i.f.
Mongolia	26 Jun 2002	26 Sep 2002

Protocol Relating to the International Convention on Load Lines, 1988
(Continued from Vol. 8 p. 192)
Entry into force: 3 February 2000
(Status as included in IMO doc. J/8687, as at 31 December 2003)

State	Cons.	E.i.f.	State	Cons.	E.i.f.
Bangladesh	18 Dec 2002		Pakistan	25 Apr 2002	25 Jul 2002
Cambodia	8 Jun 2001	8 Sep 2001	Vietnam	27 May 2002	27 Aug 2002
Korea (DPR)	8 Aug 2001	8 Nov 2001			

SOCIAL MATTERS

International Convention for the Suppression of the Circulation of and Traffic in Obscene Publications, 1923: *see* Vol. 6 p. 277.

International Convention for the Suppression of the Traffic in Women and Children, 1921: *see* Vol. 6 p. 277.

Convention for the Suppression of the Circulation of, and Traffic in, Obscene Publications, 1923, amended by Protocol in 1947: *see* Vol. 6 p. 277.

International Convention for the Suppression of the Traffic in Women of Full Age, 1933: *see* Vol. 6 p. 277.

Convention for the Suppression of the Traffic in Women and Children, 1921, amended by Protocol in 1947, *see* Vol. 6 p. 277.

Convention for the Suppression of the Traffic in Women of Full Age, 1933, amended by Protocol, 1947: *see* Vol. 6 p. 277.

International Agreement for the Suppression of the White Slave Traffic, 1904, amended by Protocol 1949: *see* Vol. 6 p. 278.

International Convention for the Suppression of the White Slave Traffic, 1910, amended by Protocol 1949: *see* Vol. 6 p. 278.

Agreement for the Suppression of the Circulation of Obscene Publications, 1910, amended by Protocol 1949: *see* Vol. 6 p. 278.

Final Protocol to the Convention for the Suppression of the Traffic in Persons and of the Exploitation of the Prostitution of Others, 1950: *see* Vol. 6 p. 278.

Convention for the Suppression of the Traffic in Persons and of the Exploitation of the Prostitution of Others, 1950
(Continued from Vol. 7 p. 340)

State	Sig.	Cons	State	Sig.	Cons
Nepal		10 Dec 2002	Tajikistan		19 Oct 2001

TELECOMMUNICATIONS

Constitution of the Asia-Pacific Telecommunity, 1976: *see* Vol. 8 p. 192.

Convention on the International Maritime Satellite Organization (INMARSAT), 1976 (as amended): *see* Vol. 8 p. 193.

Amendment to Article 11, Paragraph 2(a), of the Constitution of the Asia-Pacific Telecommunity, 1981: *see* Vol. 8 p. 193.

Amendments to articles 3(5) and 9(8) of the Constitution of the Asia-Pacific Telecommunity, 1991: *see* Vol. 9 p. 298

Agreement establishing the Asia-Pacific Institute for Broadcasting Development, 1977
(Continued from Vol. 9 p. 298)

State	Sig.	Cons
Cambodia		10 Jul 2001

Amendments to the Agreement establishing the Asia-Pacific Institute for Broadcasting Development
Islamabad, 21 July 1999
Entry into force: 14 December 2001

State	Sig.	Cons	State	Sig.	Cons
Afghanistan		23 Dec 1999	Korea (Rep.)		14 Sep 2001
Bangladesh		21 Jun 2000	Myanmar		3 Apr 2000
Bhutan		12 Oct 2000	Pakistan		17 Aug 2001
Brunei		5 Jul 2000	Singapore		10 Jan 2000
Cambodia		10 Jul 2001	Sri Lanka		20 Aug 1999
China		10 Apr 2000	Thailand		2 Jul 2001
Indonesia		23 Apr 2001	Vietnam		27 Jan 2000
Iran		30 Nov 1999			

TREATIES

Vienna Convention on the Law of Treaties Between States and International Organizations or Between International Organizations, 1986: *see* Vol. 6 p. 280.

Vienna Convention on the Law of Treaties, 1969
(Continued from: Vol. 8 p. 193)

State	Sig.	Cons.
Vietnam		10 Oct 2001

WEAPONS

Protocol for the Prohibition of the Use in War of Asphyxiating, Poisonous or other Gases, and of Bacteriological Warfare, 1925: *see* Vol. 6 p. 281.

Treaty Banning Nuclear Weapon Tests in the Atmosphere, in Outer Space and Under Water, 1963: *see* Vol. 6 p. 281.

Treaty on the Prohibition of the Emplacement of Nuclear Weapons and Other Weapons of Mass Destruction on the Sea-Bed and the Ocean Floor and in the Subsoil Thereof, 1971: *see* Vol. 6 p. 282.

Convention on the Prohibition of the Development, Production and Stockpiling of Bacteriological (Biological) and Toxin Weapons and on Their Destruction, 1972: *see* Vol. 6 p. 282.

Convention on the Prohibition of Military or any other Hostile Use of Environmental Modification Techniques, 1976: *see* Vol. 8 p. 194.

Treaty on the Non-Proliferation of Nuclear Weapons, 1968
(Continued and corrected from Vol. 6 p. 282, and dates included)

State	Sig.	Cons.	State	Sig.	Cons.
Afghanistan	1 Jul 1968	4 Feb 1970	Maldives	11 Sep 1968	5 Mar 1970
Bangladesh		31 Aug 1979	Mongolia	1 Jul 1968	14 May 1969
Bhutan		23 May 1985	Myanmar		2 Dec 1992
Brunei		26 Mar 1985	Nepal	1 Jul 1968	14 May 1969
Cambodia		2 Jun 1972	Papua New		
China		9 Mar 1992	Guinea		13 Jan 1982
Indonesia	2 Mar 1970	12 Jul 1979	Philippines	7 Jan 1968	5 Oct 1972
Iran	1 Jul 1968	2 Feb 1970	Singapore	5 Feb 1970	10 Mar 1976
Japan	3 Feb 1970	8 Jun 1976	Sri Lanka	1 Jul 1968	5 Mar 1979
Kazakhstan		14 Feb 1994	Tajikistan		17 Jan 1995
Korea (DPR)		12 Dec 1985	Thailand		2 Dec 1972
Korea (Rep)	1 Jul 1968	23 Apr 1975	Turkmenistan		29 Sep 1994
Kyrgyzstan		5 Jul 1994	Uzbekistan		2 May 1992
Laos	1 Jul 1968	20 Feb 1970	Vietnam		14 Jun 1982
Malaysia	1 Jul 1968	20 Feb 1970			

Convention on Prohibitions or Restrictions on the Use of Certain Conventional Weapons which may be Deemed Excessively Injurious or to have Indiscriminate Effects, and Protocols, 1980
(Continued from Vol. 9 p. 299)

State	Sig.	Cons.
Korea (Rep.)		9 May 2001

Convention on the Prohibition of the Development, Production, Stockpiling and Use of Chemical Weapons and on Their Destruction, 1993
(Continued from Vol. 9 p. 299)

State	Sig.	Cons.
Thailand	14 Jan 1993	10 Dec 2002

Comprehensive Nuclear Test Ban Treaty, 1996
(Continued from Vol. 8 p. 194)

State	Sig.	Cons.	State	Sig.	Cons.
Kazakhstan	30 Sep 1996	14 May 2002	Singapore	14 Jan 1999	10 Nov 2001
Philippines	24 Sep 1996	23 Feb 2001			

**Convention on the Prohibition of the Use, Stockpiling, Production and Transfer of
Anti-Personnel Mines and on their Destruction, 1997**
(Continued from Vol. 9 p. 300)

State	Sig.	Cons.
Afghanistan		11 Sep 2002

ASIA AND INTERNATIONAL ORGANIZATIONS

ASIAN-AFRICAN LEGAL CONSULTATIVE ORGANIZATION BI-ANNUAL SURVEY OF ACTIVITIES 2000-2001

including the work of its Fortieth Session held at New Delhi, 20-24 June 2001.

M.C.W. Pinto[*]

Note: The Asian-African Legal Consultative Committee (now: Organization) was established on 15 November 1956 to facilitate the exchange of views and information on legal matters of common concern to its Members. Its regular Sessions are convened annually, alternately in Asia and Africa. A Session generally takes place in the first half of a calendar year, and is known by the name of the city in which it is held. Consideration of a topic commenced at one Session may continue at subsequent Sessions, as well as inter-sessionally through seminars or expert group meetings, which retain their association with the originating Session. Reports on inter-Sessional activities may be discussed at the following Session.

By a decision adopted at its Special Session in New Delhi on 14 October 1992 (Res. SS 1997/1), the Organization's permanent headquarters were established in New Delhi.

Member States are represented at Sessions by high level delegations, which may include Chief Justices, Judges, Cabinet Ministers, Attorneys-General, and senior public officials. Sessions are routinely attended by observers from non-Member States, and inter-governmental and non-governmental organizations. The Organization maintains working relationships with the United Nations and its Specialized Agencies and Commissions, as well as with other international organizations, including the International Atomic Energy Agency, UNIDROIT, the Hague Conference on Private International Law, the Commonwealth Secretariat, the Organization of African Unity and the League of Arab States.

The present survey covers the focus of the work of the Organization's Fortieth Session, held at New Delhi, 20-24 June 2001, while containing references also to activities associated with Sessions which were covered in earlier volumes of this *Yearbook*.

---

[*] Of the Editorial Board.

Asian Yearbook of International Law, Volume 10 (B.S. Chimni *et al.*, eds.)

Information on the activities of AALCO may be obtained from:

The AALCO Secretariat, E-66, Vasant Marg., Vasant Vihar, New Delhi 110057, India,
E-mail: aalcc@del3.vsnl.net.in

1. MEMBERSHIP AND ORGANIZATION

There were forty-four Members of the Organization at the time of its Fortieth Session, held at New Delhi, India, from 20-24 June 2001: Bahrain, Bangladesh, China, Cyprus, Egypt, Gambia, Ghana, India, Indonesia, Iran, Iraq, Japan, Jordan, Kenya, Democratic People's Republic of Korea, Republic of Korea, Kuwait, Lebanon, Libya, Malaysia, Mauritius, Mongolia, Myanmar, Nepal, Nigeria, Oman, Pakistan, Palestine, Philippines, Qatar, Saudi Arabia, Senegal, Sierra Leone, Singapore, Somalia, Sri Lanka, Sudan, Syria, Tanzania, Thailand, Turkey, Uganda, United Arab Emirates, and Yemen. Botswana is an Associate Member.

2. INTER-SESSIONAL MEETINGS AND OTHER ACTIVITIES

A Meeting of Legal Advisers of AALCO Member States convened at New York on 26 October 2000, presided over by Ambassador Aboul Geit, Permanent Representative of the Arab Republic of Egypt to the United Nations. The meeting focused on the *Jurisdictional Immunities of States and their Property*, and was attended *inter alia* by Professor Gerhard Hafner, Chairman of the UN Sixth Committee's Working Group on that topic (*Report*, pages 4-7).

A Seminar on *International Humanitarian Law* was held at New Delhi on 17 November 2000 on the occasion of AALCO's 44th Constitution Day, sponsored jointly with the International Committee of the Red Cross, and presided over by H.E. Gehad Madi, Ambassador of the Arab Republic of Egypt to India (*Report*, pages 8-9).

An open-ended Working Group to finalize the revised consolidated text of AALCO's *Bangkok Principles on the Status and Treatment of Refugees* met in New Delhi, 26-27 February 2001. Dr. Mrs. Neeru Chadha, Legal Officer, Ministry of External Affairs of India, was appointed Rapporteur.

The work of AALCO's *Regional Arbitration Centres* established at Cairo, Kuala Lumpur, Lagos and Tehran is referred to at pages 14-17 of the Secretariat's Report of the Fortieth Session ("Report").

The Organization's *Data Collection Unit*, with a broader range of functions, and re-named *Centre for Research and Training* is funded by the Republic of Korea and has available a range of information on the economic laws and regulations of Member States. See *Report*, pages 12-14.

3. OFFICERS OF THE FORTIETH (NEW DELHI) SESSION

The Fortieth Session of the Organization elected Dr. P. Sreenivasa Rao as its President. Joint Secretary and Legal Adviser to the Ministry of External Affairs, India, Chief Bola Ige San, Attorney General and Minister of Justice, Nigeria, was elected Vice-President of the Session. Ms. Nelum Mayadunne, Assistant Legal Adviser to the Ministry of Foreign Affairs, Sri Lanka, was appointed Rapporteur of a Special

Meeting on *Some Legal Aspects of Migration* held on 22 June 2001 (*Report*, pages 598-645).

Organization of the Session was the responsibility of the Secretary-General of the Organization, Mr. Tang Chengyuan, who was assisted by Deputy Secretaries-General Dr. Wafik Zaher Kamil, Mr. Mohammed Reza Dabiri and Mr. Ryo Takagi, as well as by Assistant Secretaries-General and members of the Secretariat.

4. *ADMINISTRATIVE MATTERS*

By its resolution RES/40/ORG.3 dated 24 June 2001, adopted at its Fortieth Session, the Asian-African Legal Consultative Committee (AALCC) decided to change its name to *Asian-African Legal Consultative Organization (AALCO)*.

At that Session Dr. Wafik Zaher Kamil (Egypt) was appointed Secretary-General of the Organization. Dr. Kamil took office in May 2001, upon retirement of Mr. Tang Chengyuan (China).

5. *SUBJECTS DEALT WITH BY THE ORGANIZATION*

The Organization considered and adopted decisions on the subjects listed below, the order of their discussion being determined at the commencement of the Session. The references next to each subject are to the pages of the Report of the Fortieth Session issued by the Secretariat** The *Report* on each Session will, from 2002, be contained in a volume entitled *Yearbook of the Asian-African Legal Consultative Organization*.

I. Questions under consideration by the International Law Commission (*Report*, pages 169-304)

The Secretariat's report on the work of the Commission at its Fifty-second Session (2000) focussed on the Commission's work on six topics: State responsibility; International liability for injurious consequences arising out of acts not prohibited by international law; Reservations to treaties; Diplomatic protection; Unilateral acts of States; and Jurisdictional immunities of States and their property. Of particular interest from an Asian perspective are (1) *Jurisdictional immunities of States and their property*, a topic of the International Law Commission which, on the initiative of Japan at AALCO's the Cairo Session, was placed on the Organization's own agenda (*Report*, pages 305-358); and (2) *International liability for injurious consequences arising out of acts not prohibited by international law*, a topic on which the Commission's Special Rapporteur is (*Report*, pages 280-304) Dr. P. Sreenivasa Rao of India (*Report*, pages 280-304).

II. Matters referred to the Organization by Member States
1. Law of the Sea (*Report*, pages 23-64)

The Committee reviewed the work of the institutions created for giving effect to the provisions of the 1982 UN Convention on the Law of the Sea, expressing satisfaction at the adoption by the Council of the International Seabed Authority on 13 July 2000, of the *Regulations on Prospecting and Exploration for Polymetallic Nodules in the Area*, as well as at the working of the International Tribunal for the

Law of the Sea, and related dispute settlement mechanisms. Members welcomed the UN General Assembly's establishment (resolution 54/33 of 24 November 1999) of an open-ended informal consultative process (UNCIPO), with a mandate (i) to study developments in ocean affairs consistent with the legal framework provided by the UN Convention and the goals of Chapter 17 of Agenda 21, (ii) against the background of overall developments of all relevant ocean issues, to identify particular issues to be considered by the General Assembly; and (iii) to place emphasis on areas where co-ordination and co-operation at the inter-governmental and the inter-agency level were needed.

2. Status and treatment of Refugees (*Report*, pages 113-168)
The Organization completed its work on a consolidated text of the Revised Bangkok Principles (for the original text see Asian YIL, Vol 7 (1997), pages 381-7) taking into account Member States' comments. The Revised Consolidated text of the *Bangkok Principles on the Status and Treatment of Refugees* adopted by the Organization on 24 June 2001 is reproduced at **A** below.

3. Deportation of Palestinians and other Israeli practices among them the massive immigration and settlement of Jews in occupied territories in violation of international law, particularly the Fourth Geneva Convention of 1949 (*Report*, pages 445-507)
A Secretariat summary of international action on the subject (*Report*, pages 466-507) covers an Asian Meeting on the Question of Palestine 1-3 March 2000, and the Hanoi Declaration adopted there; the Vatican/PLO Agreement on Church Rights in the Holy Land and Jerusalem 15 February 2000; the work of the UN General Assembly's Committee on the Exercise of Inalienable Rights of the Palestinian People; the South Summit meeting, Havana, 10-14 April 2000 and the XIII Ministerial meeting of the Non-aligned Nations, Cartagena, 8-9 April 2000; the International Meeting in Support of Peaceful Settlement of the Question of Palestine, 23-4 May 2000; the annual Co-ordination Meeting of the Foreign Ministers of the Organization of the Islamic Conference (OIC), New York, 18 September 2000; the 10th Emergency Special Session on Illegal Israeli Actions, New York, 18 October 2000; the Extra-ordinary Arab Summit Conference, Cairo, 21-2 October 2000; UN Security Council consideration of international protection for Palestinian civilians, 31 October 2000; the Sharm El-Sheikh Understanding Fact-finding Committee, 7 November 2000; the Report of the High Commissioner for Human Rights on her visit to occupied Palestinian Territory, 8-16 November 2000; Peace Proposals by President Clinton, 23 December 2000; and the Arab League Foreign Ministers' Meeting, Cairo, 3 January 2001.

4. Legal protection of Migrant Workers (*Report,* pages 593-689)
The item was discussed extensively at a Special Meeting on *Some Legal Aspects of Migration*, held on 22 June 2001 during the Fortieth Session of the Organization, with collaboration and support from the International Organization for Migration, and other international organizations. The Report contains a summary of the dis-

cussion at the Special Meeting and the resolution adopted by the Organization (pages 598-645), as well as a Secretariat study on the topic (pages 646-689).

5. Extra-territorial application of national legislation: sanctions imposed against third parties (*Report*, pages 65-112)

Members re-affirmed views expressed at the Organization's 36th, 37th, 38th and 39th Sessions that the extra-territorial imposition of national laws violated State sovereignty and interfered with the legitimate economic interests of States. A Secretariat study on the subject and the Secretariat's report on discussion of related issues at the 55th Session of the United Nations General Assembly, are at pages 78-112.

6. Jurisdictional immunities of States and their property (*Report*, pages 305-358)

Referred to the Committee at its Cairo Session (2000) by the Delegation of Japan, consideration of this topic by the Committee takes account of the work of the International Law Commission, and discussion of it at meetings of the Sixth Committee of the UN General Assembly. With a view to collating the views of AALCO's Members States, the Secretary-General by his letter dated 3 July 2000, invited them to transmit to it national legislation, court decisions and other relevant materials on the topic. By January 2001, four countries had done so. Their responses are reproduced at **B** below.

7. International terrorism (*Report*, pages 508-552)

Referred to the Committee by the Government of India, the topic was placed on the agenda of the Fortieth Session for the first time. The Explanatory Note provided by India, and a preliminary study by the Secretariat, are reproduced at **C** below.

8. Establishing co-operation against trafficking in women and children (*Report*, pages 553-592)

Referred to the Committee by the Government of Indonesia, the topic was placed on the agenda of the Fortieth Session for the first time. The Explanatory Note provided by Indonesia, and a preliminary study by the Secretariat, are reproduced at **D** below.

III. Matters of common concern having legal implications
1. United Nations Diplomatic Conference of Plenipotentiaries on the establishment of an International Criminal Court (Rome, 15 June-17 July 1998): the work of the Preparatory Commission for an International Criminal Court (*Report*, pages 359-407)

The Secretariat's report of the work of the Preparatory Commission covers the work of the Commission's Sixth Session (27 November-8 December 2000). Notes on the initiatives of AALCO's Members in regard to signature and ratification of the Rome Statute are at pages 390-407.

2.   United Nations Conference on Environment and Development (*Report*, pages 409-444)

The Report contains the Secretariat's review of the work of the Conference of the Parties to the *UN Convention on Climate Change* at its first session (13-25 November 2000). The Report also covers the work of the fifth session of the Conference of the Parties to the *UN Convention on Biological Diversity* (1998), 15-26 May 2000; and of the fourth session of the Conference of the Parties to the *Convention to Combat Desertification*, 11-22 December 2000.

IV International Trade Law Matters (*Report*, pages 690-815)

The Secretariat continued its regular review of the work of international organizations in the field of international trade law. The review covers the work of the *United Nations Commission on International Trade Law (UNCITRAL)*, the *United Nations Conference on Trade and Development (UNCTAD) and its Commissions*, and the United Nations *Industrial Development Organization (UNIDO)*; as well as of the *International Institute for the Unification of Private Law UNIDROIT)*, the *Hague Conference on Private International Law*, and the *World Trade Organization*. A Secretariat study entitled "WTO as a Framework Agreement and Code of Conduct for World Trade" is at pages 787-815.

Article VII
Voluntary Repatriation

1.   The essentially voluntary character of repatriation shall be respected in all cases and no refugee shall be repatriated against his will.

2.   The country of asylum, in collaboration with the country of origin, shall make adequate arrangements for the safe return of refugees who request repatriation.

3.   The country of origin shall provide all necessary documents to expedite their return on receiving back refugees, facilitate their resettlement and grant them the full rights and privileges of nationals of the country, and subject them to the same obligations.

4.   Refugees who voluntarily return to their country shall in no way be penalized for having left it or for any of the reasons giving rise to refugee situations. Whenever necessary, an appeal shall be made through national information media and through the relevant universal and regional organizations inviting refugees to return home without risk and to take up a normal and peaceful life without fear of being disturbed and punished, and that the text of such appeal should be given to refugees and clearly explained to them by their country of asylum.

5.   Refugees who freely decide to return to their homeland, as a result of such assurances or on their own initiative, shall be given every possible assistance by the

country of asylum, the country of origin, the country of transit, voluntary agencies and international and intergovernmental organizations to facilitate their return.

Article VIII[1]
International Cooperation on Comprehensive Solutions[2]

1.   Voluntary repatriation, local settlement or third country resettlement, that is, the traditional solutions, all remain viable and important responses to refugee situations, even while voluntary repatriation is the pre-eminent solution. To this effect, States may undertake, with the help of inter-governmental and non-governmental organizations, development measures which would underpin and broaden the acceptance of the three traditional durable solutions.

2.   States shall promote comprehensive approaches, including a mix of solutions involving all concerned States and relevant international organizations in the search for and implementation of durable solutions to refugee problems.

3.   The issue of root causes is crucial for solutions, and international efforts should also be directed to addressing the causes of refugee movements and the creation of the political, economic, social, humanitarian and environmental conditions conducive to repatriation.

Article IX
Right to Compensation

1.   A refugee shall have the right to receive compensation from the State or the Country which he left or to which he was unable to return.[3]

---

[1]   At the Open-ended Working Group Meeting held in New Delhi 26-27 February 2001, the delegate of India maintained her Government's position to place reservation on this Article. "The Government of India expresses its reservation on including a separate Article VIII on "International cooperation and comprehensive solutions". It wants the emphasis to remain on 'voluntary repatriation'. The other solutions like 'local settlement' or 'third country resettlement', according to it, would have to be considered carefully in each case, given their political, economic or security implications, particularly in situations of mass influx. In this connection, a distinction needs to be maintained between the 'individual refugees' and 'situations of mass influx', as well as between 'convention refugees' and 'economic migrants'. Further, the implementation of these solutions and treatment of refugees is linked to the available resources and capacity of each State."

[2]   Proposition of the AALCC Secretariat and the UNHCR to change the earlier title "Other solutions" to "International Cooperation on Comprehensive Solutions", which met with the approval of the Working Group.

[3]   In view of the financial and economic implications reservations were expressed at the Manila and Tehran Meetings on the right of refugees to receive compensation. Reservations to paragraph 1 were expressed by the Governments of Sudan, Pakistan, Turkey, Jordan, and Tanzania. The Government of Tanzania also proposed a reference to some mechanism accessible by all parties in order to deal with compensation issues. During the Open-ended Working Group Meeting held

2. The compensation referred to in paragraph 1 shall be for such loss as bodily injury, deprivation of personal liberty in denial of human rights, death of the refugee or of the person whose dependant the refugee was, and destruction of or damage to property and assets, caused by the authority of the State or Country, public officials or mob violence.

3. Where such person does not desire to return, he shall be entitled to prompt and full compensation by the Government or the authorities in control of such place of habitual residence as determined, in the absence of agreement by the parties concerned, by an international body designated or constituted for the purpose by the Secretary General of the United Nations at the request of either party.

4. If the status of such a person is disputed by the Government or the authorities in control of such place of habitual residence, or if any other dispute arises, such matter shall also be determined, in the absence of agreement by the parties concerned, by an international body designated or constituted as specified in paragraph (3) above.

Article X
Burden Sharing

1. The refugee phenomenon continues to be a matter of global concern and needs the support of the international community as a whole for its solution and as such the principle of burden sharing should be viewed in that context.

2. The principle of international solidarity and burden sharing needs to be applied progressively to facilitate the process of durable solutions for refugees, whether within or outside a particular region, keeping in perspective that durable solutions in certain situations may need to be found by allowing access to refugees in countries outside the region, due to political, social and economic considerations.

3. The principle of international solidarity and burden sharing should be seen as applying to all aspects of the refugee situation, including the development and strengthening of the standards of treatment of refugees, support to States in protecting and assisting refugees, the provision of durable solutions and the support of international bodies with responsibilities for the protection and assistance of refugees.

4. International solidarity and cooperation in burden sharing should be manifested whenever necessary, through effective concrete measures where the major share shall be borne by developed countries.[4]

---

on 26-27 February 2001, upon a request from the Chairman the delegate of Tanzania promised to send a concrete draft on his suggestion to be studied by the Secretariat.

[4] During the Open-ended Working Group Meeting held in New Delhi on 26-27 February 2001, at the suggestion of the delegation of Pakistan the phrase "where [the] major share be borne by developed countries" was included.

5. In all circumstances, the respect for fundamental humanitarian principles is an obligation for all members of the international community. Giving practical effect to the principle of international solidarity and burden sharing considerably facilitates States' fulfilment of their responsibilities in this regard.

Article XI
Obligations

A refugee shall not engage in subversive activities endangering the national security of the country of refuge or any other country[5] or in activities inconsistent with or against the principles and purposes of the United Nations.

Article XII
Rights Granted apart from the Principles

Nothing in these articles shall be deemed to impair any higher rights and benefits granted or which may hereafter be granted by a State to refugees.

Article XIII
Cooperation with International Organizations

States shall cooperate with the Office of the United Nations High Commissioner for Refugees and, in the region of its mandate, with the United Nations Relief and Works Agency for Palestine Refugees in the Near East.

B. Communication Received from Member States in Response to the Letter of the Secretary General of the AALCO dated 3 July 2000

(i) **Botswana**
The State Practice of the Republic of Botswana in Relation to the Jurisdictional Immunities of States and their Properties
"As far as can be discerned, there are no decisions related to Jurisdictional Immunities of States and their Properties that have been rendered by our national courts.
With regard to national legislation, as yet, we have no set statute dealing specifically with the above mentioned area of the law. Furthermore, upon diligent research into this field it was found that regrettably, no relevant material indicative of the jurisprudence and State practice on this topic could be found." [Letter from the Attorney General's Chambers, dated 15 August 2000.]

---

[5] During the Open-ended Working Group Meeting held in New Delhi on 26-27 February 2001, the delegate of India proposed the addition of the words "or any other country" after "country of refuge". The proposal was supported by Ghana and Turkey, and approved by the Working Group.

(ii) **Japan**

Japanese State practice related to Sovereign Immunity

1. National Legislation

Japan has no legislation on Sovereign Immunity.

2. Decisions related to Sovereign Immunity rendered by the national courts (see Attachment 1).

3. Other Materials indicative of Japanese State practice (see Attachment 2).

Attachment 1

1. Decision by the Supreme Court on 28 December 1928
   Matsuryama et al. v. Republic of China

Summary of the Facts and Judgement:

The plaintiff claimed payment for the promissory note issued by the Chargé d'Affaires of the defendant State. The courts of the first and second instances decided that, since the defendant had not waived its immunities, no service of writ from the Court could be done. The (former) Supreme Court upheld the conclusion of these decisions of the lower Court, stating that "the service undertaken by the Court and its designation of the date of subpoena is tantamount to the exercise of Japan's sovereign power, and therefore, they cannot be enforced upon a foreign State which is not to be subjected to our sovereignty". The Court further states: "Since a State is not to be subject to another State except by the former's self-restraint, a foreign State does not, in principle, come under Japan's jurisdiction with regard to civil procedures excepting suits concerning immovable property. However, it is an established rule of international law that, only in the case that the foreign State in question voluntarily submits itself to our jurisdiction, it will be an exception. Such an exception could be stipulated for in a treaty or could be made as an *ad hoc* expression of its jurisdiction submission with regards to a specific suit in question. However, such an expression should always be made *vis-à-vis* the State of Japan by the said foreign State. Even if there is an agreement between the foreign State and a Japanese subject according to which the former agrees to submit itself to the jurisdiction of Japan, this does not automatically give effect to oblige the said foreign State to actually submit to our jurisdiction".

2. Decision by the District Court of Tokyo of 9 June 1954
   Limbin Hteik Tin Lat v. Union of Burma

Summary of the facts:

The claimant filed with the Court an application for provisional disposition to determine the provisional status of a piece of land to which he claimed title. The land in question, situated next to the premises of the Burmese Consulate-General in Tokyo, was actually purchased in 1944 by A (third party in the present case), father-in-law of the claimant and the then Burmese Ambassador to Japan. The claimant purchased the land in question in 1953 from the wife and daughter of A., who were his joint legal successors under Burmese law. He came to Japan, obtained delivery of the land then in the possession of the administrator, and completed the registration of the transfer on the ground of purchase.

The respondent, the Government of the Union of Burma, was of the view that the purchase of the land in question was made by A in his capacity as agent of the respondent, so that the title to the land belonged to the latter. The respondent sought a provisional disposition for the striking out of the registration, which the Court granted. The claimant thereupon filed with the Court the present application for provisional disposition in order to prevent disturbance to his title and possession of the land.

The point at issue before the Court was whether a Japanese court had jurisdiction in a case in which the respondent was a foreign State.

Excerpts from the Judgement

The respondent, the Union of Burma, is known to the Court to have achieved independence a few years ago; it has a Government and controls a certain territory and its people, and has its consuls stationed in his country. In the absence of proof of the existence of special circumstances, such as the fact that the Union does not exercise exclusive control over its territory and its people, the Union must be recognized as a foreign State for the purpose of civil proceedings, even if Japan has not recognized it.

A State is not subject to the exercise of power by another State, and thus is not subject to the jurisdiction of another State in the matter of civil proceedings. This is to be admitted as a principle of international law recognized in general. However, it need hardly be added that in cases where a foreign State has consented by agreement to submit to the jurisdiction of another State, or where a State has waived its immunities that State may be subject to the jurisdiction of another State. Again, in an action concerning an immovable, it is widely admitted that jurisdiction belongs exclusively to the State of the *situs*, and consequently it must be said that a foreign State may be subject to the jurisdiction of another State.

In general, there is as yet no clearly recognized principle of international law on the question of jurisdiction in international cases, so that each State has to determine the extent of its jurisdiction. Consequently, such a determination, even if not respected by foreign States, is nonetheless valid in the sphere of municipal law of the State making the determination, and as a result clearly gives a basis for the exercise of jurisdiction against a foreign State. However, there is in our law no provision determining the extent of such jurisdiction, and the question must be judged by international customs and other factors. In this respect, there is no denying the fact that an immovable is an object *par excellence* of the territorial sovereignty of the State of its *situs* and this fact has been regarded as worthy of respect as a matter of international comity; hence, it has come to be recognized for a long time that an action directly concerning an immovable comes within the exclusive jurisdiction of the State of the *situs*. It has to be admitted therefore that, judging from its motive and its history, this principle has been recognized as applicable in actions in which a foreign State is a party, as well as where a private person is a party.

Accordingly ... It has to be concluded that Japan has jurisdiction, and the present Court has competence over the present proceedings in which the Union of Burma is designated as respondent.

With regard to the designation of the Burmese Consul-General as an agent of the respondent, the Court said: "Although in principle [the] Consul-General is considered according to international law not to have authority to represent his State at the diplomatic level, whether he is endowed with the authority to represent his State in civil proceedings is a matter to be decided solely by reference to the legal system of the Union of Burma." The Court concluded from the evidence that he was endowed with such authority.

On the question of the propriety of serving the writ of summons on his person, the Court admitted that such service was not in general permissible if the Consul-General enjoyed diplomatic privileges and immunities. The Court continued: "In cases where the Union of Burma, as respondent, should be subjected to our jurisdiction, the exercise of jurisdiction has to that extent to be recognized, and it cannot be regarded as contrary to international custom to serve the writ on his person, even when he has privileges as head or a member of the diplomatic mission and inviolability with regard to his residence, etc."

Attachment 2
(Provisional Translation)
Notification of the Secretary General of the Supreme Court to the Presidents of the High Courts and of the District Courts amended 14 December 1996 (originally issued on 15 April 1974)
(Note: This notification was abolished on 20 April 2000)
(Inquiry about the intention of a foreign State of appearing in the proceedings in a civil suit against the State)
The following has been decided with regard to the above mentioned inquiry. The Courts are requested to be in conformity with this. The Presidents of the competent District Courts shall transmit this notification to their subordinate Summary Courts.
1.   When a civil action is instituted against a foreign State, the competent court shall in advance request the Supreme Court to inquire through the Ministry of Foreign Affairs about the intention of the defendant State of appearing in the proceedings (see annexed request format).
2.   The competent court, in making the request mentioned in paragraph 1, shall annex a document which summarizes the claims or a copy of the written complaint, accompanied by a translation, if possible, into the official language of the defendant State (if not into English).
(Letter from the Embassy of Japan in New Delhi dated 26 September 2000.)

(iii)   **Myanmar**
The State Law and Order Restoration Council
The State-owned Economic Enterprises Law
(The State Law and Order Resolution Council Law No. 9/98)
The 10th Waning Day of Tabaung, 1350 M.E. (31 March 1989)
The State Law and Order Restoration Council Hereby enacts the following law:

Chapter I
Title and Definition

1. This Law shall be called the State-owned Economic Enterprises Law.
2. The expression "Government" contained in this Law includes departments, corporations and other organizations under the Government.

Chapter II
Economic Enterprises to be Carried out Solely by the Government

3. The Government has the sole right to carry out the following economic enterprises as State-owned economic enterprises:
(a) extraction of teak and sale of the same in the country and abroad;
(b) cultivation and conservation of forest plantation with the exception of village-owned fire-wood plantations cultivated by the villagers for their personal use;
(c) exploration, extraction and sale of petroleum and natural gas and production of products of the same;
(d) exploration and extraction of pearl, jade and precious stones and export of the same;
(e) breeding and production of fish and prawn in fisheries which have been reserved for research by the Government;
(f) Postal and Telecommunications Services;
(g) Air Transport Service and Railway Transport Service;
(h) Banking Service and Insurance Service;
(i) Broadcasting Service and Television Service;
(j) exploration and extraction of metals and export of the same;
(k) Electricity Generating Services other than those permitted by law to private and cooperative electricity generating services;
(l) manufacture of products relating to security and defence, which the Government has, from time to time, prescribed by notification.

4. The Government may, by notification, permit in the interest of the Union of Myanmar any economic enterprise which is prescribed under Section 3 to be operated solely the Government to be carried out by Joint venture between the Government and any other person or any other economic organization or under conditions by any person or any economic organization subject to conditions.

5. The Government may, by notification, prohibit or prescribe conditions regarding the purchase, procurement, improvement, storage, possession, transport, sale and transfer of products derived from or produced by or used by economic enterprises which are prescribed under Section 3 to be carried out solely by the Government.

Chapter III
Right of Carrying Out Other Economic Enterprises

6. Any person shall have the right to carry out any economic enterprise other than those prescribed under Section 3 to be carried out solely by the government.

7. Without prejudice to the provision of Section 6, the Government may, in addition to those economic enterprises which are prescribed under Section 3 to be carried out solely by the Government, also carry out any other economic enterprise if it is considered necessary in the interest of the Union of Myanmar.

Chapter IV
Right to Form an Organization

8. (a) In order to carry out the economic enterprise mentioned in Section 3 and Section 7, the Government may, by notification:
   i) constitute organizations which are to undertake responsibility, and pre-scribe their duties and powers;
   ii) re-constitute, if necessary, such organizations which are in existence at the time of the commencement of this Law, amend and prescribe their duties and power;
   iii) constitute one or more bodies to supervise the organizations mentioned in such Sections (i) and (ii), if necessary, and prescribe their duties and powers.

(b) The respective organizations constituted under sub-section (a) shall be a body corporate having perpetual succession and a common seal, and shall have the right to sue and be sued in its corporate name.

Chapter V
Offences and Penalties

9. Whoever is convicted of an offence of carrying out, without the permission of the Government, any economic enterprise prescribed under Section 3 to be carried out solely by the Government, shall be punished with imprisonment for a term which may extend to a period of five years and may also be liable to a fine. Furthermore, property both movable and immovable relating to the economic enterprise may be confiscated.

10. Whoever is convicted of an offence of violating an order or any condition notified under Section 4 or Section 5 shall be punished with imprisonment for a term which may extend to a period of three years and may also be liable to a fine.

Chapter VI
Miscellaneous

11. For the purpose of carrying out the provisions of this Law, the Government may prescribe such procedures as may be necessary, and the respective Ministers may issue such orders and directives as may be necessary.

12. The Law conferring powers for Establishing the Socialist Economic System, 1965 is hereby repealed.
Sd./Saw Maun
General
Chairman
The State Law and Order Resolution Council
(Letter from H.E. the Ambassador of Myanmar in New Delhi, dated 4 September 2000)

(iv)   Mauritius
We wish to bring to His Excellency's kind attention the following provisions of the *States Proceedings Act*:
(a) Section 13 of which
   (i) broadly speaking, prevents an order for specific performance from being made against the State and instead, provides for declaratory relief in lieu of an order for specific performance to be issued;
   (ii) provides that in proceedings against the State for the recovery of land or other property, a declaration rather than order for the recovery of property may be made by a Court of Law;
(b) Section 17(4) of which precludes the Courts from issuing attachment orders against the State for enforcing the payment by the State or any Government Department of a sum of money.
   It may however be noted that the State is otherwise liable to be sued and to have judgement delivered against it just as any subject may be sued and have judgement given against him.
   Please accept, Excellency, the assurances of our highest consideration.

Sd./-
(M. Ramlall)
for Head of Mission

F.-Explanatory Note sent by the Government of India on the item entitled "International Terrorism" for inclusion as an additional item on the Agenda of the 40th Session of AALCO

Draft comprehensive Convention on International Terrorism

Introduction

It may be recalled that India circulated a draft of a Comprehensive Convention on International Terrorism in the 51st UNGA in 1996. The Resolution 53/108 on "Measures to Eliminate International Terrorism" adopted by 53rd UNGA in 1998 gave the legislative mandate to elaborate the draft Convention on a priority basis, once negotiations on draft Conventions on Nuclear Terrorism and Funding of Terrorist Activities have been completed. At the 54th UNGA in 1999, it was decided that negotiated discussions on the Indian draft would commence in the Ad Hoc Committee on International Terrorism in September 2000. Pursuant to the UNGA Resolution of 1999 on Measures to Eliminate International Terrorism, a Working Group of the Sixth Committee on International Terrorism (A/C.6/55/1), as proposed by India, from 25 September to 6 October 2000. The second round negotiations on the draft Convention took place from 12 – 23 February 2001.

Salient features of the draft Convention:
i.   The Preamble recognizes the responsibility of States for suppressing acts of international terrorism including those which are committed or supported by States, directly or indirectly.

ii.   The scope of the Convention is defined by Article 2. Under the Convention, a person commits an offence if that person, by any means, unlawfully and intentionally causes death or serious bodily injury or serious damage to property including State or Government facilities, the public transportation system or infrastructure facilities, when the purpose of such act is to intimidate a population, or to compel a Government or an international organization to do or to abstain from doing any act.

The offences covered by the draft Convention are not covered in any other Convention. The definition is comprehensive as it covers "any means" used in the commission of a terrorist offence. The expression "any means" would thus cover the entire range of devices or substances which could be used for committing terrorism. The definition also contains a threshold which separates a terrorist offence from a common street crime.

iii.   Article 2(3) of the draft Convention includes the principle of command responsibility which was already accepted by the international Convention for the Suppression of Terrorist Bombings.

iv. Article 7 lays down the duty on States to refuse the granting of asylum to those involved in the commission of offences covered by the Convention.

v. Article 5 is the political exception clause under which the offences covered in the draft Convention can under no circumstances be justified by considerations of a political, philosophical, ideological, racial, ethnic, religious or other similar nature.

vi. The responsibility of contracting States to ensure that their respective territories are not used for the establishment of terrorist installations and training camps is reflected in Article 8. Under this article the States are required to take effective measures to prohibit:
(a) the establishment and operation of installations and training camps for commission, within or outside their territories, of offences covered by the draft Convention; and
(b) illegal activities of persons, groups and organizations that encourage, organize, knowingly finance or engage in the commission of offences covered by the draft Convention.

vii. Article 14 reinforces the political exception clause and states that extradition and mutual legal assistance may not be refused solely on the grounds that it concerns a political offence or an offence inspired by political motives.

viii. The draft Convention also lays down the duty to prosecute or extradite fugitive offenders.

...

Secretariat Study: International Terrorism

Background Note

It may not be an exaggeration to say that no other issue has attracted such world-wide attention as has combating international terrorism. Its complex character involving political, ideological, racial and religious issues has defied attempts to reach any international consensus on what constitutes terrorism. Notwithstanding such a lack of legal definition of "terrorism", there are several bilateral and regional agreements, and international conventions to deal with specific situations for the suppression of terrorism which provide the legal framework to establish and promote cooperation among States to deal with this problem. The recent move to draft a comprehensive international convention on terrorism under the auspices of the United Nations is yet another opportunity for the international community to take a concerted approach to combat this menace.

It may be recalled that as early as in 1937, a Convention on Prevention and Punishment of Terrorism was negotiated under the auspices of the League of Nations; it was ratified only by India and never came into force.

In the aftermath of the Second World War, the establishment of the United Nations was a historic achievement of the twentieth century. The UN Charter set out comprehensive provisions to deal with international peace and security, economic, social, human rights, and scores of other issues. In the wake of the call of the United Nations to end colonialism, liberation movements arose towards gaining independence, but unfortunately various unrecognized groups gathered momentum in several parts of the world. The means and methods advocated by such unrecognized groups added a new dimension to the problem of defining "terrorism" and to drawing a line between these liberation movements and the terrorist groups. It gave rise to "State terrorism", either sponsored or clandestinely supported by them, and resulted in the disruption of civil aviation and maritime navigation, attacks, on diplomatic personnel and civilian targets, and hostage taking by terrorist groups. In order to deal with these emerging issues, it was felt that instead of a comprehensive approach, a sector-wise approach addressing specific situations would be more practical and result-oriented.

The General Assembly as early as in 1972 took up for consideration an item on measures to prevent international terrorism, the convening under the auspices of the United Nations of an international conference to define international terrorism and to differentiate it from the struggle of peoples for national liberation. The resolutions adopted by the General Assembly on subsequent occasions, besides condemning such acts, among other aspects drew attention to the urgency for the conclusion of special agreements on a bilateral, regional and multilateral basis.[6] Parallel to these developments, international and regional instruments were developed under the ICAO, IMO, IAEA, and some regional organizations. However, a comprehensive approach to deal with the entire gamut of problems of international terrorism remained a matter of universal concern.

Against this backdrop, a major initiative under the United Nations was the adoption of the Declaration on "Measures to Eliminate International Terrorism" on 9 December 1994 by the General Assembly at its 49th Session. It was a significant achievement in its efforts to deal with the problem of international terrorism.

The Declaration, while expressing concern over the world-wide persistence of acts of international terrorism in all its forms and manifestations, including those in which States are directly or indirectly involved, recognized the desirability for connected co-ordination and operation among States in combating crimes closely connected with terrorism, including drug trafficking, unlawful arms trade, money laundering, and the smuggling of nuclear and other potentially deadly materials. It stressed the imperative need for further international co-operation between States in order to take and adopt practical and effective measures to prevent, combat and

---

[6] The various resolutions adopted by the General Assembly include: Re.3034(XXVII) of 18 December 1972, 31/102 of 15 December 1976, 32/147 of 16 December 1977, 34/145 of 17 December 1979, 36/109 of 10 December 1981, 38/130 of 19 December 1983, 40/61 of 9 December 1985, 42/159 of 7 December 1987, 44/29 of 4 December 1989, 46/51 of 9 December 1991, 49/60 of 9 December 1994, 50/5 of 18 October 1995, 50/53 of 11 December 1995, 51/210 of 17 December 1996, 52/165 of 15 December 1997, 53/108 of 8 December 1998, 54/110 of 9 December 1999, and 55/158 of 12 December 2000.

eliminate all forms of terrorism that affect the international community as a whole. It recalled the existing international treaties relating to various aspects of the problem and welcomed the conclusion of regional agreements and declarations to combat and eliminate terrorism in all its forms and manifestations.

The solemn Declaration by States was further expanded in subsequent provisions of the Declaration. These, among others, include:

i)   Reaffirmation of unequivocal condemnation of all acts, methods and practice of terrorism as criminal and unjustifiable wherever and by whomever committed;

ii)   Taking of effective and resolute measures in accordance with relevant provisions of international law and international standards of human rights for the speedy and final elimination of international terrorism. Such measures would include: the apprehension and prosecution or extradition of perpetrators of terrorist acts, co-operation and the exchange of relevant information, and

iii) Adherence to international conventions and protocols relating to various aspects of international terrorism.

The Declaration envisaged an important role for the United Nations, the relevant specialized agencies and inter-governmental organizations and other relevant bodies in promoting measures to combat and eliminate acts of terrorism. it suggested certain practical measures which the Secretary General of the United Nations could initiate with a view to assisting in the implementation of the Declaration. These measures could include:

(a) a collection of data on the status and implementation of existing multilateral regional and bilateral agreements relating to international terrorism;

(b) the preparation of a compendium of national laws and regulations, and

(c) an analytical review of existing international legal instruments, identifying aspects not covered by those instruments which could be subjects for the development of a further comprehensive legal framework.

Finally, the Declaration urged all States to promote and implement in good faith and effectively its provisions in all aspects.

The General Assembly at its 51st Session adopted Resolution 51/210 reaffirming the 1994 Declaration and approved another Declaration as a supplement to it. The General Assembly also decided to establish an Ad Hoc Committee open to all States Members of the United Nations or member of specialized agencies or of the International Atomic Energy Agency, and mandated it to elaborate an international convention for the suppression of terrorist bombings, as well as a further convention on the suppression of acts of nuclear terrorism.

During the year 1997, the Ad Hoc Committee met twice and completed the preparation of the text of the draft international Convention for the Suppression of Terrorist Bombings. It was adopted by the General Assembly at its 52nd Session on 15 December 1997.

The Ad Hoc Committee during its Session held 17-27 February 1998 focused its discussion on matters concerning the elaboration of an international convention for the suppression of acts of nuclear terrorism. The Report of the Ad Hoc Committee containing a draft text of the Convention on the Suppression of Acts of Nuclear Terrorism was further considered by a working group of the Sixth Committee which met from 28 September to 9 October 1998, during the 53rd Session of the General Assembly. In spite of several informal consultations, the Working Group failed to arrive at a consensus on the issues concerning the scope of the Convention. The General Assembly at its 53rd Session took note of the progress of work in the Ad Hoc Committee and directed it to continue to elaborate the draft Convention for the Suppression of Acts of Nuclear Terrorism and also to initiate consideration of the draft Convention on the Suppression of Financing of Terrorism, taking as a basis for discussion the draft text submitted by the delegation of France to the Sixth Committee. During the 53rd Session, the delegation of India proposed the adoption of a comprehensive convention against international terrorism and circulated a draft text on the same.

The Ad Hoc Committee during its meetings in 1999 devoted its time to the consideration of the outstanding issues relating to the two draft conventions. This work continued within the framework of a Working Group of the Sixth Committee convened during the 54th Session of the General Assembly from 27 September to 8 October 1999. The Working Group was able to finalize the draft articles on the International Convention for the Suppression of the Financing of Terrorism, which was later adopted by the General Assembly at its 54th Session.

In its resolution adopted on 9 December 1999, the General Assembly decided that the Ad Hoc Committee, besides considering the outstanding issues relating to the elaboration of the draft Convention on the Suppression of International Terrorism, would also address the question of convening a high-level conference under the auspices of the United Nations to formulate a joint organized response of the international community on terrorism in all of its forms and manifestations, as well as the elaboration of a comprehensive convention on international terrorism.

The Fourth Session of the Ad Hoc Committee was held in New York from 14 to 18 February 2000. It elected Rohan Perera (Sri Lanka) as Chairman; Cate Steains (Australia) as Vice-Chairperson and Co-ordinator, and Ivo Jande (Czech Republic) as Rapporteur. The debate in the Ad Hoc Committee focused on matters relating to the draft Convention on the Suppression of Acts of Nuclear Terrorism and the convening of a high-level United Nations Conference to formulate a joint organized response to terrorism in all its forms. In addition, general comments were also made by delegations on the importance of preparing a comprehensive legal framework international terrorism. The Ad Hoc Committee could not complete its work on the draft Convention on the Suppression of Nuclear Terrorism. The Co-ordinator for consultations reported that the outstanding issues revolved around the "scope provision" in the text and "the differences on the substance were too fundamental and polarized".

The next round of discussions was held during the 55th Session of the General Assembly in the Working Group of the Sixth Committee, which met from 25 September to 6 October 2000. The Working Group decided to invite the representatives of the International Committee of the Red Cross (ICRC), the Commonwealth Secretariat, the European Union (EU), the League of Arab States, and the Organization of African Unity (OAU) to participate in its discussions as observers.

The Working Group continued its discussion on a revised text of the draft Convention on the Suppression of Acts of Nuclear Terrorism prepared by the friends of the Chairman, and the working document submitted by India entitled "Draft comprehensive convention on international terrorism", a revised version of its previous text, as well as proposals submitted by other delegations.

During the course of the discussions in which some delegations reiterated the convention on international terrorism, attention focused on the revised text submitted by India, especially on Article 5 (the depoliticization clause), the limitation on the granting of asylum, Article 8 (the obligation to cooperate in the prevention of terrorist acts), and Article 11 (the extradite or prosecute principle). The necessity for the inclusion of a definition of terrorism was stressed by some delegations. It was suggested that a provision should be made for the recognition of State terrorism. Others felt that the conduct of a State could not fall within the ambit of terrorism. Some delegations suggested the need for drawing a distinction between terrorism, on the one hand, and the legitimate struggle, on the other, of people in the exercise of their right to self-determination, as well as the right of self-defence against aggression and occupation. There were divergent views on the scope of the draft convention and its relationship to existing international conventions on terrorism. It was suggested that the provisions and approach adopted by the regional conventions concluded in various regions could provide useful guidance.

There were as many as 38 written proposals submitted by various delegations. Among them, the proposals submitted by AALCO Member States, besides India, included: Lebanon (Article 2); Sudan (Articles 2 and 3); the Syrian Arab Republic (Article 6, para 2(d)); Lebanon (Article 6, para 2); Sri Lanka and Turkey (Article 7); Syria (Article 11, para 2); Nigeria (Article 2, para 1); Qatar (Article 18); Lebanon and Syria (new Preamble paragraph; Lebanon and Syria (Articles 1 and 18).

The Fifth Session of the Ad Hoc Committee was held in New York from 12 to 23 February 2001; some delegations stressed the need for the speedy finalization of the text of the draft International Convention for the Suppression of Acts of Nuclear Terrorism. Elaborate discussions were held on the two other issues, namely, the question of convening a high-level conference under the auspices of the United Nations to formulate a joint organized response of the international community to terrorism in all its forms and manifestations, and the elaboration of a draft Comprehensive Convention on International Terrorism.

As regards the question of convening a high-level conference, no consensus emerged. Some delegations felt that the convening of such a conference would help expedite the conclusion of a comprehensive international convention; other delegations were of the view that prior to a decision to convene such a conference, it would be desirable first to consider carefully the objective and possible outcome of such a conference.

On the issues concerning the elaboration of a draft Comprehensive Convention on International Terrorism, the discussions were able to make good progress, despite the fact that there was no consensus on certain key issues. Among these were the scope of the conventions and the relationship of the convention to other anti-terrorism conventions.

Malaysia, on behalf of the organization of the Islamic Conference Group, proposed the inclusion of definitions of the terms "terrorism" and "terrorist crime" based on General Assembly Resolution 46/51 of 9 December 1991[7] and in accordance with the provision on the Convention of the Organization of Islamic Conference on Combating International Terrorism. Some delegations were not in favour of such a proposal. In their view, Article 2 of the revised draft text provided an operational definition as set out in the phrase "within the meaning of this convention". A suggestion was made to redraft Article 2 so that "terrorist acts" could be indicated more clearly in the text. Some delegations reiterated that the definition of terrorism must differentiate between terrorism and legitimate struggle in the exercise of the right to the self-determination and independence of all peoples under foreign occupation.

There were divergent views on the exclusion of the activities of armed forces, the application of international humanitarian law conventions, and covering acts of State-sponsored terrorism within the definition of terrorism in the proposed convention.

The discussion on the possible relationship between the proposed convention and sectoral anti-terrorism conventions already in force remained inconclusive.

As directed by the General Assembly at its 55th Session, the next round of negotiations will be held within the framework of a working group of the Sixth Committee, from 15-26 October 2001.

General Comments

There is wide support from the international community to take concerted and strong action against world-wide acts of terrorism which are criminal in nature.

---

[7] Paragraph 15 of Resolution 46/51 of 9 December 1991 "considers that nothing in the present resolution could in any way prejudice the right to self-determination, freedom or independence, as derived from the Charter of the United Nations of people forcibly deprived of that right referred to in the Declaration of the Principles of International Law concerning Friendly Relations and Cooperation among States in accordance with the Charter of the United Nations, particularly peoples under colonial and racist regimes or other forms of alien domination, or the right of these peoples to struggle legitimately to this end and to seek and receive support in accordance with the principles of the Charter, the above-mentioned Declaration and the relevant General Assembly resolution including the present resolution."

It is a matter of great satisfaction that the issues concerning international terrorism have received a good deal of attention in many other fora apart from the United Nations. The Twelfth Conference of Heads of States or Governments of Non-aligned Countries held in Durban, South Africa, on 2 and 3 September 1998 reaffirmed its collective position on terrorism and called for the convening of an international summit under the auspices of the United Nations to formulate a joint organized response of the international community to terrorism in all its forms and manifestations. The Organization of American States (OAS) at an Inter-American Specialized Conference on Terrorism adopted the Lima Declaration and Plan of Action to Prevent, Combat and Eliminate Terrorism held on 23 and 24 November 1998 at Mar del Plata, Argentina, in which the progress made subsequent to the adoption of the Lima Declaration was evaluated and the Inter-American Committee against Terrorism (CICTE) was established. More recently, the Organization of African Unity, the League of Arab States and the Organization of Islamic Conference have adopted conventions to combat terrorism.

The comprehensive international convention to combat terrorism which is being negotiated under the auspices of the United Nations would be a major step towards complementing the existing network of anti-terrorism conventions.

The draft text of the convention submitted by the Government of India has provided a sound basis for the negotiation of a comprehensive text. While considerable progress has been made in narrowing down the divergent views on many issues, there are a few key remaining issues which deserve the utmost attention.

As was the exercise to achieve consensus on the definition of "aggression", which took several years, the attempt to define "terrorism" is also a challenging task; without achieving that objective, the accomplishment of the proposed international convention on terrorism would remain incomplete.

Issues concerning "State terrorism" may be dealt with under State responsibility and violations of international law. However, the obligation not to provide a "safe haven" to terrorism by any State, nor to encourage or support such activities under any pretext, should be a core commitment under the proposed convention.

The inalienable right to self-determination and to struggle against a colonial and racist regime are well recognized principles of international, and had been endorsed by the General Assembly of the United Nations in its numerous resolutions. The Declaration on Measures to Eliminate International Terrorism adopted by the General Assembly on 9 December 1994 and the Declaration on the occasion of the Fiftieth Anniversary of the United Nations, adopted on 24 October 1995, reaffirmed the right of self-determination of all peoples, taking into account the particular situation of peoples under colonial or other forms of alien domination or foreign occupation, and recognized the right of peoples to take legitimate action in accordance with the Charter of the United Nations to realize their inalienable right of self-determination. Any attempt to undermine those rights would remain a stumbling block in achieving consensus on the convention on terrorism.

The proposed comprehensive international convention should complement the existing legal regime of the anti-terrorism conventions. Indeed, it should be a step forward and constitute an "umbrella" convention under which that regime could be further strengthened.

There are several regional conventions which set out effective provisions for promoting cooperation among States to deal with terrorism issues. Their examples and experience could benefit the on-going negotiations in the Ad Hoc Committee.

The crux of the effective implementation of the proposed convention would be to promote cooperation among the law enforcement agencies to act jointly and to take measures to prevent, detect and investigate acts of terrorism. The obligations of the States in this respect in the proposed convention should be elaborated in precise terms such that no loopholes for any subjective interpretation are left.

It is interesting to note that a Terrorism Prevention Branch of the Centre for International Crime Prevention has been established in Vienna, under the auspices of the United Nations. Since the increase in the number of terrorist groups' activities around the world and their growing capability and financial resources to obtain sophisticated weapons have made the international terrorism problem more serious, the Centre in Vienna could collect and provide useful information to the governmental agencies and other interested inter-governmental organizations involved in anti-terrorist operations. The cooperation of Interpol in this respect would further strengthen the measures to contain and eliminate international terrorism.

There are as many as 19 international and regional conventions which have been adopted over the years to deal with specific situations or in general concerning the issues of terrorism. The wider participation and increasing ratification by State which are not yet parties to those conventions should be one of the prime objectives in the meantime, until the proposed comprehensive convention sees the light of day.

The proposal to convene a high-level conference on terrorism has gained wide support. In order to gain further support, it would be desirable to prepare a precise outline of the issues for consideration. In addition, the timing and level of participation need to be considered. The idea of convening a meeting of technical and legal experts and law enforcement officials to do the preparatory work is a practical step. The holding of an international conference at a high level would demonstrate the determination of the international community to face the challenge posed by international terrorism.

The Asian-African Legal Consultative Organization, being a regional inter-governmental organization engaged in the field of international law, may also contribute to strengthening the legal framework to combat terrorism. The Member States may wish to identify the areas in which useful work can be taken up by the AALCO Secretariat. The Ad Hoc Committee at its last meeting has opened the door for participation in the ICRC, the European Union, the Commonwealth Secretariat, the OAU and the League of Arab States as observers. The AALCO may also consider representation in the meeting of the Ad Hoc Committee scheduled to be held in New York from 15 to 26 October 2001.

ANNEX

List of International and Regional Legal Instruments Related to the Prevention and Suppression of International Terrorism

A. International Conventions

(i) Convention on Offences and Certain Other Acts Committed on Board Aircraft, signed at Tokyo on 14 September 1963 (entered into force on 4 December 1969);

(ii) Convention for the Suppression of Unlawful Seizure of Aircraft, signed at The Hague on 16 December 1970 (entered into force on 14 October 1971);

(iii) Convention for the Suppression of Unlawful Acts against the Safety of Civil Aviation, signed at Montreal on 23 December 1971 (entered into force on 26 January 1973);

(iv) Convention on the Prevention and Punishment of Crimes against Internationally Protected Persons, including Diplomatic Agents, adopted by the General Assembly of the United Nations on 14 December 1973 (entered into force on 20 February 1977);

(v) International Convention against the Taking of Hostages, adopted by the General Assembly of the United Nations on 17 December 1979 (entered into force on 3 June 1983);

(vi) Convention on the Physical Protection of Nuclear Material, signed at Vienna on 3 March 1980 (entered into force on 8 February 1987);

(vii) Protocol for the Suppression of Unlawful Acts of Violence at Airports serving International Civil Aviation, supplementary to the Convention for the Suppression of Unlawful Acts against the Safety of Civil Aviation, signed at Montreal on 24 February 1988 (entered into force on 6 August 1989);

(viii) Convention for the Suppression of Unlawful Acts against the Safety of Maritime Navigation, done at Rome on 10 March 1988 (entered into force on 1 March 1992);

(ix) Protocol for the Suppression of Unlawful Acts against the Safety of Fixed Platforms Located on the Continental Shelf, done at Rome on 10 march 1988 (entered into force on 1 March 1992);

(x) Convention on the Marking of Plastic Explosive for the Purpose of Detection, signed at Montreal on 1 March 1991 (entered into force on 21 June 1998);

(xi) International Convention for the Suppression of Terrorist Bombings, adopted by the General Assembly of the United Nations on 17 December 1997;

(xii) International Convention for the Suppression of the Financing of Terrorism, 1999.

B. Regional Conventions and Instruments

(i) European Convention on the Suppression of Terrorism, concluded at Strasbourg on 27 January 1977 (entered into force on 4 August 1978);

(ii) OAS Convention to Prevent and Punish Acts of Terrorism Taking the Form of Crimes Against Persons and Related Extortion that are of International Significance, concluded at Washington, D.C. on 2 February 1971 (entered into force on 16 October 1973);

(iii) Declaration and Plan of Action of Lima to Prevent, Combat and Eliminate Terrorism, 1996;

(iv) SAARC Regional Convention on Suppression of Terrorism, signed at Kathmandu on R November 1987 (entered into force on 22 August 1988); all seven States Members of SAARC (Bangladesh, Bhutan, India, Maldives, Nepal, Pakistan and Sri Lanka) are Parties to the Convention;

(v) Arab Convention on the Suppression of Terrorism, 1999, concluded under the auspices of the Organization of Islamic Conference;

(vii) Convention on the Prevention and Combating of Terrorism, 1999, concluded under the auspices of the Organization of African Unity (OAU);

(viii) Treat on Cooperation between the Commonwealth of Independent States (CIS) in Combating Terrorism, 4 June 1999 (Azerbaijan, Georgia, Kazakhstan, Kyrgyzstan, Republic of Moldova, Russian Federation and Tajikistan).

D. Explanatory note on the item received from the Government of Indonesia

Establishing Cooperation against Trafficking in Women and Children

A. Background

Transnational organized crime is truly international in nature and has increasingly become a global concern since the menace of this crime knows no boundaries. In responding effectively to this crime, domestic legislation and law enforcement in a given country must also be followed by international cooperation among countries, both bilaterally and multilaterally. The rapid growth in the flow of people and goods as a result of globalization has brought about dramatic changes in coping with criminality. Without effective law enforcement, criminals will continue to disrupt law and order. It is a matter of common awareness that no country would be able effectively to combat transnational organized crime without fostering international cooperation.

Countries in Asia and Africa, as in other regions, are not immune from the threats inherent in this crime. Economic and social problems have very often affected the protection and welfare of women and children in this region. Women and children are also vulnerable to exploitation committed by transnational organized crime groups. Even though there are no accurate statistics, this problem has become much more alarming and serious.

In this connection, the High Level Political Signing Conference for the UN Convention against Trans-National Organized Crime and Protocol to Prevent Trafficking in Persons, especially Women and Children; and the Protocol against the Smuggling of Migrants were held in Palermo, Italy, from 12 to 15 December 2000. The Government of Indonesia signed these three legal instruments during the conference.

To combat transnational organized crime more effectively, it is necessary to focus the attention on a specific area of this crime. It is a matter of urgency for this region to deal with this matter more comprehensively, since women and children are the most vulnerable as victims of criminals in Asian and African countries. Essentially, the Protocol to Prevent Trafficking in Persons is intended to "prevent and combat" trafficking in persons and to facilitate international cooperation against such trafficking. It provides control and cooperation measures to protect and assist the victims. Trafficking in persons is intended to include a range of cases where human beings are exploited by organized groups, where there is an element of duress involved and a transnational aspect, such as the movement of people across borders or their exploitation within a country by a transnational organized group.

Due to the fact that to prevent and combat this problem effectively cooperation among countries in the Asian and African regions is needed, the Government of Indonesia, therefore, considers it necessary that during the 40th Session of the Asian African Legal Consultative Organization which will be held in Jakarta the problem of trafficking in women and children should be included in the agenda and expected the following items to be our concern, as follows:

-   Expecting that those countries who had not yet signed the Protocol to Prevent Trafficking in Women and Children to consider signing it;
-   Expecting that those countries who had already signed the Protocol to Prevent Trafficking in Women and Children to consider ratifying it pursuant to their laws and legislation;
-   Expecting the countries to implement the Protocol immediately.

Concerning that matter, we really hope to discuss these significant issues, such as:

a. The role of law enforcement in the trafficking in women and children cases;

b. Prosecutorial strategies;

c. Model legislation and international agreement;

d. Intelligence sharing;

e. Effective utilization of resources and initiatives.

B. Problem in Indonesia

Trafficking in women has emerged in Indonesia recently as a consequence of the rapid growth in the numbers of Indonesian women migrant workers abroad. Although accurate research and surveys have not yet been conducted properly, trafficking in women has frequently been reported in the press and media. The increase in Indonesian women migrant workers abroad started in 1984, and most are employed as domestic workers. The figures have significantly increased by eight to ten times higher, from 11,180 workers to 85,231 workers in 1992.

The main obstacle to prevent and combat illicit trafficking in women and children in Indonesia stems from the unavailability of exact and accurate data related to this problem. Therefore, international cooperation in information sharing is also significant and necessary in fighting this truly serious crime.

Jakarta, 12 March 2001

Secretariat Study: Establishing Cooperation Against Trafficking in Women and Children

Background Note Prepared by the Secretariat

Trafficking in Women and Children

At the recent United Nations General Assembly Millennium Summit, world leaders proclaimed freedom – from fear and from want – as one of the essential values in the twenty-first century. Yet the right to live in dignity, free from fear and want, is still denied to millions of people around the world.

"I believe the trafficking of persons, particularly women and children, for forced and exploitative labour, including for sexual exploitation, is one of the most egregious violations of human rights which the United Nations now confronts. The fate of these most vulnerable people in our world is an affront to human dignity and a challenge to every state, every people and every community. I therefore urge the Member States not only to ratify the Convention Against Transnational Organized Crime, but also the Protocol to Prevent, Suppress and Punish Trafficking in Persons, particularly trafficking in women and children, which can make a real difference in the struggle to eliminate this reprehensible trade in human beings." These words of Mr. Kofi Annan, the Secretary General of the United Nations, have focused on the problem of trafficking in women and children.[8]

Every day, around the world, women and girls are enticed with the promise of well-paid jobs, bought from their families, or abducted outright and taken to a foreign country for the purpose of sexual exploitation. Escape is nearly impossible. The women are often not allowed to leave the brothel, making communication with the

---

[8] Speech of Mr. Kofi Annan, Secretary General of the UN, delivered at the opening of the Conference for the Convention Against Trans-National Organized Crime in Palermo, Italy, 12 December 2000.

outside world difficult. If the woman is able physically to free herself, return to her home country may be impossible as pimps frequently keep the woman's only means of return: her passport, airline ticket and money. The risk of arrest and immediate deportation is always present.

For the women who do return home, prostitution, even involuntary, often carries with it a social stigma, making the women into pariahs and thus often also unmarriageable. Lacking opportunities for education or "honest" work, and with no husband or family to support them, the women are often forced into prostitution as the sole means of supporting themselves, thus continuing the cycle of degradation, humiliation and victimization.[9]

What is Trafficking?

The practice of the sexual exploitation of women continues today. When this exploitation involves the moving of women, the practice is usually termed "trafficking in women". This term was used as early as the end of the 1800s. There has, however, been confusion as to exactly what is meant by it. The confusion can be seen in the various, often contradictory, definitions and concepts used in domestic law and international conventions, as well as in on-going international debates. Ultimately, however, "trafficking in women" is a complex phenomenon that involves often extremely sensitive issues such as sex and money. According to the International Organization for Migration (IOM), trafficking occurs when:
(a) a migrant is illicitly engaged (recruited, kidnapped, sold, etc.) and moved either within national or across international borders, and
(b) intermediaries (traffickers) obtain economic or other profit by means of deception, coercion and other forms of exploitation under conditions that violate the fundamental rights of migrants.[10]

The subjects of trafficking

Why women and girls are susceptible to sex traffickers is not difficult to understand. While each woman's situation is unique, there are recurrent trends in the trafficking business. First, the vast majority of women is very poor.[11] They come from places where women and girls have fewer educational and economic opportunities than do males. Often the girls have been socialized into an ethos of female servitude and

---

[9] Trafficking in Women and Children, Diane Johnson, New England School of Law, 1999. http//www.nest.edu/annual/vol.s./johnson.htm
[10] A definition contained in the 18 January 1996 European Parliament goes beyond earlier resolutions which limited the definition of trafficking to include only women, and takes the term "trafficking in human beings" to include men: "the illegal action of someone who, directly or indirectly, encourages a citizen from a third country to enter or stay in another country in order to exploit that person by using deceit or any other form of coercion or by abusing that person's vulnerable situation or administrative status".
[11] Fourth World Conference on Women, Beijing, China, 4-15 September 1995.

self-sacrifice. These conditions, coupled with a preference for sons in many parts of the world, often lead families to sell their daughters for the promise of immediate payment.

There are commonalities on how these women are recruited and the conditions they are forced to endure. Recruitment often occurs with the promise of a good job in another country. It also occurs through false marriage offers, with the bride later sold off to a brothel. Another almost universal theme in trafficking is that most women are held under debt bondage, and are vulnerable under issues related to this form of control.

The women are subject to many risks, such as the physical consequences of prostitution. Besides rape and battery at the hands of customers and pimps, they are exposed to health risks, especially to sexually transmitted diseases including hepatitis B and HIV/AIDS. Infertility is another serious risk from the forced prostitution that can bring about so many harmful consequences.

Trafficking in children

As was rightly pointed out by Razali Ismail, President of the Third Committee (social, humanitarian and cultural) of Malaysia,[12] trafficking is an illegal and clandestine practice and, therefore, it was virtually impossible to estimate the actual numbers of women and children involved. Actual information on the incidence of children was even more fragmented. One fact remained incontrovertible: that a greater number of young girls were absorbed into the commercial sex trade where adult female prostitution existed. Even more disheartening were indications of a growing demand by male clients for sexual activities with very young girls, a trend probably associated with the HIV/AIDS pandemic. Razali Ismail said it was ironic that when globalization and market forces had been accepted as the keystones of greater freedom and prosperity, the most vulnerable women and children had themselves fallen victim to the global zeal for commodification. Despite all of the efforts of the international community, the organized crime of trafficking in women and children had continued.

Existing Legal Framework for the Prevention of Trafficking in Women and Children

At the global conferences held in Rio de Janeiro, Vienna, Cairo and Copenhagen, the importance of issues related to the improvement of the status of women was stressed. From each of these global conferences emerged a more powerful recognition of the crucial role of women in sustainable development and protecting the environment.

The Vienna Declaration and programme of action[13] proclaimed: "The human rights of women of the girl child are an inalienable, integral and indivisible part of

---

[12] GA/9189, 75th Meeting, 6 December 1996.
[13] Adopted by the World Conference on Human Rights, Vienna, 25 June 1993 (A/Conf.157/24)(Part I), Chapter III.

universal human rights. The full and equal participation of women in political, civil, economic, social and cultural life, at the national, regional and international levels, and the eradication of all forms of discrimination on grounds of sex are priority objectives of the international community".

(A)   Convention for the Suppression of Traffic in Persons and of Exploitation of the Prostitution of Others

The 1949 Convention for the Suppression of Traffic in Persons and of Exploitation of the Prostitution of Others[14] was the outcome of the concern of the international community towards the effective suppression of trafficking in women and girls which was a matter of pressing international concern.

(B)   Convention on the Elimination of All Forms of Discrimination Against Women

Another turning point was in 1979, when the General Assembly adopted the Convention on the Elimination of all Forms of Discrimination Against Women, which entered into force in 1981[15] and set an international standard for what is meant by equality between women and men.

Although the International Bill of Human Rights[16] lays down a comprehensive set of rights to which all persons, including women, are entitled, it was necessary to have a separate legal instrument for women; this is because additional means for protecting women were seen as necessary because the mere fact of their "humanity" has not been sufficient to guarantee women the protection of their rights. The preamble to the Convention on the Elimination of All Forms of Discrimination against Women explains that, despite the existence of other instruments, women still do not have equal rights with men. Discrimination against women continues to exist in every society.

The Convention was adopted by the General Assembly in 1979 to reinforce the provisions of existing international instruments designed to combat the continuing discrimination against women. It identifies many specific areas where there has been notorious discrimination against women, for example, in regards to political rights, marriage and the family, and employment. In these and other areas the Convention

---

[14] General Assembly Resolution 317 (N), Annex.

[15] The Convention has 165 parties, of which 20 are AALCO Member States: Egypt, Gambia, Ghana, India, Indonesia, Iraq, Japan, Jordan, Kenya, Kuwait, Lebanon, Libyan Arab Jamahiriya, Sierra Leone, Singapore, Sri Lanka, Thailand, Turkey, Uganda, United Republic of Tanzania, and Republic of Yemen.

[16] The International Bill on Human Rights is a term used to refer collectively to three instruments: (i) the Universal Declaration of Human Rights; (ii) the International Covenant on Economic, Social and Cultural Rights, and (iii) the International Covenant on Civil and Political Rights, and its two Protocols. Taken together, these instruments form the ethical and legal basis for all of the human rights work of the United Nations and provide the foundation upon which the international system for the protection and promotion of human rights has been developed.

spells out specific goals and measures that are to be taken to facilitate the creation of a global society in which women enjoy full equality with men and thus full realization of their guaranteed human rights.

To combat gender-based discrimination, the Convention requires States Parties to recognize the important economic and social contribution of women to the family and to society as a whole. It emphasizes that discrimination will hamper economic growth and prosperity. It also expressly recognizes the need for a change in attitudes, through the education of both men and women, to accept equality of rights and responsibilities, and to overcome prejudices and practices based on stereotyped poles. Another important feature of the Convention is its explicit recognition of the goal of actual, in addition to legal, equality, and of the need for temporary special measures to achieve that goal.[17]

Article 6 of that Convention deals with suppressing the exploitation of women; it urges States to take all appropriate measures to combat trafficking in women and exploitative prostitution. In addressing these problems, it is essential for States to consider and act upon the conditions which are at the root of female prostitution: underdevelopment, poverty, drug abuse, illiteracy, and the lack of training, education and employment opportunities. States Parties should also provide women with alternatives to prostitution by creating opportunities through rehabilitation, job-training and job-referral programmes.

States that tolerate the existence of exploitative prostitution, girl-child prostitution and pornography, and other slave-like practices are in clear violation of their obligations under this Article. It is not enough to enact laws against such injustices: in order adequately to discharge their responsibilities, States Parties must ensure that measures are taken to implement penal sanctions fully and effectively.

(C)   Convention on the Rights of the Child

The Convention on the Rights of the Child was adopted by the General Assembly in 1989 and entered into force on 2 September 1990, in accordance with its Article 49. By December 1995, no fewer than 185 countries had ratified the Convention.[18]

The Convention on the Rights of the Child has the same meaning for people in all parts of the world. While laying down common standards, the Convention takes into account the different cultural, social, economic, and political realities of individual States so that each State may seek its own means to implement the rights common to all.

---

[17] Discrimination against women: the Convention and Committee, Human Rights Fact Sheet 22, p.4.

[18] As of December 2000, 191 countries had ratified the Convention, and 32 Member States of the AALCO were Parties to the Convention: India, Indonesia, Islamic Republic of Iran, Iraq, Japan, Jordan, Kenya, Kuwait, Lebanon, Libyan Arab Jamahiriya, Malaysia, Mauritius, Mongolia, Myanmar, Nepal, Nigeria, Pakistan, Philippines, Qatar, Republic of Korea, Saudi Arabia, Senegal, Sierra Leone, Singapore, Sri Lanka, Sudan, Syrian Arab Republic, Thailand, Turkey, Uganda, United Republic of Tanzania, Republic of Yemen.

There are four general principles enshrined in the Convention. These are meant to help with the interpretation of the Convention as a whole and thereby guide national programmes of implementation. The four principles are formulated, in particular, in Articles 2, 3, 6 and 12.

Non-discrimination (Article 2): States Parties must ensure that all children within their jurisdiction enjoy their rights. No child should suffer discrimination. This applies to every child, "irrespective of the child's or his or her parent's or legal guardian's race, colour, sex, language, religion, political or other opinion, national, ethnic or social origin, property, disability, birth or other status".

The essential message is equality of opportunity. Girls should be given the same opportunities as boys. Refugee children, children of foreign origin, children of indigenous or minority groups should have the same rights as all others. Children with disabilities should be given the same opportunity to enjoy an adequate standard of living.

Best interests of the child (Article 3): When the authorities of a State take decisions which affect children, the best interests of children must be a primary consideration. This principle relates to decisions by courts of law, administrative authorities, legislative bodies, and both public and private social welfare institutions. This is, of course, a fundamental message of the Convention, the implementation of which is a major challenge.

The right to life, survival and development (Article 6): The right-to-life Article includes formulations about the right to survival and to development, which should be ensured "to the maximum extent possible". The term "development" in this context should be interpreted in a broad sense, adding a qualitative dimension: not only is physical health intended, but also mental, emotional, cognitive, social, and cultural development.

The views of the child (Article 12): Children should be free to have opinions in all matters affecting them, and those views should be given due weight "in accordance with the age and maturity of the child". The underlying idea is that children have the right to be heard and to have their views taken seriously, including in any judicial or administrative proceedings affecting them.

The articles which specifically deal with the suppression of trafficking in children are: Article 33 of the Convention which requires States Parties to take all appropriate measures, including legislative, administrative, social and educational measures, to protect children from the illicit use of narcotic drugs and psychotropic substances as defined in the relevant international treaties, and to prevent the use of children in the illicit production and trafficking of such substances.

Article 34 requires States Parties to protect the child from all forms of sexual exploitation and sexual abuse. For these purposes States Parties shall in particular take all appropriate national, bilateral and multilateral measures to prevent: (a) the inducement or coercion of a child to engage in any unlawful sexual activity; (b) the exploitative use of children in prostitution or other unlawful sexual practices, and (c) the exploitative use of children in pornographic performances and materials.

(D)   United Nations Convention against Transnational Organized Crime

The United Nations Convention against Transnational Organized Crime was adopted by the General Assembly at its Millennium meeting in November 2000. It was opened for signature at a high-level conference in Palermo, Italy, in December 2000. It is the first legally binding UN instrument in the field of crime. It must be signed and ratified by 40 countries before it comes into force.

Of the 189 Member States of the UN, 124[19] had signed this landmark Treaty, with close to 80 of them also signing the Treat's two accompanying Protocols: one to prevent, suppress and punish trafficking in persons, especially women and children, and the other against the smuggling of migrants by land, sea and air.

States Parties to the Convention would be required to establish in their domestic laws four criminal offences: participation in an organized criminal group; money laundering; corruption, and obstruction of justice.

The new instrument spells out how countries can improve cooperation on such matters as extradition, mutual legal assistance, transfer of proceedings, and joint investigations. It contains provisions for victim and witness protection and shielding legal markets from infiltration by organized criminal groups. Parties to the Treaty would also provide technical assistance to developing countries to help them take the necessary measures and upgrade their capacities for dealing with organized crime.

It is hoped that upon ratification the Convention will emerge as the main tool of the international community for fighting transnational crime.

(E)   The Protocol to Prevent, Suppress and Punish Trafficking in Persons

Some of the important aspects of the Protocol have been summarized as follows:

Part I – Purpose, scope and criminal sanctions (Articles 1 – 3)

Articles 1 and 2 set out the basic purpose and scope of the Protocol. Essentially, the Protocol is intended to "prevent and combat" trafficking in persons as criminal offences, and to require control and cooperation measures against traffickers. It also provides some measures to protect and assist the victims. Some issues remain open with respect to the application of the Protocol to purely domestic activities (e.g., the movement of victims within a country) which support international trafficking.

"Trafficking in person" is intended to include a range of cases where human beings are exploited by organized crime groups where there is an element of duress involved and a transnational aspect, such as the movement of people across borders or their exploitation within a country by a transnational organized crime group.

---

[19] Out of these 124 signatory parties, 22 AALCO Member States have signed either the Convention or its Protocols: Arab Republic of Egypt, China, Cyprus, The Gambia, Indonesia, Iran Iraq, Japan, Republic of Korea, Kuwait, Mauritius, Nigeria, Pakistan, The Philippines, Saudi Arabia, Senegal, Singapore, Sri Lanka, Sudan, Syria, Thailand, Republic of Yemen.

The key definition of "trafficking in persons" (Article 2 bis) is not yet finalized, but there is general agreement about core elements. Trafficking is the "... recruitment, transportation, transfer, harbouring or receipt of persons..." if this uses improper means, such as force, abduction, fraud, or coercion, for an improper purpose, such as forced or coerced labour, servitude, slavery or sexual exploitation. The Protocol also contains language to include cases where those who have custody or control over another person, often a child, transfer custody in exchange for improper payments. Countries which ratify the Protocol are obliged to enact domestic laws making these activities criminal offences, if such laws are not already in place (Article 3).

This has been a difficult exercise in drafting and negotiation because of the wide variety of activities many of the countries involved are seeking to control. Some of the more difficult issues which have had to be addressed include the following: Some States have taken the position that, since the major abuses of trafficking involve women and children and these are most in need of protection, the Protocol should be limited to them to focus domestic efforts accordingly. Others felt that abuses against all "persons" should be included. As presently worded, the Protocol applies to all "persons", but generally refers to "... persons, especially women and children ...". Finding language to capture a wide range of coercive means used by organized crime has also proven difficult. With the exception of children, who cannot consent, the intention is to distinguish between consensual acts or treatment and those in which abduction, force, fraud, deception or coercion are used or threatened. As with the Convention, the nature and degree of international and organized crime involvement that should be required before the Protocol applies has also been the subject of extensive discussions, some of which are still ongoing. Generally, cases in which there is little or no international involvement can be dealt with by domestic officials without recourse to the Protocol or Convention for the assistance of other countries. On the other hand, requiring too direct a link might make it impossible to use the Protocol provisions in cases where purely domestic offences were committed by foreign offenders or as part of a larger transnational organized crime scheme.

Part II – Protection of Trafficked Persons (Articles 4 – 6)

In addition to taking action against traffickers, the Protocol requires States which ratify it to take some steps to protect and assist trafficked persons. Trafficked persons would be entitled to confidentiality and have some protection against offenders, both in general and when they provide evidence or assistance to law enforcement agencies or appear as witnesses in prosecutions or similar proceedings. Some social benefits, such as housing, medical care and legal or other counselling are also provided for.

The legal status of trafficked persons and whether they would eventually be returned to their respective countries of origin has been the subject of extensive negotiations. Similar discussions have taken place with respect to the return of smuggled migrants in the Protocol dealing with them. Generally, developed countries to which persons are often trafficked have taken the position that there should not be a right to remain in their countries as this would provide an incentive both for trafficking and for illegal migration. Countries whose nationals were more likely to be trafficked wanted as much protection and legal status for trafficked persons as possible. The negotiations are still ongoing, but the text presently requires States "to consider" laws which would allow trafficked persons to remain, temporarily or permanently, "in appropriate cases" (Article 5). States would also agree to accept and facilitate the repatriation of their own nationals (Article 6).

Part III – Prevention, Cooperation and other Measures (Articles 7 – 11)

Generally, the law enforcement agencies of countries which ratify the Protocol would be required to cooperate in such matters as the identification of offenders and trafficked persons, sharing information about the method of offenders, and the training of investigators, enforcement and victim-support personnel (Article 7). Countries would also be required to implement security and border controls to detect and prevent trafficking. These include strengthening their own border controls, imposing requirements on commercial carriers to check passports and visas (Article 8), setting standards for the technical quality of passports and other travel documents (Article 9), and cooperation in establishing the validity of their own documents when used abroad (Article 6, para (3)). Cooperation between States who ratify is generally mandatory. Cooperation with States who are not parties to the Protocol is not required, but is encouraged (Article 11). Social methods of prevention, such as research, advertising, and social or economic support are also provided for, both by governments and in collaboration with non-governmental organizations (Article 10).

(vi)   General Comments

Trafficking in women and children has no doubt become a global business generating huge profits for traffickers and organized crime syndicates. Out of the 15 to 30 million irregular migrants world-wide, 700,000 women and children are trafficked yearly across borders, numbers which are alarming.[20]

Out of the Fourth World Conference of Women held in Beijing, China, 1995 emerged a Platform of Action which acknowledged that "Human rights and fundamental freedoms are the birthright of all human beings; their protection and promotion is the first responsibility of governments". The Platform of Action also reaffirmed that all human rights – civil, cultural, economic, political and social, including the right to development, are universal, indivisible, interdependent and interrelated, as expressed in the Vienna Declaration and Programme of Action adopted by the World Conference of Human Rights. The Conference reaffirmed that the human rights of women and the girl-child are an inalienable, integral and indivisible part of universal human rights. The full and equal enjoyment of all human rights and fundamental freedoms by women and girls is a priority for Governments and the United Nations, and is essential in the advancement of women.

---

[20] IOM counter-trafficking services: http//www.iom.int

It is encouraging to note that most of the AALCO Member States are already parties to the Convention on the Elimination of all Forms of Discrimination Against Women, as well as the Convention on the Rights of the Child. This could help considerably in addressing these issues effectively and systematically throughout relevant bodies and mechanisms.

What is needed at this point is, as has rightly been mentioned in the explanatory note of the Government of Indonesia, the early ratification of the recent United Nations Convention Against Transnational Organized Crime and its Protocols, especially the Protocol to Prevent, Suppress and Punish Trafficking in Persons, especially in women and children, adopted by the United Nations General Assembly on 15 November 2000 and which will come into force after 40 countries have ratified it.

Another significant step for protection against trafficking in women and children could be the formulation of a model legislation, as suggested in the Indonesian proposal. This task could be accomplished with the technical assistance of the AALCO's new partner, the International Organization for Migration (IOM), with whom a Cooperation Agreement was signed on 6 October 2000. Of significant importance also would be more effective cooperation with the United Nations High Commissioner for Human Rights.

One of the programme activities of the AALCO Secretariat is to promote wider acceptance of International Conventions among the AALCO Member States. The preparation of a model legislation as a first step could facilitate the consideration by Member States of becoming Parties to the UN Convention Against Transnational Organized Crime, and its Protocols. Subsequently, the issues related to (a) the role of law enforcement in the trafficking in women and children; (b) prosecutorial strategies; (c) intelligence sharing, and (d) effective resources utilization and initiatives can be discussed. The Member States may wish to direct the Secretariat about the future course of action in this regard.

CHRONICLE

CHRONICLE OF EVENTS AND INCIDENTS RELATING TO ASIA WITH RELEVANCE TO INTERNATIONAL LAW
July 2000 – June 2002

Ko Swan Sik[*]

TABLE OF HEADINGS

---

[*] Of the Editorial Board. For the considerations underlying the Chronicle, *see* the "Editorial Introduction" in 1 Asian YIL (1991) 265.

Asian Yearbook of International Law, Volume 10 (B.S. Chimni *et al.,* eds.)
© 2005 Koninklijke Brill NV. Printed in The Netherlands, pp. 333-405.

Regional security
Rivers
Sanctions
Self-determination
Special territories within a state:
Kashmir
State liability
Straits

Terrorism
United Nations
World Bank
World War II
World Trade Organization

AFGHAN WAR
See also: International humanitarian law; Inter-state relations etc.: Afghanistan-US

Succession of government

When it became clear that the US and its allies would start military operations in Afghanistan which eventually would topple the Taleban government, representatives of the UN, the US, Afghans in exile and reigning warlords began building alliances and laying the groundwork for a successor government. [The factual, Taleban, government had been recognized by no more than three states, among which Pakistan, while other states had maintained recognition of the predominantly United Front ("Northern Alliance") government under president Rabbani, which also held the Afghan seat in the UN. *See* 7 Asian YIL 402 *et seq.*] Although Pakistan was no longer allied to the Taleban rule in Afghanistan, it remained anxious to ensure that the non-Pashtun "Northern Alliance" would not replace the Taleban. Pakistan and the US agreed to aim at the creation of a broad-based Afghan government that could include moderate elements of the Taleban movement.

The issue was also the object of discussion between the US and the UN and there had been some UN-sponsored forums in Geneva to discuss the shape of a future government in Afghanistan. (IHT 16-10, 17-10-01) Efforts to build a political altern-ative to the Taleban government remained, however, in disarray for some time, due to inter-Afghan as well as international differences in interest.

The following "processes" could be distinguished: (1) the so-called "Rome process", centering on an elevated role for the former king and backed by the US but opposed by Iran; (2) a process based in Cyprus, including anti-monarchist Afghans who emphasized Islamic interests; (3) an initiative organized by exiled Pashtuns in Peshawar (Pakistan) and backed by Pakistan; (4) a "working group" of the US, Italy, Iran and Germany, meeting at Geneva; (5) the "Afghan Support Group" comprising mostly European and Western-leaning states; (6) the "Six Plus Two" group of the six states bordering Afghanistan plus the US and Russia. India, on its part, was interested in cooperative links between the United Front ("Northern Alliance") and the ex-king, so as to prevent any residual Taleban role. (IHT 02-11-01)

US initiatives aimed at the forming of a "coalition of the willing" to prepare the ground for an interim government formed the centrepiece of the UN Security Council debates on 12 November 2001 and those among ministers of the "Six plus Two" countries. A declaration issued after this meeting endorsed efforts by the UN envoy for Afghanistan "to facilitate efforts by Afghan groups committed to a free and peaceful Afghanistan to establish a broad-based Afghan administration on an urgent basis". [Afghanistan had become a rough-knit patchwork of fiefdoms and localities under the sway of warlords or provincial chiefs.] The ministers backed a political solution providing for a "broad-based, multi-ethnic, politically balanced, freely chosen" government that would be at "peace with its neighbours". (IHT 13-11-01)

Kabul was seized by the "Northern Alliance" on 13 November 2001, a fact which alarmed Pakistan because it feared that a hostile regime would take power. It therefore strongly urged that, *inter alia*, an international force composed of Muslim troops be sent to maintain order and establish a demilitarized zone. (IHT 15-11-01) The next day the UN Security Council adopted resolution 1378 in which it, *inter alia*, "[e]xpress[ed] its strong support for the efforts of the Afghan people to establish a new and transitional administration leading to the formation of a government ..." and "[e]ncourage[d] Member States to support efforts to ensure the safety and security of Afghanistan no longer under Taleban control ...".

As part of the endeavours to form a new government the UN sponsored talks focused on planning Afghanistan's post-Taleban future. These talks started on 27 November 2001 in Bonn, Germany, and were attended by four of the Afghan factions: the "Northern Alliance"; the faction loyal to the former king; the "Peshawar group", based in Pakistan, and the "Cyprus group", close to Iran. The talks aimed at producing a transitional executive administration of 15 to 20 people and a temporary council, the Supreme National Council. Under the UN plan, these temporary institutions would function for a few months, when an emergency *loya jirga* or "great council" would meet to name a provisional administration and council which would serve for some two years and write a new constitution. Then, a new *loya jirga* would meet to ratify the constitution and new elections would be held.

The Afghan factions finally signed their agreement on 5 December 2001 (*Agreement on provisional arrangements in Afghanistan pending the re-establishment of permanent government institutions, see* UN doc.S/2001/1154), creating an "Interim Authority" dominated by members of the Northern Alliance yet led by Hamid Karzai, a Pashtun leader whose name had already been mentioned quite early in the process.

While regional and ethnic factions were asserting control over vast areas of Afghanistan, the newly appointed prime minister warned the US to never again "walk away from Afghanistan", promising that his country would be "a good friend and trusted friend and an ally" in the US-led fight against terrorism.

The UN plan also provided for a multinational security force (as distinct from the existing US-led forces in Afghanistan) to be deployed especially in and around Kabul, and to help train an all-Afghan police and army. The setting up of the force was construed as resulting from a request for assistance from the Afghan authorities who would formally have responsibility for law and order. The idea of such an internationally composed force was initially rejected though later accepted by the Northern Alliance provided it operated under the UN. The US was opposed to the idea as being premature.

On 20 December 2001 the UN Security Council adopted resolution 1386, acting under Chapter VII of the UN Charter, authorizing (for six months) the deployment of a (British-led) *International Security Assistance Force* (ISAF) "to assist the Afghan Interim Authority in the maintenance of security in Kabul and its surrounding areas". Because of the extent of the existing needs the new government soon attempted to have the limited territorial competence of ISAF expanded, but this was refused by the US which instead preferred the build-up of a new Afghan army. In view of the long time needed to build an army it was expected that the US forces would have to remain in the country for several years. The US side also said the military campaign would continue and the US military would stay for as long as it would take to rid the country of Al Qaeda and achieve political stability even if the Afghan government were to ask for a halt.

The commission set up by the government to lay down rules for the organization of the projected *loya jirga*, to be convened from 10 to 16 June 2002 and which would choose a new government for the next 18 months, completed its preparations in late March 2002 and the former king, Mohammed Zahir Shah, arrived back in the country on 18 April 2002 after a 29-year exile. Belonging to the Durrani dynasty, his 40-year reign had ended in 1973 when he was overthrown by a cousin, Mohammed Daud.

The *loya jirga* convened on 11 June 2002 and overwhelmingly expressed itself in favour of the sitting interim government leader Hamid Karzai to become transitional head of state and government for the next 18 months until national elections were to be held. This was in conformity with existing expectations, not only because of his strong backing from the former king and his solidified ties with several powerful former leaders of the Northern Alliance, but especially because of the enormous influence of American backing and the latter's money and military clout as the ultimate source of power. (IHT 21-11, 27-11, 01/02-12, 04-12, 05-12, 06-12, 11-12, 21-12, 27-12, 29/30-12-01, 31-12-01 / 01/01-02, 18-01, 26/27-01, 28-01, 15-03, 01-04, 02-04, 09-04, 19-04, 27-05, 12-06, 14-06-02)

The course of the war

The main war operations were announced by the US president and started with heavy air assaults on military targets and suspected terrorist camps across Afghanistan on 7 October 2001. (IHT 08-10-01) Besides, the US also notified the UN Security Council that counter-terrorism attacks might be extended "beyond Afghanistan". (IHT 09-10-01)

After over a week of persistent bombings there were increasing signs of international restiveness resulting in criticisms from Saudi Arabia, Pakistan, Indonesia, and Iran, and also signs of doubt and impatience over the breadth and duration of the attacks. The Indonesian president urged adherence to international norms and said "No one group or state should make its own rules in the use of force and then attack others". (IHT 16-10-01) The war also started stoking tensions among the Southeast Asian population, and polarizing and radicalizing Muslims in the region. (IHT 31-10-01)

It turned out to be impossible to complete the military campaign within a short time. (IHT 29-10-01) The first US combat forces appeared on the ground in late October 2001 supporting anti-Taleban forces in northern Afghanistan. Meanwhile, it was reported that Pakistani volunteers entered Afghanistan to come to the assistance of the Taleban, and that Pakistan was increasingly being pushed into the uncomfortable position of supporting the US-led war and confronting ever stronger domestic challenges. (IHT 31-10, 03/04-11, 05-11-01)

In March 2002 the president of Pakistan said that the war was over when the "legitimate government" had returned to Kabul, but the US, on the contrary, was hesitant to declare the conflict ended and vowed to wage an open-ended "war on terrorism". It was said that, as a "last resort", US forces might cross the border into Pakistan in moving against Qaeda and Taleban sanctuaries, but would do so only with the approval of Pakistan. These speculations gave rise to unambiguous warnings by leaders from the Pakistani tribal areas concerned which share a 720-kilometre border with Afghanistan.
(IHT 15-03, 18-03, 22-03-02)

ALIENS: PROTECTION

Kidnappings in the Philippines

In April and July 2000 Philippine rebel groups had kidnapped hostages from, *inter alia*, a Malaysian diving resort and had brought them to their hide-out on Jolo Island in the Philippines. Among them were nationals of foreign countries whose governments pressed the Philippines to end the crisis quickly but without force, so as not to threaten the hostages' safety. Meanwhile, the Philippine government divulged that foreign agencies and governments were paying huge amounts to obtain their respective citizens' freedom.

After the release of some of the hostages in July, nine others were to be freed in mid-August in a deal financed by Libya. Libyan sources said the amounts paid would go towards development projects in the Philippines. [Libya had acted as a mediator between Muslim rebels and the Philippine government, and had contributed to development work in the past. (*See, inter alia,* Asian YIL Vol.4:451, Vol.5:426, Vol.6:390) The intended release was not, however, carried out exactly as planned, but left a number of hostages still in the rebels' hands.

After new kidnappings took place in September 2000, the Philippine authorities considered tougher steps *(see* Asian YIL Vol 5:426, Vol.6:390). The Philippine vice-president called for a US-led multinational blockade of the southern Philippine Sea to thwart any further rebel attempts to seize hostages from tourist resorts in neighbouring countries and spirit them to their jungle hide-outs in Philippine territory. However, the president played down the possibility of military intervention.

When the Philippine government finally started military operations against the rebels on 16 September, the French president issued a statement expressing his disapproval, adding that he held the Philippines responsible for the two remaining French hostages. Malaysia also expressed its concern about the remaining Malaysian hostages, but said it was a Philippine prerogative to mount a military rescue.

As to the fact that the French and the only remaining US hostage had in fact voluntarily sought the company of the *Abu Sayyaf* rebels, the US Defense Secretary said that how the American hostage had ended up in *Abu Sayyaf* custody was "quite irrelevant" and that "he should be released, immediately and safely". The man was freed when Philippine forces raided a rebel hide-out. (IHT 14-07, 18-07, 24-07, 09-08, 17-08, 24-08, 29-08, 11-09, 14-09, 16/17-09, 18-09-00, 13-04-01)

Murder of UN workers in Indonesian province of West Timor

An armed mob on 6 September 2000 killed three unarmed UN workers in Atambua, West Timor; the local office of the UNHCR was then demolished and looted. The Indonesian president blamed supporters of a militia leader and promised to send troops to reassert control in the territory. The UN Secretary General condemned the incident and underlined the dangers facing unarmed humanitarian UN workers in conflict or post-conflict situations. The UN High Commissioner of Refugees called it the worst security incident ever involving the agency. The remaining UNHCR employees were evacuated to East Timor, and the High Commissioner said they would not return until their security was assured. (IHT 07-09-00)

The UN Security Council convened and on 8 September 2000 adopted resolution 1319 (2000), *inter alia* "insist[ing] that ... Indonesia take immediate ... steps, in fulfilment of its responsibilities, to disarm and disband the militia" blamed for killing the UN workers. It welcomed the intention of the president of Indonesia to conduct a full-scale investigation and to take firm measures against those found guilty.

The Security Council also considered sending an ambassadorial mission to investigate violence in East and West Timor, but Indonesia suggested a postponement of the visit, proposing that a number of Jakarta-based ambassadors instead visit West Timor. It promised to act quickly to resolve the militia violence. The US said that failure to do so could threaten economic aid, while Indonesia urged the lifting of a US military embargo (*see supra* at 352) depriving the Indonesian military of the equipment it needs to control the militia. (IHT 14-09, 19-09, 21-09-00)

ASIA-PACIFIC ECONOMIC COOPERATION FORUM (APEC)

Annual meeting 2000

The annual summit meeting was held at Bandar Seri Bagawan, Brunei, in November 2000.

It was said that APEC seemed to have begun backing away from liberalization in favour of less controversial "business facilitation", dealing with areas such as customs administration, technical regulation and standards (nevertheless, over the previous 12 years the unweighted tariff rates of the members had fallen from an average of 15 to eight per cent).

Meanwhile, a new development seemed to emerge among some of the member states, in the form of bilateral free trade agreements. Japan and Singapore planned to conclude such an agreement by the end of 2001; similar agreements were planned between Singapore and New Zealand, the US, Australia and Chile. Japan and South Korea had also agreed to explore the possibility of such an agreement, while South Korea was also considering similar agreements with countries outside Asia. (IHT 13-11, 22-12-00)

Acting on a South Korean proposal the meeting agreed to grant North Korea the right to participate in APEC working groups. The organization had had a moratorium on new members until 2007. (IHT 17-11-00)

Summit meeting 2001

In preparing its 2001 summit meeting at Shanghai on 20-21 October there were plans to devote the meeting to the commitment to fighting terrorism and the US had prepared a draft declaration on terrorism. At the same time there were signs of concern about the increasing focus on terrorism instead of on economic issues; there were even suggestions that controls to prevent terrorism flew in the face of the APEC efforts to promote free trade and investment. (IHT 15-10, 16-10-01)

APEC's initiative for trade liberalization had slowed down considerably since the East Asian financial crisis in 1997/1998. Members had failed to specify complete timetables for eliminating trade barriers and trade-distorting measures by 2010 and 2020, despite pledging to do so at Bogor, Indonesia, in 1994 (*see* 5 Asian YIL 391). As a result some member states had decided to conclude their own bilateral or sub-regional free trade agreements (*see supra*). (IHT 19-10-01)

The meeting produced an "APEC Leaders Statement on Counter-Terrorism" The statement included a condemnation of the attacks on the US, classifying terrorist acts in all forms as threats to the peace, prosperity and security of all people, faiths and nations. In the "Statement" the leaders committed themselves to preventing and suppressing terrorist acts "in accordance with the Charter of the United Nations and other international law", pledged to implement UN Security Council resolutions 1368 and 1373 (on terrorism) "faithfully and immediately", called for increased cooperation to bring perpetrators to justice, and called for early signing and ratification of the basic universal anti-terrorist conventions. The statement failed to include a definition of "terrorism". (www.apecsec.org)

ASIAN DEVELOPMENT BANK

Membership for North Korea

North Korea applied for membership of the Bank in late August 2000, with South Korean support. However, the US and Japan ruled out even observer status for North Korea unless the latter addressed concerns about its sponsoring terrorism. The issue was referred to the Bank's shareholders. (IHT 2/3-09-00)

ASSOCIATION OF SOUTH EAST ASIAN NATIONS (ASEAN)

Composition of ASEAN Regional Forum

The Regional Forum (*see* Asian YIL Vol.4:505, Vol.5:484) meeting held in July 2000 was the first one in which North Korea participated. Until then it had shunned an invitation to join. (IHT 27-07-00)

ASEAN + 3

The grouping consisting of the ASEAN member states together with the Northeast Asian countries China, Japan and South Korea held their first formal meeting of foreign ministers on 26 July 2000. This was followed by the ASEAN Fourth Informal Summit of November 2000 which agreed to study the idea of turning the existing informal summit meeting known as the "ASEAN plus Three" (*see* 8 Asian YIL 256) into a formal East Asia summit meeting. The heads of state of the grouping had already held a ground-breaking summit meeting before, in Manila in November 1999, on the fringes of the ASEAN Third Informal Summit (*see* 9 Asian YIL 386-387). (IHT 25-07, 25/26-11-00)

In October 2001 the deputy prime minister of Thailand, who was then the incoming WTO director-general, recalled the ongoing efforts towards having the three Northeast Asian countries join the ASEAN low-tariff bloc in 2010 (*see* 9 Asian YIL 386), which would have the effect of integrating those large economies more closely with the developing countries in the region. The pursuit was confirmed at the ASEAN Seventh Summit at Bandar Seri Begawan on 5 November 2001. (IHT 19-10, 06-11-01)

The ASEAN Fourth Informal Summit meeting in November 2000 at Singapore supported a proposal by China to set up an expert group for the study of how economic cooperation and free trade relations between ASEAN and China could be deepened.

Some industrialized countries, including the US, were reported to have voiced concern that regional free-trade agreements, which are proliferating in Asia, might undermine moves to begin another global round of liberalization under the WTO (*see*: World Trade Organization); on the other hand, there was a Chinese warning against double standards, evidently referring to the North American Free Trade Agreement (NAFTA). (IHT 24-11-00)

The ASEAN countries and China reached agreement on 6 November 2001 for the creation of a free trade area (ASEAN-China FTA) within ten years. (IHT 07-11-01)

ASEAN Free Trade Area

The annual foreign ministers meeting in July 2000 agreed on a statement announcing that rules were being worked out enabling countries "experiencing real difficulties" in meeting their commitments under the AFTA agreement temporarily to withdraw sensitive sectors from the free-trade agreement . In May 2000 the economic ministers had already agreed to consider a request from Malaysia to delay by at least two years, until January 2005, the opening of its automotive industry. It was understood that Malaysia wanted to protect its national car industry against competition from, especially, Thailand which had become a regional centre for car manufacturers from outside the region.

In October 2000 the economic ministers agreed on an additional protocol under which the country asking for a delay was to agree on compensation for the affected members. If no agreement was reached, the affected states would have the right to retaliate by withdrawing some of their own goods from the free-trade regime.

AFTA, with maximum five per cent tariffs, became effective for the six original ASEAN members on 1 January 2002. (IHT 26-07, 7/8-10-00, 03-01-02)

ASEAN – EU

Relations between ASEAN and the European Union were troubled in the past few years because of the EU sanctions against Myanmar, an ASEAN member since 1997. The EU had boycotted ministerial meetings with ASEAN since Myanmar had become an ASEAN member. However, it appeared in 2000 that the EU countries were following a modified policy by easing their pressure on Myanmar and muting their criticism of the military rulers of Myanmar. Myanmar would thus no longer be banned from taking part in ASEAN-EU cooperation. It was alleged that the EU flexibility stemmed from its concern about losing investment opportunities in Asia.

The new flexibility lead to the decision to have the next, thirteenth, ASEAN-EU ministerial meeting (11-12 December 2000) at Vientiane, Laos, instead of in Europe as scheduled, in order to avoid the European ban on the entry of Myanmar officials. Meanwhile, ASEAN told the European Union that it would abandon high-level talks with the EU if the latter continued to press for the exclusion of Myanmar on human rights grounds. (IHT 01-08, 29-11, 11-12-00)

ASEAN involvement in Myanmar labour conditions

(*See also:* Sanctions)

ASEAN decided to send a team of experts to Myanmar to achieve the compliance of Myanmar with ILO labour standards. This was in fact ASEAN's first serious involvement in Myanmar domestic affairs, despite the ASEAN principle of not interfering in the internal affairs of its members. (IHT 01-08-00)

Seventh Summit Meeting, November 2001

The meeting which was held at Bandar Seri Begawan, Brunei, dealt, among other things, with the pursuit of an enlarged East Asia trade bloc (*see supra*), the conflict in Afghanistan (*see infra*), the plans for a railway link and other mega-infrastructure projects and programs on the combat of regional epidemics. (IHT 06-11-01)

ASEAN Declaration on Joint Action to Counter Terrorism

The Declaration adopted at the Seventh Summit meeting, besides *condemning* the 11 September attacks on the US, *extending* sympathy and condolences, *viewing* terrorism "in all its forms and manifestations, committed wherever, whenever and by whomever" as a "profound threat to international peace and security", and *rejecting* attempts to link terrorism with religion or race, also contained the commitment to prevent and suppress terrorist acts "in accordance with the Charter of the United Nations and other international law" and the assurance that the counter-terrorism measures taken should be "in line with specific circumstances in the region and in each member country". (www.aseansec.org)

ASYLUM
See: Diplomatic and consular immunity and inviolability

BORDERS, BORDER DISPUTES AND BORDER INCIDENTS

Bangladesh – Myanmar

A dispute had arisen between the two countries over Myanmarese efforts to build a dam near the south-eastern border of Bangladesh. The dam was to be built on the Naaf River at Totardia, 100 kilometres south-east of Cox's Bazaar. If built, the dam might flood or cause erosion in Bangladesh and damage shrimp cultivation projects. Both countries sent troop reinforcements to the border region after talks failed to resolve the dispute.

In 1967 the border forces of the two countries fought a brief battle over a similar Myanmarese attempt at building a dam. (IHT 08-01-01)

Bangladesh – India

There were clashes between Bangladeshi and Indian border troops, fighting over a patch of land along the northern Kurigram-Dhuburi frontier near the north-east corner of Bangladesh and the Indian state of Assam. This followed a weekend incident in which Bangladesh seized a frontier post from India. (IHT 19-04, 20-04-01) India later invited Bangladesh for talks to resolve their border dispute (IHT 02-05-01)

Myanmar – Thailand

There were clashes in February 2001 between Thai and Myanmarese soldiers near the Thai northern border at the border crossing between Mae Sai in Thailand and Tachilek in Myanmar. According to Thai sources the incident was the result of an attack by Myanmarese soldiers and their allies from the so-called Wa State Army against ethnic rebels in the area. (IHT 14-02-01)

CENTRAL ASIA
See also: Insurgents

United States presence

When the air war in Afghanistan started to wane (*see*: Afghan War) there were indications that the US was preparing a long-term military presence in Central Asia that could last for years. Among other factors, an air base was built in Kyrgyzstan that would be a "transportation hub" to house up to 3,000 soldiers and to accommodate warplanes and support aircraft. Furthermore, bases in Uzbekistan and Pakistan were improved in many respects.

It was said that a significant US military presence was needed around Afghanistan since the interim government did not seem intent on rooting out the remnants of Al Qaida and Taleban forces. On the other hand it was recognized that a too large or too long-term US military presence could alarm Russia and China, and anger the Afghans. (IHT 10-01-02)

CIVIL WAR
See also: Insurgents

Afghanistan
(*See also:* Cultural matters)

Taleban control

A series of military victories in late September 2000 resulted in Taleban control over more than 95 per cent of the country, "about as close as any party has ever gotten in ruling that deeply divided country". (IHT 04-10-00)

China-Taleban relations

In November 2000 a delegation from the China Institute of Contemporary International Relations visited Kabul and Kandahar. It was later reported in September 2001 that China and the Taleban regime in Afghanistan had signed a memorandum of understanding for economic and technical cooperation. (IHT 13-09-01)

CULTURAL MATTERS

Demolition of Buddhist statues

The Taleban rulers in Afghanistan in late February 2001 ordered the destruction of all statues being worshipped, including the two giant Buddha statues at Bamiyan, west of Kabul. Statues were considered not to conform to Islamic prohibitions against depicting the human form in pictures or statues. (IHT 27-02-01) Responding to international condemnation the Taleban leader said, "All we are breaking are stones." The demolition started in early March 2001. (IHT 27-02, 28-02, 3/4-03-01)

DEMOCRACY

Iranian speech in the UN General Assembly

In his speech before the UN General Assembly the president of Iran referred to the issue of democracy, saying that no form of democracy was unique and that the demands of a few power-holders should not supersede the interests of humanity. He also said: "No particular form of democracy can be prescribed as the only and final version." (IHT 07-09-00)

DIPLOMATIC AND CONSULAR FUNCTIONS

Consular access to detainees

The Taleban authorities in Afghanistan had detained 24 aid workers on 5 August 2001 on charges of promoting Christianity and proselytizing. Among them were German, US and Australian citizens. According to the Afghan (Taleban) deputy ambassador to Pakistan, the German-based *Shelter Now International* organization had been warned before to refrain from such activities.

The foreign countries concerned had sought permission for consular access to the detainees. On 9 August the Afghan authorities said that diplomats from the countries concerned would be granted visas and allowed to meet their detained nationals, but this was later denied by the foreign minister. (IHT 09-08, 10-08, 13-08-01)

DIPLOMATIC AND CONSULAR IMMUNITY AND INVIOLABILITY

Immunity of Chairman of the National People's Congress of China from service of court summons

The Chairman of the Chinese NPC, a former prime minister, was served a court summons at a New York hotel when on a visit to the US in late August 2000. The summons was handed by a process server to an employee of the US State Department who was guarding the Chinese official. The State Department said it was not in a position to accept such a document on behalf of a foreign official, but a judge had ruled earlier that a (US) federal employee guarding such an official could accept the summons, given the difficulty of reaching the foreign official himself. China later blamed the US for not properly protecting the Chinese visitor from the summons. (IHT 2/3-09, 04-09-00)

Refuge in foreign consulates

Since March 2002 there has been an increasing number of cases of North Koreans attempting to gain political asylum in foreign, such as US, Japanese, Canadian and Spanish, embassies and consulates in China, often organized by people with links to South Korea's Christian community and their aid organizations.

In a case in the northern Chinese city of Shenyang, where on 8 May 2002 such refugees were caught and detained by Chinese police while already on the premises of the Japanese consulate, the Japanese diplomatic mission lodged a protest with the Chinese foreign ministry, claiming that the Chinese police had entered the Japanese compound to carry out the arrest. The Japanese foreign minister spoke of "a clear violation of international law" and demanded the release of the asylum seekers and a formal apology. China refused, saying that its police guards had been acting to protect Japanese diplomats from "unidentified persons" and had received permission from consulate staff to seize the persons concerned. Efforts to have the persons expelled to a third country were successful when China on 22 May 2002 released the refugees and sent them to South Korea, doing so via Manila to avoid angering North Korea.

There was a hardening of the Chinese attitude when North Koreans began breaking into South Korean consulates. This culminated in a demand to South Korea on 28 May 2002 to hand over some North Koreans who had broken into the South Korean consulate in Beijing. The foreign ministry spokesman was quoted as saying: "We believe that according to international and Chinese laws, foreign embassies have no right to grant asylum to citizens of a third country." On 13 June 2002 this position was confirmed when the government announced that it had sent notes to all diplomatic missions in Beijing, reiterating its demand that North Koreans must be handed over.

On the same day an incident occurred when South Korean diplomatic staff tried to prevent Chinese police from arresting a North Korean man who, according to the South Korean side, had been dragged by guards assigned by the host state out of the consulate building and taken to a guard-house outside the consulate. It was reported that in their efforts the police who had then arrived had punched, kicked and shoved the diplomats out of the way when the latter tried to prevent the arrest of the man. The South Korean embassy issued a formal protest and called the incident a violation of international law. The Chinese side rejected both protest and accusation, emphasizing that the persons who had entered the consulate and dragged out the North Korean were private security guards and not police officers, hence there was no breach of the Vienna Convention. On the other hand the South Korean diplomats were accused of having tried to prevent the police from taking the man away and thus of having acted in a way incompatible with their diplomatic status and with international law.

A sudden reversal of the Chinese policy took place when China decided on 23 June 2002 to allow 26 North Korean refugees to leave the country for South Korea, *via* third countries. Meanwhile, it was said that the decision might risk starting a flood of refugees. Reference was being made to the Hungarian example, when the Hungarian government decided in 1989 to allow East German refugees to go to the West. [China was said to have a treaty with North Korea that commits it to returning any North Korean who illegally enters China.](IHT 09-05, 11/12-05, 29-05, 14-06, 15/16-06, 24-06-02)

DIPLOMATIC AND CONSULAR RELATIONS
See also: Inter-state relations etc: North Korea – EU, North Korea – Myanmar and Thailand

Afghanistan – Pakistan

In November 2001 the Taleban government of Afghanistan was represented by an embassy in Pakistan, with consulates in Karachi, Quetta and Peshawar. Pakistan was the only country left at that time that recognized the Taleban as the government of Afghanistan.

In view of the US attacks on Afghanistan the Afghan embassy had been the scene of frequent news conferences at which the US attacks were strongly denounced. In early November 2001 the Pakistani government asked the ambassador to stop holding such briefings, reminding him that foreign embassies were not permitted to make public statements "against a third country". (IHT 08-11-01) On 8 November 2001 Pakistan ordered the Taleban government to close its consulate in the city of Karachi. (IHT 09-11-01)

Reacting to the seizure of Kabul by the "Northern Alliance" the Pakistani foreign minister affirmed Pakistan was no longer doing business with the Taleban ("We don't have relations, we don't conduct business between the government of Pakistan and whatever is left of the Taleban government") but would permit its embassy to remain open for the time being. (IHT 20-11-01)

On 22 November 2001 Pakistan, bowing to US pressure and the changed "situation on the ground", finally ordered the Taleban to close the embassy and announced the expulsion of Taleban diplomats. (IHT 23-11-01)

Iran – United Kingdom

Iran had turned down the UK's choice of an ambassador to Tehran, against which Britain retaliated by downgrading the status of the Iranian ambassador in London. Iranian newspapers wrote that the British ambassadorial candidate was a Jew and attached to the British intelligence service, but these allegations were denied by Britain. The spokesman of the Iranian foreign ministry expressed surprise at the British reaction and reminded the UK that whether or not to accept a proposed person as ambassador is the natural right of the host country.

The two states had re-started the exchange of ambassadors in July 1999 after a decade-long break since Ayatollah Khomeini issued a *fatwa* in 1989 urging people to kill the British author Salman Rushdie because of the allegedly blasphemous character of his book "The Satanic Verses". Formal relations were restored in 1998 when the *fatwa* was lifted (*see* 8 Asian YIL 261). (IHT 09/10-02-02)

Japan – North Korea
(*See*: Inter-state relations etc.)

North Korea

The Philippines established diplomatic relations with North Korea on 12 July 2000. *Canada* stated on 26 July 2000 that it would recognize the Democratic People's Republic of Korea. Discussions would then be started on the establishment of diplomatic relations, possibly by the end of the year. *New Zealand*, too, had started discussions with North Korea on relations that would probably lead to full diplomatic relations in 2000. As part of the same effort to end its isolation, North Korea reached agreement with *Cambodia* on an exchange of trade missions. North Korea also established official relations with *Italy, Australia* and *Kuwait* in 2000. In October 2000 *the UK* as well as *Germany* announced that they would soon establish diplomatic relations with North Korea. The relations with *the UK* commenced in December 2000. (IHT 27-07, 20-10, 13-12-00) According to North Korean sources North Korea and *the Netherlands* had agreed on the establishment of diplomatic relations on 15 January 2001. (IHT 17-01-01)

DISARMAMENT AND ARMS CONTROL
See also: Regional security

Chinese response to US withdrawal from ABM Treaty

Taking the changes in the world as the basis for their argument, the US on 12 December 2001 announced its withdrawal from the 1972 US-Soviet Anti-Ballistic Missile Treaty. The US president said to have come to the conclusion that the treaty "hinders our government's ways to protect our people from future terrorist or rogue state missile attacks". (IHT 14-12-01)

China reacted critically, but the reaction was muted. It expressed concern that the move could precipitate a new arms race. The US said that the US withdrew from the treaty to develop a missile defence system primarily to defend itself against "rogue" states and emphasized that China was not an intended target. The Chinese foreign ministry issued a statement re-stating its worries, stressing "the importance of safeguarding international military control and the disarmament system and the stability of global strategy in the current circumstances". (IHT 18-12-01)

(NON-)DISCRIMINATION

Espionage trial of Iranian Jews

The trial of ten Iranian Jews convicted of spying for Israel in Iran attracted international attention, with countries such as the US and France as well as human rights organizations and Jewish groups urging Iran to ensure that the trial was fair. US and Israeli officials were reported to have vehemently denied that any of the Jews were involved in intelligence-gathering for any government. The Iranian president said that the government would not interfere in the case. He also said: "If instead of these Jews they were Christians, would the world still react as it does today?" On 21 September 2000 an appeals court reduced the sentences handed down by the court below. The verdict apparently disappointed the US as falling short of what US officials said they had been led to believe would occur and allegedly reneging on a behind-the scenes diplomatic pledge. European and US officials were reported to have said that the Iranian foreign minister had "promised more" in private discussions. On his part the latter said that in his conversations on the matter he had "underscored the separation of powers in the Islamic Republic". (IHT 08-09, 22-09, 23/24-09, 25-09-00) A further appeal was rejected in early February 2001. (IHT 08-02-01)

DISSIDENTS

Myanmar: Aung San Suu Kyi

The opposition leader had held a nine-day roadside protest outside the city of Yangon after being stopped by the authorities when en route to a meeting with members of her party. (When Aung San Suu Kyi was freed from house arrest in 1995, she was forbidden to travel beyond Yangon.) The Myanmar government on

3 September 2000 forced her to return home, tightening restrictions on her movements and those of other leading members of her party, but on 14 September allowed diplomats to see her and practically lifted the home-confinement orders. (IHT 05-09, 15-09-00)

It was reported by the UN in January 2001 that thanks to UN mediation the military government and the opposition leader had begun reconciliation talks in October 2000 and planned later to start substantive discussions on national reconciliation. (IHT 10-01, 23-01-01) By way of gesture of support of the talks between the government and the opposition, Japan approved an aid package which was the largest since the crack-down of 1988. (IHT 26-04-01)

Aung San Suu Kyi was officially released from house arrest on 6 May 2002. (IHT 07-05-02)

DIVIDED STATES: CHINA

Appeal for cross-Strait talks

The new Taiwanese president on 31 July 2000 appealed to the Chinese government to reopen negotiations. He argued that dialogue could lead to exchanges, which in turn could lead to consensus. However, he brushed aside the Chinese government's demand that Taiwan first acknowledge a single China, of which Taiwan is part. Instead, he referred to "the spirit of 1992" (*see* 3 Asian YIL 366; 491), the negotiations in which the two sides agreed to disagree about the meaning of "one China". (IHT 01-08-00)

Direct Taiwan – mainland links

With Taiwanese permission Taiwanese ships for the first time in 51 years made a legal voyage from Taiwan to mainland China on 2 January 2001. This signalled the beginning of the so-called "three small links": direct trade, postal and transportation links between a number of tiny outlying islands under Taiwanese control and the mainland. The Chinese government called for such links for the whole of Taiwan. (IHT 03-01, 04-01-01)

Taiwanese request for weapons

According to signals from Taiwan the government might ask the US to buy guided missile destroyers equipped with the "Aegis" radar system to counter China's recently purchased Russian-made destroyers. It would be the most significant weapons transfer by the US to Taiwan since the sale of 150 fighter aircraft in 1992 (*see* 3 Asian YIL 346). (IHT 09-01-01) The Taiwanese request was met with a Chinese warning to the US that the supply of these advanced armaments would have grave consequences. (IHT 07-03-01) The Chinese foreign ministry cited the violation of Chinese sovereignty, threat to Chinese state security, aggravation of tension in the Taiwan Strait and disruption in Sino-US relations. (IHT 14-03-01) A key Chinese concern appeared to be that in an upgraded version the system would give the ships the first ballistic missile defence capability and would encourage the Taiwanese in their wish to declare independence from China. On the other hand it was said by the US side that Chinese missile deployments might determine the US sale of anti-missile systems to Taiwan opposed by China. The argument was that "there will be a point at which that missile build-up will threaten the sufficient defence of Taiwan and which it is the US policy to maintain". (IHT 16-03-01) The Aegis system had great political significance because of its association with American plans for a regional missile defence system. It would be able to detect and track more than 100 missiles, aircraft or surface vessels at a time. (IHT 21/22-04-01)

In its objections to US arms supplies to Taiwan, China was singling out three items as particularly objectionable: the Aegis system, submarines, which the US had never yet sold to Taiwan, and the Patriot anti-missile system. (IHT 02-04-01)

Remarkably, there were also reports about divisions among Taiwan government and armed forces circles on the expediency of the purchase of, especially, the Aegis-system because of the potential cost in terms of money and relations among China, the US and Taiwan. (IHT 21/22-04-01)

Finally, the US decided in April 2001 on a $5 billion arms package which did not include the weaponry to which China had objected most strongly: the Aegis system, but for the first time did include offensive weapons: diesel submarines, which, however, the US no longer manufactures and had not operated since 1990.

Besides, the US president said, on the following day, 25 April 2001, that if China attacked Taiwan, the US would "do whatever it took to help Taiwan defend itself". This appeared to represent a clear step beyond the decades-old US policy, under the (US) Taiwan Relations Act (*see* 2 Asian YIL 302), of assuring Taiwan that the US would provide Taiwan needed weaponry, without explicitly going beyond that pledge. The long-term balancing act between on the one hand offering weapons support to Taiwan to deter any Chinese attack, while on the other leaving the eventual US response vague to discourage independence-minded Taiwanese politicians, is known as "strategic ambiguity", allegedly crucial to regional stability. (IHT 25-04, 26-04-01)

Proposal for Taiwan UN seat

El Salvador, Senegal, the Dominican Republic, Gambia, Burkina Faso, Nicaragua, Chad, Tuvalu, Palau, and Belize submitted a proposal for Taiwan to join the UN. Similar proposals had been submitted in the past nine years, but consistently failed to be included in the UN General Assembly's agenda. (IHT 10-08-01)

Taiwanese direct investments in China

The Taiwan authorities on 7 November 2001 lifted long-standing restrictions on direct investment in the Chinese mainland, a milestone in the economic relationship between the two territories. The decision included the abolition of a $50-million limit on individual investments and automatic approval for investments of less than $20 million. The new rules would enable Taiwanese companies to invest directly in China, rather than through third countries. (IHT 08-11-01)

Change in Chinese policy

On 24 January 2002 the Chinese deputy vice-premier issued a statement which implied a softening of China's policy toward Taiwan. He said China would welcome members of Taiwan's majority party visiting the mainland, and called for renewed dialogue and stronger economic ties across the Taiwan Strait. In early February China dropped its precondition of recognition of the "one-China" principle before the opening of direct shipping, trade and mail links (the "three links") without government involvement. (IHT 25-01, 06-02-02)

US policy toward Taiwan

According to US officials and analysts, as reported in early May 2002, the US government was embracing a closer political and military relationship with Taiwan than had any previous US government in decades, as a way of endorsing democracy on the island and deterring a Chinese military threat across the Taiwan Strait.

Whereas in the past the US had maintained "strategic ambiguity" towards Taiwan (*see supra*), a stance meant to discourage Taiwan from declaring independence while keeping China guessing about how the US would respond to a Chinese offensive, the current US president once said that the US would do "whatever it took" (*see supra*) to help Taiwan defend itself. (IHT 02-05-02)

DIVIDED STATES – KOREA
See also: Inter-state relations: North Korea – US; Nuclear energy matters

Four-party talks

The sixth round of the four-party talks between North and South Korea, China and the US in Geneva, August 1999 (9 Asian YIL 392), ended with the US and South Korea resisting North Korean efforts to put the issue of US troops on the agenda. It was reported that since that time there has been reluctance from the side of North Korea to have another round of talks. (IHT 09-11-00)

Family reunions

North and South Korea on 30 June 2000 agreed on the first reunions in fifteen years (in 1985) of relatives divided by the Korean War. The breakthrough in the talks came two weeks after the South Korean president returned from his three-day meeting with the North Korean leader (*see* 9 Asian YIL 393).

North Korea dropped its demand that South Korea return more than 50 former political prisoners held there for many years as spies before the first exchange of family members on 15 August, the national day for the celebration of Korean liberation from Japanese rule. It was reported that South Korea promised to let the prisoners go to North Korea in early September if they wished. (IHT 1/2-07-00)

After a second reunion in December 2000 a third one was agreed in late January 2001, to take place in February. (IHT 30-01-01) However, no further reunions took place.

Other agreements

Talks between the two Koreas in late July 2000 in Seoul succeeded in reaching a series of agreements by way of implementation of the joint declaration of 15 June 2000. Among the agreements reached were those on the establishment of liaison offices, the resumption of railway services, and access to South Korea for North Korea passport holders residing in Japan. However, the parties agreed neither on a military hot line nor on talks about reducing tensions engendered by the huge number of troops facing each other on either side of the cease-fire line. Discussion was also avoided on the issue of guarantees for South Korean investments in North Korea and on double taxation issues.

The parties agreed to continue, in late August 2000, the dialogue "in accordance with the spirit of the South-North joint declaration". On 1 September 2000 they reached agreement on dialogue between military officials to ease military tensions. The joint statement read: "The South and North will exert efforts to ease tension and guarantee peace. In this regard consultations will be held for military authorities of both sides to open a dialogue as soon as possible." (IHT 31-07, 01-08, 01-09, 2/3-09-00) In January 2001 the two sides agreed to resume talks on reuniting families (*see supra*) and on economic matters. These would be the first full-scale talks after those following the summit meeting in 2000. (IHT 23-01-01) On 8 February 2001 a 41-point agreement was reached on arrangements to reconnect a cross-border railroad and on a military hotline. The rail-link agreement included an arrangement on mine-clearing. (IHT 09-02-01)

Unfortunately, the two governments did not talk with each other in the following months and it was said in mid-2001 that the "sunshine policy" was foundering in the shadow of the US's tougher approach to North Korea and the sullen response from North Korea, which was unwilling to move ahead with South Korea unless such a move would result in better ties with the US. (IHT 15-08-01)

There were indications of a North Korean proposal in early September 2001 for a resumption of the talks, and a brief meeting took place on 16 September. (IHT 03-09, 17-09-01) Meanwhile, various projects were said to have bogged down because of North Korean lack of funds. (IHT 08-10-01) After a last ministerial meeting in November 2001 the talks stalled, until North Korea and South Korea announced on 25 March 2002 that they would resume their dialogue. (IHT 26-03-02)

Reduced South Korean – US military exercise

In line with the growing improvement and the conciliatory mood in relations between the two Koreas the annual military exercises were reduced in scale. (IHT 22-08-00)

EMBARGO
See also: Sanctions

US arms embargo against Indonesia

(*See also*: Military cooperation)

The US enacted an arms embargo against Indonesia, together with a suspension of military training assistance (*see* 9 Asian YIL 407), after the violence in connection with the East Timorese conflict (*see* 9 Asian YIL 413). It was said that the Indonesian military relied on US logistics support for 70 per cent of its modern equipment. (IHT 05-07-00)

US embargo on Israeli export of dual-use technology to China

Under a Sino-Israeli transaction the Israel Aircraft Industries would supply a *Phalcon* early warning radar system to China. However, the US government expressed its concern that China could use the radar system against US forces in the Taiwan Strait, and the US House of Representatives Appropriation Committee called on Israel to terminate the process. There were even references to a possible cut in US aid to Israel if it did not comply. On 12 July 2000 Israel cancelled the deal. (IHT 1/2-07, 13-07-00)

It was reported in November 2000 that Russia appeared ready to sell its own weaker version of the system to China. The system would allow the air force using it to coordinate scores of fighters and bombers, increase the accuracy of its missiles and provide the ability to see over the horizon. (IHT 20-11-00)

Renunciation of US-Russian agreement on arms sales to Iran

Russia informed the US on 3 November 2000 that it planned to withdraw from the (secret) US-Russian agreement of 1995 in which it pledged not to sell conventional weapons to Iran. This was affirmed in a joint Iranian-Russian announcement on 28 December 2000. (IHT 23-11, 29-12-00) On 12 March 2001 the Russian government announced that it would resume the sale of conventional weapons, which was criticized by the US. (IHT 15-03, 16-03-01)

ENVIRONMENTAL POLLUTION AND PROTECTION

Whaling

Japan decided to broaden its whale hunting to more categories of whales in July 2000. These categories were protected under US law, and consequently the US announced it would ban Japan from future access to fishing in US waters and threatened economic sanctions if Japan did not curtail its expanded hunting of whales. On the other hand, Japan warned it would file a complaint with the WTO if the US took action. (IHT 14-09-00)

The International Whaling Commission on 23 May 2002 voted down a Japanese proposal which would pave the way for lifting a 1986 moratorium on commercial whale hunts. The proposal would have set up a framework for a commercial whaling management program. Of the Commission's 45 voting members, 16 backed the proposal, 25 voted against and three abstained. (IHT 24-05-02)

Other Japanese efforts were its (failed) attempts to re-admit Iceland, a country that had refused to stop commercial whaling. Meanwhile, the pro-whaling bloc, including Japan and Norway, was enlarged by the inclusion of West African and Caribbean countries (environmental NGOs accused the Fisheries Agency of Japan of vote buying). (IHT 27-05-02)

Caspian Sea sturgeon

The states parties to the Convention on International Trade in Endangered Species in their meeting in June 2001 banned the fishing of sturgeon from most of the Caspian Sea and its rivers as of 2002, hitting chiefly Russia, Kazakhstan, Turkmenistan, and Azerbaijan. It left Iran with a monopoly on legal caviar since two thirds of Iran's catch were of a species that spent its entire life along the Iranian coastline. (IHT 22-06-01)

Japanese initial disavowal and later ratification of Kyoto Protocol

In mid-2001 the Japanese prime minister told the US president that Japan would not implement the 1997 Kyoto Protocol without US participation. Nevertheless, Japan ratified the Protocol on 4 June 2002, a few days after the 15 member states of the European Union had done so. Japan is the fourth-largest emitter of carbon dioxide, after the US, the EU and Russia. [The Kyoto Protocol was the first multilateral treaty requiring industrial countries to reduce emissions of gases linked to global warming. The position of the EU was that it would pursue ratification and enactment even without the US; the latter had announced its opposition in March 2001 because the required reductions could harm the US economy. The US on 19 July 2001 affirmed its decision not to ratify the Kyoto Protocol. Despite US abstention the protocol would, under its complicated requirements, take effect if it were to be ratified by the EU, Russia, Japan, and either Canada or Poland.]
(IHT 02-07-01, 05-06-02)

ESPIONAGE

Bugging of Chinese aircraft

According to newspaper reports Chinese intelligence officers had found spying devices hidden in a US-built aircraft that was bought by China in June 2000 and refitted in the US to become a presidential aircraft. It appeared that both governments wanted to play down the incident and to resolve it quietly. (IHT 21-01-02)

FOREIGN INVESTMENT

Iran

The Iranian parliament for the first time passed legislation authorizing and protecting foreign investment in Iran. Previous law dating from many decades ago prevented foreigners from holding more than 49 per cent of companies, although full international investment had been allowed within certain constructions in the energy sector. (IHT 24-08-00)

HAND-OVER FOR PENAL PURPOSES

Demand to turn over Osama bin Laden

The UN Security Council, in its resolution 1267(1999) of 15 October 1999, acting under Chapter VII of the UN Charter, inter alia "[deplored] the fact that the Taleban continues to provide a safe haven to Usama bin Laden and to allow him ... to operate a network of terrorist training camps from Taleban-controlled territory and to use Afghanistan as a base from which to sponsor international terrorist operations", and "[demanded] that the Taleban turn over Usama bin Laden without further delay to appropriate authorities in a country where he has been indicted ...".

On 5 November 2000 a Taleban spokesman was quoted as saying that Afghanistan would not expel the person in question, even if evidence linked him to the 1998 bombings of US embassies in Africa, and that any trial he could face would be in Afghanistan. (IHT 06-11-00)

Pakistan-US practice

In connection with the kidnapping and murder in Pakistan of a US journalist in January 2002, Pakistan agreed in principle to surrender to the US the chief suspect who was a British-born militant Muslim. There was no extradition treaty between the two countries, yet they had worked closely together in the past in the hand-over from Pakistan to the US of several top terrorist suspects.

Since the Afghan war following the September 2001 attacks on the US, Pakistan had handed over scores of Taleban and Al Qaeda fighters who were detained in Pakistan as they fled from Afghanistan. It was said that these handings-over were carried out on the basis of an agreement with the US specifically meant to apply to the Afghan crisis. (IHT 26-02, 27-02-02)

Asian collusion with US "rendition" policies

According to newspaper reports various countries, among which Asian ones, had been cooperating with US policies for the past several years and increasingly after the September 2001 attacks on the US, in the hand-over of criminal suspects from one country to another while bypassing national as well as international rules on the matter. Such "renditions" were preferred in order to prevent legal complications and publicity. They sometimes took place to countries other than the US, in order to avoid the application in the US of interrogation tactics which are illegal in the US and, generally, to prevent anti-US reactions.

Among the reported cases was that of Mohammed Saad Iqbal Madni, said to be in possession of an Egyptian and a Pakistani passport, who went to Indonesia from Pakistan in November 2001. In January 2002 the USCIA was said to have informed the Indonesian intelligence agency that Iqbal was an Al Qaeda suspect and to have urged Indonesia to apprehend him. This was followed by an Egyptian request for his hand-over ("Egypt just provided the formalities"), allegedly on charges of terrorism. He was then, allegedly at US request, detained by the Indonesian authorities, expelled because of visa violations, and hustled aboard a US-registered plane and flown to Egypt.

Another reported example was that of a Yemeni, who was wanted (by the US) in connection with the attack on the US destroyer *Cole* in Yemen in October 2000. He was detained in Pakistan and there surrendered to US authorities who flew him to Jordan. (IHT 12-03-02)

HUMAN RIGHTS
See: International and municipal law

INSURGENTS
See also: Protection of foreign nationals

Sri Lankan civil war

The Sri Lankan government on 3 August 2000 proposed a new constitution that would give greater political autonomy to the minority Tamil population, in order to help end the 17-year war. But the main Tamil insurgent group rejected the proposed constitution on grounds that nothing short of an independent state would satisfy them. On its part, the main opposition party voted against it, believing that the measure would give the Tamils too much power and could lead to a division of the country, making its passage in Parliament improbable. (IHT 04-08-00)

In November 2000 the separatist Tamil Tiger rebels announced that the group was ready for unconditional peace talks with the government, calling on the government to end its economic blockade and to de-escalate the war. The peace overture came in response to mediation efforts by Norway which had acted to "facilitate" talks since 2000. Although the prime minister said that the government planned to carry on the war "until the enemy is totally eliminated", the rebels nevertheless declared a unilateral, month-long cease-fire on 21 December 2000. They voiced the hope that the government would reciprocate and that the peace talks of 1995 that broke down after eight months, could be resumed. (*see* 6 Asian YIL 391-392). The cease-fire was extended several times. The government did not reciprocate and began a new offensive instead, although operations were slowed down and several attempts were made, with the help of Norway, to bring the parties to the negotiating table. (IHT 28-11, 22-12, 23/24-12-00, 13-04-01) In April 2001 the rebels announced they would not further extend the unilateral cease-fire which was scheduled to expire, but would continue to support Norwegian attempts to broker peace. (IHT 24-04-01) The rebels' period of relative quiescence ended on 24 July 2001 by an attack on the country's main airport. (IHT 07-08-01)

After the Tamil Tigers said for the first time that they would consider settling for less than a separate state, the rebels and the newly elected government, on the proposal of Norwegian mediators, agreed in principle on 21 February 2002 to a long-term cease-fire, preparing the ground for peace talks. Mistrust between the Tamil Tigers and the large Muslim minority in the east of the country could, as an additional factor, derail progress toward a settlement. (IHT 26-12-01, 22-02, 10-04-02)

Philippine Muslim insurgents
(*See also:* Military cooperation: Philippines – US)

The 1996 peace agreement between the government and the MNLF (*see* 7 Asian YIL 429) and the election of the MNLF leader Nur Misuari as governor of the newly constituted Autonomous Region of Muslim Mindanao had not brought the hoped-for peace. The surrender of arms promised in the peace agreement was not implemented; there was an increased standing of the *Moro Islamic Liberation Front* (MILF) and the *Abu Sayyaf* grouping (named after its founder, Abdul Rasul Abu Sayyaf) which engaged in kidnapping and hostage-taking. All this resulted in increased military operations and a sceptical appraisal of the merits of a cease-fire. (IHT 5/6-08-00) In February 2001 the president declared a suspension of military operations against the Muslim separatist rebels in an effort to revive the stalled peace talks. However, there would be no withdrawal of government forces from guerrilla bases seized by the government troops in 2000, and the idea of a separate Islamic state was ruled out. (IHT 21-02-01) In March 2001 the MILF accepted the offer. (IHT 15-03-01) Negotiations were held in Malaysia with the assistance of the Malaysian government and a cease-fire agreement was signed in Malaysia on 7 August 2001, building on a preliminary accord reached in Libya in June. The cease-fire was to be monitored by the members of the Organization of the Islamic Conference. Parallel to this agreement another document reunifying the MILF with the MNLF was agreed upon and signed on the same day. (The two factions broke apart in 1978.) (IHT 04/05-08, 08-08-01)

Indonesian province of Aceh

Police had fired on people trying to reach a pro-independence rally in the provincial capital in November 2000, resulting in a refusal by the rebels to attend any further peace talks (*see* 9 Asian YIL 394) until the escalation of violence against civilians had stopped. (IHT 13-11, 23-11 -00) However, on 8 January 2001 the parties agreed to extend by one month the "moratorium on violence" or "humanitarian pause" that was agreed in May 2000 and due to expire on 10 January 2001. (IHT 11-01-01)

Indonesian province of Irian Jaya

The Indonesian government in early December 2000 abandoned its policy of trying to persuade the separatist groups (*see* 9 Asian YIL 394) to accept a regime of liberal autonomy, and ordered a severe crackdown. [The outermost eastern province has a population of 2 million and dozens of indigenous tribes. The island is of great economic importance, being the location of among the world's largest copper and gold mines, which are operated by a US company.] (IHT 04-12-00)

Nepal

In 1994 the election commission barred the Communist alliance, once the third-largest party in Parliament, from taking part in the parliamentary elections. The following year the Communist Party of Nepal (Maoist) was formed; in 1996 it issued forty demands, including radical land reform and the abolition of the monarchy. When they did not get their way, they declared war against the state and an armed insurgency started.

Just days after the Maoist insurgents began their most fierce offensive since 1996 they said in spring 2001 they were prepared to enter into talks with the government. (IHT 09-04, 02-05-01) However, after the palace massacre on 1 June 2001 they again stepped up their attacks. The government and rebels eventually announced a cease-fire on 23 July 2001. (IHT 24-07-01)

In the wake of a guerrilla attack on 25 November 2001 in which tens of police officers were killed, the King declared a state of emergency. (IHT 27-11-01) The rebels staged their deadliest assault ever on 17 February 2002 after which the state of emergency was extended. (IHT 18-02, 22-02, 25-04-02)

Central Asia

(*See also*: Inter-state relations etc.: Shanghai Cooperation Organization)

There were regular attacks into Kyrgyzstan and Uzbekistan by Islamic insurgents, operating from Tajikistan and Afghanistan and known as the *Islamic Movement of Uzbekistan*, and allegedly financed from Afghanistan. Their alleged goal was said to be carving an Islamic state in the Fergana Valley, which stretches across parts of Uzbekistan, Kyrgyzstan and Tajikistan, and the overthrow of the Uzbek government. Russian military units took part in anti-terrorist exercises and border patrols in Kyrgyzstan and Tajikistan. (IHT 04-05-01)

INTERNATIONAL AND MUNICIPAL LAW
See also: International crimes and their adjudication

Chinese interpretation of treaty obligation

China ratified the International Covenant on Economic, Social and Cultural Rights on 28 February 2001, but accompanied it by issuing a statement to the effect that it would assume the obligations prescribed in Article 8 item 1(a) [on freedom in the field of trade unions] in line with relevant provisions of the Chinese constitution, trade union law and labour law. (IHT 01-03-01)

INTERNATIONAL CRIMES AND THEIR ADJUDICATION

Cambodian tribunal for trial of Khmer Rouge leaders

The Cambodian National Assembly on 2 January 2001 approved the creation of a tribunal for the trial of Khmer Rouge leaders on charges relating to the mass killings during their regime. The tribunal was to be structured according to a formula agreed by the UN (*see* 9 Asian YIL 396). The Assembly specified that only "those persons who are most responsible" could be brought before the tribunal. The Senate approved the bill on 15 January; the Constitutional Council did so on 12 February. After a revision in late February, necessary because of a number of inconsistencies in the draft, the law was signed by the King on 10 August 2001.

Before the tribunal could actually convene, an agreement on the details was to be concluded between Cambodia and the UN, ensuring that the tribunal would adhere to minimum international standards. (IHT 03-01, 16-01, 13-02, 24/25-02, 17-07, 11/12-08-01)

On 8 February 2002, however, the UN pulled out of the preparatory work, mainly because the Cambodian government insisted that Cambodian law should take precedence over the projected agreement. The UN legal counsel said that it had been the UN's consistent position that the tribunal cannot be bound by a national law. On the other hand, the Cambodian prime minister was reported to have said: "If I don't follow Cambodian law, the National Assembly will vote to remove me. So I have to follow Cambodian law." (IHT 09/10-02-02)

UN indictments for East Timor crimes

A special panel for serious crimes set up under the UN Transitional Administration for East Timor (UNTAET) issued the first indictments on 11 December 2000 in connection with the violence that broke out after the popular vote for independence from Indonesia. Under these indictments ten members of a pro-Indonesia militia group and one Indonesian army officer were charged with crimes against humanity that occurred in and around the town of Los Palos. Two months later another indictment was issued concerning five persons for crimes against humanity by murder, rape, torture, unlawful deprivation of liberty, inhumane and degrading treatment, and persecution.

Earlier in the year the UN and Indonesia, represented by its attorney-general, had signed an agreement to cooperate on investigative matters, but UN prosecutors were reported to have encountered difficulties in gathering evidence from Indonesian citizens. (IHT 12-12-00, 07-02-01)

Another four (pro-Jakarta) East Timorese militiamen were indicted for crimes against humanity in August 2001. (IHT 10-08-01)

Indonesian trials for crimes in East Timor

Indonesia on 14 March 2002 convened its first trials of senior officials accused of crimes against humanity in East Timor committed in 1999. (*See* State practice, *supra* at 180) Indonesia hoped the proceedings would satisfy demands for an international war crimes tribunal along the lines of the former Yugoslavia and Rwanda tribunals. It also hoped that they would lead the US to overturn a ban on military assistance (*see infra* at 382).

Eighteen persons would be tried although the Indonesian Commission on Human Rights had found 15 other officials implicated. Many people expected most of the suspects to receive relatively light sentences out of concern that stiff penalties could prompt a backlash from the military, which contended that its actions were justified in order to prevent the country from splitting apart. (IHT 14-03-02)

INTERNATIONAL ECONOMIC AND TRADE RELATIONS
See also: Asia Pacific Economic Cooperation; Association of South East Asian Nations; World Trade Organization

Vietnam – US trade agreement

After nearly four years of negotiations, Vietnam and the US in July 2000 reached agreement on the issue of unfettered commerce between the two countries, for the first time since the Vietnam War and after having restored full diplomatic ties in 1995. The US Congress gave its approval in September-October 2001, the Vietnamese National Assembly in November. The agreement extended "permanent normal trade relations" status (PNTR, formerly referred to as Most-Favoured Nation status: MFN) to Vietnam and completed the process of Vietnamese-US normalization of relations. (IHT 14-07-00, 10-04, 05-10, 29-11-01)

Asia-Pacific bilateral free-trade agreements

Malaysia renewed its criticism of moves by Asia-Pacific countries towards the conclusion of bilateral free-trade agreements. It informed Singapore that it would oppose attempts to allow Australia and New Zealand entry to the ASEAN Free Trade Agreement (AFTA) through their eventual free-trade arrangements with Singapore. [Singapore has virtually no import tariffs and relatively painlessly concluded a free-trade agreement with New Zealand, while negotiating or planning to negotiate similar agreements with Australia, the US, Japan, Canada, Mexico and the four-member (Switzerland, Norway, Iceland, Liechtenstein) "European Free Trade Association" (EFTA). It was ready to exclude agriculture from a deal with Japan and include measures linking trade to labour and environmental standards in a deal with the US.] (IHT 22-02-01)

Japan, while having long been a staunch multilateralist, started pursuing a parallel policy of negotiating bilateral free-trade agreements. In October 2001 it concluded its first bilateral agreement, with Singapore, and it was said that similar agreements with Mexico, Australia, Canada, Chile, South Korea and Taiwan could be envisaged. Dwindling trade surpluses were mentioned as one of the major causes of the policy change. (IHT 09-11-01)

However, after having concluded the agreement with Singapore Japan did not plan to negotiate any more free trade deals with other countries in the region for the next few years, because of the expected large agricultural imports to Japan as a result of such agreements (even in the case of Singapore where farm products amounted to a tiny 1.8 per cent of annual two-way trade with Japan, the modest goldfish exports were excluded from the tariff cuts. Furthermore, the agreement was not called a free trade agreement but "Economic Agreement for a New Age Partnership"). Even without free trade arrangements, however, Japan was importing over $9 billion in farm goods from Southeast Asia annually, including about 20 per cent of the Thai and Vietnamese exports to Japan and ten per cent of the Philippine exports. Japan's food self-sufficiency had gradually declined over the last 30 years to under 40 per cent (compared with more than 90 per cent in the case of the US and Europe). (IHT 16-01-02)

European Union phase-out of trade barriers

The EU decided to phase out trade barriers on everything except military weapons from 48 least-developed countries. The phase-out nature was a compromise, lasting until 2009, for barriers to sensitive products like bananas, rice and sugar. The practical result of the measure would be reflected in increased imports from the poorest countries substituting for those from less poor developing countries. (IHT 01-03-01)

INTERNATIONAL HUMANITARIAN LAW
See also: World War II

No Gun Ri incident (Korean War)

South Korea had long been contending that US soldiers fired into a crowd of unarmed refugees near the village of No Gun Ri in the early days of the Korean War in July 1950. In December 2000 news emerged of a later report from the US Army's inspector general in which the conclusion was drawn that the soldiers had panicked in the midst of a chaotic retreat and had indeed fired into the crowd, believing North Korean troops were posing as refugees. The report also stated that there had been no conclusive evidence about orders to shoot the civilians, but there was difference of opinion on this point. There was also disagreement on the question whether the US should pay compensation to the families of those killed in the shooting. It was the first formal acknowledgement by the US military of its involvement in the massacre.

South Korean and US officials discussed the findings in early December 2000 when preparing a memorandum of "common understanding", but failed to reach agreement on the crucial element of whether the US troops were ordered to fire. (IHT 07-12-00, 04-01-01)

On 11 January 2001 the US president stated in a written statement: "On behalf of the United States of America, I deeply regret that Korean civilians lost their lives at No Gun Ri in late July 1950. ... To those Koreans who lost loved ones at No Gun Ri, I offer my condolences. Many Americans have experienced the anguish of innocent casualties of war." However, the statement fell short of an admission of guilt and there were no apologies, nor any offer of compensation to the relatives of the dead. (IHT 12-01, 13/14-01-01)

Germ warfare in World War II

In 1997 a suit had been filed in the Tokyo District Court by 180 Chinese citizens alleging that crimes against humanity were committed by a medical experimentation unit of the Japanese army ("Unit 731") in northeast China during the Second World War. It was alleged that the unit had tested and developed biological weapons, spreading bubonic plague, cholera and typhus. The case had dragged on and no decision was expected before the end of 2001.

The Japanese government had denied the jurisdiction of the court and had insisted that it did not know what the army unit in question had done. (IHT 10/11-03-01)

US treatment of prisoners taken in the Afghan War

The US had transferred several prisoners, captured in the course of the war in Afghanistan, out of Afghan territory, such as to US warships at sea. On 10 January 2002 the US started to transfer a group of Al Qaeda and Taleban detainees, termed by US officials as "the worst of the worst", out of the country to a camp ("Camp X-Ray") at the US Navy base at Guantanamo Bay, territory under US jurisdiction that was leased from Cuba in 1903.

The captives were initially named "battlefield detainees" and later described by the US as "unlawful combatants". They were not recognized by the US as prisoners of war, and consequently not accorded a status that would give them per se the legal rights under the Convention Relative to the Treatment of Prisoners of War, among which eventual trial through court-martial or civilian courts, not special military tribunals (this denial of prisoner-of-war status was affirmed in a US presidential decision of 18 January 2002). Nor were they charged with any criminal activity. They were in fact allowed limited rights, including the right to practise their religion, but they were not allowed legal representation during interrogation. Determination as prisoner of war would limit the possibilities of the US military to interrogate the detainees. On the other hand, their classification as "unlawful combatants" would make the Conventional obligation to release them when the military campaign terminates inapplicable. Besides all this the US Secretary of Defense rejected the criticism voiced against this treatment by saying that the detainees were being treated vastly better than they themselves treated anybody else.

The US government based its refusal to accord the status of prisoner of war to the detainees on the nature of their method of warfare, which allegedly did not meet the requirements of the laws of war and the Geneva Convention, such as those about uniforms, military hierarchy and the conduct of operations. (IHT 11-01, 18-01, 28-01-02)

Responding to protests from among its allies the US president decided on 7 February 2002 that the US would grant the protection of the Geneva Convention to detainees who had fought for the Taleban but not to members of the Al Qaeda network. The US spokesman said: "Although the US does not recognize the Taleban as the legitimate Afghan government, the president determined that the Taleban members are covered under the treaty because Afghanistan is a party to the convention. ... Al Qaeda is an international terrorist group and cannot be considered a state party to the Geneva Convention." But the US held to the view that nevertheless Taleban supporters would still not be considered "prisoners of war". [It was said that the decision was meant to meet concerns that denying the protection to detainees from Afghanistan could be used as a precedent that would result in mistreatment of captured US soldiers at some future point in the war on terrorism.] (IHT 08-02-02)

The International Red Cross reacted to the decision by saying that it fell short of international law and that people "in a situation of international conflict [i.e. including Taleban and Al Qaeda fighters] are considered to be prisoners of war unless a competent tribunal decides otherwise". (IHT 09/10-02-02)

It was reported in May 2002 that one of the detainees was transferred from Guantanamo Bay to a prison in Virginia in April 2002 after it was discovered that the person had been born in the US and might be a US citizen. Lawsuits filed on behalf of Guantanamo detainees were frustrated by the fact that US federal courts have no jurisdiction over Guantanamo (Cuban) territory. A 1950 Supreme Court decision denied captured foreign combatants overseas the right to have their case heard in a US federal court. (IHT 15-05-02)

A petition was filed in January 2002 in the US District Court at Los Angeles against the detentions, alleging that the detainees were held in violation of the Geneva Convention and the US Constitution. It wanted, *inter alia*, due-process guarantees. The judge would first have to decide on his/her jurisdiction and on whether the California plaintiffs had legal standing to pursue a case involving prisoners held at a US facility in Cuba. (IHT 22-01-02)

British treatment of prisoners taken in the Afghan War

According to information from British sources dating from 2002 prisoners taken by British forces in Afghanistan were not handed over directly to US authorities, but were turned over to the Afghan government. British officials acknowledged that "under international law every single person arrested would have to be put before a British tribunal", yet "our forces in the region simply don't have enough bodies there to do that"; therefore, captives were turned over to the Afghan authorities while notifying the US military commander concerned of this. (IHT 02-05-02)

INTER-STATE RELATIONS: GENERAL ASPECTS

Shanghai Cooperation Organization

(*See also:* Regional security)

A regional security summit meeting took place in Dushanbe, Tajikistan, in early July 2000, with the participation of China, Russia, Kazakhstan, Kyrgyzstan, and Tajikistan.

The five countries met again in June 2001 in Shanghai, admitted a sixth member, Uzbekistan, and changed the name of the forum into "Shanghai Cooperation Organization", with a focus on combating Islamic militancy in Central Asia and with the "Islamic Movement of Uzbekistan" as their chief concern. (IHT 15-06-01)

Conference on Interaction and Confidence-Building Measures in Asia

An initiative of the president of Kazakhstan at the General Assembly session of the UN in 1992 led to the founding of the Conference on Interaction and Con-fidence-Building Measures in Asia (CICA). The Conference aimed at the creation of a security framework for Asia along the same lines as the Organization for Security and Cooperation in Europe (OSCE). In the course of the following years the foreign ministers of the interested states worked out cornerstone principles, resulting in the signing, in Almaty on 4 September 1999, of a *Declaration on the Principles Guiding Relations* among the CICA states.

The Declaration laid down seven fundamental principles which should govern the relations among the Conference states and would constitute the legal basis of a system of security for Asia.: (1) Sovereign equality and respect for rights inherent in sovereignty; (2) Refraining from the threat or use of force; (3) Territorial integrity of the Member States; (4) Peaceful settlement of disputes; (5) Non-intervention in internal affairs; (6) Economic, social and cultural cooperation, and (7) Human rights and fundamental freedoms.

The membership of the Conference consists of 16 states: Azerbaijan, Afghanistan, China, Egypt, India, Iran, Israel, Kazakhstan, Kyrgyzstan, Mongolia, Pakistan, Palestine National Administration, Russia, Tajikistan, Turkey, and Uzbekistan.

A summit meeting of heads of state took place for the first time in early June 2002 at Almaty. It issued a declaration committing the participating countries to working together to make Asia peaceful and safe from terrorism and other threats. (IHT 04-06, 05-06-02; www.kazakhembus.com/CICA)

Afghanistan – Iran

After the establishment of the Afghan interim government in December 2001 there were reports about meddling from the Iranian side in some provinces through the distribution of money, goods, and even weapons. Nevertheless, the interim Afghan prime minister visited Iran and praised Iran for standing by Afghans in their struggles against Soviet occupation and terrorists, thereby referring to bonds of "a common culture and language" which had "made our friendship eternal". (IHT 25 –01, 08-02, 26-02-02)

Afghanistan – Pakistan
(*See also:* Pakistan – US)

After having supported the Islamic resistance that fought and drove the Soviet occupation force from Afghanistan in the 1980s, Pakistan shifted its backing to the Taleban movement which took Kabul in 1996 (*see* 7 Asian YIL 402). In October 2001, however, Pakistan started taking sides with the US in support of the latter's campaign against terrorism. In early April 2002 the Pakistani president went to visit Afghanistan, where he pledged brotherly support for the new Afghan government. (IHT 03-04-02)

Afghanistan – US
(*See also:* Terrorism)

In connection with the attack on the US destroyer *Cole* in Yemen on 12 October 2000 newspaper reports were speculating that the US might take military action against Afghanistan because of suspicions that Osama bin Laden, who had moved his main base to Afghanistan, was involved in the attack. [In 1998 the US launched cruise missiles against sites in Afghanistan where Osama bin Laden was suspected of operating guerrilla training camps, about two weeks after bombs had exploded at two US embassies in East Africa. Although the Taleban had seized power in 1996, Afghanistan was never put on the US list of terrorist-sponsoring countries, apparently reflecting the US focus on its various other interests rather than on the threat of terrorism.] (IHT 03-11-00, 06-11-01)

The US took a similar attitude when the attacks of 11 September 2001 on New York and Washington took place. It claimed to have evidence linking Osama bin Laden to the attacks, and vowed to strike the group to which the attackers belonged as well as any country that harboured them.

The Taleban denied that Osama bin Laden was behind the New York and Washington plane crashes, and pleaded with the US for restraint.(IHT 14-09-01) It called Osama bin Laden a guest and, consequently, rejected the Pakistani warning to surrender him (*see*: Pakistan – US, *infra* at 377) and took the position that handing him over could be considered only when convincing evidence of his involvement was provided. [This evidence was never provided, allegedly for reasons of intelligence confidentiality. Meanwhile, US officials admitted they had no "smoking gun" showing that Osama bin Laden had personally ordered the attacks nor one that definitively linked him to the attackers. IHT 26-09-01] Eventual evidence would have to be presented to the *Shura*, the supreme organ of the Taleban (or, according to later reports, to the Afghan Supreme Court or to clerics of three Islamic countries) for judgment. Besides, the handing-over would have to be approved by the *Organization of the Islamic Conference*, and if a trial of Osama bin Laden took place outside Afghanistan, at least one of the judges must be a Muslim.

Meanwhile the US rejected a suggestion to urge (but not force) Osama bin Laden to leave Afghanistan voluntarily, and demanded that he, together with other figures living in Afghanistan who were suspected of being members of the alleged network Al Qaeda, must be surrendered to "responsible authorities" . A more or less formal ultimatum along these lines was announced in a US presidential speech on 21 September 2001 that proclaimed a "war on terror". In this speech it was said: "Either you are with us or you are with the terrorists. ... From this day forward, any nation that continues to harbor or support terrorism will be regarded by the US as a hostile regime." Specifically, it was said: "The Taleban must act and act immediately. ... They will hand over the terrorists, or they will share in their fate."

It was reported on 28 September 2001 that US and UK forces had begun operating inside Afghanistan in the first phase of military offensive. (IHT 15/16-09, 18-09, 19-09, 20-09, 21-09, 22/23-09, 29/30-09-01) (*see further*: Afghan War)

In what seemed to be a reversal of policy the US president on 17 April 2002 called for a plan for Afghanistan analogous to the Marshall Plan devised for post-war Germany and for Japan. He described a long-term involvement that would extend beyond the battlefield into infrastructure building and the re-invigoration of the economy. However, he did not say what kinds of resources the US was prepared to devote to the task. (IHT 18-04-02)

China – Afghanistan
(*See*: Civil War)

China – Japan

Mutual distrust

The Japanese foreign minister, speaking at the Central Party School in Beijing, warned in late August 2000 of increasing distrust between Japan and China. He cited Chinese reports claiming a revival of Japanese militarism and Japanese suspicions of rising military spending and an expanding missile arsenal in China. (IHT 31-08-00)

Prime ministers' visits

The Chinese prime minister visited Japan in October 2000. It was expected that the visit would soothe the tension that existed during the 1998 visit by the Chinese president (*see* 8 Asian YIL 274). Though recalling the pain caused by Japanese militarism the prime minister said that the Japanese people had also been victims and should, therefore, not be held responsible. He said that China "highly evaluated" Japan's economic assistance during the past 20 years.

The prime ministers of both countries agreed to speed up efforts to work out a mutual notification system for maritime activities in waters between the two countries, such as the Chinese maritime research activities in Japan's 200-mile exclusive economic zone. (IHT 14/15-10-00)

The Japanese prime minister visited China in early October 2001, just as the US had started military operations against Afghanistan. (*see*: Afghan War) Until shortly before the visit, China had objected to it until the Japanese prime minister had expressed his remorse for past Japanese aggression (*see infra*: Japan – East Asia). The prime minister started his visit with a trip to the Marco Polo Bridge near Beijing and an adjacent museum dedicated to the war against Japan, where he made a public expression of contrition. (IHT 09-10-01)

Japanese visa for former Taiwanese president

The granting of a visa to a former Taiwanese president in April 2001 caused China to launch a protest, saying that the grant "undermined the basis of bilateral relations" as the person in question (who, formally, was going to Japan for a medical check-up) was viewed as an advocate of Taiwan's independence. The Japanese foreign minister admitted that he was "a very influential person politically" and said: "I think we are about to enter a difficult period in our diplomatic relations with China" although "[w]e will strive to make China understand that our decision was made on the basis of humanitarian concerns" and "[t]his decision will not affect Japan's stance on Taiwan". (IHT 21/22-04-01) There was a possibility that the cancellation of a visit to Japan planned by the Chairman of the Chinese National People's Congress for May 2001 was, at least partially (*see infra*: Japan – East Asia), the result of the visa incident. (IHT 26-04-01)

China – Russia

The Russian president visited China in July 2000 to cement the good relations between the two countries. One year later, in July 2001, the Chinese president visited Russia, culminating in a treaty of friendship and cooperation of 16 July 2001, the first such pact since 1950. The treaty contained 25 articles and would have a validity of twenty years.

It was emphasized that the treaty neither founded a military alliance nor was it aimed at "any third country". Yet the treaty joined the two countries formally in opposition against US missile defence plans and rejected the kind of humanitarian intervention that NATO undertook in the Balkans in 1999. It said the two countries "stand for strict observance of the generally recognized principles and norms of international law against any actions aimed at forced pressure or at interference, under any pretext, into domestic affairs of sovereign states". It reflected the deep concerns shared by both countries about a new world order dominated by the US and its European allies. Instead, the two presidents expressed the hope for a "just and rational new international order".

The border between the two countries had shrunk from 4,500 miles in Soviet times to 2,550 miles as a result of the emergence of the new Central Asian republics. Old enmities had faded and the two countries had forged a tactical partnership to oppose US and European ascendancy. Both countries chafed at NATO's intervention in the Balkans; both had worked to ease UN sanctions on Iraq, and both sold weapons and nuclear technology to Iran. (IHT 15-01, 07-03, 16-07, 17-07-01)

It was reported in late June 2002 that China was negotiating to buy eight submarines from Russia, being part of a billion-dollar package of weapons that Russia had committed itself to provide to China over the next four or five years. (IHT 25-06-02)

China – US

(*See also:* Divided states: China (Taiwanese request for weapons), Regional security)

Military cooperation

By way of the latest step in a gradual rekindling of bilateral military ties severed in 1999 after the bombing of the Chinese embassy at Belgrade a US warship entered the harbour of Qingdao on 2 August 2000 for a visit. It followed a visit by the US defense secretary to China in July. (IHT 03-08-00)

Another visit by US warships, this time to Hong Kong, took place in August 2001 and again this was interpreted as a sign of improvement in Sino-US relations after the warplane collision incident of April 2001 (*see infra*). (IHT 21-08-01)

Missile technology export

On US insistence China in November 2000 agreed to adopt municipal export control laws halting the supply of missile technology to other countries. This came instead of accession to the Missile Technology Control Regime (1 Asian YIL 270), for which China was not prepared. It considered the MTCR to amount to a cartel in which the countries that already have missile capability prevent other countries from acquiring it.

Later (on 1 September 2001) the US imposed sanctions by way of trade restrictions, barring both a major Chinese arms manufacturer from importing US items for dual purposes, and the issuance of licenses for US companies to launch their satellites on Chinese rockets. These sanctions would be lifted only if four conditions were fulfilled, i.e., halting exports of missile technology to Pakistan, refraining from helping other countries develop missiles capable of delivering nuclear weapons, broadening the scope of the 2000 agreement to include pre-November 2000 contracts, and establishing a system of export controls to regulate the transfer of sensitive technology. (IHT 06-10-00, 03-09-01) China accused the US of having acted on erroneous intelligence and the Chinese company in question said its exports to Pakistan consisted of machine tools and parts for civil use only. (IHT 07-09-01)

In late February 2002 it was announced that China would send its top arms control negotiator to the US to continue talks on the above issues. (IHT 27-02-02)

Hainan warplane collision

A Chinese fighter jet and a US surveillance plane collided 50 nautical miles south of Hainan Island above the South China Sea on 1 April 2001, resulting in the crash of the Chinese plane and the US plane being forced to make an emergency landing on Hainan Island. The collision occurred when two Chinese fighter planes intercepted the US aircraft when the latter approached Chinese airspace. Surveillance and reconnaissance flights by US aircraft near Chinese airspace had been taking place since at least the 1970s.

Blaming the US for the incident China launched a protest, while the US, concerned about Chinese access to the military technology in the American aircraft, emphasized its immunity and urged China to "respect the integrity of the aircraft", while requesting the immediate return of the aircraft and crew. It also requested access to the plane and crew (in Chinese custody) by its diplomats, a request which was granted the next day. The US ambassador to China said that China had no jurisdiction over the US crew and that the plane's immunity status barred China from boarding, searching, seizing or detaining it without US consent. [In past comparable cases the US had often rejected similar appeals. In 1976 in the case of a Soviet pilot who defected to Japan, US authorities spent nine weeks taking his airplane apart and inspecting it before sending the plane back to the Soviet Union, in packing crates. But some analysts distinguished between an aircraft brought in by defectors and the case of one in distress.] (IHT 02-04, 03-04-01)

The US president and the Secretary of State expressed regret over the presumed death of the pilot of the Chinese aircraft, without, however, issuing a formal apology as demanded by China. It was the US position that it had done nothing wrong and that apparently the Chinese plane had manoeuvred too closely underneath the slower spy plane, while the Chinese side argued that the US plane had violated the rules by turning suddenly and colliding, and by making a landing without permission.

While the US urged that the aircraft and crew be returned immediately, the Chinese authorities wanted time to "complete their investigation". US circles described the Chinese attitude to be "intransigent" and "violating norms of decent behaviour". The case was compared to that of the spy-ship "*Pueblo*" which gathered intelligence off the coast of North Korea in January 1968 and was captured by the North Korean military and never returned, while the crew was held captive for eleven months. (IHT 05-04, 06-04-01)

A solution to the problem was sought in the exchange of letters that would express regrets for the collision, establish an investigatory body, and pave the way for the release of the American crew. It was said that a 1998 Sino-US Military Maritime Consultation Agreement might be used as a forum to reach new procedures to prevent collisions in the future. (IHT 7/8-04, 11-04-01)

On 11 April 2001 China announced it would release the US crew since the US had declared, in a letter from the US ambassador to the Chinese foreign minister, that it was "very sorry" that the entering of Chinese airspace and the landing of the US plane [at Hainan Island] did not have verbal clearance, and for the death of the Chinese pilot. The difference between the Chinese translation of the term "very sorry" by the Americans and the Chinese was significant. The crew members were flown out of China on 12 April 2001.

The two sides subsequently met several times to discuss the other aspects of the case, such as the release of the plane, the causes of the incident, recommendations on the prevention of collisions in the future, and a plan for the return of the US aircraft. From the beginning China had also demanded that the US stop conducting surveillance flights near the Chinese coast, but the US said it would continue since it considered these flights important for security in the region, particularly for Taiwan. In fact, the US resumed surveillance flights in early May. On its part the US side asked China to be less aggressive and more careful when its fighter planes intercept US surveillance planes, citing standard procedures worked out by the US and the Soviet Union during the Cold War. For some time the parties were unable to reach agreement on any of these matters. (IHT 12-04, 13-04, 20-04, 08-05-01)

In the course of the negotiations China allowed a US team to inspect the damaged plane, and the parties were considering US payments to China. (IHT 30-04, 02-05-01) Meanwhile China would not allow the plane to be flown out of the country in case of its return to the US. (IHT 09-05-01) The disassembled parts of the plane were finally packed in a cargo aircraft and flown off Hainan Island on 3 July 2001. (IHT 04-07-01)

The US rejected a Chinese claim of $1 million for the expenses relating to the 24-day stay of the US crew and the dismantling of the aircraft, while reaffirming its readiness to consider payment of the costs directly associated with the process of returning the aircraft, offering $34,567, which was considered unacceptable by China "both in its contents and form". (IHT 09-07, 21/22-07, 11/12-08, 13-08-01)

US meeting with the Dalai Lama

The US president had a "private meeting" with the Dalai Lama on 23 May 2001, the fiftieth anniversary of the 1951 agreement between China and Tibetan leaders that, from the Chinese perspective, marked the liberation of Tibet. In a later statement he offered his strong support to the Dalai Lama and the latter's efforts to initiate a dialogue with the Chinese government. China had been demanding that the Dalai Lama should first accept Tibet as being a part of China before launching talks. (IHT 23-05, 24-05-01)

US president's visit

During the US president's visit to China in February 2002 the US and China reached agreement neither on US policy relating to Iraq, nor on Chinese controls of weapons supply to other countries, nor on the lifting of US sanctions barring US companies from launching satellites on Chinese rockets. (IHT 22-02-02)

China – Vatican/Holy See

China attacked the Vatican over the latter's plans to canonize 120 Roman Catholic "martyrs" killed in China between 1648 and 1930. A spokesman asserted that many of these people committed "monstrous crimes against the Chinese people" and were executed for violation of Chinese laws during the invasion of China in the nineteenth century by imperialists and colonialists, especially the invasion by eight European powers in 1900 to suppress the anti-foreign, anti-Christian Boxer movement, or were killed during the Opium War (1839-1842). The canonizations took place on 1 October 2000.

China severed diplomatic relations with the Vatican in 1951 because the Vatican maintained its recognition of the Kuo Min Tang (Nationalist Party) government. It was reported, however, that the Vatican had already signalled its willingness to move its embassy from Taiwan to Beijing in exchange for a resumption of diplomatic relations. (IHT 27-09, 02-10-00)

In a message addressed to a symposium in Rome on Matteo Ricci, the 17th-century Jesuit missionary, the Pope on 24 October 2001 apologized for errors of the colonial past and pleaded for the establishment of diplomatic relations. The Chinese responded by saying it would earnestly study the Pope's plea. The foreign ministry spokesman reiterated the two principles on the matter to which China adhered: first, termination of the Vatican's diplomatic ties with Taiwan and recognition of the People's government at Beijing as the sole government of China; second, a promise not to interfere in China's internal affairs, including under the pretext of religious activities. [Some have referred to the Vietnamese compromise model, under which the Vatican agreed to appoint bishops in consultation with the government.] (IHT 25-10, 26-10-01)

India – Pakistan
See: Special territories within a state: Kashmir

India – Russia

On the occasion of a visit by the Russian president to India in early October 2000 the two countries signed a "Declaration of Strategic Partnership" on 3 October, pledging not to join any military or political blocs and also to avoid treaties or agreements that would infringe on each other's territorial integrity or sovereignty. The two sides would also inform each other of planned foreign policy initiatives and hold regular political consultations. They were also committed to close cooperation at the UN, to working together for the reduction and eventual elimination of nuclear weapons, and to halting nuclear proliferation. (IHT 04-10-00)

India – US

US missile defence and sanctions

To the surprise of many India said, in May 2001, that the US plans responded to "a strategic and technological inevitability". On its part India wanted the sanctions of 1998 (*see* 8 Asian YIL 303) lifted and the US to encourage Pakistan to rein in militants in Kashmir. It would also, it was said, eventually like to be able to buy nuclear reactors for civilian use from the US. (IHT 07-05-01)

The US law relating to the sanctions imposed on India in its original version already included a presidential competence to grant a waiver; in October 1999 the president was granted authority to remove all the sanctions imposed in 1998, on the condition that the president determine and certify to the Congress "that the application of the restriction would not be in the national security interests of the US". Whereas the previous president predicated a complete lifting on Indian signature of the Comprehensive Test Ban Treaty, its agreement not to deploy nuclear weapons and a freeze on fissile material followed by signature of the Fissile Material Cut-Off Treaty, the US attitude changed in 2001 when, in view of the Indian change of attitude (*see supra*), the US government decided to lift most of the sanctions, opening the doors to Indo-US military cooperation and to transfers of military and dual use technology. It was said that this policy shift amounted to a watershed and resulted from an altered appreciation of the Chinese threat to US hegemony in Asia. (IHT 03-09-01) A further lifting of sanctions took place in late September, apparently in appreciation of Indian help in the terrorism crisis resulting from the attacks in the US. (IHT 24-09-01)

Military and political ties
(*See*: Terrorism)

Iran – Europe

The EU foreign ministers on 17 June 2002 gave their agreement in principle to the opening of formal trade and cooperation negotiations with Iran without imposing explicit conditions, such as an improvement of the latter's human rights record. The EU also emphasized its opposition to extending US sanctions on Iran and Libya for five years. Apart from political and economic reasons, the EU pursuit of improved relations also resulted from the need for cooperation in the field of narcotics trade and for stemming the flow of refugees from the region, environmental issues, and the prevention of the spread of nuclear weapons. (IHT 19-06-02)

Iran – Japan

Japan and Iran reached a landmark agreement on 1 November 2000, giving negotiation rights to Japanese oil companies for appraisal and development of a specific area of the Azadegan oil field which has a potential production of 400,000 barrels of crude oil per day. The Japanese had been cautious in investing in Iran because under the (US) Iran-Libya Sanctions Act the US could impose sanctions on non-US companies that invest in Iran and Libya. (IHT 02-11-00)

Iran – Palestine

In early January 2002 a ship, the *"Karine A"*, which was laden with 50 tons of mortars, rockets, missiles and explosives and that apparently came from Iran heading towards Palestinian territory, was intercepted and seized by the Israelis in the Red Sea. The two parties denied allegations made by US and Israeli intelligence sources according to which a new agreement had been concluded between Iran and the Palestinians involving the supply of weapons and money. (IHT 25-03-02)

Responding to Western accusations that it armed and otherwise supported or even directed the Hezbollah militia in Lebanon, Iran repeated its standing denial by way of its foreign minister who emphasized in April 2002 that "Hezbollah is an independent organization and does not take orders from Iran. It makes decisions based on its own judgments". As to the legitimacy of *Hezbollah*'s activities he added: "It is Hezbollah's legitimate right to continue resisting until it liberates the remaining territories under occupation. … Only through resistance can one ward off aggression by Israeli aggressors." Iran admitted only providing political and financial backing to the organization. (IHT 17-04-02)

Iran – Russia

Following a Russian decision in November 2000 to restart arms sales to Iran the two countries concluded a military cooperation agreement on 2 October 2001, citing the promotion of the struggle against terrorism.

Russia suspended arms sales to Iran in 1995 under a secret US-Russian agreement in exchange for alternative deals with the US which, however, seemed not to have materialized. (IHT 03-10-01)

Iran – US

Mutual dissatisfaction

On the occasion of his presence in New York for participation in the UN Millennium Summit (September 2000) the Iranian president said in a news conference, *inter alia*, that relations between Iran and the US would improve only if the US apologized for past policies in Iran. In February 2000 the US Secretary of State had admitted that Iranians had reason to resent US intervention in the 1953 coup on behalf of the Shah [and for the overthrow of the government under Mohammed Mossadegh], but she did not apologize.

The US had somewhat relaxed its sanctions against Iran, but insisted that Iran end its support for militant Islamic groups, such as *Hezbollah*, although Iran emphasized that it had halted funding of the group years ago. The US also claimed that Iran had been seeking to develop weapons of mass destruction, in particular long-range missiles. (IHT 08-09-00)

The US explorations of closer ties with Iran were put to an end by the US president's inclusion of Iran in his "axis of evil" (*see infra* at xxx) The efforts also met setbacks by the incident in January 2002 involving the interception of the *"Karina A"* (*see infra* at 399) and when the US started accusing Iran of supplying arms, money and training to an Afghan militia commander in western Afghanistan (*see supra*: Afghanistan – Iran). (IHT 05-02-02)

Sanctions

Among the variety of US sanctions against Iran (*see* Asian YIL Vol.7:474, Vol.8:304) were those imposed by executive order, some which were mandated as a result of Iran's classification as a supporter of terrorism, and those imposed by the Iran-Libya Sanction Act (intended to level the playing field for US oil companies by extending to foreign companies the bans already imposed on US corporations). The latter act was to expire in August 2001.

In the past the US government had issued a waiver allowing some European investment in the Iranian energy industry, and in 2000 a small gesture was made by lifting a ban on the import of caviar, pistachio nuts and rugs. (IHT 12/13-05-01)

Alleged Iranian involvement in "Khobar Towers" bombing
(*See also:* 9 Asian YIL 401)

An indictment was issued in the US in the case concerning the "Khobar Towers" bombing of a US military housing complex in Saudi Arabia in 1996 which killed a number of US service members. While not naming any members of the Iranian government it was unambiguous about Iranian involvement. The US attorney general said Iranians had "inspired, supported and supervised" the action though admitting that there was insufficient evidence to make a case against any Iranians that would stand up in court. Iran rejected the allegations of involvement. (IHT 22-06, 23/24-06-01)

US attack on Iranian vessel

US speedboats attacked an Iranian-registered Saudi oil tanker in the Gulf on 19 December 2001. The tanker had been on its way to the southwestern Iranian port of Abadan when it came under attack. The Swiss ambassador in Tehran, whose country represented US interests in Iran, told that the US speedboats had mistaken the tanker for an Iraqi vessel smuggling oil. (IHT 20-12-01)

Japan – Africa

The Japanese prime minister in January 2001 visited several African countries, the first visit by a Japanese prime minister to sub-Saharan Africa. He said in South Africa that development support and conflict prevention would be the main features of Japan's support for the continent. Of the annual more than $10 billion Japanese development aid almost $1 billion was allocated to Africa, with Kenya, Tanzania and Zambia the biggest recipients. In 1987 Japan overtook the US as South Africa's leading trading partner. (IHT 10-01-01)

Japan – East Asia

Revisionist textbook issue

The government approval of a revisionist junior school history textbook, the *Junior High School Social Studies New History Textbook*, raised continued angry reaction and deep hostility from various East Asian countries, South Korea in particular. According to its critics the book sought to justify and play down Japan's Asian conquests. A group of revisionist Japanese historians had written the book, wanting to reawaken the pride of young people in their nation, but according to the critics the book distorted the truth.

The South Korean government presented thirty-five changes it wanted made in this and other books, and members of the South Korean parliament filed a suit in the Tokyo District Court seeking an injunction to prevent the textbook from being published. North Korea had also harshly condemned the book, and China had cancelled a planned visit by its second-highest leader while also presenting its own list of demanded changes. The Japanese government said that the book did not represent Japan's official view of history and resisted pressure to revise it. (IHT 19/20-05, 07-06, 10-07-01) In retaliation South Korea cancelled military exchanges and the introduction of Japanese cultural imports, and even recalled its ambassador in Japan by way of protest. (IHT 10-04-01) [It was reported that the school districts in Japan were one by one rejecting the use of the disputed history text.] (IHT 10-04, 13-07, 14-08-01)

Prime minister's attitude toward pacifism; visits to Yasukuni shrine

The new Japanese prime minister had made proposals toward breaking with official pacifism and revising the post-war constitution which barred Japan from raising an army. He also repeated an earlier announcement of April 2001 on his intention to visit the Shinto *Yasukuni* shrine in Tokyo, dedicated to Japan's war dead, on 15 August, the anniversary of the official end of World War II, a decision that enraged China and Korea. An especially stern warning, one that could even be considered as implying a lack of respect, to call off the visit was given by the Chinese foreign minister on the sidelines of the annual ASEAN meeting at Hanoi on 25 July 2001. (IHT 21-06, 26-07-01)

The controversial visit to the shrine took place on 13 August 2001. The prime minister made a gesture to the Chinese and Korean warnings by not going on 15 August which is the anniversary of the Japanese surrender in World War II. The visit was seen by the surrounding countries as paying homage to (the Japanese) war criminals. The prime minister sought to offset that appearance by stating that Japan had caused "immeasurable disaster and pain and left a still incurable scar on many people in the region. Japan should never again walk on the path to war. ... I wish, in light of our country's regrettable history, to take this to heart, to express my deepest regret and remorse toward all the victims of war."

[One Japanese prime minister had earlier made an "official" visit to the shrine, in 1985; others had made visits that they described as "private". The present prime minister declined to characterize his visit.]

Despite the Japanese attempts to mitigate its significance, the visit gave rise to renewed angry reactions from Korea and China. The South Korean government said that if the Japanese prime minister were "willing to cultivate genuine friendship and cooperation" with Japan's neighbours, he should "respect the positions and national sentiments of the countries concerned, based on a correct understanding of history." The Chinese government said the central question was whether the Japanese side could sincerely regret that aggressive period of history and comprehend "the feelings of the people of the Asian countries that suffered". (IHT 14-08-01)

After the visit and the reactions from other countries the Japanese prime minister said he wanted to meet those countries' leaders to try to mend ties, but there was a negative response (*see supra*: China-Japan; *infra*: Japan-South Korea) (IHT 25/26-08-01)

To the indignation of China and Korea the Japanese prime minister paid another visit to the shrine on 21 April 2002. (IHT 22-04-02)

Japan – North Korea

In August 2000 North Korea sent negotiators to Japan for a second round of talks (the first took place in April 2000, *see* 9 Asian YIL 401) aimed at establishing diplomatic relations. It demanded Japanese compensation and an apology for the past Japanese colonization, while Japan demanded information on alleged kidnappings in the past and guarantees that North Korea's missile program would not constitute a threat to it. The parties continued their negotiations in October 2000.

Early October Japan surprisingly announced a five-fold increase in its rice aid to North Korea, as a gesture to try to spur normalization talks. (IHT 27-07, 29/30-07, 31-07, 22-08, 25-08, 06-10, 18-10, 31-10, 01-11-00) [Negotiations between Japan and North Korea had been stalled for a decade. They began in 1991 but broke down after eight sessions (*see* Asian YIL Vol.2:330, Vol.3:399) and were resumed only in 2000.]

Japan – South Korea

In an attempt to calm down South Korean dissatisfaction with Japanese behaviour (*see supra*: Japan – East Asia) the Japanese prime minister apologized profusely during his visit in mid-October 2001 for former Japanese imperialism. (IHT 16-10-01)

Japan – South Asia

The Japanese prime minister paid a visit to India, Pakistan, and Nepal in August 2000, the first such visit in ten years. (IHT 16-08, 21-08-00)

Japan – US

Relations between the two countries suffered a setback when a collision of a US submarine with a Japanese fishing boat near Hawaii on 9 February 2001 resulted in the sinking of the fishing boat and the death of nine of its passengers. (IHT 12-02, 13-02-01)

Malaysia – Singapore
See: Straits

Myanmar – European Union

At a meeting in Laos in December 2000 between ministers from the EU and ASEAN, Myanmar agreed in principle to allow an EU mission to visit the country, without restrictions on whom the delegation could meet. The visit took place in late January. (IHT 17-01, 23-01-01)

North Korea – European Union

At the suggestion of the South Korean president the European Union despatched their own team of mediators to help invigorate the reconciliation process between North and South Korea and fill the breach left by the US's attitude of non-interest in talks with North Korea *(see infra:* South Korea – US). A delegation led by the Swedish prime minister had meetings in North Korea in early May. This move was accompanied by another step, namely, the establishment of diplomatic relations between the EU and North Korea. (IHT 26-03, 28-03, 31-3/01-04, 03-05, 15-05-01).

North Korea – Myanmar and Thailand

Myanmar remained the only ASEAN member state which refused to (re-)establish diplomatic relations with North Korea. The reason for this was the incident of 9 October 1983 when North Korean agents blew up the Martyrs' Mausoleum in Yangon in a bid to assassinate the visiting South Korean president. Myanmar thereupon severed relations and had not been willing to change its attitude before North Korea had admitted its act of terrorism and had officially apologized.

Thai-North Korean relations were disturbed in 1999 when North Korea sent a hit squad to Thailand to kidnap a defecting diplomat and his family. Diplomatic ties were, however, not severed, even though no official apology was offered. (IHT 27-07-00)

North Korea – Russia

The Russian president paid a visit to North Korea in July 2000, the first Russian leader (including preceding Soviet leaders) ever to do so. The visit marked some reversal in Russia's Korea policy since the Soviet Union made a policy shift in 1990 when the Soviet Union announced that it would enter diplomatic relations with South Korea and would demand hard currency from North Korea in payment for oil and other supplies. The policy shift resulted in a $3 billion South Korean loan to the Soviet Union. (IHT 20-07-00)

The North Korean leader visited Russia in July-August 2001. The meeting with the Russian president produced a joint declaration in which the two leaders gave expression to their views about various current issues. The declaration stated, *inter alia*, that the North Korean side "reiterated its position that the withdrawal of American troops from South Korea will endure no delay" and that "the Russian side expressed understanding of this position". (IHT 26-07, 07-08-01)

North Korea – US
(*See also:* Divided states: Korea; Nuclear energy matters)

Meetings

The chairman of the North Korean Supreme People's Assembly who was on his way to attend the UN Millennium Summit in early September 2000 in New York, where he was expected to have sideline talks with the South Korean and US sides, had to undergo a strip search at Frankfurt airport before boarding a US airline flight. In reaction to this incident the North Korean envoy decided to return home. The North Korean foreign ministry referred to the incident as having hurt the dignity of the North Korean people, and the North Korean ambassador to the UN said that "all these facts clearly show that the US is a rogue state." (IHT 06-09, 07-09-00)

In early October 2000 the two sides held talks at the UN on the issue of negotiations aimed at ending a stalemate over North Korea's development and export of missiles, followed by a meeting of the US president and the vice-chairman of the North Korean National Defence Commission on 10 October at Washington.

A joint communique issued after the meeting read, *inter alia*, that the two sides "have decided to take steps to fundamentally improve their bilateral relations in the interests of enhancing peace and security in the Asia-Pacific region", and that "[as] a first step ... neither government would have hostile intent toward the other", confirming "the commitment of both governments to make every effort in the future to build a new relationship free from past enmity". With regard to the specific US concern of North Korean missiles the communique read that North Korea "informed the US that it will not launch long-ranch missiles of any kind while talks on the missile issue continue".

It was said that by acting as host to the high North Korean official and agreeing on a return visit by the Secretary of State the US was trying to regain the initiative on Korea negotiations that it lost to South Korea as a result of the inter-Korean summit in the summer of 1999. Such a development would also, it was said, fulfil North Korea's ambition of dealing directly and bilaterally with the US. (IHT 04-10, 11-10, 13-10-00) The US Secretary of State went to visit North Korea on 22 October 2000, raising expectations of a subsequent visit by the US president. (23-10-00)

In the last few months of 2000 North Korea offered a complete halt to its exports of missiles and related technology and a freeze to the development of new missiles, but the parties could not resolve the issue of verification, and were not then able to discuss the question whether North Korea would destroy its existing stocks of missiles. (IHT 30/31-12-00/01-01-01)

Further developments

During the first couple of months of 2001 the newly elected US administration ruled out the possibility of resuming the negotiations begun under the previous US administration, pending a policy review, citing problems of verification of agreements on the freeze of the production, testing or export of missiles. This was interpreted as indicating a shift in US policy, although the US president wrote to his South

Korean counterpart that the US would "strongly support the South's engagement policy on the North". (IHT 10-05-01)

The US announced on 6 June 2001 that discussions would be resumed with the aim of restricting North Korean missile development, halting its missile exports, tightening inspections of nuclear facilities and easing military tension along the border with South Korea. It was reported that the policy review implied that an accord on the missile issue was no longer sufficient and that improved relations would have to include a comprehensive program on limiting the North Korean military potential. (IHT 08-06, 04-07-01)

The first meeting took place in New York on 13 June 2001. (IHT 15-06-01) The US wanted the negotiations to include the issue of conventional troop deployment before the removal of the 37,000 US troops from South Korea, and verifiability of any missile control agreement. Repeating its earlier position that it would not accept conditions for the resumption of talks, North Korea dismissed the US wish which marked a significant departure from previous US policy that focused almost exclusively on eliminating the threat of nuclear weapons and ending the testing and sale of ballistic missiles. (IHT 19-06, 10-07-01)

During his visit to South Korea in February 2002 the US president assured that, despite his designation of North Korea as part of an "axis of evil", the US had no intentions of invading or attacking the country. On the contrary: he said he fully supported the sunshine policy of reunification adhered to by the South Korean president (giving rise to the saying that Washington and Seoul were sleeping in the same bed but dreaming very different dreams), (IHT 21-02-02) and during his following visit to China the US president asked the Chinese president to convey to North Korea the US willingness to have talks. From the other side there was an offer in early April 2002 for a resumption of dialogue with the KEDO organization (*see* 5 Asian YIL 545 et seq. and *infra* at 386) and a further thaw set in, thanks to South Korean efforts, through a North Korean statement of willingness to receive a US envoy. (IHT 22-02, 04-04, 08-04, 11-04, 30-04-02)

Pakistan – US
(*See also*: China – US)

The US had been pressing Pakistan for months to play a greater role in efforts to dislodge Osama bin Laden from Afghanistan. The US had asked, *inter alia*, for the secret deployment of US special forces in northern Pakistan for the purpose of conducting operations inside Afghanistan to capture him. Having resisted for some time Pakistan agreed to meet a number of demands for cooperation under immense US pressure following the September 2001 attacks on the US. Among other things it consented to opening Pakistani airspace to possible missile attacks and aerial bombardments against Afghanistan. Pakistan would also share intelligence with the US on Osama bin Laden's operations and would try to tighten the illegal movement of supplies across Pakistan's borders into Afghanistan. It was later reported that Pakistan also permitted military logistical and technical personnel to operate at Pakistani air bases, naval ports and some other locations. The compliance with the US requests was seen as an effort to prevent retaliatory action against Pakistan and to restore international credibility since Pakistan was the state that was most instrumental in the Taleban's rise to power (*see* Asian YIL Vol.5:397, Vol.6:350). In fact, the Taleban had been useful to Pakistan, providing an ally on its western flank as balancing a perceived threat from India on its eastern flank. In a speech on 19 September the military ruler of Pakistan explained that he was facing a US ultimatum and that he felt that the country's very survival was at risk.

The issue of a joint US-Pakistani effort to force the Taleban to turn over Osama bin Laden had been discussed for more than a year. In an effort to demonstrate its compliance with UN sanctions against the Taleban (*see infra* at 391) Pakistan had frozen the accounts of the Afghan government in the State Bank of Pakistan as well as accounts being used by religious organizations in Pakistan to help finance the Taleban. It had also urged the Taleban to surrender Osama bin Laden in order to defuse US threats of retaliation. (*see supra*: Afghanistan – US) The message, repeated on 17 September 2001, also contained the prospect that if the surrender took place and if the training camps were closed down, the Taleban would be left to continue in power. On 4 October 2001 Pakistan even acknowledged that the US had produced strong enough evidence to indict Osama bin Laden.

On its part Pakistan was trying to have the existing US sanctions against Pakistan lifted and to obtain US support for international financial aid for Pakistan. The US sanctions against Pakistan and India imposed in 1998 were indeed eased in late September 2001.

During a visit to Pakistan in mid-October 2001 by the US Secretary of State (*see supra*: Afghan War) it was announced that the US planned to provide another $550 million in economic aid to Pakistan on top of the $50 million it dispersed shortly after the September attacks on the US, when Pakistan was asked to open its airspace and provide logistic support and basing facilities. Pakistan would also receive nearly $100 million to help control its borders and cope with an eventual refugee crisis. Besides, however, Pakistan wanted more debt relief than the already approved rescheduling of a $379 million debt. However, as late as April 2002 the US had been slow to deliver on promises of police assistance, and had not removed duties and quotas on Pakistani textiles. (IHT 14-09, 15/16-09, 17-09, 18-09, 20-09, 26-09, 03-10, 05-10, 12-10, 17-10-01, 02-04-02)

South Korea – Russia
(*See also:* North Korea – Russia)

The Russian president visited South Korea in late February 2001, the first time since 1992. (IHT 27-02-01)

In a joint communiqué the two presidents criticized the US for falling behind in its commitments to reduce the threat from nuclear weapons by failing to ratify relevant treaties. The South Korean president adhered to the Russian view that the 1972 Anti-Ballistic Missile Treaty was incompatible with the idea of a national anti-missile shield and was a "cornerstone of strategic stability". He also identified with the concerns among European powers that the US endeavours for a missile defence system were likely to spark a new round of nuclear competition. However, when pressed by US officials for an explanation the South Korean foreign ministry drew a careful distinction between endorsement of the 1972 Treaty and any conclusion that South Korea would view a system of missile defence as inevitably violating that Treaty.

The meeting also dealt with the Russian debt of $1.8 billion and the rehabilitation of a rail line connecting South Korea's ports and industrial centres with the Russia's Far East. (IHT 28-02, 01-03, 02-03-01)

South Korea – US
(*See also:* North Korea – US)

Status of Forces Agreement
Newspaper reports referred to long-standing South Korean irritation at the behaviour of US military in South Korea resulting in the desire to have the 1965 Status of Forces Agreement (SOFA) between the two states revised again (a previous revision took place in 1991). Such revision should abolish discrimination against South Koreans and should give South Korea the same powers as Japan had under the Japan-US SOFA.

Under the latter agreement custody of a US soldier who is indicted for a crime is automatically transferred to the Japanese authorities. Under the Korean SOFA, however, the defendant is not turned over to local authorities until after conviction or the exhaustion of all appeals. In addition, if a Japanese court acquits the US suspect, Japanese prosecutors have the right to appeal, whereas in the Korean case South Korean prosecutors did not have the same right. Conversely, by way of explanation of other differences from the Japanese SOFA, it was said that the US traditionally tried not to agree to deviations in Korean court practice from traditional US constitutional rights, such as the ban on double-jeopardy trials and the right to confront an accuser, neither of which was said to be protected under South Korean law. Similar concessions were indeed made in the Japanese SOFA because at the time the US was desperate to rush troops to Japan to be deployed to fight in the Korean War.

Early August 2000 agreement was reached on increased South Korean jurisdiction. Henceforth custody of US criminal suspects was to be transferred at the time of indictment. (IHT 25-07, 04-08-00)

Handling of the North Korean issue
The South Korean president visited the US in early March 2001 trying to persuade the new US president to give complete support to his "sunshine policy" with North Korea and to ask for US commitment to reconciliation with North Korea. For that purpose he would unqualifiedly endorse the South Korea-US security alliance which was called a comprehensive partnership.

There was a clear contrast between the South Korean approach of the issue of North Korea and that preferred by the then newly installed US government. South Korea was eager to engage North Korea in all respects, whereas the US preferred to keep distance and put pressure. (IHT 3/4-03, 06-03-01)

South Korea – Vietnam

The South Korean defence minister visited Vietnam in December 2000 for the first time since the Vietnam War. In that war South Korea fought alongside the US. (IHT 19-12-00)

(NON-)INTERVENTION
See: Inter-state relations etc.: China – Russia

JAPAN'S MILITARY ROLE
See also: Terrorism: Asian attitudes

Deployment of "Self-Defence Force"

In order to be able to contribute effectively to the US efforts in combating terrorism (*see infra* at 397) the Japanese government called on Parliament to enact a seven-point plan to allow the Japanese "Self-Defence Forces" to provide rearguard support for a US military action beyond "areas surrounding Japan" (*see* 8 Asian YIL 290). The changes proposed would give those forces much greater leeway for a broad range of rearguard roles. (IHT 28-09-01)

The legislation was passed by the Lower Chamber of Parliament on 18 October and by the Upper House on 29 October 2001, permitting the deployment of the Self-Defense Force to provide "logistic support" to US military operations against "terrorism" not necessarily in areas surrounding Japan. This essentially meant an extension of the initial "self-defence" restriction imposed on the Force, allowing the military to take part in war. Significantly the permission was limited to two years only.

On 8 November 2001 the Japanese government announced that it was sending two warships to the Indian Ocean for "information gathering" in support of US military operations in Afghanistan. (IHT 19-10, 09-11-01)

JURISDICTION
See: International humanitarian law: US treatment etc.; Inter-state relations etc.: China – US; State liability

KOREAN WAR
See: International humanitarian law

LABOUR
See: Association of South East Asian Nations; Sanctions

MILITARY ALLIANCE

Asia-Pacific alliances

At the end of 2000 the US had formal security agreements with five states in the Asia-Pacific area: Australia, Japan, South Korea, the Philippines, and Thailand.

The idea of a US-Pacific alliance was discussed in Canberra between Australian and US officials. It related to a US-led security alliance including the US, Australia, Japan and Korea. Such an alliance would resemble an Asian version of NATO and would be directed at containing China. It was said to reflect the Australian desire to keep the US militarily engaged in East Asia and to prompt Japan to play a greater role in maintaining regional security. (Straits Times 01-08-01)

MILITARY COOPERATION

Philippine – US cooperation
(*See also:* Insurgents; Terrorism)

US training and other cooperation with Philippine troops

The US in September 2000 offered to give counter-terrorism training to Philippine troops. About 200 US elite troops were then already in the Philippines to take part in "joint exercises", not "in response to the current hostage situation" *(see infra* at 398) The US was considering expanding the schedule of such exercises in the future, since "increased military cooperation between our countries is going to improve the bilateral security of both the Philippines and the US and contribute to regional security".

The "shoulder-to-shoulder" exercise by more than 600 US soldiers with the Philippine forces formally started late January 2002 (newspaper reports in mid-2002 already mentioned a number of 1,200). There were reports of last-minute negotiations over the so-called "terms of reference", dealing with, *inter alia*, who should be in command and what limits should be placed on the US forces. The "training" of Philippine forces by US military special forces would be completed in June 2002, yet turned out not even to have started in April when a proposal was discussed on assigning US special forces with Philippino troops at the company level (instead of at the previous, higher, battalion level). (IHT 16/17-09-00, 28-01, 30-01, 01-04, 26-04,10-06-02)

Subic Bay for rent

More than a decade after the US military bases were handed back to the Philippines (*see* 2 Asian YIL 345) it was reported that the Philippine government was considering transforming the Subic Bay deepwater port into a naval base for hire and inviting foreign navies, including that of the US, to dock, service and repair warships for a fee. (IHT 13-07-01)

China – US

The relationship between the US and Chinese military goes back to 1979, soon after the formal resumption of diplomatic relations, first focusing on bolstering the Chinese military against the Soviet Union, in exchange for intelligence concerning the Soviet invasion of Afghanistan. It included high-level military visits, port visits, exchanges between defence colleges and other cooperation. The program suffered a series of setbacks, such as the 1989 Tiananmen incident which lead to a suspension of the contacts, and the 1999 bombing of the Chinese embassy in Belgrade.

In the period under review mutual visits by high military officers took place, but in early May 2001 the US decided to downgrade its military contacts with China by reviewing them individually. (IHT 01-11, 03-11-00, 04-05-01)

India – US
(*See also:* Terrorism)

As a consequence of the war on terrorism the two countries built closer military ties. By early December 2001 a team of Indian and US military officials was scheduled to begin meeting as the "Defense Policy Group" to discuss ways of cooperating over the coming decades. (IHT 06-11-01) In mid-2002 there were already reports of the US sale of military equipment to India, Indian troops going to the US for exercises in Alaska, and US and Indian ships jointly patrolling the Strait of Malacca. (IHT 11-06-02)

Indonesia – US

Following moves in 2000 (*see* 9 Asian YIL 407) the participation by US warships in a joint exercise with the Indonesian navy in May 2001 sent another signal that the US wanted to restore closer links with the Indonesian armed forces and constituted a departure from the ban on military links imposed by the US in 1999 (*see* 9 Asian YIL 413). (IHT 19/20-05-01)

In late December 2001 the US legislature created a loophole to resume military training with Indonesia by way of setting aside an amount in the Defense Department Appropriations Act for establishing regional counter-terrorism training programs, bypassing the 1991 ban on military education and training for Indonesia retained in the Foreign Operations Appropriations Act. (IHT 27-12-01)

Iran – Russia
(*See*: Inter-state relations: Iran-Russia)

MISSILE TECHNOLOGY

Restrictions on Chinese export of missiles
(*See also:* Inter-state relations etc.: China-US)

After having been suspended for more than a year following the US bombing of the Chinese embassy in Belgrade, the high-level negotiations over missile exports were resumed, since November 1998.

In the US Senate the Thompson-Torricelli bill would require the government to monitor developments and would impose automatic sanctions on companies or states if there was "credible evidence" of certain exports, even though China had not signed the so-called Missile Technology Control Regime (*see* 1 Asian YIL 270; www.mtcr.info). There was the possibility that the government would have to accept the bill in order to win passage through the US Senate of a bill on permanent normal trading relations with China, part of the package of enabling China's entry into the WTO. (IHT 03-07, 05-07-00)

However, in November 2000 the US government announced a waiver of penalties against China after China had formally pledged on 21 November to end the supply of the suspected missile parts. The "waiver" meant that China would be exempted from sanctions even though the US government had determined that such exports had taken place. The Chinese declaration read: "China has no intention to assist, in any way, any country in the development of ballistic missiles that can be used to deliver nuclear weapons." There would be a formal system of export controls, including restrictions on "dual use" technology. (IHT 23-11-00)

However, when the US Secretary of State visited China in July 2001 the US formally protested to China about continued exports of missiles and related technology to Pakistan and other countries despite the Chinese pledge. But China said it had "kept to the letter" of its promises. (IHT 28/29-07, 09-08-01)

Iranian medium-range missile

Iran confirmed US reports in late May 2002 that it had conducted a test flight of the "Shahab-3", a missile with a range of 800 miles and capable of reaching Israel. Such test-flights had, however, already been reported much earlier, in July 2000. (The original version of the Shahab was tested in 1998.) (IHT 17-07-00, 27-05-02)

Iran – Israel

Israel accused Iran on 3 February 2002 of having supplied the *Hezbollah* organization in Lebanon with 8,000 missiles that could hit Israeli cities, and contended that North Korea had supplied Iran with a medium-range missile. Iran denied the Israeli assertion. (IHT 04-02, 06-02-02)

Iran – North Korea

On the occasion of a visit by the president of Iran to Japan the Iranian foreign minister on 31 October 2000 dismissed concerns voiced by Japan that it was developing missiles with technology provided by North Korea. He emphasized that Iran was developing missiles on its own. [Iran began an arms development program during its 1980-1988 war with Iraq to compensate for shortages caused by a US embargo.] (IHT 01-11-00, 27-05-02)

North Korea

(*See also:* Inter-state relations etc.: North Korea – US; Regional security)

A demand by North Korea to receive $1 billion annually in exchange for the dismantling of North Korea's missile export program was rejected by the US in July

2000 at three-day talks at Kuala Lumpur. Instead, the US negotiator said that North Korea could expect unspecified "benefits" from what was called the "normalization process". The US suspected North Korea of being a leading exporter of missile equipment and technology to countries such as Pakistan and Iran. (IHT 13-07-00)

On 19 July 2000 the Russian president divulged a North Korean proposal offering to abandon its missile program if it were provided with rockets to launch satellites into space. North Korea had been insisting that it had no program to develop long-range missiles for military purposes, and that its rockets were intended only to launch satellites and carry out space research. It had in fact halted flight tests as part of an understanding with the US. [North Korea tried to put a satellite in orbit in 1998 by using a three-stage Taepodong-1 missile. More recently it reportedly abandoned work on this missile in favour of a newer Taepodong-2 two-stage missile.] (IHT 20-07-00) The US seemed to reject the idea of making rocket boosters available, but was willing to consider launching satellites for North Korea from outside North Korean territory. (IHT 21-07, 22/23-07-00). The details of the idea constituted the subject of the talks between North Korean and US officials in Kuala Lumpur in early November, but these talks ended with no clear result although they were described as "detailed, constructive and very substantive". (IHT 29/30-07, 5/6-08, 02-11, 4/5-11, 06-11-00)

On 3 May 2001 North Korea promised to extend its 1999 moratorium on test-firing missiles (*see* 9 Asian YIL 408) until 2003 [the year when the five-year term of the South Korean president Kim Dae Jung would end] (IHT 04-05-01) but said it could not afford to stop selling missiles as "part of trade". The extension of the moratorium was promised despite the US freeze of talks (*see supra* at 376) which had in fact broken the 1999 understanding that the test moratorium was predicated on continued dialogue. [The 1999 moratorium came after the US promised to ease economic sanctions.] (IHT 05/06-05-01)

During a visit to Russia in July-August 2001 the North Korean leader repeated the above promise, saying in a joint declaration that North Korea's missile program "does not present a threat to nations respecting North Korea's sovereignty". (IHT 06-08-01)

South Korean missile plans

South Korea had expressed its wish to develop missiles within the limits of the Missile Technology Control Regime (MTCR) to which it was not a signatory but by the conditions of which it had promised to abide. Under this Regime the maximum range allowed is 300 kilometres. In the past the US was averse to South Korean proposals concerning missiles with a range beyond 180 kilometres, referring to a US-South Korean agreement of late 1979 under which that range was one of the conditions for US recognition of the government of General Chun Doo Hwan. In the aftermath of the North-South Korean summit meeting of June 2000, however, the US indicated its willingness to endorse the South Korean wishes. A range of 300 kilometres would enable South Korean missiles to reach most of North Korea. The South Korean plans were confirmed in January 2001.

The MTCR had 32 members. Among the non-members were the Middle Eastern countries, India, Pakistan, China, and North Korea. (IHT 13-07, 15/16-07-00, 18-01-01)

MONETARY MATTERS

Currency safety net

The efforts to set up an Asian currency safety net, the so-called "Chiang Mai initiative" *(see* 8 Asian YIL 293-294, 9 Asian YIL 409) were continued on the sidelines of the annual meeting of the Asian Development Bank in May 2001 at Hawaii.

Meanwhile, Japan has set up a system of bilateral agreements consisting of a $3-billion currency swap facility with Thailand, a $2-billion agreement with South Korea, and a $1-billion swap facility with Malaysia, all aimed at supplementing an existing $1-billion swap fund among ASEAN members and linking the foreign-exchange reserves of the ASEAN countries with those of Japan, China, and South Korea. The Japanese swap agreements were in addition to a $2.5-billion swap deal with Malaysia and a $5-billion agreement with South Korea, both part of a $30-billion "Miyazawa Initiative" (named after the Japanese finance minister of the time). (IHT 11-05-01; FEER 12-07-01)

NUCLEAR ENERGY MATTERS
See also: Inter-state relations: North Korea – US

Iran – Russia

During a visit by the Iranian president to Russia in March 2001 Russia repeated its intention to assist in completing the long-stalled nuclear power plant at Bushehr *(see* 5 Asian YIL 477). It was further reported that Iran would sign up for a second Russian-built nuclear reactor. (IHT 16-03-01)

Myanmar nuclear ambitions

It was reported that Myanmar was negotiating the building of a research nuclear reactor with Russian financial and technical help. The project would be built in accordance with IAEA guidelines and could not easily be transformed to produce nuclear weapons. The agreement in principle was already reached in early 2001.

Myanmar had been member of the IAEA since 1957, had acceded to the non-proliferation treaty in 1992 and had agreed to a protocol allowing inspections in 1995. (IHT 14/15-07-01)

North Korean complex at Kumchangri

It was reported that the second US inspection of the site in May 2000 *(see* 9 Asian YIL 410) confirmed earlier findings that it did not constitute a violation of North Korea's commitment to freeze its plutonium reprocessing. (IHT 07-08-00)

The 1994 Agreed Framework and the Korean Peninsula Energy Development Organization (KEDO)

It was reported by analysts that the US was "wearying of its role as the major power behind KEDO" and "just wants to stop the project. They are looking for excuses." In line with these rumours it was reported that the two main (South Korean) contractors were being liquidated. (IHT 09-11-00) From the US side the following problems were raised: (1) The power grid in North Korea was too outdated and too severely damaged to be able to deal with the output of the projected reactors; (2) the unwillingness of North Korea to halt the spread of nuclear weapons which constituted a prerequisite for the US to supply the material and technology needed for the reactors; (3) the possibility for North Korea to extract weapons-grade material from the reactors; (4) the withdrawal by North Korea of half of its workers from the site, demanding a huge increase in their pay beyond the amount agreed upon, and its failure to cooperate on training workers and technicians to man the project, and (5) the tripling of the price over the past five years for the heavy fuel oil the US agreed to provide until the reactors were ready for use. Besides, the US had sought to persuade North and South Korea to build just one reactor instead of two and replace the second with a conventional power plant. There were also reports that the US even wanted to abandon the whole idea of nuclear plants and build conventional plants instead. These considerations led to pronouncements according to which the whole project was "close to being dead" and that implementation was "at a glacial pace". It was said that under these circumstances the reactors could not go into operation for at least another ten years. (IHT 26-02-01)

Impatient with hints by the new US government that had recently taken office about the need for a policy review with respect to North Korea (*see supra* at **xxx**), the latter threatened on 22 February 2001 to abrogate the Agreed Framework by way of retaliation: "If the United States does not fulfill the agreed framework, we don't have to be bound by it any longer." (IHT 23-02-01)

In early March 2001 the US official who negotiated the Agreed Framework in 1994 also suggested that the agreement should be revised so as to provide conventional rather than nuclear power plants, while South Korea responded with alarm to calls by members of the US Congress and US administration for such a review. (IHT 08-03-01) On 8 March 2001 the US Secretary of State, testifying before the US Senate Foreign Relations Committee, said the US government had reservations about the 1994 agreement and said it might want to "revisit or change" some of its provisions. (IHT 09-03-01) Later in the month a bipartisan group on Korea of the (US) Council on Foreign Relations urged the president to consider such revision, contending that the agreement "deferred the difficult dismantling of North Korea's nuclear program". (IHT 27-03-01) On the other side North Korea accused the US of failing to live up to its obligation of completing the reactors by 2003 (*see* 5 Asian YIL 556, Art.III of the Agreed Framework). North Korea asked for compensation for the delays and had threatened to resume work on its frozen reactors unless such compensation was paid, but the US dismissed these requests, denying any binding date for the completion in the agreement. Meanwhile, the IAEA and North Korea held talks in late May 2001 on verification of Korean compliance with the 1994 agreement. (IHT 25-05, 07-06-01)

In March 2002 the US government for the first time since 1994 refused to certify that North Korea was complying with its commitments under the 1994 accord, but nonetheless decided to continue fulfilling the US obligations under the agreement. It was emphasized that by refusing the certification the US was not accusing North Korea of violating the agreement. (IHT 21-03-02) It was reported in April 2002 that the building of the two promised nuclear power reactors would reach the stage of pouring concrete. (IHT 20/21-04-02)

OIL AND GAS
See also: Inter-state relations etc.: Iran – Japan

East Timor – Australia

After the break of East Timor from Indonesia negotiations between UNTAET on behalf of East Timor and Australia started in 2000 in order to come to new though provisional revenue-sharing rules for the oil and gas fields between northern Australia and East Timor which were determined as a Joint Petroleum Development Area. The aim was an agreement that would give East Timor much greater resources than the 1989 Timor Gap Treaty awarded to Indonesia, and which would generate annual revenue of between $100 million and $500 million for the new state. The *Timor Sea Treaty* was finally signed on 20 May 2002, the first day of East Timor independence. It awarded East Timor 90 per cent of the profits of exploitation. Besides the treaty other arrangements were also made regarding the conditions for the exploitation of other oil and gas fields.

East Timor and Australia were, furthermore, to start negotiations over a redrawing of the sea-bed boundaries. Such redrawing in accordance with the principles as contained in the UN Convention on the Law of the Sea would greatly favour East Timor. In view of its interests Australia announced on 25 March 2002 that it would henceforth exclude its disputes on maritime boundaries from the jurisdiction of the International Court of Justice and the International Tribunal for the Law of the Sea. (IHT 21-05-01, 17-05, 21-05-02)

ORGANIZATION OF THE ISLAMIC CONFERENCE

Position on terrorism

At the initial suggestion of Iran the OIC held a one-day conference at Doha, Qatar on 10 October 2001. The meeting produced a policy statement which "rejected the targeting of any Islamic or Arab State under the pretext of fighting terrorism", but made no criticism of the ongoing bombing campaign. In that spirit the OIC called for future battles against terrorism to be waged under the UN flag, and to be defined narrowly so as to exclude Palestinian and Lebanese fighters. The OIC rejected any linking between terrorism, on the one hand, and the rights of Islamic and Arab people "to self-determination, self-defence, sovereignty" and "resistance against Israel and foreign occupation", on the other. There was no determination of what action the member states would take in the event of a US assault on other states (the foreign minister of the host state acknowledged: "We don't have a strategy") and the brevity of the meeting was said to have reflected the decision not to take up controversial proposals.

From 1 to 3 April 2002 the OIC held an extraordinary session of foreign ministers at Kuala Lumpur on the topic of terrorism. At this meeting the Malaysian prime minister focused on the importance of defining the concept of terrorism and identifying the identity of terrorists, and the necessity of distinguishing between acts of terrorism and people's struggle for independence. He objected to the linking of Muslims to terrorism, and called on Muslims everywhere to "condemn terrorism once it is clearly defined". He also called for examining the causes of terrorism in order to eliminate its motives, foremost among which are poverty, injustice and oppression. The *Iranian* delegate argued that it was not the responsibility of Muslims to define terrorism, but that the international community should start a process of defining.

The conference produced a declaration, the *Kuala Lumpur Declaration on International Terrorism*, of 3 April 2002, according to which the participants pledged, *inter alia*, to "work towards the early conclusion of a Comprehensive Convention on International Terrorism" and to "work towards an internationally agreed definition of terrorism and terrorist acts, which shall be differentiated from the legitimate struggle and resistance of peoples under colonial or alien domination and foreign occupation for national liberation and self-determination". [The OIC was founded in response to a 1969 arson attack on Al Aqsa Mosque in Jerusalem, carried out by an Australian tourist.] (IHT 08-10, 11-10-01, 02-04, 03-04-02; www.oic-oci.org; www.nationalreview.com)

PIRACY

Relevance for Asia

According to the International Maritime Bureau (maritime) pirate attacks rose by more than 63 per cent worldwide in the first nine months of 2000, with more than two-thirds occurring in Asian waters, most of which in Indonesian sea-lanes. This was to be seen against the backdrop that 33 per cent of all shipping moved through Southeast Asian waters, with over 600 vessels a day passing the Malacca Straits and the South China Sea.

It was said that many countries in the region seemed to be unwilling to prosecute offenders for acts of piracy committed in international waters and prefer instead to deport them. [As late as 1999 only four Asian states adhered to the 1988 Convention for the Suppression of Unlawful Acts Against the Safety of Maritime Navigation, namely China, India, Japan, and Turkmenistan. Of these India had not yet given its consent to be bound. (*see* Asian YIL Vol.6:256, Vol.8:183). States parties to the Convention are entitled to prosecute persons caught in their territorial waters for acts of piracy committed within another country's jurisdiction.]

REFUGEES
See also: Diplomatic and consular immunity

Afghan refugees to Pakistan

Pakistan closed its borders to refugees from Afghanistan after two decades of providing shelter. A deluge of new refugees had swelled the number of Afghan refugees in the country to 2.1 million. Pakistani officials said they simply could no longer handle the influx, in terms of money as well as of resources. A secondary reason for the closure was security concerns, following a series of unexplained bombings in Pakistani cities in 2000. Pakistan (as well as Iran) wanted the Afghans to return to their country. It was conceded, however, that it would be difficult to seal the mountainous border between Pakistan and Afghanistan. (IHT 11/12-11-00)

Refugees from Myanmar

Both the Thai and Myanmarese governments were of the opinion that the civil war in Myanmar involving the ethnic minorities had ended and that it was safe to repatriate refugees. Although the Thai government accordingly agreed in late July 2001 to send all Myanmarese refugees in Thailand back, the UN urged a reconsideration in view of continued fighting between Karen National Union fighters and the Myanmar army. Consequently, the repatriation was temporarily suspended. (FEER 06-09-01)

REGIONAL SECURITY

Asian attitudes toward US plans for anti-missile defence system

During a visit to Italy in early July 2000 the Chinese premier said that the US plan for a "theater missile defence (TMD) system" in East Asia would draw Taiwan into its sphere of protection, which would be an interference in Chinese affairs and a resumption of the US military alliance with Taiwan that was abrogated in the 1970s. On the occasion of a visit by the US Defense Secretary later in the month China repeated its demand that the US drop its plans for an anti-missile defence system, warning that it would link its disarmament policy to the US decisions on the system. It was said this implied that if the US would export technology for a "theater missile-defense system" [to be distinguished from the so-called "*national* missile-defence system" or NMD, meant for the protection of the US national territory] on the island of Taiwan, China would continue to engage in missile-technology sales to Pakistan and possibly other countries. It was said that North Korea on its part also said that it would link a decision to curb its missile exports to whether the US dropped its missile-defence plans.

It was reported that China found spurious the US arguments for its plans according to which the missile defence system would be a way to defend the US and US forces abroad against attack from states such as Iran, Iraq, and North Korea. Conversely, the Chinese argument was that the defensive missiles would cancel out

China's nuclear deterrent consisting of a small force of long-range missiles and compel it to build a stronger strike force.

Because of the missile-defence issue China had also taken steps to block US-backed disarmament proposals. Among other comments it was said that at the UN Disarmament Conference China had upheld talks on a treaty to cut off the production of fissile material and instead wanted the conference to focus on a treaty to limit or control space-based weapons systems.

At a foreign ministers' meeting of the G-8 countries in July 2000 in Japan participants in the meeting warned that a US national missile defence system would not be welcomed by key US allies. They feared a missile proliferation as the 'domino' result of such a system. Instead they urged the preservation of the 1972 Anti-Ballistic Missile Treaty as a "cornerstone of strategic stability". This stand was also taken by the Chinese and Russian presidents during a regional Central Asian summit meeting early July 2000 in Tajikistan (*see supra* at 362). (IHT 07-07, 10-07, 12-07, 14-07-00)

In May 2001 a US envoy was sent to China to try to convince the Chinese that the missile defence project would not be directed against China, but against smaller, worrisome countries, yet leaving open the possibility of protecting Taiwan against a missile attack. (IHT 15-05-01)

Visit of US naval unit to "enhance peace and security within the region"

In light of militia activity in West Timor resulting in the destruction of the UNCHR premises and the killing of, *inter alia*, three UN refugee workers (*see supra* at 338), three US amphibious assault ships and a guided missile cruiser arrived off East Timor on 14 September 2000. The fleet carried 4,000 soldiers and marines. A US Marine Corps statement said the visit was designed to enhance "peace and security within the region". (IHT 16/17-09-00)

RIVERS

Mekong (Lancang) River navigation

The 1995 Agreement on Cooperation for the Sustainable Development of the Mekong River Basin (*see* Asian YIL Vol.5:591, Vol.6:446) had been followed on 20 April 2000 by an agreement between China, Laos, Myanmar and Thailand on commercial navigation. The agreement would open a major shipping route from Simao in the Chinese province of Yunnan to Thailand, via Myanmar and Laos. The work required for such a shipping route would have to deal with falling water levels, shoals and rapids and the Khone Falls in southern Laos. (IHT 31-07-01)

Danav River dam project

India had begun to dam the Danav River at a place just a few hundred metres from the Nepalese border south of Lumbini in order to manage the river's flow, mainly for irrigation purposes. Nepal had asked for the project to be stopped as it allegedly threatened to flood villages in the area including Buddha's birthplace. India responded early August 2001 by stopping the construction of the river embankment. (IHT 01-08, 02-08-01)

SANCTIONS

See also: Environmental protection; Inter-state relations etc.: China – US, Iran – US

US sanctions

(*See also*: Inter-state relations etc.: Iran – US)

The start of a new US presidency in January 2001 offered an opportunity for the presentation of the following data on US sanctions with relevance to Asian countries: about 75 countries were subject to US sanctions. The reasons for these sanctions ranged from mislabelling cans of tuna to engaging in egregious human rights violations and narcotics trafficking. Almost half of the 125 unilateral economic sanctions imposed by the US since World War I were started between 1993 and 1998. In contrast, the UN enforced sanctions against fewer than a dozen countries. One of the sets of UN sanctions promoted by the US were those against Afghanistan. (IHT 23-01-01)

In July 2001 the US Congress voted overwhelmingly to extend the 1996 sanctions against Iran and Libya (*see* 7 Asian YIL 474) for another five years. The sanction law gave the president the authority to bar or reduce imports of goods from foreign companies that invest in Iran or Libya. He could also block such companies from selling to the US government or obtaining more than $10 million a year in American bank loans. The new House of Representatives and Senate bills also amended and tightened the existing law by lowering the maximum allowable investment in Iran from $40 million to $20 million. (IHT 27-07-01)

UN Security Council sanctions against Afghanistan

Sanctions were imposed under UN Security Council resolution 1267(1999) (*see supra*: Hand-over for penal purposes). A report of mid-August 2000 by the UN relief office for Afghanistan said that the embargo was having a tangible negative effect on the country and on efforts to help the Afghan people. (IHT 30-08-00)

The Taleban movement vowed on 10 December 2000 to shut down UN offices if the UN would impose more sanctions on Afghanistan. (IHT 11-12-00) Despite UN concerns of the consequences of further sanctions the Council on 19 December adopted resolution 1333 (2000) as proposed by the US and Russia, with China and Malaysia abstaining from a vote. The resolution, which was adopted under Chapter VII of the UN Charter, demanded, *inter alia*, compliance with the previous resolution 1267, especially the turn-over of Osama bin Laden and the closure of "camps where terrorists are trained". (IHT 20-12-00) The Taleban responded by pulling out of UN-mediated peace talks on ending the civil war and ordering a boycott of products from the US and Russia. (IHT 21-12-00)

ILO sanctions against Myanmar
See also: ASEAN, *supra* p. 341

The governing body of the International Labour Organisation agreed on 16 November 2000 that countries go ahead with sanctions against Myanmar because of the country's use of forced labour. However, fifty-two out of the fifty-six members opposed the move, and it was reported in June 2001 that not a single country had responded to the call with any concrete action. The reason given for this negative response was that sanctions like a ban on textile exports would as such violate WTO rules. The sanctions would be applied under an article of the ILO constitution that had never been used before in ILO history for that purpose. (IHT 17-11-00, 06-06-01)

SELF-DETERMINATION

East Timor
The territory of East Timor became an independent state on 20 May 2002.

SPECIAL TERRITORIES WITHIN A STATE: KASHMIR

Cease-fires, talks and tensions
The main Islamic guerrilla group in Indian-administered Kashmir, the Hizbul Mujahidin, held talks with the Indian government on 3 August 2000, vowing to implement the cease-fire which was unilaterally declared by the group on 24 July 2000. The talks started a day after a wave of shootings left more than hundred people dead. It was the first such meeting since 1989 when militants began their war for independence or for accession to Pakistan. The *Hizbul Mujahidin* consisted largely of local Kashmiri youth and was led by former Kashmiri politicians. When it announced its truce, it was expelled by the umbrella association of guerrilla factions, the *United Jihad Council*.

The group demanded that India began joint talks with Pakistan and the militants over the future of Kashmir which was rejected by India. The rebels then called off the cease-fire on 8 August and the spiral of violence started again. (IHT 25-07, 04-08, 14-08-00)

On 19 November 2000 India surprisingly announced a unilateral cease-fire for the Muslim vasting month of Ramadhan, but this was snubbed by both the militant groups and Pakistan. The *Hizbul Mujahidin* said the cease-fire meant nothing unless it included a pledge to begin talks with both the Kashmiris and Pakistan (India resisted Pakistani participation until it stopped its alleged military support to the guerrillas). (IHT 21-11-00)

Although the cease-fire was holding, the *Hizbul Mujahidin* on 29 November reiterated the group's condition for peace talks: the release of prisoners, the inclusion of Pakistan in negotiations and the withdrawal of Indian soldiers from Kashmir to the pre-1989 level. (IHT 30-11-00) In early December the Pakistani foreign ministry stated that Pakistan would accept bilateral talks between India and the Kashmiri provided they would lead to three-way negotiations. (IHT 05-12-00)

On 20 December both India and Pakistan announced steps to lessen tensions. India announced an extension of its unilateral cease-fire and Pakistan announced a partial withdrawal of troops along the Line of Control. (IHT 21-12-00) A further one-month extension of the cease-fire was announced in late January 2001 despite a series of sensational attacks by Pakistan-based Islamic militants. As to talks the Indian side said that a resumption of the talks that broke off in 1999 (*see* 8 Asian YIL 277, 308) after a Pakistan-backed incursion into Kashmir still awaited a more "conducive atmosphere". (IHT 24-01-01) A further Indian extension of the cease-fire on 21 February was, however, rejected by the guerrilla groups. (IHT 22-02-01).

On 23 May 2001 India called off its cease-fire and instead invited the Pakistani president for talks, the first such offer since the war over the Himalayan region in 1999 (*see* 9 Asian YIL 417). (IHT 24-05-01) The response was positive and a summit meeting started at Agra, India, on 15 July 2001. (IHT 21-06, 16-07-01) The two-day summit failed to produce agreement on the Kashmir dispute, but the parties agreed to continue the dialogue. (IHT 17-07-01)

Guerrilla violence surged from September 2001; on 1 October a suicide bombing and subsequent fighting occurred at the state legislature building of the Indian part of Kashmir, resulting in growing tensions between the two countries. (IHT 16-10-01)

On 13 December 2001 a group which India believed to be members of a Pakistan-based militant organization carried out a suicide attack on the Indian Parliament building in New Delhi. (IHT 15/16-12-01) India demanded that Pakistan take steps against the organizations while Pakistan denied that it or the organizations were involved. It committed itself to take action against anyone whose involvement could be proven, but even where steps were contemplated it was said that the government had to move cautiously because the organizations enjoyed broad popular support. [When the Kashmiri insurgency entered a violent phase 12 years ago, it was mostly indigenous. Pakistan first gave only political support to the separatists, but it was said that over the years it increasingly provided military support, drawing on the 80,000 fighters whom Pakistan had trained and armed to fight the Soviet Union in Afghanistan. (IHT 28-05-02)]

Signalling its anger over the attack India recalled its High Commissioner in Islamabad, for the first time in 30 years, and suspended bus and train services between the two countries. (IHT 22/23-12-01) Escalating tensions led to the deployment of large military forces along the border and the reciprocal imposition of sanctions, such as a ban of each other's aircraft to use the national airspace and the expulsion of part of each other's diplomatic mission. (IHT 28-12-01) There was even an exchange of mortar fire at the cease-fire line dividing Kashmir. (IHT 29/30-12-01)

In an effort to defuse tension Pakistan on 30 December 2001 arrested the head of one of the organizations accused by India of having carried out the 13 December attack, and on 12 January 2002 the Pakistani president, vowing that Pakistan would not be used as a staging ground for terrorism in the name of the Kashmiri cause, held a speech announcing a broad ban on militant groups among which two that had been accused of fomenting violence against India. Besides, more than 1,500 Islam activists were arrested. On the other hand, the Pakistani president reiterated his pledge that Pakistan would never give up its support for the "freedom struggle" in Kashmir. For its part India ruled out a troop withdrawal before Pakistan had curbed "cross-border terrorism" and handed over 20 alleged criminals wanted by India. India justified its tough stance as part of the international war against terrorism (*see infra* at 395 et seq.).

On 14 May 2002 another deadly attack took place on the outskirts of the Indian state of Jammu and Kashmir. Pakistan denied involvement but made a conciliatory gesture by arresting the head of the militant groups allegedly involved.The incident seriously added to the existing tensions to such an extent that Pakistani military circles expected an Indian attack across the Line of Control. At the same time, however, they took the position that because Kashmir was a disputed territory, an attack would not be taken as a breach of an international boundary and therefore would fall short of all-out war. Yet the deteriorating situation led to Indian and Pakistani troops' starting to trade heavy fire across the border in the south of Jammu and Kashmir and the expulsion of the Pakistani ambassador by India..

In the following days, while conducting a series of missile tests after advance notice to India, the president of Pakistan announced that infiltration of Islamic militants into Indian-held Kashmir had stopped and on 6 June 2002 pledged to permanently halt the infiltration of Islamic guerrillas into Indian Kashmir. At the same time, however, it accused India of sponsoring terrorism in Pakistan and demanded a renewal of direct talks with India. On the Indian part the defence minister said that large numbers of Al Qaeda members and Taleban fighters had retreated into Pakistan-controlled Kashmir.

De-escalation of the tension between the two countries set in thanks to US mediation and pressure, which was followed by the lifting of a five-month-old Indian ban on Pakistani commercial aircraft flying over India and the selection of a new ambassador to Pakistan. (IHT 31-12-01/01-01, 14-01, 15-01, 16-01, 02-04, 11/12-05, 15-05, 17-05, 18/19-05, 20-05, 25/26-05, 27-05, 28-05, 29-05, 11-06-02)

STATE LIABILITY

US court verdicts against Iran

A US District Court awarded damages to the estate and family of a person who had been held hostage in Lebanon by a group that the Court classified as having been founded and controlled by the Iranian government and the Iranian Ministry of Information and Security. (IHT 04/05-08-01)

In another case US citizens who were held hostage in Tehran in 1979 had brought a lawsuit before a US federal court against Iran in 2000. Iran did not contest the suit on, the grounds of alleged lack of jurisdiction of the US court, resulting in a default verdict for the plaintiffs in August 2001. The US government subsequently asked the federal judge to throw out the case. (IHT 17-10-01)

STRAITS

Johor Strait Bridge project

In 2001 Malaysia and Singapore agreed in principle to build a new suspension bridge over the strait to replace the existing bridge (causeway) which blocks shipping and bars access to Malaysian ports in Johor state. There were, however, obstacles to the effectuation of the project due to disagreements on other matters such as the price of the Malaysian water supply to Singapore. According to news reports Singapore alleged the existence of an agreement to build the suspension bridge by 2007 while the Malaysian side was said to deny the existence of such agreement.

Consequently Malaysia drafted a plan of its own, consisting of the building of a 1.1 kilometre, steep and sweeping curved bridge segment to replace its half of the existing causeway, including a railway bridge. The bridge would be high enough to allow ships to pass underneath and offer complete access through the strait, enabling ships to bypass Singapore in proceeding to Northeast Asia. It may also cause the return of a great amount of Malaysian cargo to Malaysian ports from being ferried through Singapore ports in order to circumvent the causeway. It might thus create the possibility for Malaysia to develop the port of Tanjung Pelepas at the southwestern tip of Johor state as a cargo and transshipment hub, competing with Singapore.

Land reclamation

Singapore had been carrying out land-reclamation projects since 2001. They would provide 4,900 hectares of land within the limits of its current territorial waters.

Malaysia charged that these activities would narrow the shipping lanes between Singapore Island and Johor state which form the entry to the Malaysian ports of Tanjung Pelepas and Pasir Gudang. Singapore denied this and emphasized that the reclamation work would neither degrade the water quality in the strait, nor change the width or depth of navigation channels, affect the water flow, cause flooding or harm fishing. (FEER 21-02, 18-4-2002)

TERRORISM
See also: Asia Pacific Economic Cooperation; Association of South East Asian Nations; Inter-state relations etc.: Afghanistan – US; Organization of the Islamic Conference; Protection of foreign nationals

Asia and the US "war on terrorism"
(*see also*: Inter-state relations: Afghanistan-US, Pakistan-US)

On 14 September 2001 the US State Department summoned foreign ambassadors and presented them with a four-point message about terrorism. The ambassadors from various various parts of the world, among which Asian countries, were told that the US expected their countries to arrest terrorists, to prevent terrorists from moving across their borders, to speak out forcefully against the kind of violence unleashed on 11 September 2001 and to join international efforts to combat terrorism. Avoiding any distinction between politically different categories of states it was said: "We will not rule out the possibility of any country working with the US and the international community in the fight against terrorism." (IHT 17-09-01)

The Taleban regime in *Afghanistan* vowed on 16 September to continue to shelter Osama bin Laden and announced it would declare war on any country that cooperated in an attack against Afghanistan.

Most Asian states, however, expressed sympathy with the US in connection with the "11 September" attacks and announced support in its "war against terrorism".

India welcomed the US decision to use military might against terrorists and the states that harbour them, and eagerly offered military cooperation. It was expected to share intelligence on the location of Afghan and Pakistani training camps, and offered access to Indian military bases for the refuelling of US aircraft. It was said that India would even allow US troops and equipment temporarily to be based on Indian soil, for the first time in the country's history. On the other hand, India asked the US to outlaw the Pakistan-based militant group *Jaish-e-Mohammed*, which was accused of an attack in the Indian state of Jammu and Kashmir on 1 October 2001 (*see supra* at 393), and freeze its assets, as the US had done with other "terrorist organizations" since the 11 September attacks in the US. Although the US froze the assets of *Lashkar-e-Taiba* in December 2001, branding it as "a stateless sponsor of terrorism", it was reported that India became increasingly concerned over US efforts to pamper Pakistan. The growing tensions between India and Pakistan since late 2001 and the first half year of 2002 gave rise to an intriguing question for the US in light of its pursuit of a global campaign against terror: what should it do when two important allies exchange accusations of terrorism?

A *Russian-Central Asian* initiative was unveiled at a meeting at Dushanbe, Tajikistan, of senior officials from India, Iran, Uzbekistan, Tajikistan, Russia, and the Afghan Northern Alliance (which was still recognized by most states as the legitimate Afghan government). The Dushanbe group sought a global alliance to reconcile the warring factions in Afghanistan, a government of national unity through elections and stopping the inflow of arms and close down the training camps.

The cooperation of the US with *Uzbekistan* in conducting joint covert operations against the Taleban and its terrorist allies had in fact existed since well over a year before the September 11 attacks. A detailed agreement was concluded in October 2001, allowing the US to station ground troops and airplanes at an Uzbek air base.

Also *Tajikistan* had granted permission for US warplanes to use its airfields (with Russian blessing), and it was reported in early November 2001 that Tajikistan had also reached tentative agreement with the US on military cooperation that could lead to US air strikes from Tajik territory.

Pakistan on 15 September 2001 pledged its "full support" in the hunt for the perpetrators of the attacks on the US, but carefully avoided any specific commitment to provide bases in Pakistan for ground operations or for direct Pakistani participation in military strikes. Yet the Pakistani president said that his country risked "very grave consequences" if it did not back a US-led campaign and that such policy could "endanger our very existence". On 28 March 2002 US FBI agents in fact joined

Pakistani police in raids against Al Qaeda and Taleban fugitives in northern Pakistan. While the raids were described as a Pakistani operation with US cooperation, they were in fact US-driven with the local authorities informed only hours before. The arrested persons were turned over to the US (*see supra* at 354) (IHT 30/31-03, 02-04-02). In late April 2002 it was even reported (though denied by Pakistani military circles) that covert US military units had been conducting operations within Pakistan and had participated in attacks on suspected Al Qaeda hideouts. But it was reported that Pakistan resisted US pressure to mount large-scale attacks against remaining concentrations of Al Qaeda fighters in western Pakistan. (IHT 26-04, 30-04, 02-05, 13-05, 14-06-02)

The *Japanese* prime minister said that, constrained by its constitution, the country would not be able to join military action alongside the US but he had nevertheless pledged "all possible and necessary cooperation" to the US. In this context it would take action for the amendment of a controversial law of 1999 (*see* 8 Asian YIL 290) in order to enable Japanese logistic support for US military operations beyond "areas surrounding Japan" (*see supra* at 380). The prime minister said that in case of military action, Japanese ships would be sent to help the US gather intelligence, deliver supplies, and provide medical services and humanitarian relief. Among the non-military measures there was a plan to provide emergency economic aid to Pakistan and India as part of efforts to solicit their cooperation.

On 18 September 2001 *China* issued a statement supporting a US war against terrorism and suggesting that such a war would include China's fight against separatism in Taiwan, Tibet and Xinjiang. China held that discussions on combating terrorism must be taken up at the UN Security Council and not unilaterally or within NATO, and that military action in retaliation for the attacks on the US would need concrete evidence, should not hurt civilians and should be conducted within international law. As did many other countries, China hoped to wrest policy changes from the US in exchange for support of a US war against terrorism. Generally Chinese support for a worldwide campaign against terrorism was qualified by its expectation that the UN be consulted.

South Korea said it would back the US response by allowing its own armed forces, airports, seaports and military bases be used if needed. Following the beginning of the US main military operations against Afghanistan (*see*: Afghan War) the South Korean president said that "[t]he actions by the international society led by the US are justified" and condemned terror as "the enemy of all mankind".

North Korea issued a statement on 25 September 2001 calling the attacks on the US "very regretful and tragic", and an editorial by the official press agency said: "It may be a right option … to make a due contribution to the efforts of the international community to eliminate the root cause of this terrorism."

Thailand reacted more cautiously, probably in view of its Muslim Southeast Asian neighbours. It wanted the terrorism problem to be solved within the framework of the UN and wanted the US to have clear proof of those who perpetrated the attacks before taking any military reprisals.

In *Iran* officials said that any assault on terrorism must include efforts to rein in Israeli attacks on Palestinians. In this it joined a long list of Muslim and Arab countries which had expressed their willingness to join the campaign against terrorism if the approach was evenhanded. Yet it had issued a strong statement of condemnation following the attacks on New York and Washington and expressed its opposition to the Taleban (*see* Asian YIL Vol.7: 404, Vol.8: 272-273). But Iran's supreme religious leader, while condemning terrorism in general and calling the world struggle against it "a holy war", declared on 26 September 2001 that Iran would not take part in any measure led by the US whom he accused of trying to gain a foothold in Central Asia. He said: "It is wrong to say that those who are not with us are with the terrorists", referring to countries which are US allies but which committed terrorist acts. "No, we are not with you and we are not terrorists." [Iran is listed by the US as an active state sponsor of terrorism because of its support for anti-Israeli groups.]

Meanwhile Iran attempted to rally other countries behind a unified Islamic stance on terrorism and for that purpose called for a meeting of the Organization of the Islamic Conference (*see supra* at 387). The foreign minister did not condemn the military campaign in Afghanistan explicitly but said that it was "unacceptable" as it was open-ended, without clear purpose and causing civilian casualties. Iran prohibited US flights over its airspace which was accepted by the US. Yet Iran agreed on 8 October that it would rescue US military personnel in distress in its territory.

In *Indonesia* the president condemned the attacks in the US, but was pressed to give only limited backing to the US coalition in light of existing strong Muslim militant groups. At the ASEAN summit meeting in early November 2001 Indonesia as well as Malysia called for a halt to the air assault against Afghanistan.

Malaysia said it would support action "to destroy terrorism, which has become a menace to free and democratic governments" and was willing to rally Islamic countries to take part in an international summit meeting (*see*: Organization of the Islamic Conference) on terrorism. However, the prime minister flatly opposed military action against Afghanistan as it would "only bring disaster to the country without overcoming terrorism".

Early October 2001 *Turkmenistan* was still ambivalent about assisting the US in retaliatory strikes against Afghanistan and said only that its airspace might be used for humanitarian flights.

The president of the *Philippines* said that as the leader of a nation that had fought back against Islamic militants, she was prepared to "go every step of the way" with the US. She offered logistical and intelligence support, and the use of Philippine airspace and the former US military bases, Clark and Subic Bay. Alone among Asian countries the Philippines also offered combat troops, albeit pending parliamentary consent. On the other hand the president said she hoped that the US would help the Philippines fight the *Abu Sayyaf* rebels (*see* 9 Asian YIL 395) which organization was put on a list of "terrorist organizations" by the US (*see supra* at 356). (IHT 17-09, 18-09, 19-09, 20-09, 21-09, 24-09, 25-09, 26-09, 27-09, 03-10, 04-10, 08-10, 09-10, 11-10, 15-10, 17-10, 06-11, 12-11, 22/23-12-01)

The parliament of *Kyrgyzstan* on 6 December 2001 voted in favour of allowing the US-led coalition in Afghanistan to use air bases in Kyrgyzstan for one year. (IHT 07-12-01)

The US "war on terror" and Asia

The US response to the September 2001 attacks had been from the beginning that their campaign against the groups linked to "Al Qaida" and Osama bin Laden is global and may last for years. It was said in this context that among the likely targets of future covert and overt US actions were groups based in the Philippines, Indonesia and Malaysia. During a UN Security Council meeting on the issue of the military action in Afghanistan the US ambassador said that the US, acting in self-defence after the September 11 attacks, may take "further actions with respect to other organizations and other states". (IHT 11-10-01)

Southeast Asian states, such as the Philippines, Indonesia and Malaysia, made known, however, that while US offers to assist in countering terrorism in the region were helpful, sending in soldiers would not be.

The *Indonesian* foreign ministry spokesman said that sending US troops to Indonesia was out of the question as it would face sovereignty problems.

A *Malaysian* defence official confirmed that "we have training with US forces … but having American troops on Malaysian soil on a much more permanent basis … is quite out of the question. It would be inconsistent with our policy."

When the US president during a meeting with the *Philippine* president offered to send soldiers to help fight the *Abu Sayyaf* rebels, the latter immediately declined. With regard to the US promise to provide training, equipment and maintenance support it was said the Philippine president "firmly believe[d] that the US advisers should not be armed, or their deployment would fall into the gray area that can be classified as foreign troops on Philippine soil" which was prohibited by the constitution. Nevertheless, however, the contemplated 600 US special operations forces concerned would be armed when accompanying the Philippine troops in operations (called "exercises") and authorized to fire in self-defence (*see supra* at 381). (IHT 14-12-01, 17-01-02)

China and terrorism

In meetings with the US president and the US Secretary of State on 21 September 2001 the Chinese foreign minister referred to unrest in certain regions of China and said that "China is also a victim of terrorist attacks", pledging support for battling terrorism. Later China estimated that Chinese Muslims had trained in camps run by Osama bin Laden in Afghanistan. (IHT 24-09, 12-11-01)

However, in responding to suicide bombings and other violent acts in Israel and Palestine the Chinese government refused to characterize them as terrorism, instead criticizing both parties for the use of violence and calling for renewed peace talks. Israel expressed displeasure on hearing "the Chinese position regarding what were so obviously acts of terrorism". (IHT 05-12-01)

US classification of Iran and North Korea as forming part of an "axis of evil"

In his "state of the union" address on 30 January 2002 the US president vowed to turn the US fight against terrorism next against "an axis of evil" among which he counted Iran, Iraq and North Korea, singled out for allegedly seeking "weapons of mass destruction". Iran said the assertion betrayed a desire for world dominance and North Korea said it saw in the pronouncements evidence of a "policy of aggression". (IHT 31-01-02) [North Korea was included on the US Department of State's list of states that sponsor terrorism from 1988, after North Korean agents blew up a South Korean airliner.]

UNITED NATIONS

UN seat for Taleban

The Taleban, which controlled about 90 per cent of Afghanistan in 2000, followed up its major victory with the demand for the UN seat for Afghanistan. The seat was held by the former government under the presidency of Rabbani which was still recognized as the legitimate government by most states (*see* 8 Asian YIL 260). (IHT 07-09-00)

Japan's candidacy for permanent Security Council membership

Japan called for an end to the inconclusive debate on whether the Council should be expanded and asked that major states come to concrete agreement on its future shape. It formally recommended an expansion to 24 members and a restriction on the use of the veto. Japan was paying 20 per cent of the UN budget.

Of the 189 UN member states 155 had committed themselves to a larger Council. The issue had been in the hands of a working group for the past seven years. (IHT 18/19-11-00)

Alleged racial biases

A Malaysian diplomat had resigned as chief of staff of the UN Transitional Administration in East Timor (UNTAET), charging that it "had become very much a 'white' mission, an Eastern mission with a Western face". It was reported by a Malaysian newspaper that as a result the Malaysian foreign minister had urged the UN to investigate these claims. (IHT 10-01-02)

WORLD BANK

Rejection of anti-poverty project by wealthy countries' directors

The World Bank abandoned an anti-poverty project after the directors from several major donor countries, including the US and Japan, rejected the management's recommendations for it. The plan would include financing of the resettlement of ethnic Han-Chinese in the western Chinese province of Qinghai, an area once dominated by Tibetan nomads. It was said that critics had argued that this would contribute to the "sinification" of the territory and might have reinforced China's claims to lands which some Tibetans claim is part of their homeland. But those in favour of the project argued that Qinghai was already predominantly Han Chinese.

The case was a test of the power of developing countries to resist pressure from rich countries and private lobbying groups when allocating funds. It also tested the

Bank's internal procedures for approving projects and the power of rich donor countries to determine the interpretation of the applicable rules. (IHT 8/9-07-00)

WORLD WAR II
See also: International humanitarian law

Comfort women and other slave workers file law suit in the US

It was reported that fifteen Asian women from Korea, China, Taiwan, and the Philippines had filed a class-action suit against Japan in a US federal court in September 2000, seeking compensation and an apology for being forced to work as sex slaves in the 1930s and 1940s. (IHT 20-09-00)

Besides, Chinese, Philippine, and Korean men who served as forced labourers for Japanese companies during the war filed lawsuits in California, USA, claiming an apology and compensation from the companies. They sued under a 1999 Californian law allowing victims who had been unable to pursue their claims elsewhere, to file suit in California state courts against those companies concerned that have subsidiaries in the US. The law suit of the Chinese was filed by way of class-action suit by two persons, one who had worked for *Mitsubishi* and one who had worked for *Mitsui*. (IHT 03-10-00)

Compensation settlement

A landmark settlement was reached in Tokyo on 29 November 2000 in the case brought in 1995 by eleven Chinese who were kidnapped and forced to work in Manchuria during World War II. The District Court had thrown out the case on grounds of the expiry of the statute of limitations, but the appellate court urged the defendant to reach a settlement.

Kajima, the largest Japanese general contractor, agreed to establish a 500-million-yen fund to compensate survivors and relatives of those who died at its Hanaoka copper mine during the war. The fund would be administrated by the Chinese Red Cross, which would have discretion over how the money would be disbursed.

The settlement was probably the largest-ever in Japan, where the law often limits the amount of compensation that can be awarded in legal disputes.

It was said that the settlement was extremely significant because other companies which were similarly accused were likely to set up similar funds.

The case was the first one on compensation for a violation of the 1907 Hague Convention. Three other cases on compensation for forced labour had also been settled; it related to persons from Korea which was a Japanese colony at the time. (IHT 30-11-00)

War victims' claims rejected by Japanese court

The Tokyo High (appellate) Court on 6 December 2000 rejected demands from Philippine (former "comfort") women for compensation and an apology. It upheld a lower court ruling that the government had no obligation to pay damages to the 80 women and their relatives. The High Court referred to international law and held that individuals were not allowed to sue a government for human right abuses. Besides, the statute of limitations had expired. (IHT 07-12-00)

The Tokyo District Court on 26 March 2001 rejected demands from eight women, 16 (former) soldiers and 16 relatives of other persons, members of the South Korean-based Association of Pacific War Victims and Bereaved Families, who were forced into service by the Japanese Army during the Japanese colonization. The plaintiffs had argued that Japan's wartime behaviour should be considered among crimes against humanity. The defendant Japanese state contended that international law did not grant such a claim to individuals and that the matter had been settled by bilateral treaties. (IHT 27-03-01)

Comfort women compensated from private fund

The Japanese Asian Women Fund had paid compensation to 78 Dutch women who were forced into sex slavery by the Japanese military during World War II in Indonesia, then a Dutch colony.

The foundation was funded partly by the Japanese government and partly by donations from Japanese citizens, former soldiers and their families. It had set up compensation projects in Indonesia, Taiwan, South Korea, and the Philippines. (IHT 14/15-07-01)

WORLD TRADE ORGANIZATION
See also: Environmental protection; International economic and trade relations

China's membership

[After a candidate member has reached bilateral agreement with each of the existing members on the tariffs to be applicable in their mutual trade, these commitments and concessions are laid down in one multilateral, comprehensive document which is annexed ("schedule") to the agreement of accession to be concluded between the WTO and the candidate member.]

The US Senate approval of the bill granting China "permanent normal trading status" (*see* 9 Asian YIL 398) essentially removed all US obstacles to China's WTO membership.

Difficulties arose in the final stage of the process of China's candidacy because of conflicts over the formulation of the schedule. China complained that the US and some European countries tried to gain new market concessions not agreed in the preceding bilateral agreements (The US Senate on 19 September 2000 had approved the bill granting China "permanent normal trading status", thus removing all US obstacles to Chinese membership of the WTO) while the other side demanded that China clearly determine the means of implementation of its commitments. (IHT 20-09-00, 11-10-00)

On 9 June 2001 the US and China announced agreement on several issues that had been blocking China's entry into the WTO. (*see* 9 Asian YIL 398) China had insisted that it be allowed to join the WTO as a developing country which would, *inter alia*, include the right to provide farm subsidies equal to ten per cent of its agricultural output. For developed countries the limit is five per cent. The two sides finally agreed on 8.5 per cent, while China agreed not to provide subsidies that would act as incentives to produce certain crops. (IHT 11-06, 28-06-01)

On 20 June 2001 China reached agreement with the EU on their outstanding differences in connection with China's pursuit of WTO membership. The differences included disagreement about the number of licenses for European insurance companies to operate in China. (IHT 21-06-01)

The WTO working group on China approved the Chinese application on 17 September 2001 followed by approval by the WTO Ministerial Conference on 10 November 2001. The agreement was subject to ratification by China. (IHT 05-09, 17-09, 18-09, 12-11-01)

Taiwan membership

One day after China's entry into the WTO, Taiwan followed under the name "Separate Customs Territory of Taiwan, Jinmen and Matsu", or "Chinese Taipei", the name under which it has been known in other international organizations in which it is holding membership.

Asian attitudes towards the impending 2001 Doha meeting

It was reported that Asian countries were wary of putting on the agenda items that could be considered "extraneous" to trade, such as labour standards and protection of the environment. In face of these controversies *Malaysia* suggested the introduction of a provision allowing countries to "opt out" of contentious issues. *India* insisted that a new negotiation round could be held only after the developed countries met their commitments on implementing matters discussed in previous rounds. (IHT 30-10-01)

The forthcoming WTO meeting at Doha gave rise to various items that emphasized the gap between rich and poor countries, and endangered the outcome of the meeting..

In connection with its concern about the possibility of terrorist attacks with chemical weapons the US had forced the drugs manufacturer Bayer A.G. to sharply reduce the price of its anthrax drug. This emboldened developing countries, such as India and Brazil, to insist on a broad "public health" exception to international patent rules for other drugs. This position was strongly opposed by countries like Switzerland, Canada, Japan, and the US which defended strict preservation of intellectual property protection.

On another matter the special trading rights granted by the US to Pakistan's textile and apparel industry in the context of the cooperation of the two countries in fighting terrorism, lead many countries, among which India and Nigeria, to argue that the liberalization measure should apply to similar industries in all developing countries. (IHT 06-11-01)

In preparing an agenda for the Doha meeting India threatened to block an agreement if it failed to provide expanded access for Indian textile exports to Western markets. The interested developing countries in this respect were led by India,

Pakistan, and Bangladesh, the opponents were mainly the US and Canada. (IHT 14-11-01) An agreement was finally achieved. (IHT 15-11-01)

Doha Round

The Doha Round of global trade talks started in December 2001 and was scheduled to complete in January 2005. At the start the negotiations were directed especially towards the question whether the chair of the "trade negotiations committee" would be held on a rotating basis among the 144 member states (preferred by the developing states) or by the director-general (preferred by the industrialized states). The developing countries were of the opinion that chairmanship by the director-general would put too much power in the WTO headquarters which are, they said, subject to pressure by the big trading powers. (IHT 30-01-02)

Sino-Japanese tariffs dispute

Japan in April 2001 attempted to protect its farmers by imposing temporary tariffs on a host of Chinese goods (spring onions, shiitake mushrooms, rushes used in tatami mats), arguing that the curbs were allowed under WTO rules. China in June retaliated by imposing punitive tariffs on Japanese cars, phones and air conditioners. Japan argued that the Chinese measure violated WTO rules as retaliatory measures were not allowed without first taking the dispute to arbitration

The two countries met in early July 2001 to try resolve the dispute. This was not successful until early November 2001 when Japan announced that it would for the time being lift the temporary tariffs and continue studying the effects of the low-priced Chinese imports.

The two countries settled the dispute on 21 December 2001 as China agreed to retract its 100 per cent tariffs, and Japan backed down from its threat to extend its import limits for as long as four years. (IHT 20-06, 02-07, 09-11, 22/23-12-01)

US tariffs on foreign steel

The US announced in March 2002 that it would impose tariffs of up to 30 per cent on a range of foreign steel imports to support its struggling domestic steel mills, thereby invoking a WTO "safeguard" rule that allows countries to provide temporary protection to industries hit by surges in imports. The EU considered itself to be the main victim because the US decision focused on the higher end of the steel market where European companies were particularly strong, and because it expected, as a result, an increase from Asia and other regions in steel imports which might be priced out of the US market. It consequently responded by lodging a complaint with the WTO.

China on 15 March 2002 called for talks on the US decision and said it would make its first complaint to the WTO if the negotiations failed (a position shared by *South Korea*); on 24 May China took measures to exclude the import of steel that was diverted from the US as a result of the US tariffs. *Japan* asked the US to be compensated under WTO rules by lowered tariffs on unspecified non-steel imports from Japan, and threatened that it would, otherwise, take retaliatory action. (IHT 07-03, 16/17-03, 29-04, 29-05-02) [The "safeguard" exception is meant to allow a country to head off a sudden wave of imports without its having to wait for the outcome of a trade-dispute resolution process. This preference for unilateral measures may also exist in the case of retaliatory action against safeguard measures, for the taking of such retaliatory action justification is sought in the above legal limitation of the safeguard right. Accordingly prompt retaliation may be allowed if the imports meant to be limited by the safeguard tariffs have been falling rather than rising.]

LITERATURE

BOOK REVIEWS*

World Trade Governance and Developing Countries: The GATT/WTO Code Committee System, by KOFI OTENG KOFUOR, Blackwell Publishing, 2004, ISBN 1-405-116781 in hardback (£50.00/ $64.95) and ISBN 1-405-116773 in paperback (£19.99/$29.95).

This concise monograph appears in the Chatham House Papers series of the Royal Institute of International Affairs. The series aims to address contemporary issues of intellectual importance in a scholarly yet accessible way. This study has undoubtedly achieved this goal.

The book positions itself as adhering to the liberal theory of international relations, and its choice of analytical tools is determined by this position. The author analyses the institutional framework and decision-making procedures of the GATT/WTO Code Committee System. He rightly identifies these as a *lacuna* in the literature and sets out to address the role of developing countries in four selected GATT/WTO Code Committees, relating to antidumping, textiles, agriculture, and trade and environment. The choice of these committees is justified by their importance to developing countries' interests.

After the introductory foray into the political science theories inspiring the development and understanding of the international trading system, the book in its second chapter discusses the role of developing countries in the committees under GATT. The author puts an interesting argument regarding the increasing understanding of developing countries of the committee system and the latter's importance in the formulation and refinement of international trade rules and procedures. He recasts the general understanding of the driving forces behind shifts in the GATT period in the GATT Committees on Antidumping Practice, away from the importance of publicly understood high politics relating to the New International Economic Order and the ensuing special and differential treatment in the GATT towards these much more pragmatic reasons. The disjunction between, on the one hand, rules and practice in these Committees and, on the other, the legal framework that is used as a backdrop for often illegal but advantageously flexible arrangements for developing countries offers a compelling explanation of the use price arrangement and voluntary export restraints.

The Committees on Antidumping in the GATT period are thus shown as having important secondary importance for developing countries, yet little direct practical use. In the textiles sector, it is shown that the relevant committees were both weak and were controlled by the developed countries; the internal divisions among developing countries did not facilitate the reaching of a common position of strength in their attempts to change the direction. Both in textiles and in the agriculture sector, Kofuor argues that the weakness of these committees was partly due to the strategic choice of certain developing countries who considered their interests could be better defended through other methods.

The developments after the Tokyo Round form the subject of the third chapter, which provides lucid access to a complex set of circumstances that changed the outlook of developing countries in the international trading system and that dissolved the communality of their outlook. The circumstances include the end of

---

* Edited by Surya P. Subedi, General Editor.

Asian Yearbook of International Law, Volume 10 (B.S. Chimni *et al.,* eds.)
© 2005 Koninklijke Brill NV. Printed in The Netherlands, pp. 409-417.

the Soviet Union and the loss of credibility of the planned economy as a model; the example of rapid economic growth of the Newly Industrialized Countries that relied on open markets; and the realignment of developing countries with positions traditionally taken by industrialized countries. The reconfiguration of the international trading system in the WTO and the changed positions of its Members have increased the tensions in the system such that the author ponders whether the breaking point might be reached where the hegemon considers its interests are no longer served by its supporting the system.

The final chapter investigates the current practice in the 1995 WTO Committee on Antidumping Practices, the Textiles Monitoring Body, the Committee on Agriculture, and the Committee on Trade and Environment. A general trend that repeats in the assessment of these committees is the impact on the developing countries of the integrated dispute settlement system of the WTO. This system has changed the role and dynamic of these committees.

Although developing countries are generally active participants in these committees, the process of shifting the priorities within them is cumbersome as, firstly, they are based from the outset on developed countries' interests and, secondly, developed countries' interests are entrenched in the processes and procedures. A nice example is brought to light in the section on the Committee on Agriculture where 'creative calculations and interpretations of their obligations' and 'subjective methodologies' ensure that developed countries largely maintain their protected position. The final section on the Committee on Trade and Environment tells a different story of a committee where the circumstances have come together to ensure that developing countries can play an active and influencing role and can engage individually in the work of the committee in avoiding green protectionism.

In his recommendations, Kofuor calls on developing countries to work together in a pragmatic manner to ensure that their interests are fully represented in the committees, and to forge stronger links with non-governmental organizations. He acknowledges the problems associated with such cooperative efforts and offers suggestions to alleviate these. To ensure that the representatives in the committees increase their legitimacy with their respective home constituencies and are not overtaken by non-governmental organizations, Kofuor concludes that they need to become better communicators that can link communities and 'rewire' to national economic and social interests.

This study analyses a side of the GATT/WTO system that has not received the attention it deserves. Kofuor shows the reader the reality of decision-making lying behind the legal rules and procedures, and offers realistic perspectives for improvement. Thus, this book is an important contribution to a growing body of critical research that goes beyond the rules to reveal the practice. Without understanding the code committee system, it is possible to understand neither the functioning of the WTO nor the role played by developing countries in the WTO. This study offers the required insights and is, as such, required reading.

KIM VAN DER BORGHT
School of Law, University of Hull

Institutionalizing International Environmental Law by BHARAT H. DESAI, Transnational, Ardsley, NY, 2004, ISBN 1-57105-313-1, pp xiii, 378, $115

This book examines "[t]he interface between the two streams" of international environmental law and institutional law to help "in explaining the process of 'institutionalization' of international environmental law". (p. xii) In so doing, it makes accessible the core issues of international organization and international environmental law. It also provides a *tour d'horizon* of a number of issues that face other areas of international law, such as the role and transformation of soft law, the problem of sovereignty, unequal international power distribution, reform of the United Nations, and relations among international organizations.

The first part of the book provides a useful primer on international institutions: what the terms mean, the history of international organizations, the tension with state sovereignty, functions of international organizations, aspects of institutions' governance, etc. The author sees institutions as both outcomes of a state-driven "process", and tools. The "international institution building process is an organic process

directly geared to the needs of states. ... [I]nsti-
tutions are essentially tools, operating within
legal parameters, for states to address the global
problematique". (p. xiii) "Institutions are
products of a complex process of 'institutionalization' and they engage in norm-building in
various complex areas of interdependence." (p.
xii) Anyone wanting a short (63-page) introduction to the subject of international institutions, whether as part of an international environmental law course or otherwise, would be
well served by reading this section.

Although the book examines international
environmental law, the author admits that there
is controversy over the existence of international
environmental law as a separate branch of international law. The lack of agreement on basic
legal principles, dispute over fundamental
scientific issues, the *ad hoc* nature of rule creation, and the patchwork state of treaty ratification support the argument against the existence
of a coherent body of law. However, the author
concludes that "the existence of a distinct branch
of international environmental law has now
come to be widely accepted in the international
academic circles as well as practicing community and the judicial forums". (p. 69) Perhaps
all could agree that "international law had to
devise a *framework* to regulate the 'environmental' behaviour of states" (p. 71, emphasis added).

The history of the development of international environmental law is charted to provide
"an idea essentially about the changes as well
as tools and techniques used in the process of
international legal regulation protection of the
environment" (p. 71). This lucid section (pp. 70-
104) reviews the reports, declarations, statements, principles, strategies, action plans, resolutions, charters, covenants, protocols, programmes, frameworks, expert groups, forums,
summits, processes, etc. which have kept environmental matters on the international agenda
(and conference circuit), especially after 1968.
"Over the years, [international environmental
law] has changed from confining itself to limited
concerns for protection of species of [*sic*]
resources, to much broader and complex
challenges, having a long-term effect on human
welfare and survival." (p.104) "The web of
multilateral environmental regulatory framework
is gradually thickening in terms of its range as
well as content, notwithstanding its partial and
uneven growth." (p. 107)

Taking "emerging principles of international
environmental law" (p. 96) as his case-study,
the author analyses a situation which is often
encountered when "[i]n the heat of the moment,
most of the states want to be seen on the right
side", whether it be environment, economics,
trade or security. "Mere incorporation of some
of these principles in a multilateral agreement
may not necessarily elevate them to the status
of an established norm of international environmental law. The presentation of something in
the formative stage *as law* creates a miasma. In
such cases, what needs to be deciphered is the
content rather than the *form*. ... [T]he *soft*
character of some of these principles, depicts the
political dilemma of the states. In fact consistent
adherence in *actual practice* on the part of states
and acceptance as an obligation, (*sic*) confers
legitimacy on such soft norms as *hard* obligations." (p. 97, emphases in original)

Capturing some of the flavour of the way
in which environmental institutions have
evolved, there is a reference to the "'atmos-
pherics' and 'posturing' witnessed during negotiations for multilateral environmental agreements" (p. 70). The author is aware that even
highly touted international agreements on environmental matters such as the Framework
Convention on Climate Change and the Convention on Biological Diversity can contain "soft
obligations couched in the hard treaty form"
which states have signed because "they felt it
was politically convenient to go for the carefully
crafted consensus" which reflects "the politically
convenient 'lowest common denominator'
approach". (p. 96)

The author makes an interesting analysis
of how "hard [that is, treaty] law" can be made
"soft". "In many cases such soft obligations
[which comprise, for example, hortatory principles or discretionary provisions] are injected
into the text of an agreement as a compromise
formula or sheer calculated ambiguity to gain
elusive consensus (which may be on account of
lack of political will among negotiating states
or lack of concrete scientific evidence or uncertainty) on an issue among negotiating states,
with no immediate intention of making them
effective. Such a consciously built-in contradiction, in the form of a hard treaty shell with
its soft underbelly, mainly seeks to woo recalcitrant states to enter the framework as well as
avoids potential 'hold-out' problems." (p. 117)

This feature should not be taken as being necessarily detrimental. "As the recent practice of designing 'framework' conventions reveals, negotiating states explicitly do not intend to lay down hard commitments in the first round. ... [This] ensures gradual evolution of a legal regime as the political consensus materializes." (p. 118) The 1985 Vienna Convention on the Depletion of the Ozone Layer and the 1989 Basel Convention on Transboundary Movements of Hazardous Wastes and their Disposal are given as examples of framework agreements with soft obligations which evolved into harder provisions as scientific uncertainty decreased and political will increased. "[T]he process of law-making on most of the sectoral environmental issues has been generally linked to scientific evidence on the issue in question." (p. 106)

The kernel of the book lies in Chapter 5, "International Environmental Institutions" (pp. 133-218), and the "nucleus" comprises fifty pages in which the United National Environment Programme (UNEP), the Commission on Sustainable Development (CSD), the Global Environment Facility (GEF), regime-specific institutions, and multilateral development banks are reviewed. "As a logical corollary to the process of development of international environmental law, institutional structures have also taken shape. These international environmental institutions cater to the needs of the states for interdependence in addressing the environmental challenge." (p.104) The guided tour through the international environmental institutions is excellent, giving the reader a solid understanding of the bases, powers, constraints, relationships and possibilities of the various institutions.

"[W]hile international environmental institutions are products of the need for institutionalized international cooperation, once these institutions are set up, generally, they acquire their own momentum in catalyzing international environmental law. ... [I]nstitutions constitute a product of the process as well as a contributor to it. ... The multilateral environmental negotiations remain essentially a state-centric process in spite of the active role played and influence exerted by the civil society groups at the conference venues and outside. As a result, it is the sovereign states which still remain the final arbiters for the creation and functioning of international environmental institutions. The efficacy

of institutions has thus to be measured by the expectations of states." (p. xi-xii) In this context, we can draw our conclusions about the cause of "[t]he problem of institutional fragmentation, especially since the international environmental law-making process largely remains *ad hoc*, piecemeal and sectoral in nature, [which] has contributed to making the process complex and cumbersome." (p. 104) "International institutions ... inherit certain weaknesses and inadequacies from their birth. Some of these 'genetic disorders' are especially bequeathed by the states in the course of working out consensus among the negotiating states as well as through expression of their consent." (p. 63)

There have been many suggestions for coordinating or strengthening international environmental institutions and/or law-making, so a section of the book which proffers a "blueprint" might be off-putting, especially in light of the otherwise hard-headed and realistic approach. However, this final section continues to examine the situation in the light of practical reality, noting that proposals for reform must "be treated cautiously" (p. 269) and that "political courage" will be required for true reform (p. 273).

Three appendices provide the UN General Assembly resolutions establishing UNEP (1972) and the Commission of Sustainable Development (1992), and the rather longer instrument establishing the restructured Global Environment Facility (1994), the three institutions on which the book the most strongly focuses.

The book ends with an impressive "Select" Bibliography, which if anything is overly inclusive: there is no need to include the inscription on the Jefferson Memorial or the *Collected Works of Mahatma Gandhi* in a Select Bibliography on institutionalizing international environmental law. It is sometimes difficult to guess at what is the alphabetical principle, particularly for the "primary sources", and "the" is not conventionally a word on which to sort.

Dr JAMES J. BUSUTTIL
Queen Mary, University of London

CITES, Implementation in Nepal & India, Law Policy & Practice by RAVI SHARMA ARYAL, Bhrikuti Academic Publications, Kathmandu, Nepal, April 2004.

Mainly doctrinal, the book is a detailed and complete commentary examining the legal perspective of 'The Convention on International Trade In Endangered Species of Wild Flora and Fauna (CITES) 1973', in protecting endangered species from extinction and particularly its implementation in Nepal and India.

Additionally, and possibly intentionally, the author - while analyzing CITES from both the Nepalese and the Indian perspectives - recommends a three-fold objective, *viz.*, regulating trade (in the scheduled species) along with the long-term protection of their natural wealth and habitat, through a deft application of the CITES treaty in combination with the existing laws in both countries.

Flora and fauna comprise an irreplaceable part of natural systems that must be protected for the biodiversity of our planet to be maintained; towards this purpose the CITES lends itself to international cooperation for the protection and exploitation of certain species of flora and fauna which suffer the risk of extinction. Both India and Nepal are countries that have exceptionally rich natural wealth and this wealth is revered not only in their myths and cultures, but also in their religions.

Notwithstanding these traditions, the lack of constitutional provisions and legislation haunts both countries. Extinction happens more often through man-made alterations of, and forms of destruction of, the environment and less through the process of evolution. CITES, unfortunately, deals only with regulating trade in scheduled species of plants and animals, and consequently it does not seek to protect all species directly; nor does it contain provisions to protect the habitat.

This book therefore aims to discuss the resources of flora, fauna and the habitat, in both Nepal and India, their significance in maintaining the bio-diversity balance for the ecosystem as well as for the species, and the associated legal issues from the perspective of CITES and also from current laws in force in the two countries. Furthermore, issues inextricably intertwined with the environment, ranging across administrative, political, socioeconomic, legal and technical fields, are also dealt with in the light of existing legal principles and practices. Juxtaposition of the issues relevant to CITES with aspects of the local legislation, such as state practice, judicial pronouncements, and international norms, is then done.

While both India and Nepal are signatory parties to the CITES, enforcement has been inadequate, most often due to an inappropriate understanding of the law, its policies and its enforceability. There are obvious gaps in its implementation mechanism and a crying need to plug these.

CITES seeks international co-operation in protecting scheduled wild-life species from threats of extinction and other forms of exploitation, particularly their trade. Importantly, the book examines CITES in comparison with the two dominant environmental protection laws: the 'The National Parks and Wildlife Conservation Act 1973, of Nepal' and 'The Wildlife (Protection) Act 1972, of India'. In so doing it is able to identify the gaps in the legislation between CITES and the local laws in both countries. In spite of its structured doctrinal approach the book is loaded in favour of the practical implementability of CITES considering the limitation of the weakness of environmental laws and their enforcement in both countries.

Enforcement officials, agencies and interested parties would be able to use the book almost as a handbook because of its detailed citation of the list of protected flora and fauna, the CITES treaty text, pertinent Supreme Court judgments, and other decisions of adjudicating bodies in India and Nepal.

Ms CHRISTABEL SILVA
Middlesex University, London

Essays on the Future of the WTO: Finding a New Balance, by KIM VAN DER BORGHT (Editor), ERIC REMACLE and JARROD WIENER (Associate Editors), London, Cameron May, 69-71 Bondway, London SW8 1SQ, 2003. ISBN 1-874-698-49-X, pp 360, £125.00/$212.00

Pascal Lamy, the EU trade commissioner, described the WTO as "an island of governance in the sea of globalisation", as evidenced by its binding dispute settlement mechanism. Still, he attributed the failure of Cancun in September 2003 to the fact that the WTO is not a perfect model of economic governance (Journal of Common Market Studies Annual Lecture, London, 28 October 2003). This book examines some of the most burning underlying problems of the WTO and suggests ways in which to tackle them by finding a new balance.

This collection of essays was inspired by a seminar series held in 2000 at the Vrije Universiteit Brussel culminating in a conference entitled "The Millennium Round: Europe and the World". Two of the contributions for this collection were written by participants in the conference and lectures, while the others are invited contributions.

The book is in twelve chapters. Four of these address "horizontal" issues: the role and function of the WTO in international governance, the decision-making process in the WTO, the position of developing countries in the multilateral trading system, and the integration of non-commercial values in the world trade system. The remaining eight chapters focus on "vertical" or linkage issues: the protection of labour standards in a globalized economy, the relationship between investment and trade regulation, agriculture and the WTO, the conflict between environmental protection and free trade and, finally, the impact of WTO accession on China. The arrangement of the contributions does not necessarily reflect this dichotomy, given that the chapter on labour standards appears among the more general chapters.

The opening chapter by Kim Van der Borght sets out the unifying theme of this book in particularly clear terms. There are two conflicting perceptions of the role to be performed by the WTO, which also find expression in the preamble to the Marrakech Agreement; some expect the WTO to promote the ideals of the international community: human rights, environmental protection, economic and social development, while others see the WTO as nothing more than a mechanism for creating open markets. If anything, economic liberalization will in itself cater for these vulnerable values. The ever-increasing inequality in the world and the hard reality of poverty in the developing countries have disproved the second view, hence the need for a new balance between the developed, and the developing and least-developed countries. This balance can be achieved only if the world trade system finally acknowledges the different starting-points of the WTO members and adopts more equitable rules.

The chapter by Dencho Georgiev is an insightful analysis of the decision-making process in the World Trade Organization. Decision-making in the WTO is by consensus. This is favoured by developed and developing countries alike, since it allows them to block decisions inimical to their own interests. In order to facilitate negotiations and the making of compromises, delegations often resort to closed consultations with restricted participation and last-minute proposals during Ministerial Conferences. However, these practices call seriously into question the internal transparency of decision-making in the WTO. The author argues that the dilemma between transparency and effective decision-making is artificial. Enhanced transparency and effective decision-making can and should be pursued simultaneously.

The following chapter by I. Mataitonga is a penetrating analysis of the inequalities suffered in the world trade system by developing countries. The promised enhanced access to developed world markets for agricultural products and textiles has not materialized. Trade liberalization has been imposed on developing countries prematurely and without their having been involved in the drafting of the rules in place, trapping these countries in a vicious circle of instability, debt and recession. The author argues that the trading system needs to be instilled with a new global ethic and to accommodate wider development issues.

Michael Hansenne addresses the challenges faced by the ILO in the age of globalization in a chapter based on long experience. How is it possible to ensure a minimum of social justice in the world when conventions relating to labour are not universally ratified and when the market is dominated by ruthless multinational corporations? He places his faith in the ILO Declaration relating to the principles and fundamental rights of work from 1998, and urges for more cooperation between the WTO and the ILO to transform the objectives of the Declaration into reality.

Alan Rosas, in the last of the "horizontal" contributions, examines the extent to which non-commercial values can be protected by means of Art. XX GATT. He argues that even though there is scope for trade sanctions in Art. XX, the adoption of international standards is preferable. Unilateral, extraterritorial trade sanctions should be imposed only if exhaustible natural resources are seriously under threat.

Surya Subedi's analysis of the regulation of foreign investment is particularly stimulating.

Regulating foreign investment is unthinkable without the regulation of multinational enterprises (MNEs). He argues that regulation would benefit not only the developing world, but also multinationals, as these would be faced with a uniform set of rules. However, the rejection of the multilateral agreement on investment (MAI) drafted by the OECD in the late 1990s has shown that a modern international law of foreign investment needs to reflect the interests of both home and host countries in a balanced way so as to be approved by the international society.

Jürgen Kurtz takes up in his article the issue of trade and investment by looking closely at the investment provisions of the new Vietnam-US Bilateral Trade Agreement (BTA). He examines their relationship, firstly, to the Vietnamese system of foreign investment; secondly, to Vietnam's current commitments as a member of ASEAN and its prospective ones after accession to the WTO. Kurtz finds that the BTA will necessitate the removal of sensible developmental parameters from Vietnam's *doi moi* legislation. Also, it may pre-empt the outcome of the new round of WTO negotiations to the detriment of developing countries.

A common criticism levelled at compilations is that they lack coherence. Such a criticism cannot be made of this collection of essays. Its unifying theme is the search for a balance between trade liberalization, on the one hand, and the attainment of broader aims of development, environmental protection and social justice on the other. The contributions have been carefully chosen to shed light on this very important and topical question from different angles. The chapter by Thomás García Azcárate and Marina Mastrostefano argues that the EU is willing to encompass social, environmental and consumer issues while taking the multifunctional character of agriculture into account. Melaku Geboye Desta addresses the bias of the current rules of agricultural trade in favour of the developed world, and finds that more than empty words and promises is needed to redress the balance.

The chapter by Sandrine Maljean-Dubois examines the areas of conflict between the Cartagena Protocol on Biosafety and the WTO framework. In interesting counterpoint to Alan Rosas' analysis, Yun Zhao suggests that in cases of impending irreversible damage to the environment, environmental protection should override

procedural considerations such as the improper manner of application of a measure. The only chapter perhaps less sharply focused on the common theme is the final, timely contribution on China's entry into the WTO.

This collection represents a welcome contribution to the debate on the future of the WTO. It unites in one volume the voices of leading academic experts from Australia, France, Hong Kong and the United Kingdom, senior government officials from Bulgaria, China and the Fiji Islands, and in-house experts from the Commission and the ILO. It provides a balanced and rounded treatment of a wide range of topical issues; the compilation adds up to more than the sum of its parts. Its greatest value lies in alerting readers to the disparity between the objectives of the world trade system and those of the international community. It will therefore be of great interest to academics, to students of the world trade system, and also to practitioners entrusted with shaping the future face of the WTO.

IRINI KATSIREA
Middlesex University Law School, London

International Human Rights; A Practical Approach, by JAVAID REHMAN, Pearson, London, 2003, ISBN 0 582 43773 3, pp 520, £27.99.

At a time of recent wars in Iraq and Afghanistan and interventions in countries such as the former Yugoslavia, Rwanda and East Timor, the world community and the mass media have begun to take an interest in issues to do with the promotion and protection of Human Rights. The use of torture, war crimes, the rights of minorities, and the rights to self determination have been given great prominence. Attempts to try and to convict perpetrators of breaches of human rights, such as ex-Presidents Pinochet and Milosevic, have meant that this renewed interest has spread beyond the few and now attracts widespread comment. Rather appropriately, as the decade of education relating to Human Rights comes to an end shortly (in 2005), there has also been an enormous growth in those wishing to learn about and even practise in this field of law.

If one considers, in addition, the impact of the Human Rights Act of 1998 in the UK whereby from October 2000, the whole jurisprudence of the European Convention of Human Rights has been made applicable to the activities of public authorities, it is clear that textbooks on this topic were needed. There exist lengthy and erudite texts in English on the subject by such as Alston and Steiner, and Robertson and Merrills. Also required were books that could introduce students on undergraduate and postgraduate courses to an overview of the main themes and topics of study in this area. This book, together with others, for example, that by Rhona Smith, has attempted to meet such a need. In its clear and practical exposition of the subject Rehman has admirably succeeded.

The approach of the author is, after an overview and introduction to the types and sources of international law, to explore the short history of the law of International Human Rights, correctly identifying it as a distinct subject of study and practice apart from Public International Law generally. In the second part of the book he then considers in some detail the major international sources of human rights law and their means of enforcement. He argues strongly for the equality in law of economic, social and cultural rights with those of political and civil rights, but concedes that implementation remains a major problem for the former especially. He also raises the position and importance of the NGO actors in developing the law, but again notes their traditional reluctance to move forward more effectively on the non-political and civil rights agenda.

The third part of the book then considers the regional dimension of international human rights. This section provides a very useful summary of the European, Inter- American and African systems for the protection and promotion of human rights. The review of the institutions concerned, as well as a comparison between the rights protected in each of these systems, is particularly useful for students. It enables them to see to what extent there is a different approach and to some extent the relative political and cultural aspects of such a topic. The clear explanation of the relationship among the Council of Europe Convention on Human Rights, the developing EU approach to human rights and the EU Charter of Fundamental Rights is likely to assist the beginner in their understanding of this complex relationship. However, for this reviewer, it seems a little unfortunate that there is virtually no mention of

the attempts in other parts of the world to develop a regional system such as the three discussed. It would have been helpful, perhaps, to consider briefly the situation in Asia and in Arab countries, with some comment as to how these are dealing with the abuses which have occurred in their regions.

The author in the final parts seeks to add in this text something different from the standard books. In the fourth part of the book he has, in some detail, dealt with the problems of the protection of Group rights. In addition to the rights of women and children he has devoted space to a critical review of the rights of minorities and indigenous peoples, issues with which International law has traditionally had some difficulty in the past. In particular, in the final part, he has added a chapter on issues in relation to terrorism, an aspect few others have attempted. It remains a difficult task to assess how the law deals with international terrorism, especially in relation to definitional issues. However, he has assembled all the relevant legal instruments and has carefully yet critically reviewed their possible effectiveness.

It is perhaps due to the familiar problem of space that although this book adopts a fairly critical, if ultimately optimistic stance, in relation to the growth of international human rights law, some discussion of the reasons for this quite recent development has been omitted. There is some useful detail in the appendices about those states and which international legal instruments have been ratified, with similar information in relation to the regional treaties. There are numerous references in the Chapters, but in these times it would have been useful to provide at the end of each chapter further reading, as well as relevant web sites for students to facilitate their wider background research.

Strangely, this text comes to a rather sudden halt. It would have felt more satisfactory to this reviewer if after the main exposition there had been some sort of overall conclusion regarding the past development of this area of law. Equally, perhaps, reflection on the ways in which this field may further progress in the coming years could have been of assistance, particularly in the light of recent events at the United Nations and in Iraq. However, these are minor points that in no way detract from an excellent introductory book, which can be recommended to and will be well used by those

students at both undergraduate and postgraduate
levels starting out in this fascinating and rapidly
growing area of law.

STEPHEN HOMEWOOD
Centre for Legal Research
Middlesex University

SURVEY OF INTERNATIONAL LAW LITERATURE PUBLISHED IN 2003 WITH SPECIAL RELEVANCE TO ASIA

Compiled and Edited by Bimal N. Patel[*]

Areas of international law:

Air and space
Arms control and disarmament
Conflict and disputes
Criminal law and terrorism
Development
Economic relations and International
Finance
Environment
General
Individuals, groups of persons – human rights

Peace-keeping, peace-making and peace-building
Sea, rivers and water-resources
States and groups of states
United Nations and other international/regional organizations and regional laws
War, peace and neutrality, armed conflict, international humanitarian law

Air and space

ABEYRATNE, RUWANTISSA, The carriage by air of invasive alien species: regulatory and legal issues, Air Space Law (2) 196-208

CHAN, YU-CHUN and WILLIAMS, GEORGE, Prospects for changing airline ownership rules, 67 Journal of Air Law and Commerce (2) 233-240

FERRAO, PETER, Developing a system of dispute settlement for commercial activi-ties in outer space, 68 Arbitration (3) 250-252

Arms control and disarmament

MEHMOOD, AMNA, American policy of non-proliferation towards Pakistan: a post-cold war perspective In 56 Pakistan horizon (1) 35-58

VARKEY, SHAJI, Nuclear restraint and peace in South Asia In G. Gopa Kumar (ed.) International terrorism and global order in the twenty first century, 213-224

---

[*] Bimal N. Patel, BSc, MA (International Relations), LLM (International Law), PhD candidate, Nijmegen University, the Netherlands. Staff member, Verification Division, Organization for the Prohibition of Chemical Weapons, The Hague.

Asian Yearbook of International Law, Volume 10 (B.S. Chimni *et al.,* eds.)
© 2005 Koninklijke Brill NV. Printed in The Netherlands, pp. 419-433.

Conflict and disputes

CHALK, PETER, Non-military security in
the wilder Middle East In 26 Studies in
conflict and terrorism (3) 197-214

FINKELSTEIN, NORMAN G., Image and
reality of the Israel-Palestine conflict,
Verso (London), 287p.

GIOIA, ANDREA, The development of the
international law relating to the protection
of cultural property in the event of armed
conflict: the second protocol to the 1954
Hague Convention In 11 Italian Yearbook
of International Law, 25-57

KRISTJÁNSDÓTTIR, EDDA, Resolution of
water disputes: lessons from the Middle
East In International Bureau of the Permanent Court of Arbitration (ed.), Resolution of international water disputes,
351-370

ODGAARD, LISELOTTE, The South China
Sea: ASEAN's security concerns about
China In 34 Security dialogue (1) (PRIO)
11-24

NONNEMAN, GERD, A European view of
the US role in the Israeli-Palestinian
conflict In Martin Ortega (et. al), The
European Union and the crisis in the
Middle East, 33-46

SCHABAS, WILLIAM A., Punishment of
non-state actors in non-international
armed conflict In 26 Fordham International Law Journal (4) 907-933

SHIJIAN MO, JOHN, Settlement of trade
disputes between mainland China and the
separate customs territory of Taiwan
within the WTO In 2 Chinese Journal of
International Law (1) 145-173

TO, LEE LAI, China, the USA and the South
China Sea conflicts In 34 Security dia-

logue (1) Security dialogue (1) (PRIO)
25-39

VAN DYKE, JON M., VALENCIA, MARK
J. and GARMENDIA, JENNY MILLER,
The North-South Korea boundary dispute
in the Yellow (West) Sea In 27 Maritime
Policy (2) 143-158

WALDMAN, ADIR, Arbitrating armed con-
flict: decisions of the Israel-Lebanon
Monitoring Group, Huntington, NY:
Juris, 320p.

Criminal law and terrorism

AKANDE, DAPO, The jurisdiction of the
International Criminal Court over
nationals of non-parties: legal basis and
limits In 1 Journal of International Criminal Justice (3) 618-650

ALVAREZ JOSE E., The Security Council's
war on terrorism: problems and policy
options In Erika de Wet and Andre Noll-
kaemper (eds.), Review of the Security
Council by member states, 119-145

ARBOUR, LOUISE, Will the ICC have an
impact on universal jurisdiction? In 1
Journal of International Criminal Justice
(3) 585-588

ASSADI, MUZAFFAR, Globalization and
the changing forms of international terrorism In G. Gopa Kumar (ed.) International
terrorism and global order in the twenty
first century, 19-30

BAHGAT, GAWDAT, Iran, the United
States, and the war on terrorism In 26
Studies in conflict and terrorism (2) 93-
104

BIN, LI and ZHIWEI, LIU, The contribution
of arms control to fighting nuclear terrorism In 2 Disarmament forum (2003) 17-
22

BOOT-MATTHIJSSEN, MACHTELD, The International Criminal Court and international peace and security In 11 Tilburg foreign law rev. (2) 517-536

BREDEL, RALF, The UN's long-term conflict prevention strategies and the impact of counter-terrorism In 10 International Peacekeeping (2) 51-70

CHENUMOLU, SIREESHA, Revamping international securities laws to break the financial infrastructure of global terrorism In 31 Georgia journal of international and comparative law (2) 385-421

DAVID, ERIC, The contribution of international tribunals to the development of international criminal law In Mark Lattimer and Philippe Sands (eds.) Justice for crimes against humanity, 31-45

DENZA, EILEEN, The 2000 Convention on Mutual assistance in Criminal Matters In 40 Common Market Law Review (5) 1047-1074

HALBERSTAM, MALVINA, The evolution of the United Nations position on terrorism: from exempting national liberation movements to criminalizing terrorism wherever and by whomever committed In 41 Columbia Journal of Transnational Law (3) 573-584

JOSHI, K.C., The International Criminal Court: a hope against hope? In 45 Journal of the Indian Law Institute (2) 239-252

KASTENBERG, JOSHUA E., The right to assistance of counsel in military and war tribunals: an international and domestic law analysis In 14 Indiana International & Comparative Law Review (1) 175-225

KRASKA, JAMES C., The International Criminal Court, national security, and compliance with international law In 9

ILSA Journal of International & Comparative Law (2) 407-411

MANI, V.S., International terrorism and the quest for legal controls In 40 International studies (1) 41-67

PALOMBINO, FULVIO MARIA, The overlapping between war crimes and crimes against humanity in international criminal law In 12 Italian Yearbook of International Law, 123-145

PATEL-KING, FAIZA and SWAAK-GOLDMAN, OLIVIA, The applicability of international humanitarian law to the "war against terrorism" In 15 Hague Yearbook of International Law, 39-49

ROMANO, CESARE, P.R., Mixed jurisdictions for East Timor, Kosovo, Sierra Leone and Cambodia: the coming of age of internationalized criminal bodies? In The global community (1) 97-138

ROSAND, ERIC, Security Council Resolution 1373, the Counter-Terrorism Committee, and the fight against terrorism In 97 American Journal of International Law (2) 333-341

SCHAPER, ANNETT, Nuclear terrorism: risk analysis after 11 September 2001 In 2 Disarmament Forum (2003), 7-16

SHAJI, VARKEY Nuclear restraint and peace in South Asia In G. Gopa Kumar (ed.) International terrorism and global order in the twenty first century, 213-224

SREEKANTAN NAIR, R., Terrorism and strategic options for India In G. Gopa Kumar (ed.) International terrorism and global order in the twenty first century, 241-249

SUDHAKAR, E., War on terrorism and its impact on South Asia In G. Gopa Kumar (ed.) International terrorism and global order in the twenty first century, 225-240

SUNNY, K.C., Prevention of terrorism: the approach of the legal systems in UK and India In G. Gopa Kumar (ed.) International terrorism and global order in the twenty first century, 81-88

TIWARI, G.S., Drugs trade and terrorism: an assault on human rights In 45 Journal of the Indian Law Institute (1) 25-37

WIERDA, MARIEKE, Procedural developments in international criminal courts In 2 The Law and Practice of International Courts and Tribunals (2) 347-367

Development

AHN, DUKGEUN, Korea in the GATT/WTO dispute settlement: legal battle for economic development In 6 Journal of International Economic Law (3) 597-633

CHADHA, RAJESH, Computational analysis of the impact on India of the Uruguay Round and the Doha development agenda negotiations In Aaditya Mattoo and Robert M. Stern (eds.) India and the WTO, 13-46

KRASKA, JAMES, Sustainable development is security: the role of transboundary river agreements as Confidence Building Measure (CBM) in South Asia In 28 Yale Journal of International Law (2)465-503

RAJAGOPAL, BALAKRISHNAN, International law from below: development, social movements, and Third World resistance, Cambridge University Press, 343p.

WEINER, ANDY, The forest and the trees: sustainable development and human rights in the context of Cambodia In 151 University of Pennsylvania Law Review (4) 1543-1598

Economic relations and International Finance

BAYNE, NICHOLAS and WOOLCOCK, STEPHEN, The new economic diplomacy: decision-making and negotiation in international economic relations, Ashgate, 314p.

BIRNIE, PATRICIA, Impact on the development of international law on cooperation: the United Nations law of the sea, straddling stocks and biodiversity conventions In Myron H. Nordquist, John Norton Moore and Said Mahmoudi (eds.) The Stockholm declaration and law of the marine environment, 85-98

BRONCKERS, MARCO and GOYETTE, MARTIN, The EU's special safeguard clause in respect of China: (how) will it work? In 30 Legal Issues of Economic Integration (2) 123-131

CALDAROLA, MARIA CRISTINA and PATTLOCH, THOMAS, Legal material related to Asian intellectual property on the World Wide Web In Christopher Heath, Intellectual property law in Asia, 473-499

CHOI, WON-MOG, Regional economic integration in East Asia: prospect and jurisprudence In 6 Journal of International Economic Law (2) 49-77

COSSA, RALPH A., US approaches to multilateral security and economic organizations in the Asia-Pacific In Rosemary Foot, S. Neil MacFarlane, and Michael Mastanduno (eds.) US hegemony and international organizations, 193-214

EL-GAMAL, MAHMOUD A., "Interest" and the paradox of contemporary Islamic law and finance In 27 Fordham International Law Journal (1) 108-149

GAO, HENRY S., Legal issues under WTO rules on the Closer Economic Partnership Arrangement (CEPA) between mainland China and Hong Kong In 2 Chinese Journal of International Law (2), 629-648

GIROUARD, ROBERT J., Water export restrictions: a case study of WTO dispute settlement strategies and outcomes In 15 The Georgetown International Environmental Law Review (2) 247-289

HANSEN, MICHAEL W., Managing the environment across borders: a survey of environmental management in transnational corporations in Asia In 12 United Nations Transnational corporations (1) 27-52

HAUSWALDT, CHRISTIAN, Problems under the EC-Israel Association Agreement: the export of goods produced in the West Bank and the Gaza Strip under the EC-Israel Association Agreement In 14 European Journal of International Law (3) 591-611

HESELTINE, COLIN, Asia-Pacific Economic Cooperation: institutional evolution and the factors driving ongoing change In Michael Wesley (ed.) The regional organizations of the Asia-Pacific, 60-75

INGCO, MERLINDA D. (ed.), Agriculture, trade, and the WTO in South Asia, World Bank, 244p.

JUNG, YOUNGJIN and HAO, QIAN, The new economic constitution in China: a third way for competition regime? In 24 Northwestern Journal of International Law & Business (1) 107-171

HEATH, CHRISTOPHER (ed.), Intellectual property law in Asia, Kluwer Law International, Max Planck series on Asian intellectual property law, 520p.

KANEHARA, ATSUKO, The incident of an unidentified vessel in Japan's exclusive economic zone In 45 The Japanese Annual of International Law, 116-126

KIM, KWANG-ROK, Settling business disputes with North Koreans in the advent of the external economic arbitration law In 16 The Transnational Lawyer (2) 401-409

KNELLER, ROBERT, University-industry cooperation and technology transfer in Japan compared with the United States: another reason for Japan's economic malaise? In 24 University of Pennsylvania Journal of International Economic Law (4) 329-449

LEE, CATHERINE H., To thine own self be true: IMF conditionality and erosion of economic sovereignty in the Asian financial crisis In 24 University of Pennsylvania Journal of International Economic Law (4) 875-904

LEMIERRE, JEAN, Central Asian economic development and the implications for social and political stability: the role of the EBRD In 14 Helsinki Monitor (3) 232-241

MATTOO, AADITYA, China's accession to the WTO: the services dimension In 6 Journal of International Economic Law (2) 299-339

MUSHKAT, RODA, Potential impacts of China's WTO accession on its approach to the Trade-Environment Balancing Act In 2 Chinese Journal of International Law (1) 227-264

PAHUJA, SUNDHYA, Globalization and international economic law In Catherine Dauvergne (ed.) Jurisprudence for an interconnected globe, 71-91

PAUL, JOEL R., Do international trade institutions contribute to economic growth and development? In 44 Virginia journal of international law (1) 285-340

PURI, HARDEEP, How and under what conditions can developing countries be enabled to receive a better share of a benefit of trade facilitation? In United Nations Economic Commission for Europe (ed.) Sharing the gains of globalization in the new security environment, 29-35

RAJAN, RAMISHEN, S. and SEN, RAHUL, Liberalization of financial services in Southeast Asia under the ASEAN Framework Agreement on Services (AFAS), 18 Journal of International Banking Law and Regulation (3) 132-135

SORNARAJAH, M., Economic neo-liberalism and the international law on foreign investment In Antony Anghie et.al The Third World and international order, 172-190

TOVIAS, ALFRED and AL KHOURI, RIAD, An empirical estimation of the economic effects of a bilateral free trade area agreement between Israel and Jordan in the context of the Euro-Mediterranean partnership, San Domenico: European University Institute, EUI working papers (No. 2003/11) 48p.

WAKEFORD, DAVID, Possible approach for a trade facilitation agreement in the World Trade Organization In United Nations Economic Commission for Europe (ed.) Sharing the gains of globalization in the new security environment, 120-126

WEBBER, KATHRYN J., The economic future of Afghan women: the interaction between Islamic law and Muslim culture In 24 University of Pennsylvania Journal of International Economic Law (4) 959-992

WEERAWORAWIT, WEERAWIT, The harmonization of intellectual property rights in ASEAN In Christopher Heath, Intellectual property law in Asia, 247-266

Environment

ALI, SALEEM H., Mining, the environment, and indigenous development conflicts, University of Arizona Press, 254p.

BALKIN, ROSALIE P., Some future developments in liability and compensation for environmental damage at sea In Myron H. Nordquist, John Norton Moore and Said Mahmoudi (eds.), The Stockholm declaration and law of the marine environment, 437-454

JHA, VEENA, Trade and environment: Doha and beyond In Aaditya Mattoo and Robert M. Stern (eds.) India and the WTO, 299-325

MENSAH, THOMAS A., Protection and preservation of the marine environment and the dispute settlement regime in the United Nations Convention on the Law of the Sea In Andree Kirchner (ed.) International marine environmental law, 9-18

PEGG, SCOTT, Globalization and natural-resource conflicts In 56 Naval War College Review (4) 82-96

ROTHWELL, DONALD R. The International Tribunal for the Law of the Sea and Marine Environmental Protection: expanding the horizons of international oceans governance In 17 Ocean yearbook, 26-55

TANAKA, MAKI, Bridging the gap between Northern NGO's and the Southern sovereigns in the trade-environment debate: the pursuit of democratic dispute settlements in the WTO under the Rio Principles In 30 Ecology law quarterly (1) 113-188

ZERNER, CHARLES (ed.), Culture and the question of rights: forests, coasts, and seas in Southeast Asia, Duke University Press, 289p.

General

ANDERSON, JOHN, Constitutional change in Central Asia In Sally N. Cummings (ed.), Oil, transition and security in Central Asia, 75-83

ANTONS, CHRISTOPH, Legal culture and history of law in Asia In Christopher Heath, Intellectual property law in Asia, 13-35

FOX, HAZEL, International law and restraints on the exercise of jurisdiction by national courts of states In Malcolm D. Evans (ed.) International law, 357-385

KHOURY, AMIR H., The development of modern trademark legislation and protection in Arab countries of the Middle East In 16 The Transnational Lawyer (2) 249-343

MAJID, SALEH and MAJID, FARIS, Application of Islamic law in the Middle East: interest and Islamic banking In 20 The international construction law review (1) 177-196

MILLER, DAWN J. Holding states to their convention obligations: the United Nations Convention against Torture and the need for a broad interpretation of state action In 17 Georgetown Immigration Law Journal (2) 299-323

MUGRABY, MUHAMAD, Some impediments to the rule of law in the Middle East and beyond In 26 Fordham International Law Journal (3) 771-784

Individuals, groups of persons – human rights

ABEYSEKERA, SUNILA, Maximizing the achievement of women's human rights in conflict-transformation: the case of Sri Lanka In 41 Columbia Journal of Transnational Law (3) 523-540

AGARWAL, H.O., International law & human rights, Central Law Publications, 920p.

AHMAD, FURQAN, Protective judiciary in aid of human rights in India In 43 Indian Journal of International Law (2) 349-359

BADERIN, MASHOOD A., International human rights and Islamic law, Oxford University Press, 279p.

BENGWAYAN, MICHAEL A., Intellectual and cultural property rights of indigenous and tribal peoples in Asia: Minority Rights Group International, 39p.

BERWEEN, MOHAMED, International bills of human rights: an Islamic critique In 7 The International Journal of Human Rights (4) 129-142

BREEN, CLAIRE, The right to education of persons with disabilities: disabled in interpretation and application In 21 Netherlands Quarterly on Human Rights (1) 7-37

COLLIER, NIAMH, The development of human rights in Irish foreign policy – case study: Ireland and Burma In 14 Irish Studies in International Affairs, 107-128

DADWAL, LALIT, Position of human rights: an Indian profile In 39 Civil & military law journal on rule of law, military jurisprudence and legal aid (4) 221-229

EL DIN HASSAN, BAHEY, Regional protection of human rights in the Arab states in *statu nascendi* In Janusz Symonides (ed.) Human rights: international protection, monitoring, enforcement, 239-253

FRYNAS, JEDRZEJ and PEGG, SCOTT, Transnational corporations and human rights, Palgrave Macmillan, 223p.

GREENWOOD, SCOT W., Lessons from conflict: the role of a strong judiciary and the international community in protecting human rights for successful humanitarian aid In 31 Denver Journal of International Law and Policy (4) 551-578

HAPPOLD, MATTHEW and ANDERSON, MICHAEL (eds.), Constitutional human rights in the Commonwealth , British Institute of International and Comparative Law, 232p.

HITCHCOCK, ROBERT K. Human rights and indigenous peoples in Africa and Asia In David P. Forsythe and Patrice C. McMahon (eds.) Human rights and diversity, 205-228

MENDES, ERROL and LALONDE-ROUSSY, ANIK (eds.) Bridging the global divide on human rights: a Canada-China dialogue, Ashgate, 373p.

GHANDHI, P. R., The Human Rights Committee and the death row phenomenon In 43 Indian Journal of International Law (1) 1-66

HUNG, VERON MEI-YING, Improving human rights in China: should re-education through labor be abolished? In 41 Columbia Journal of Transnational Law (2) 303-326

KATZENSTEIN, SUZANNE, Hybrid tribunals: searching for justice in East Timor In 16 Harvard Human Rights Journal (spring) 245-278

KHAN, MAIMUL AHSAN, Human rights in the Muslim world: fundamentalism, constitutionalism, and international politics, Carolina Academic Press, 489p.

KHAN, AMJAD MAHMOOD, Persecution of the Ahmadiyya Community in Pakistan: an analysis under international law and international relations In 16 Harvard Human Rights Journal (spring) 217-244

KLABBERS, JAN, Redemption song?: Human rights versus community-building in East Timor In 16 Leiden Journal of International Law (2) 367-376

KRISHNAN, JAYANTH K., The rights of the new untouchables: a constitutional analysis of HIV jurisprudence in India In 25 Human Rights Quarterly (3) 791-819

KUITENBROUWER, MAARTEN, Colonialism and human rights: Indonesia and the Netherlands in comparative perspective In 21 Netherlands Quarterly on Human Rights (2) 203-224

LANE, JENNIFER, The mass graves at Dasht-e Leili: assessing U.S. liability for human rights violations during the war in Afghanistan In 34 California Western International Law Journal (1) 145-170

LEVIN, SCOTT A., Sexual exploitation of refugee children by U.N. peacekeepers In 19 New York Law School Journal on Human Rights (3) 833-842

MACDONALD, NEIL, More harm than good?: human rights considerations in international commercial arbitration In 20 Journal of International Arbitration (6) 523-538

MAZZESCHI, RICCARDO PISILLO, Reparation claims by individuals for state breaches of humanitarian law and human rights: an overview In 1 Journal of International Criminal Justice (2) 339-347

MIGRET, FRIDIRIC and HOFFMANN, FLORIAN, The UN as a human rights violator?: some reflections on the United Nations changing human rights responsibilities In 25 Human rights quarterly (2) 314-342

MONSHIPOURI, MAHMOOD, WELCH CLAUDE E. and KENNEDY, EVAN T., Multinational corporations and the ethics of global responsibility: problems and possibilities In 25 Human rights quarterly (4) 965-989

MONSHIPOURI, MAHMOOD, Human rights and child labor in South Asia In David P. Forsythe and Patrice C. Mc-Mohan (eds.), Human rights and diversity, 182-204

MOUANGUE KOBILA, JAMES, Comparative practice on human rights: North-South In Jean-Marc Coicaud, Michael W. Doyle and Anne-Marie Gardner (eds.) The globalization of human rights, 89-115

NARULA, SMITA, Overlooked danger: the security and rights implications of Hindu nationalism in India In 16 Harvard Human Rights Journal (spring) 41-68

NIRMAL, B.C., An ancient Indian perspective of human rights and its relevance In 43 Indian Journal of International Law (3) 445-478

OTHMAN, MOHAMED, East Timor: a critique of the model of accountability for serious human rights and international humanitarian law violations In 72 Nordic Journal of International Law (4) 449-482

PALTIEL, JEREMY, To whom must we answer?: exploring the relationship between sovereignty, the rule of law and human rights in Chinese and Canadian practice In Errol Mendes and Anik La-

londe-Roussy (eds.) Bridging the global divide on human rights, 53-75

PATIL, V.T., Human rights developments in South Asia, Authors Press, 334p.

PETERSEN, CAROLE J., The Paris Principles and human rights institutions: is Hong Kong slipping further away from the mark? In 33 Hong Kong Law Journal (3) 513-522

RAJ KUMAR, C., National human rights institutions: good governance perspectives on institutionalization of human rights In 19 The American University International Law Review (2) 259-300

—, Corruption and human rights: promoting transparency in governance and the fundamental right to corruption-free service in India In 17 Journal of Asian Law (1) 31-72

RAZDAN, VINOD K., Expanding dimensions of human rights: global and Indian position In 39 Civil & military law journal on rule of law, military jurisprudence and legal aid (4) 165-177

RENREN, GONG, Implementing international human rights treaties in China In Errol Mendes and Anik Lalonde-Roussy (eds.) Bridging the global divide on human rights, 99-109

RUBIN, BARNETT, Transitional justice and human rights in Afghanistan In 79 International Affairs (3) 567-581

RUIZ RUIZ, FLORENTINO, The succession of states in universal treaties on the protection of human rights and humanitarian law In 7 The international journal of human rights (2) 42-96

SAHLIYEH, EMILE, The status of human rights in the Middle East: prospects and challenges In David P. Forsythe and

Patrice C. McMahon (eds.) Human rights and diversity, 252-275

SARKIN, JEREMY and PIETSCHMANN, MAREK, Legitimate humanitarian intervention under international law in the context of the current human rights and humanitarian crisis in Burma (Myanmar) In 33 Hong Kong Law Journal (2) 371-415

SHAH, MEGHANA, Rights under fire: the inadequacy of international human rights instruments in combating dowry murder in India In 19 Connecticut Journal of International Law (1) 209-229

SIDIQI, NAEEM and COLEMAN, TRAVIS, Human rights in Pakistan since the 1970s, Grid Foundation, 48p.

SUBBIAN, A., Human rights complaints system: international and regional, Deep & Deep Publishers, 268p.

THELLE, HATLA, Social rights and the Chinese work unit system In 7 The International Journal of Human Rights (3) 27-48

WAWRYNEK, CHRISTINE, World War II comfort women: Japan's sex slaves or hired prostitutes? In 19 New York Law School Journal of Human Rights (3) 913-922

WEINER, ANDY, The forest and the trees: sustainable development and human rights in the context of Cambodia In 151 University of Pennsylvania Law Review (4) 1543-1598

WHITING, AMANDA, Situating Suhakam: human rights debates and Malaysia's National Human Rights Commission In 39 Stanford Journal of International Law (1) 59-98

WISEBERG, LAURIE S., The role of Non-Governmental Organizations (NGO's) in the protection and enforcement of human rights In Janusz Symonides (ed.) Human rights: international protection, monitoring, enforcement, 347-372

Peace-keeping, peace-making and peace-building

DOBSON, HUGO, Japan and United Nations peacekeeping: new pressures, new responses, Routledge Curzon, 188p.

SMITH, MICHAEL and DEE, MOREEN, Peacekeeping in East Timor: the path to independence, Rienner, International Peace Academy occasional paper series, 214p.

Sea, rivers and water-resources

ABDULLAH ELMI, MOHAMED, Joint development and cooperation in international water resources In Mikiyasu Nakayama (ed.) International waters in Southern Africa, 209-248

ANTYPAS, ALEXIOS and STEC, STEPHEN, Towards a liability regime for damages to transboundary waters by industrial accidents: a new protocol in the UNECE region In 14 The Journal of Water Law (4) 185-193

BENVENISTI, EYAL, Water conflicts during the occupation of Iraq In 97 The American Journal of International Law (4) 860-872

BOYLE, ALAN, Central Asian water problems: the role of international law In Sally N. Cummings (ed.) Oil, transition and security in Central Asia, 203-215

CAPONERA, DANTE A., National and international water law and administration: selected writings, Kluwer Law International, 446p.

DIBA, BAHMAN AGHAI, The law & politics of the Caspian Sea in the twenty-first century: the positions and views of Russia, Kazakhstan, Azerbaijan, Turkmenistan, with special reference to Iran, Bethesda, 182p.

ECKSTEIN, GABRIEL and ECKSTEIN, YORAM, A hydrogeological approach to transboundary ground water resources and international law In 19 The American University International Law Review (2) 201-258

HELTZER, GREGORY E., Stalemate in the Aral Sea Basin: will Kyrgyzstan's new water law bring the downstream nations back to the multilateral bargaining table? In 15 The Georgetown International Environmental Law Review (2) 291-320

INTERNATIONAL BUREAU OF THE PERMANENT COURT OF ARBITRATION (ed.), Resolution of international water disputes: papers emanating from the Sixth PCA International Law Seminar, November 8, 2002, 453p.

KANG, JOON-SUK, The United Nation convention on the law of the sea and fishery relations between Korea, Japan and China In 27 Maritime Policy (2) 111-124

KEYUAN, ZOU, Management of marine nature reserves in East Asia: the case of the People's Republic of China In Andree Kirchner (ed.) International Marine Environmental Law, 193-209

—, Sino-Japanese joint fishery management in the East China Sea In 27 Maritime Policy (2) 125-142

—, China's efforts in deep sea-bed mining: law and practice In 18 International Journal of Maritime Coast Law (4) 481-508

KRASKA, JAMES, Sustainable development is security: the role of transboundary river agreements as Confidence Building Measure (CBM) in South Asia In 28 Yale Journal of International Law (2) 465-503

KRISTJÁNDÓTTIR, EDDA, Resolution of water disputes: lessons from the Middle East In International Bureau of the Permanent Court of Arbitration (ed.) Resolution of international water disputes, 351-370

NARDONE, RONA, Like oil and water: the WTO and the world's water resources In 19 Connecticut Journal of International Law (1) 183-207

PYO KIM, SUN, The UN convention on the law of the sea and new fisheries agreements in north East Asia In 27 Maritime Policy (2) 97-109

RAMANGKURA, VARAMON, Thai shrimp, sea turtles, mangrove forests and the WTO: innovative environmental protection under the international trade regime In 15 The Georgetown International Environmental Law Review (4) 677-708

SERDY, ANDREW, How long has the United Nations Fish Stocks Agreement been in force? In 34 Ocean Development and International Law (1) 29-40

SUBEDI, SURYA P., Resolution of international water disputes: challenges for the 21st century In International Bureau of the Permanent Court of Arbitration (ed.) Resolution of international water disputes, 33-47

THORSON, JOHN E., Visions of sustainable interstate water management agreements In 43 Natural Resources Journal (2) 347-371

VALENCIA, MARK J. and AMAE, YOSHIHISA, Regime building in the East China Sea In 34 Ocean Development and International Law (2) 189-208

WOUTERS, PATRICIA, Universal and regional approaches to resolving international water disputes: what lessons learned from state practice In International Bureau of the Permanent Court of Arbitration (ed.) Resolution of international water disputes, 111-154

YETIN, M., Governing international rivers of the Middle East In 166 World Affairs (2) 81-94

States and groups of states

ABU JABER, KAMEL S., The democratic process in Syria, Lebanon, and Jordan In Amin Saikal and Albrecht Schnabel (eds.) Democratization in the Middle East, 127-141

BOSI, DOMENICA, Post-conflict reconstruction: the United Nations' involvement in Afghanistan In 19 New York Law School Journal of Human Rights (3) 819-831

GHAI, YASH, LATTIMER, MARK, SAID, YAHIA and VAN DER STOEL, MAX et al, Building democracy in Iraq, Minority Rights Group International, 44p.

HOFMANN, RAINER, International law and the use of military force against Iraq In 45 German Yearbook of International Law, 9-34

PIOTROWICZ, RYSZARD, The use of force and the force of law in Iraq In 77 Australian Law Journal (5) 283-289

POLLACK, JONATHAN D., The United States, North Korea and the end of the agreed framework In 56 Naval War College Review (3) 11-49

QUARTERMAN, MARK, UN leverage in East Timor: inducing Indonesian compliance through international law In Jean Krasno, Bradd C. Hayes and Donald C.F. Daniel (eds.) Leveraging for success in United Nations peace operations, 141-168

RAMMREZ, JORGE ALBERTO, Iraq war: anticipatory self-defense or unlawful unilateralism? In 34 California Western International Law Journal (1) 1-27

ROBERT, ADAMS, Law and the use of force after Iraq In 45 Survival (2) (London), 31-56

SAIKAL, AMIN, Democracy and peace in Iran and Iraq In Amin Saikal and Albrecht Schnabel (eds.) Democratization in the Middle East,166-182

WEITZ, RICHARD, Why Russia and China have not formed an anti-American alliance In 56 Naval War College Review (4) 39-61

YOO, JOHN, International law and the war in Iraq In 97 The American Journal of International Law (3) 563-576

United Nations and other international/ regional organizations and regional laws

ABAD, M.C. JR., The Association of Southeast Asian Nations: challenges and responses In Michael Wesley, The regional organizations of the Asia-Pacific, 40-59

BOHR, ANNETTE, Regional cooperation in Central Asia: mission impossible? In 14 Helsinki Monitor (3) 254-268

BOSI, DOMENICA, Post-conflict reconstruction: the United Nations' involvement in Afghanistan In 19 New York Law School Journal of Human Rights (3) 819-831

CHOI, WON-MOG, Regional economic integration in East Asia: prospect and jurisprudence, In 6 Journal of International Economic Law (Oxford) (1) 49-77

COSSA, RALPH A., US approaches to multilateral security and economic organizations in the Asia-Pacific In Rosemary Foot, S. Neil MacFarlane, and Michael Mastanduno (eds.) US hegemony and international organizations, 193-214

EMMERS, RALF, Cooperative security and the balance of power in ASEAN and the ARF, Routledge Curzon, 197p.

FISCHER, THOMAS C., A commentary on regional institutions in the Pacific rim: do APEC and ASEAN still matter? In 13 Duke Journal of Comparative & International Law (2) 337-380

FUKUSHIMA, AKIKO, The ASEAN Regional Forum In Michael Wesley (ed.) The regional organizations of the Asia-Pacific, 76-93

FUNABASHI, YOICHI (ed.), Reconciliation in the Asia-Pacific, United States Institute of Peace Press, 238p.

HESELTINE, COLIN, Asia-Pacific Economic Cooperation: institutional evolution and the factors driving ongoing change In Michael Wesley (ed.) The regional organizations of the Asia-Pacific, 60-75

MORIKAWA, KOICHI, Japan's legal responses to United Nations Security Council resolutions In 45 The Japanese Annual of International Law, 34-52

RAJAN RAMKISHEN and SEN, RAHUL, Liberalization of financial services in Southeast Asia under the ASEAN Framework Agreement on Services (AFAS) In 18 Journal of International Banking Law and Regulation (3) 132-135

SALTFORD, JOHN, The United Nations and the Indonesian takeover of West Papua, 1962-1969: the anatomy of betrayal, Routledge Curzon, 228p.

THAKUR, RAMESH, Reforming the United Nations: changing with and for the times In 10 International Peacekeeping (4) 40-61

WESLEY, MICHAEL (ed.), The regional organizations of the Asia-Pacific: exploring institutional change, Palgrave Macmillan, 247p.

War, peace and neutrality, armed conflict, international humanitarian law

BHATIA, MICHAEL V. War and intervention: issues for contemporary peace operations, Kumarian Press, 222p.

CABALLERO-ANTHONY, MELY, The regionalization of peace in Asia In Michael Pugh and Waheguru Pal Singh Sidhu (eds.) The United Nations & regional security, 195-211

CHETAIL, VINCENT, The contribution of the International Court of Justice to international humanitarian law In 85 Rev. int. Croix-Rouge (850) 235-269

CHIMNI, B.S., Post-conflict peace-building and the return of refugees: concepts, practices and institutions In Edward Newman and Joanne van Selm (eds.) Refugees and forced displacement, 195-220

CLOONEY, FRANCIS X., Pain but not harm: some classical resources toward a Hindu just war theory In Paul Robinson (ed.) Just war in comparative perspective, 109-125

GIRI, T.N., Refugee problems in Asia and Africa: role of the UNHCR, Manak Publishers, 302p.

DONOVAN, DANIEL KEMPER, Joint U.N.-Cambodia efforts to establish a Khmer Rouge Tribunal In 44 Harvard International Law Journal (2), 551-576

GASSER, HANS-PETER GASSER and STEIN, TORSTEN, International humanitarian law and human rights law in non-international armed conflict: joint venture or mutual exclusion? In 45 German Yearbook of International Law, 149-165

GHOSCH, SUCHETA, Crisis in the kingdoms: refugee question between Bhutan and Nepal In Omprakash Mishra and Anindyo J. Majumdar (eds.) The elsewhere people, 169-182

GREENWOOD, CHRISTOPHER, The law of war (international humanitarian law) In Malcolm D. Evans (ed.) International law, 789-823

GURHARPAL SINGH, Sikhism and just war In Paul Robinson (ed.) Just war in comparative perspective, 126-136

HARRIS, ELIZABETH, J. Buddhism and the justification of war: a case study from Sri Lanka In Paul Robinson (ed.) Just war in comparative perspective, 93-108

HEINSCH, ROBERT W., Possibilities to prosecute war crimes committed in Iraq: the different forum options In 16 Humanitäres Völkerrecht (3) 132-138

KANE, THOMAS M., Inauspicious tools: Chinese thought on the morality of warfare In Paul Robinson (ed.) Just war in comparative perspective, 139-152

KASHIMA, TETSUDEN, Judgment without trial: Japanese American imprisonment during World War II, University of Washington Press, 316p.

KEI, USHIMURA, Beyond the "judgment of civilization": the intellectual legacy of the Japanese war crimes trials, 1946-1949, International House of Japan (Japan), 336p.

LI, PETER (ed.), Japanese war crimes: the search for justice, New Brunswick, 339p.

KELSAY, JOHN, War, peace and the imperatives of justice in Islamic perspective: what do the 11 September 2001 attacks tell us about Islam and the just war tradition? In Paul Robinson (ed.) Just war in comparative perspective, 76-89

KU, CHARLOTTE and BRUN, JOAQUIN CACERES, Neutrality and the ICRC contribution to contemporary humanitarian operations In 10 Int. peacekeeping (1) 56-72

MEHTA, JAGAT, Humanitarian law and diplomacy In 43 Indian Journal of International Law (1) 85-92

METTRAUX, GUINAKL, US courts-martial and the armed conflict in the Philippines (1899-1902): their contribution to national case law on war crimes In 1 Journal of international criminal justice (1) 135-150

OTHMAN, MOHAMED, East Timor: a critique of the model of accountability for serious human rights and international humanitarian law violations In 72 Nordic Journal of International Law (4) 449-482

PARKER, TOM, The proportionality principle in the war on terror In 15 Hague Yearbook of International Law, 3-15

PIETSCHMANN, MAREK and SARKIN, JEREMY, Legitimate humanitarian intervention under international law in the context of the current human rights and humanitarian crisis in Burma (Myanmar) In 33 Hong Kong Law Journal (2) 371-415

QUIGLEY, JOHN, The Afghanistan war and self-defense In 37 Valparaiso University Law Review (2) 541-562

SARKIN, JEREMY and PIETSCHMANN, MAREK, Legitimate humanitarian intervention under international law in the context of the current human rights and humanitarian crisis in Burma (Myanmar) In 33 Hong Kong Law Journal (2) 371-415

SCHMITT, MICHAEL N., Counter-terrorism and the use of force in international law In 32 Israel Yearbook of Human Rights, 53-116

SEN, SUMIT, The Refugee Convention and practice in South Asia: a marriage of inconvenience? In Joanne van Selm *et al* The Refugee Convention at fifty, 203-217

SLUITER, GVRAN, The surrender of war criminals to the International Criminal Court In 25 Loyola of Los Angeles International & Comparative Law Review (3) 605-651

SNYDER, ANNA C., Setting the agenda for global peace: conflict and consensus building, Ashgate, 153p.

SOUTHGATE, EDWARD J.L, From Japan to Afghanistan: the U.S.-Japan joint security relationship, the war on terror, and the ignominious end of the pacifist state In 151 University of Pennsylvania law review (4) 1599-1638

STEIN, TORSTEN, The war against Iraq and the "*jus ad bellum*" In 42 Revue de droit militaire et de droit de la guerre (3-4) 459-465

THOMAS, RAJU G.C., Wars, humanitarian intervention and international law: perceptions and reality In Raju G.C. Thomas (ed.) Yugoslavia unravelled, 165-203

TROMBLEY, FRANK R., The Arabs, the Byzantine State and the Islamic law of war (fiqh al-jihad) (7th-10th centuries CE) In Paul Robinson (ed.) Just war in comparative perspective, 153-166

VAN HOFTEN, DEREK, Declaring war on the Japanese constitution: Japan's right to military sovereignty and the United States' right to military presence in Japan In 26 Hastings International and Comparative Law Review (2) 289-307

VAN SLIEDREGT, ELISABETH, The criminal responsibility of individuals for violations of international humanitarian law, T.M.C. Asser Press, 437p.

INDEX

GENERAL INFORMATION

Editorial address:

ASIAN YEARBOOK OF INTERNATIONAL LAW

c/o Professor S.P. SUBEDI,
    6 Manorside,
    Barnet, London EN5 2LD, UK.
    Fax: *44 113 343 5056; *E-mail:* s.p.subedi@leeds.ac.uk

or:

    Professor M. MIYOSHI,
    Aichi University Faculty of Law,
    370 Kurozasa, Miyoshi-cho,
    Aichi 470-0296, Japan.
    E-mail: mmiyoshi@vega.aichi-u.ac.jp

or:

    Professor B.S. CHIMNI,
    . Dept. of International Law,
    School of International Studies,
    Jawaharlal Nehru University,
    New Delhi 110067, India.
    E-mail: bschimni@hotmail.com

Contributions to the Yearbook

The Yearbook invites contributions in the form of:

– articles (5,000 words or more) on topics of public or private international law, either with special reference to Asia or of general relevance;

– (shorter) notes and comments;

– translated versions of articles originally written in a language other than English;

– materials in the field of municipal or international state practice of Asian states and organizations, with relevance to international law;

– data on events and incidents relating to Asia and Asian countries and with relevance to international law and relations;

– information on literature and documents (in any language) either concerning international law in Asia or concerning international law in general and published or issued in Asia.

Contributors of articles and notes will receive 25 offprints free of charge. Contributors of other materials will receive 10 offprints of the section of the *Yearbook* in which their materials are included.

Submission of manuscripts and other materials

The regular schedule of the Yearbook provides for publication in June of each year.

Submission of a manuscript should be accompanied by information whether it has been published, submitted, or accepted elsewhere, and whether it is a translation.

Submission of manuscripts implies the readiness to consider editorial suggestions for change and, as the case may be, to introduce revisions. It also implies the author's agreement with linguistic revision by native speakers so far as these services are available to the Editors.

Authors are requested to have their manuscript processed by Word under Windows 95 or higher on a PC and saved as a Word (6/95 or 7/95) file, and to submit their manuscript (1) by mail on a 3.5" disk or (2) by e-mail, as an attached file. Additional hard copies are optional though much appreciated.

SATA INTERNATIONAL LAW PRIZE 2006
OF
THE ASIAN YEARBOOK OF INTERNATIONAL LAW

The *Asian Yearbook of International Law* is pleased to invite the submission of original essays of excellent quality written by young scholars of Asian nationality residing anywhere in the world on a topic of public or private international law for consideration of the award of the Sata International Law Prize of 2006. The value of the Prize is US$2,000 and is named after Mr. Sata Yasuhiko (through the University of Tokyo) of Tokibo Ltd., Japan, whose generous gift has made it possible to establish this annual Prize.

The winning essay will be published in the Asian Yearbook of International Law. Participants must not be over the age of 40 years on the submission date. Each essay should be accompanied by the curriculum vitae of the author. Essays must be written in English, and the length should be between 8,000 and 14,000 words excluding footnotes.

The Editors of the *Yearbook* will determine the winning essay and notify the competitors of the results not later than 31 October 2006. The decisions taken by the Editors will be final. Essays for the Sata 2006 Prize must be received by the Editors of the *Yearbook* not later than 31 July 2006 by e-mail at: s.p.subedi@leeds.ac.uk or by post at the following address:

Professor Surya P. Subedi, General Editor
Asian Yearbook of International Law
6 Manorside
Barnet, London EN5 2LD, UK.